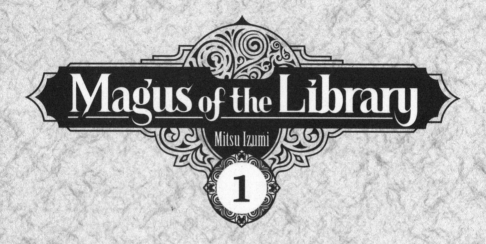

Magus of the Library

Mitsu Izumi

1

Based on *Kafna of the Wind*
Written by Sophie Schwimm • Translated by Hiroto Hamada

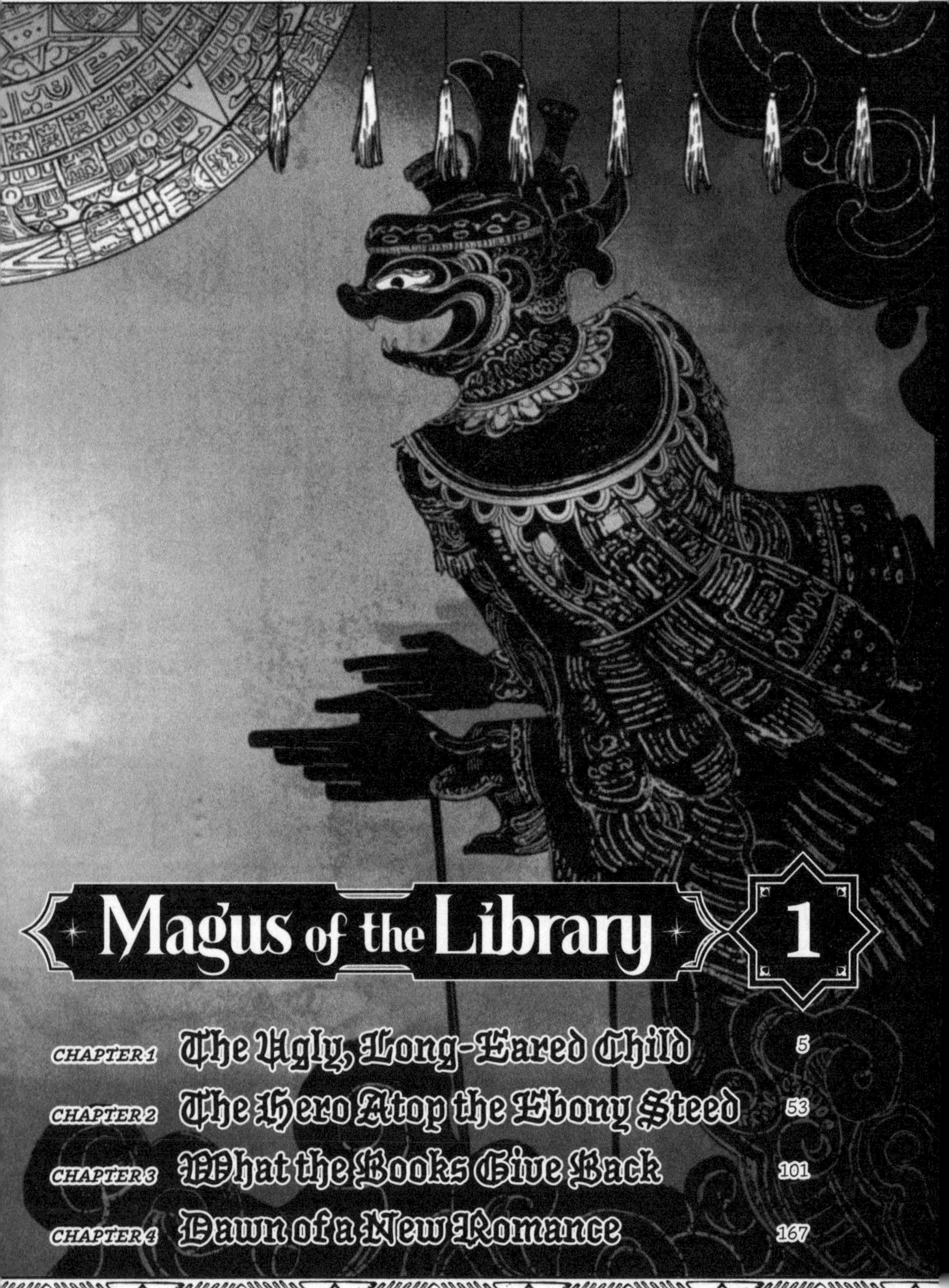

Magus of the Library 1

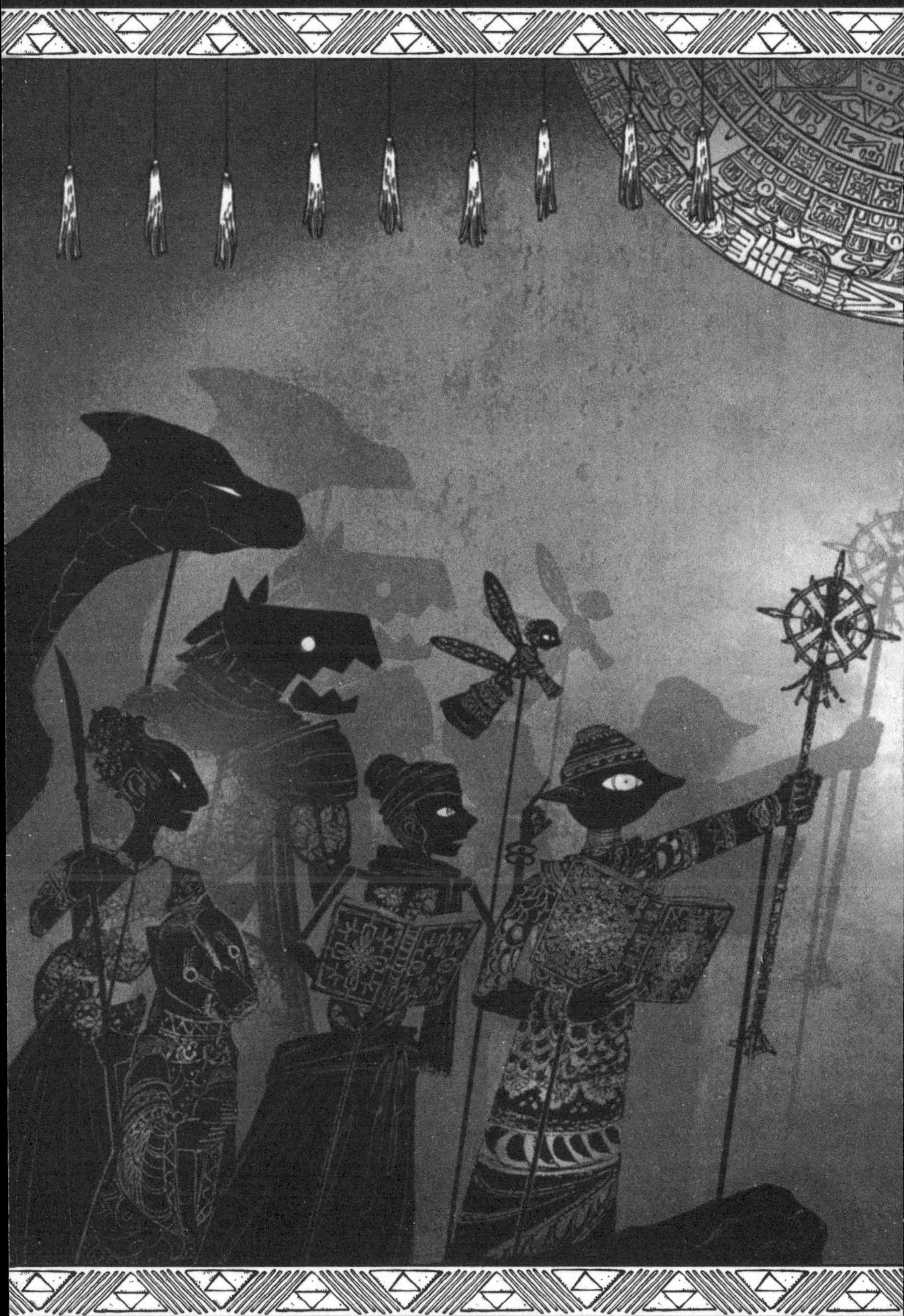

"This story is dedicated to my champion."

—Sophie Schwimm
Opening line of ***Kafna of the Wind***

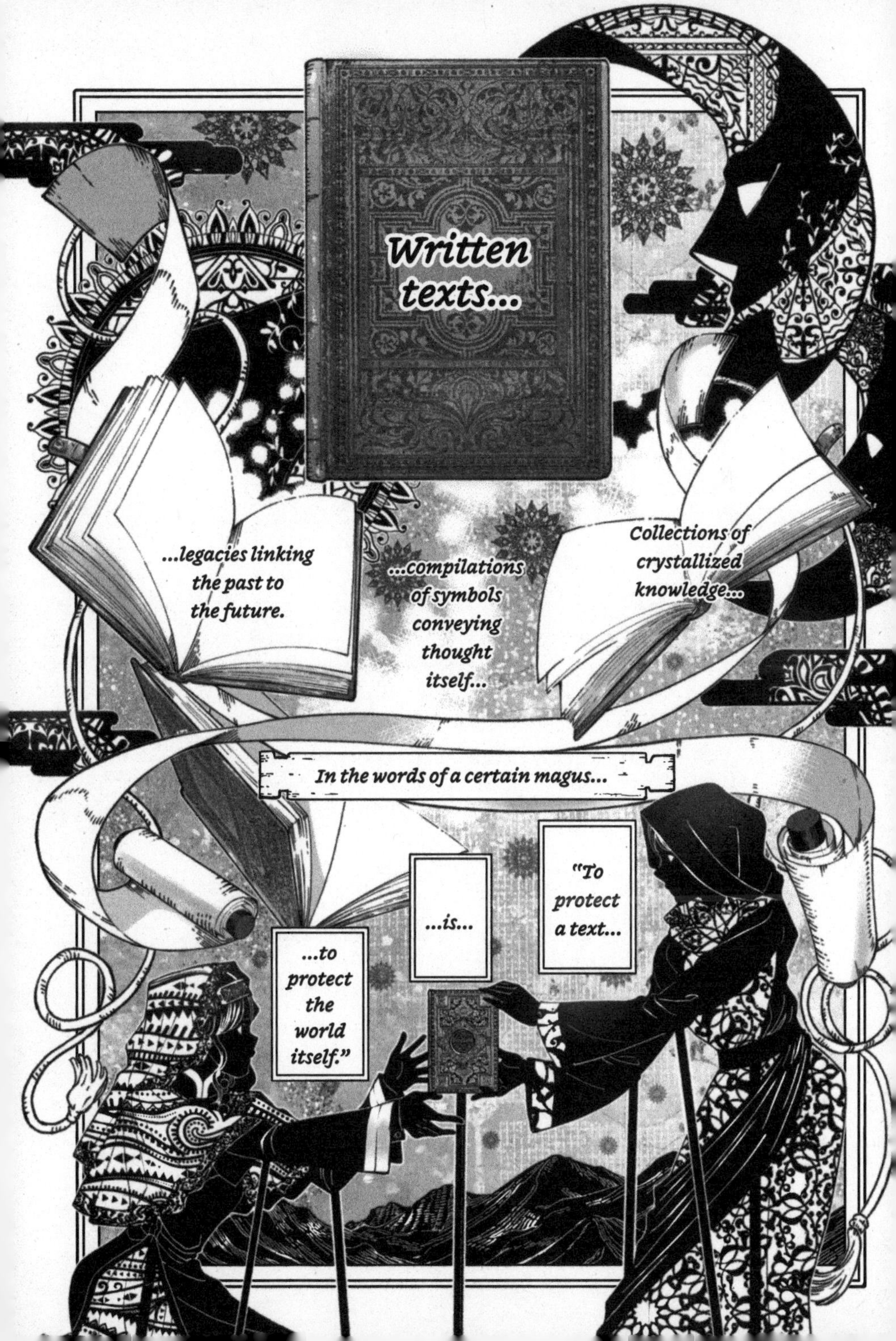
Written texts...
Collections of crystallized knowledge...
...compilations of symbols conveying thought itself...
...legacies linking the past to the future.
In the words of a certain magus...
"To protect a text...
...is...
...to protect the world itself."

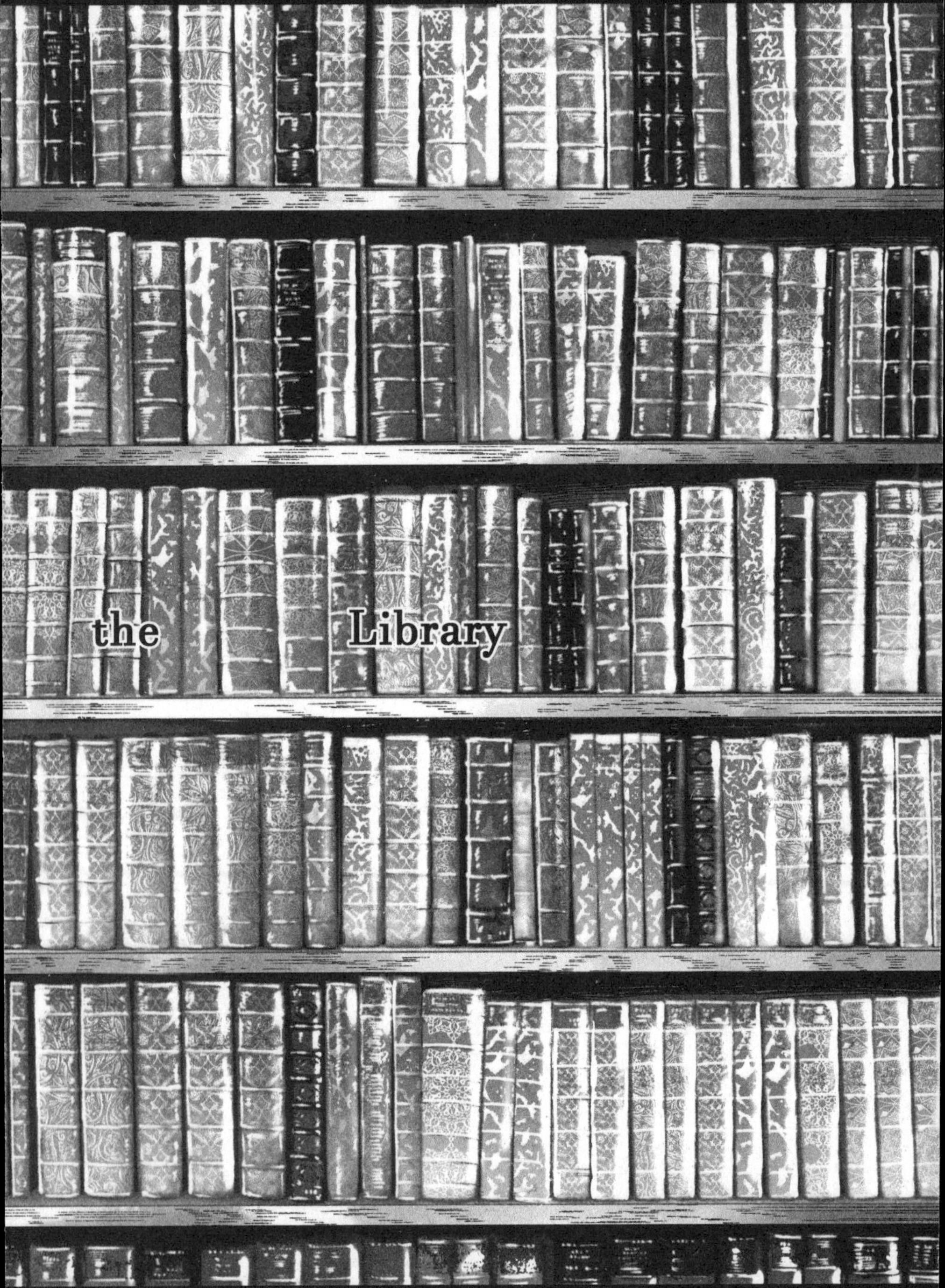
the Library

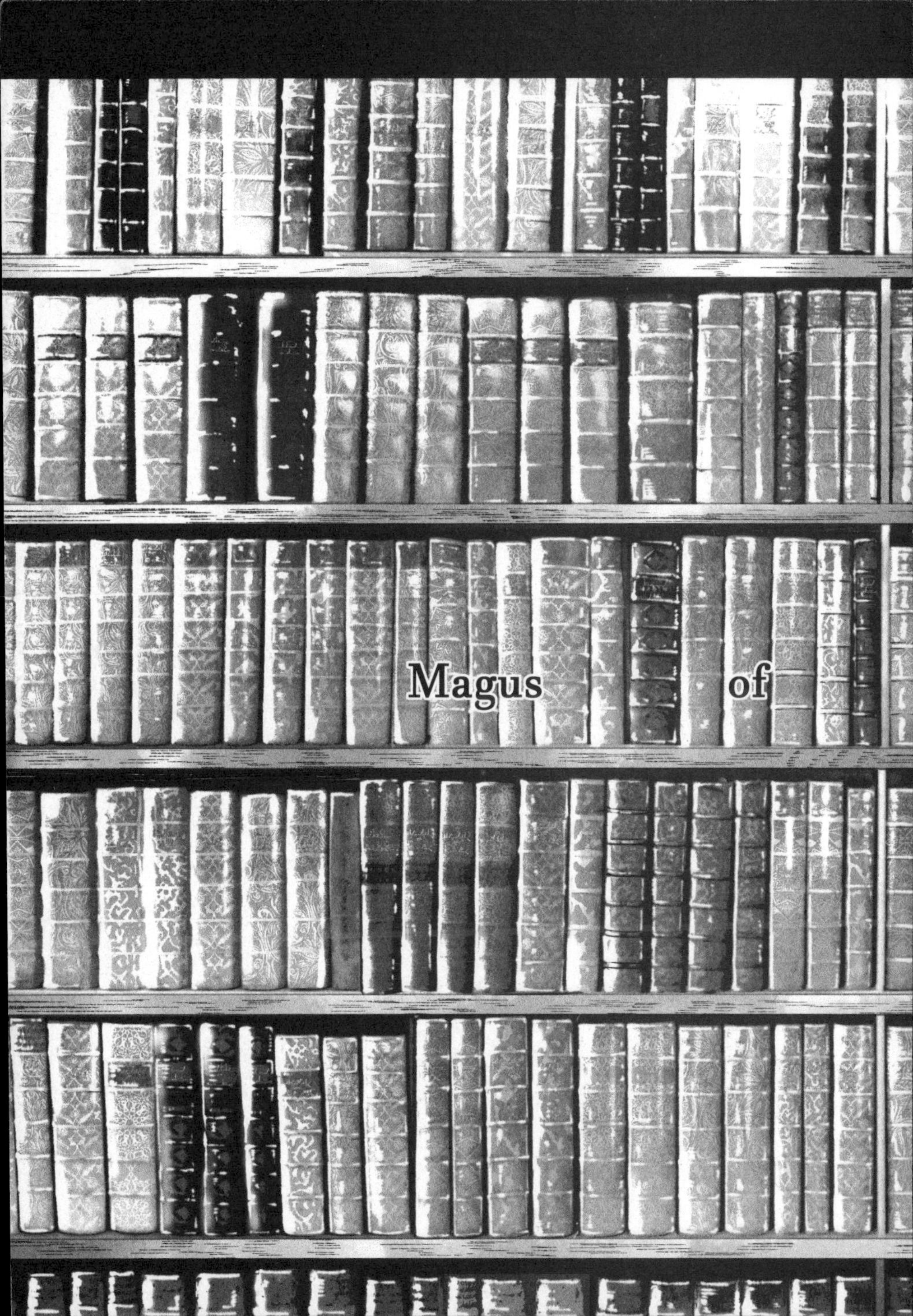
Magus
of

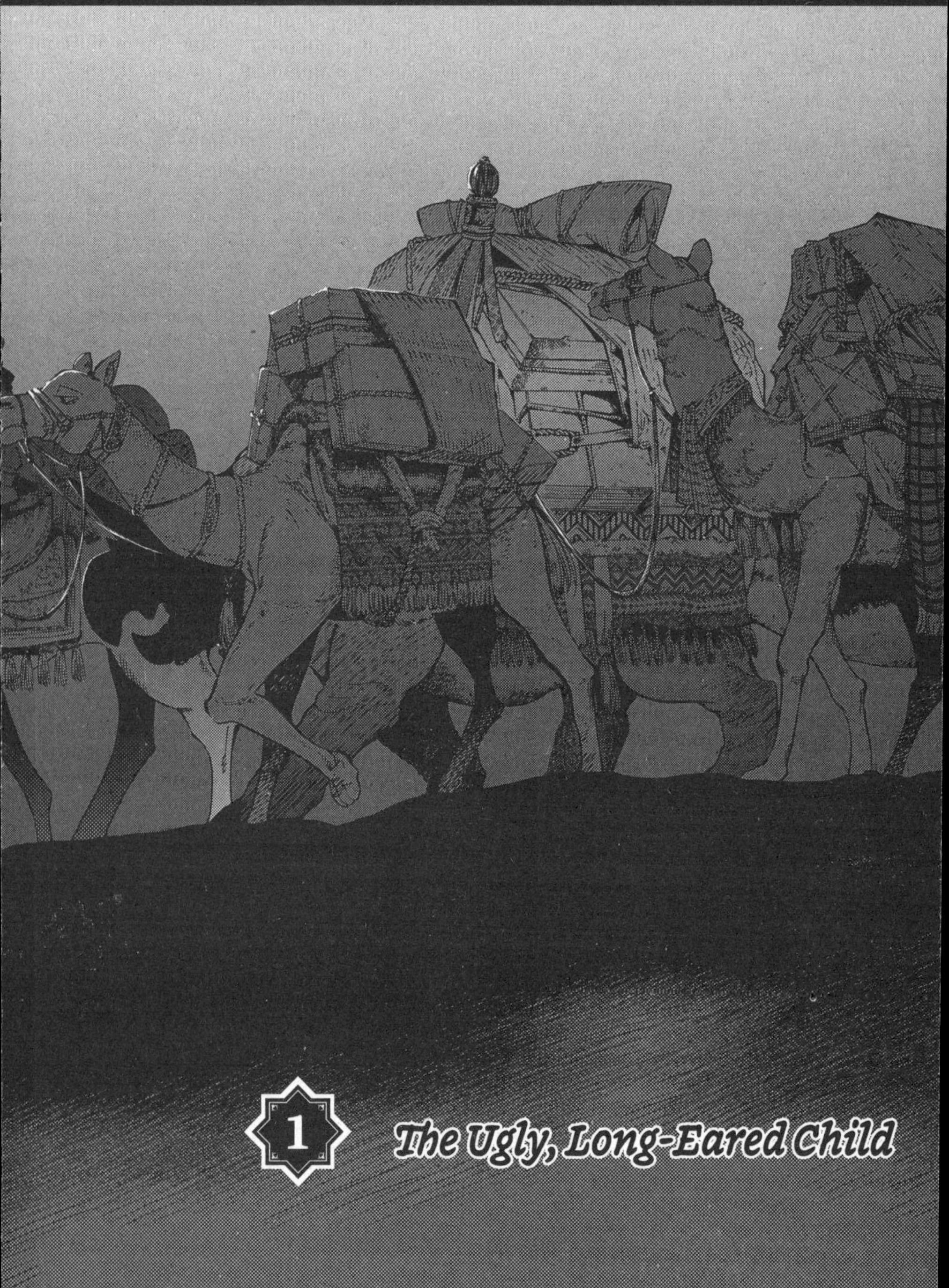

1 The Ugly, Long-Eared Child

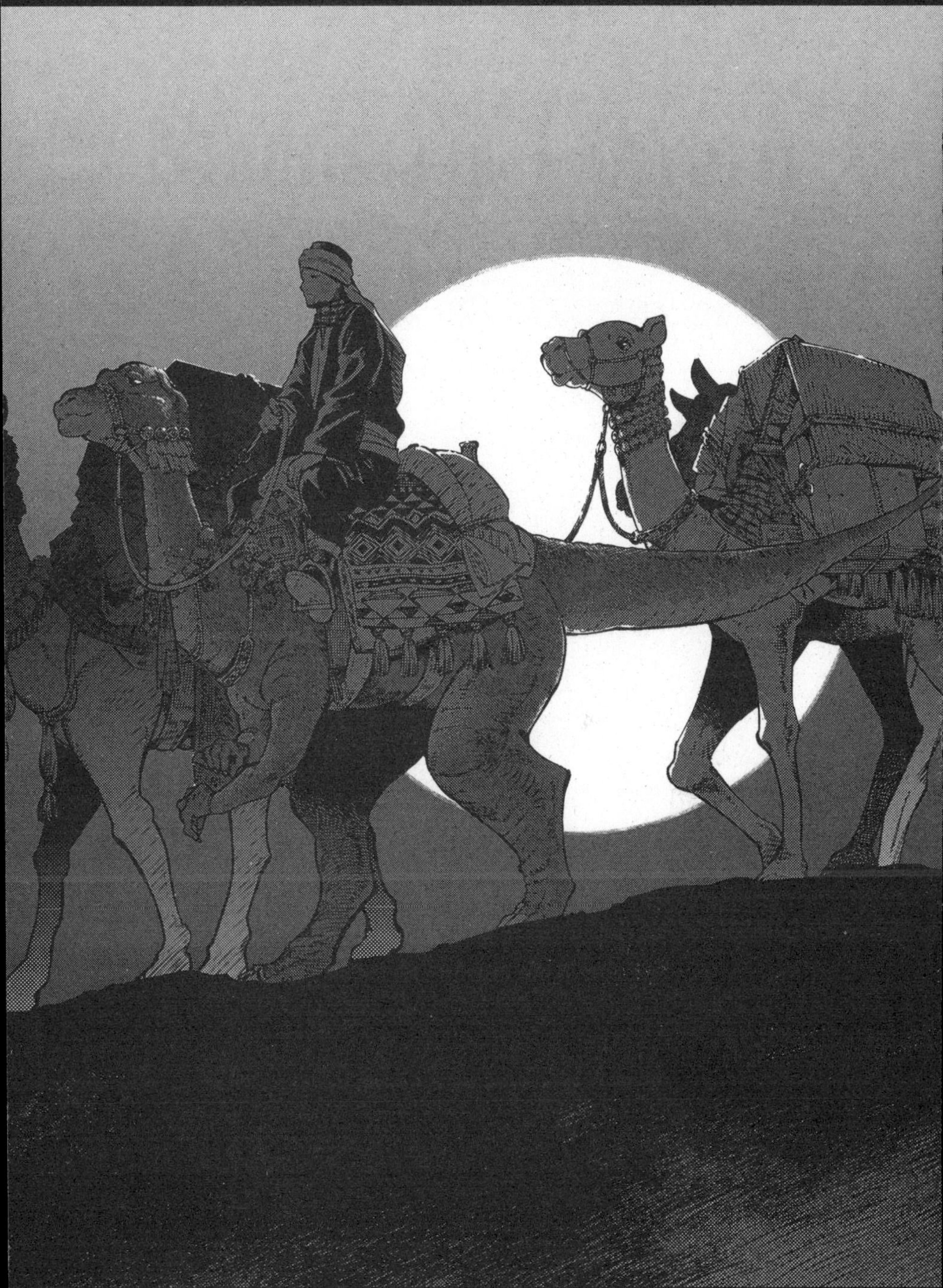

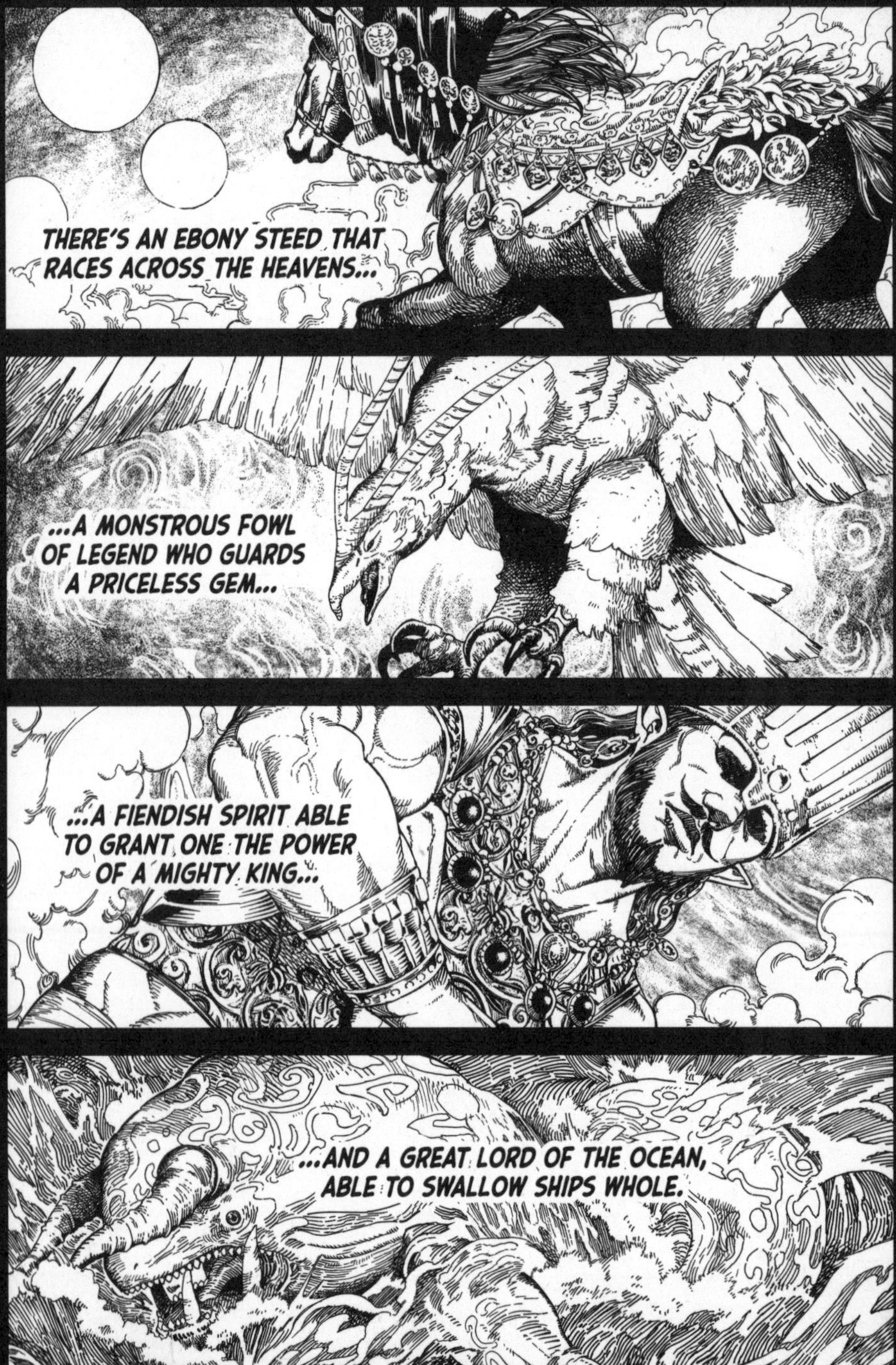
THERE'S AN EBONY STEED THAT RACES ACROSS THE HEAVENS...
...A MONSTROUS FOWL OF LEGEND WHO GUARDS A PRICELESS GEM...
...A FIENDISH SPIRIT ABLE TO GRANT ONE THE POWER OF A MIGHTY KING...
...AND A GREAT LORD OF THE OCEAN, ABLE TO SWALLOW SHIPS WHOLE.

AND SOMEWHERE BEYOND THE SEA...
...LIES A FORTUNE VAST ENOUGH TO RULE THE WORLD.

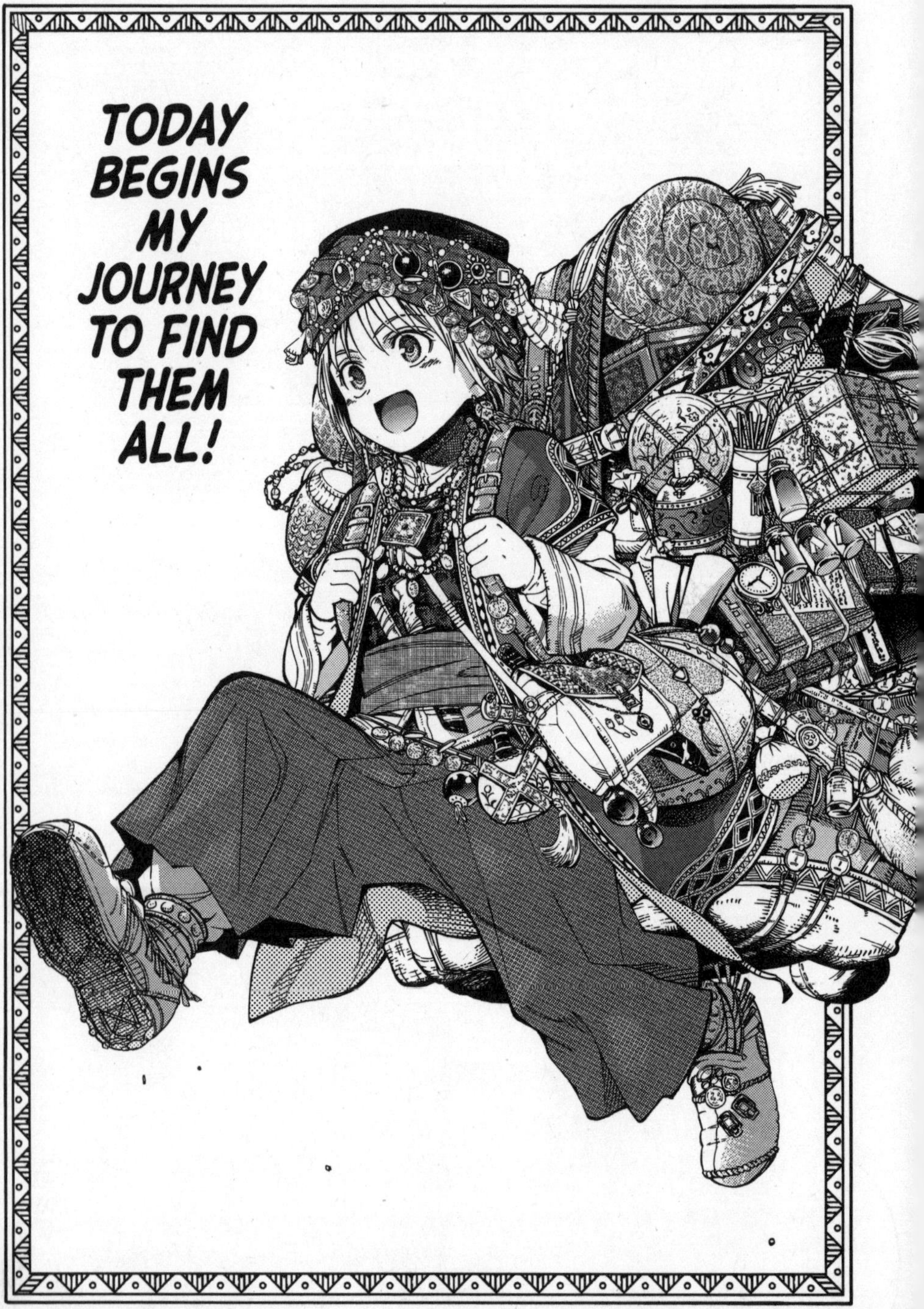
TODAY BEGINS MY JOURNEY TO FIND THEM ALL!

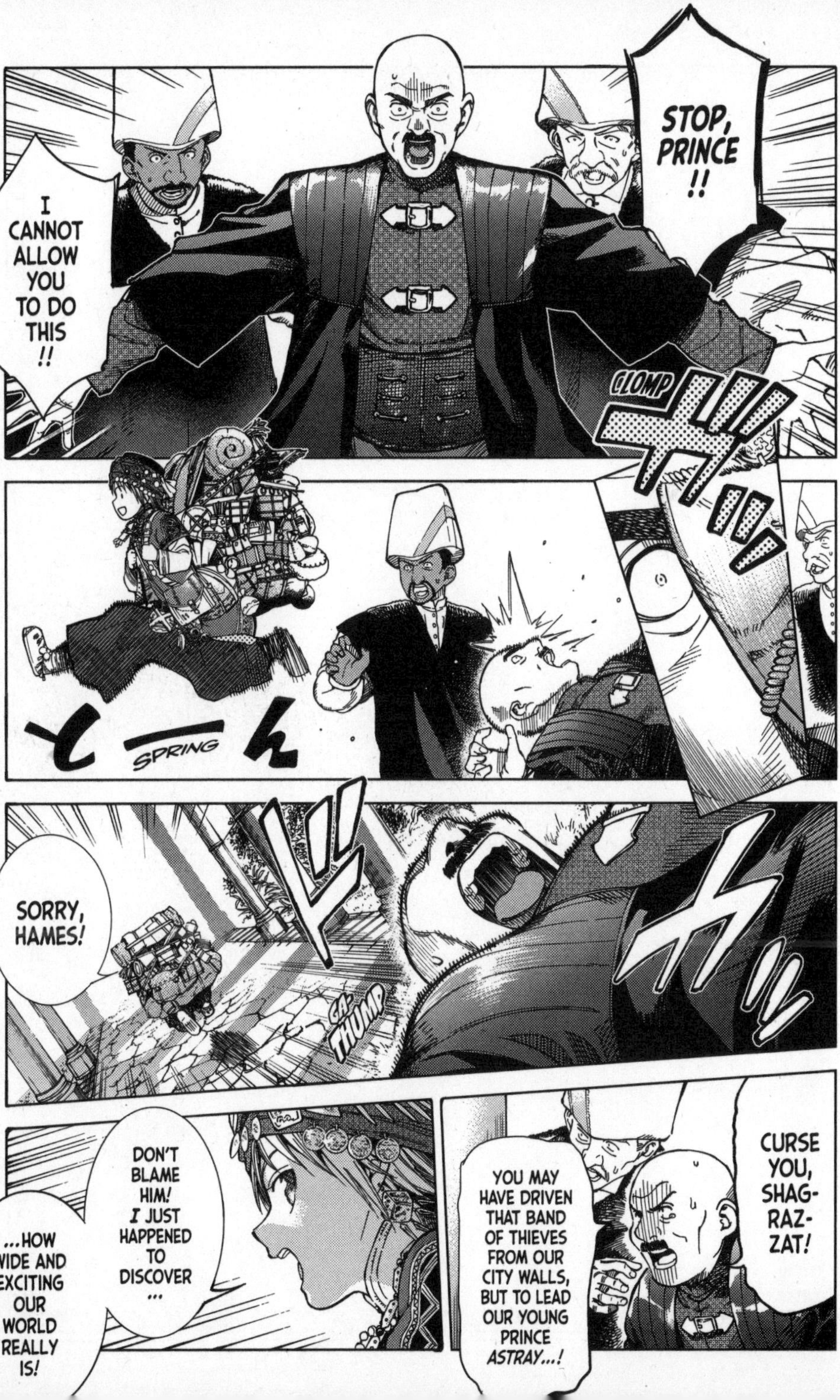
STOP, PRINCE!!
I CANNOT ALLOW YOU TO DO THIS!!
CLOMP
SPRING
GA-THUMP
SORRY, HAMES!
CURSE YOU, SHAG-RAZ-ZAT!
YOU MAY HAVE DRIVEN THAT BAND OF THIEVES FROM OUR CITY WALLS, BUT TO LEAD OUR YOUNG PRINCE *ASTRAY*...!
DON'T BLAME HIM! *I* JUST HAPPENED TO DISCOVER...
...HOW WIDE AND EXCITING OUR WORLD REALLY IS!

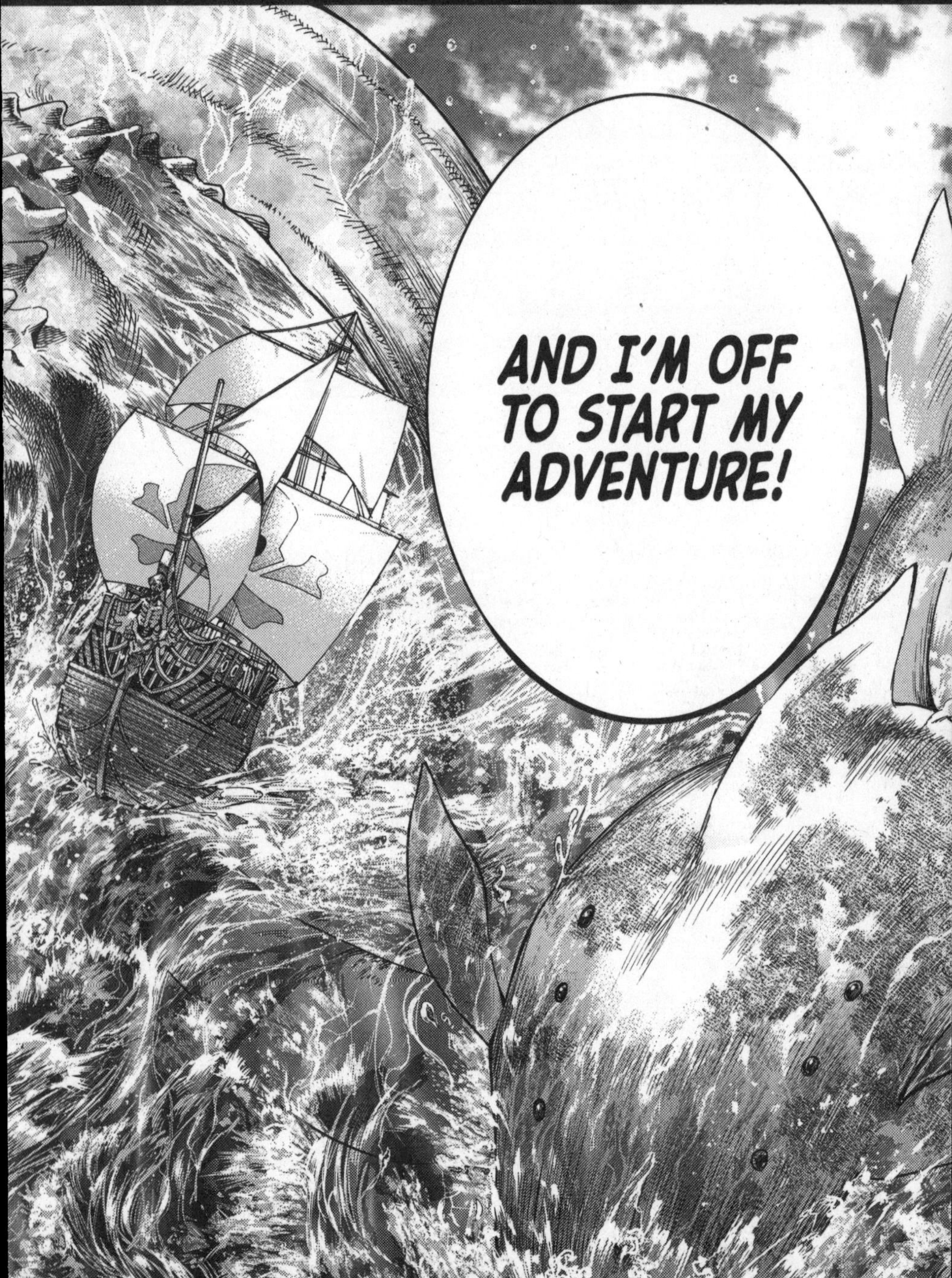
AND I'M OFF TO START MY ADVENTURE!

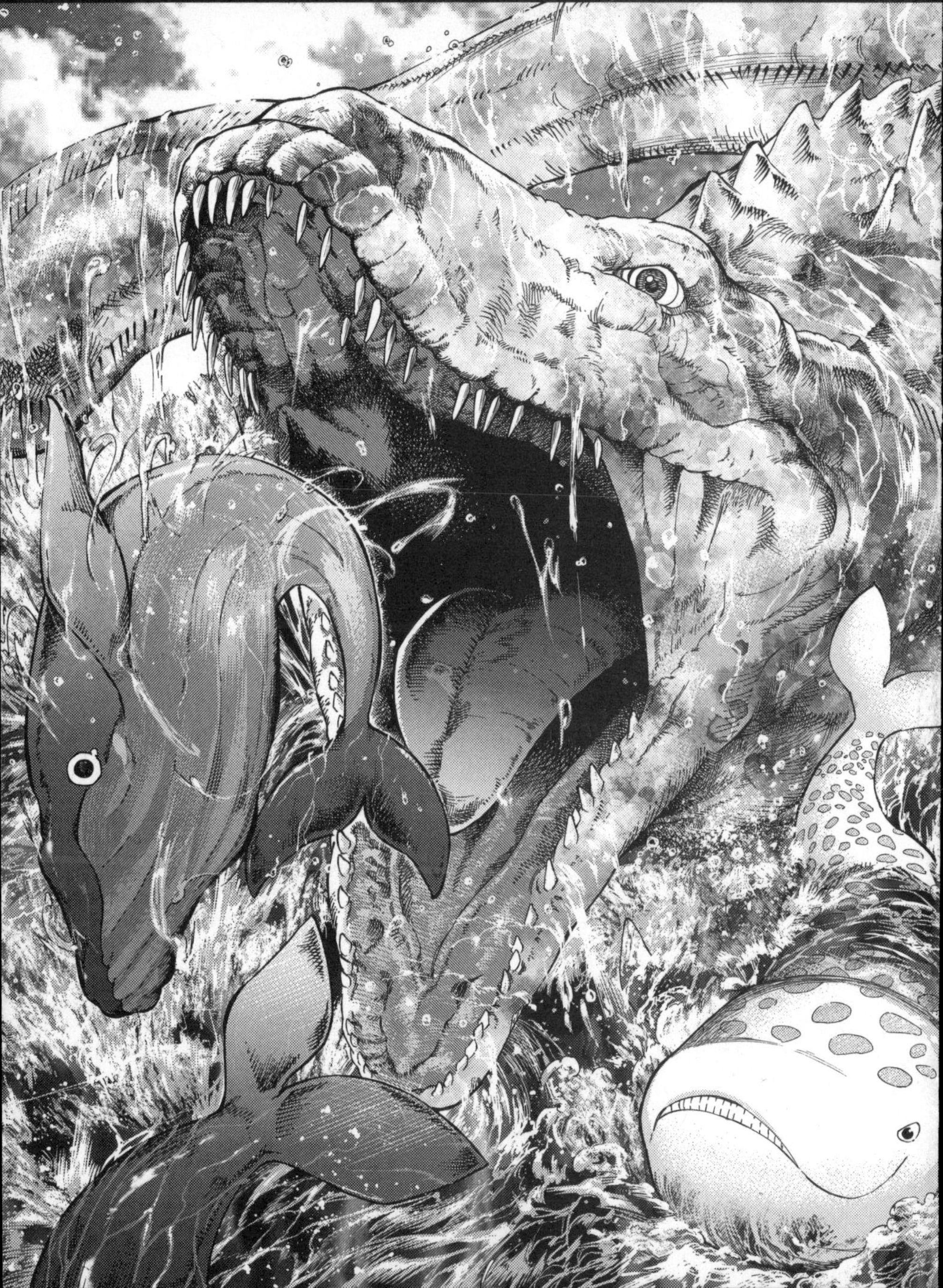

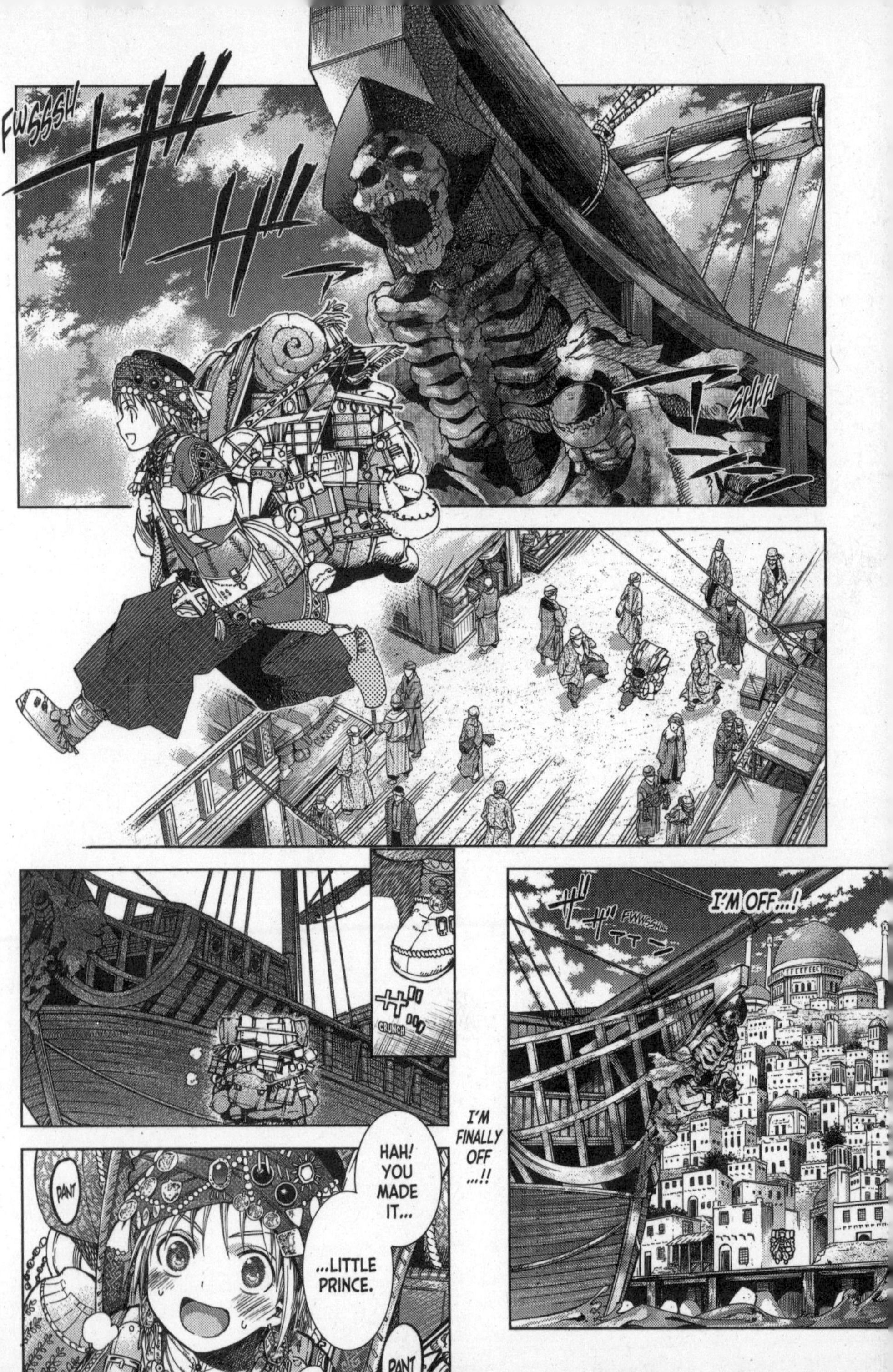
FWSSSH
I'M OFF...!
FWWSSH...
I'M FINALLY OFF ...!!
CRUNCH
PANT
HAH! YOU MADE IT...
...LITTLE PRINCE.
PANT

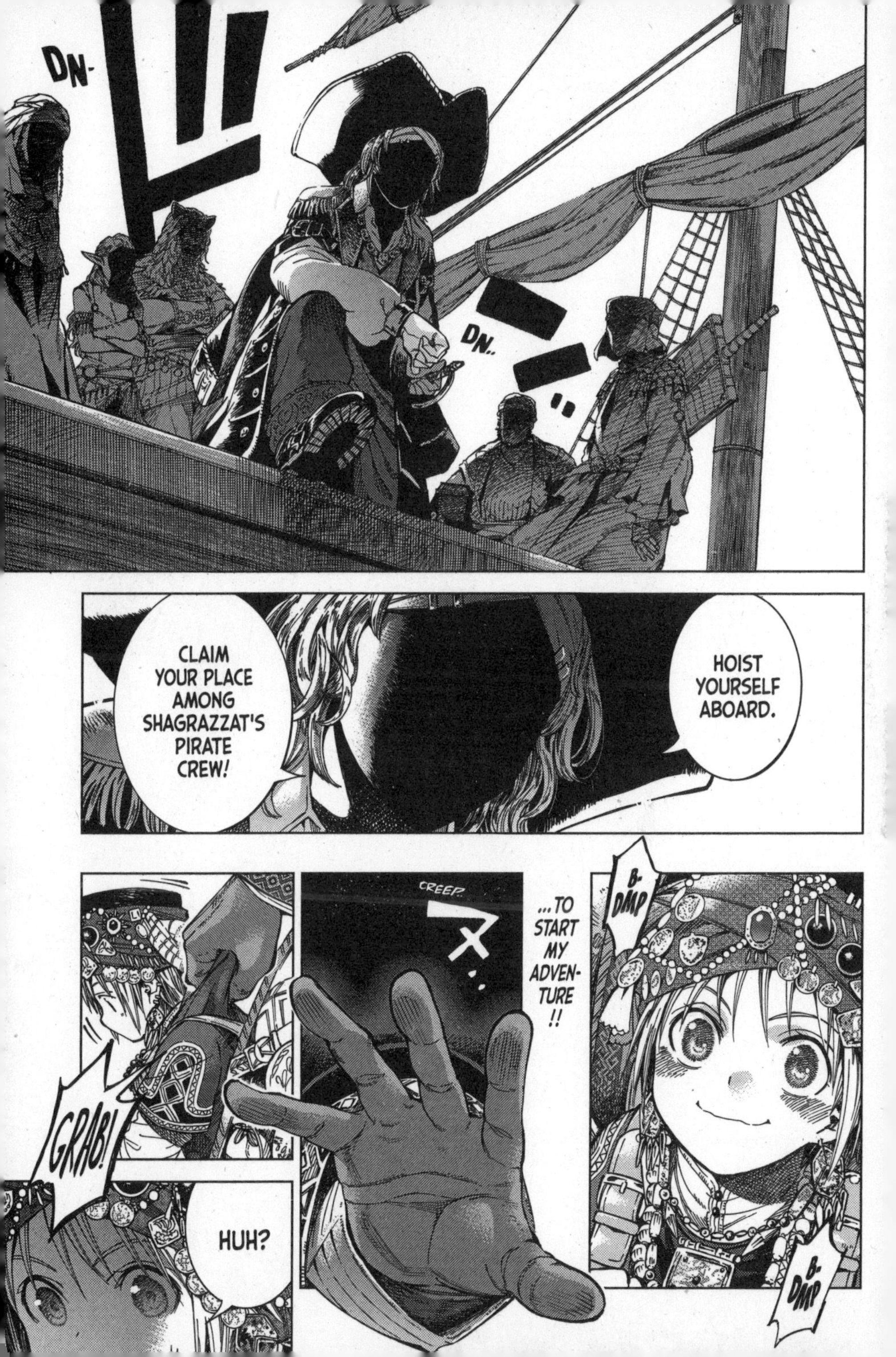

DN-
DN..
HOIST YOURSELF ABOARD.
CLAIM YOUR PLACE AMONG SHAGRAZZAT'S PIRATE CREW!
B-DMP
B-DMP
...TO START MY ADVENTURE !!
CREEP..
GRAB!
HUH?

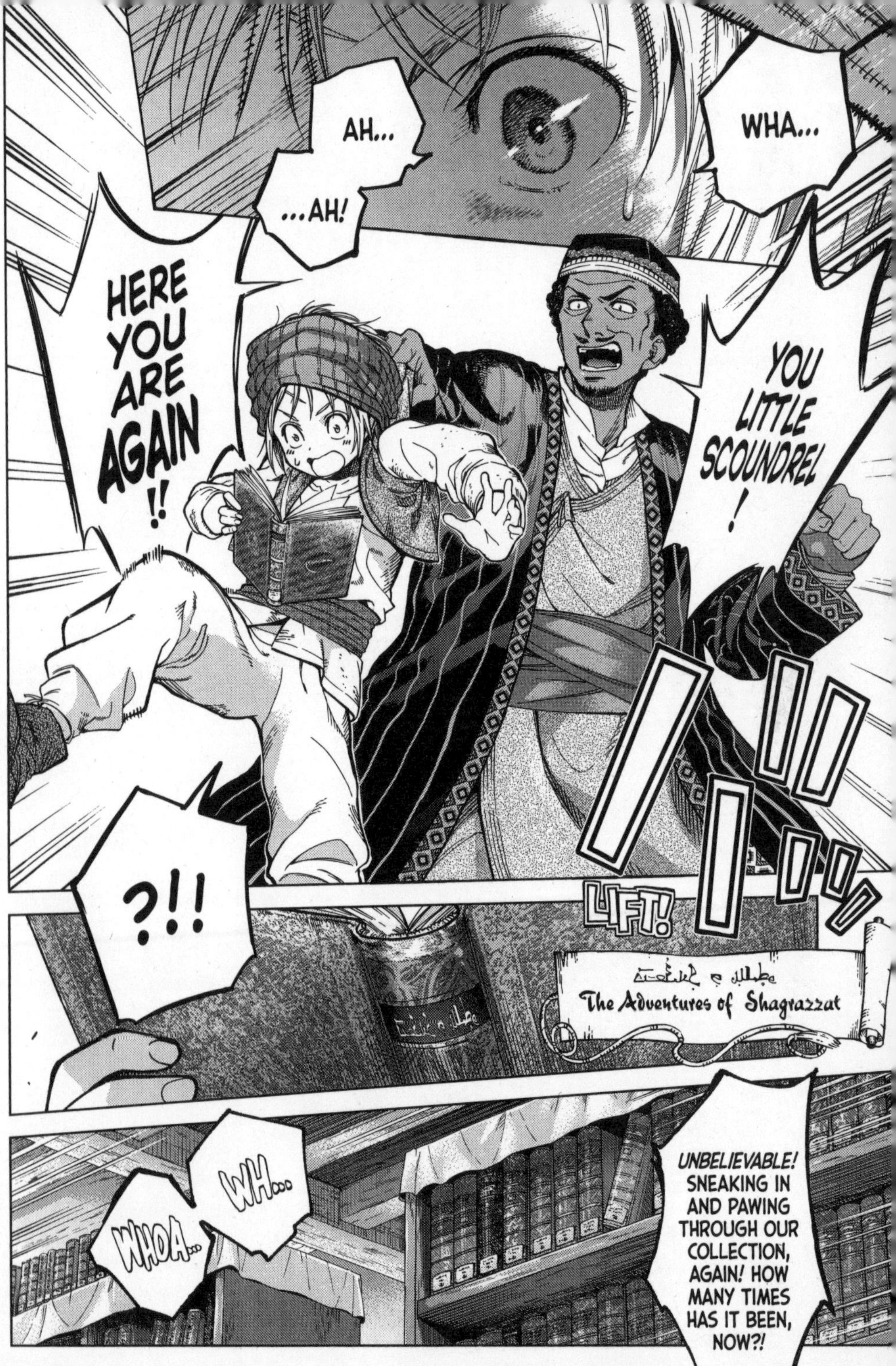
WHA...
AH...
...AH!
YOU LITTLE SCOUNDREL!
HERE YOU ARE AGAIN!!
LIFT!
The Adventures of Shagrazzat
?!!
UNBELIEVABLE! SNEAKING IN AND PAWING THROUGH OUR COLLECTION, AGAIN! HOW MANY TIMES HAS IT BEEN, NOW?!
WH...
WHOA...

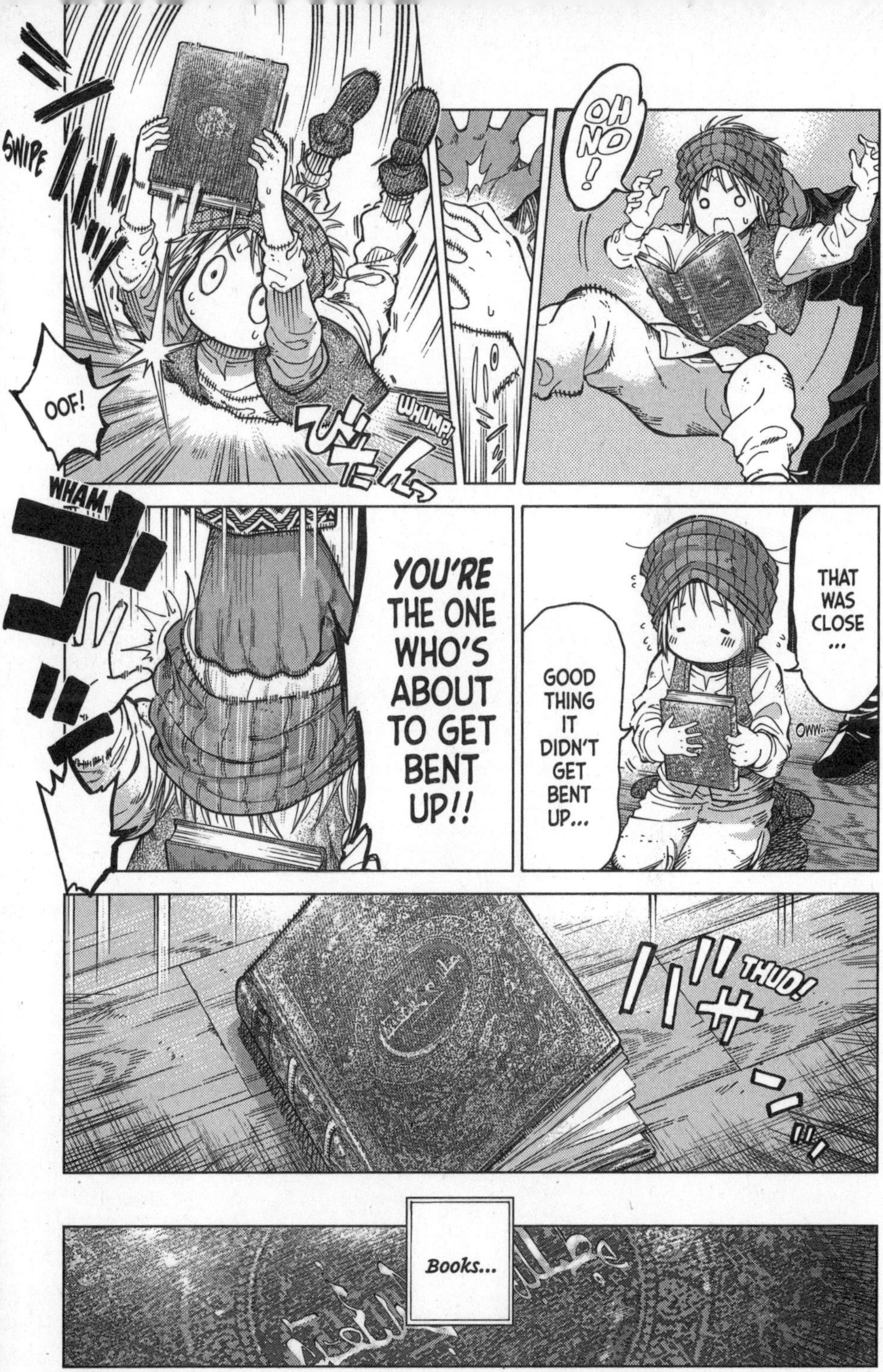
OH NO!
SWIPE
OOF!
WHUMP!
WHACK
THAT WAS CLOSE...
GOOD THING IT DIDN'T GET BENT UP...
OWW...
YOU'RE THE ONE WHO'S ABOUT TO GET BENT UP!!
WHAM
THUD!
Books...

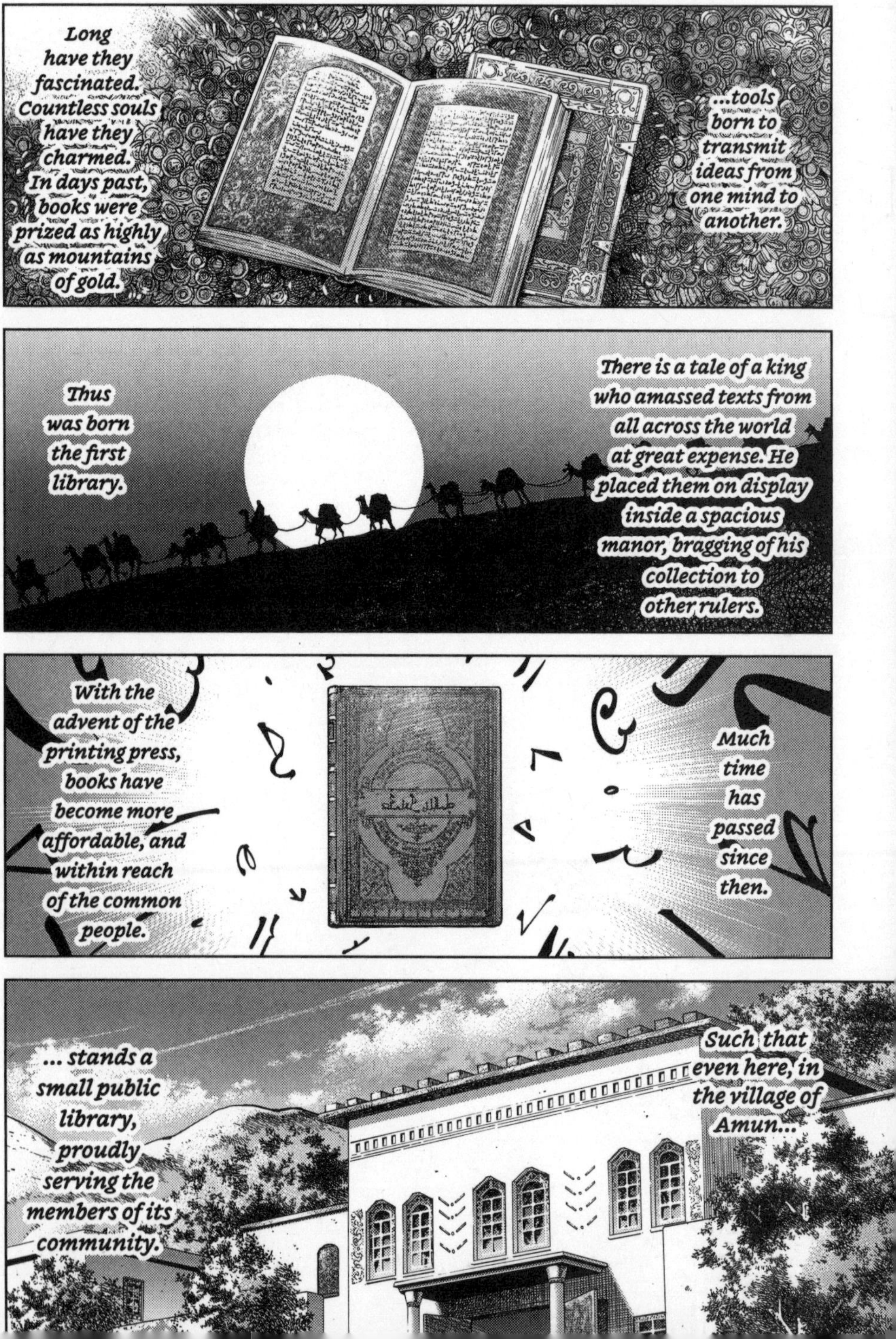
...tools born to transmit ideas from one mind to another.
Long have they fascinated. Countless souls have they charmed. In days past, books were prized as highly as mountains of gold.
There is a tale of a king who amassed texts from all across the world at great expense. He placed them on display inside a spacious manor, bragging of his collection to other rulers.
Thus was born the first library.
Much time has passed since then.
With the advent of the printing press, books have become more affordable, and within reach of the common people.
Such that even here, in the village of Amun...
... stands a small public library, proudly serving the members of its community.

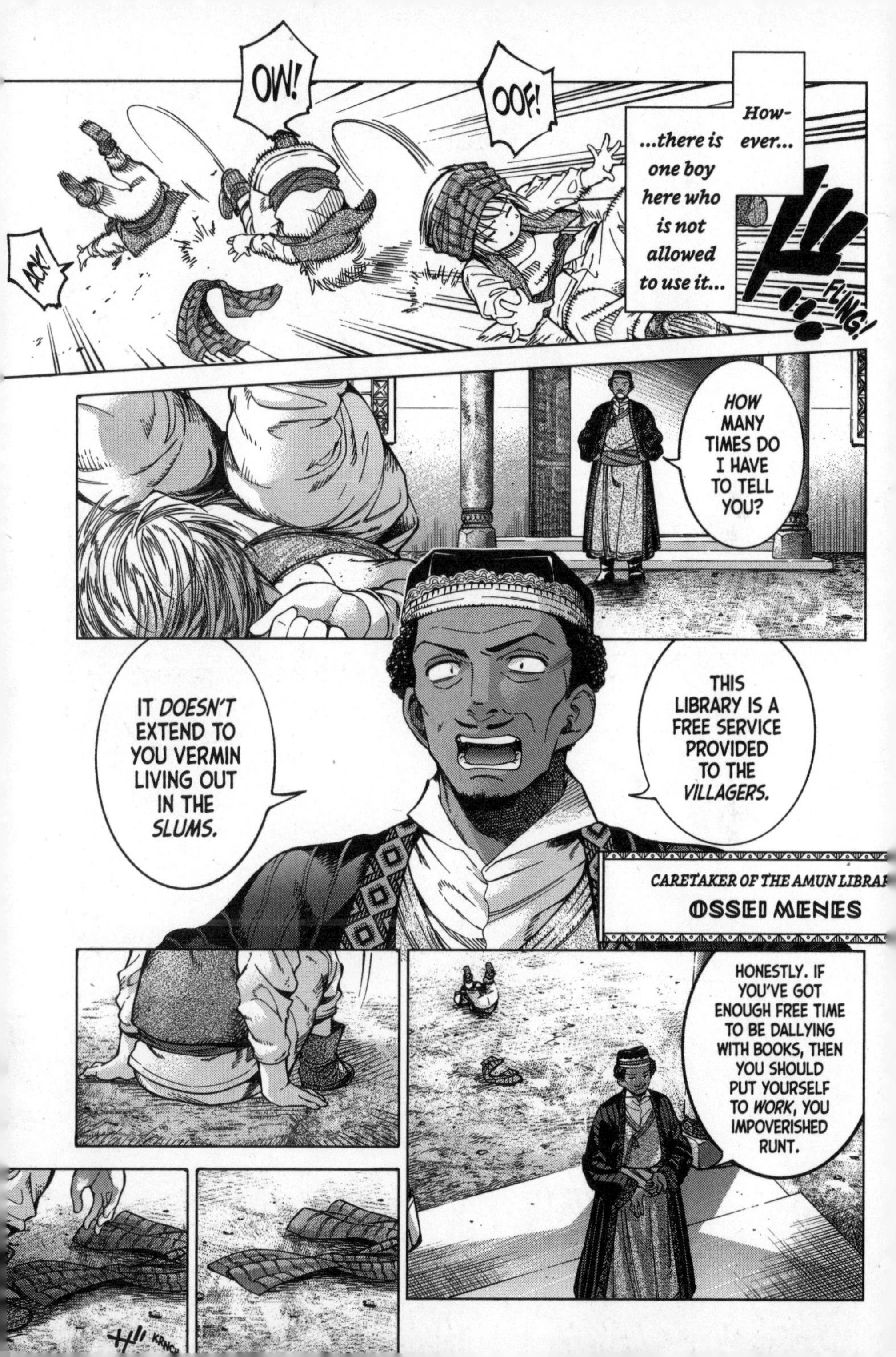
How- ever...
...there is one boy here who is not allowed to use it...
FLING!
OOF!
OW!
ACK!
HOW MANY TIMES DO I HAVE TO TELL YOU?
THIS LIBRARY IS A FREE SERVICE PROVIDED TO THE VILLAGERS.
IT DOESN'T EXTEND TO YOU VERMIN LIVING OUT IN THE SLUMS.
CARETAKER OF THE AMUN LIBRA
OSSEI MENES
HONESTLY. IF YOU'VE GOT ENOUGH FREE TIME TO BE DALLYING WITH BOOKS, THEN YOU SHOULD PUT YOURSELF TO WORK, YOU IMPOVERISHED RUNT.

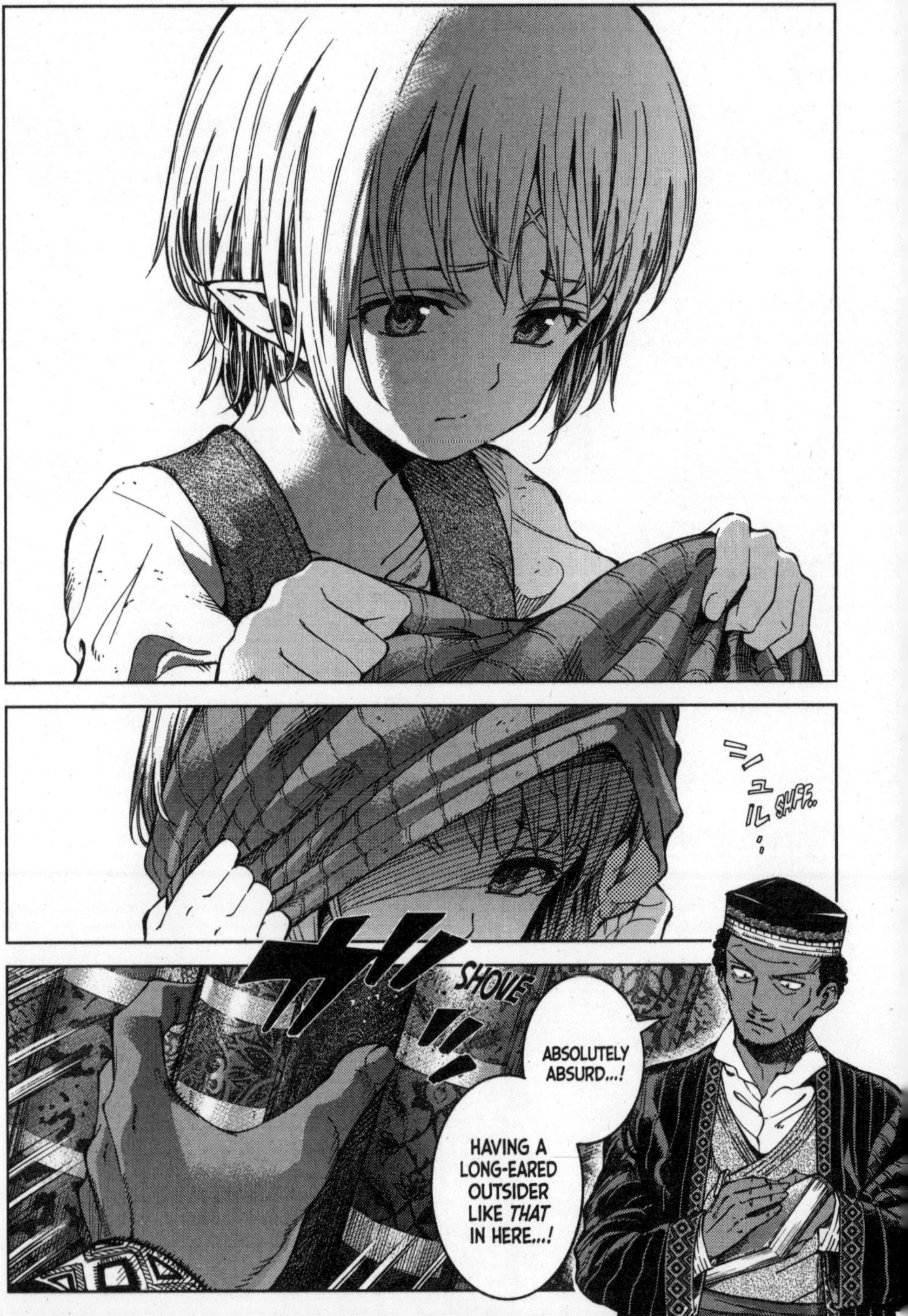
SHFF..
SHOVE
ABSOLUTELY ABSURD...!
HAVING A LONG-EARED OUTSIDER LIKE *THAT* IN HERE...!

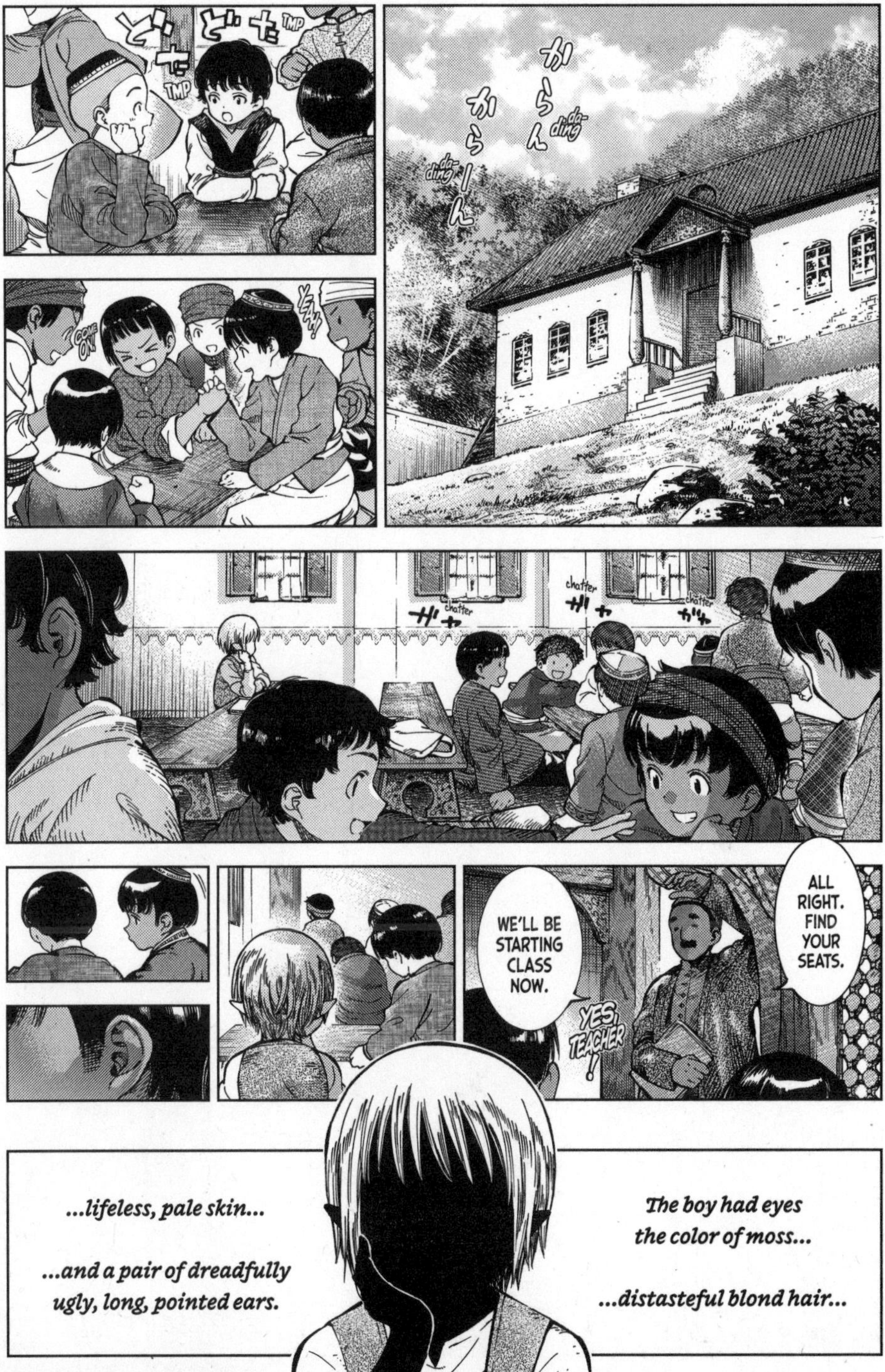

からん
da-ding
からーん
da-ding
どた
TMP
どた
TMP
COME ON
YEAH!
ガヤ
chatter
ガヤ
chatter
ALL RIGHT. FIND YOUR SEATS.
WE'LL BE STARTING CLASS NOW.
YES, TEACHER!
The boy had eyes the color of moss...
...distasteful blond hair...
...lifeless, pale skin...
...and a pair of dreadfully ugly, long, pointed ears.

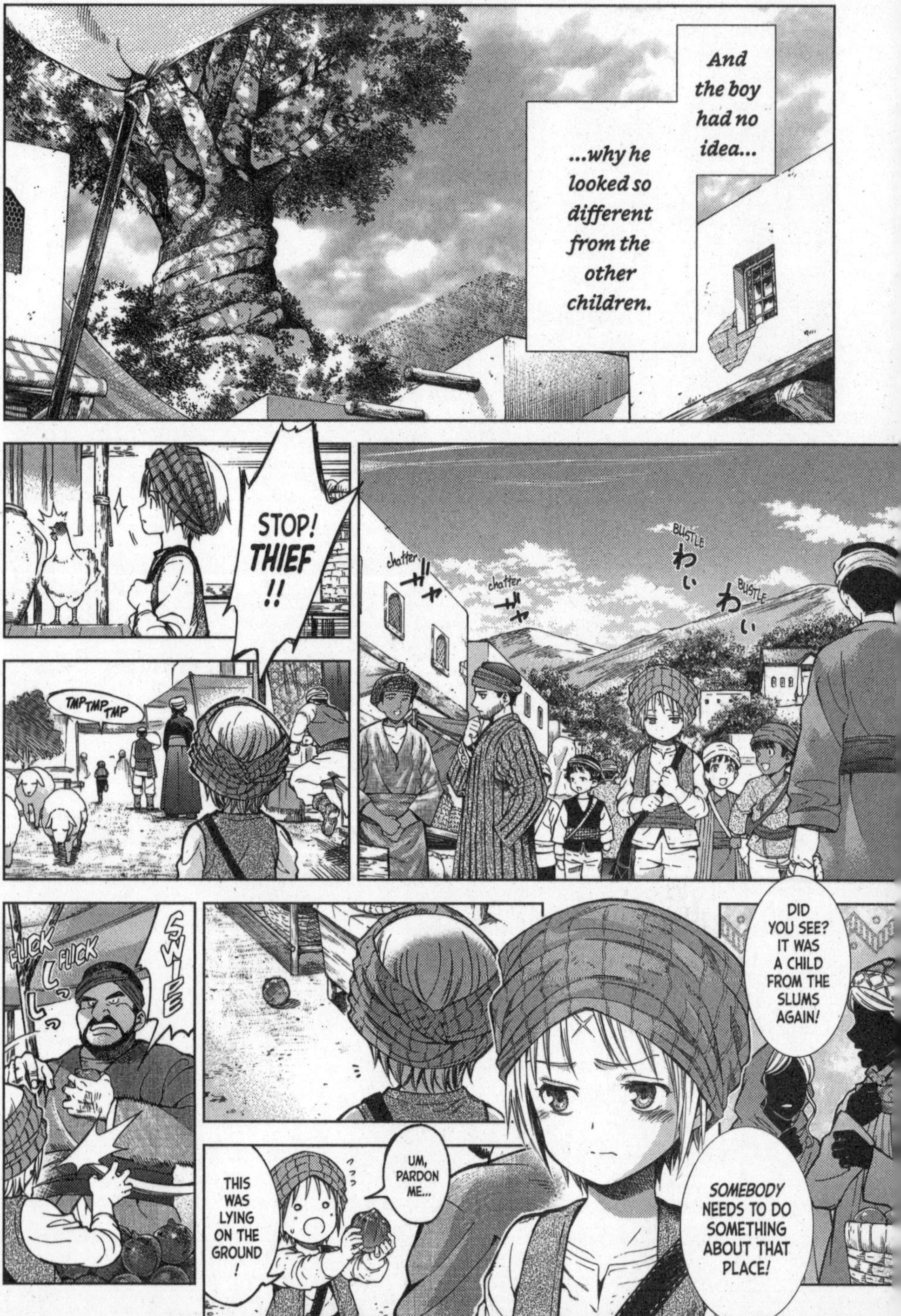
And the boy had no idea...
...why he looked so different from the other children.
BUSTLE わい
BUSTLE わい
chatter ザワ
chatter ザワ
STOP! THIEF !!
TMP TMP TMP
DID YOU SEE? IT WAS A CHILD FROM THE SLUMS AGAIN!
SOMEBODY NEEDS TO DO SOMETHING ABOUT THAT PLACE!
UM, PARDON ME...
THIS WAS LYING ON THE GROUND!
FLICK しっ
FLICK しっ
SWIPE

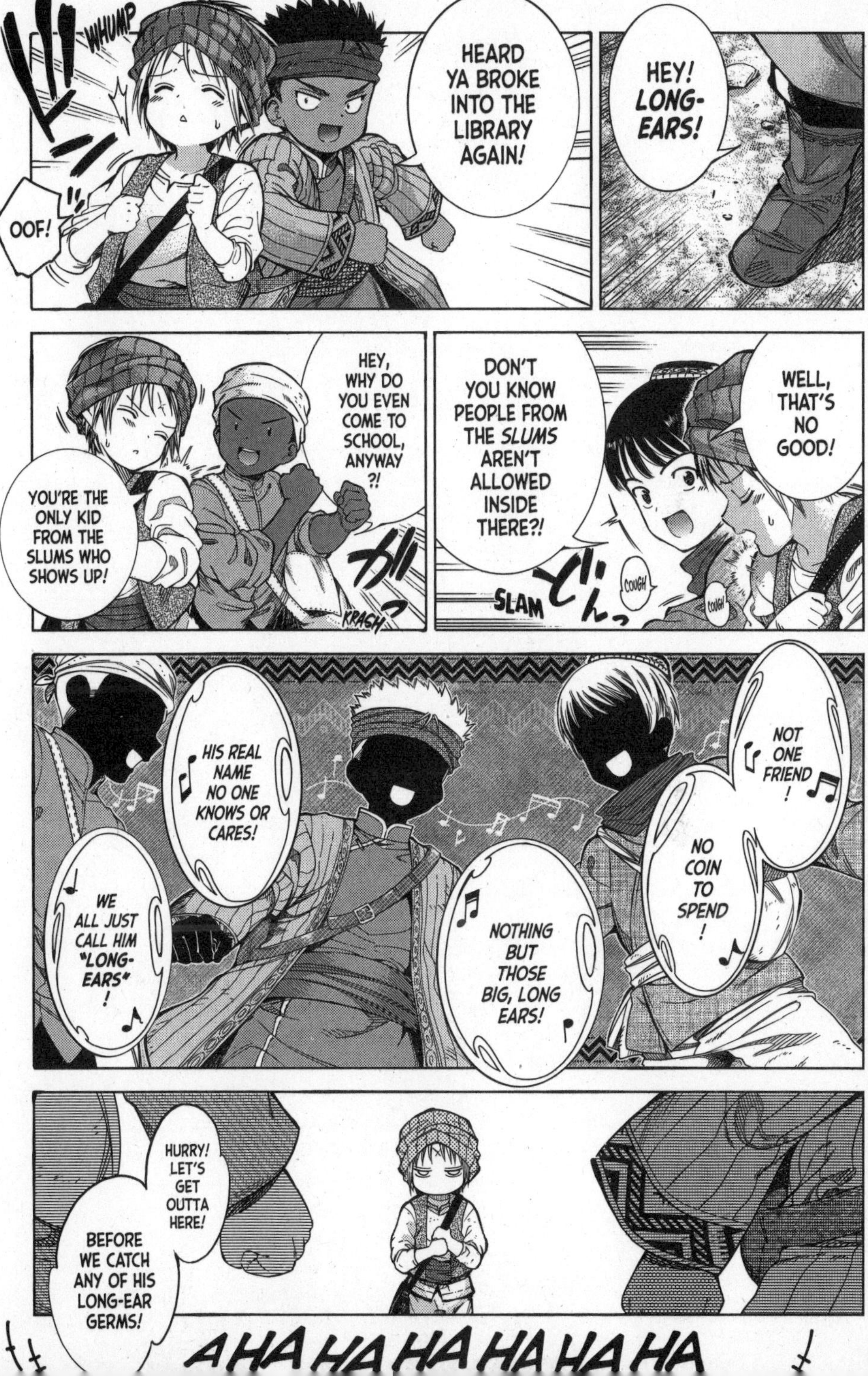
HEY! LONG-EARS!
HEARD YA BROKE INTO THE LIBRARY AGAIN!
WHUMP
OOF!
WELL, THAT'S NO GOOD!
DON'T YOU KNOW PEOPLE FROM THE SLUMS AREN'T ALLOWED INSIDE THERE?!
COUGH
COUGH
SLAM
HEY, WHY DO YOU EVEN COME TO SCHOOL, ANYWAY?!
YOU'RE THE ONLY KID FROM THE SLUMS WHO SHOWS UP!
KRASH
NOT ONE FRIEND!
NO COIN TO SPEND!
HIS REAL NAME NO ONE KNOWS OR CARES!
NOTHING BUT THOSE BIG, LONG EARS!
WE ALL JUST CALL HIM "LONG-EARS"!
HURRY! LET'S GET OUTTA HERE!
BEFORE WE CATCH ANY OF HIS LONG-EAR GERMS!
AHAHAHAHAHAHAHAHA

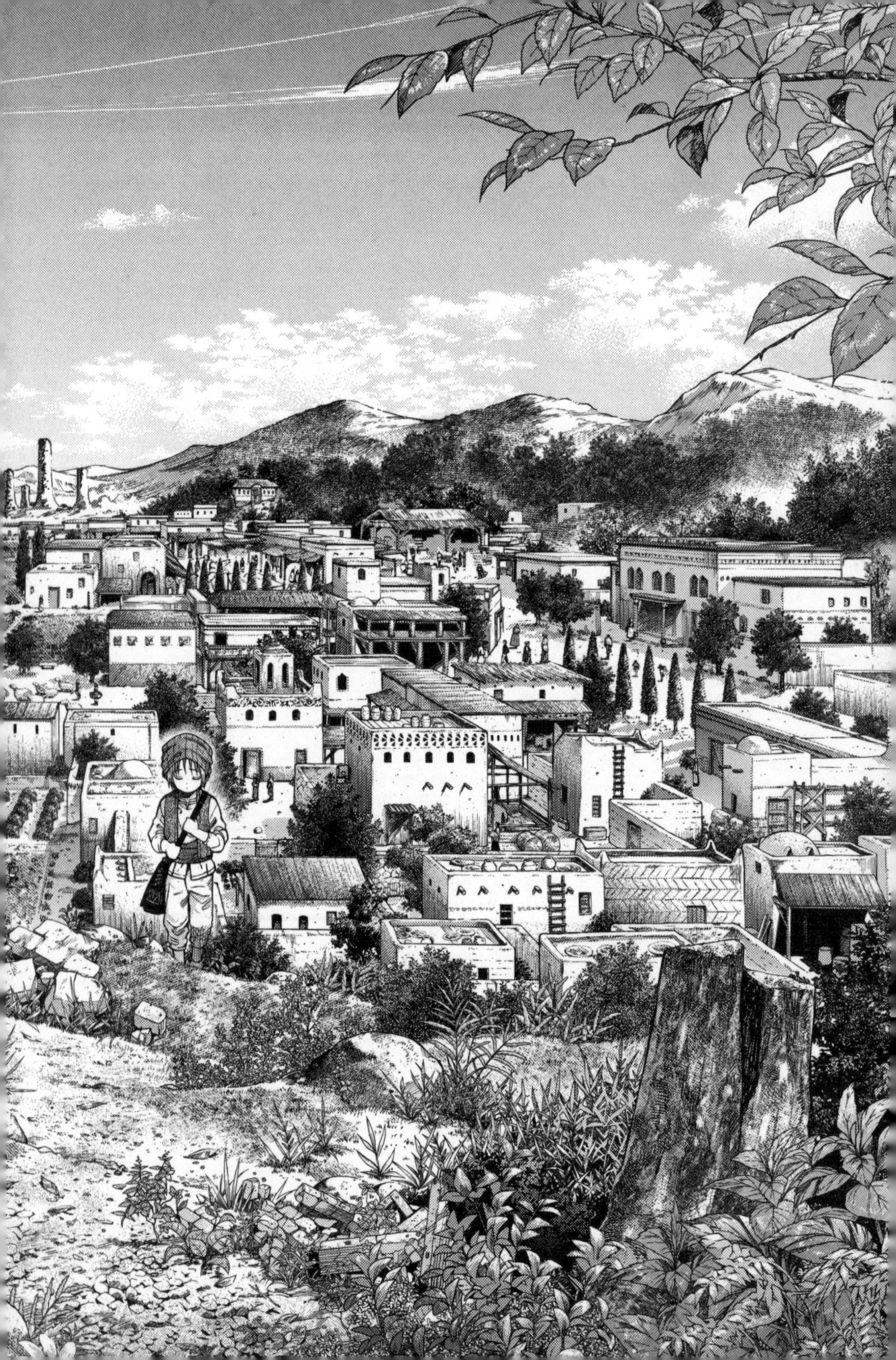

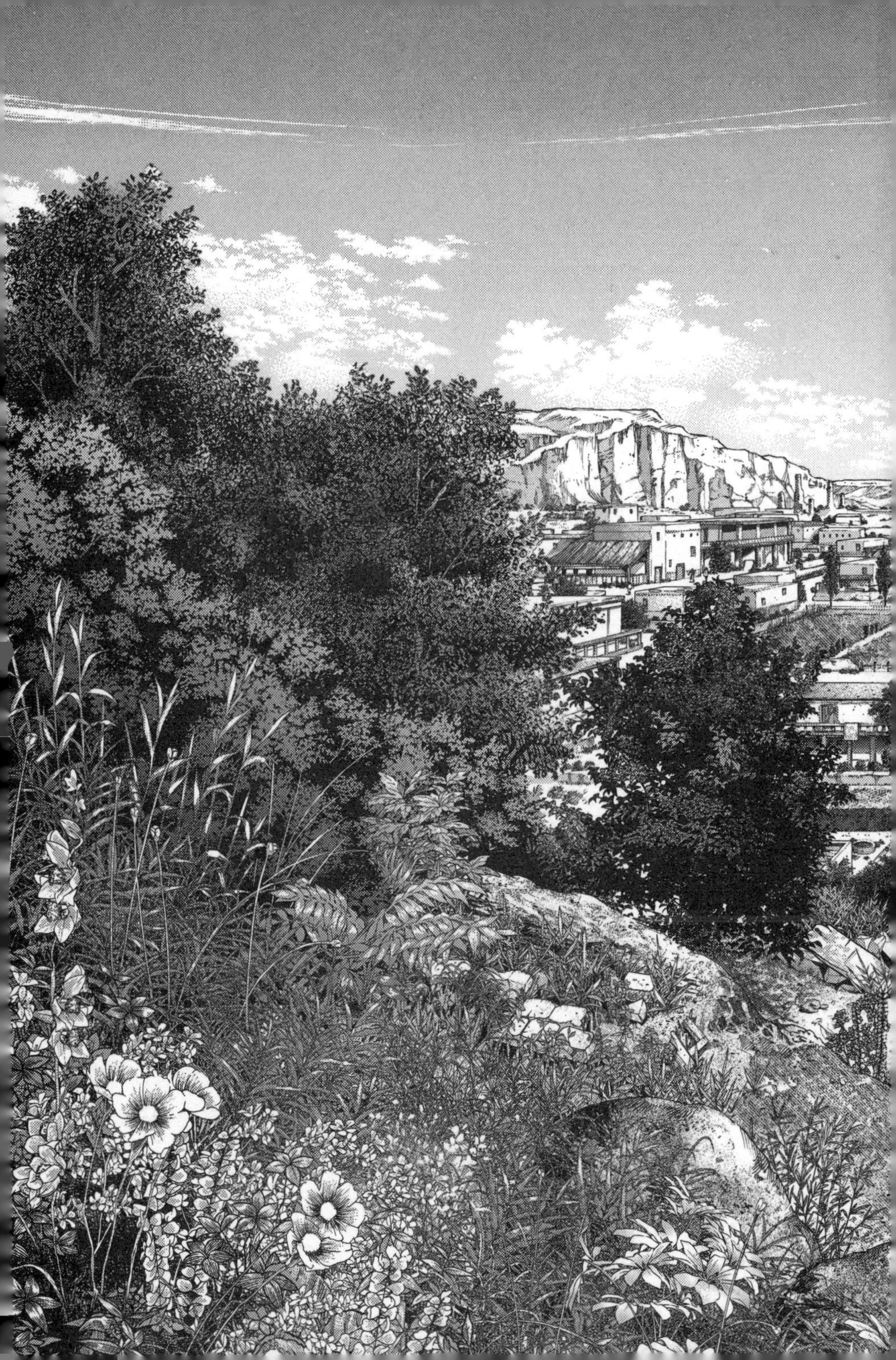

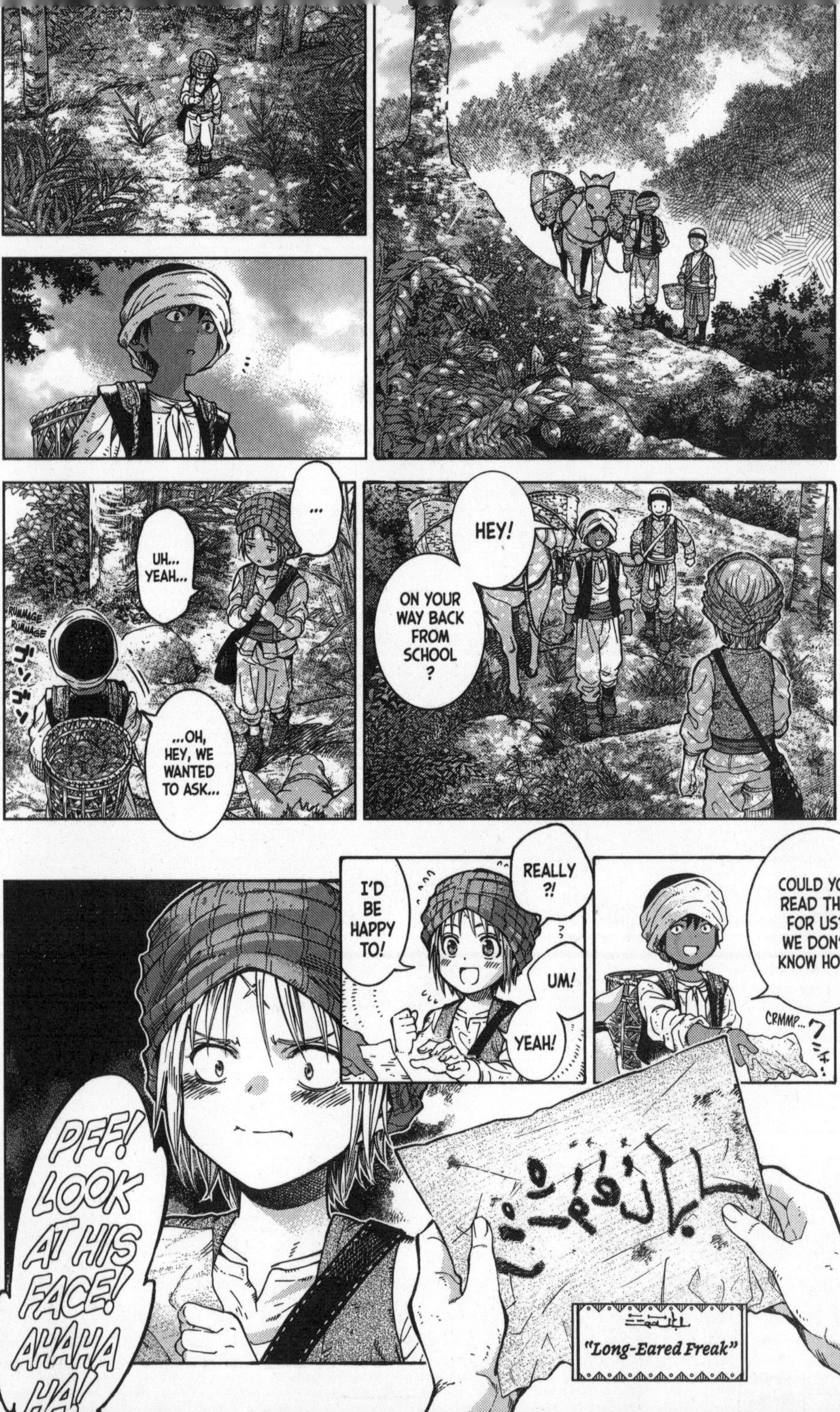
HEY!
ON YOUR WAY BACK FROM SCHOOL ?
...
UH... YEAH...
RUMMAGE RUMMAGE
...OH, HEY, WE WANTED TO ASK...
COULD YOU READ THIS FOR US? WE DON'T KNOW HOW.
CRMMP...
REALLY ?!
I'D BE HAPPY TO!
UM!
YEAH!
PFF! LOOK AT HIS FACE! AHAHAHA!
"Long-Eared Freak"

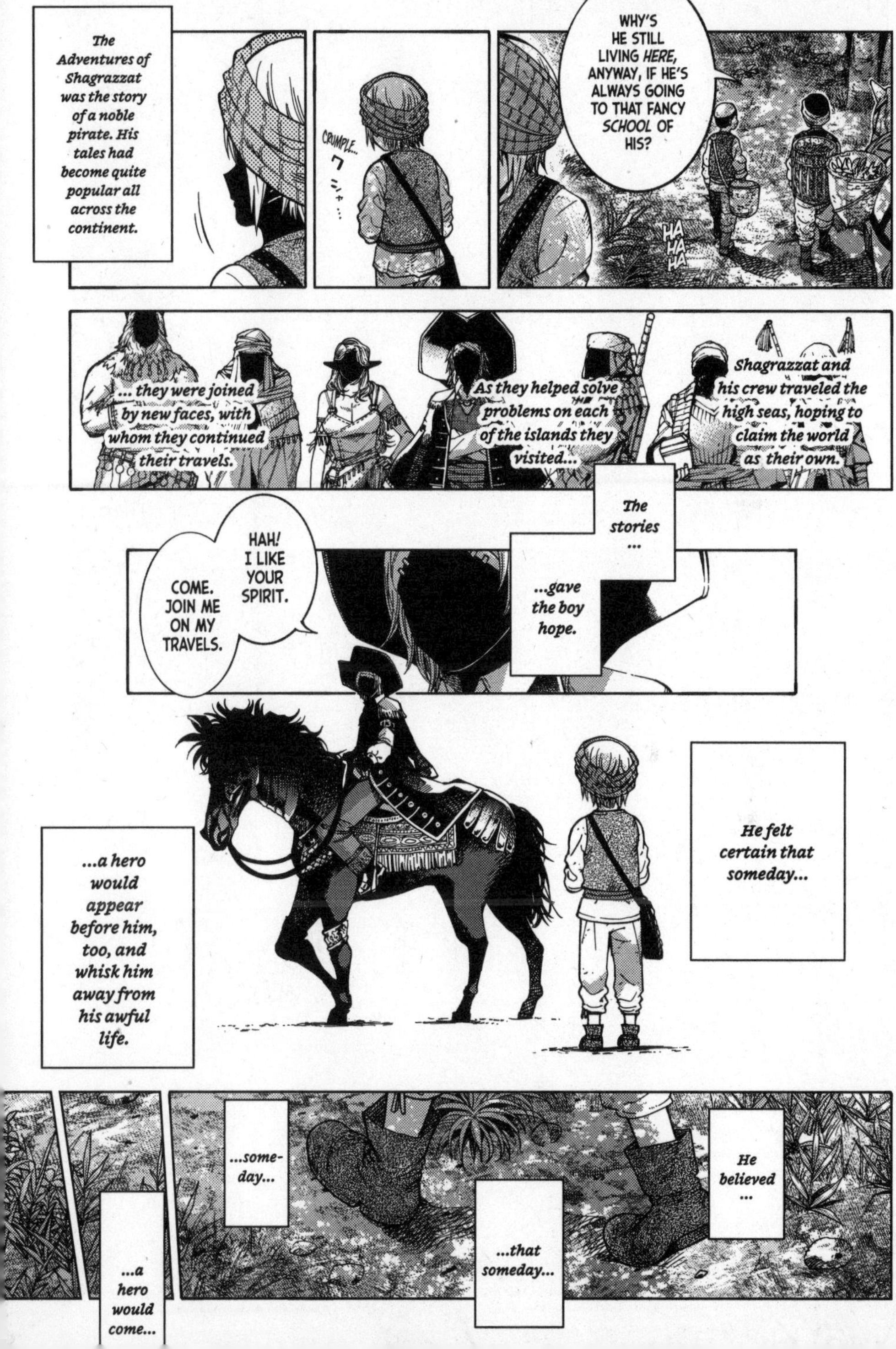
WHY'S HE STILL LIVING *HERE*, ANYWAY, IF HE'S ALWAYS GOING TO THAT FANCY *SCHOOL* OF HIS?
HA HA HA
CRUMPLE...
The Adventures of Shagrazzat was the story of a noble pirate. His tales had become quite popular all across the continent.
Shagrazzat and his crew traveled the high seas, hoping to claim the world as their own.
As they helped solve problems on each of the islands they visited...
... they were joined by new faces, with whom they continued their travels.
The stories ...
...gave the boy hope.
HAH! I LIKE YOUR SPIRIT.
COME. JOIN ME ON MY TRAVELS.
He felt certain that someday...
...a hero would appear before him, too, and whisk him away from his awful life.
He believed ...
...that someday...
...some-day...
...a hero would come...

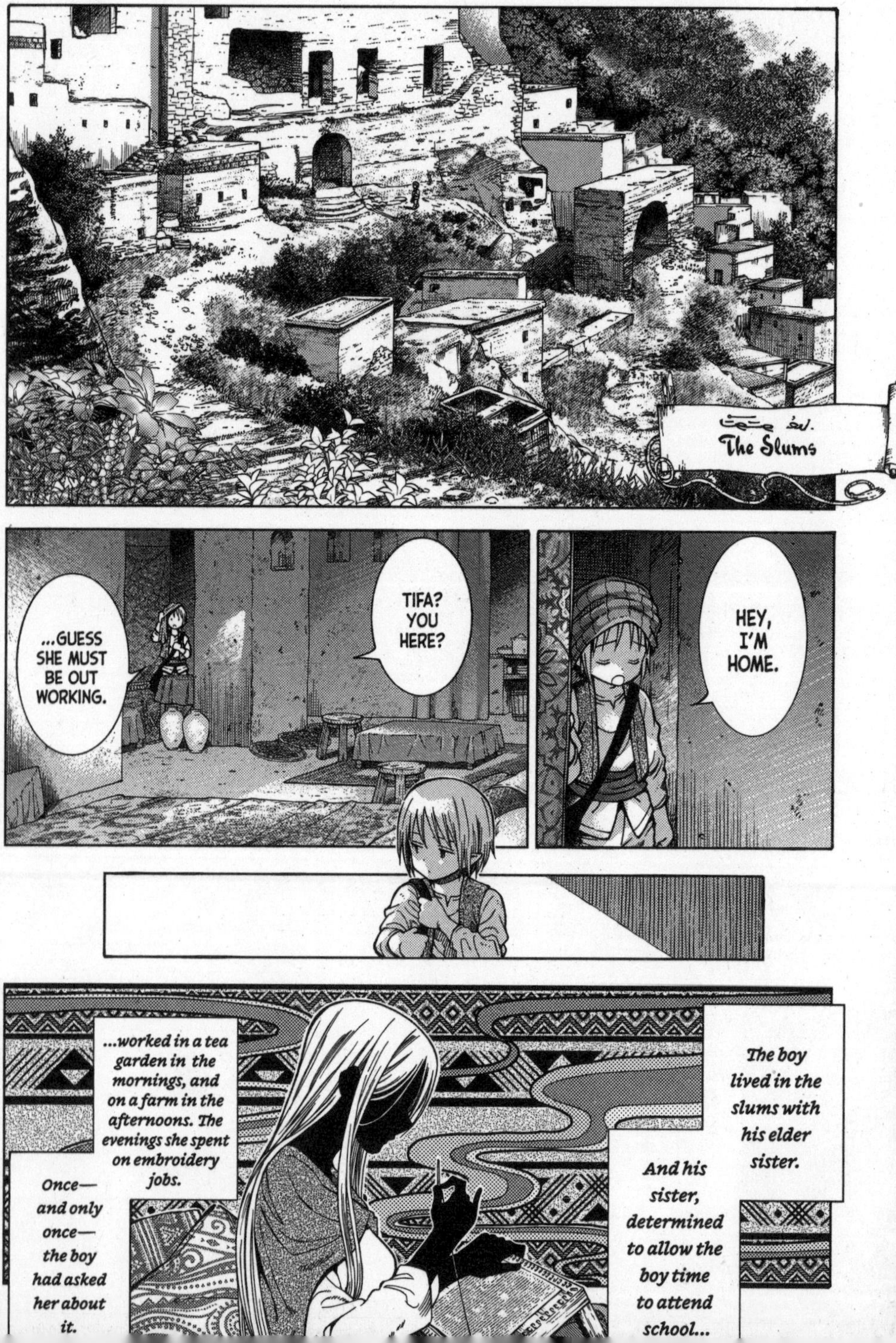
The Slums
HEY, I'M HOME.
TIFA? YOU HERE?
...GUESS SHE MUST BE OUT WORKING.
The boy lived in the slums with his elder sister.
And his sister, determined to allow the boy time to attend school...
...worked in a tea garden in the mornings, and on a farm in the afternoons. The evenings she spent on embroidery jobs.
Once—and only once—the boy had asked her about it.

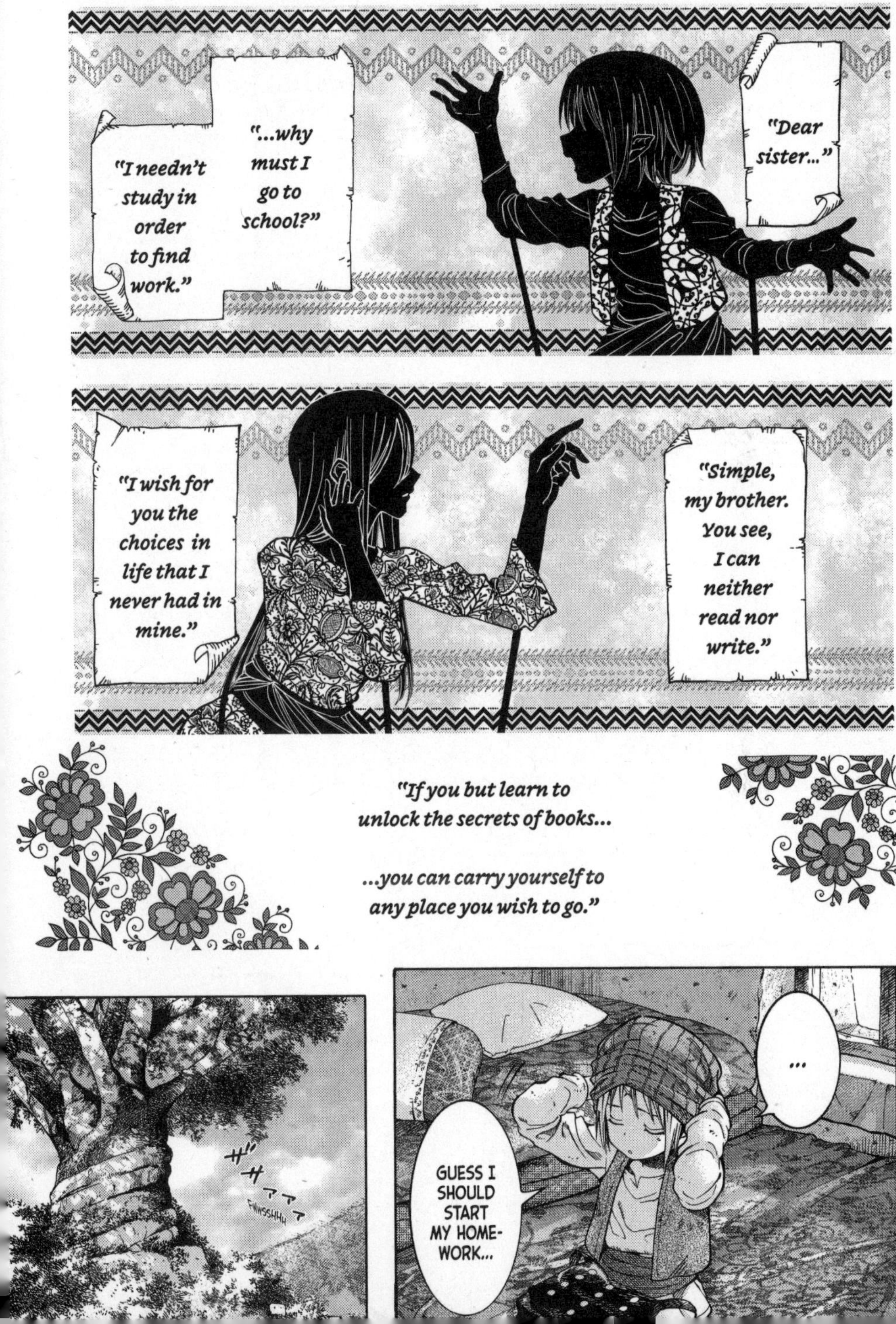
"Dear sister..."
"...why must I go to school?"
"I needn't study in order to find work."
"Simple, my brother. You see, I can neither read nor write."
"I wish for you the choices in life that I never had in mine."
"If you but learn to unlock the secrets of books...
...you can carry yourself to any place you wish to go."
...
GUESS I SHOULD START MY HOME-WORK...
ザザァァァ
FWWSSHHH

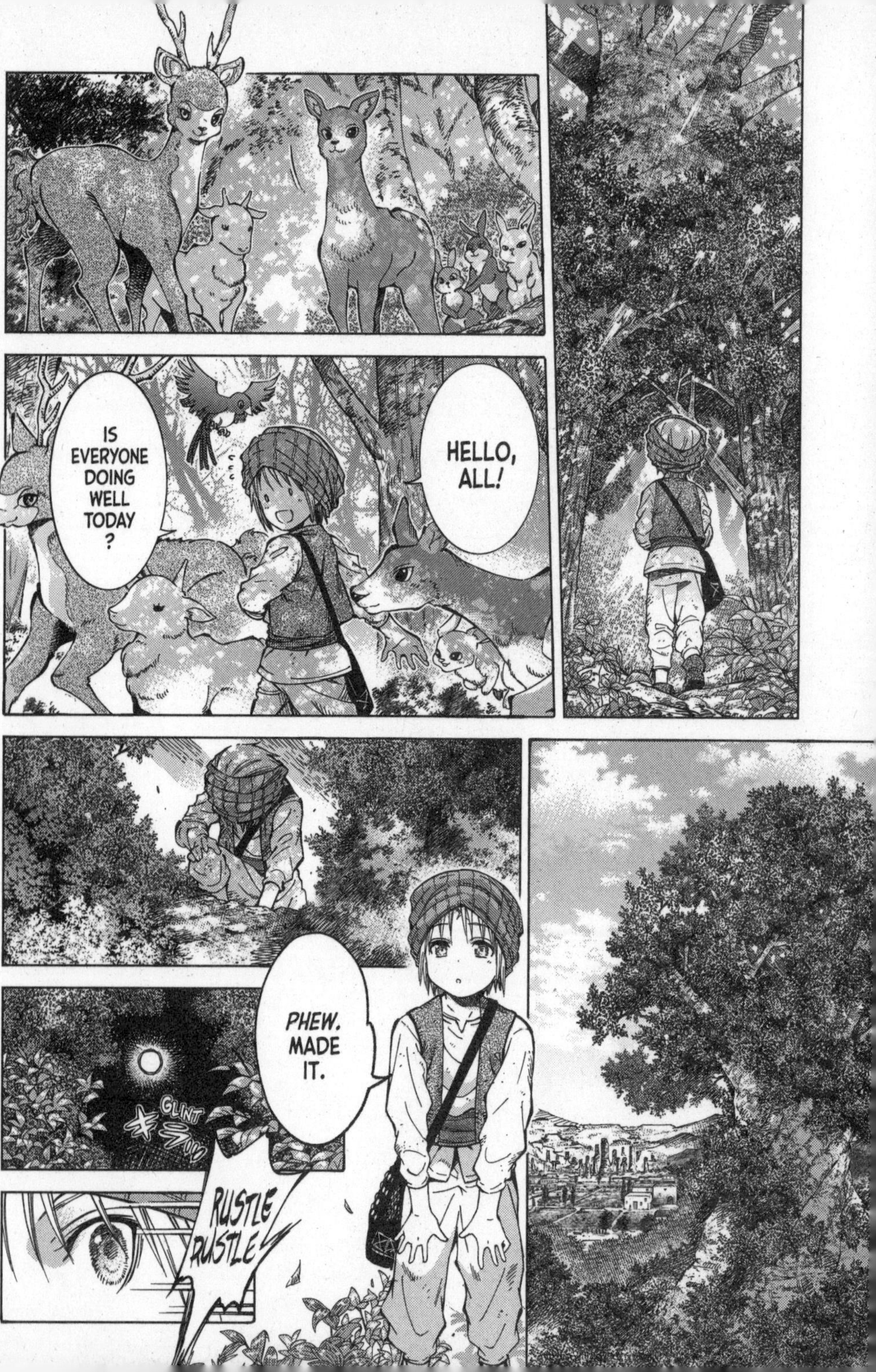
HELLO, ALL!
IS EVERYONE DOING WELL TODAY?
PHEW. MADE IT.
GLINT
RUSTLE RUSTLE

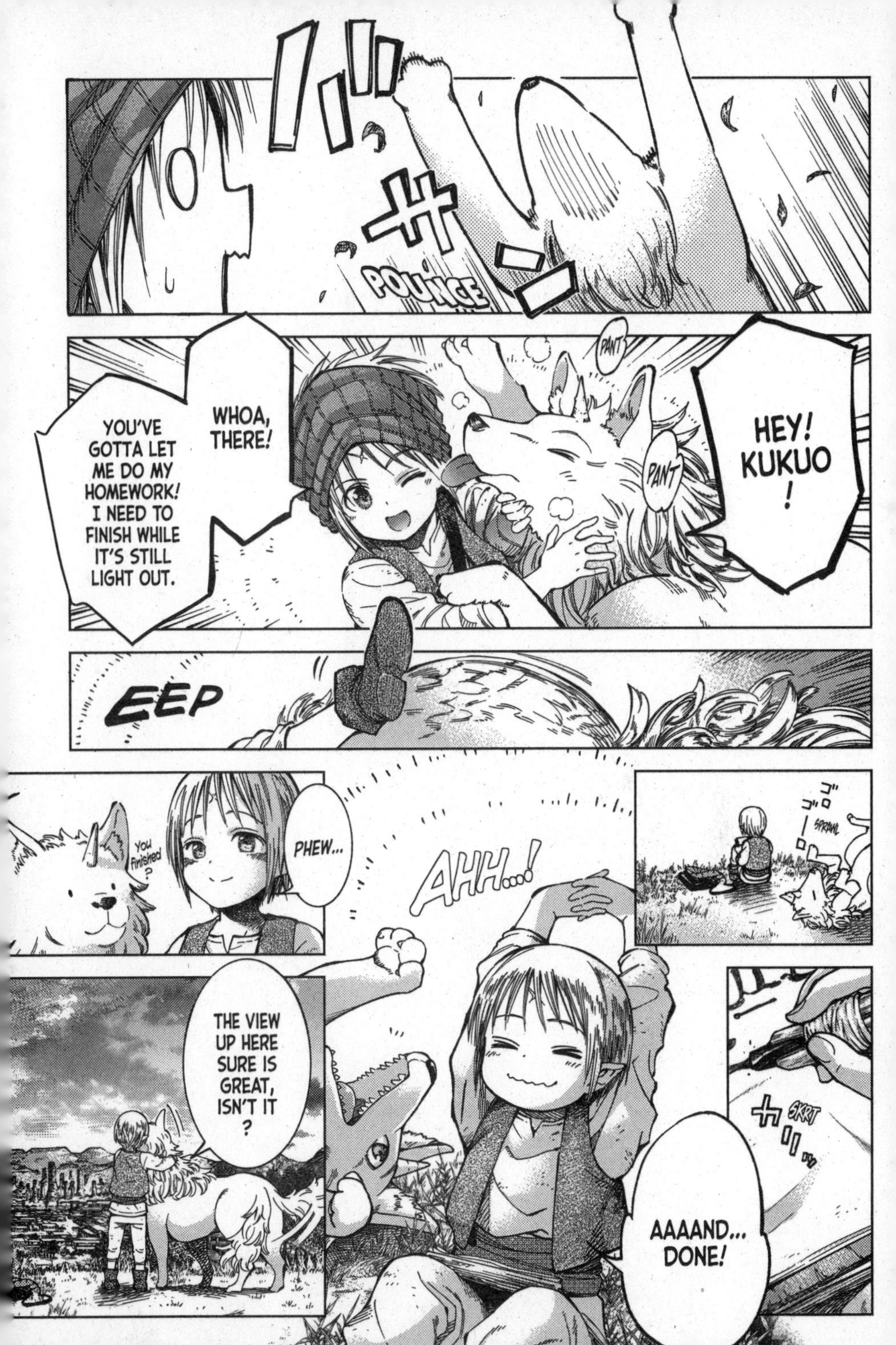

POUNCE
HEY! KUKUO!
PANT
PANT
WHOA, THERE!
YOU'VE GOTTA LET ME DO MY HOMEWORK! I NEED TO FINISH WHILE IT'S STILL LIGHT OUT.
EEP
SPRAWL
SKRT
AAAAND... DONE!
AHH...!
PHEW...
You Finished?
THE VIEW UP HERE SURE IS GREAT, ISN'T IT?

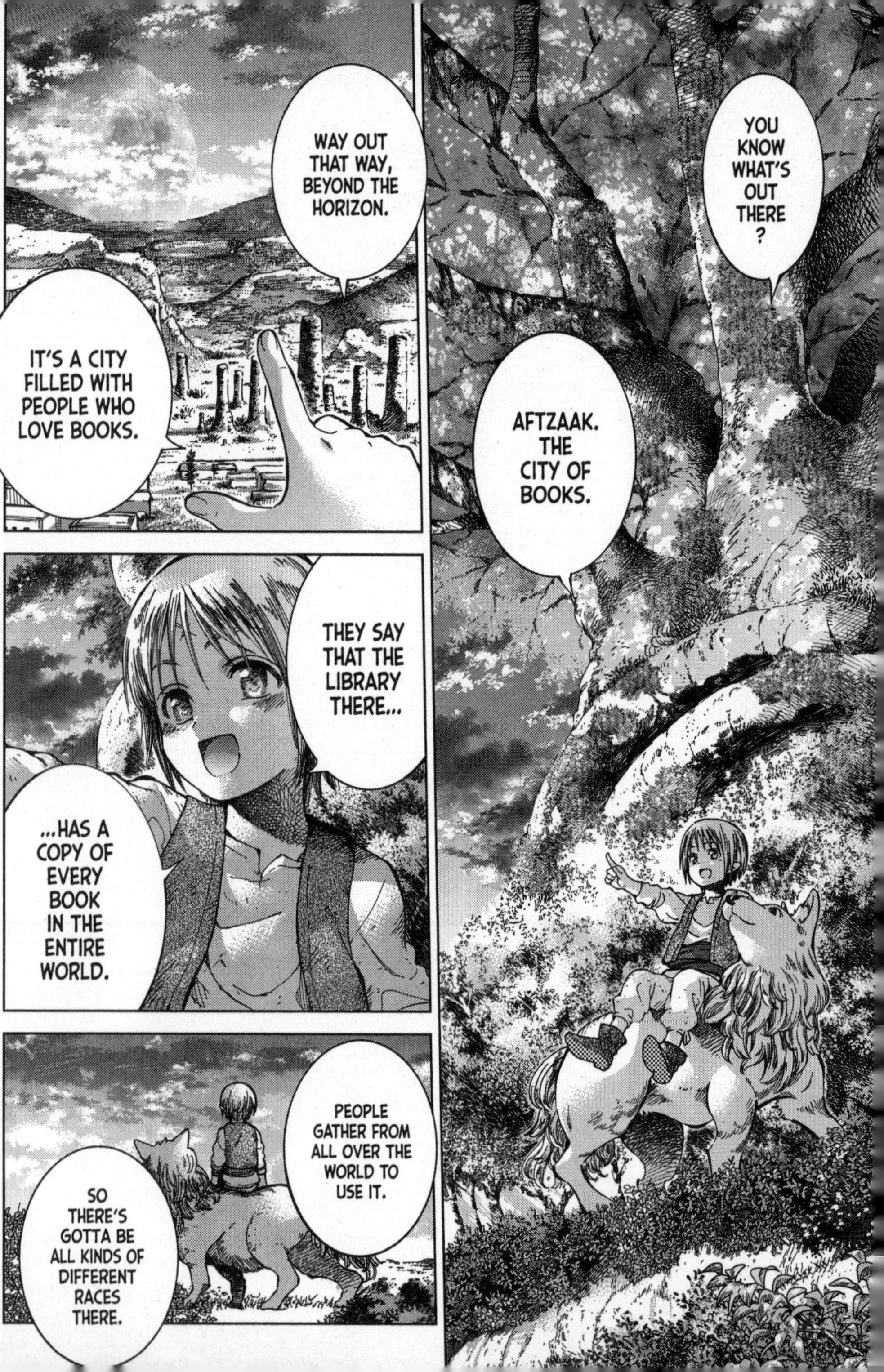
YOU KNOW WHAT'S OUT THERE?
AFTZAAK. THE CITY OF BOOKS.
WAY OUT THAT WAY, BEYOND THE HORIZON.
IT'S A CITY FILLED WITH PEOPLE WHO LOVE BOOKS.
THEY SAY THAT THE LIBRARY THERE...
...HAS A COPY OF EVERY BOOK IN THE ENTIRE WORLD.
PEOPLE GATHER FROM ALL OVER THE WORLD TO USE IT.
SO THERE'S GOTTA BE ALL KINDS OF DIFFERENT RACES THERE.

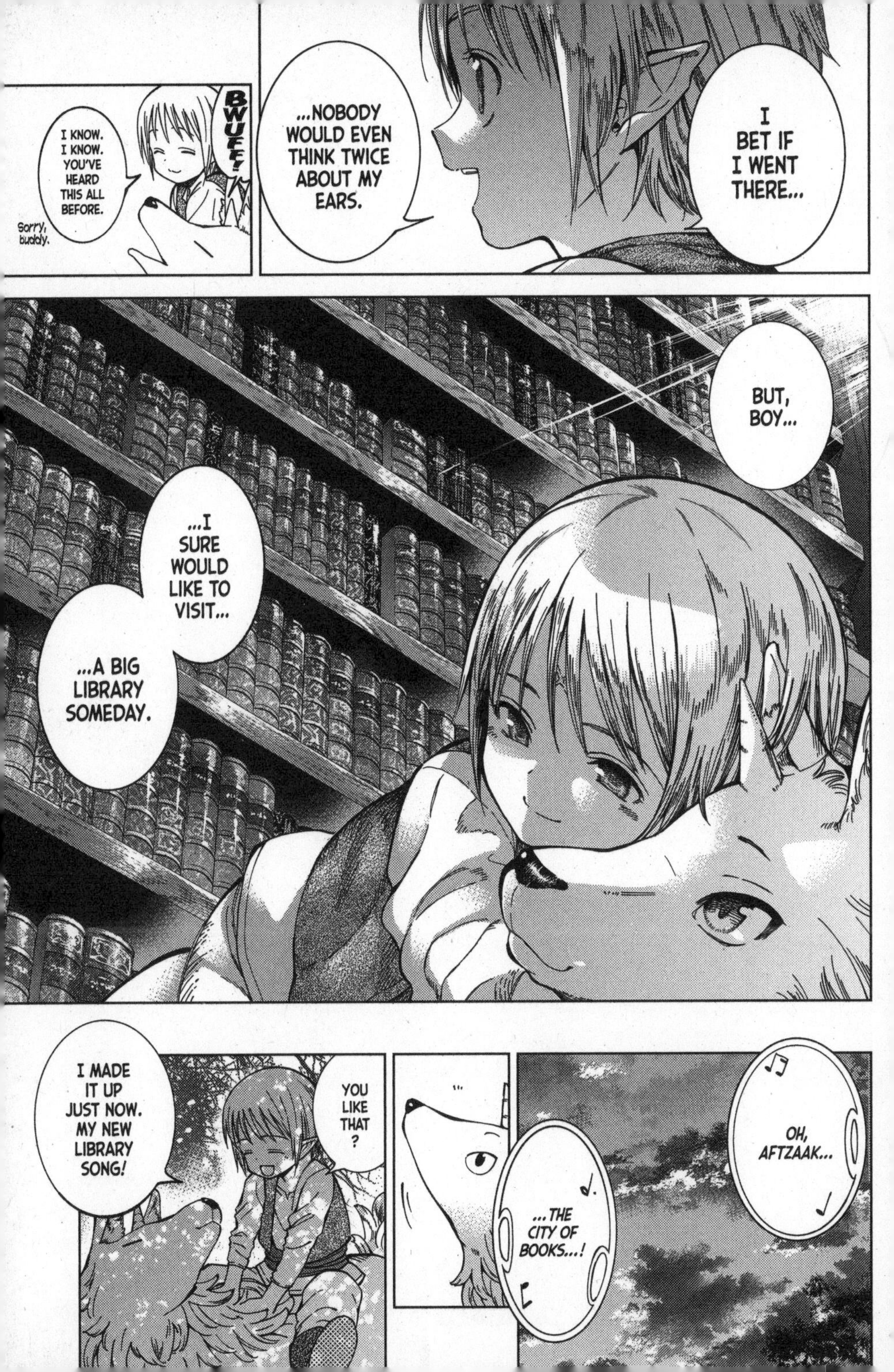
I BET IF I WENT THERE...
...NOBODY WOULD EVEN THINK TWICE ABOUT MY EARS.
BWUFF!
I KNOW. I KNOW. YOU'VE HEARD THIS ALL BEFORE.
Sorry, buddy.
BUT, BOY...
...I SURE WOULD LIKE TO VISIT...
...A BIG LIBRARY SOMEDAY.
OH, AFTZAAK...
...THE CITY OF BOOKS...!
...
YOU LIKE THAT?
I MADE IT UP JUST NOW. MY NEW LIBRARY SONG!

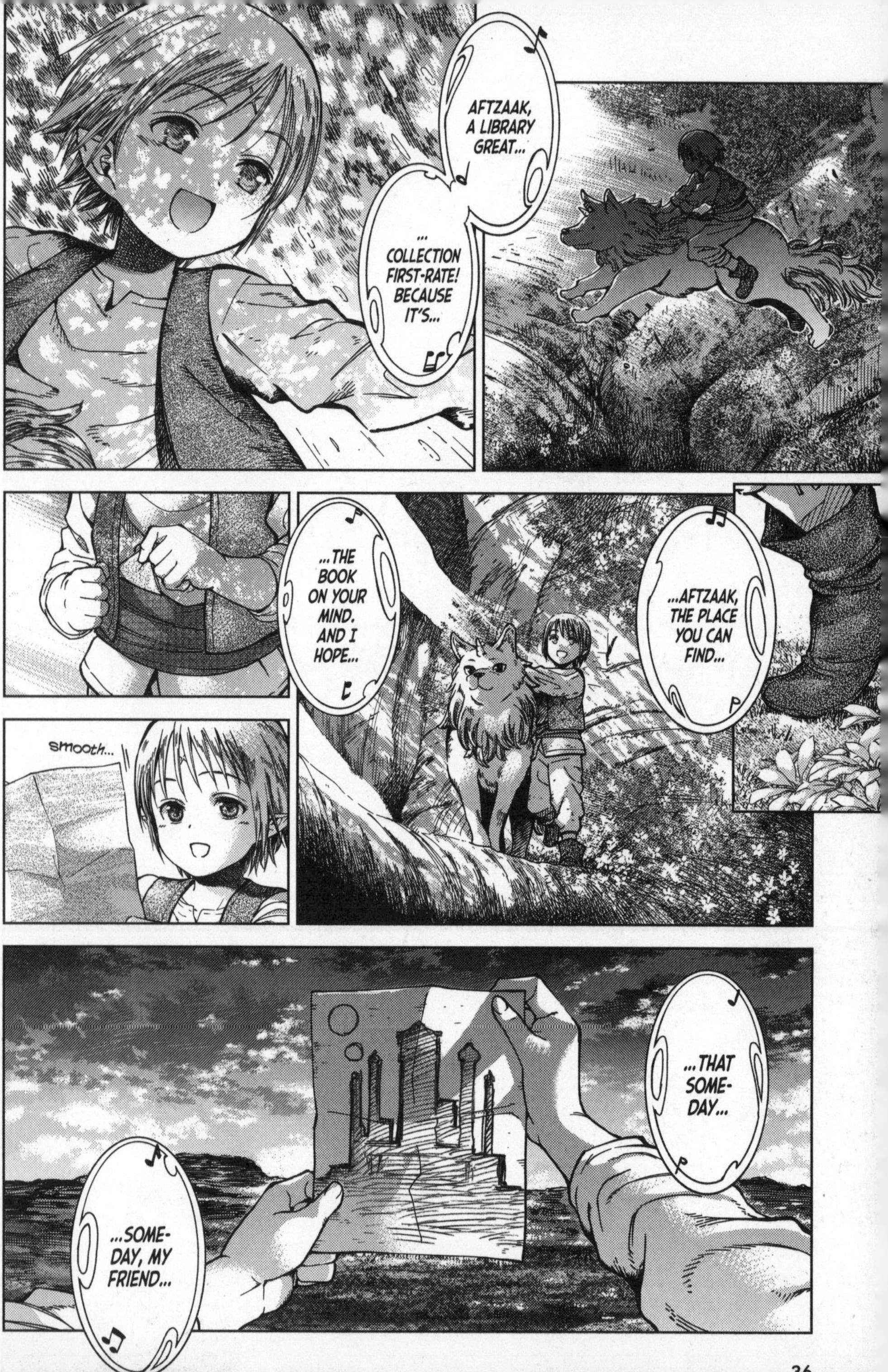
AFTZAAK, A LIBRARY GREAT...
...COLLECTION FIRST-RATE! BECAUSE IT'S...
...AFTZAAK, THE PLACE YOU CAN FIND...
...THE BOOK ON YOUR MIND. AND I HOPE...
smooth...
...THAT SOME-DAY...
...SOME-DAY, MY FRIEND...

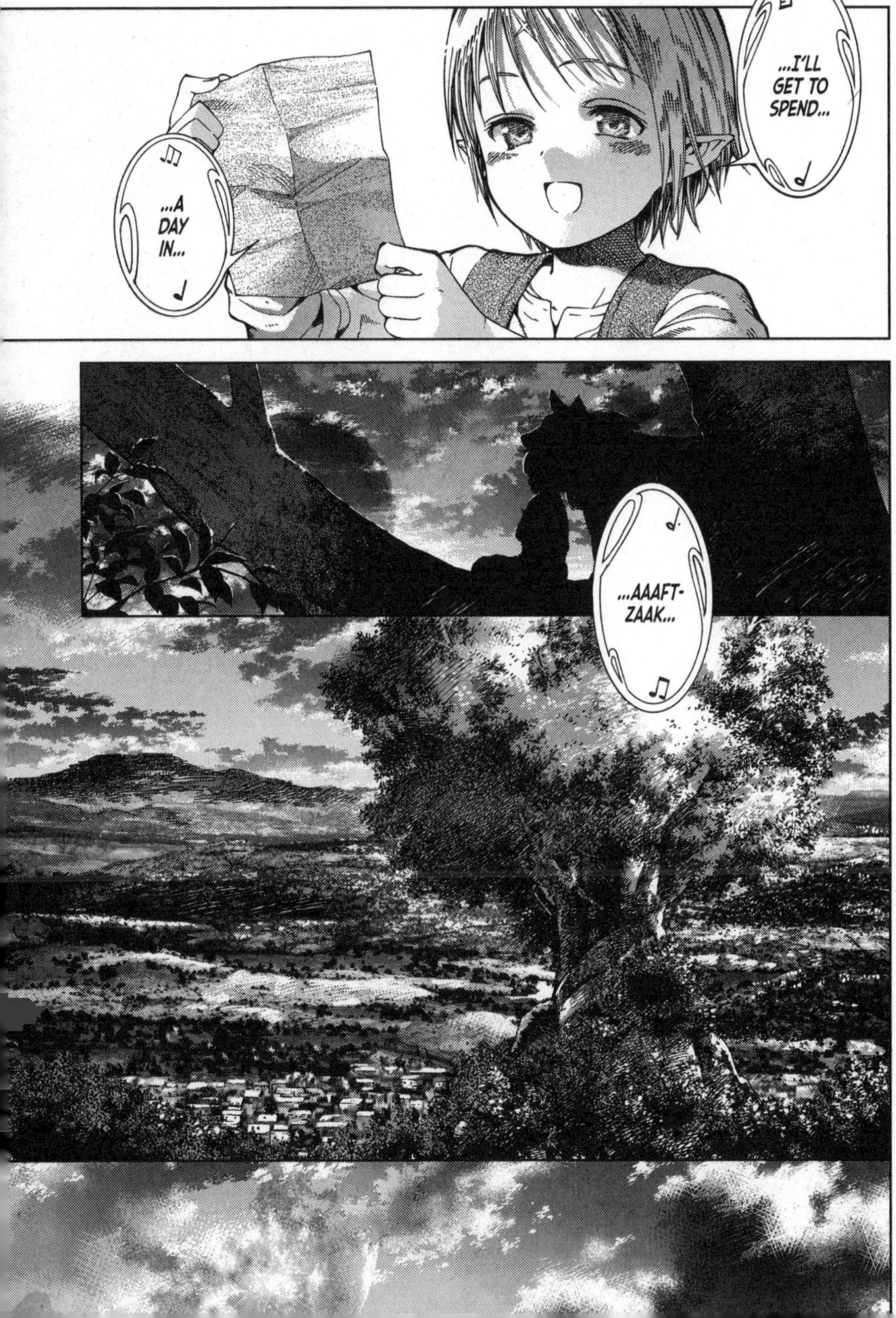
...I'LL GET TO SPEND...
...A DAY IN...
...AAAFT-ZAAK...

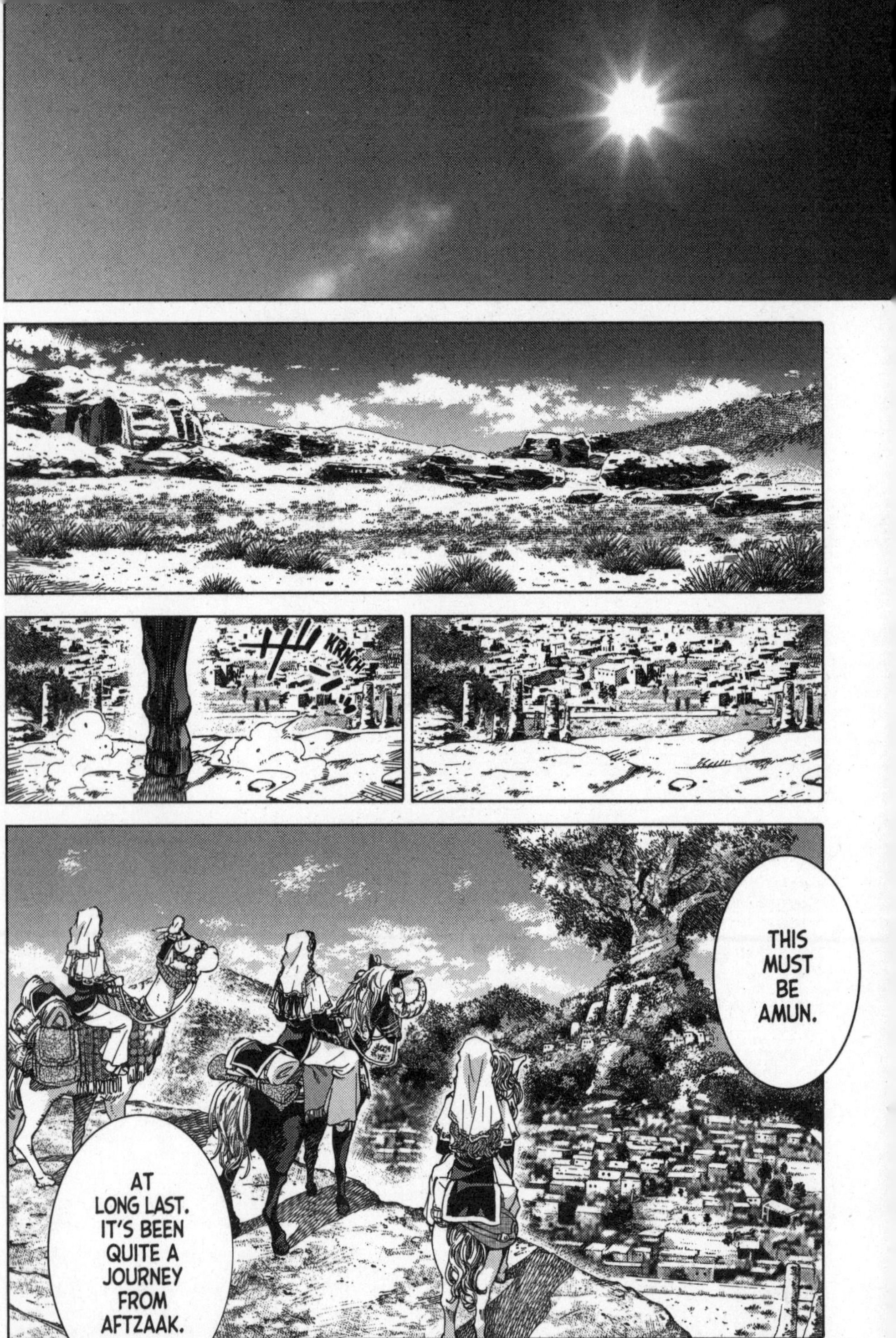
KRNCH
THIS MUST BE AMUN.
AT LONG LAST. IT'S BEEN QUITE A JOURNEY FROM AFTZAAK.

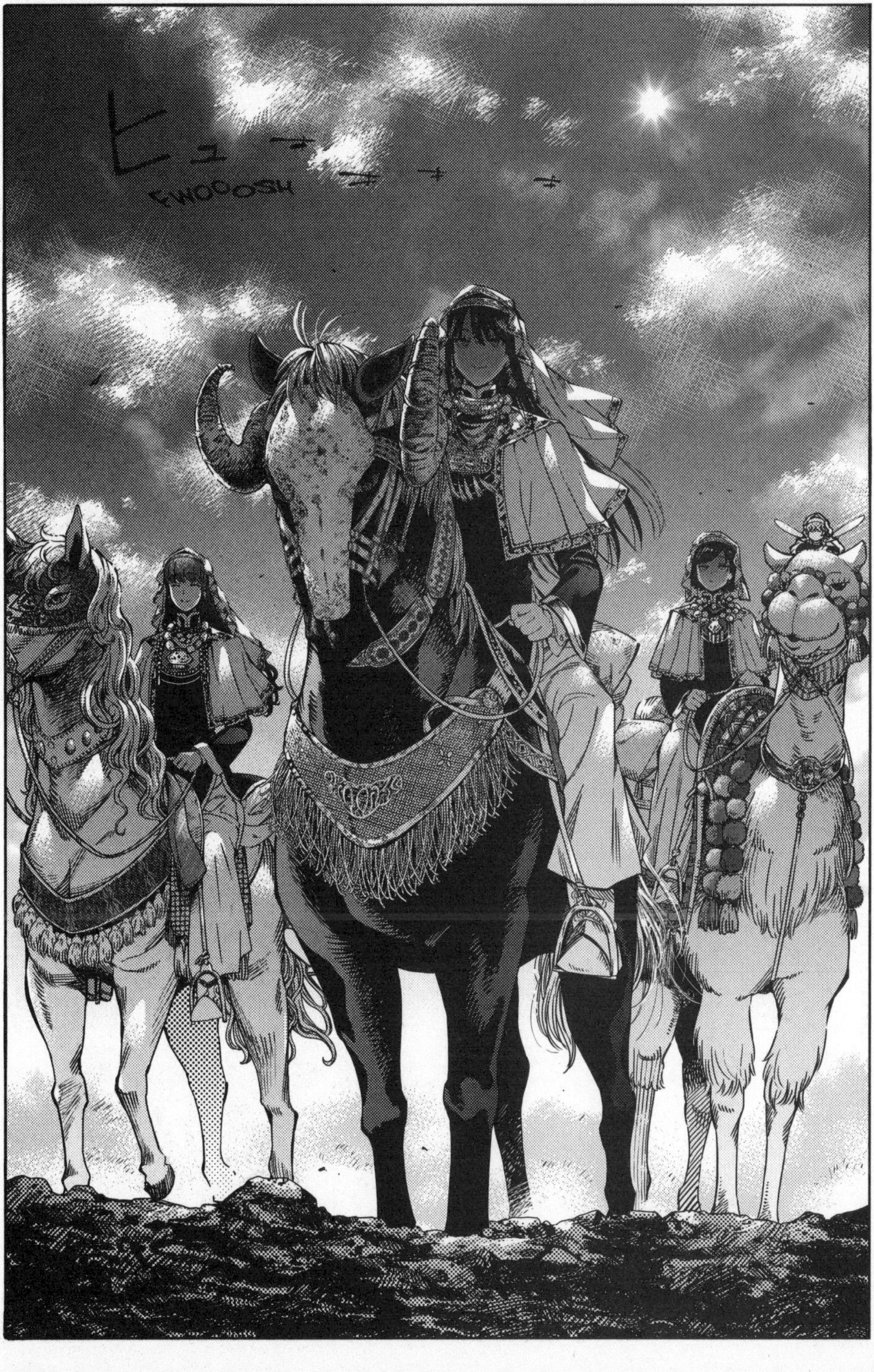
ヒューォォォォ
SWOOOSH

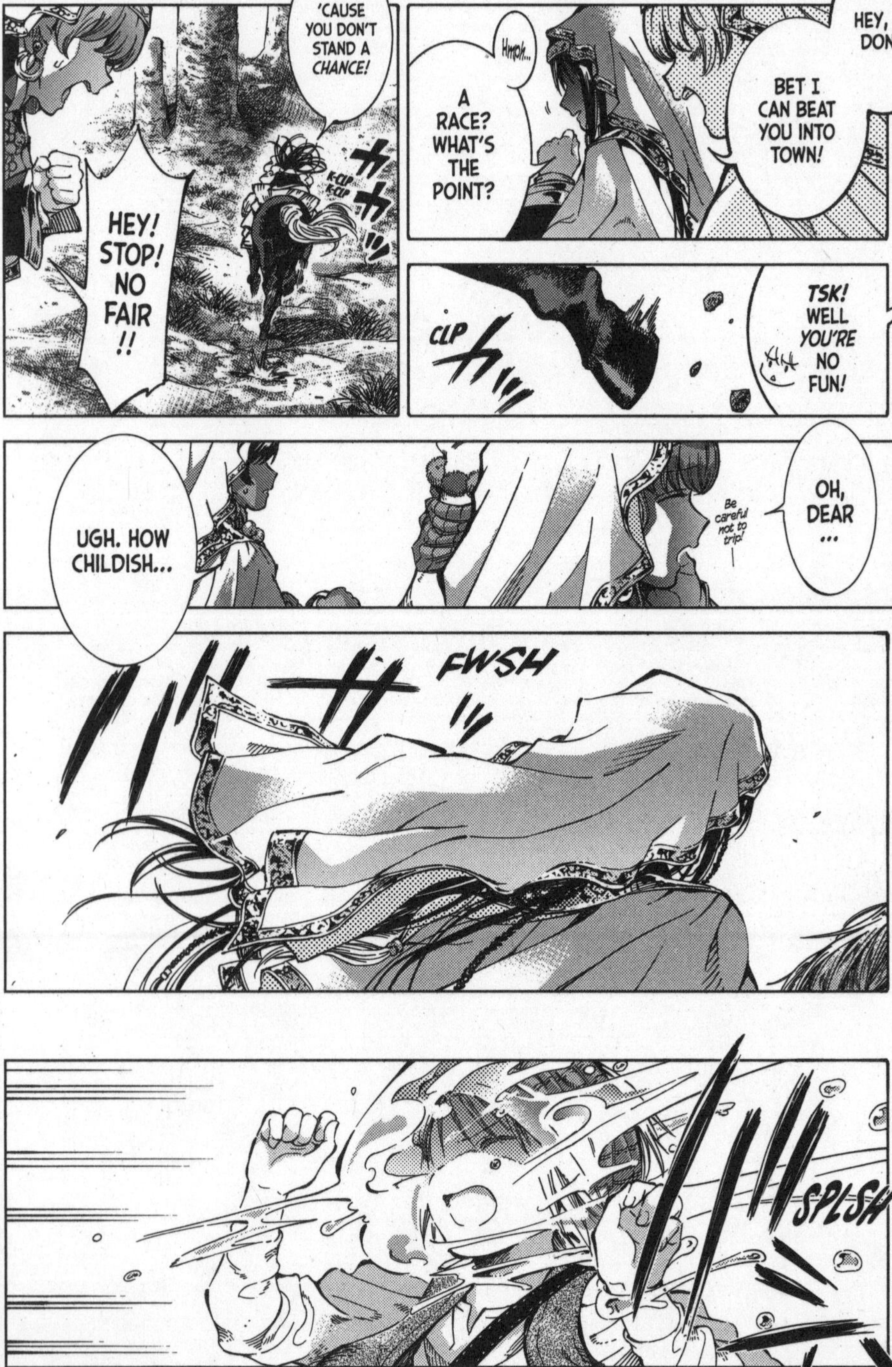
HEY, SE-DONA!
BET I CAN BEAT YOU INTO TOWN!
Hmph...
A RACE? WHAT'S THE POINT?
TSK! WELL YOU'RE NO FUN!
CLP
'CAUSE YOU DON'T STAND A CHANCE!
K-CLP K-CLP
HEY! STOP! NO FAIR!!
GRRR! GET BACK HERE!!!
OH, DEAR...
Be careful not to trip!
UGH. HOW CHILDISH...
FWSH
SPLSH

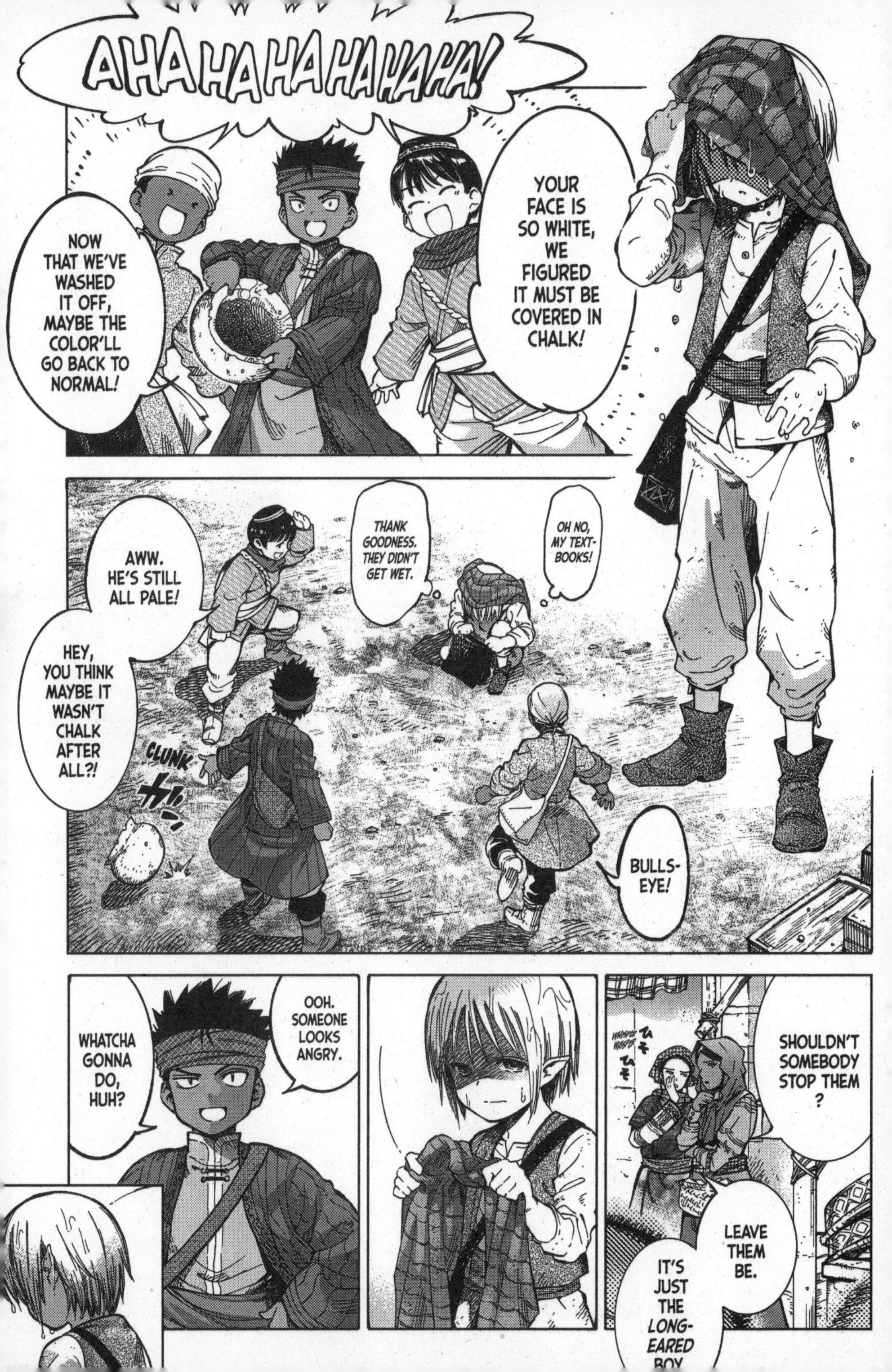
AHAHAHAHAHAHAHA!
YOUR FACE IS SO WHITE, WE FIGURED IT MUST BE COVERED IN CHALK!
NOW THAT WE'VE WASHED IT OFF, MAYBE THE COLOR'LL GO BACK TO NORMAL!
BULLS-EYE!
OH NO, MY TEXT-BOOKS!
THANK GOODNESS. THEY DIDN'T GET WET.
AWW. HE'S STILL ALL PALE!
HEY, YOU THINK MAYBE IT WASN'T CHALK AFTER ALL?!
CLUNK
SHOULDN'T SOMEBODY STOP THEM ?
WHISPER WHISPER
LEAVE THEM BE.
IT'S JUST THE LONG-EARED BOY
OOH. SOMEONE LOOKS ANGRY.
WHATCHA GONNA DO, HUH?

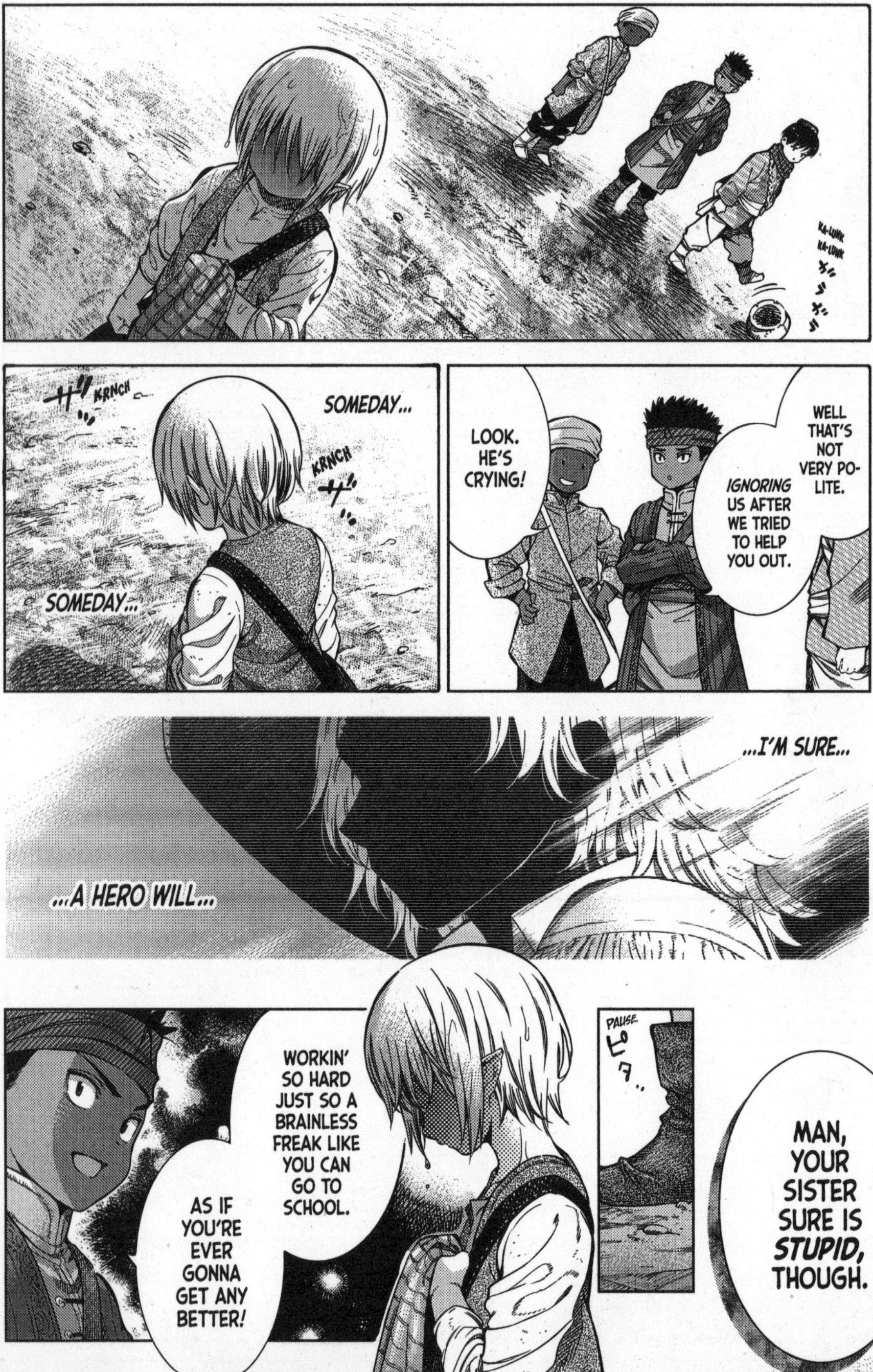
KA-LUNK KA-LUNK
WELL THAT'S NOT VERY PO-LITE.
IGNORING US AFTER WE TRIED TO HELP YOU OUT.
LOOK. HE'S CRYING!
SOMEDAY...
KRNCH
KRNCH
SOMEDAY...
...I'M SURE...
...A HERO WILL...
MAN, YOUR SISTER SURE IS STUPID, THOUGH.
PAUSE
WORKIN' SO HARD JUST SO A BRAINLESS FREAK LIKE YOU CAN GO TO SCHOOL.
AS IF YOU'RE EVER GONNA GET ANY BETTER!

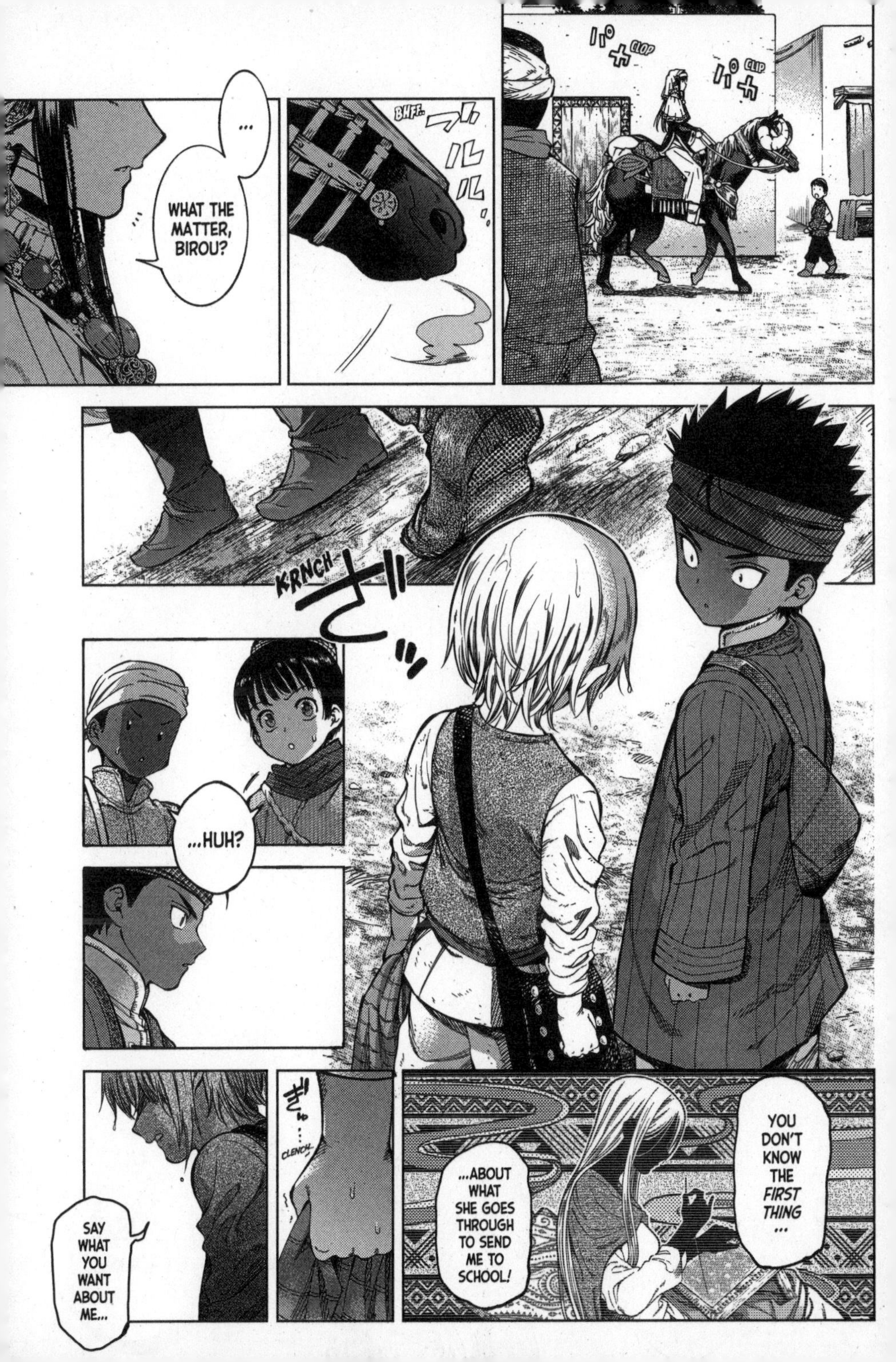
CLOP
CLIP
BHFF..
...
WHAT THE MATTER, BIROU?
KRNCH
...HUH?
YOU DON'T KNOW THE FIRST THING...
...ABOUT WHAT SHE GOES THROUGH TO SEND ME TO SCHOOL!
CLENCH
SAY WHAT YOU WANT ABOUT ME...

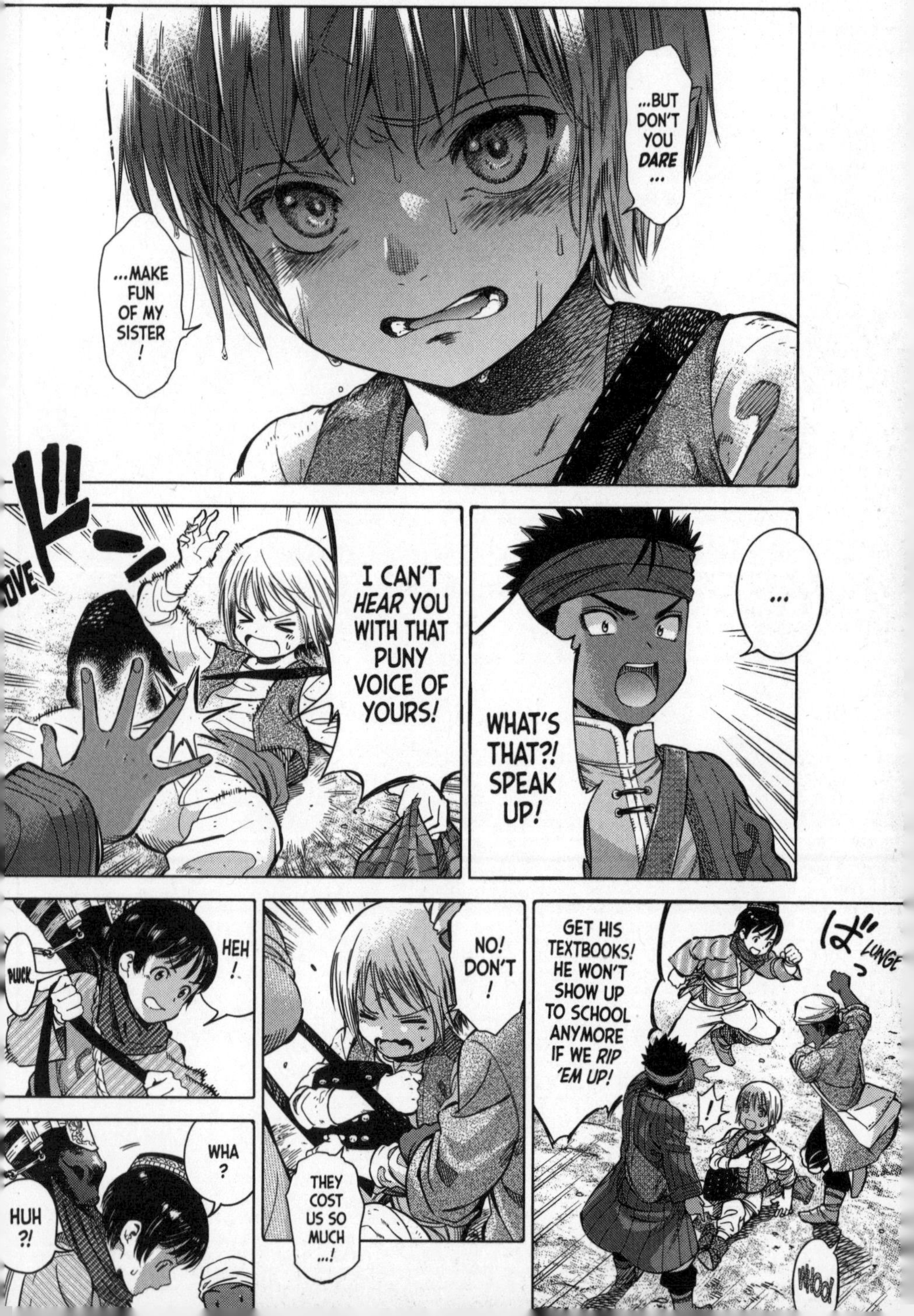
...BUT DON'T YOU DARE ...
...MAKE FUN OF MY SISTER!
...
WHAT'S THAT?! SPEAK UP!
ド
OVE
I CAN'T HEAR YOU WITH THAT PUNY VOICE OF YOURS!
ばっ
LUNGE
GET HIS TEXTBOOKS! HE WON'T SHOW UP TO SCHOOL ANYMORE IF WE RIP 'EM UP!
!
WHOO!
NO! DON'T!
THEY COST US SO MUCH ...!
HEH!
PLUCK...
WHA?
HUH?!

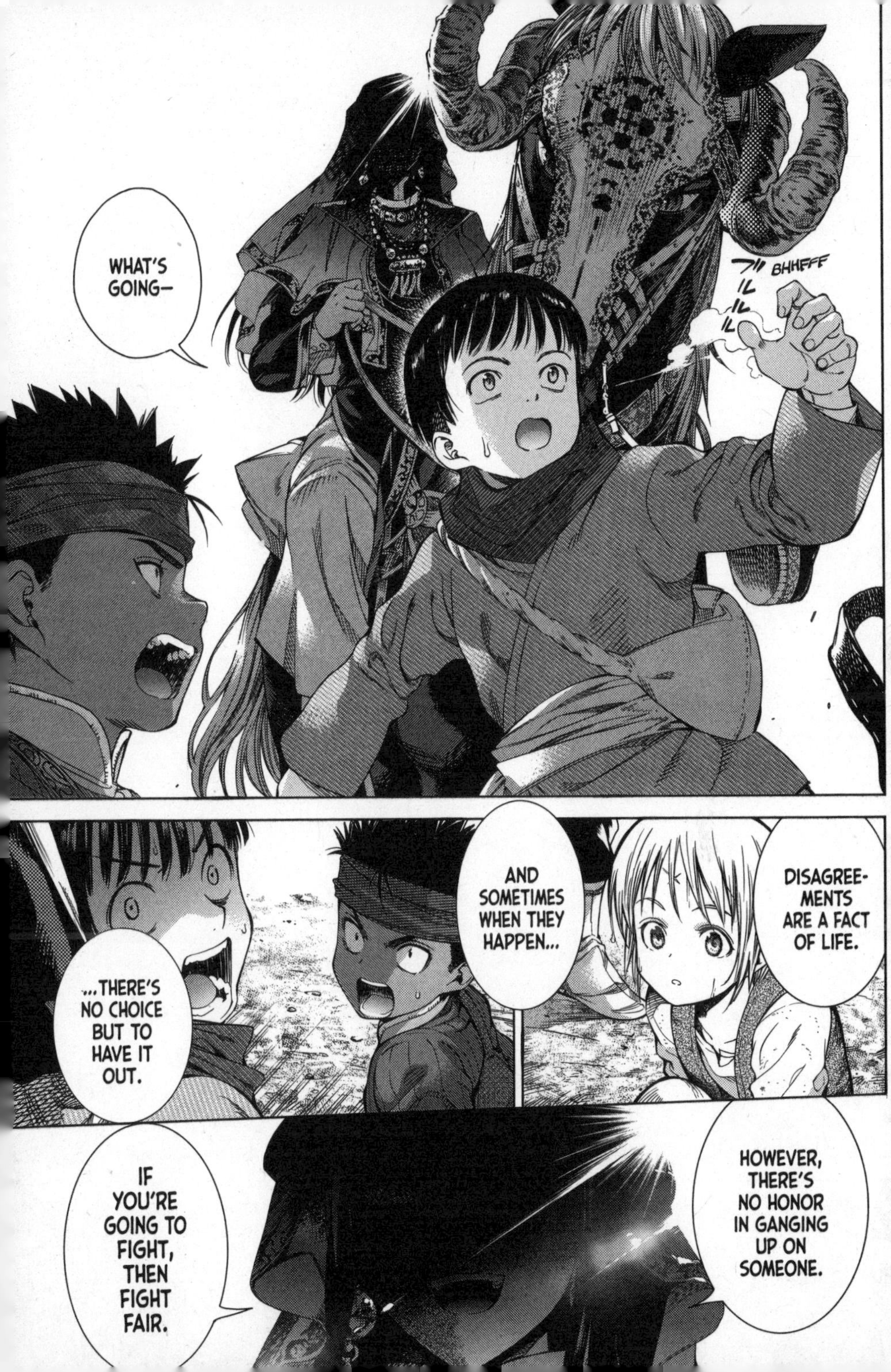
ブルルル BHHEFF
WHAT'S GOING—
DISAGREE-MENTS ARE A FACT OF LIFE.
AND SOMETIMES WHEN THEY HAPPEN...
...THERE'S NO CHOICE BUT TO HAVE IT OUT.
HOWEVER, THERE'S NO HONOR IN GANGING UP ON SOMEONE.
IF YOU'RE GOING TO FIGHT, THEN FIGHT FAIR.

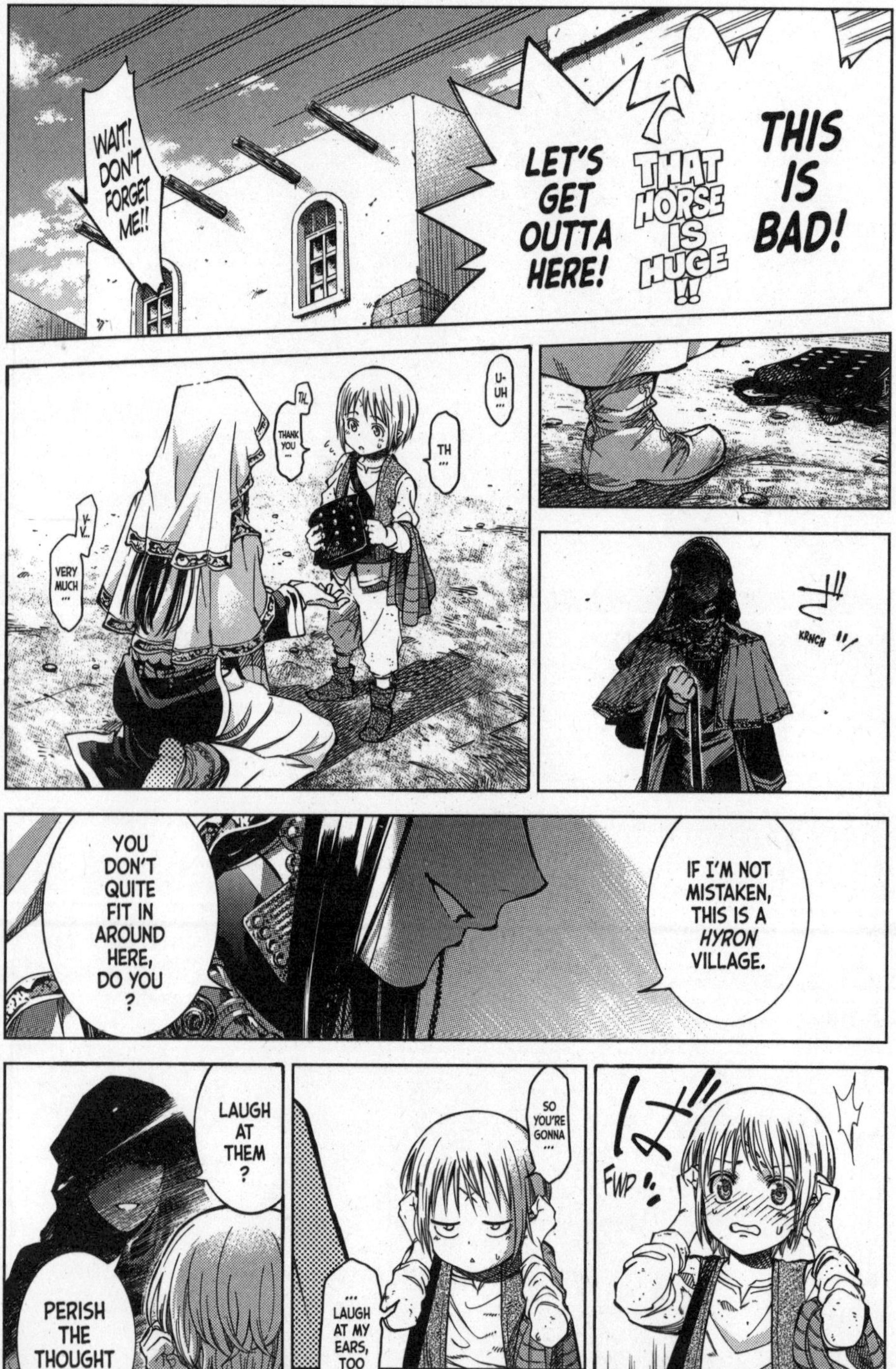
THIS IS BAD!
THAT HORSE IS HUGE!!
LET'S GET OUTTA HERE!
WAIT! DON'T FORGET ME!!
KRNCH
U-UH...
TH...
TH... THANK YOU...
V-V... VERY MUCH...
IF I'M NOT MISTAKEN, THIS IS A HYRON VILLAGE.
YOU DON'T QUITE FIT IN AROUND HERE, DO YOU?
FWP
SO YOU'RE GONNA...
...LAUGH AT MY EARS, TOO?
LAUGH AT THEM?
PERISH THE THOUGHT!

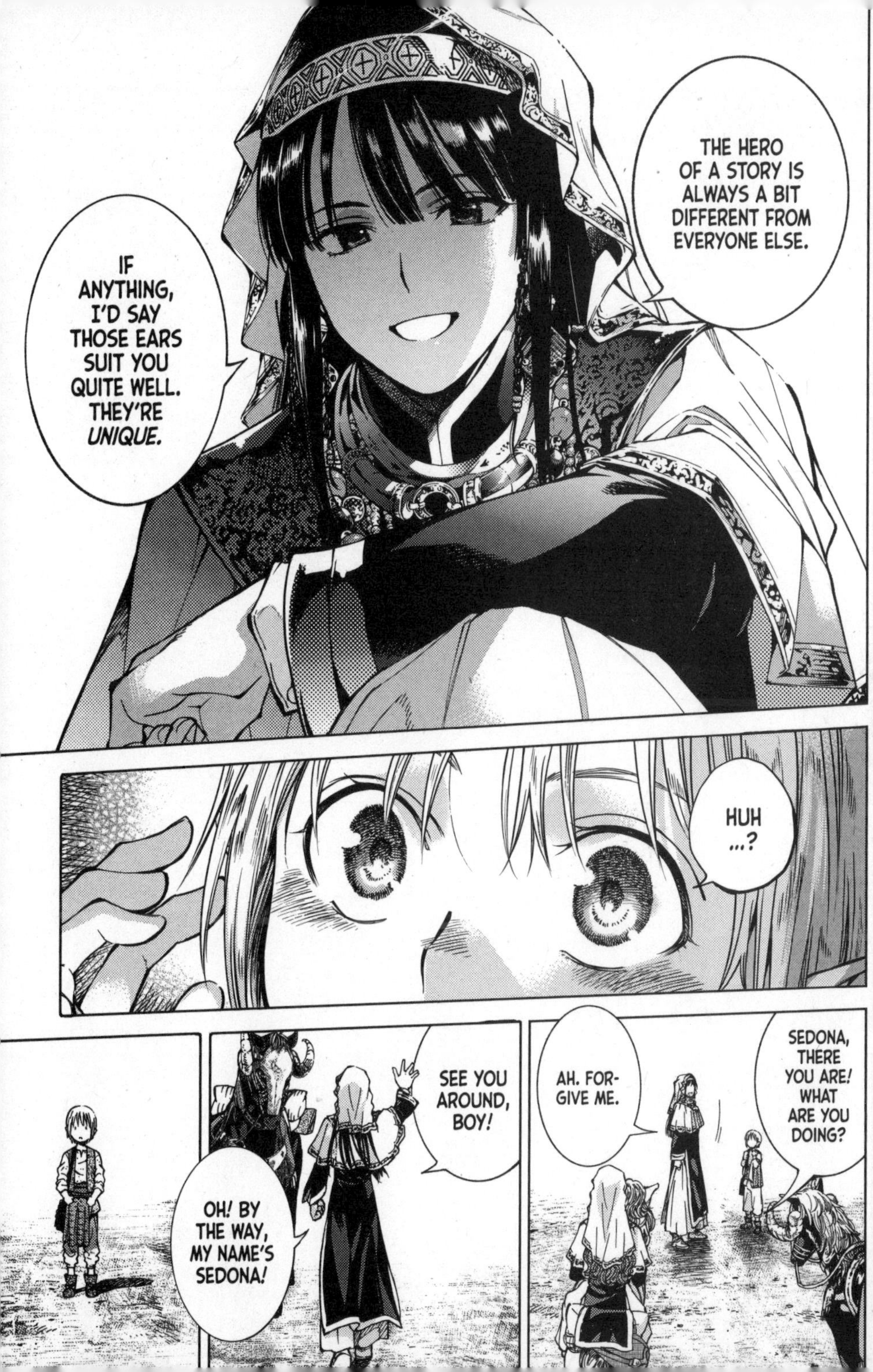
THE HERO OF A STORY IS ALWAYS A BIT DIFFERENT FROM EVERYONE ELSE.
IF ANYTHING, I'D SAY THOSE EARS SUIT YOU QUITE WELL. THEY'RE *UNIQUE.*
HUH ...?
SEDONA, THERE YOU ARE! WHAT ARE YOU DOING?
AH. FOR-GIVE ME.
SEE YOU AROUND, BOY!
OH! BY THE WAY, MY NAME'S SEDONA!

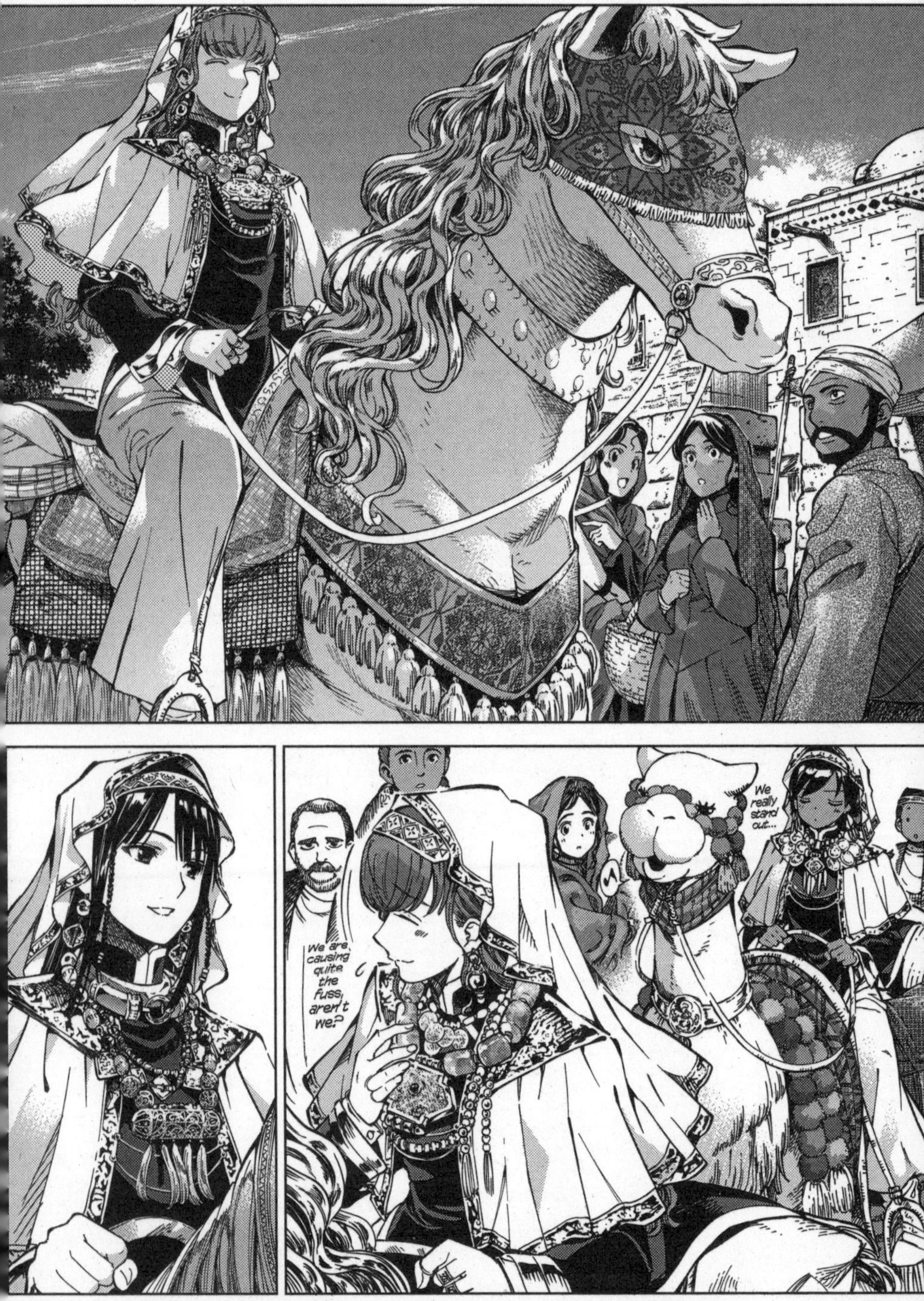
We really stand out...
We are causing quite the fuss, aren't we?

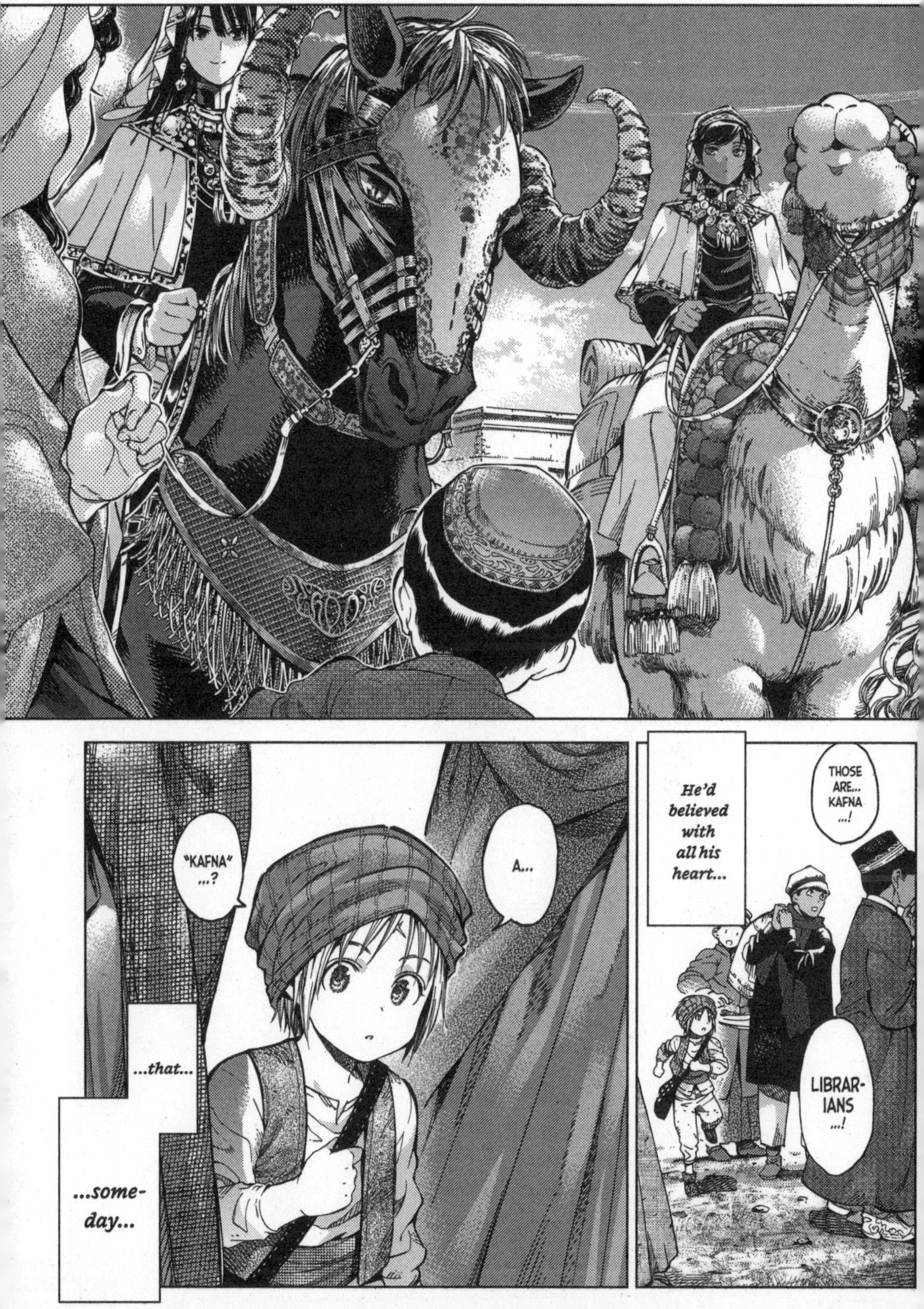
He'd believed with all his heart...
THOSE ARE... KAFNA ...!
LIBRARIANS ...!
A...
"KAFNA" ...?
...that...
...someday...

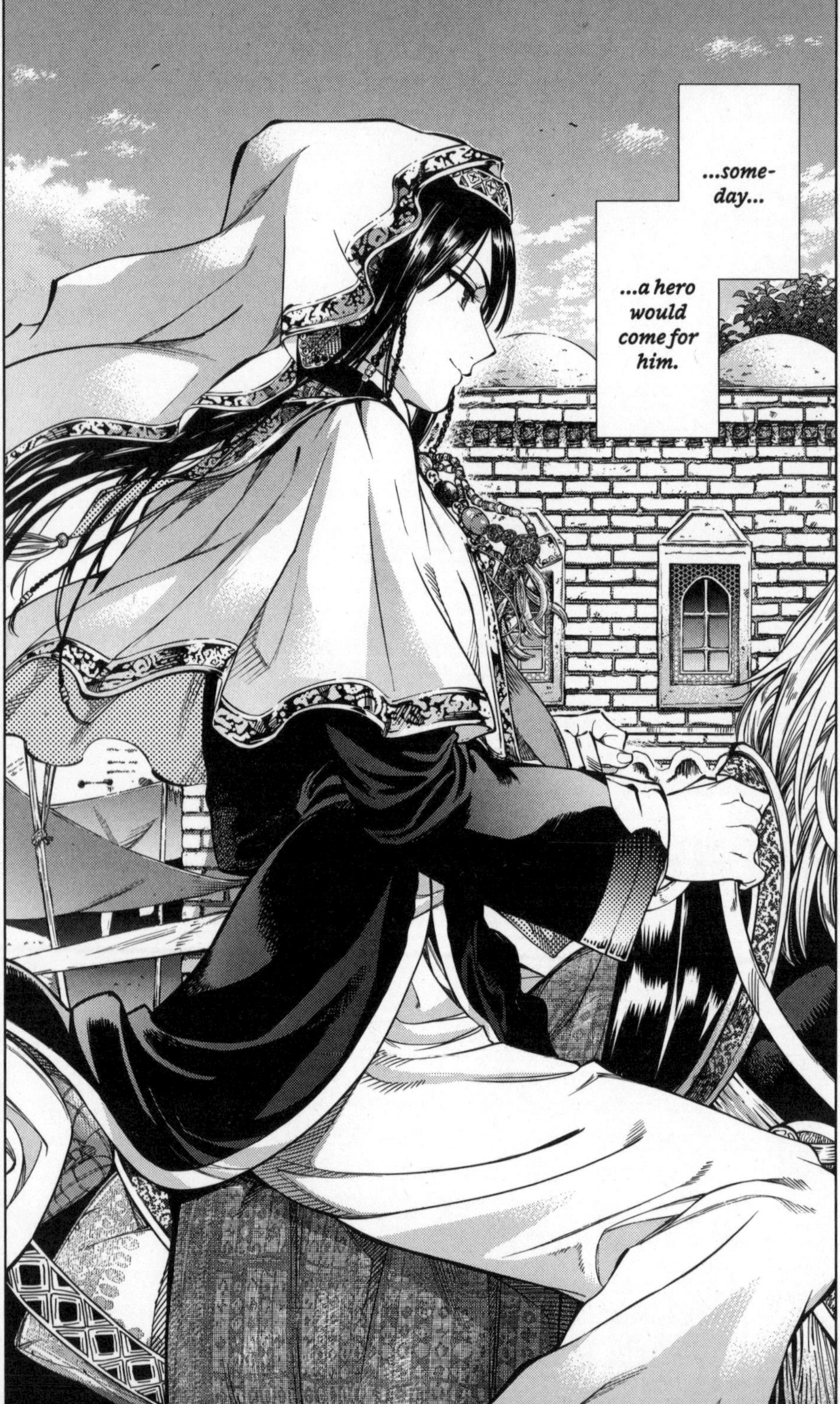
...some-
day...
...a hero
would
come for
him.

Magus of the Library

Kukuo

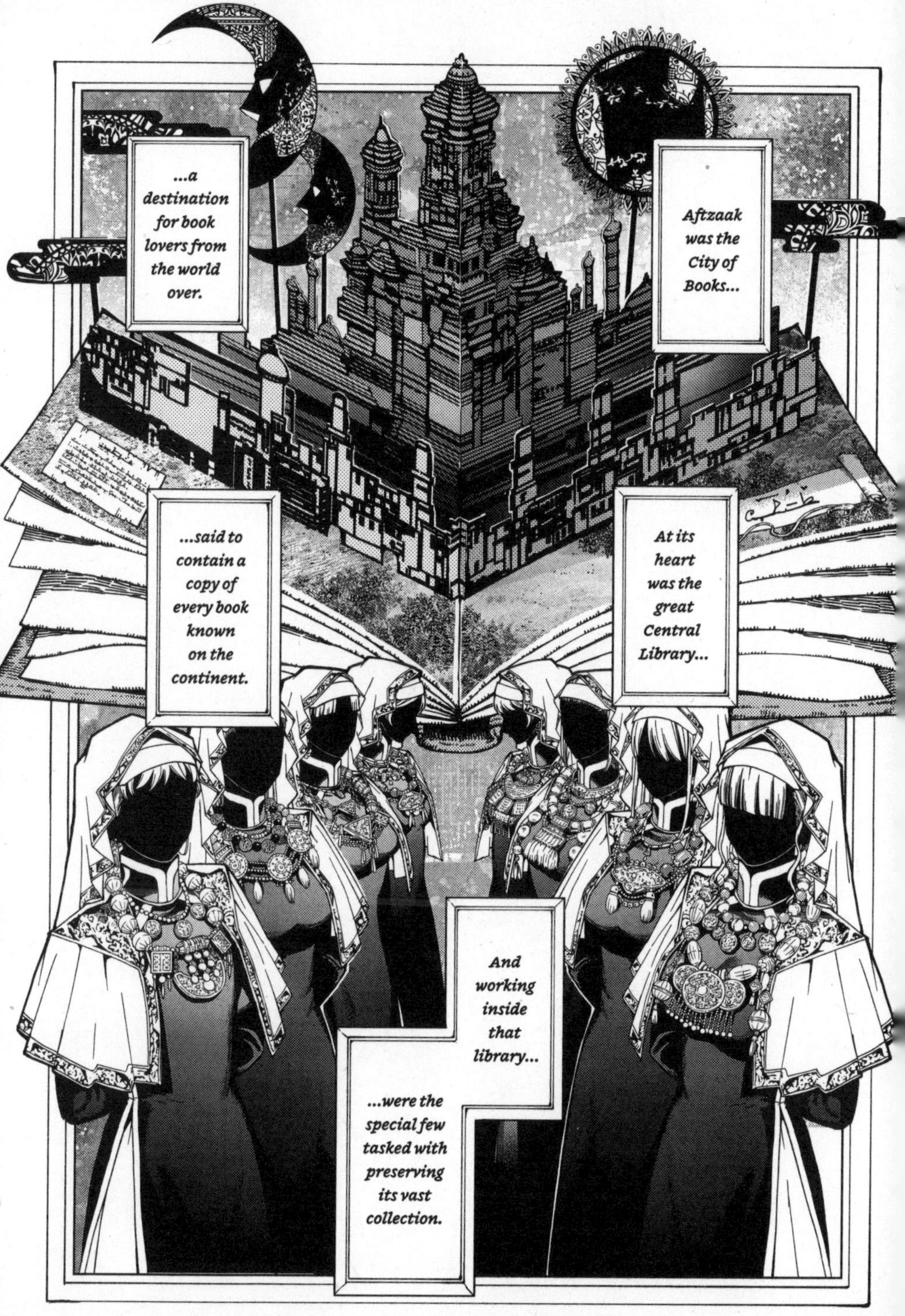
Aftzaak was the City of Books...
...a destination for book lovers from the world over.
At its heart was the great Central Library...
...said to contain a copy of every book known on the continent.
And working inside that library...
...were the special few tasked with preserving its vast collection.

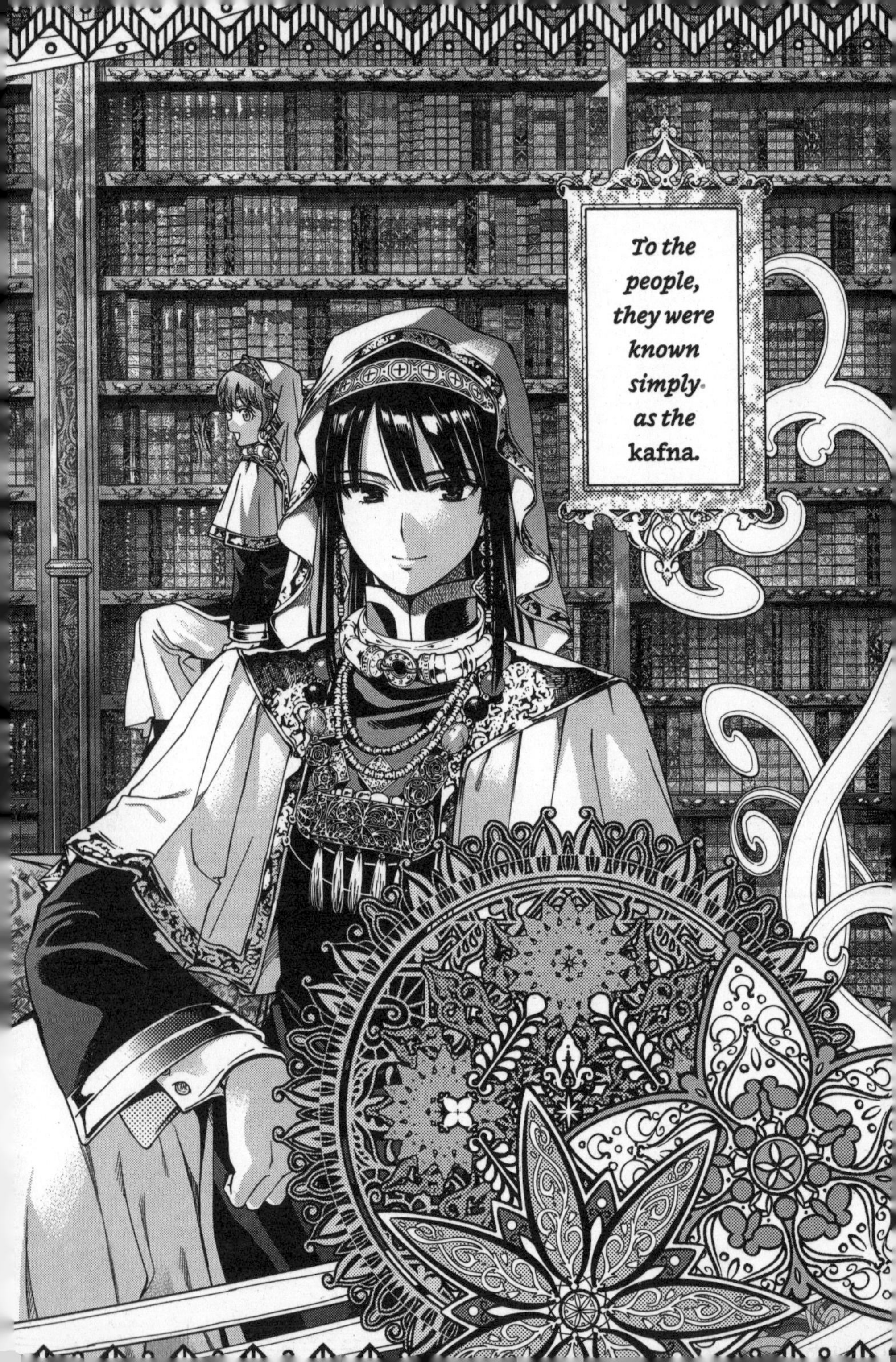
To the people, they were known simply as the kafna.

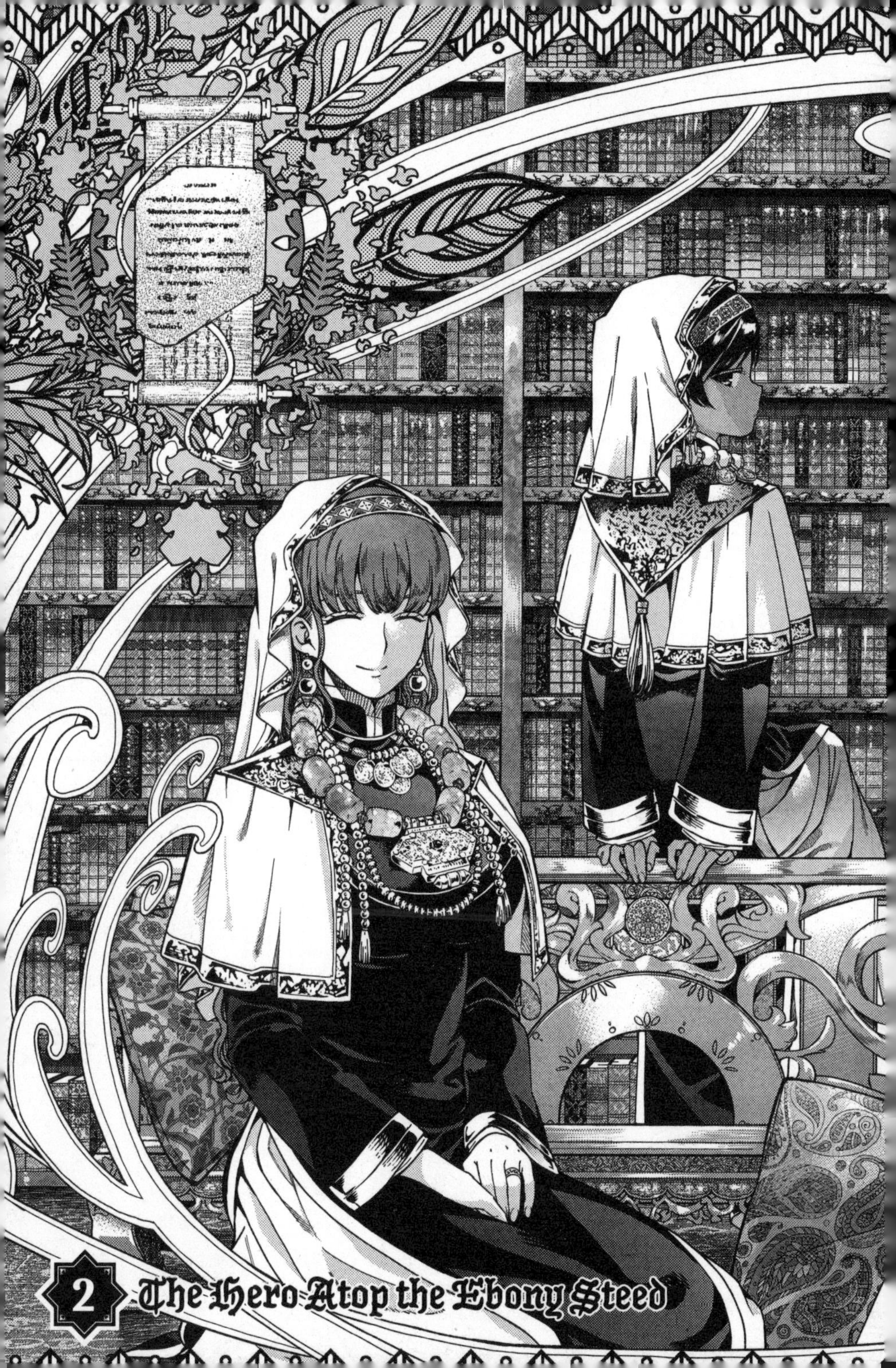
2
The Hero Atop the Ebony Steed

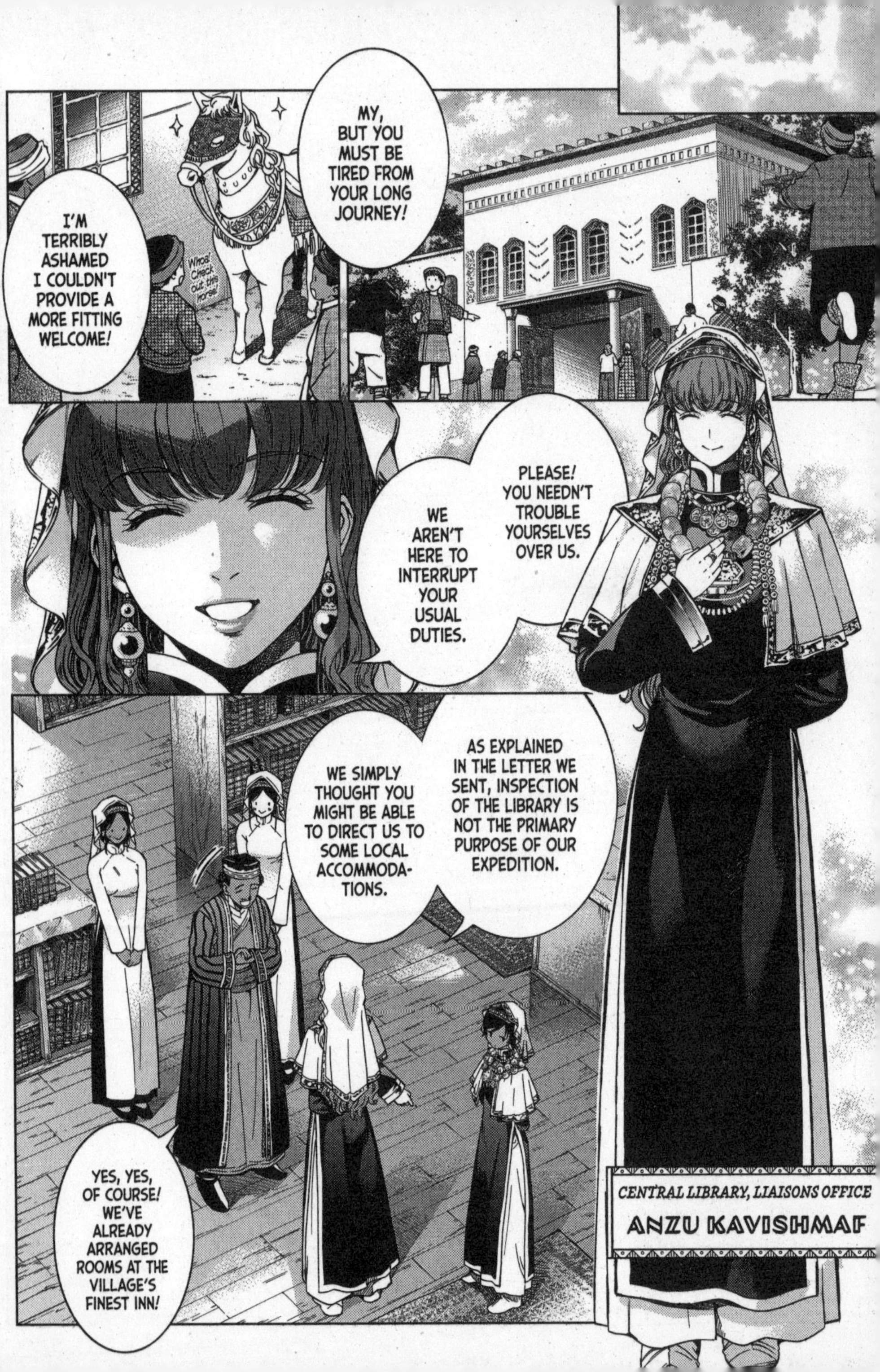
MY, BUT YOU MUST BE TIRED FROM YOUR LONG JOURNEY!
I'M TERRIBLY ASHAMED I COULDN'T PROVIDE A MORE FITTING WELCOME!
Whoa! Check out this horse!
PLEASE! YOU NEEDN'T TROUBLE YOURSELVES OVER US.
WE AREN'T HERE TO INTERRUPT YOUR USUAL DUTIES.
AS EXPLAINED IN THE LETTER WE SENT, INSPECTION OF THE LIBRARY IS NOT THE PRIMARY PURPOSE OF OUR EXPEDITION.
WE SIMPLY THOUGHT YOU MIGHT BE ABLE TO DIRECT US TO SOME LOCAL ACCOMMODA-TIONS.
YES, YES, OF COURSE! WE'VE ALREADY ARRANGED ROOMS AT THE VILLAGE'S FINEST INN!
CENTRAL LIBRARY, LIAISONS OFFICE
ANZU KAVISHMAF

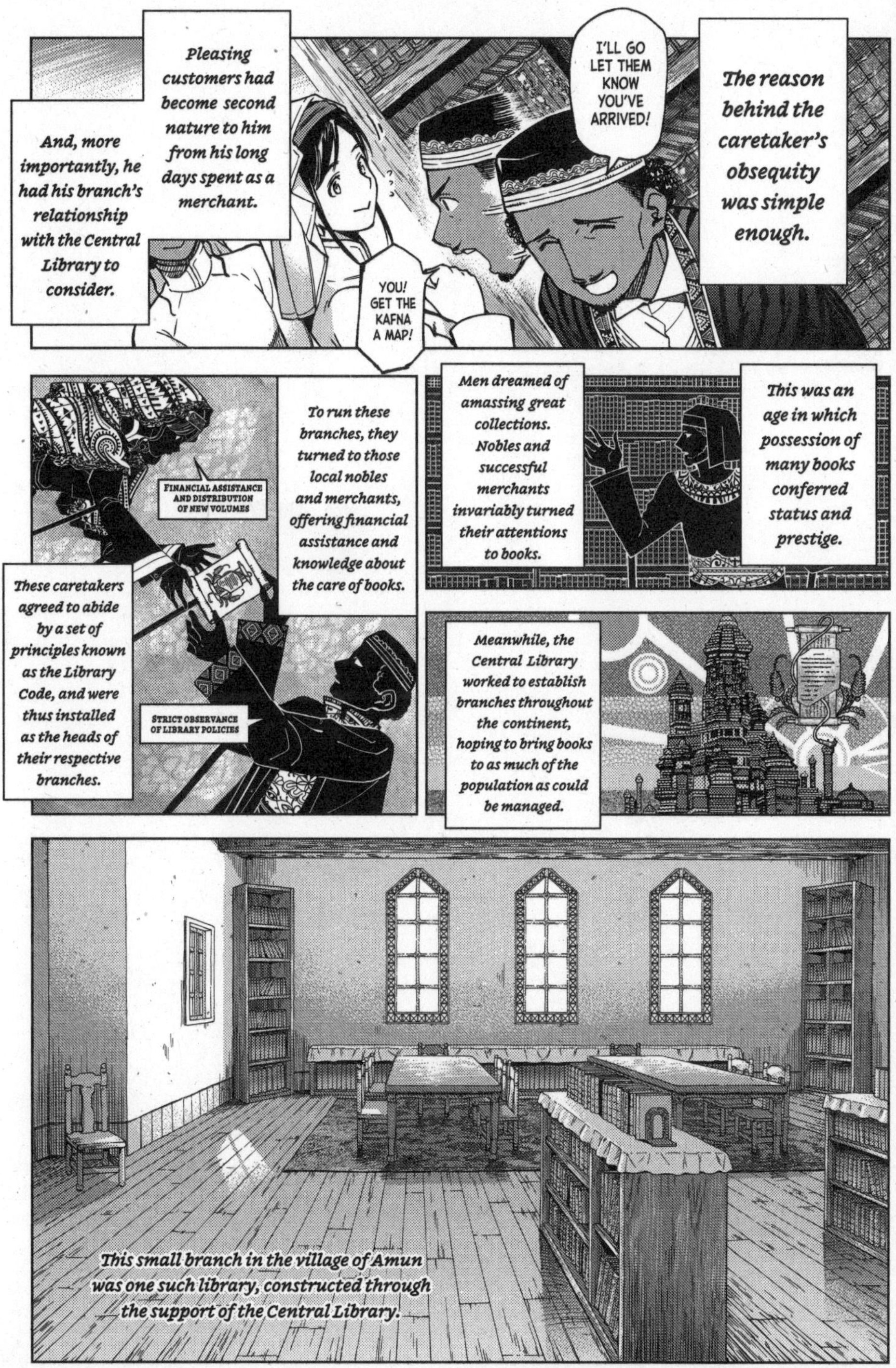
The reason behind the caretaker's obsequity was simple enough.
I'LL GO LET THEM KNOW YOU'VE ARRIVED!
Pleasing customers had become second nature to him from his long days spent as a merchant.
And, more importantly, he had his branch's relationship with the Central Library to consider.
YOU! GET THE KAFNA A MAP!
This was an age in which possession of many books conferred status and prestige.
Men dreamed of amassing great collections. Nobles and successful merchants invariably turned their attentions to books.
Meanwhile, the Central Library worked to establish branches throughout the continent, hoping to bring books to as much of the population as could be managed.
To run these branches, they turned to those local nobles and merchants, offering financial assistance and knowledge about the care of books.
FINANCIAL ASSISTANCE AND DISTRIBUTION OF NEW VOLUMES
STRICT OBSERVANCE OF LIBRARY POLICIES
These caretakers agreed to abide by a set of principles known as the Library Code, and were thus installed as the heads of their respective branches.
This small branch in the village of Amun was one such library, constructed through the support of the Central Library.

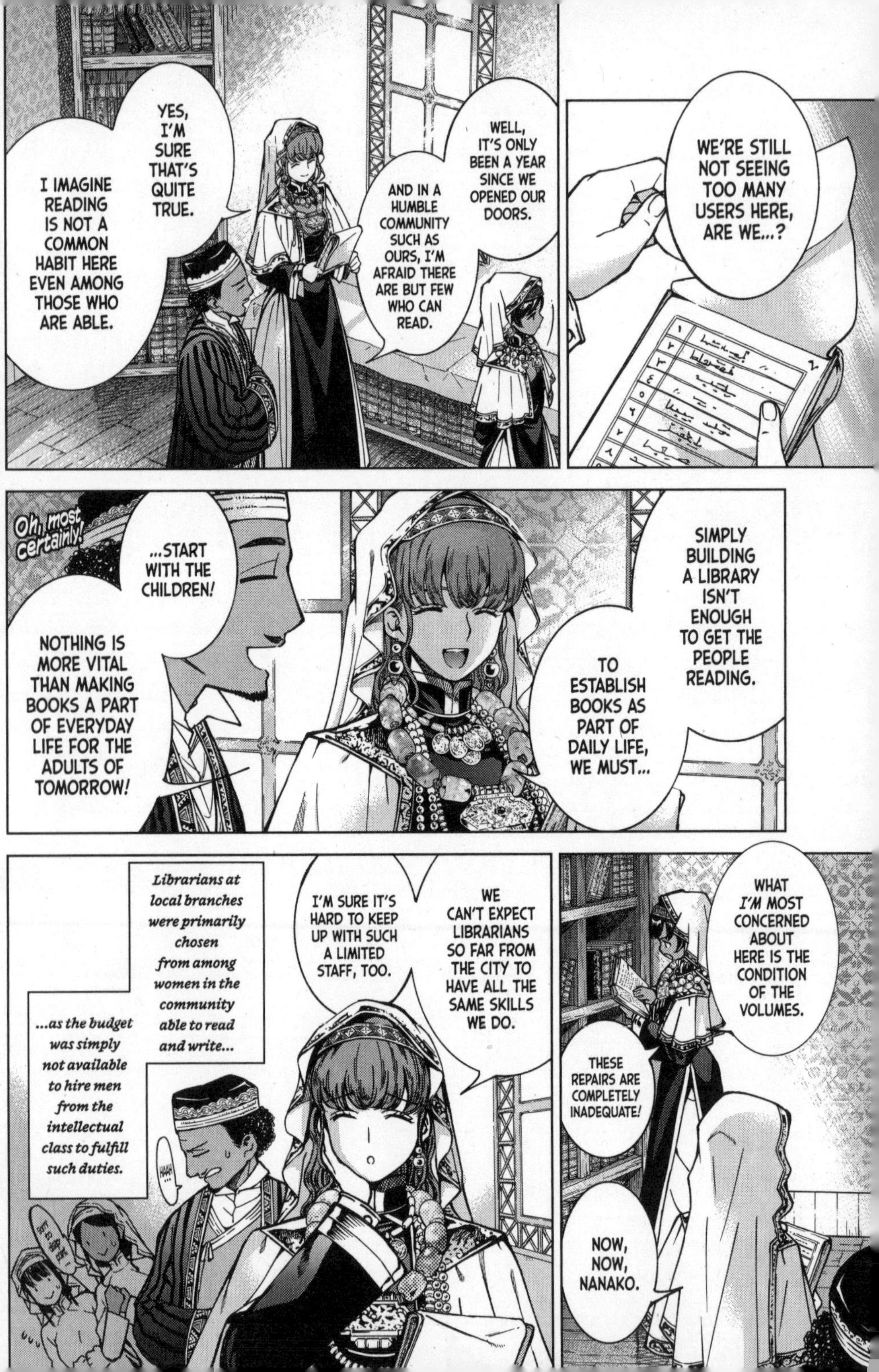
WE'RE STILL NOT SEEING TOO MANY USERS HERE, ARE WE...?
WELL, IT'S ONLY BEEN A YEAR SINCE WE OPENED OUR DOORS.
AND IN A HUMBLE COMMUNITY SUCH AS OURS, I'M AFRAID THERE ARE BUT FEW WHO CAN READ.
YES, I'M SURE THAT'S QUITE TRUE.
I IMAGINE READING IS NOT A COMMON HABIT HERE EVEN AMONG THOSE WHO ARE ABLE.
SIMPLY BUILDING A LIBRARY ISN'T ENOUGH TO GET THE PEOPLE READING.
TO ESTABLISH BOOKS AS PART OF DAILY LIFE, WE MUST...
...START WITH THE CHILDREN!
Oh, most certainly!
NOTHING IS MORE VITAL THAN MAKING BOOKS A PART OF EVERYDAY LIFE FOR THE ADULTS OF TOMORROW!
WHAT *I'M* MOST CONCERNED ABOUT HERE IS THE CONDITION OF THE VOLUMES.
THESE REPAIRS ARE COMPLETELY INADEQUATE!
NOW, NOW, NANAKO.
WE CAN'T EXPECT LIBRARIANS SO FAR FROM THE CITY TO HAVE ALL THE SAME SKILLS WE DO.
I'M SURE IT'S HARD TO KEEP UP WITH SUCH A LIMITED STAFF, TOO.
Librarians at local branches were primarily chosen from among women in the community able to read and write...
...as the budget was simply not available to hire men from the intellectual class to fulfill such duties.
HAAH...

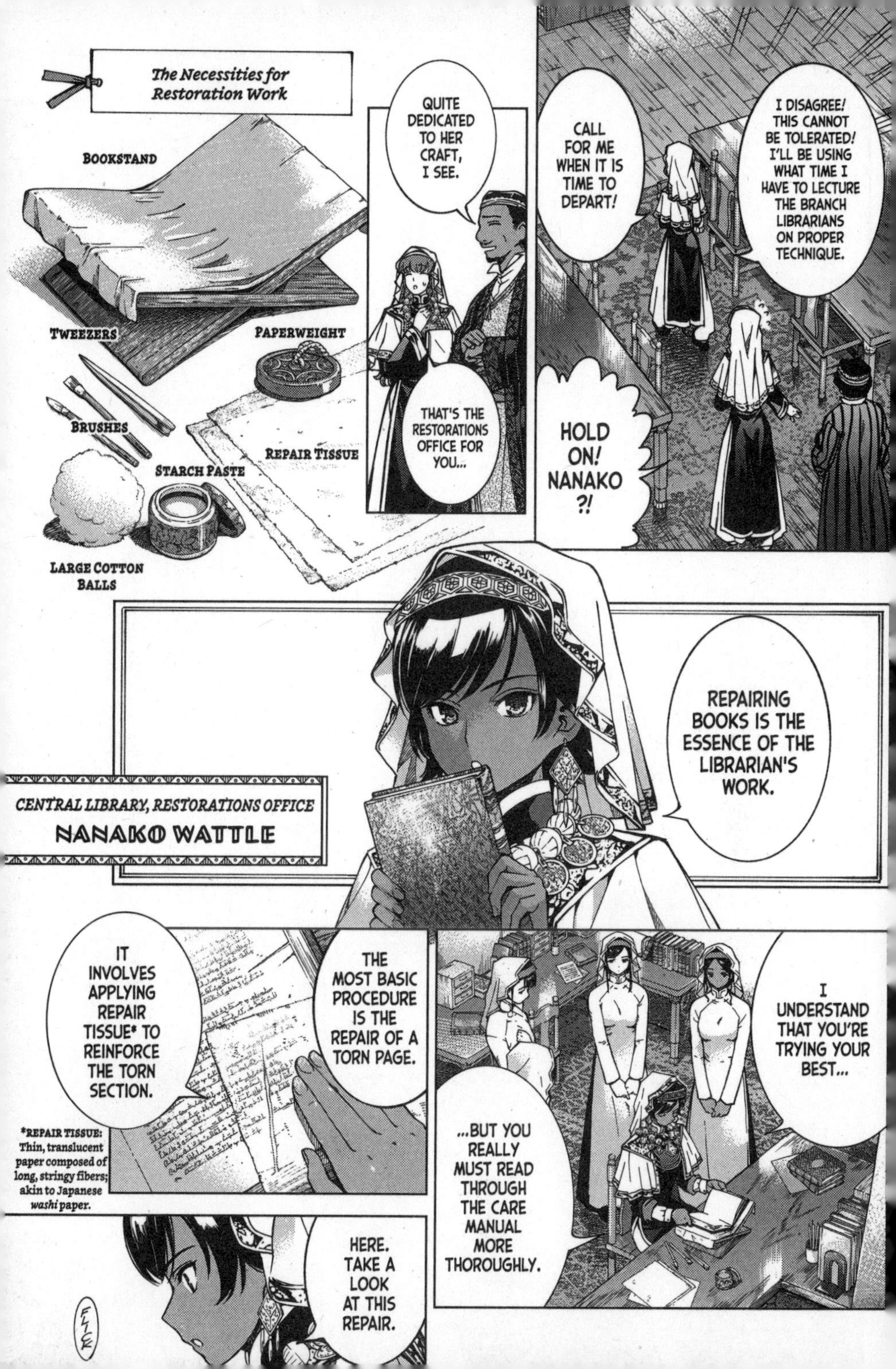
I DISAGREE! THIS CANNOT BE TOLERATED! I'LL BE USING WHAT TIME I HAVE TO LECTURE THE BRANCH LIBRARIANS ON PROPER TECHNIQUE.
CALL FOR ME WHEN IT IS TIME TO DEPART!
HOLD ON! NANAKO ?!
QUITE DEDICATED TO HER CRAFT, I SEE.
THAT'S THE RESTORATIONS OFFICE FOR YOU...
The Necessities for Restoration Work
BOOKSTAND
TWEEZERS
PAPERWEIGHT
BRUSHES
REPAIR TISSUE
STARCH PASTE
LARGE COTTON BALLS
REPAIRING BOOKS IS THE ESSENCE OF THE LIBRARIAN'S WORK.
CENTRAL LIBRARY, RESTORATIONS OFFICE
NANAKO WATTLE
I UNDERSTAND THAT YOU'RE TRYING YOUR BEST...
...BUT YOU REALLY MUST READ THROUGH THE CARE MANUAL MORE THOROUGHLY.
THE MOST BASIC PROCEDURE IS THE REPAIR OF A TORN PAGE.
IT INVOLVES APPLYING REPAIR TISSUE* TO REINFORCE THE TORN SECTION.
*REPAIR TISSUE: Thin, translucent paper composed of long, stringy fibers; akin to Japanese washi paper.
HERE. TAKE A LOOK AT THIS REPAIR.
FLICK

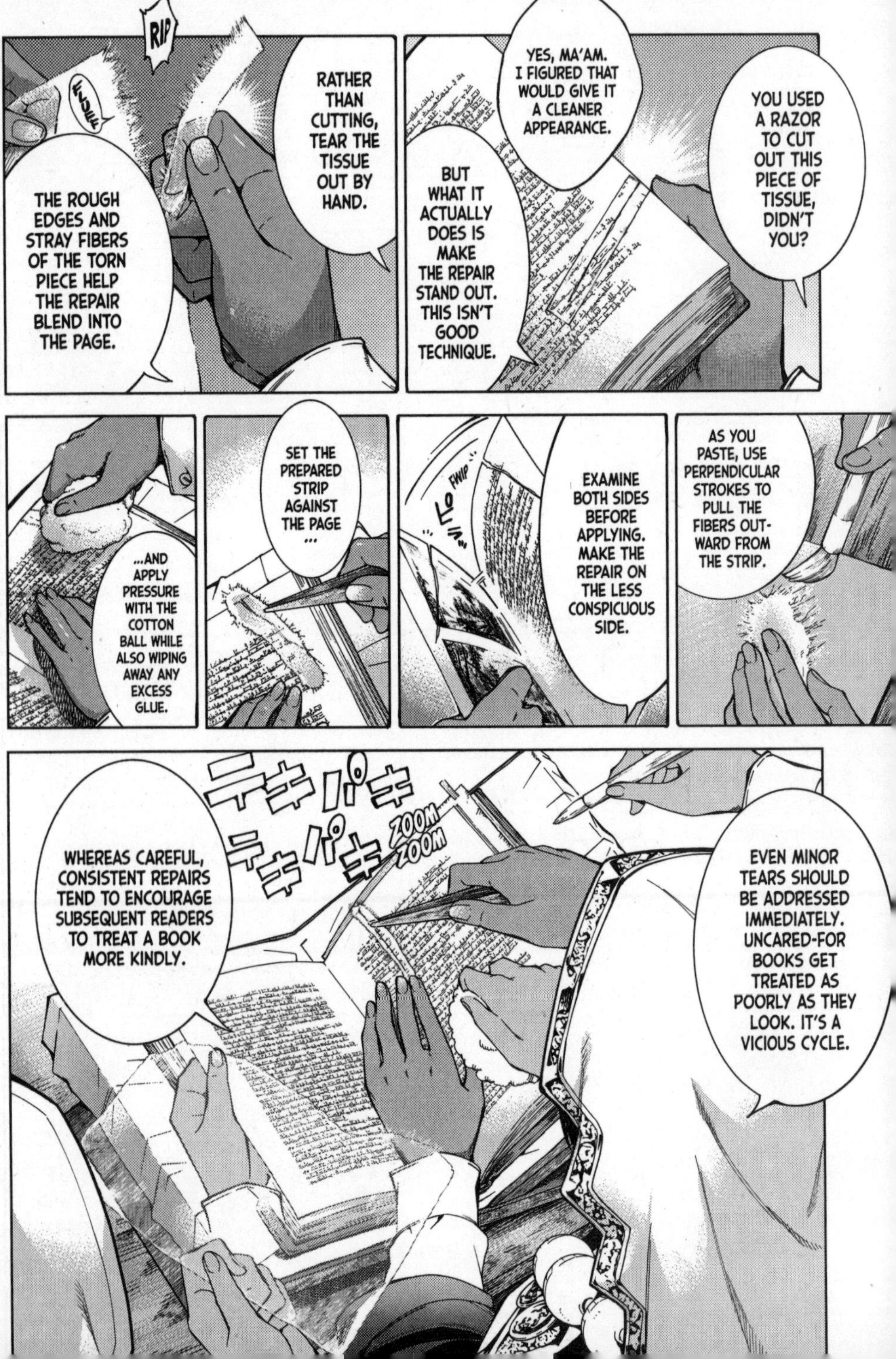
YOU USED A RAZOR TO CUT OUT THIS PIECE OF TISSUE, DIDN'T YOU?
YES, MA'AM. I FIGURED THAT WOULD GIVE IT A CLEANER APPEARANCE.
BUT WHAT IT ACTUALLY DOES IS MAKE THE REPAIR STAND OUT. THIS ISN'T GOOD TECHNIQUE.
RIP
RATHER THAN CUTTING, TEAR THE TISSUE OUT BY HAND.
THE ROUGH EDGES AND STRAY FIBERS OF THE TORN PIECE HELP THE REPAIR BLEND INTO THE PAGE.
AS YOU PASTE, USE PERPENDICULAR STROKES TO PULL THE FIBERS OUTWARD FROM THE STRIP.
FWIP
EXAMINE BOTH SIDES BEFORE APPLYING. MAKE THE REPAIR ON THE LESS CONSPICUOUS SIDE.
SET THE PREPARED STRIP AGAINST THE PAGE...
...AND APPLY PRESSURE WITH THE COTTON BALL WHILE ALSO WIPING AWAY ANY EXCESS GLUE.
EVEN MINOR TEARS SHOULD BE ADDRESSED IMMEDIATELY. UNCARED-FOR BOOKS GET TREATED AS POORLY AS THEY LOOK. IT'S A VICIOUS CYCLE.
テキパキ
テキパキ
ZOOM ZOOM
WHEREAS CAREFUL, CONSISTENT REPAIRS TEND TO ENCOURAGE SUBSEQUENT READERS TO TREAT A BOOK MORE KINDLY.

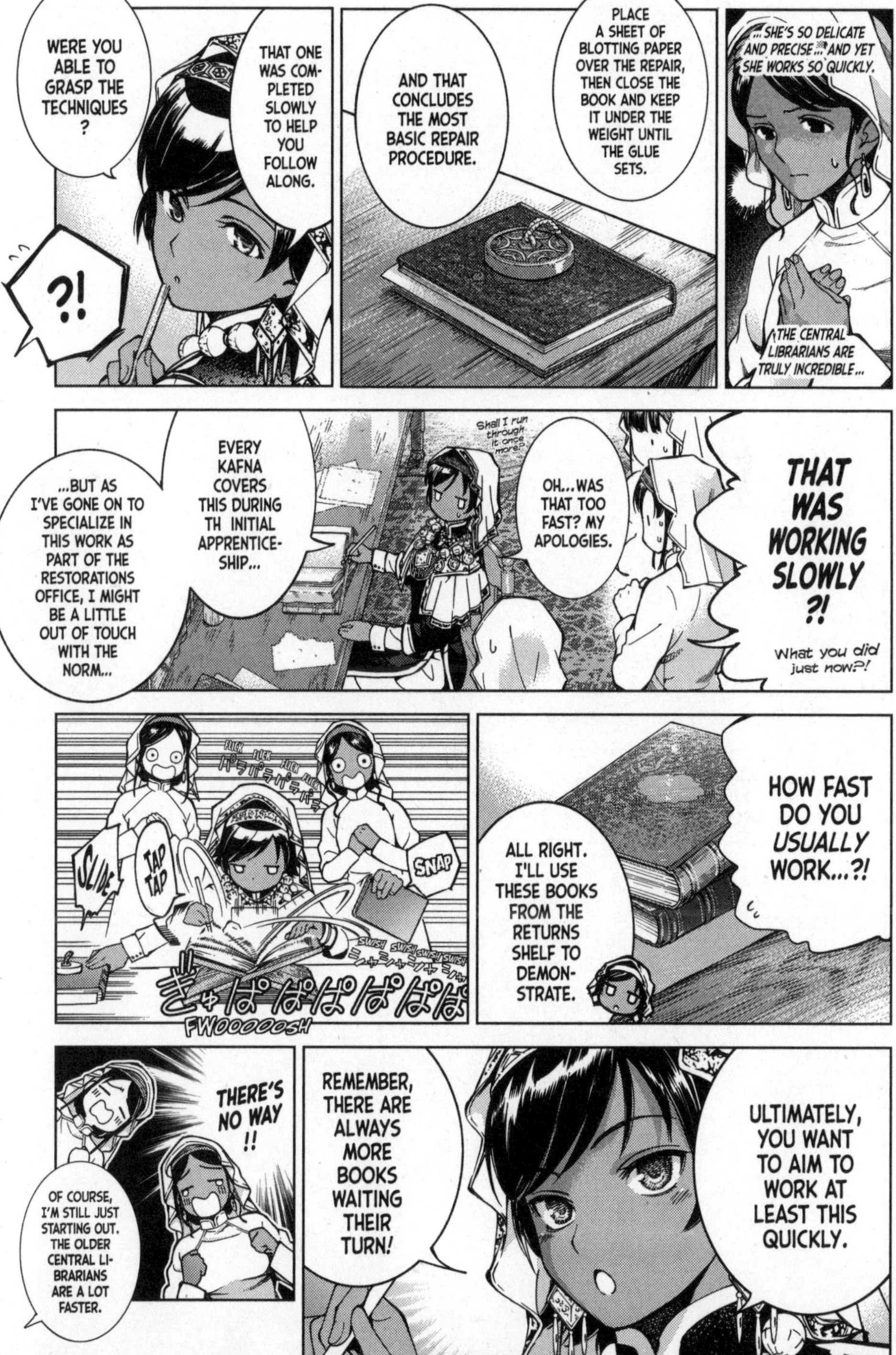
...SHE'S SO DELICATE AND PRECISE... AND YET SHE WORKS SO QUICKLY.
THE CENTRAL LIBRARIANS ARE TRULY INCREDIBLE...
PLACE A SHEET OF BLOTTING PAPER OVER THE REPAIR, THEN CLOSE THE BOOK AND KEEP IT UNDER THE WEIGHT UNTIL THE GLUE SETS.
AND THAT CONCLUDES THE MOST BASIC REPAIR PROCEDURE.
THAT ONE WAS COMPLETED SLOWLY TO HELP YOU FOLLOW ALONG.
WERE YOU ABLE TO GRASP THE TECHNIQUES?
?!
THAT WAS WORKING SLOWLY?!
What you did just now?!
OH...WAS THAT TOO FAST? MY APOLOGIES.
Shall I run through it once more?
EVERY KAFNA COVERS THIS DURING TH INITIAL APPRENTICESHIP...
...BUT AS I'VE GONE ON TO SPECIALIZE IN THIS WORK AS PART OF THE RESTORATIONS OFFICE, I MIGHT BE A LITTLE OUT OF TOUCH WITH THE NORM...
HOW FAST DO YOU USUALLY WORK...?!
ALL RIGHT. I'LL USE THESE BOOKS FROM THE RETURNS SHELF TO DEMONSTRATE.
FLICK FLICK FLICK FLICK
SNAP
TAP TAP
SLIDE
SWISH SWISH SWISH SWISH
FWOOOOOSH
ULTIMATELY, YOU WANT TO AIM TO WORK AT LEAST THIS QUICKLY.
REMEMBER, THERE ARE ALWAYS MORE BOOKS WAITING THEIR TURN!
THERE'S NO WAY!!
OF COURSE, I'M STILL JUST STARTING OUT. THE OLDER CENTRAL LIBRARIANS ARE A LOT FASTER.

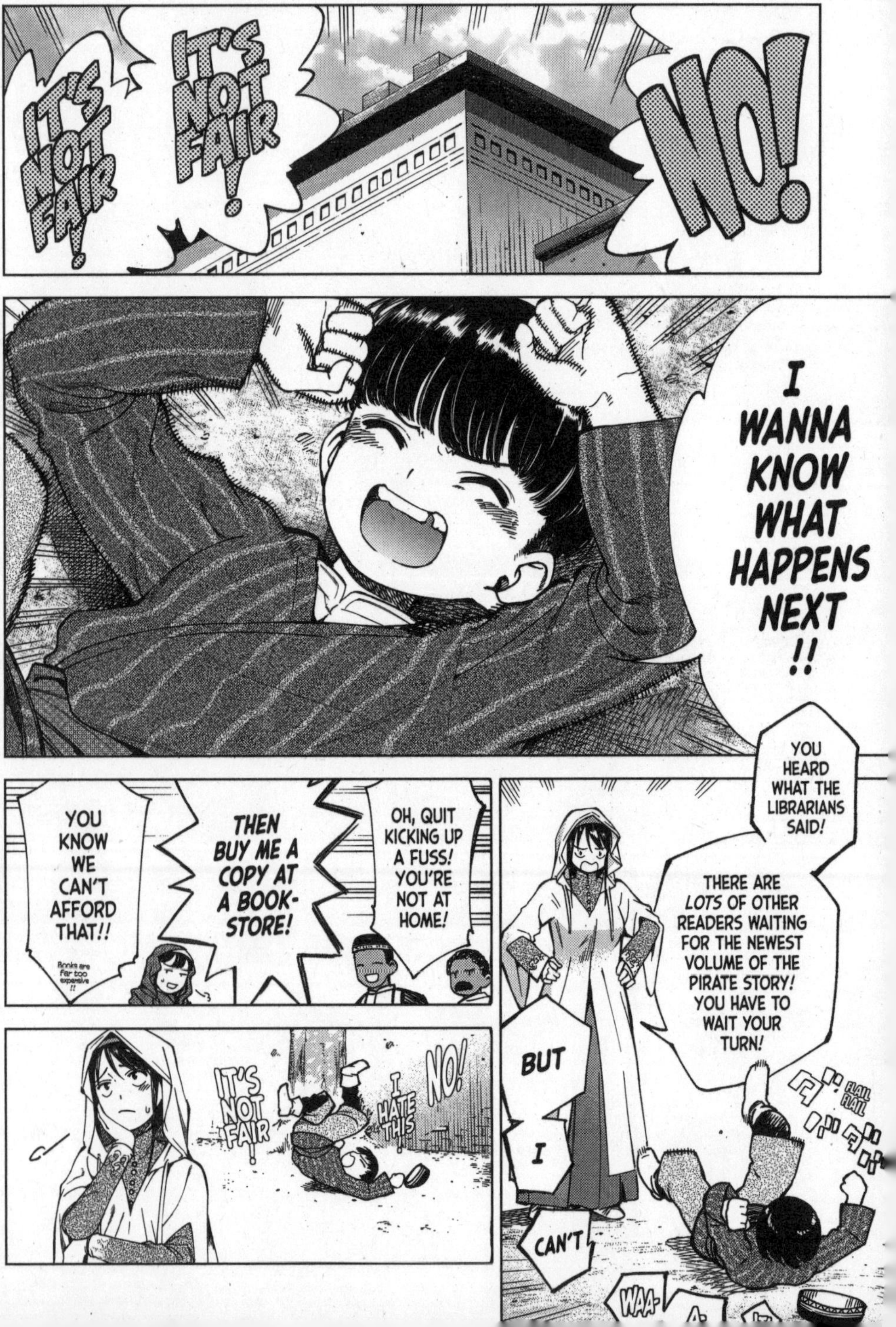
NO!
IT'S NOT FAIR!
IT'S NOT FAIR!
I WANNA KNOW WHAT HAPPENS NEXT!!
YOU HEARD WHAT THE LIBRARIANS SAID!
THERE ARE LOTS OF OTHER READERS WAITING FOR THE NEWEST VOLUME OF THE PIRATE STORY! YOU HAVE TO WAIT YOUR TURN!
FLAIL FLAIL
BUT
I
CAN'T
WAA-
OH, QUIT KICKING UP A FUSS! YOU'RE NOT AT HOME!
THEN BUY ME A COPY AT A BOOK-STORE!
YOU KNOW WE CAN'T AFFORD THAT!!
Books are far too expensive!!
NO!
I HATE THIS
IT'S NOT FAIR!

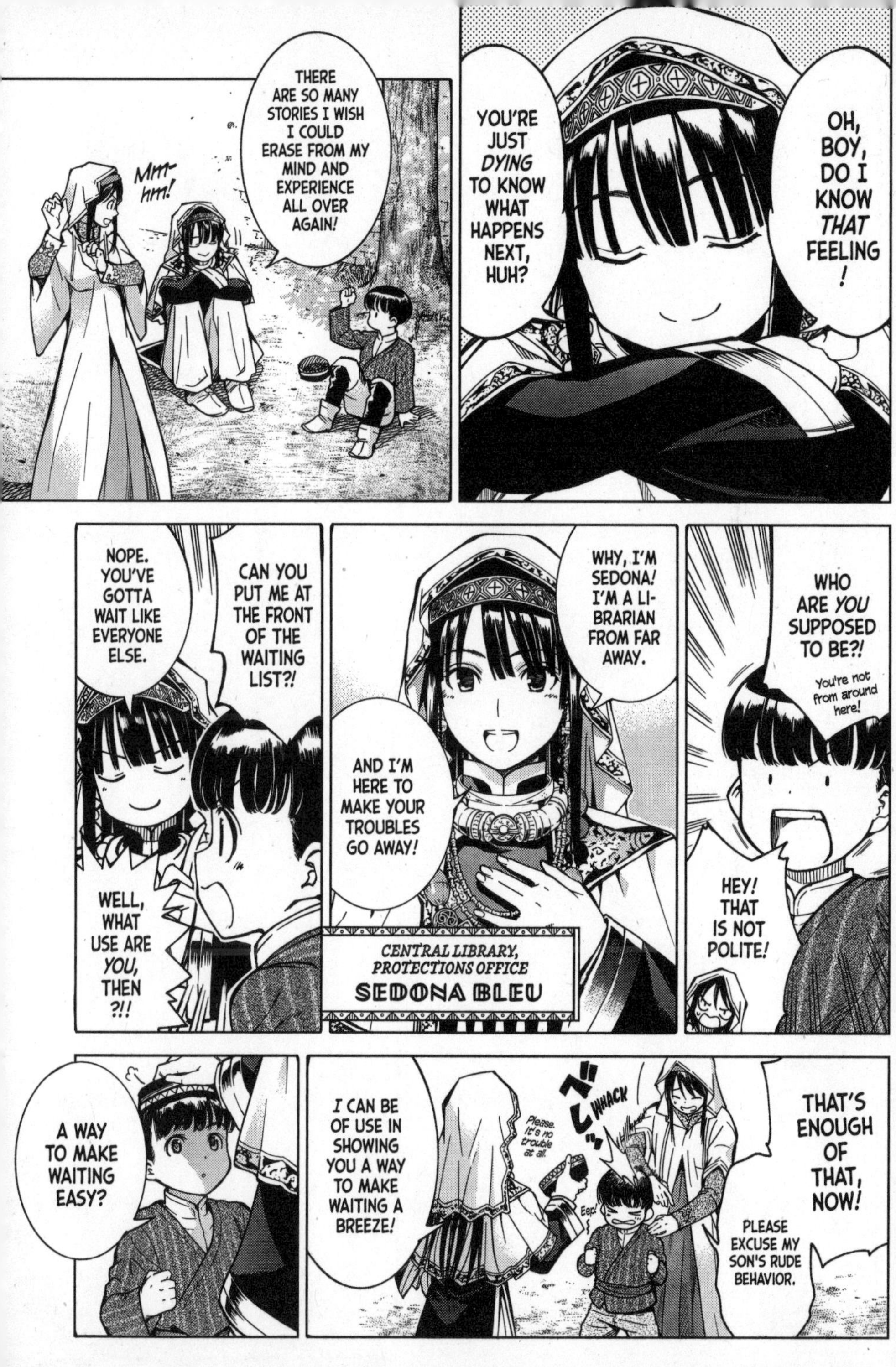
OH, BOY, DO I KNOW *THAT* FEELING!
YOU'RE JUST *DYING* TO KNOW WHAT HAPPENS NEXT, HUH?
THERE ARE SO MANY STORIES I WISH I COULD ERASE FROM MY MIND AND EXPERIENCE ALL OVER AGAIN!
Mm-hm!
WHO ARE *YOU* SUPPOSED TO BE?!
You're not from around here!
HEY! THAT IS NOT POLITE!
WHY, I'M SEDONA! I'M A LIBRARIAN FROM FAR AWAY.
AND I'M HERE TO MAKE YOUR TROUBLES GO AWAY!
CENTRAL LIBRARY, PROTECTIONS OFFICE
SEDONA BLEU
CAN YOU PUT ME AT THE FRONT OF THE WAITING LIST?!
NOPE. YOU'VE GOTTA WAIT LIKE EVERYONE ELSE.
WELL, WHAT USE ARE *YOU*, THEN?!!
THAT'S ENOUGH OF THAT, NOW!
PLEASE EXCUSE MY SON'S RUDE BEHAVIOR.
WHACK
Eep!
Please. It's no trouble at all.
I CAN BE OF USE IN SHOWING YOU A WAY TO MAKE WAITING A BREEZE!
A WAY TO MAKE WAITING EASY?

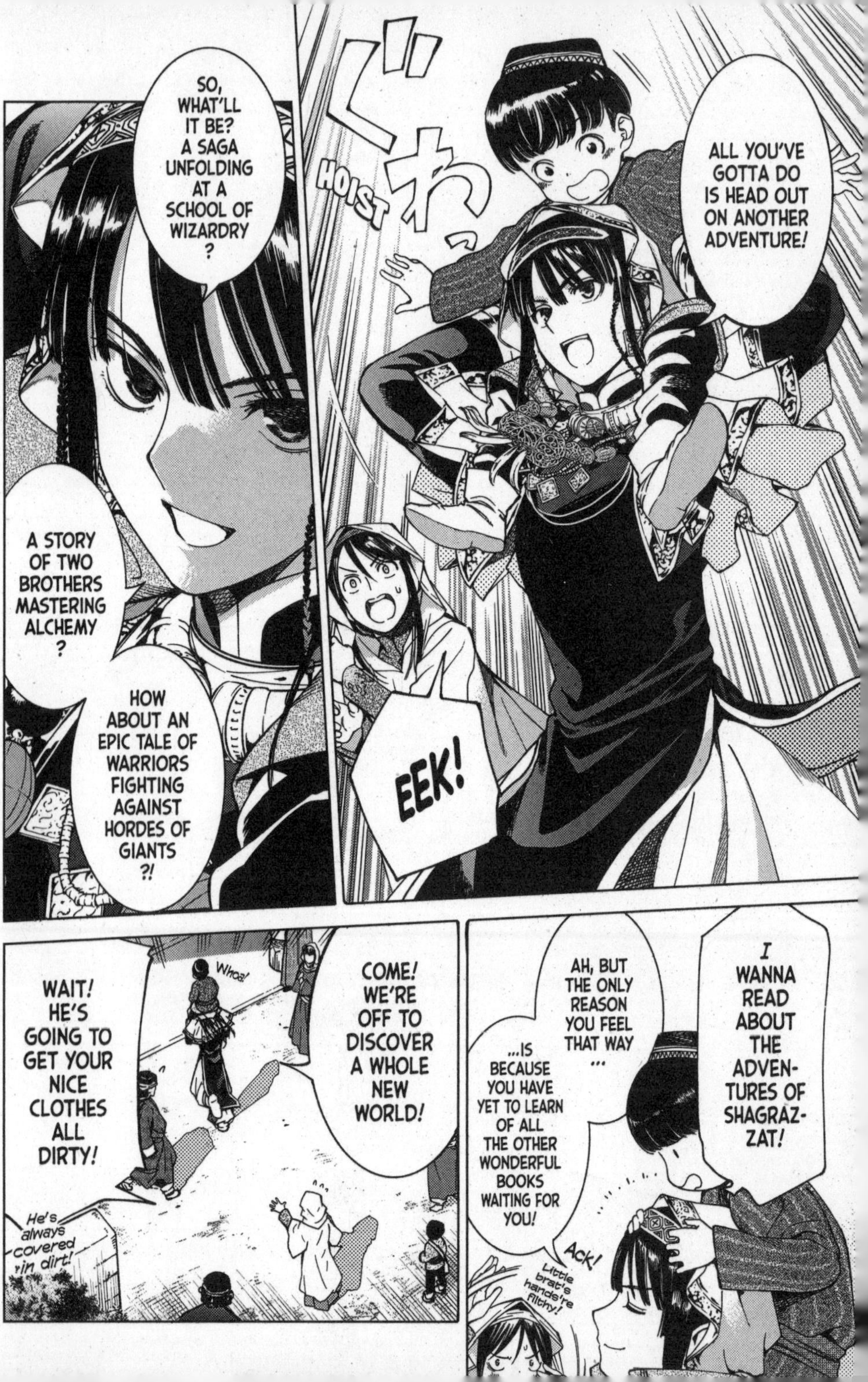
ALL YOU'VE GOTTA DO IS HEAD OUT ON ANOTHER ADVENTURE!
ぐわっ
HOIST
EEK!
SO, WHAT'LL IT BE? A SAGA UNFOLDING AT A SCHOOL OF WIZARDRY?
A STORY OF TWO BROTHERS MASTERING ALCHEMY?
HOW ABOUT AN EPIC TALE OF WARRIORS FIGHTING AGAINST HORDES OF GIANTS?!
I WANNA READ ABOUT THE ADVEN-TURES OF SHAGRAZ-ZAT!
AH, BUT THE ONLY REASON YOU FEEL THAT WAY...
...IS BECAUSE YOU HAVE YET TO LEARN OF ALL THE OTHER WONDERFUL BOOKS WAITING FOR YOU!
ACK!
Little brat's hands're filthy!
COME! WE'RE OFF TO DISCOVER A WHOLE NEW WORLD!
Whoa!
WAIT! HE'S GOING TO GET YOUR NICE CLOTHES ALL DIRTY!
He's always covered in dirt!

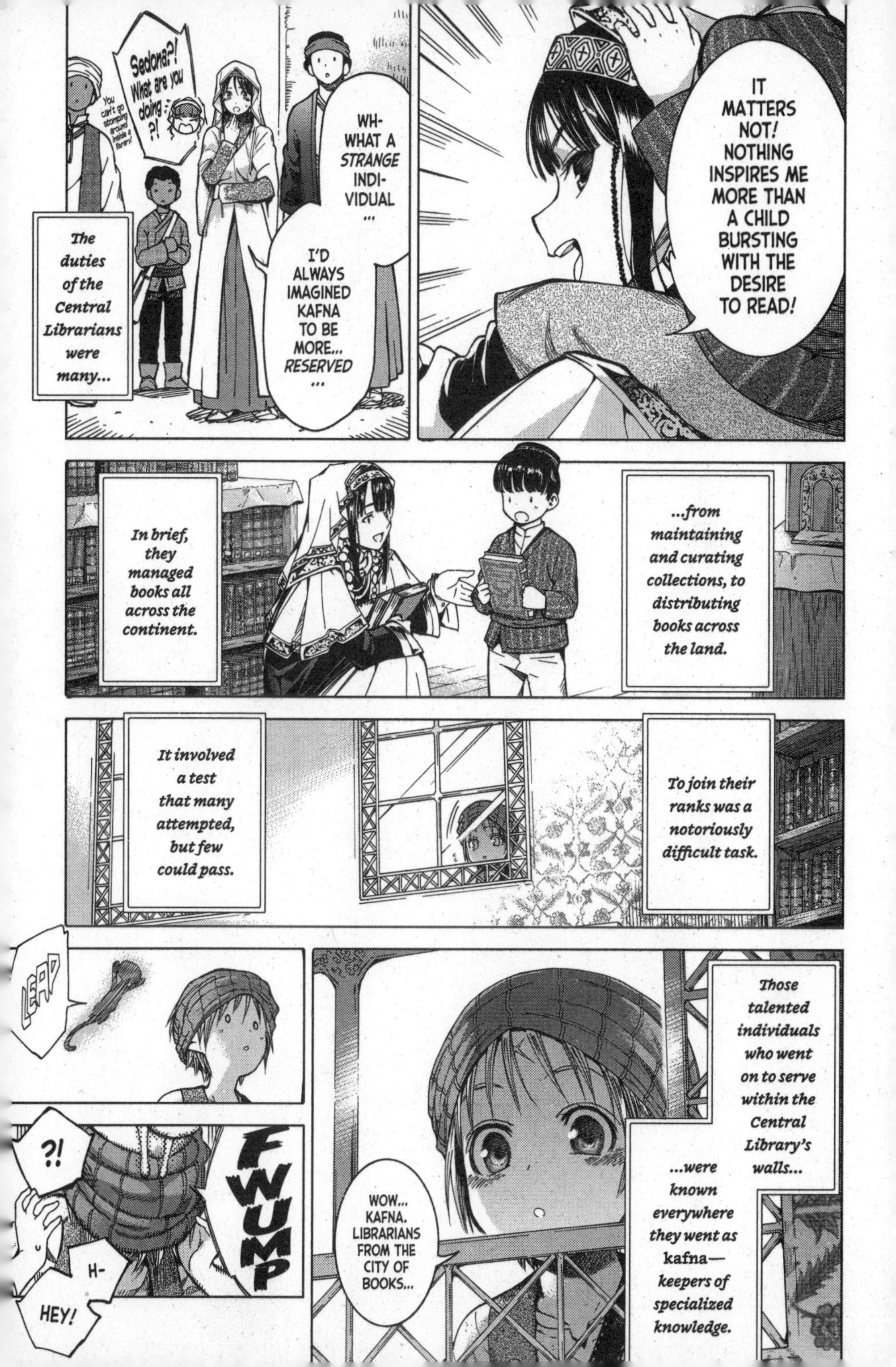
IT MATTERS NOT! NOTHING INSPIRES ME MORE THAN A CHILD BURSTING WITH THE DESIRE TO READ!
Sedona?! What are you doing ?!
You can't go stomping around inside a library!
WH- WHAT A STRANGE INDIVIDUAL ...
I'D ALWAYS IMAGINED KAFNA TO BE MORE... RESERVED ...
The duties of the Central Librarians were many...
In brief, they managed books all across the continent.
...from maintaining and curating collections, to distributing books across the land.
To join their ranks was a notoriously difficult task.
It involved a test that many attempted, but few could pass.
Those talented individuals who went on to serve within the Central Library's walls...
...were known everywhere they went as kafna—keepers of specialized knowledge.
WOW... KAFNA. LIBRARIANS FROM THE CITY OF BOOKS...
LEAP
?!
FWUMP
H-
HEY!

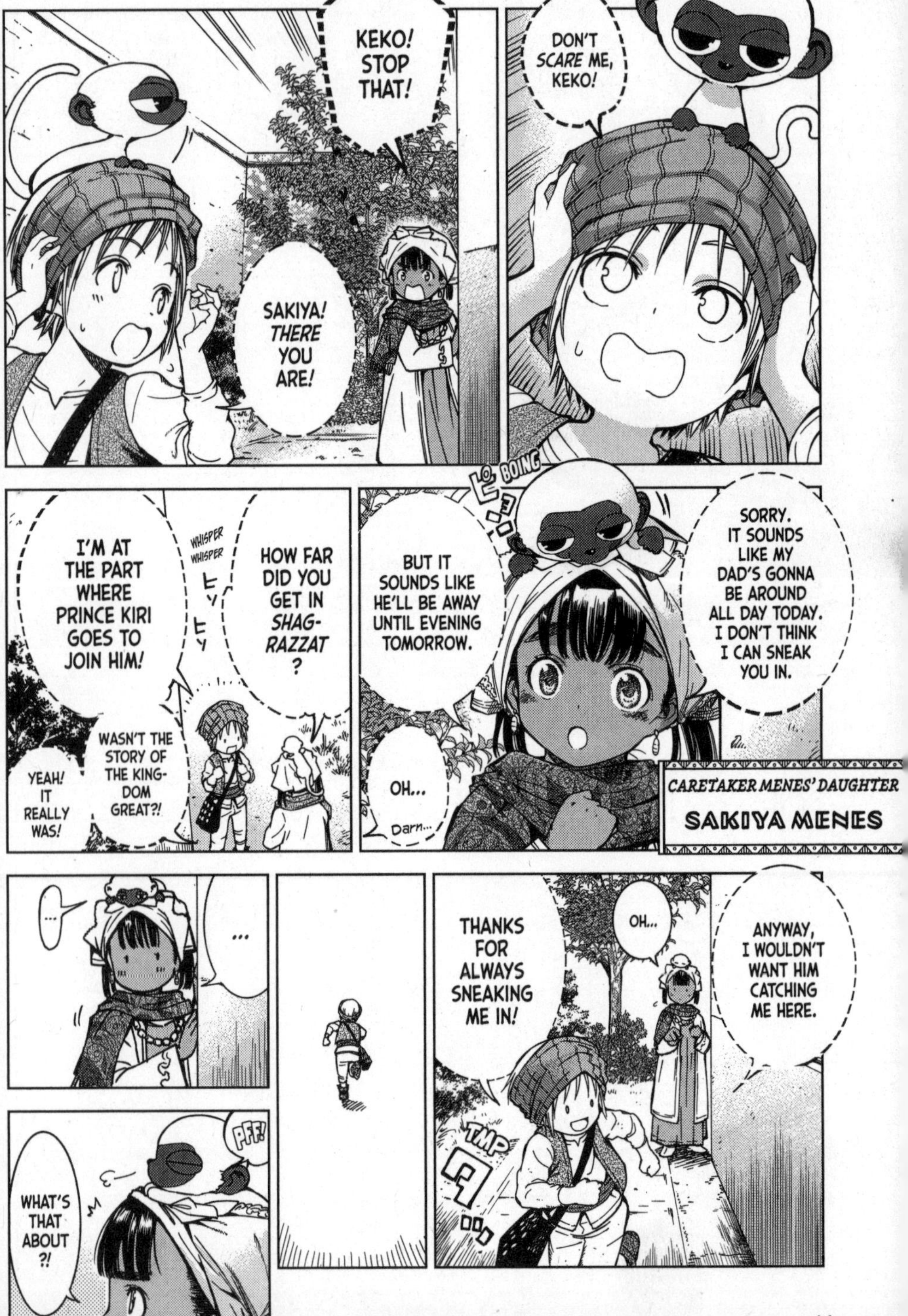
DON'T *SCARE* ME, KEKO!
KEKO! STOP THAT!
SAKIYA! *THERE* YOU ARE!
BOING
SORRY. IT SOUNDS LIKE MY DAD'S GONNA BE AROUND ALL DAY TODAY. I DON'T THINK I CAN SNEAK YOU IN.
BUT IT SOUNDS LIKE HE'LL BE AWAY UNTIL EVENING TOMORROW.
OH...
Darn...
CARETAKER MENES' DAUGHTER
SAKIYA MENES
HOW FAR DID YOU GET IN *SHAG-RAZZAT*?
WHISPER WHISPER
I'M AT THE PART WHERE PRINCE KIRI GOES TO JOIN HIM!
WASN'T THE STORY OF THE KING-DOM GREAT?!
YEAH! IT REALLY WAS!
ANYWAY, I WOULDN'T WANT HIM CATCHING ME HERE.
OH...
THANKS FOR ALWAYS SNEAKING ME IN!
TMP
...
...
PFF!
WHAT'S THAT ABOUT?!

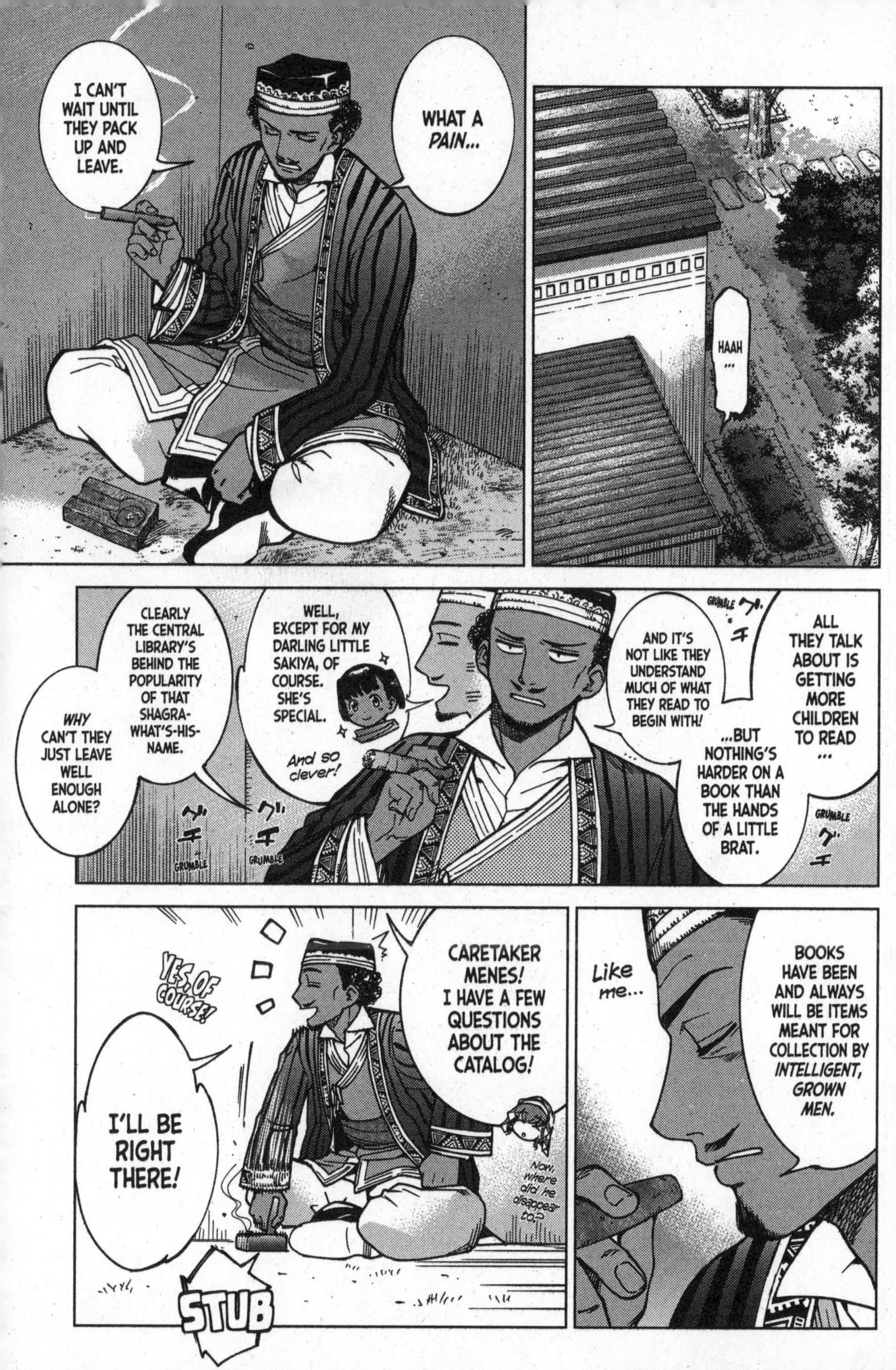
HAAH...
WHAT A PAIN...
I CAN'T WAIT UNTIL THEY PACK UP AND LEAVE.
GRUMBLE
ALL THEY TALK ABOUT IS GETTING MORE CHILDREN TO READ...
AND IT'S NOT LIKE THEY UNDERSTAND MUCH OF WHAT THEY READ TO BEGIN WITH!
...BUT NOTHING'S HARDER ON A BOOK THAN THE HANDS OF A LITTLE BRAT.
GRUMBLE
WELL, EXCEPT FOR MY DARLING LITTLE SAKIYA, OF COURSE. SHE'S SPECIAL.
And so clever!
CLEARLY THE CENTRAL LIBRARY'S BEHIND THE POPULARITY OF THAT SHAGRA-WHAT'S-HIS-NAME.
WHY CAN'T THEY JUST LEAVE WELL ENOUGH ALONE?
GRUMBLE
GRUMBLE
BOOKS HAVE BEEN AND ALWAYS WILL BE ITEMS MEANT FOR COLLECTION BY INTELLIGENT, GROWN MEN.
Like me...
CARETAKER MENES! I HAVE A FEW QUESTIONS ABOUT THE CATALOG!
YES, OF COURSE!
Now, where did he disappear to?
I'LL BE RIGHT THERE!
STUB

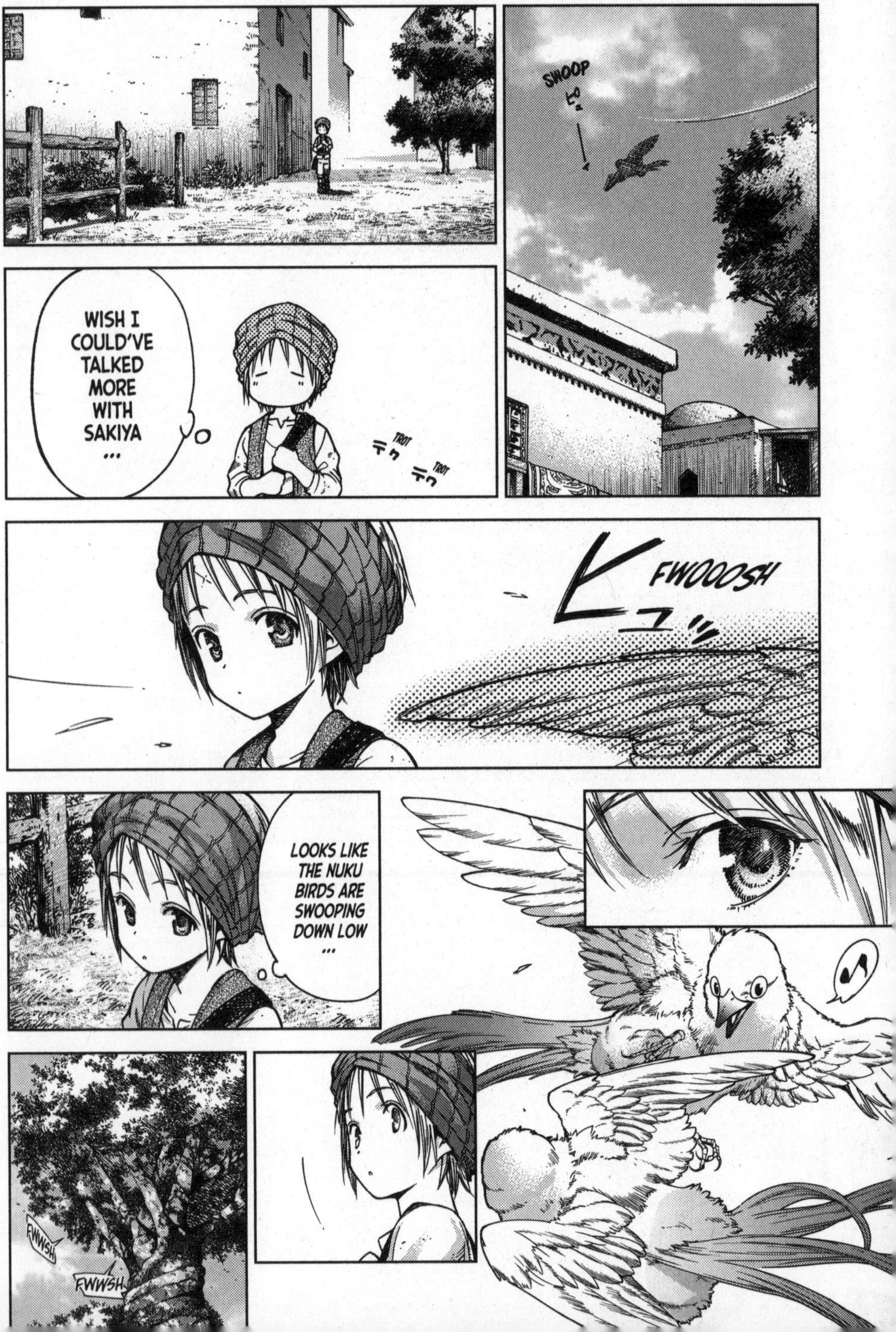
SWOOP
ピュ
WISH I COULD'VE TALKED MORE WITH SAKIYA ...
TROT
テク
TROT
テク
FWOOOSH
LOOKS LIKE THE NUKU BIRDS ARE SWOOPING DOWN LOW ...
♪
FWWSH
FWWSH

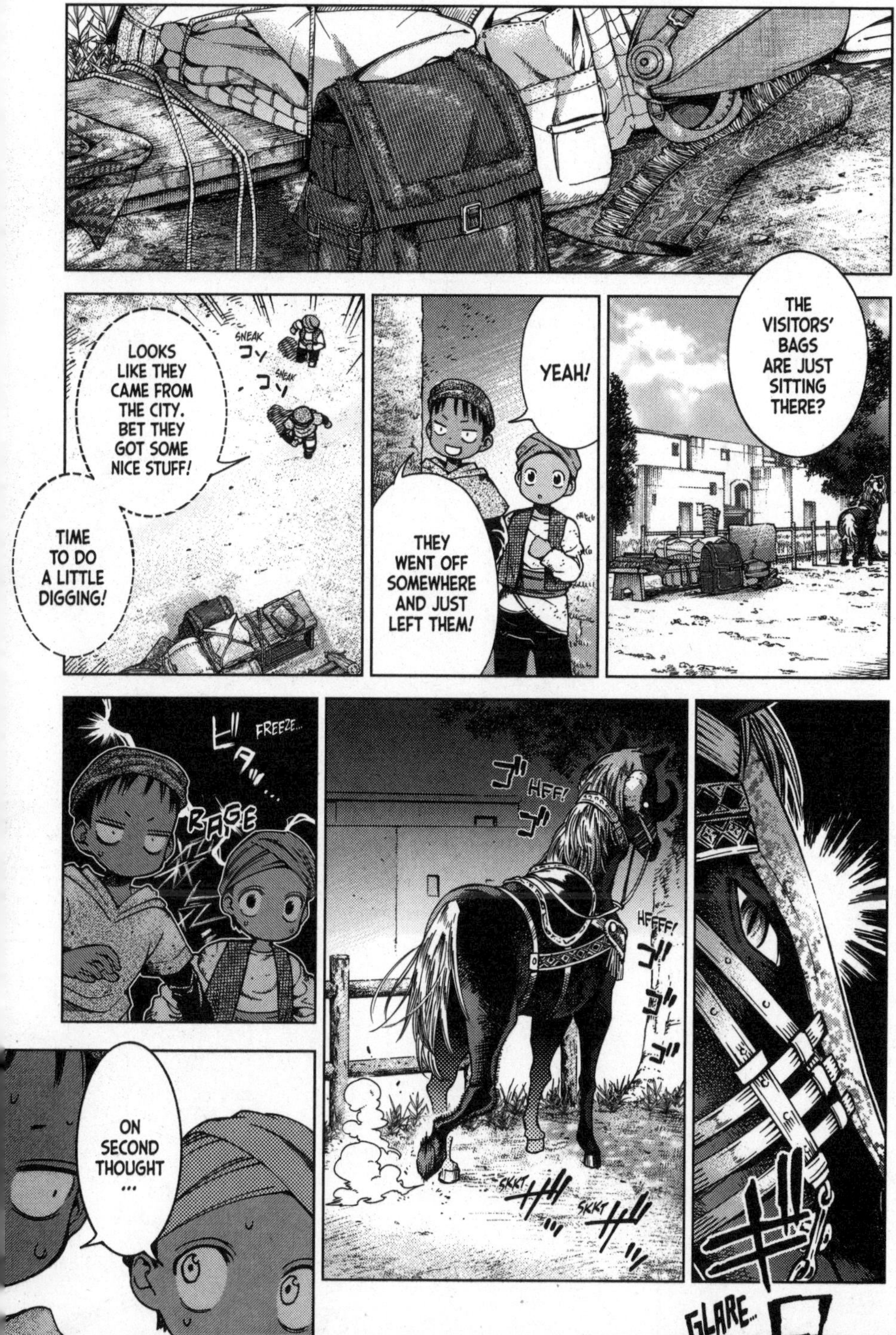
THE VISITORS' BAGS ARE JUST SITTING THERE?
YEAH!
THEY WENT OFF SOMEWHERE AND JUST LEFT THEM!
SNEAK
SNEAK
LOOKS LIKE THEY CAME FROM THE CITY. BET THEY GOT SOME NICE STUFF!
TIME TO DO A LITTLE DIGGING!
GLARE...
HFF!
HFFFF!
SKKT
SKKT
FREEZE...
RAGE
ON SECOND THOUGHT ...

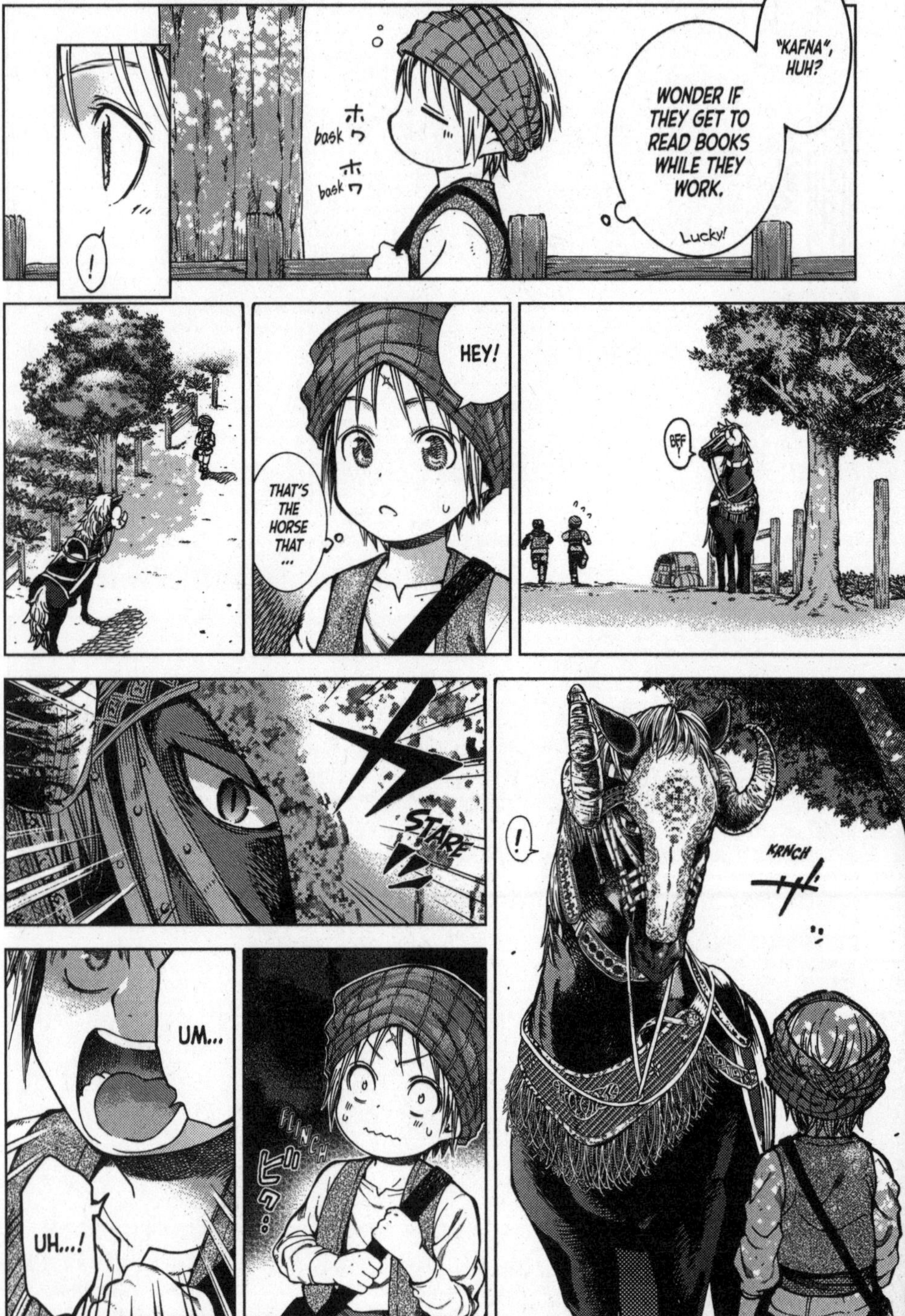
"KAFNA", HUH?
WONDER IF THEY GET TO READ BOOKS WHILE THEY WORK.
Lucky!
bask
bask
!
BFF!
HEY!
THAT'S THE HORSE THAT ...
!
KRNCH
STARE
FLINCH
UM...
UH...!

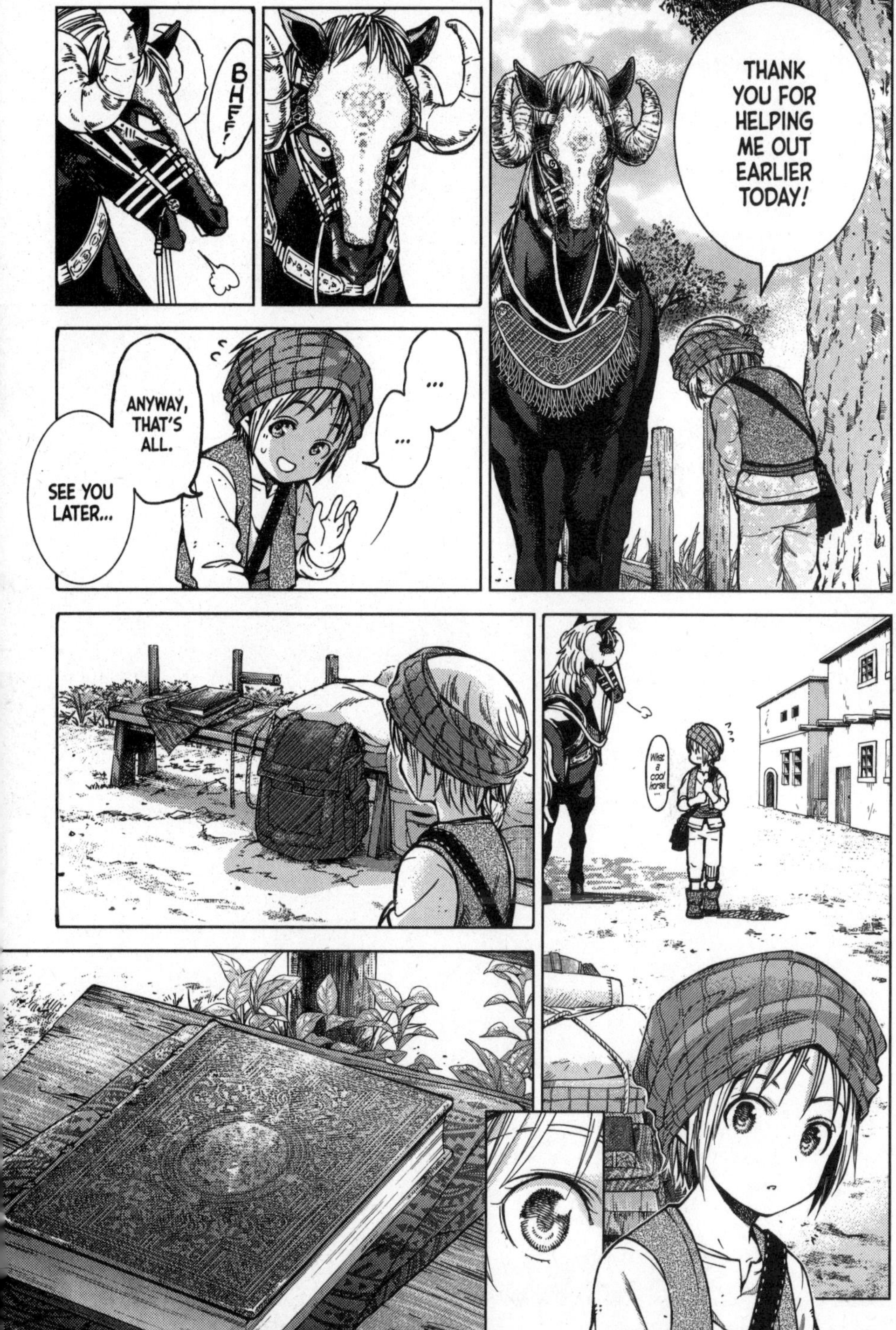
THANK YOU FOR HELPING ME OUT EARLIER TODAY!
BHFF!
...
...
ANYWAY, THAT'S ALL.
SEE YOU LATER...
What a cool horse...

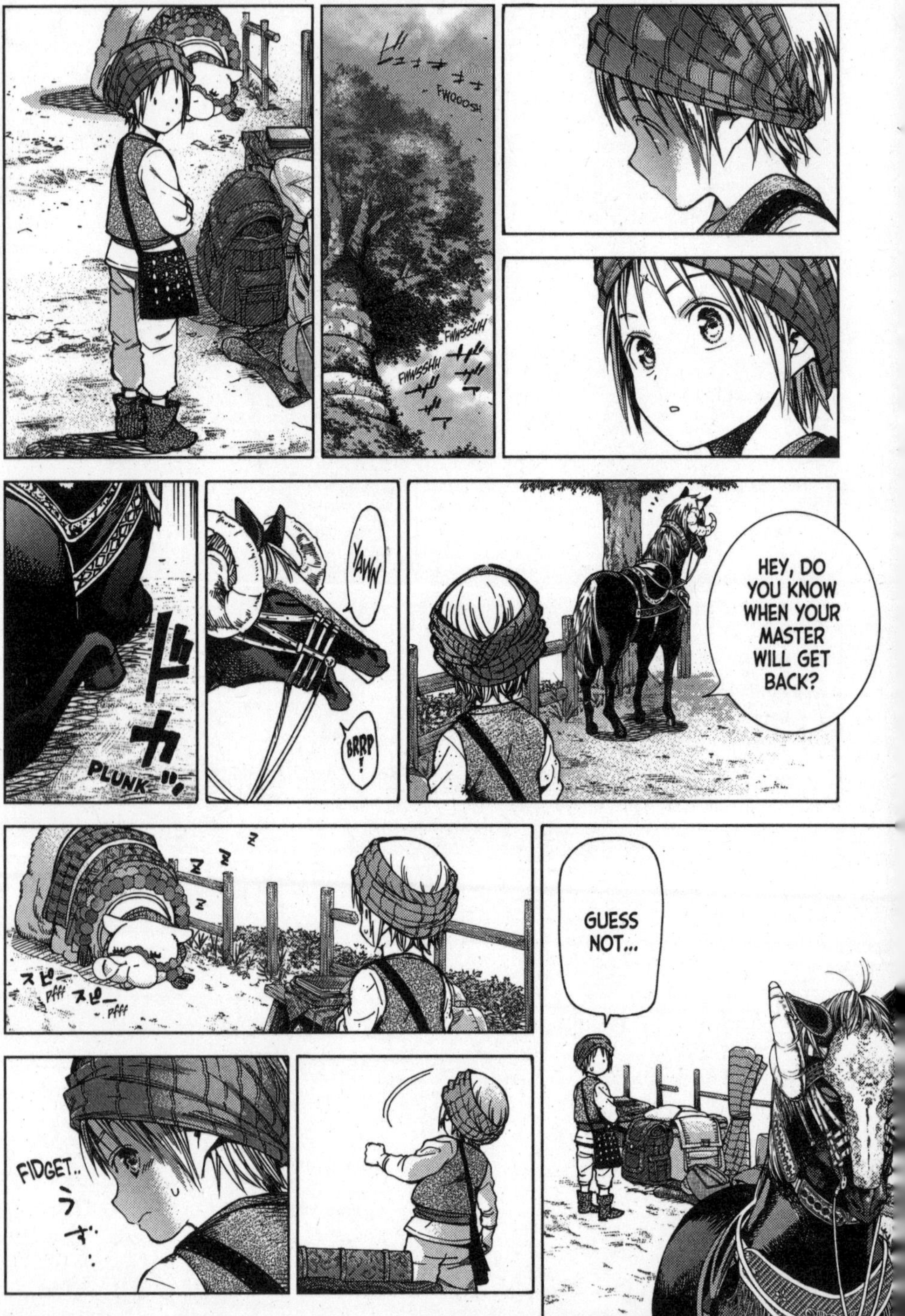
ビュォォォ
FWOOOSH
FWWSSHH
ザザ
FWWSSHH
ザザ
HEY, DO YOU KNOW WHEN YOUR MASTER WILL GET BACK?
YAWN
BRRP!
ドカ
PLUNK
GUESS NOT...
Z
Z
Z
Z
スピー
pfff
スピー
pfff
FIDGET..
うず..

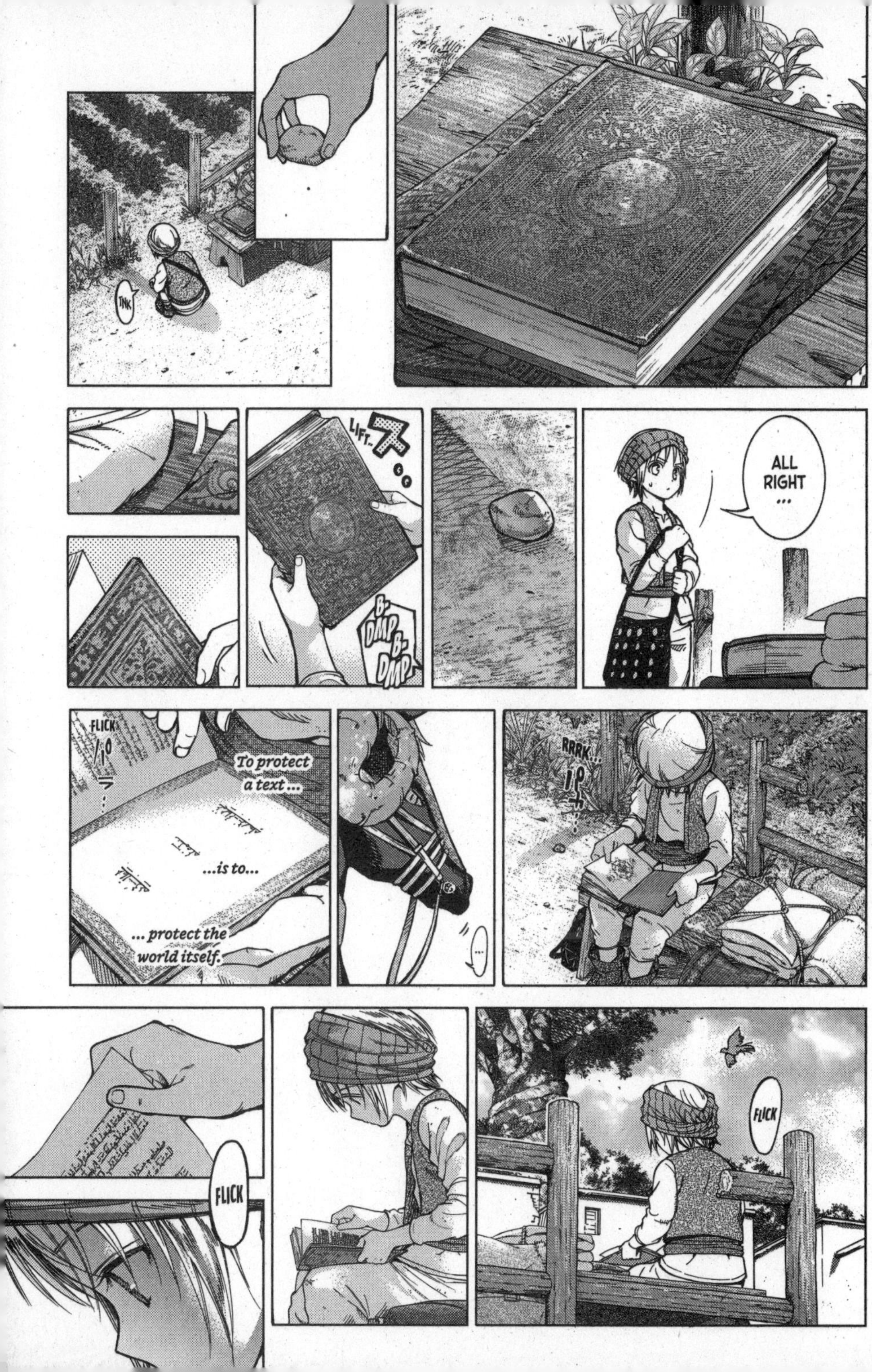
TINK
ALL RIGHT ...
LIFT..
B-DMP B-DMP
RRRK...
...
FLICK
To protect a text ...
...is to...
... protect the world itself.
FLICK
FLICK

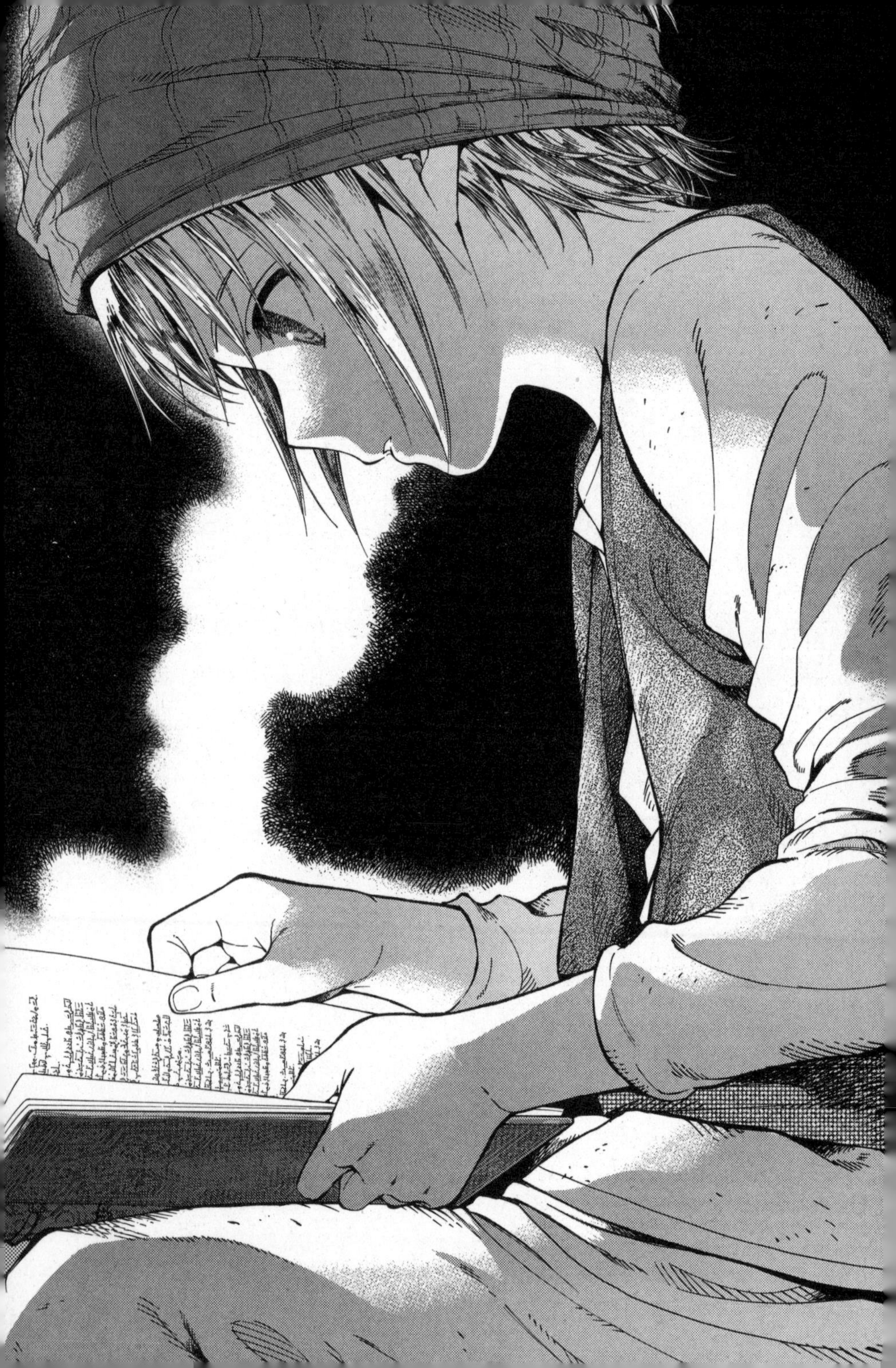

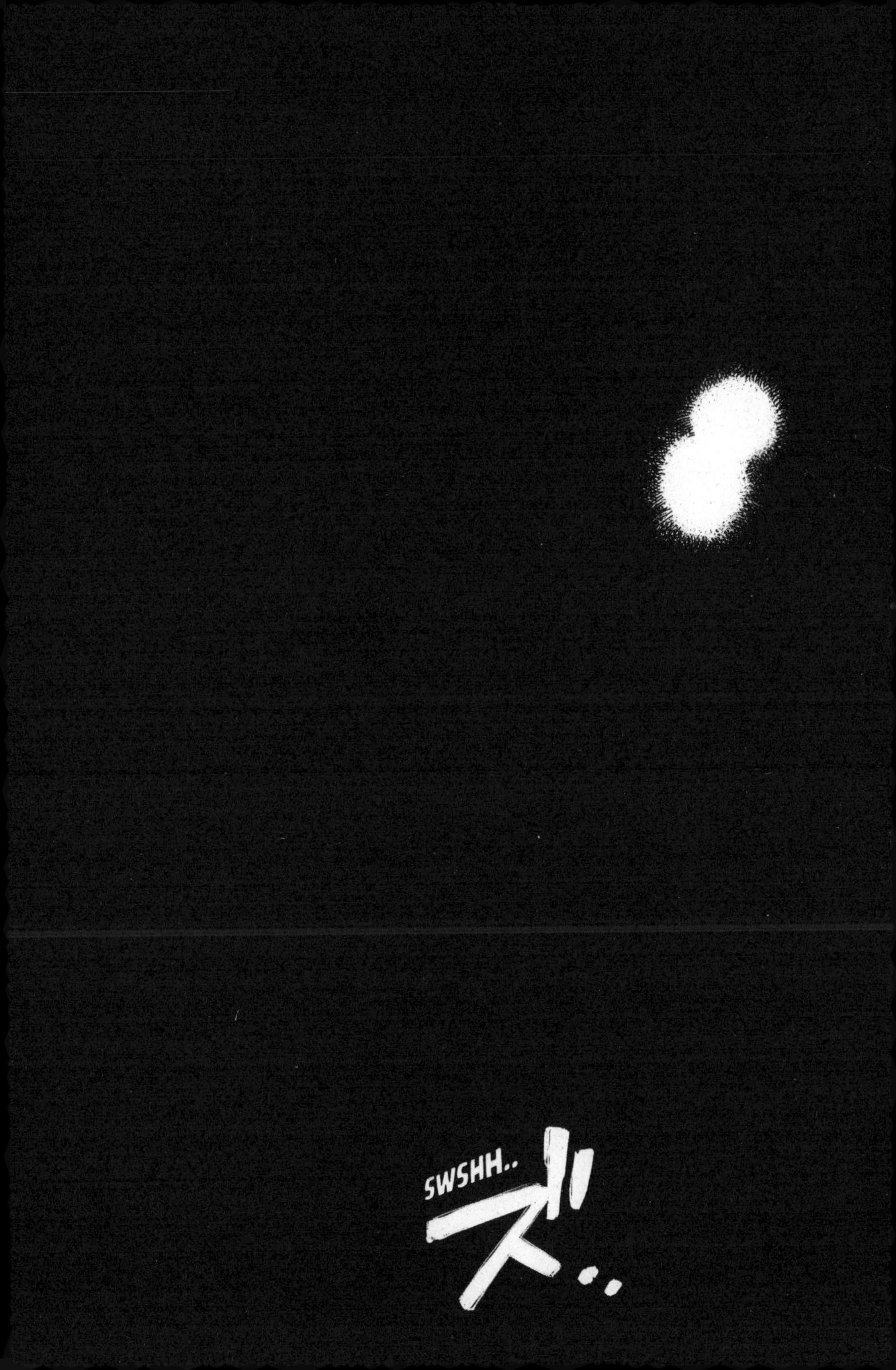
SWSHH..
ズ..

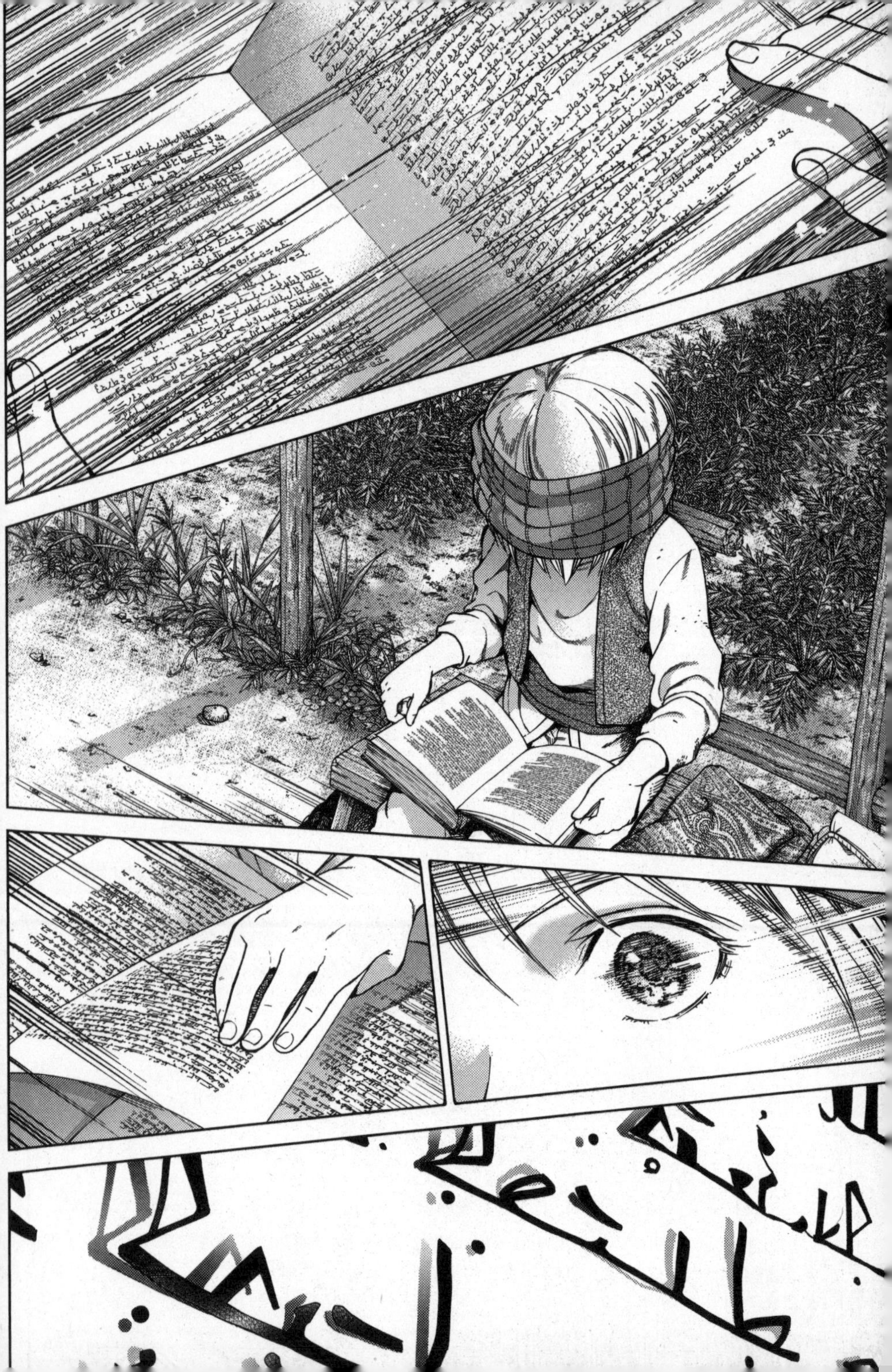

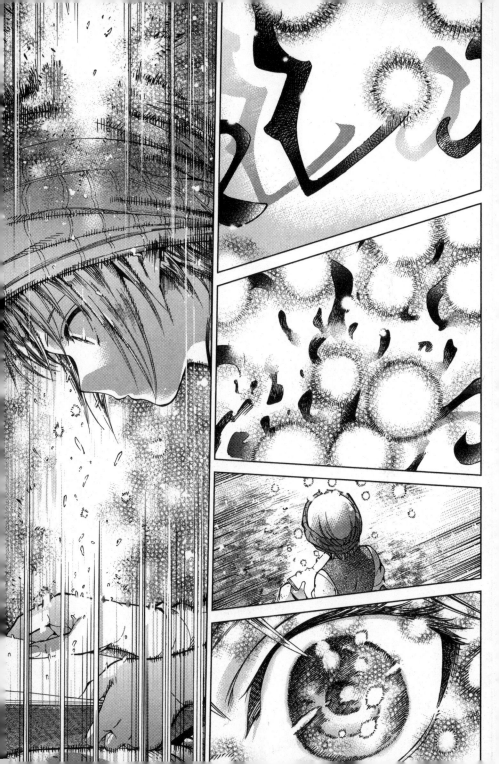

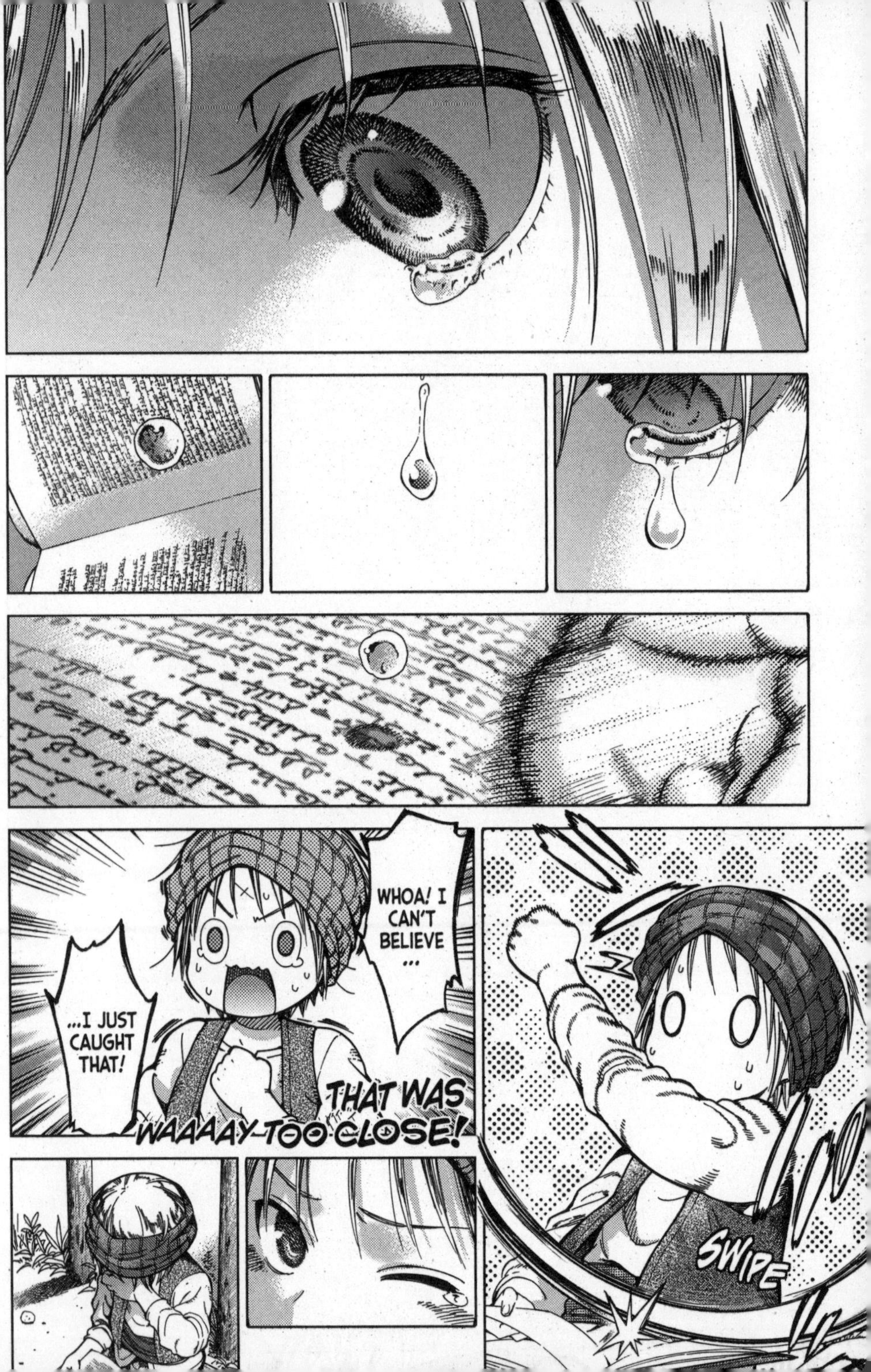
SWIPE
WHOA! I CAN'T BELIEVE ...
...I JUST CAUGHT THAT!
THAT WAS WAAAAY TOO CLOSE!

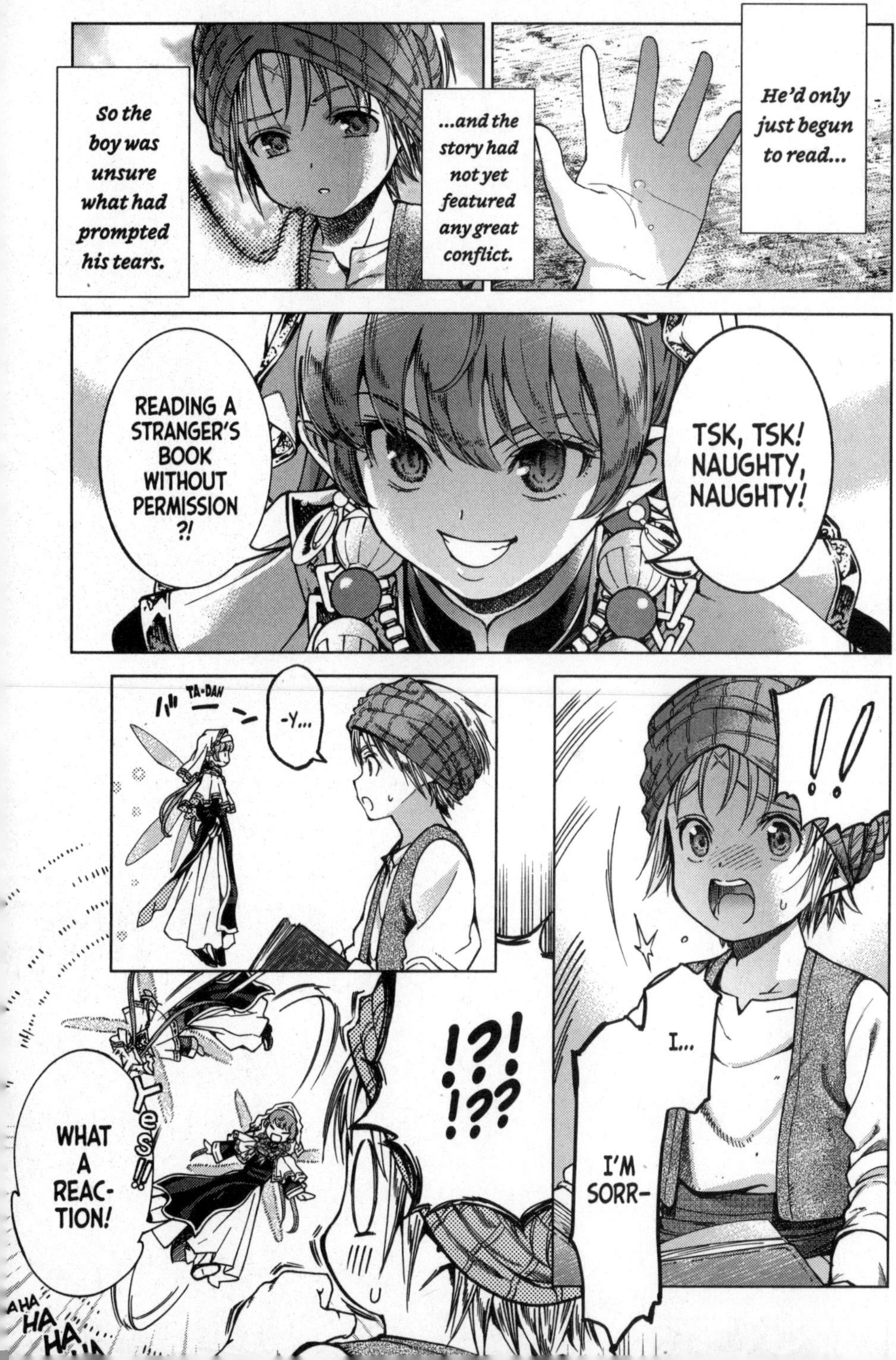
He'd only just begun to read...
...and the story had not yet featured any great conflict.
So the boy was unsure what had prompted his tears.
TSK, TSK! NAUGHTY, NAUGHTY!
READING A STRANGER'S BOOK WITHOUT PERMISSION ?!
!!
I...
I'M SORR-
TA-DAH
-Y...
!?! !??
Yes!!
WHAT A REAC-TION!
AHA HA HA

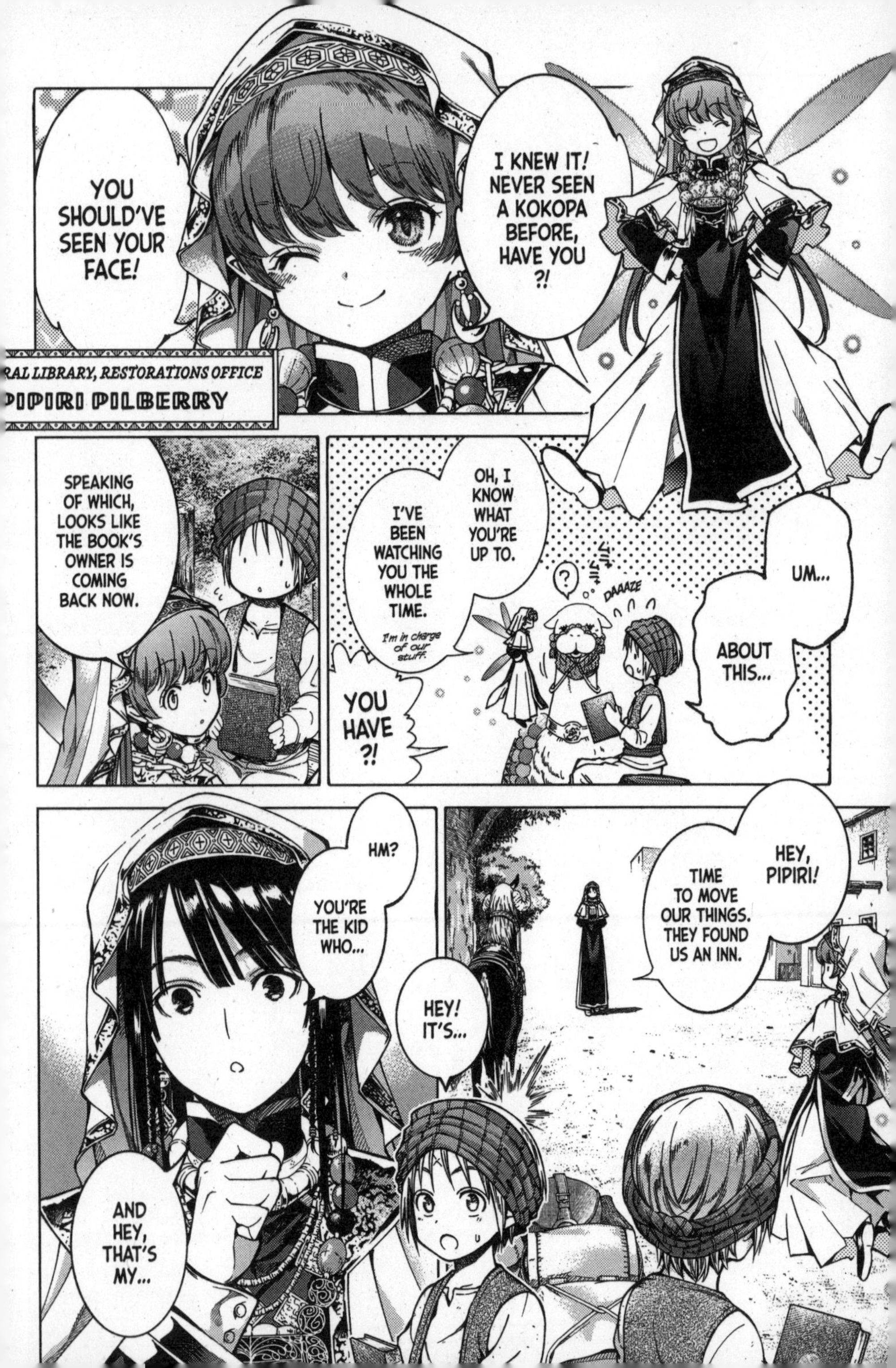

I KNEW IT! NEVER SEEN A KOKOPA BEFORE, HAVE YOU ?!
YOU SHOULD'VE SEEN YOUR FACE!
RAL LIBRARY, RESTORATIONS OFFICE
PIPIRI PILBERRY
UM...
ABOUT THIS...
DAAAZE
OH, I KNOW WHAT YOU'RE UP TO.
I'VE BEEN WATCHING YOU THE WHOLE TIME.
I'm in charge of our stuff.
YOU HAVE ?!
SPEAKING OF WHICH, LOOKS LIKE THE BOOK'S OWNER IS COMING BACK NOW.
HEY, PIPIRI!
TIME TO MOVE OUR THINGS. THEY FOUND US AN INN.
HM?
YOU'RE THE KID WHO...
HEY! IT'S...
AND HEY, THAT'S MY...

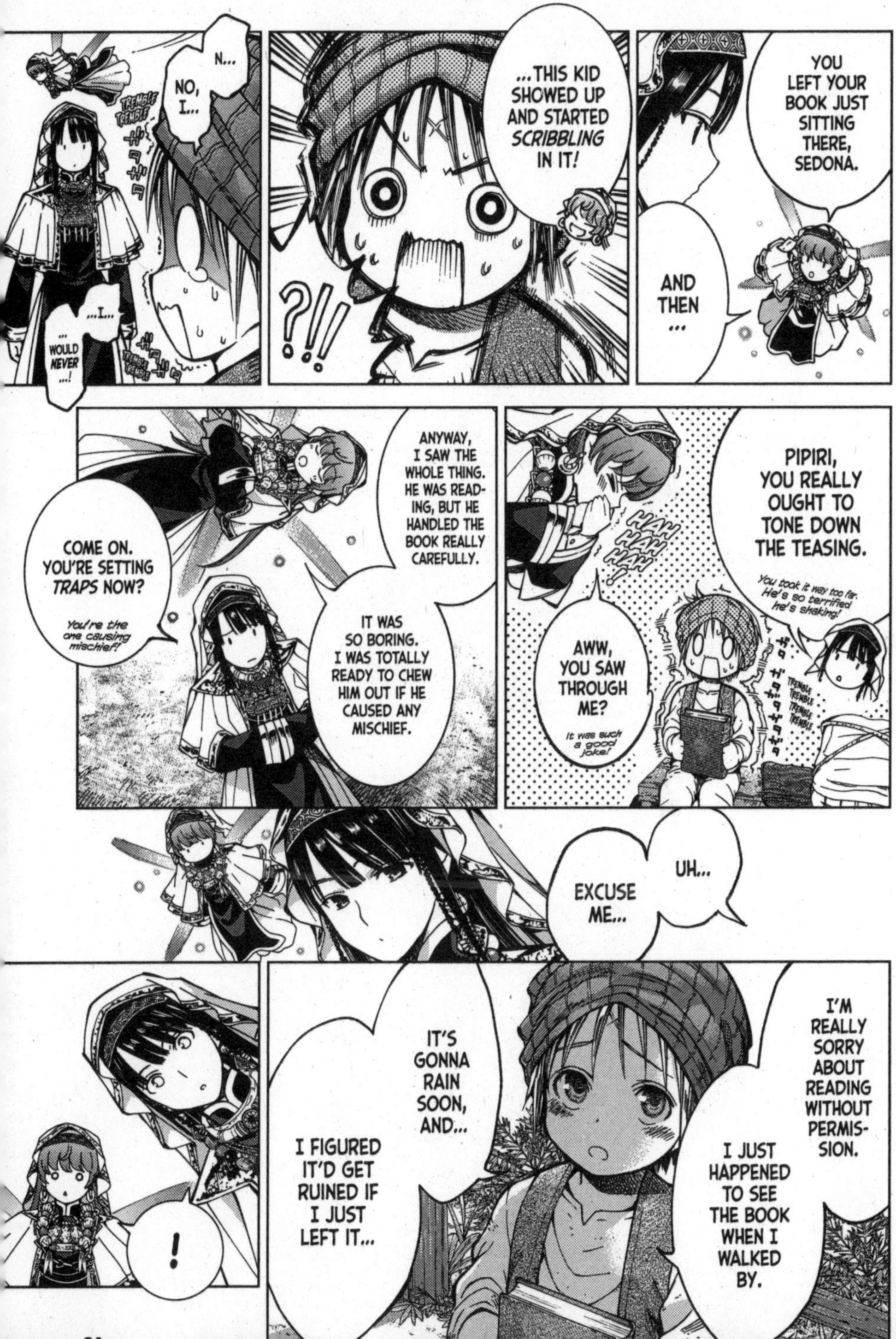
YOU LEFT YOUR BOOK JUST SITTING THERE, SEDONA.
AND THEN...
...THIS KID SHOWED UP AND STARTED *SCRIBBLING* IN IT!
?!!
N...
NO, I...
TREMBLE TREMBLE
...I...
...WOULD *NEVER* ...!
TREMBLE TREMBLE
PIPIRI, YOU REALLY OUGHT TO TONE DOWN THE TEASING.
You took it way too far. He's so terrified he's shaking!
HAH HAH HAH!
AWW, YOU SAW THROUGH ME?
It was such a good joke!
TREMBLE TREMBLE TREMBLE TREMBLE
ANYWAY, I SAW THE WHOLE THING. HE WAS READ-ING, BUT HE HANDLED THE BOOK REALLY CAREFULLY.
IT WAS SO BORING. I WAS TOTALLY READY TO CHEW HIM OUT IF HE CAUSED ANY MISCHIEF.
COME ON. YOU'RE SETTING *TRAPS* NOW?
You're the one causing mischief!
UH...
EXCUSE ME...
I'M REALLY SORRY ABOUT READING WITHOUT PERMIS-SION.
I JUST HAPPENED TO SEE THE BOOK WHEN I WALKED BY.
IT'S GONNA RAIN SOON, AND...
I FIGURED IT'D GET RUINED IF I JUST LEFT IT...
!

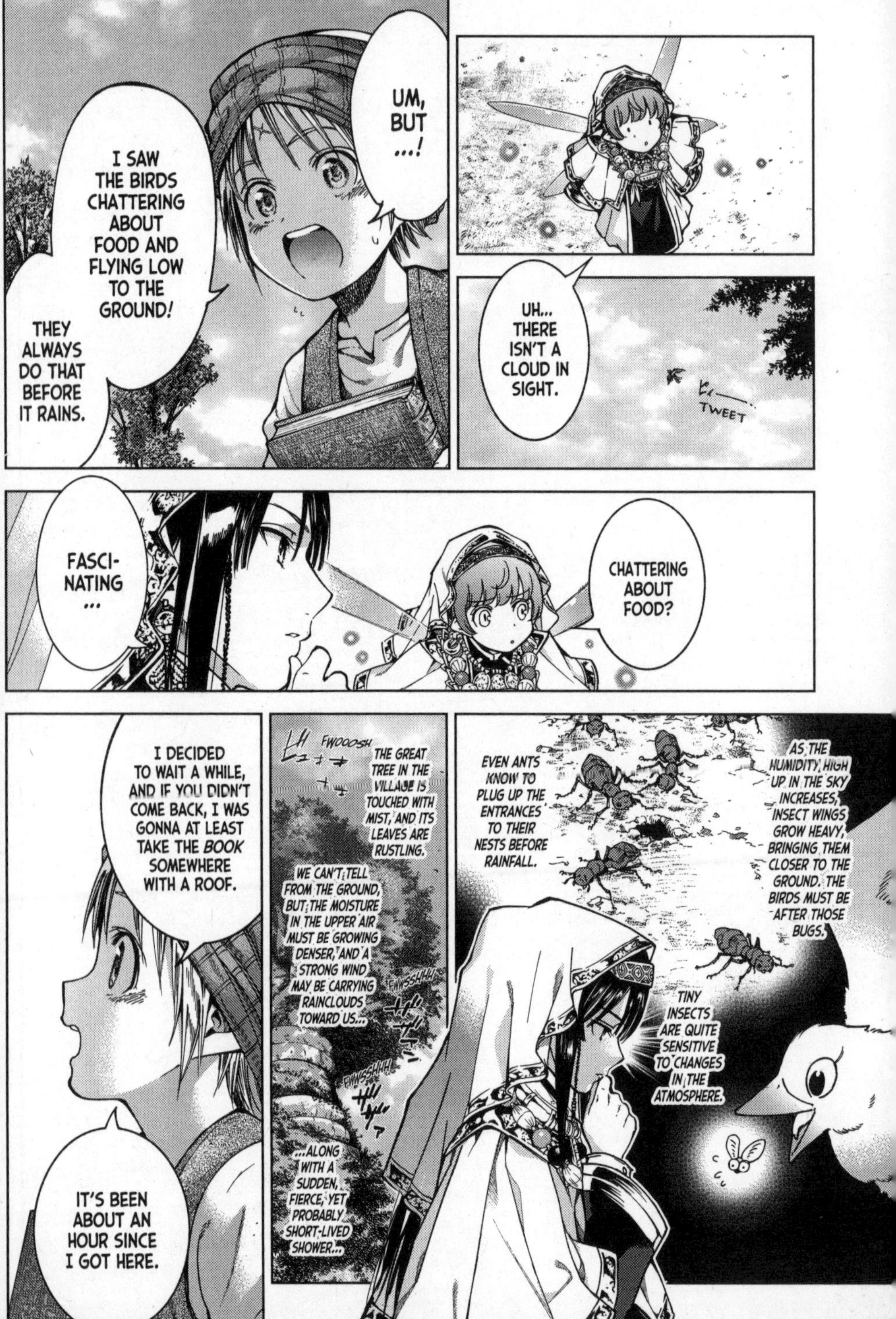
UH... THERE ISN'T A CLOUD IN SIGHT.
TWEET
UM, BUT ...!
I SAW THE BIRDS CHATTERING ABOUT FOOD AND FLYING LOW TO THE GROUND!
THEY ALWAYS DO THAT BEFORE IT RAINS.
CHATTERING ABOUT FOOD?
FASCINATING ...
AS THE HUMIDITY HIGH UP IN THE SKY INCREASES, INSECT WINGS GROW HEAVY, BRINGING THEM CLOSER TO THE GROUND. THE BIRDS MUST BE AFTER THOSE BUGS.
EVEN ANTS KNOW TO PLUG UP THE ENTRANCES TO THEIR NESTS BEFORE RAINFALL.
TINY INSECTS ARE QUITE SENSITIVE TO CHANGES IN THE ATMOSPHERE.
FWOOOSH
THE GREAT TREE IN THE VILLAGE IS TOUCHED WITH MIST, AND ITS LEAVES ARE RUSTLING.
WE CAN'T TELL FROM THE GROUND, BUT THE MOISTURE IN THE UPPER AIR MUST BE GROWING DENSER, AND A STRONG WIND MAY BE CARRYING RAINCLOUDS TOWARD US...
FWSSHH!
FWSSHH!
...ALONG WITH A SUDDEN, FIERCE, YET PROBABLY SHORT-LIVED SHOWER...
I DECIDED TO WAIT A WHILE, AND IF YOU DIDN'T COME BACK, I WAS GONNA AT LEAST TAKE THE BOOK SOMEWHERE WITH A ROOF.
IT'S BEEN ABOUT AN HOUR SINCE I GOT HERE.

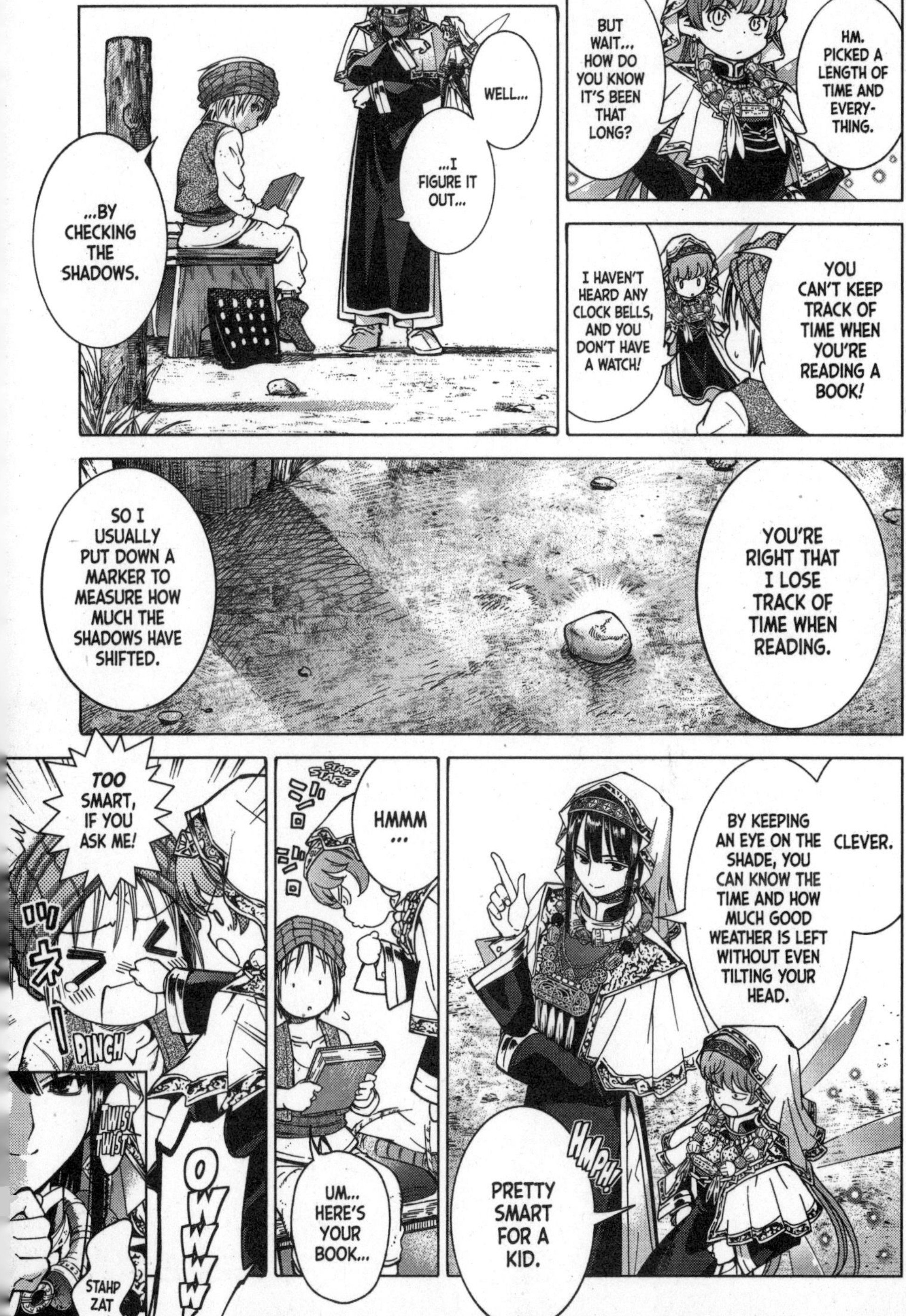
HM. PICKED A LENGTH OF TIME AND EVERY-THING.
BUT WAIT... HOW DO YOU KNOW IT'S BEEN THAT LONG?
YOU CAN'T KEEP TRACK OF TIME WHEN YOU'RE READING A BOOK!
I HAVEN'T HEARD ANY CLOCK BELLS, AND YOU DON'T HAVE A WATCH!
WELL...
...I FIGURE IT OUT...
...BY CHECKING THE SHADOWS.
YOU'RE RIGHT THAT I LOSE TRACK OF TIME WHEN READING.
SO I USUALLY PUT DOWN A MARKER TO MEASURE HOW MUCH THE SHADOWS HAVE SHIFTED.
CLEVER.
BY KEEPING AN EYE ON THE SHADE, YOU CAN KNOW THE TIME AND HOW MUCH GOOD WEATHER IS LEFT WITHOUT EVEN TILTING YOUR HEAD.
HMPH!
PRETTY SMART FOR A KID.
STARE STARE
HMMM...
UM... HERE'S YOUR BOOK...
TOO SMART, IF YOU ASK ME!
PINCH
TWIST TWIST
OWWWWW!
STAHP ZAT...!

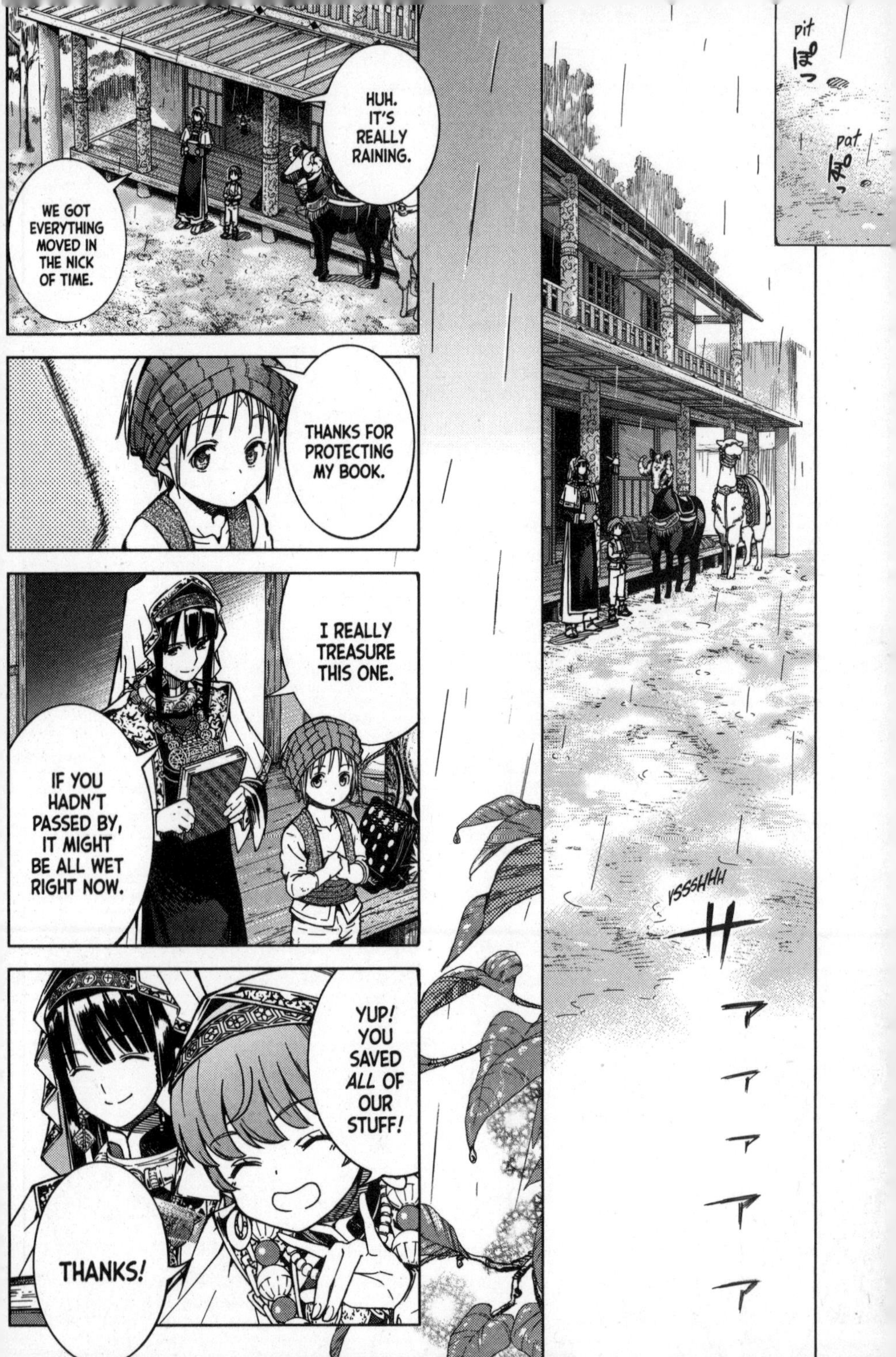
pit
ぽっ
pat
ぽっ
VSSSHHH
ザァァァァァ
HUH. IT'S REALLY RAINING.
WE GOT EVERYTHING MOVED IN THE NICK OF TIME.
THANKS FOR PROTECTING MY BOOK.
I REALLY TREASURE THIS ONE.
IF YOU HADN'T PASSED BY, IT MIGHT BE ALL WET RIGHT NOW.
YUP! YOU SAVED ALL OF OUR STUFF!
THANKS!

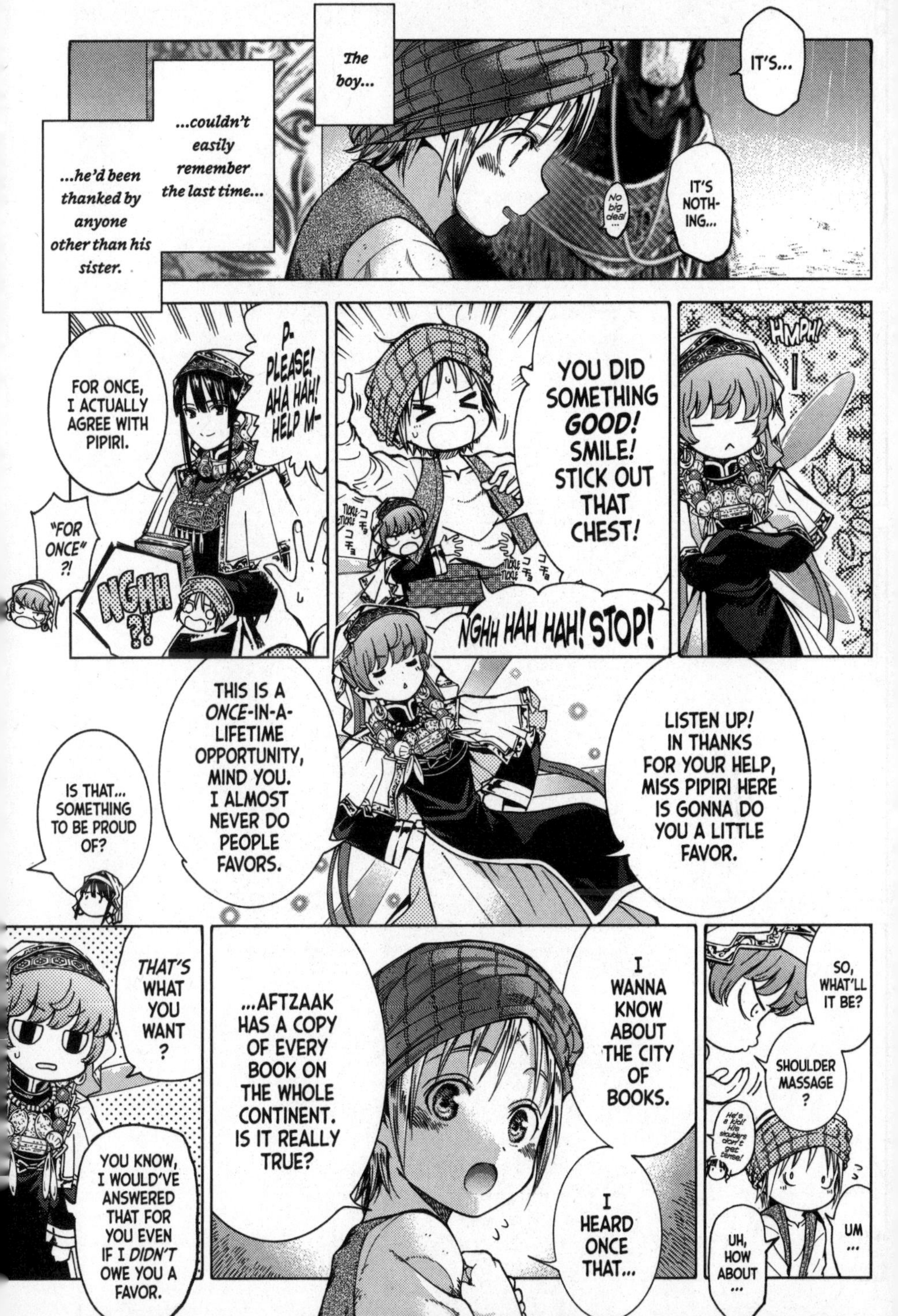
IT'S...
IT'S NOTHING...
No big deal...
The boy...
...couldn't easily remember the last time...
...he'd been thanked by anyone other than his sister.
HMPH!
YOU DID SOMETHING GOOD! SMILE! STICK OUT THAT CHEST!
TICKLE TICKLE
TICKLE TICKLE
NGHH HAH HAH! STOP!
P-PLEASE! AHA HAH! HELP M-
FOR ONCE, I ACTUALLY AGREE WITH PIPIRI.
"FOR ONCE"?!
NGHH?!
LISTEN UP! IN THANKS FOR YOUR HELP, MISS PIPIRI HERE IS GONNA DO YOU A LITTLE FAVOR.
THIS IS A ONCE-IN-A-LIFETIME OPPORTUNITY, MIND YOU. I ALMOST NEVER DO PEOPLE FAVORS.
IS THAT... SOMETHING TO BE PROUD OF?
SO, WHAT'LL IT BE?
SHOULDER MASSAGE?
He's a kid! His shoulders don't get tense!
UM...
UH, HOW ABOUT...
I WANNA KNOW ABOUT THE CITY OF BOOKS.
I HEARD ONCE THAT...
...AFTZAAK HAS A COPY OF EVERY BOOK ON THE WHOLE CONTINENT. IS IT REALLY TRUE?
THAT'S WHAT YOU WANT?
YOU KNOW, I WOULD'VE ANSWERED THAT FOR YOU EVEN IF I DIDN'T OWE YOU A FAVOR.

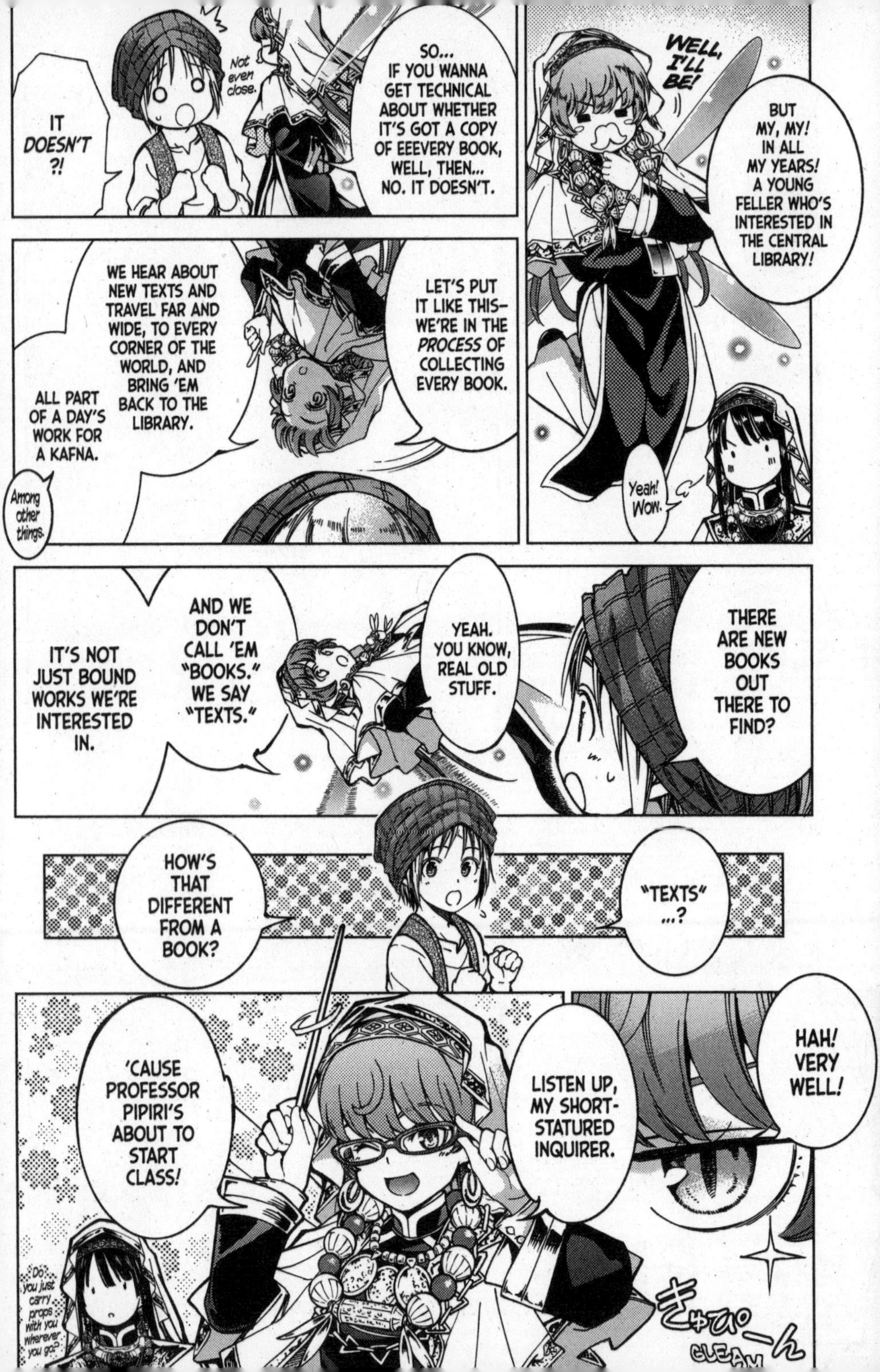
WELL, I'LL BE!
BUT MY, MY! IN ALL MY YEARS! A YOUNG FELLER WHO'S INTERESTED IN THE CENTRAL LIBRARY!
Yeah! Wow.
SO... IF YOU WANNA GET TECHNICAL ABOUT WHETHER IT'S GOT A COPY OF EEEVERY BOOK, WELL, THEN... NO. IT DOESN'T.
Not even close.
IT *DOESN'T* ?!
LET'S PUT IT LIKE THIS— WE'RE IN THE *PROCESS* OF COLLECTING EVERY BOOK.
WE HEAR ABOUT NEW TEXTS AND TRAVEL FAR AND WIDE, TO EVERY CORNER OF THE WORLD, AND BRING 'EM BACK TO THE LIBRARY.
ALL PART OF A DAY'S WORK FOR A KAFNA.
Among other things.
THERE ARE NEW BOOKS OUT THERE TO FIND?
YEAH. YOU KNOW, REAL OLD STUFF.
AND WE DON'T CALL 'EM "BOOKS." WE SAY "TEXTS."
IT'S NOT JUST BOUND WORKS WE'RE INTERESTED IN.
"TEXTS" ...?
HOW'S THAT DIFFERENT FROM A BOOK?
HAH! VERY WELL!
LISTEN UP, MY SHORT-STATURED INQUIRER.
'CAUSE PROFESSOR PIPIRI'S ABOUT TO START CLASS!
Do you just carry props with you wherever you go?
きゅぴーん
GLEAM

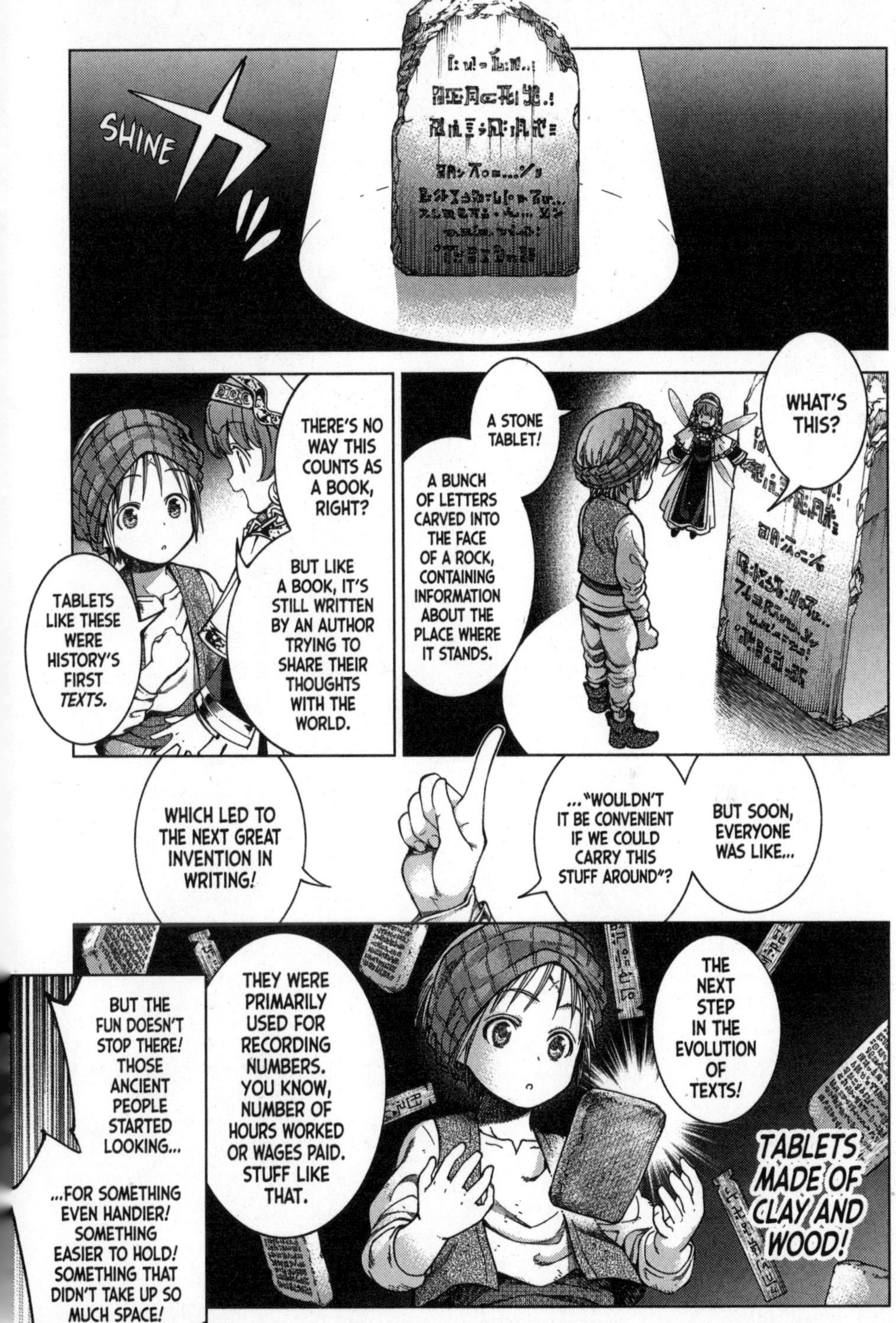
SHINE
WHAT'S THIS?
A STONE TABLET!
A BUNCH OF LETTERS CARVED INTO THE FACE OF A ROCK, CONTAINING INFORMATION ABOUT THE PLACE WHERE IT STANDS.
THERE'S NO WAY THIS COUNTS AS A BOOK, RIGHT?
BUT LIKE A BOOK, IT'S STILL WRITTEN BY AN AUTHOR TRYING TO SHARE THEIR THOUGHTS WITH THE WORLD.
TABLETS LIKE THESE WERE HISTORY'S FIRST *TEXTS*.
BUT SOON, EVERYONE WAS LIKE...
..."WOULDN'T IT BE CONVENIENT IF WE COULD CARRY THIS STUFF AROUND"?
WHICH LED TO THE NEXT GREAT INVENTION IN WRITING!
THE NEXT STEP IN THE EVOLUTION OF TEXTS!
TABLETS MADE OF CLAY AND WOOD!
THEY WERE PRIMARILY USED FOR RECORDING NUMBERS. YOU KNOW, NUMBER OF HOURS WORKED OR WAGES PAID. STUFF LIKE THAT.
BUT THE FUN DOESN'T STOP THERE! THOSE ANCIENT PEOPLE STARTED LOOKING...
...FOR SOMETHING EVEN HANDIER! SOMETHING EASIER TO HOLD! SOMETHING THAT DIDN'T TAKE UP SO MUCH SPACE!

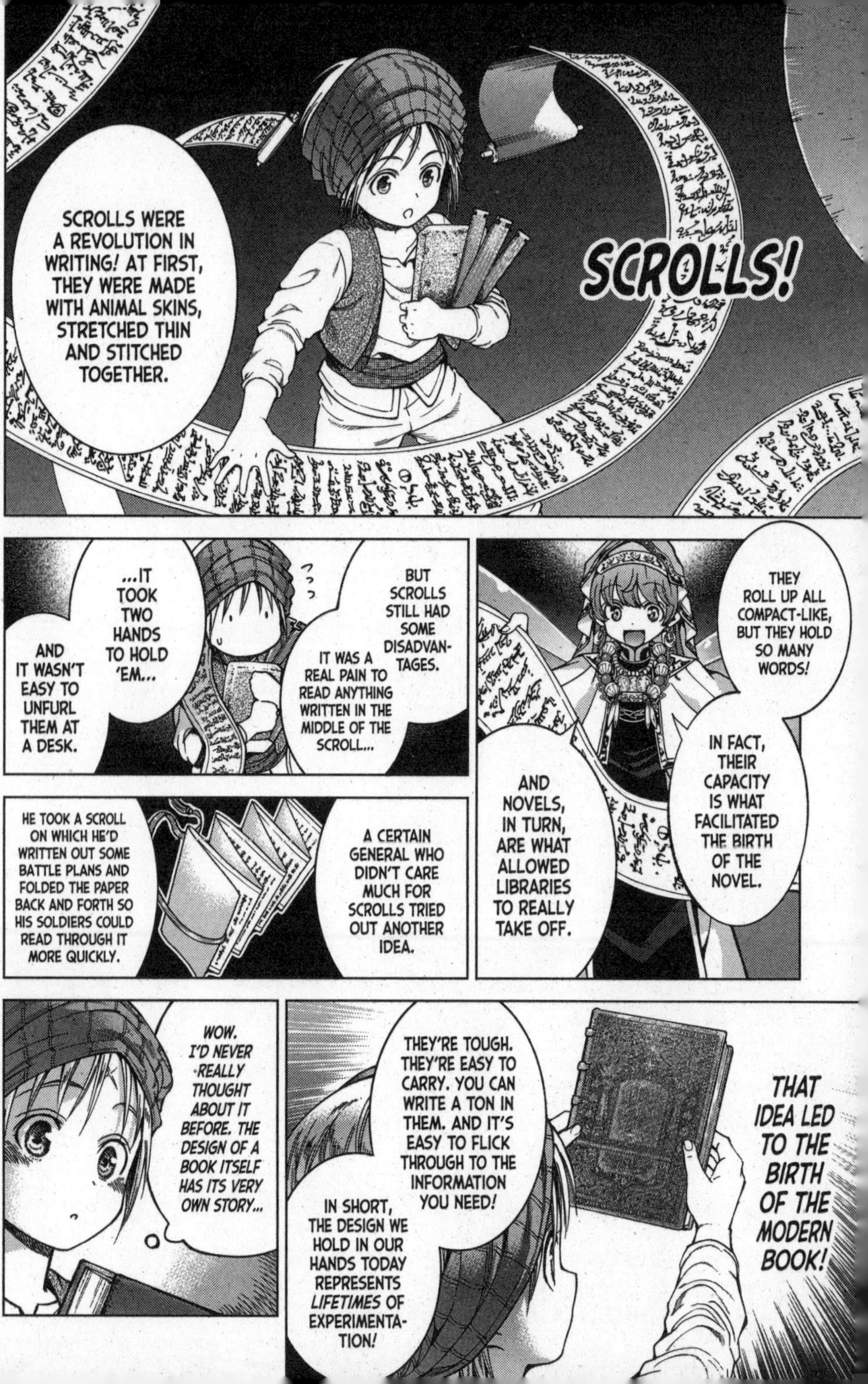
SCROLLS!
SCROLLS WERE A REVOLUTION IN WRITING! AT FIRST, THEY WERE MADE WITH ANIMAL SKINS, STRETCHED THIN AND STITCHED TOGETHER.
THEY ROLL UP ALL COMPACT-LIKE, BUT THEY HOLD SO MANY WORDS!
IN FACT, THEIR CAPACITY IS WHAT FACILITATED THE BIRTH OF THE NOVEL.
AND NOVELS, IN TURN, ARE WHAT ALLOWED LIBRARIES TO REALLY TAKE OFF.
BUT SCROLLS STILL HAD SOME DISADVANTAGES.
IT WAS A REAL PAIN TO READ ANYTHING WRITTEN IN THE MIDDLE OF THE SCROLL...
...IT TOOK TWO HANDS TO HOLD 'EM...
AND IT WASN'T EASY TO UNFURL THEM AT A DESK.
A CERTAIN GENERAL WHO DIDN'T CARE MUCH FOR SCROLLS TRIED OUT ANOTHER IDEA.
HE TOOK A SCROLL ON WHICH HE'D WRITTEN OUT SOME BATTLE PLANS AND FOLDED THE PAPER BACK AND FORTH SO HIS SOLDIERS COULD READ THROUGH IT MORE QUICKLY.
THAT IDEA LED TO THE BIRTH OF THE MODERN BOOK!
THEY'RE TOUGH. THEY'RE EASY TO CARRY. YOU CAN WRITE A TON IN THEM. AND IT'S EASY TO FLICK THROUGH TO THE INFORMATION YOU NEED!
IN SHORT, THE DESIGN WE HOLD IN OUR HANDS TODAY REPRESENTS LIFETIMES OF EXPERIMENTATION!
WOW. I'D NEVER REALLY THOUGHT ABOUT IT BEFORE. THE DESIGN OF A BOOK ITSELF HAS ITS VERY OWN STORY...

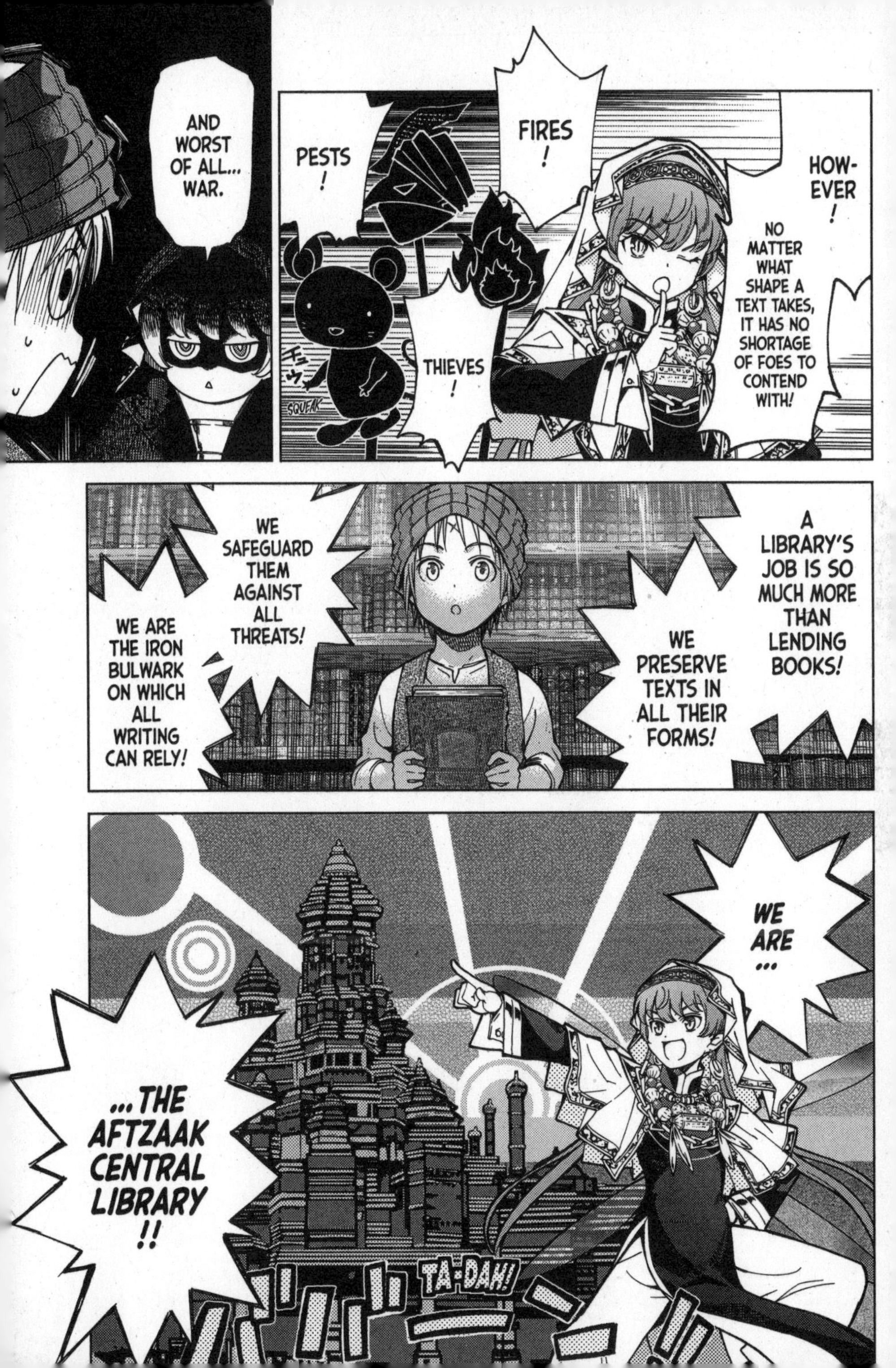
HOW-EVER!
NO MATTER WHAT SHAPE A TEXT TAKES, IT HAS NO SHORTAGE OF FOES TO CONTEND WITH!
FIRES!
PESTS!
THIEVES!
SQUEAK
AND WORST OF ALL... WAR.
A LIBRARY'S JOB IS SO MUCH MORE THAN LENDING BOOKS!
WE PRESERVE TEXTS IN ALL THEIR FORMS!
WE SAFEGUARD THEM AGAINST ALL THREATS!
WE ARE THE IRON BULWARK ON WHICH ALL WRITING CAN RELY!
WE ARE...
TA-DAH!
...THE AFTZAAK CENTRAL LIBRARY!!

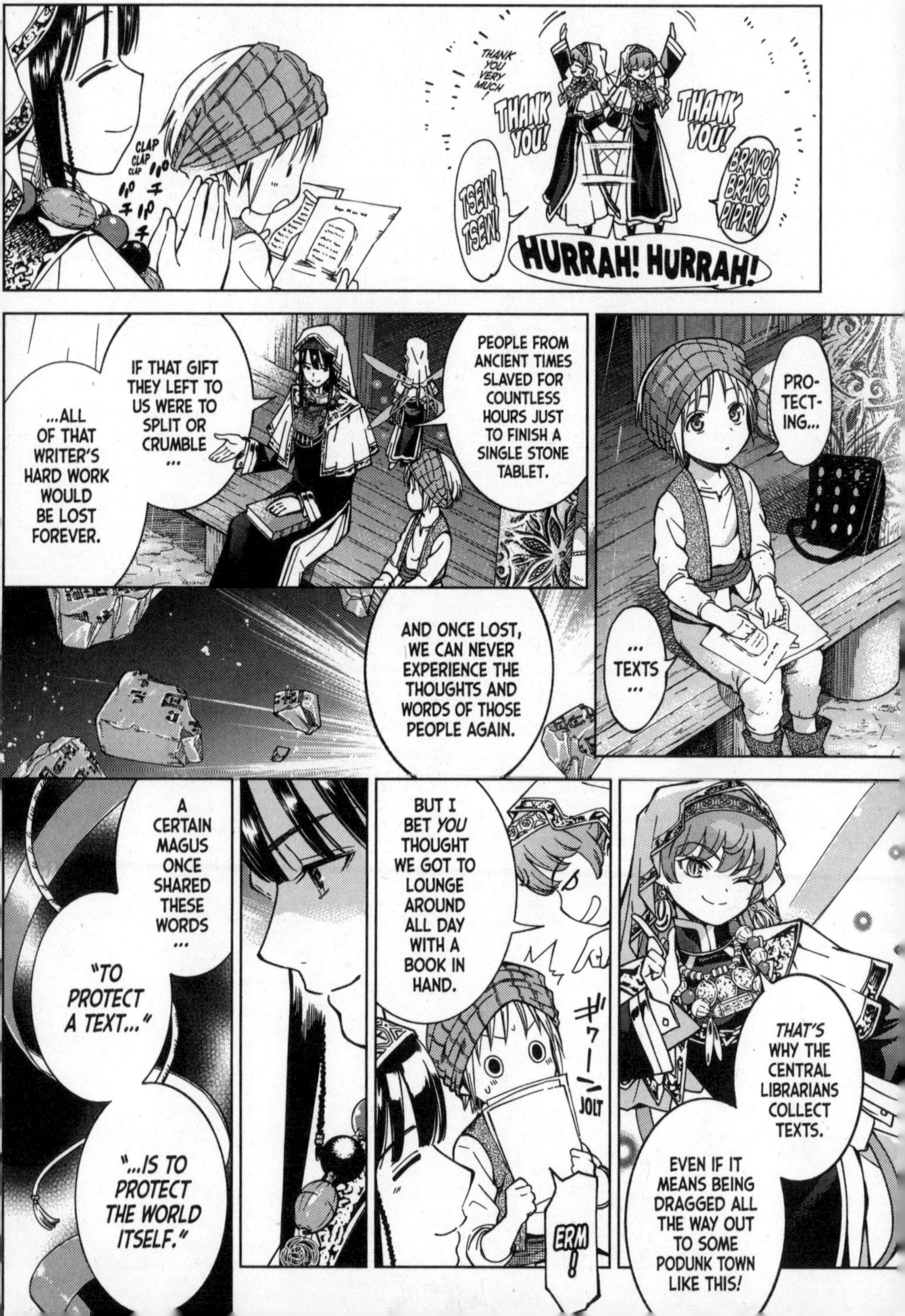
BRAVO! BRAVO, PIPIRI!
THANK YOU!
THANK YOU!
THANK YOU VERY MUCH!
TSEN! TSEN!
HURRAH! HURRAH!
CLAP CLAP CLAP
PRO-TECT-ING...
...TEXTS...
PEOPLE FROM ANCIENT TIMES SLAVED FOR COUNTLESS HOURS JUST TO FINISH A SINGLE STONE TABLET.
IF THAT GIFT THEY LEFT TO US WERE TO SPLIT OR CRUMBLE...
...ALL OF THAT WRITER'S HARD WORK WOULD BE LOST FOREVER.
AND ONCE LOST, WE CAN NEVER EXPERIENCE THE THOUGHTS AND WORDS OF THOSE PEOPLE AGAIN.
THAT'S WHY THE CENTRAL LIBRARIANS COLLECT TEXTS.
EVEN IF IT MEANS BEING DRAGGED ALL THE WAY OUT TO SOME PODUNK TOWN LIKE THIS!
BUT I BET *YOU* THOUGHT WE GOT TO LOUNGE AROUND ALL DAY WITH A BOOK IN HAND.
JOLT
ERM!
A CERTAIN MAGUS ONCE SHARED THESE WORDS...
"TO PROTECT A TEXT..."
"...IS TO PROTECT THE WORLD ITSELF."

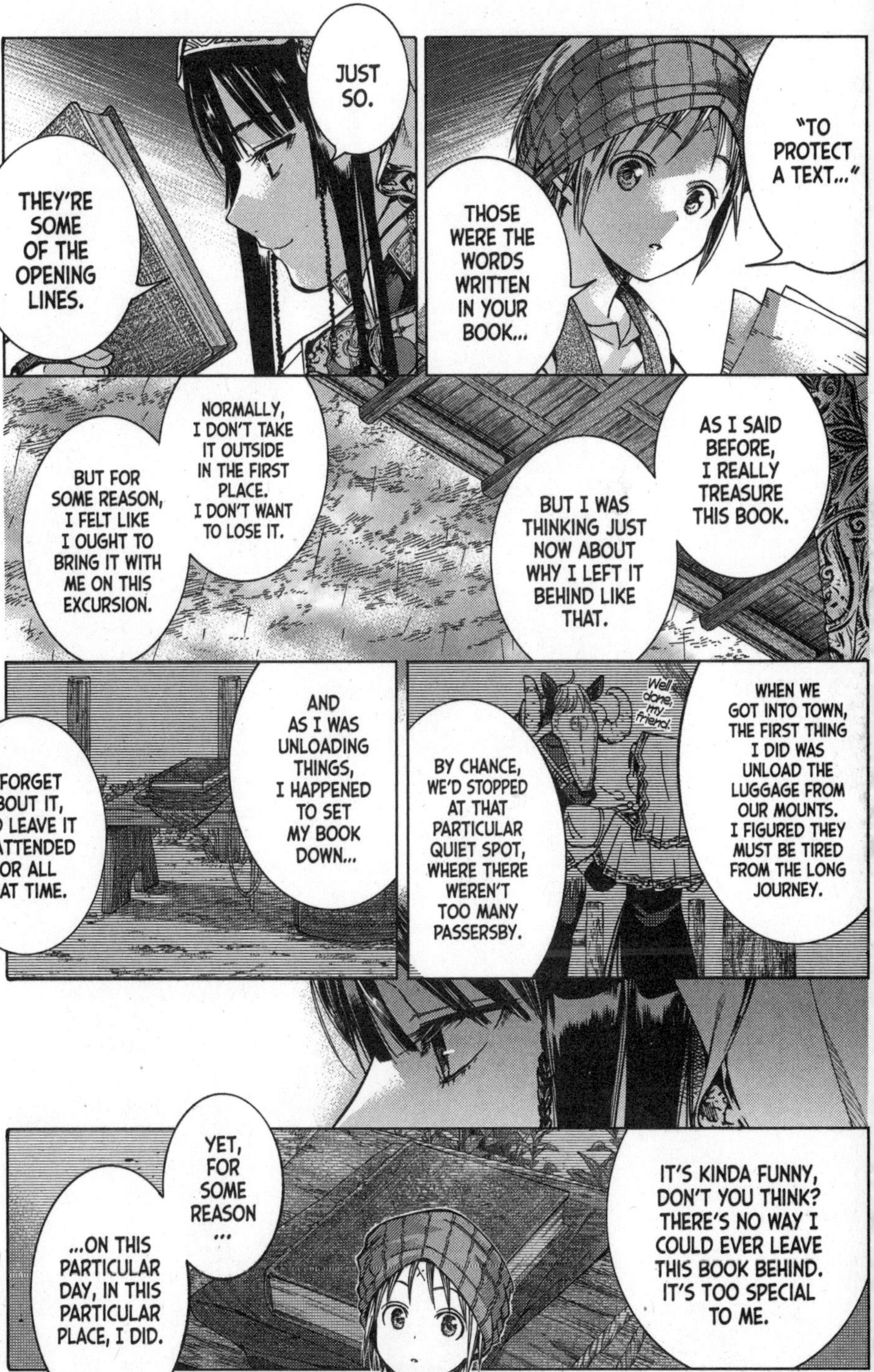
"TO PROTECT A TEXT..."
THOSE WERE THE WORDS WRITTEN IN YOUR BOOK...
JUST SO.
THEY'RE SOME OF THE OPENING LINES.
AS I SAID BEFORE, I REALLY TREASURE THIS BOOK.
BUT I WAS THINKING JUST NOW ABOUT WHY I LEFT IT BEHIND LIKE THAT.
NORMALLY, I DON'T TAKE IT OUTSIDE IN THE FIRST PLACE. I DON'T WANT TO LOSE IT.
BUT FOR SOME REASON, I FELT LIKE I OUGHT TO BRING IT WITH ME ON THIS EXCURSION.
WHEN WE GOT INTO TOWN, THE FIRST THING I DID WAS UNLOAD THE LUGGAGE FROM OUR MOUNTS. I FIGURED THEY MUST BE TIRED FROM THE LONG JOURNEY.
Well done, my friend.
BY CHANCE, WE'D STOPPED AT THAT PARTICULAR QUIET SPOT, WHERE THERE WEREN'T TOO MANY PASSERSBY.
AND AS I WAS UNLOADING THINGS, I HAPPENED TO SET MY BOOK DOWN...
...FORGET ABOUT IT, AND LEAVE IT UNATTENDED FOR ALL THAT TIME.
IT'S KINDA FUNNY, DON'T YOU THINK? THERE'S NO WAY I COULD EVER LEAVE THIS BOOK BEHIND. IT'S TOO SPECIAL TO ME.
YET, FOR SOME REASON ...
...ON THIS PARTICULAR DAY, IN THIS PARTICULAR PLACE, I DID.

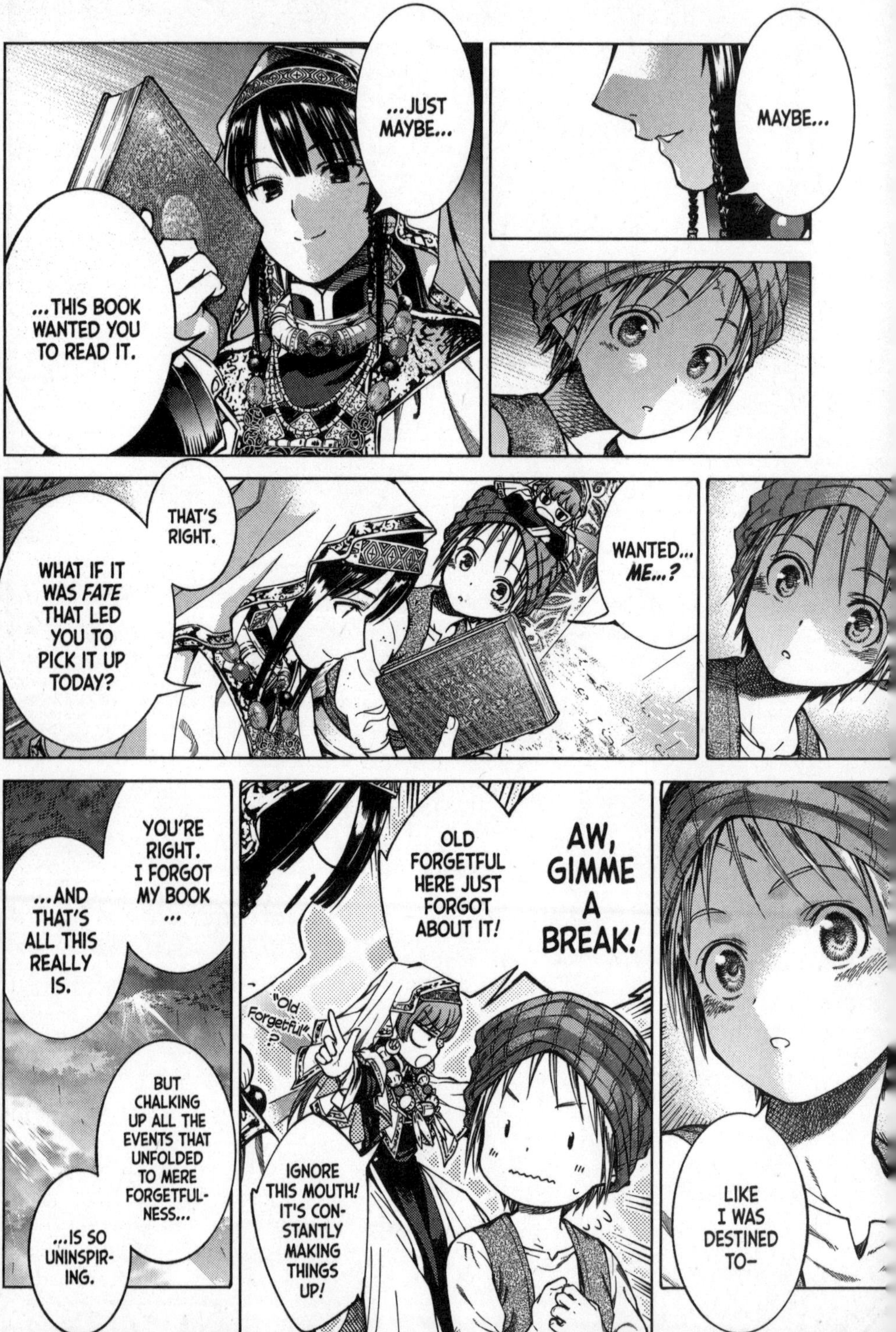
MAYBE...
...JUST MAYBE...
...THIS BOOK WANTED YOU TO READ IT.
WANTED... *ME...?*
THAT'S RIGHT.
WHAT IF IT WAS *FATE* THAT LED YOU TO PICK IT UP TODAY?
LIKE I WAS DESTINED TO—
AW, GIMME A BREAK!
OLD FORGETFUL HERE JUST FORGOT ABOUT IT!
"Old Forgetful"?
IGNORE THIS MOUTH! IT'S CON-STANTLY MAKING THINGS UP!
YOU'RE RIGHT. I FORGOT MY BOOK...
...AND THAT'S ALL THIS REALLY IS.
BUT CHALKING UP ALL THE EVENTS THAT UNFOLDED TO MERE FORGETFUL-NESS...
...IS SO UNINSPIR-ING.

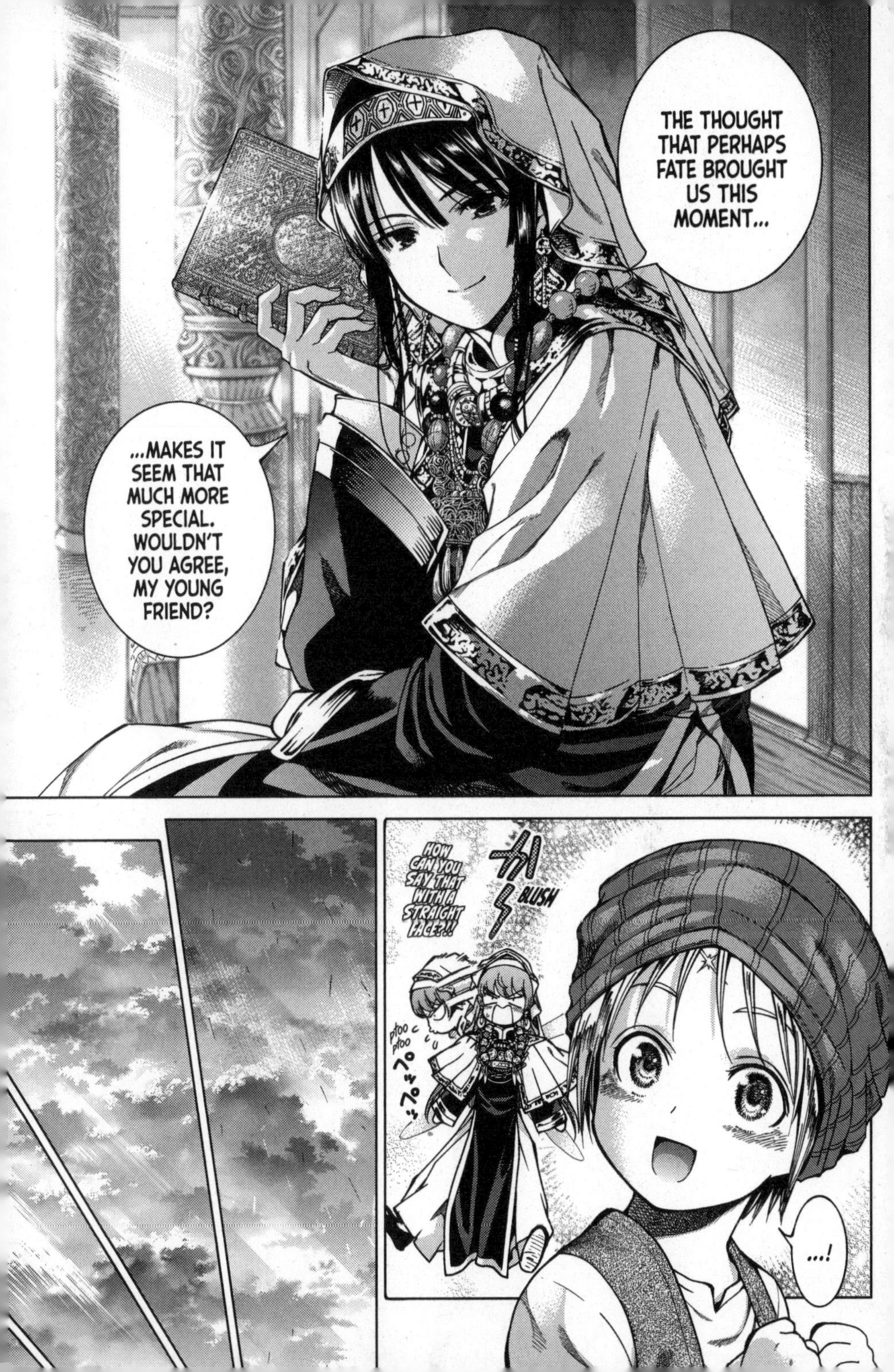
THE THOUGHT THAT PERHAPS FATE BROUGHT US THIS MOMENT...
...MAKES IT SEEM THAT MUCH MORE SPECIAL. WOULDN'T YOU AGREE, MY YOUNG FRIEND?
BLUSH
HOW CAN YOU SAY THAT WITH A STRAIGHT FACE?!!
ptoo ptoo
...!

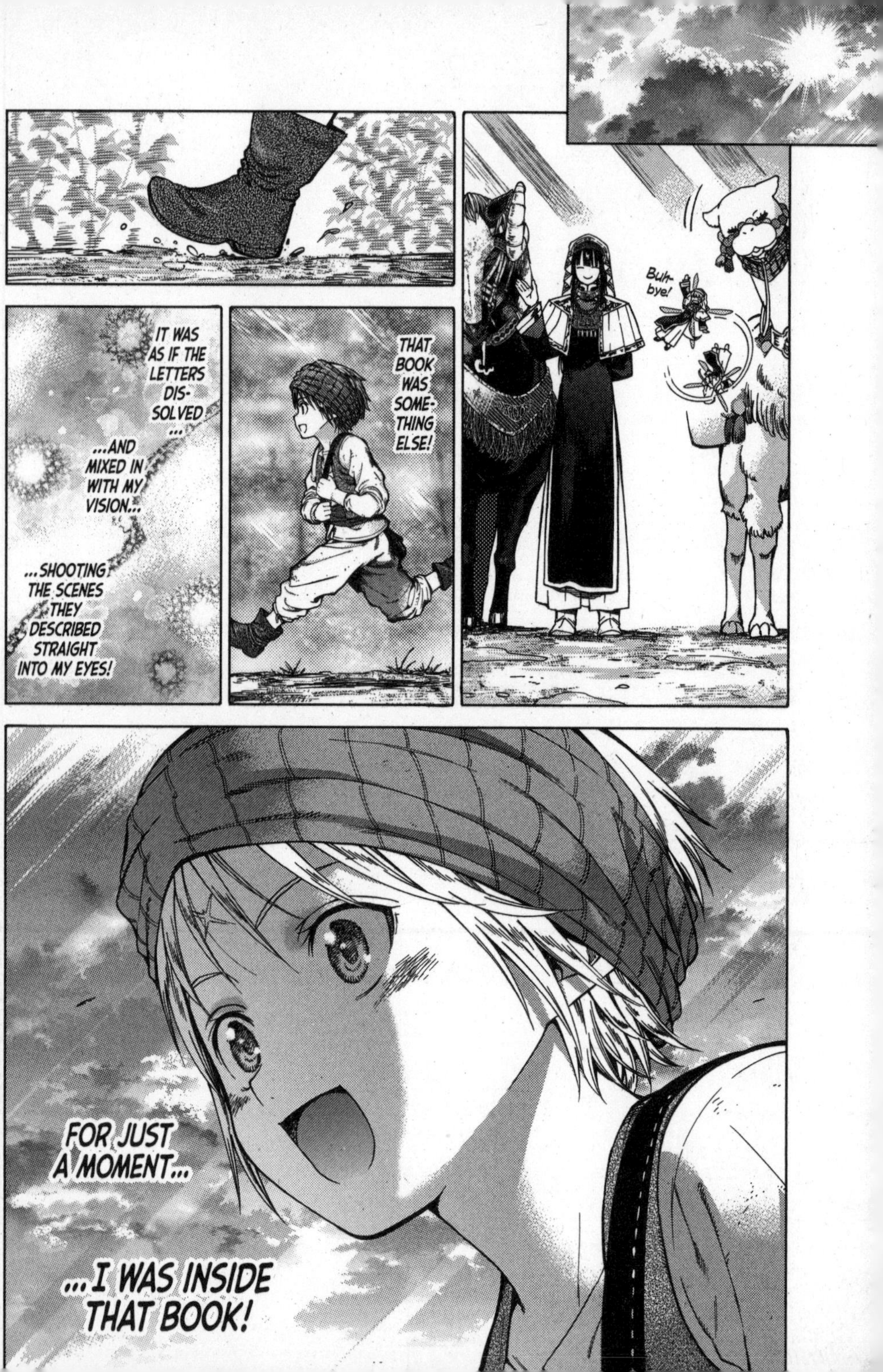
Buh-bye!
THAT BOOK WAS SOME-THING ELSE!
IT WAS AS IF THE LETTERS DIS-SOLVED...
...AND MIXED IN WITH MY VISION...
...SHOOTING THE SCENES THEY DESCRIBED STRAIGHT INTO MY EYES!
FOR JUST A MOMENT...
...I WAS INSIDE THAT BOOK!

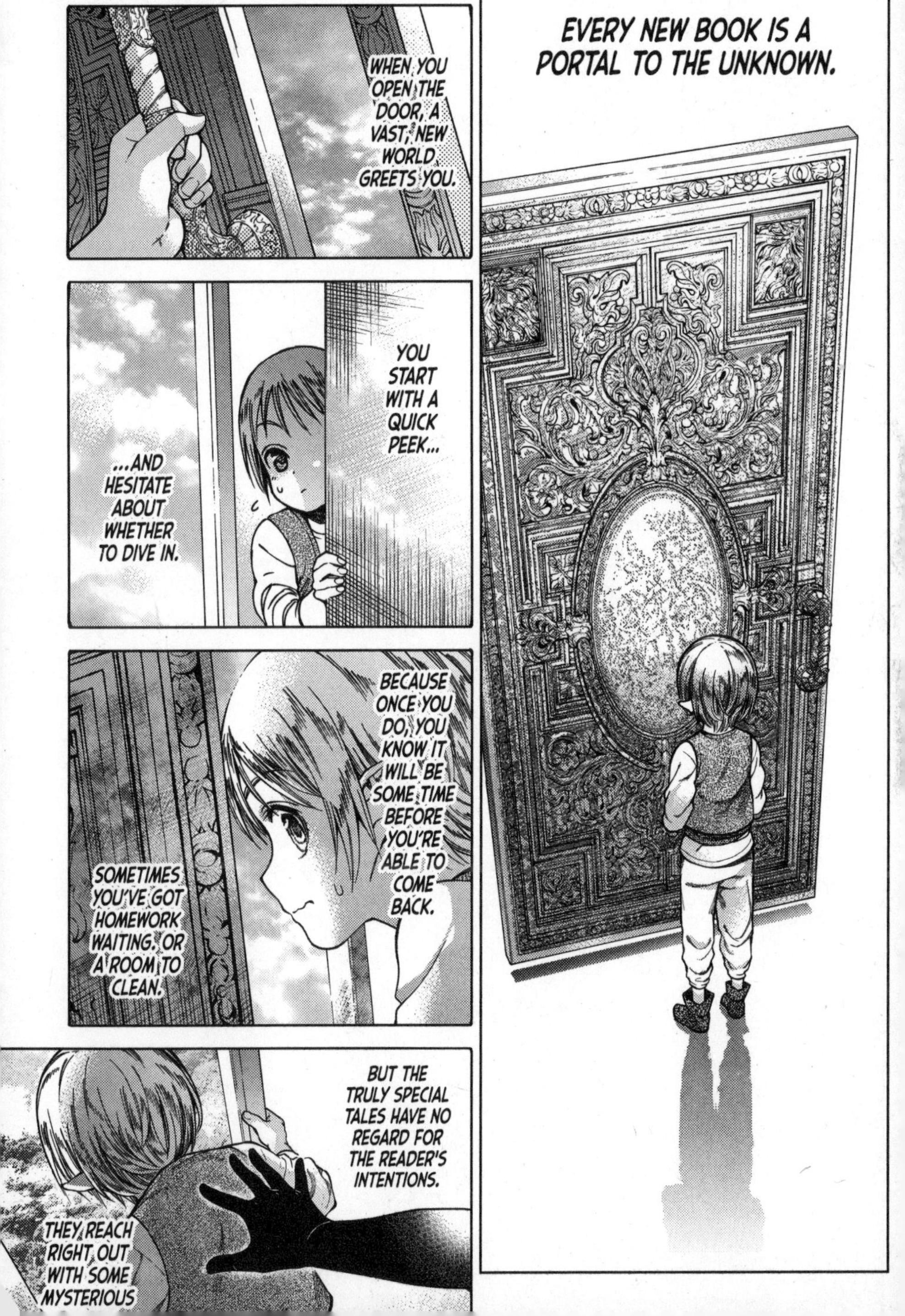
EVERY NEW BOOK IS A PORTAL TO THE UNKNOWN.
WHEN YOU OPEN THE DOOR, A VAST, NEW WORLD GREETS YOU.
YOU START WITH A QUICK PEEK...
...AND HESITATE ABOUT WHETHER TO DIVE IN.
BECAUSE ONCE YOU DO, YOU KNOW IT WILL BE SOME TIME BEFORE YOU'RE ABLE TO COME BACK.
SOMETIMES YOU'VE GOT HOMEWORK WAITING. OR A ROOM TO CLEAN.
BUT THE TRULY SPECIAL TALES HAVE NO REGARD FOR THE READER'S INTENTIONS.
THEY REACH RIGHT OUT WITH SOME MYSTERIOUS

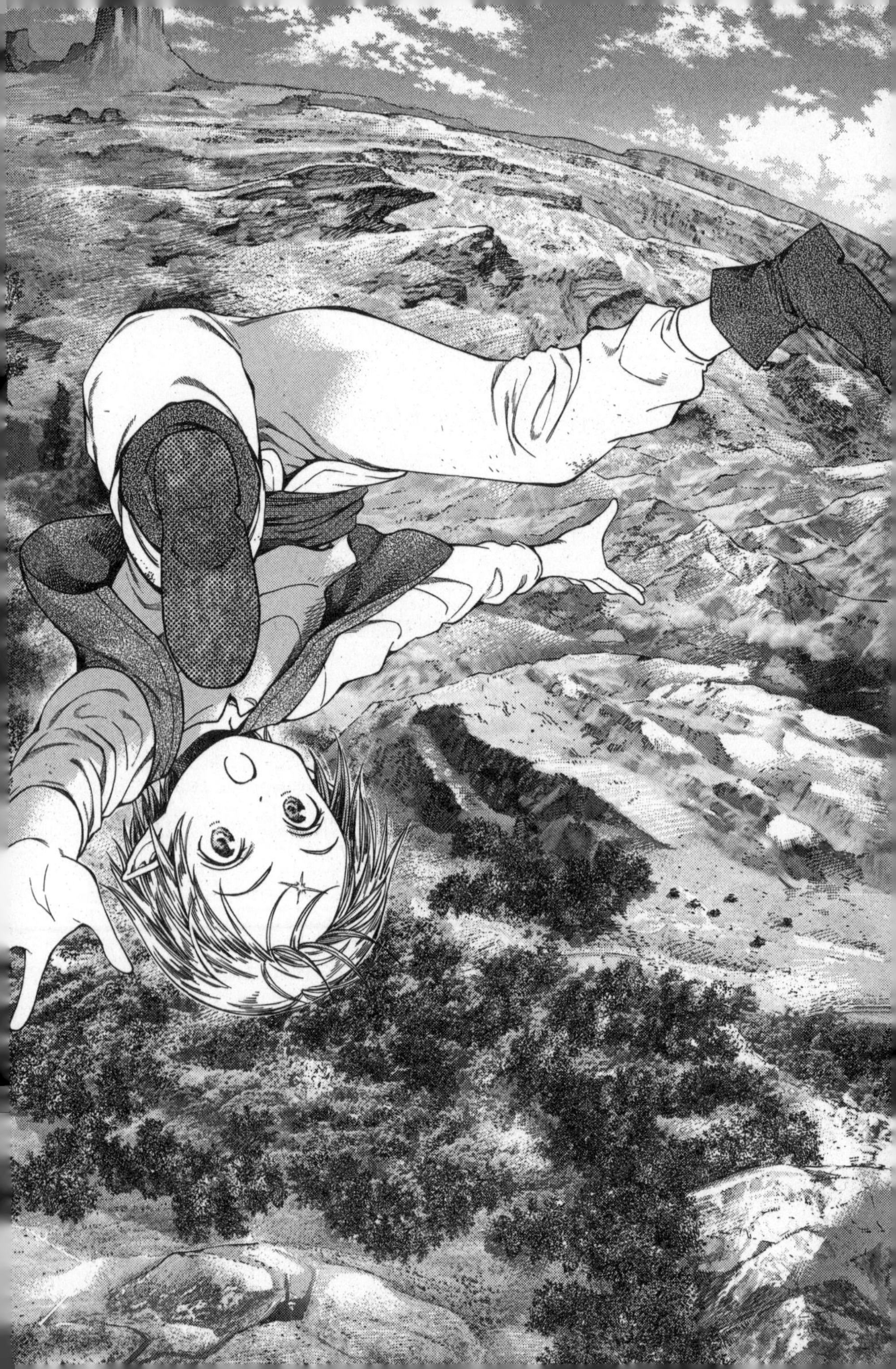

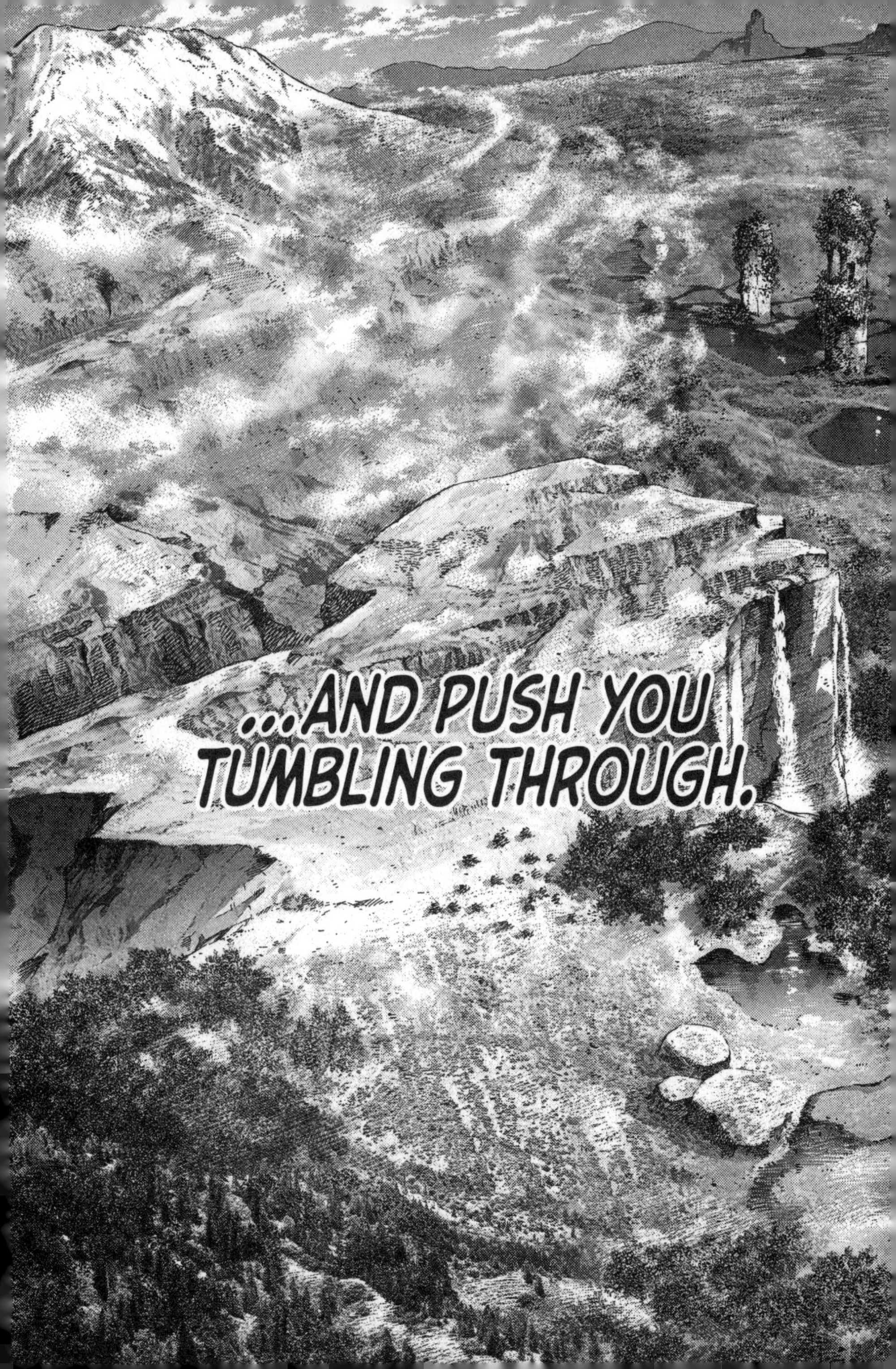
...AND PUSH YOU TUMBLING THROUGH.

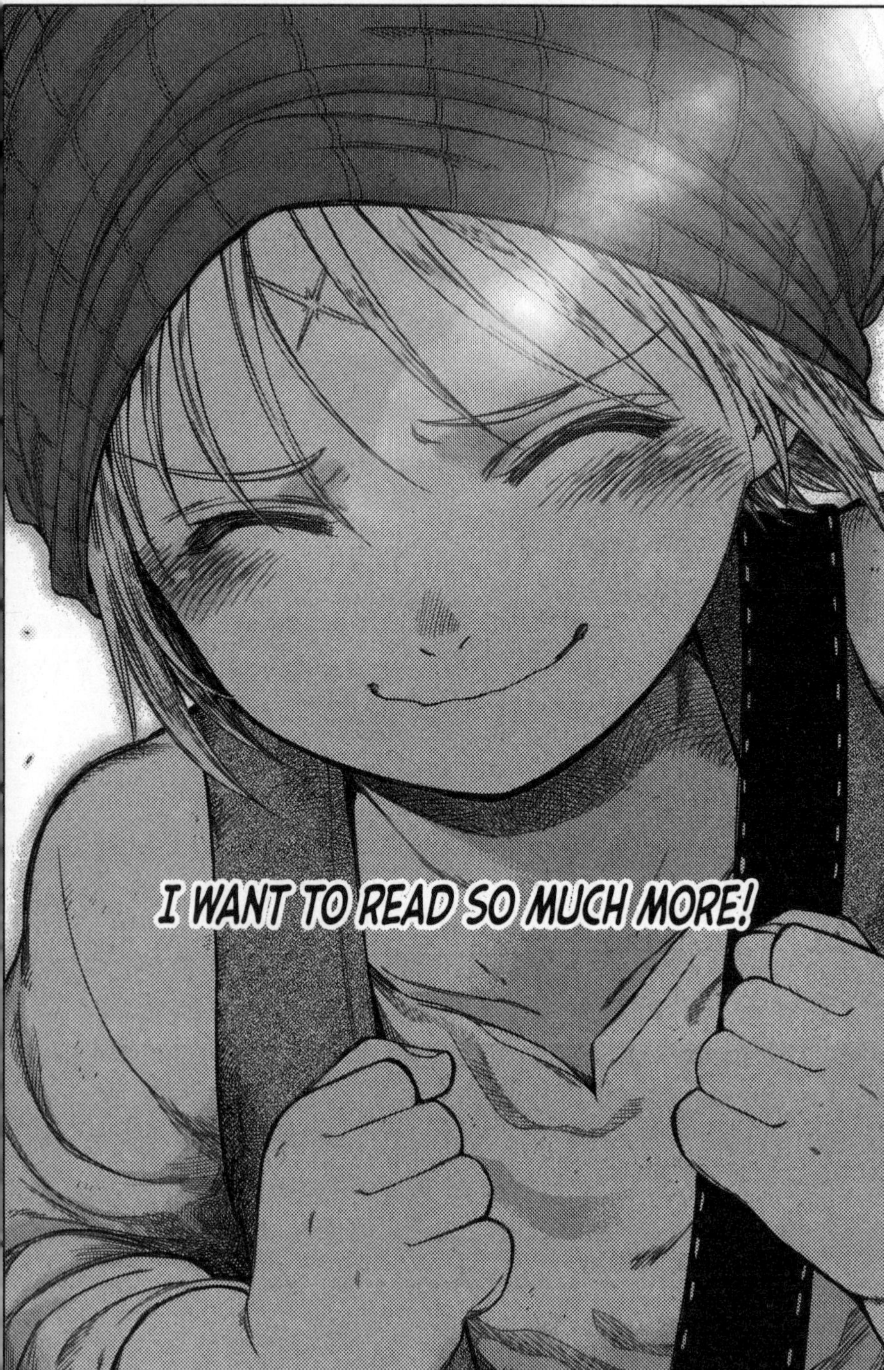
I WANT TO READ SO MUCH MORE!

Magus of the Library

Keko

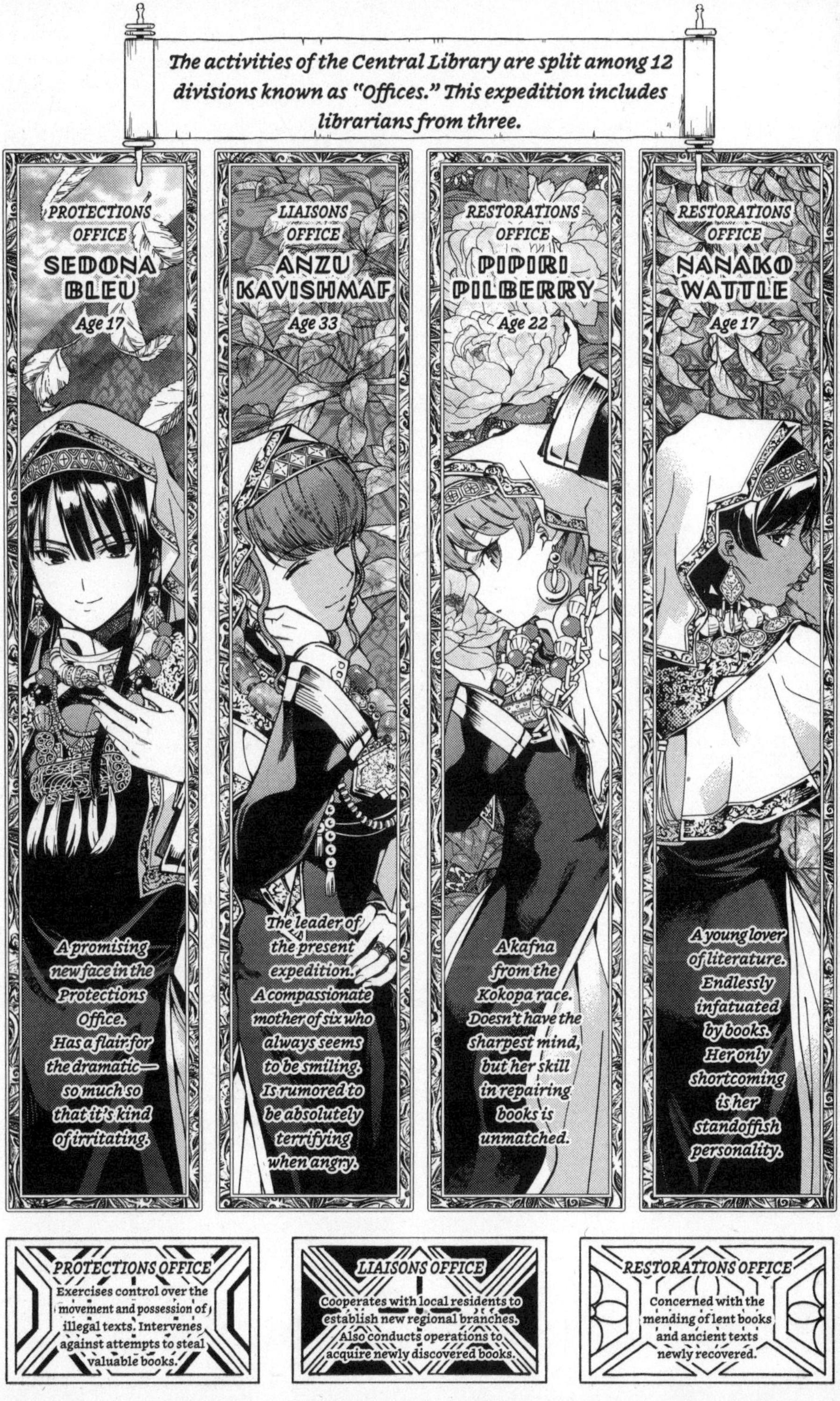
The activities of the Central Library are split among 12 divisions known as "Offices." This expedition includes librarians from three.
RESTORATIONS OFFICE
NANAKO WATTLE
Age 17
A young lover of literature. Endlessly infatuated by books. Her only shortcoming is her standoffish personality.
RESTORATIONS OFFICE
PIPIRI PILBERRY
Age 22
A kafna from the Kokopa race. Doesn't have the sharpest mind, but her skill in repairing books is unmatched.
LIAISONS OFFICE
ANZU KAVISHMAF
Age 33
The leader of the present expedition. A compassionate mother of six who always seems to be smiling. Is rumored to be absolutely terrifying when angry.
PROTECTIONS OFFICE
SEDONA BLEU
Age 17
A promising new face in the Protections Office. Has a flair for the dramatic—so much so that it's kind of irritating.
RESTORATIONS OFFICE
Concerned with the mending of lent books and ancient texts newly recovered.
LIAISONS OFFICE
Cooperates with local residents to establish new regional branches. Also conducts operations to acquire newly discovered books.
PROTECTIONS OFFICE
Exercises control over the movement and possession of illegal texts. Intervenes against attempts to steal valuable books.

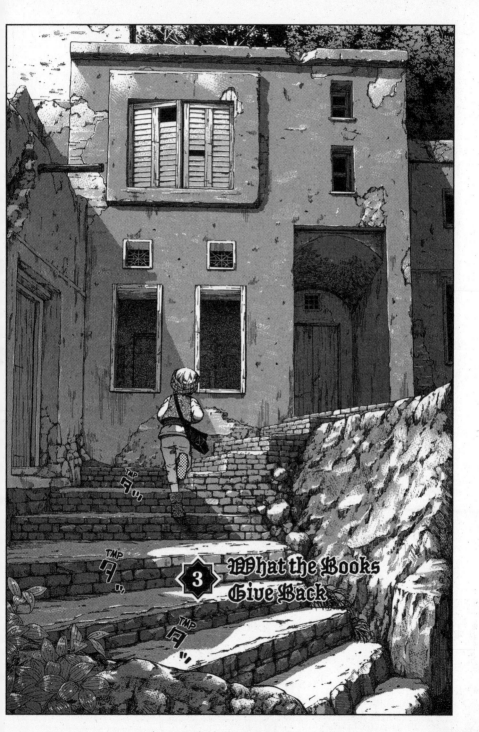

❸ What the Books Give Back

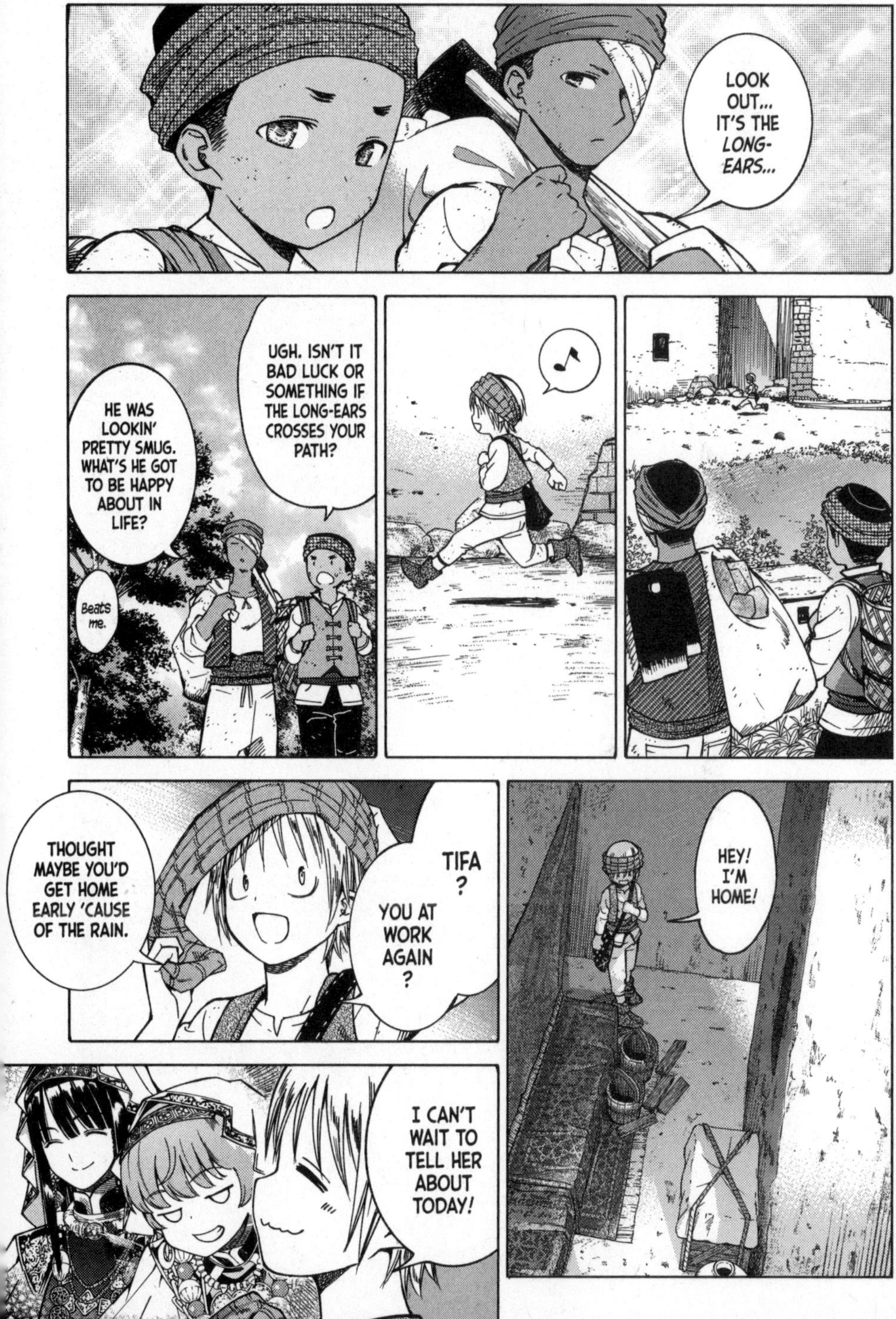

LOOK OUT... IT'S THE *LONG-EARS*...
♪
UGH. ISN'T IT BAD LUCK OR SOMETHING IF THE LONG-EARS CROSSES YOUR PATH?
HE WAS LOOKIN' PRETTY SMUG. WHAT'S HE GOT TO BE HAPPY ABOUT IN LIFE?
Beats me.
HEY! I'M HOME!
TIFA?
YOU AT WORK AGAIN?
THOUGHT MAYBE YOU'D GET HOME EARLY 'CAUSE OF THE RAIN.
I CAN'T WAIT TO TELL HER ABOUT TODAY!

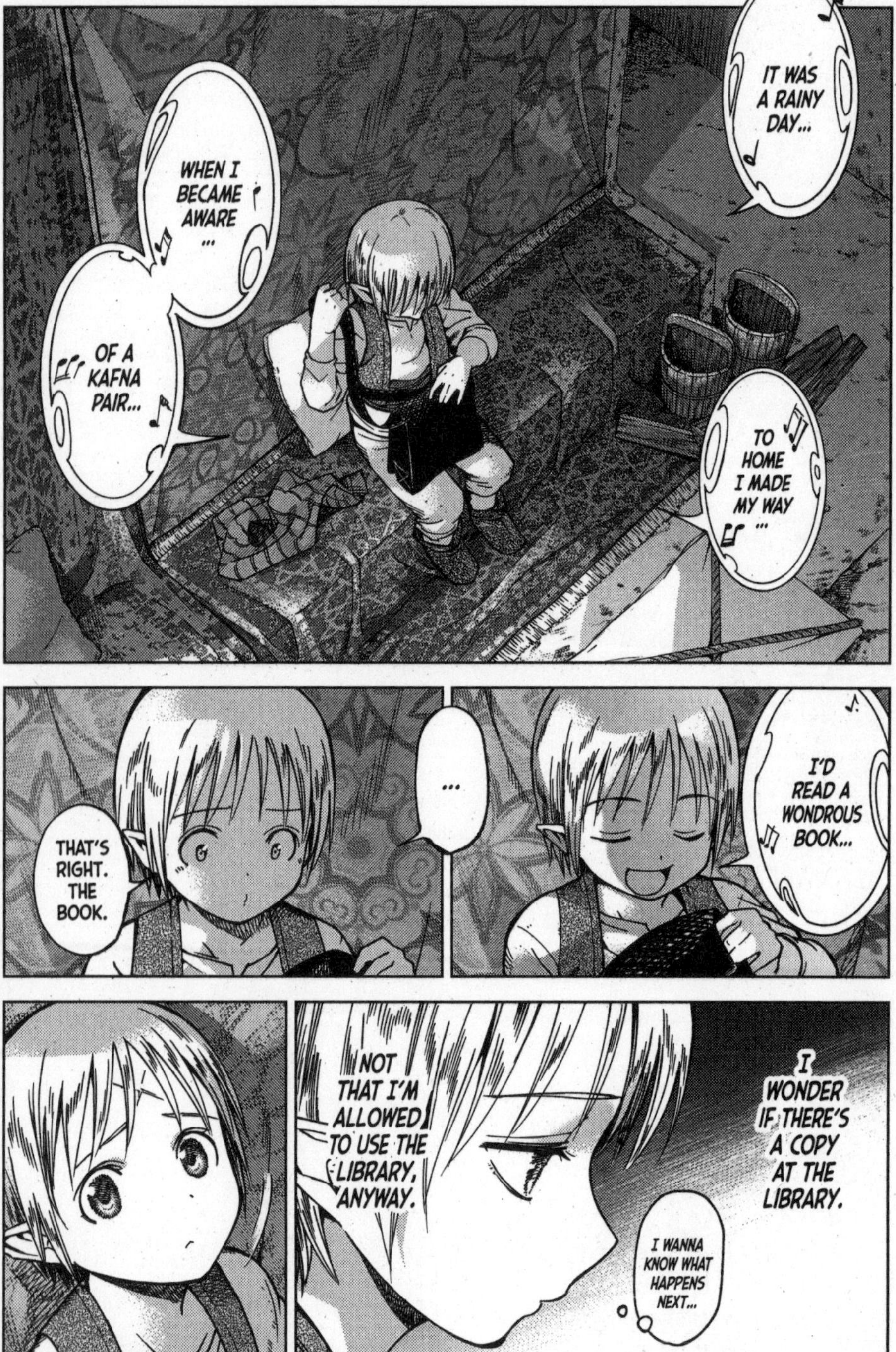

IT WAS A RAINY DAY...
TO HOME I MADE MY WAY ...
WHEN I BECAME AWARE ...
OF A KAFNA PAIR...
I'D READ A WONDROUS BOOK...
...
THAT'S RIGHT. THE BOOK.
I WONDER IF THERE'S A COPY AT THE LIBRARY.
NOT THAT I'M ALLOWED TO USE THE LIBRARY, ANYWAY.
I WANNA KNOW WHAT HAPPENS NEXT...

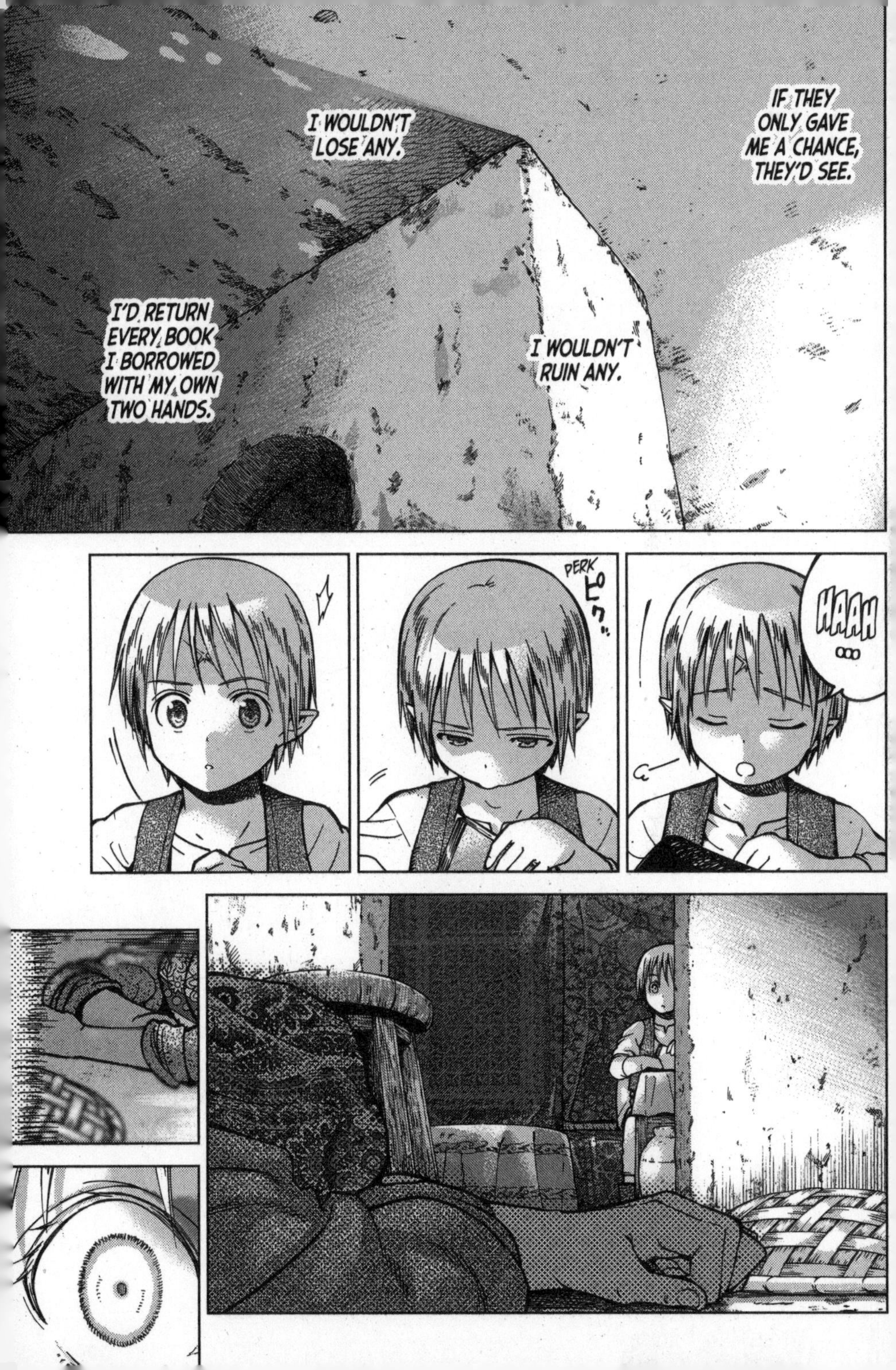
IF THEY ONLY GAVE ME A CHANCE, THEY'D SEE.
I WOULDN'T LOSE ANY.
I WOULDN'T RUIN ANY.
I'D RETURN EVERY BOOK I BORROWED WITH MY OWN TWO HANDS.
HAAH...
PERK
ピクッ

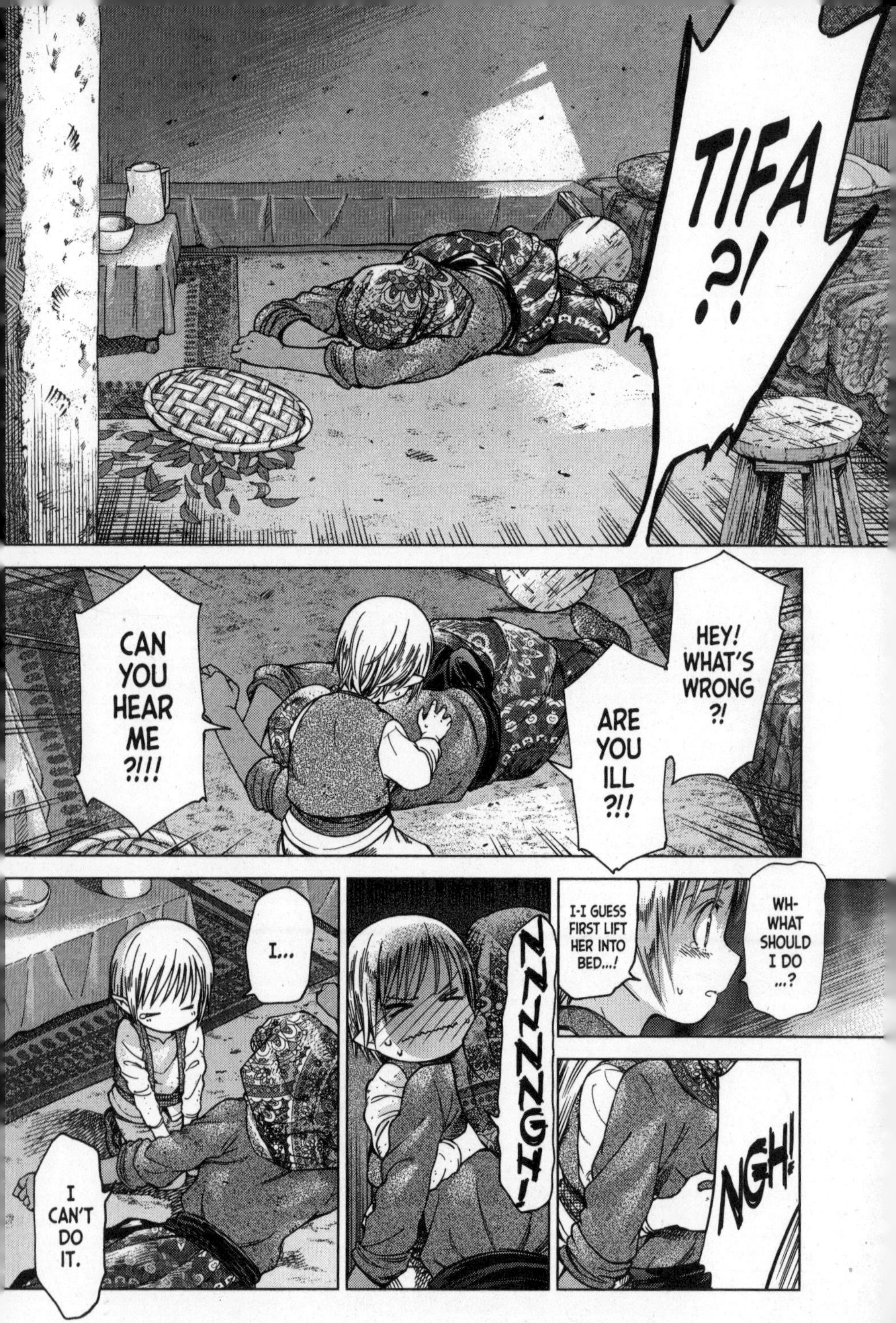
TIFA ?!
HEY! WHAT'S WRONG ?!
ARE YOU ILL ?!!
CAN YOU HEAR ME ?!!!
WH- WHAT SHOULD I DO ...?
I-I GUESS FIRST LIFT HER INTO BED...!
NGH!
NNNNNGH!
I...
I CAN'T DO IT.

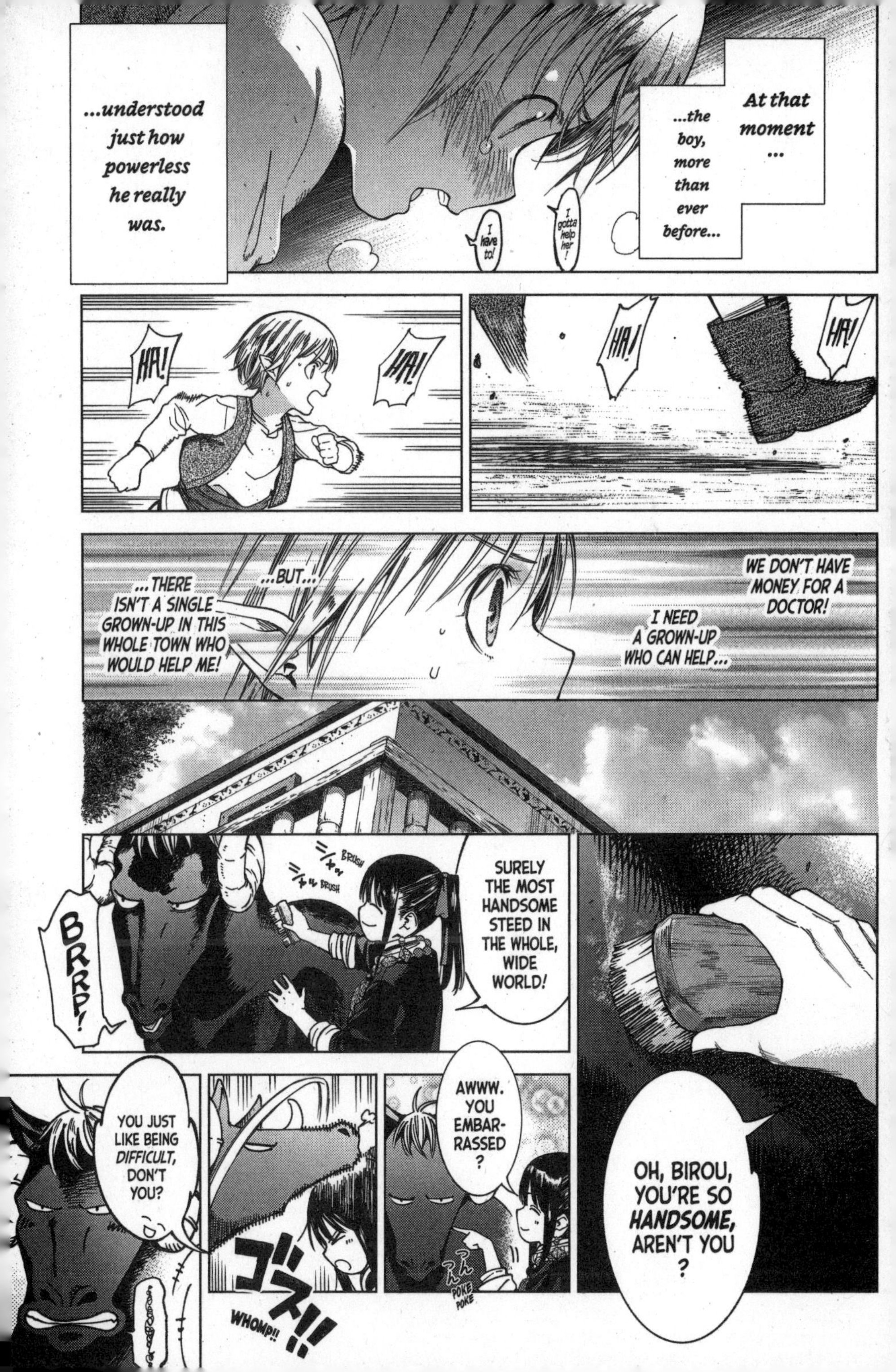
At that moment...
...the boy, more than ever before...
I gotta help her!
I have to!
...understood just how powerless he really was.
HA!
HA!
HA!
HA!
WE DON'T HAVE MONEY FOR A DOCTOR!
I NEED A GROWN-UP WHO CAN HELP...
...BUT...
...THERE ISN'T A SINGLE GROWN-UP IN THIS WHOLE TOWN WHO WOULD HELP ME!
OH, BIROU, YOU'RE SO HANDSOME, AREN'T YOU?
BRUSH
BRUSH
SURELY THE MOST HANDSOME STEED IN THE WHOLE, WIDE WORLD!
BRRP!
AWWW. YOU EMBARRASSED?
POKE POKE
YOU JUST LIKE BEING DIFFICULT, DON'T YOU?
WHOMP!!

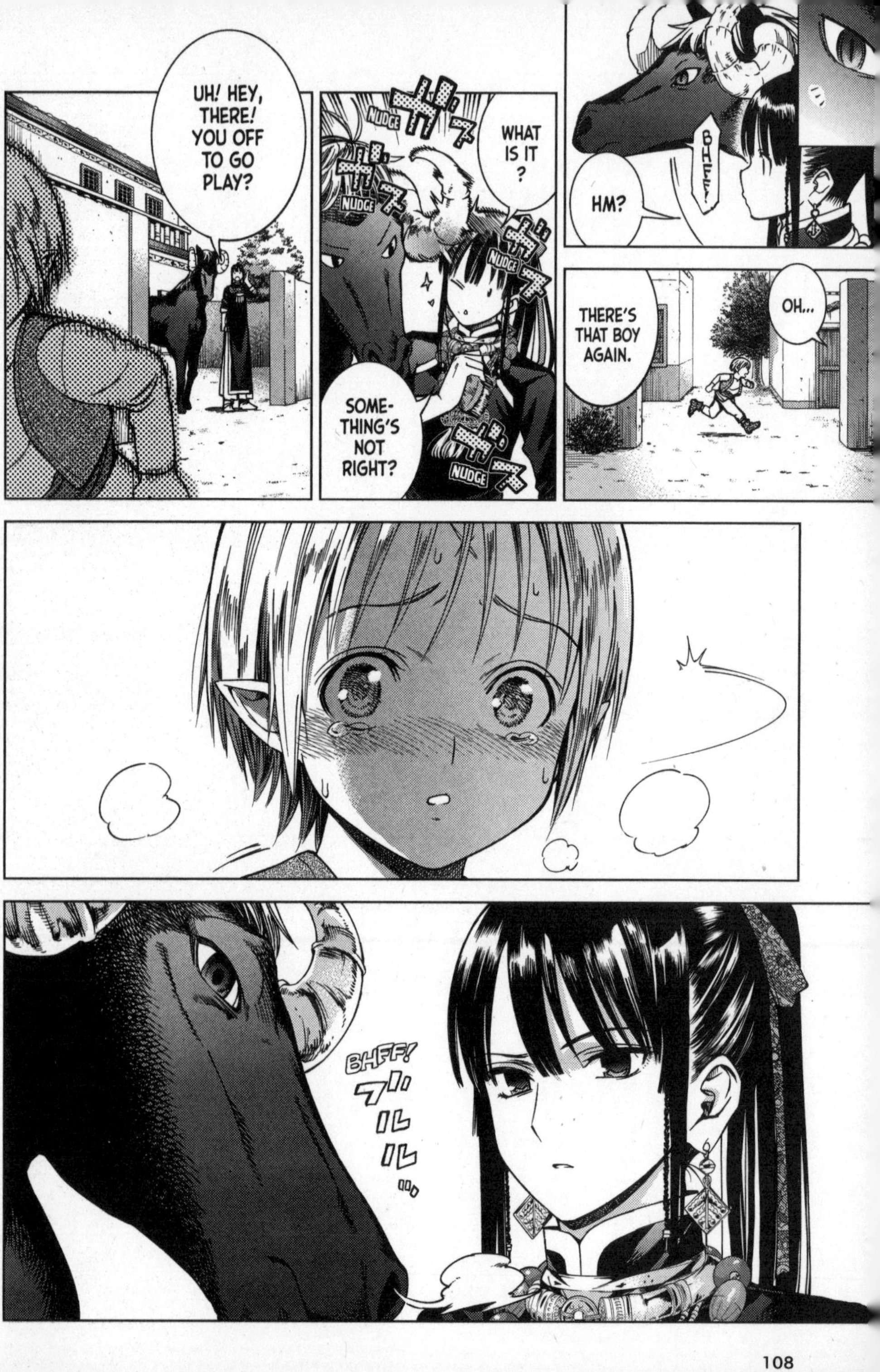
...
BHEFF!
HM?
OH...
THERE'S THAT BOY AGAIN.
NUDGE
NUDGE
WHAT IS IT ?
NUDGE
NUDGE
SOME-THING'S NOT RIGHT?
UH! HEY, THERE! YOU OFF TO GO PLAY?
BHFF!
フルルル

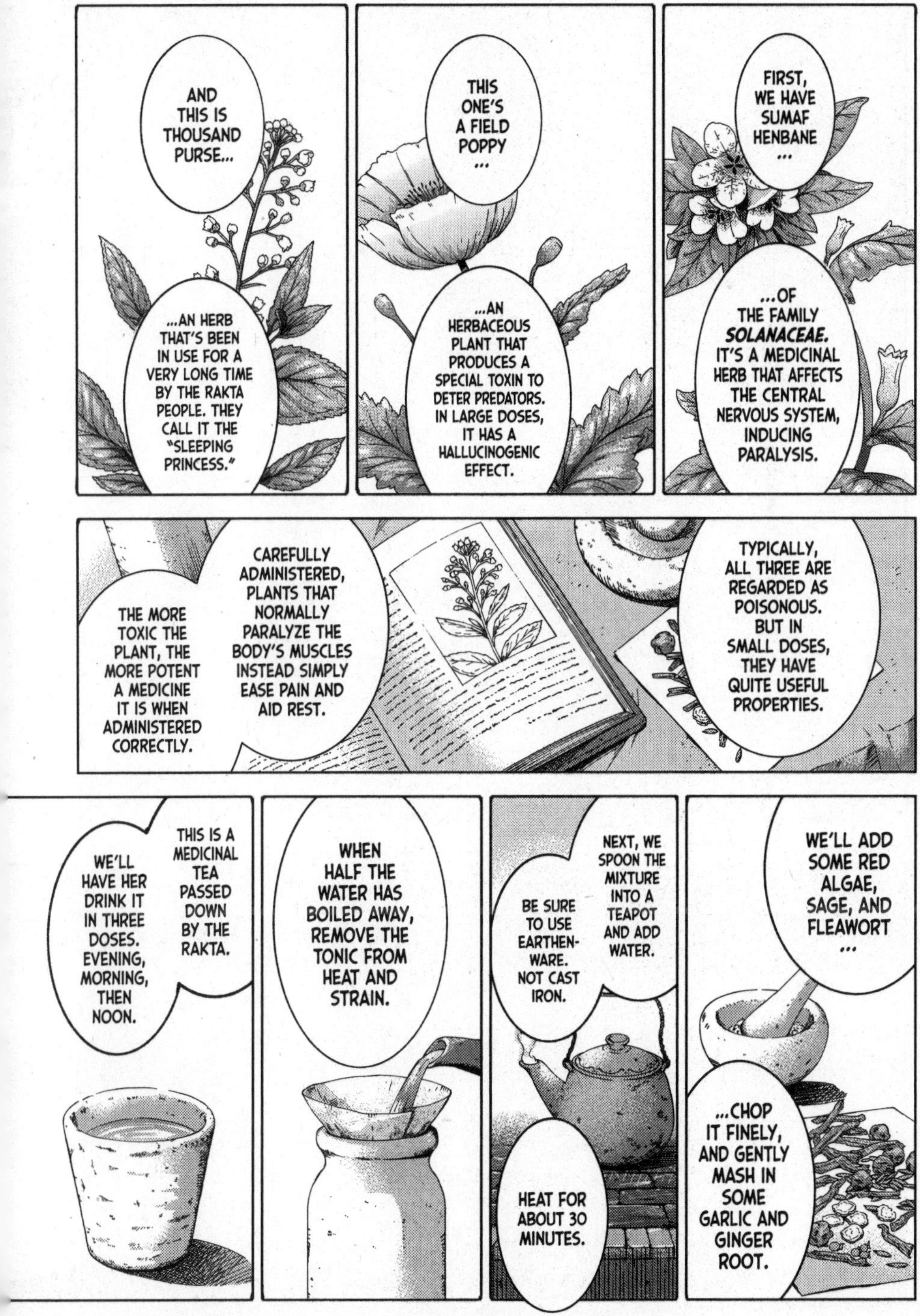
FIRST, WE HAVE SUMAF HENBANE ...
...OF THE FAMILY *SOLANACEAE.* IT'S A MEDICINAL HERB THAT AFFECTS THE CENTRAL NERVOUS SYSTEM, INDUCING PARALYSIS.
THIS ONE'S A FIELD POPPY ...
...AN HERBACEOUS PLANT THAT PRODUCES A SPECIAL TOXIN TO DETER PREDATORS. IN LARGE DOSES, IT HAS A HALLUCINOGENIC EFFECT.
AND THIS IS THOUSAND PURSE...
...AN HERB THAT'S BEEN IN USE FOR A VERY LONG TIME BY THE RAKTA PEOPLE. THEY CALL IT THE "SLEEPING PRINCESS."
TYPICALLY, ALL THREE ARE REGARDED AS POISONOUS. BUT IN SMALL DOSES, THEY HAVE QUITE USEFUL PROPERTIES.
CAREFULLY ADMINISTERED, PLANTS THAT NORMALLY PARALYZE THE BODY'S MUSCLES INSTEAD SIMPLY EASE PAIN AND AID REST.
THE MORE TOXIC THE PLANT, THE MORE POTENT A MEDICINE IT IS WHEN ADMINISTERED CORRECTLY.
WE'LL ADD SOME RED ALGAE, SAGE, AND FLEAWORT ...
...CHOP IT FINELY, AND GENTLY MASH IN SOME GARLIC AND GINGER ROOT.
NEXT, WE SPOON THE MIXTURE INTO A TEAPOT AND ADD WATER.
BE SURE TO USE EARTHEN-WARE. NOT CAST IRON.
HEAT FOR ABOUT 30 MINUTES.
WHEN HALF THE WATER HAS BOILED AWAY, REMOVE THE TONIC FROM HEAT AND STRAIN.
THIS IS A MEDICINAL TEA PASSED DOWN BY THE RAKTA.
WE'LL HAVE HER DRINK IT IN THREE DOSES. EVENING, MORNING, THEN NOON.

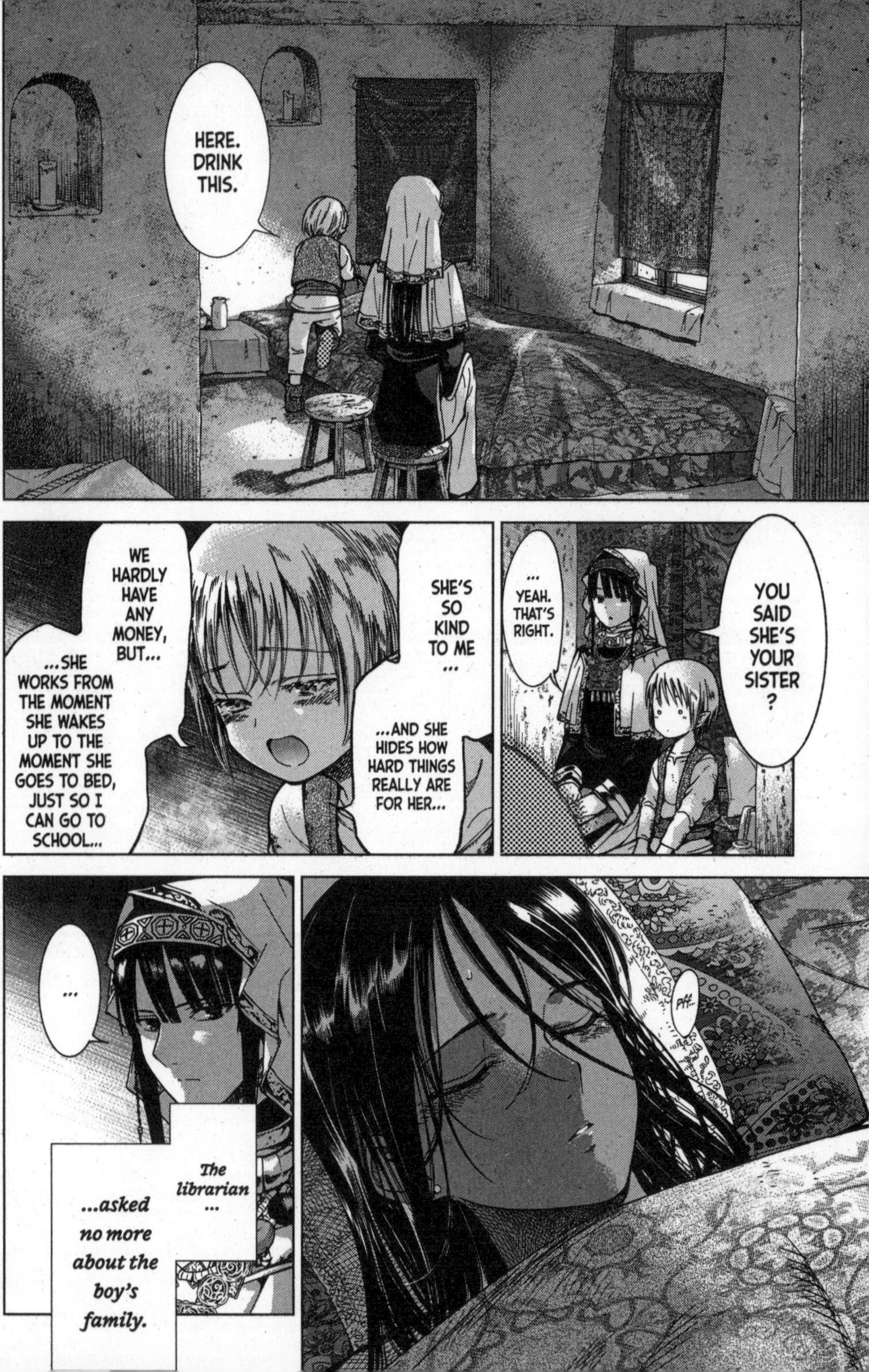
HERE. DRINK THIS.
YOU SAID SHE'S YOUR SISTER?
... YEAH. THAT'S RIGHT.
SHE'S SO KIND TO ME ...
...AND SHE HIDES HOW HARD THINGS REALLY ARE FOR HER...
WE HARDLY HAVE ANY MONEY, BUT...
...SHE WORKS FROM THE MOMENT SHE WAKES UP TO THE MOMENT SHE GOES TO BED, JUST SO I CAN GO TO SCHOOL...
Pff...
...
The librarian ...
...asked no more about the boy's family.

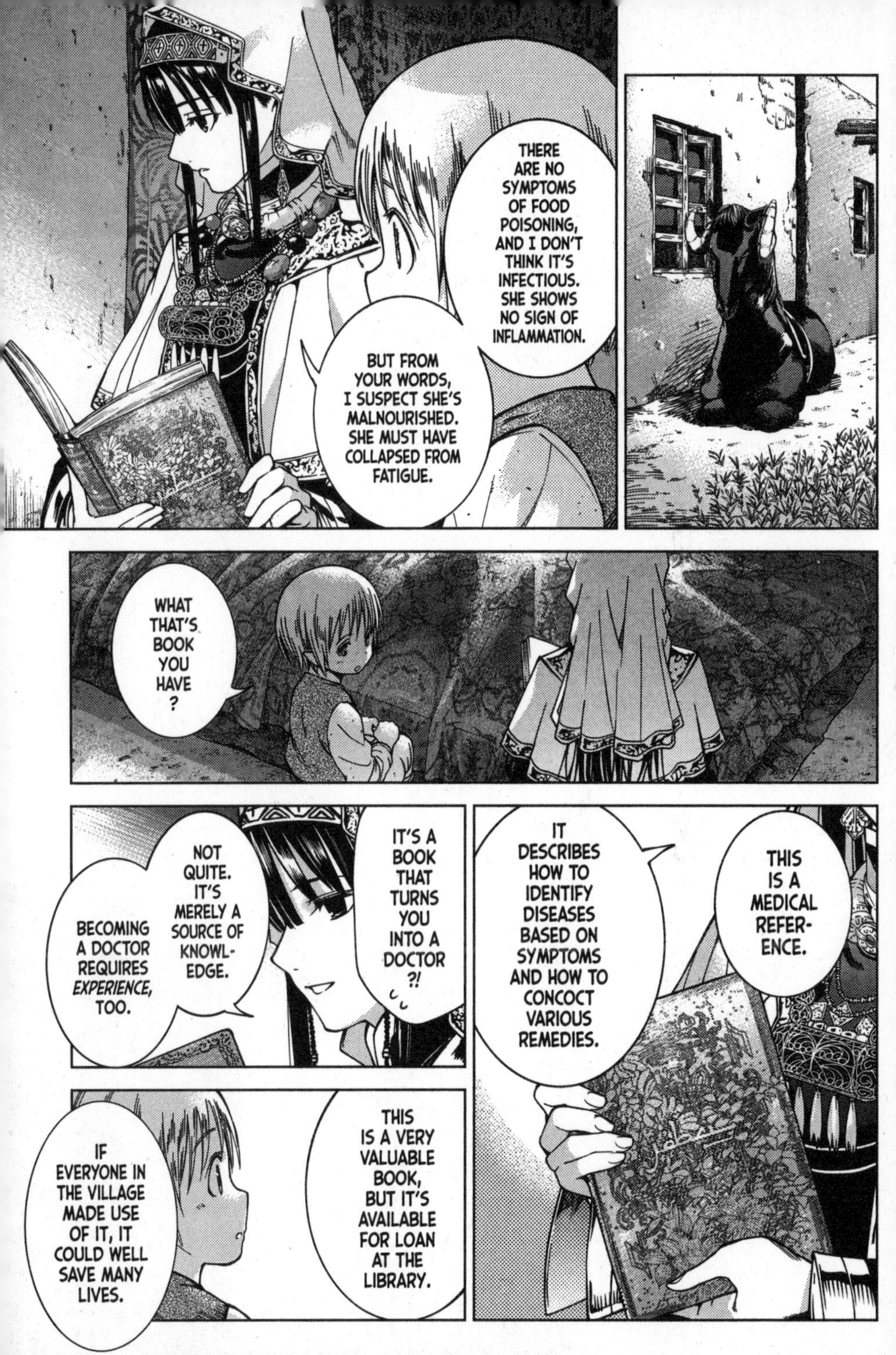
THERE ARE NO SYMPTOMS OF FOOD POISONING, AND I DON'T THINK IT'S INFECTIOUS. SHE SHOWS NO SIGN OF INFLAMMATION.
BUT FROM YOUR WORDS, I SUSPECT SHE'S MALNOURISHED. SHE MUST HAVE COLLAPSED FROM FATIGUE.
WHAT THAT'S BOOK YOU HAVE ?
THIS IS A MEDICAL REFER-ENCE.
IT DESCRIBES HOW TO IDENTIFY DISEASES BASED ON SYMPTOMS AND HOW TO CONCOCT VARIOUS REMEDIES.
IT'S A BOOK THAT TURNS YOU INTO A DOCTOR ?!
NOT QUITE. IT'S MERELY A SOURCE OF KNOWL-EDGE.
BECOMING A DOCTOR REQUIRES *EXPERIENCE*, TOO.
THIS IS A VERY VALUABLE BOOK, BUT IT'S AVAILABLE FOR LOAN AT THE LIBRARY.
IF EVERYONE IN THE VILLAGE MADE USE OF IT, IT COULD WELL SAVE MANY LIVES.

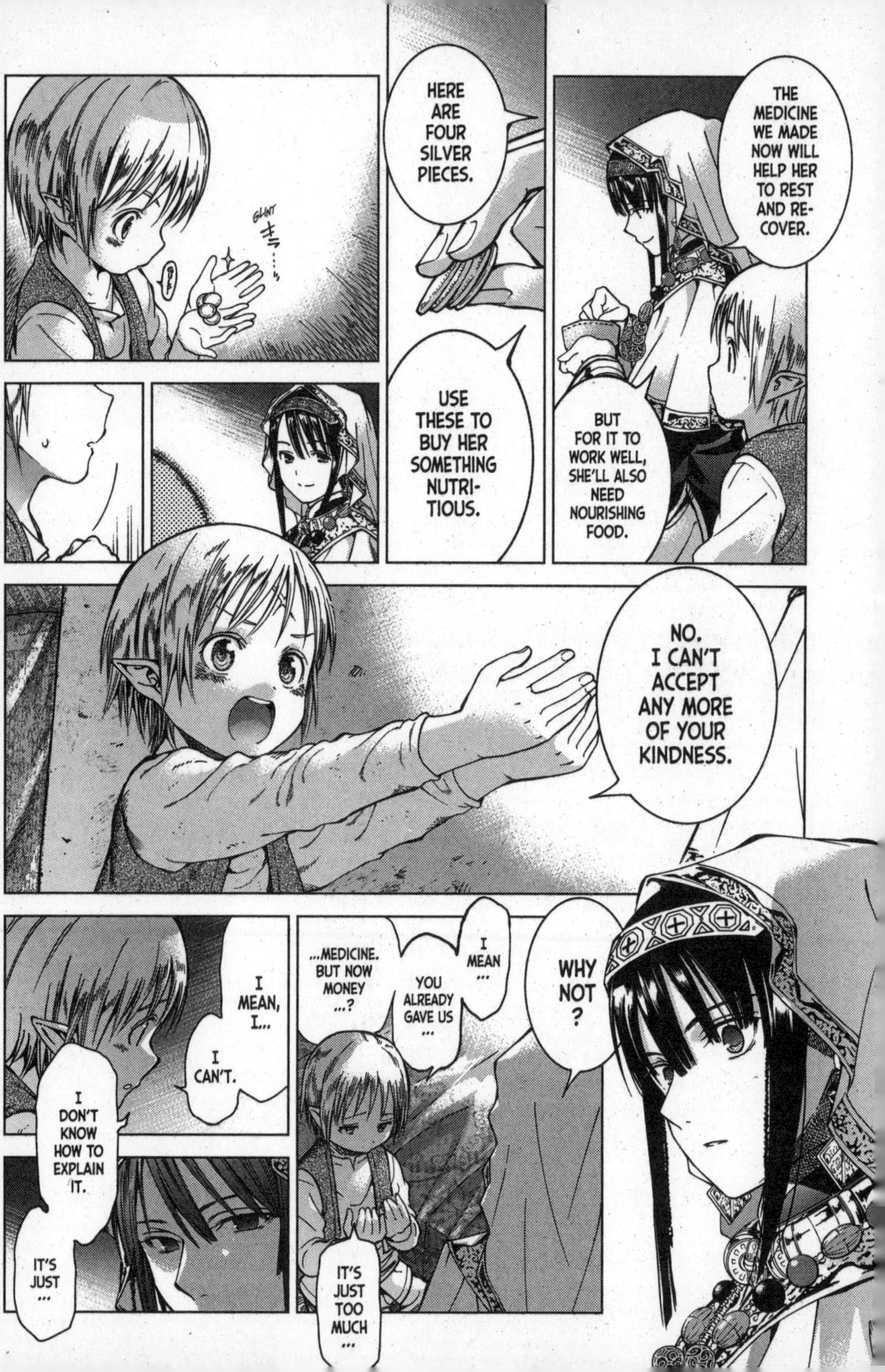
THE MEDICINE WE MADE NOW WILL HELP HER TO REST AND RE-COVER.
BUT FOR IT TO WORK WELL, SHE'LL ALSO NEED NOURISHING FOOD.
HERE ARE FOUR SILVER PIECES.
USE THESE TO BUY HER SOMETHING NUTRI-TIOUS.
GLINT
NO. I CAN'T ACCEPT ANY MORE OF YOUR KINDNESS.
WHY NOT?
I MEAN...
YOU ALREADY GAVE US...
...MEDICINE. BUT NOW MONEY...?
IT'S JUST TOO MUCH...
I MEAN, I...
I CAN'T.
I DON'T KNOW HOW TO EXPLAIN IT.
IT'S JUST...

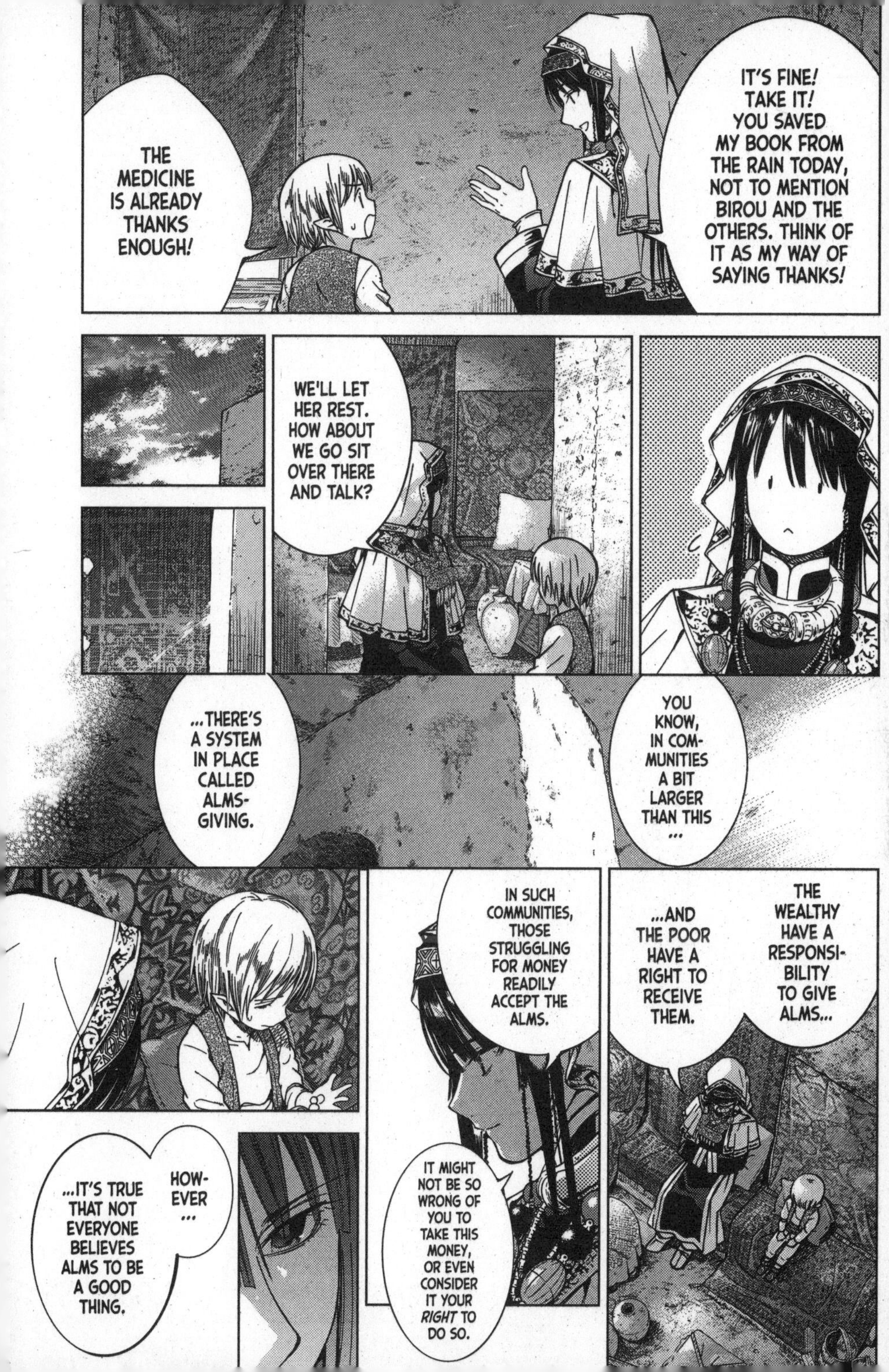
IT'S FINE! TAKE IT! YOU SAVED MY BOOK FROM THE RAIN TODAY, NOT TO MENTION BIROU AND THE OTHERS. THINK OF IT AS MY WAY OF SAYING THANKS!
THE MEDICINE IS ALREADY THANKS ENOUGH!
WE'LL LET HER REST. HOW ABOUT WE GO SIT OVER THERE AND TALK?
YOU KNOW, IN COM-MUNITIES A BIT LARGER THAN THIS ...
...THERE'S A SYSTEM IN PLACE CALLED ALMS-GIVING.
THE WEALTHY HAVE A RESPONSI-BILITY TO GIVE ALMS...
...AND THE POOR HAVE A RIGHT TO RECEIVE THEM.
IN SUCH COMMUNITIES, THOSE STRUGGLING FOR MONEY READILY ACCEPT THE ALMS.
IT MIGHT NOT BE SO WRONG OF YOU TO TAKE THIS MONEY, OR EVEN CONSIDER IT YOUR *RIGHT* TO DO SO.
HOW-EVER ...
...IT'S TRUE THAT NOT EVERYONE BELIEVES ALMS TO BE A GOOD THING.

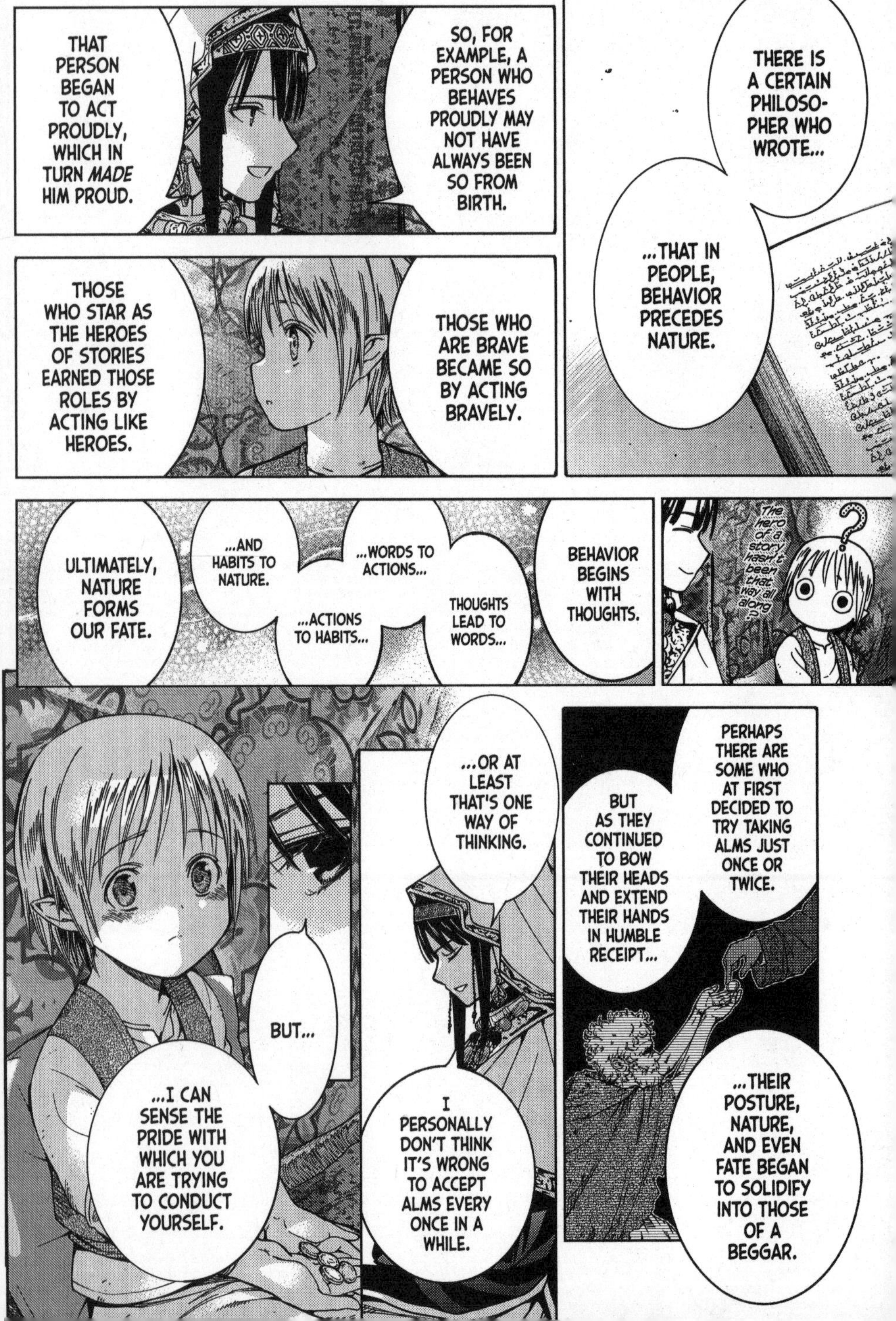
THERE IS A CERTAIN PHILOSOPHER WHO WROTE...
...THAT IN PEOPLE, BEHAVIOR PRECEDES NATURE.
SO, FOR EXAMPLE, A PERSON WHO BEHAVES PROUDLY MAY NOT HAVE ALWAYS BEEN SO FROM BIRTH.
THAT PERSON BEGAN TO ACT PROUDLY, WHICH IN TURN *MADE* HIM PROUD.
THOSE WHO ARE BRAVE BECAME SO BY ACTING BRAVELY.
THOSE WHO STAR AS THE HEROES OF STORIES EARNED THOSE ROLES BY ACTING LIKE HEROES.
The hero of a story hasn't been that way all along?
BEHAVIOR BEGINS WITH THOUGHTS.
THOUGHTS LEAD TO WORDS...
...WORDS TO ACTIONS...
...ACTIONS TO HABITS...
...AND HABITS TO NATURE.
ULTIMATELY, NATURE FORMS OUR FATE.
PERHAPS THERE ARE SOME WHO AT FIRST DECIDED TO TRY TAKING ALMS JUST ONCE OR TWICE.
BUT AS THEY CONTINUED TO BOW THEIR HEADS AND EXTEND THEIR HANDS IN HUMBLE RECEIPT...
...THEIR POSTURE, NATURE, AND EVEN FATE BEGAN TO SOLIDIFY INTO THOSE OF A BEGGAR.
...OR AT LEAST THAT'S ONE WAY OF THINKING.
I PERSONALLY DON'T THINK IT'S WRONG TO ACCEPT ALMS EVERY ONCE IN A WHILE.
BUT...
...I CAN SENSE THE PRIDE WITH WHICH YOU ARE TRYING TO CONDUCT YOURSELF.

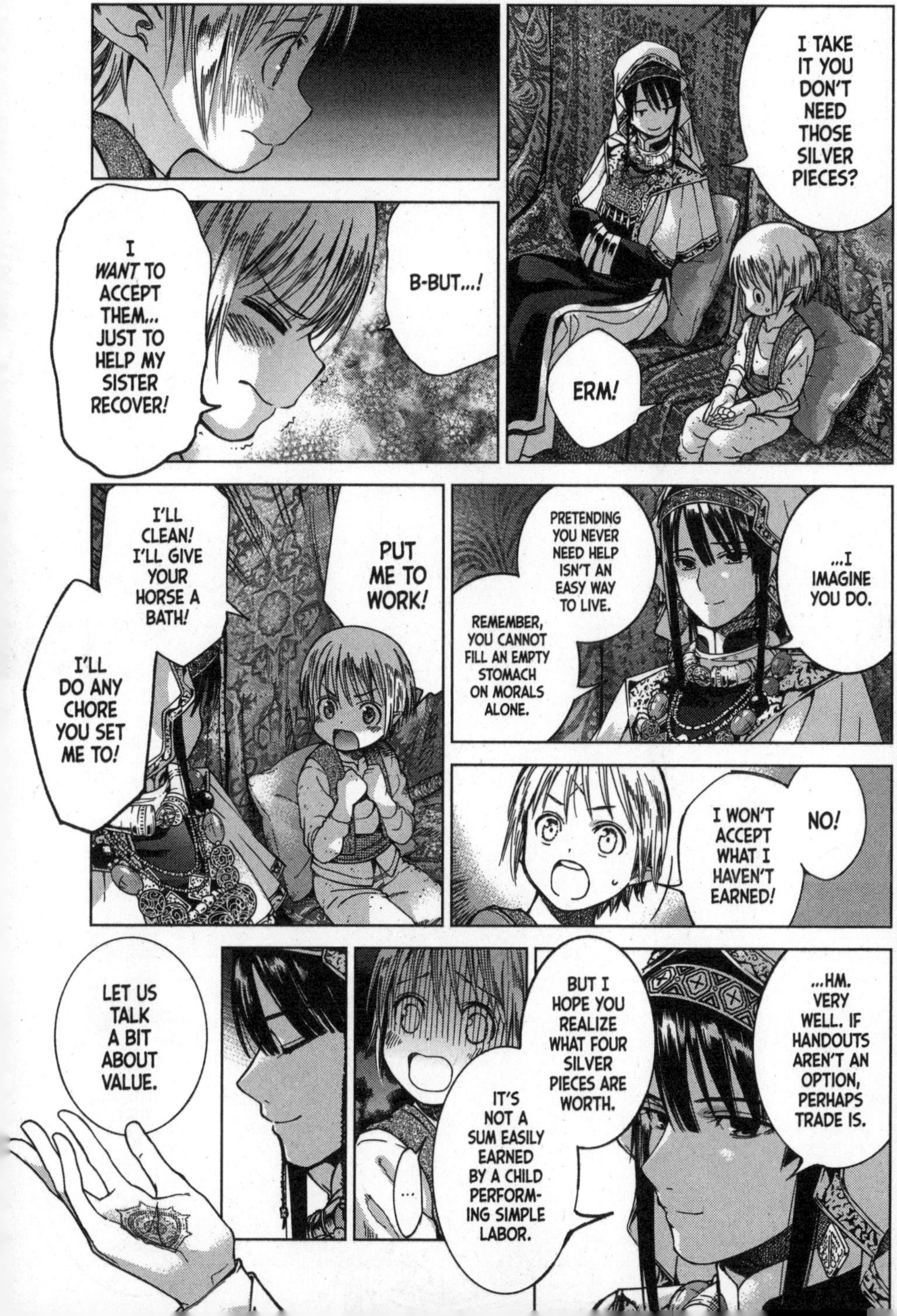
I TAKE IT YOU DON'T NEED THOSE SILVER PIECES?
ERM!
B-BUT...!
I *WANT* TO ACCEPT THEM... JUST TO HELP MY SISTER RECOVER!
...I IMAGINE YOU DO.
PRETENDING YOU NEVER NEED HELP ISN'T AN EASY WAY TO LIVE.
REMEMBER, YOU CANNOT FILL AN EMPTY STOMACH ON MORALS ALONE.
NO!
I WON'T ACCEPT WHAT I HAVEN'T EARNED!
PUT ME TO WORK!
I'LL CLEAN! I'LL GIVE YOUR HORSE A BATH!
I'LL DO ANY CHORE YOU SET ME TO!
...HM. VERY WELL. IF HANDOUTS AREN'T AN OPTION, PERHAPS TRADE IS.
BUT I HOPE YOU REALIZE WHAT FOUR SILVER PIECES ARE WORTH.
IT'S NOT A SUM EASILY EARNED BY A CHILD PERFORMING SIMPLE LABOR.
...
LET US TALK A BIT ABOUT VALUE.

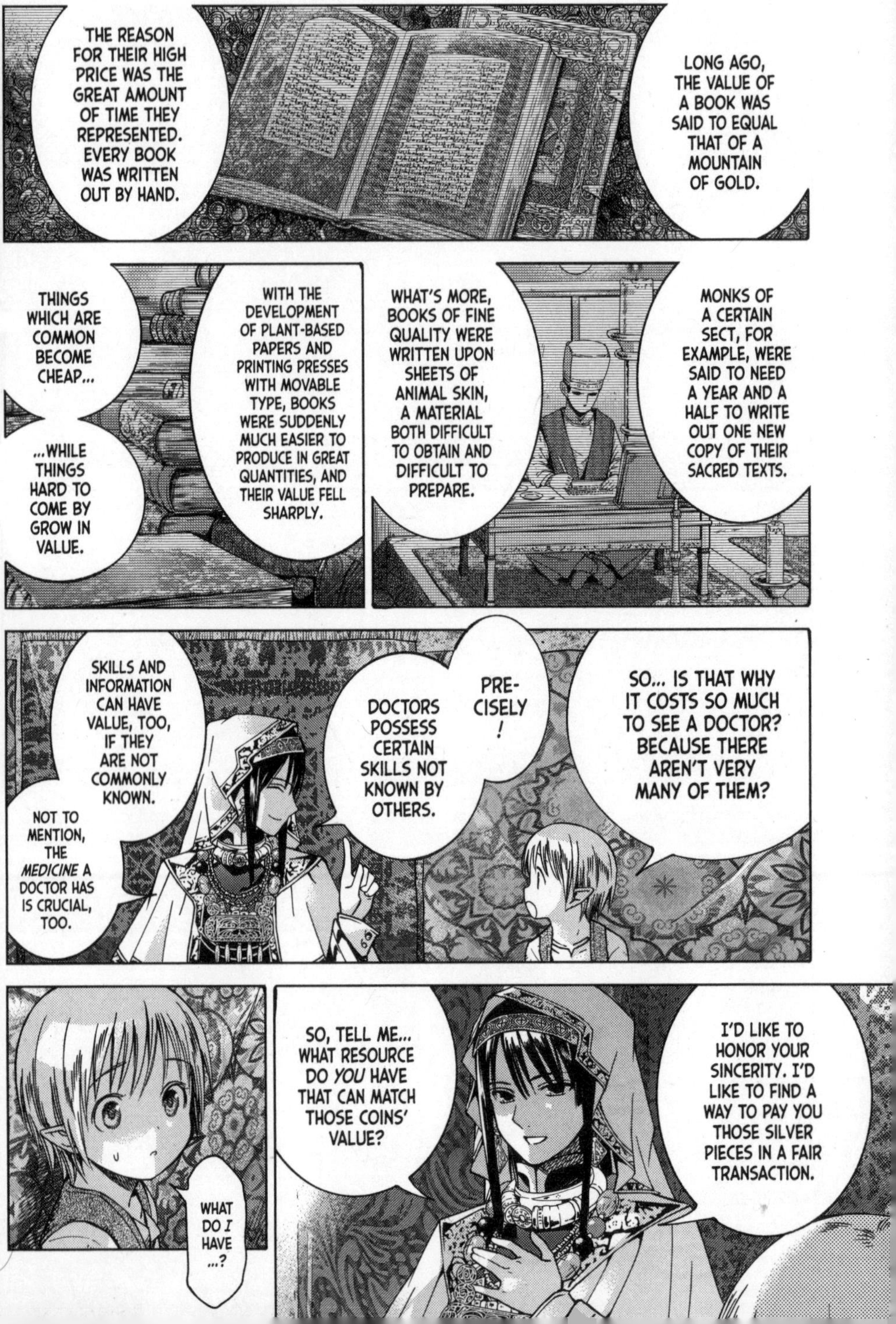
LONG AGO, THE VALUE OF A BOOK WAS SAID TO EQUAL THAT OF A MOUNTAIN OF GOLD.
THE REASON FOR THEIR HIGH PRICE WAS THE GREAT AMOUNT OF TIME THEY REPRESENTED. EVERY BOOK WAS WRITTEN OUT BY HAND.
MONKS OF A CERTAIN SECT, FOR EXAMPLE, WERE SAID TO NEED A YEAR AND A HALF TO WRITE OUT ONE NEW COPY OF THEIR SACRED TEXTS.
WHAT'S MORE, BOOKS OF FINE QUALITY WERE WRITTEN UPON SHEETS OF ANIMAL SKIN, A MATERIAL BOTH DIFFICULT TO OBTAIN AND DIFFICULT TO PREPARE.
WITH THE DEVELOPMENT OF PLANT-BASED PAPERS AND PRINTING PRESSES WITH MOVABLE TYPE, BOOKS WERE SUDDENLY MUCH EASIER TO PRODUCE IN GREAT QUANTITIES, AND THEIR VALUE FELL SHARPLY.
THINGS WHICH ARE COMMON BECOME CHEAP...
...WHILE THINGS HARD TO COME BY GROW IN VALUE.
SO... IS THAT WHY IT COSTS SO MUCH TO SEE A DOCTOR? BECAUSE THERE AREN'T VERY MANY OF THEM?
PRE-CISELY!
DOCTORS POSSESS CERTAIN SKILLS NOT KNOWN BY OTHERS.
SKILLS AND INFORMATION CAN HAVE VALUE, TOO, IF THEY ARE NOT COMMONLY KNOWN.
NOT TO MENTION, THE *MEDICINE* A DOCTOR HAS IS CRUCIAL, TOO.
I'D LIKE TO HONOR YOUR SINCERITY. I'D LIKE TO FIND A WAY TO PAY YOU THOSE SILVER PIECES IN A FAIR TRANSACTION.
SO, TELL ME... WHAT RESOURCE DO *YOU* HAVE THAT CAN MATCH THOSE COINS' VALUE?
WHAT DO *I* HAVE ...?

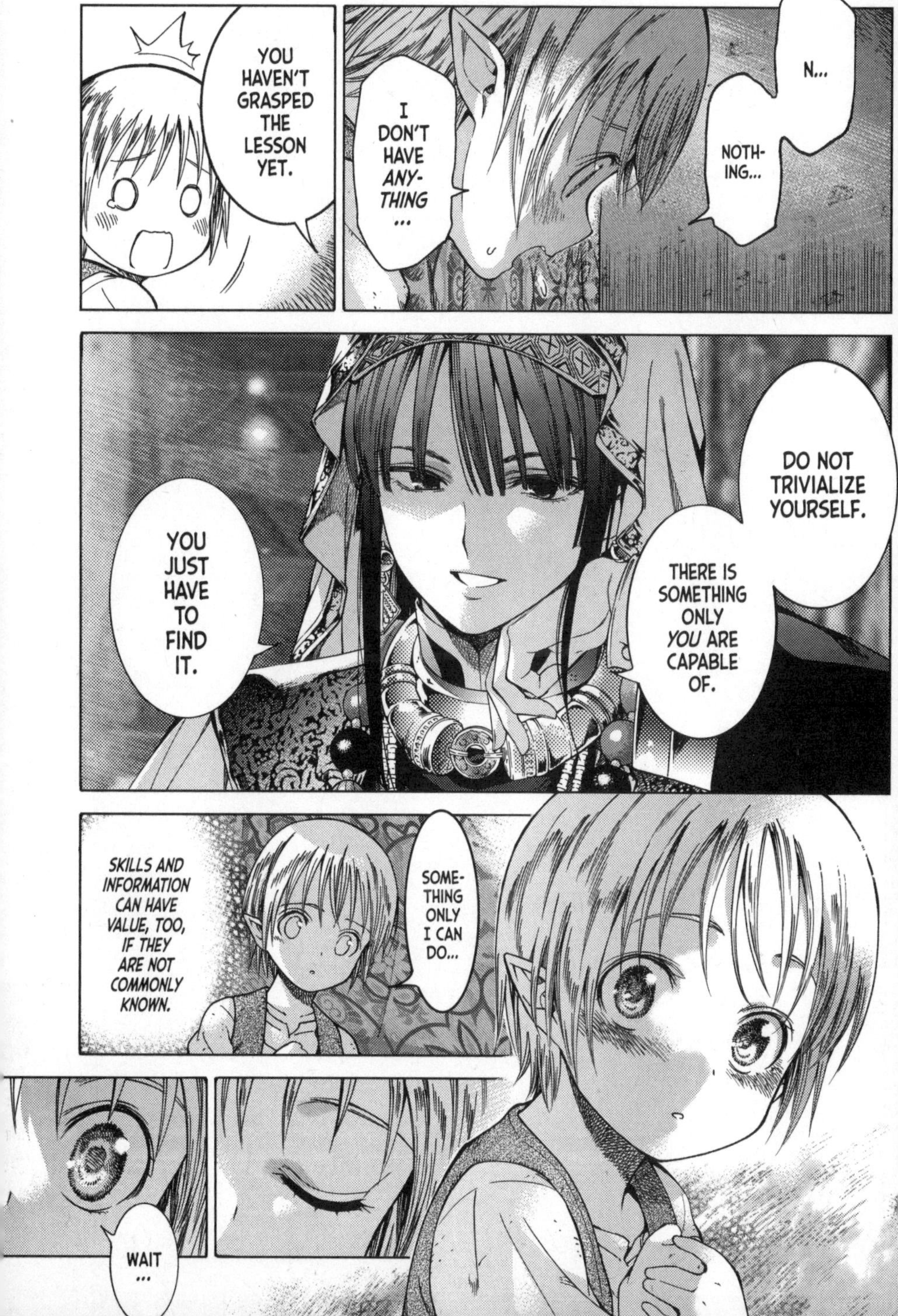
N...
NOTHING...
I DON'T HAVE *ANYTHING*...
YOU HAVEN'T GRASPED THE LESSON YET.
DO NOT TRIVIALIZE YOURSELF.
THERE IS SOMETHING ONLY *YOU* ARE CAPABLE OF.
YOU JUST HAVE TO FIND IT.
SOMETHING ONLY I CAN DO...
SKILLS AND INFORMATION CAN HAVE VALUE, TOO, IF THEY ARE NOT COMMONLY KNOWN.
WAIT...

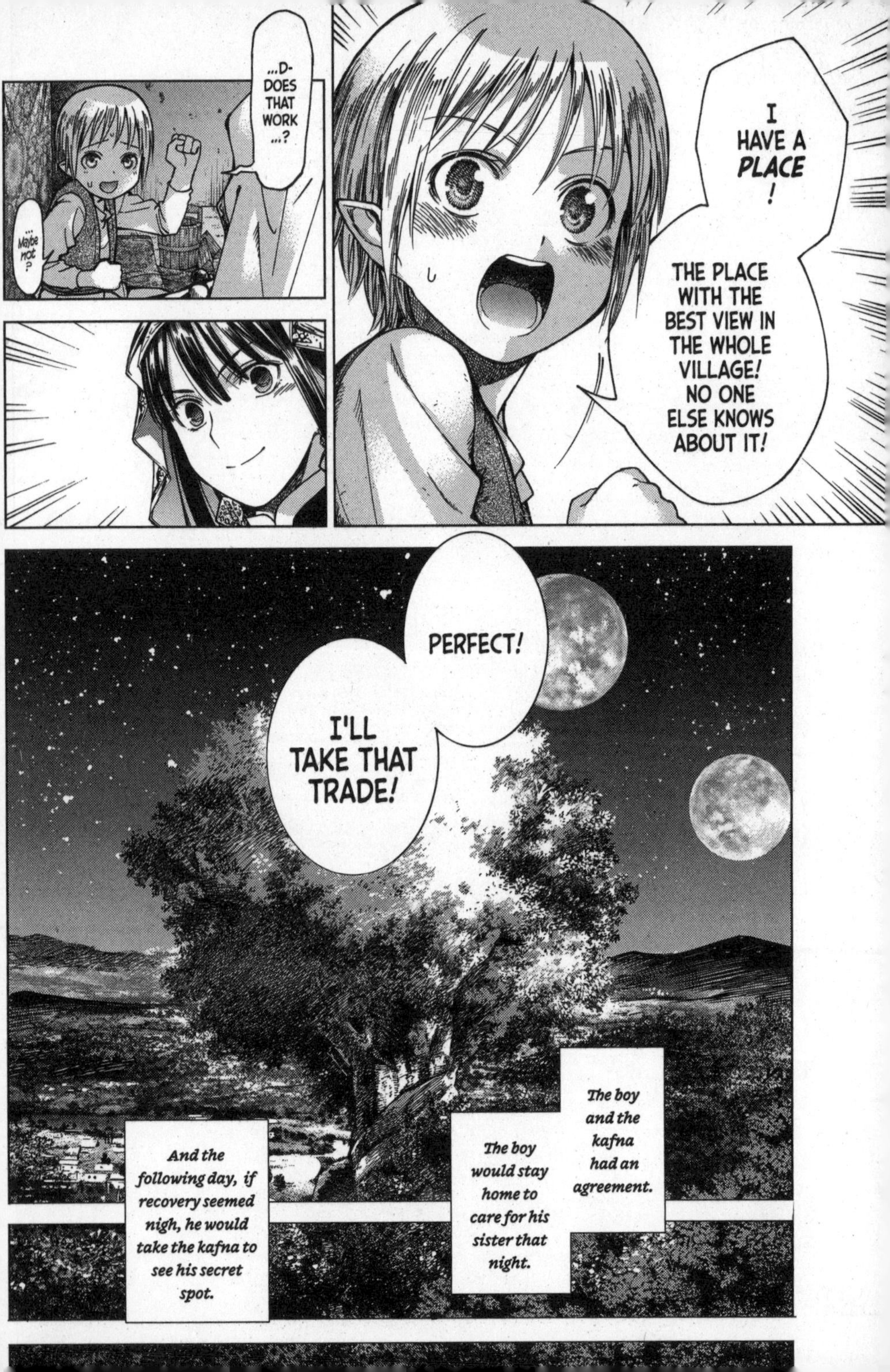
I HAVE A PLACE!
THE PLACE WITH THE BEST VIEW IN THE WHOLE VILLAGE! NO ONE ELSE KNOWS ABOUT IT!
...D-DOES THAT WORK...?
...Maybe not?
PERFECT!
I'LL TAKE THAT TRADE!
The boy and the kafna had an agreement.
The boy would stay home to care for his sister that night.
And the following day, if recovery seemed nigh, he would take the kafna to see his secret spot.

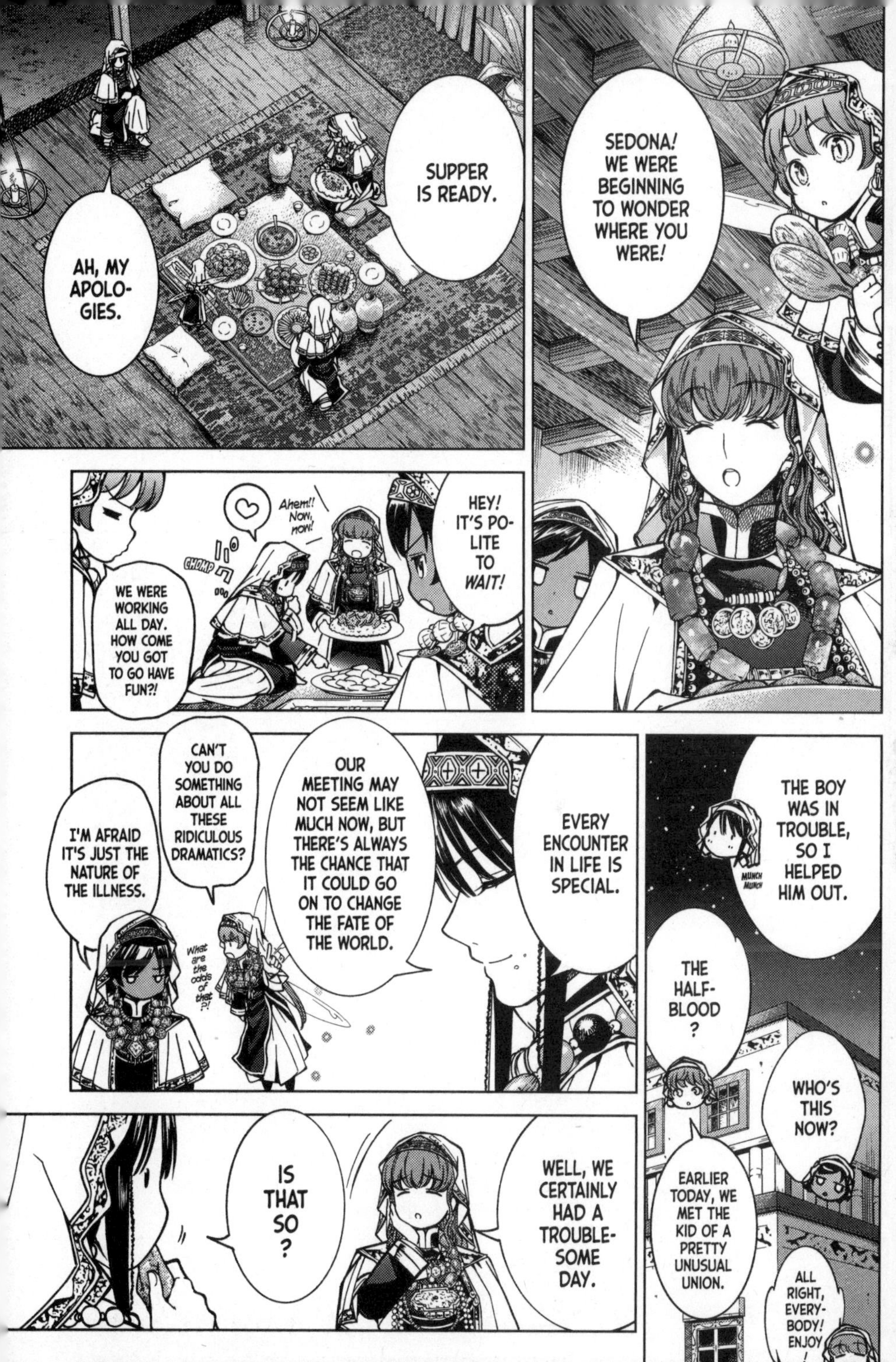
SEDONA! WE WERE BEGINNING TO WONDER WHERE YOU WERE!
SUPPER IS READY.
AH, MY APOLOGIES.
HEY! IT'S POLITE TO WAIT!
Ahem!! Now, now!
CHOMP
WE WERE WORKING ALL DAY. HOW COME YOU GOT TO GO HAVE FUN?!
THE BOY WAS IN TROUBLE, SO I HELPED HIM OUT.
MUNCH MUNCH
THE HALF-BLOOD?
WHO'S THIS NOW?
EARLIER TODAY, WE MET THE KID OF A PRETTY UNUSUAL UNION.
ALL RIGHT, EVERYBODY! ENJOY!
EVERY ENCOUNTER IN LIFE IS SPECIAL.
OUR MEETING MAY NOT SEEM LIKE MUCH NOW, BUT THERE'S ALWAYS THE CHANCE THAT IT COULD GO ON TO CHANGE THE FATE OF THE WORLD.
CAN'T YOU DO SOMETHING ABOUT ALL THESE RIDICULOUS DRAMATICS?
I'M AFRAID IT'S JUST THE NATURE OF THE ILLNESS.
What are the odds of that?!
WELL, WE CERTAINLY HAD A TROUBLESOME DAY.
IS THAT SO?

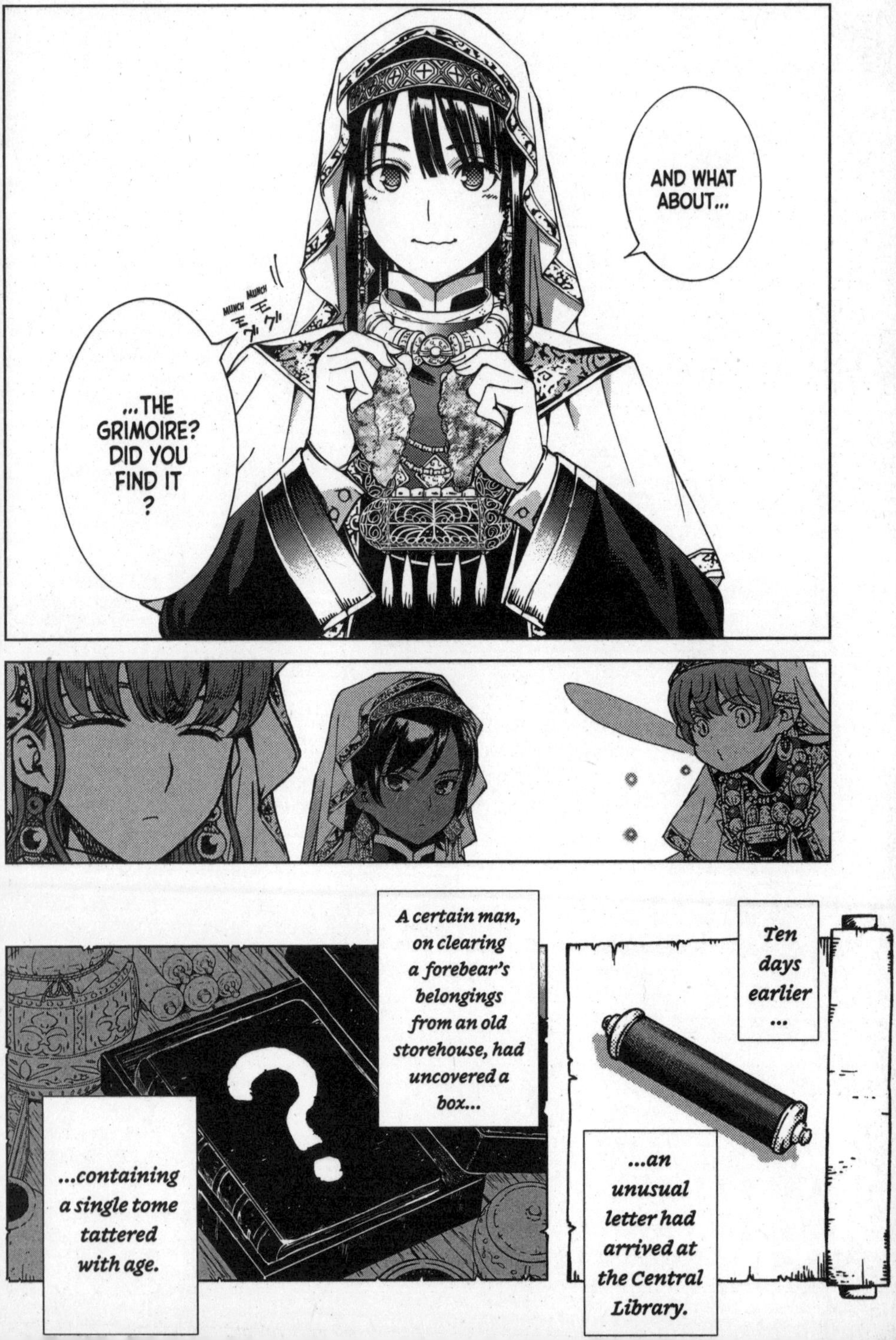
AND WHAT ABOUT...
MUNCH MUNCH
...THE GRIMOIRE? DID YOU FIND IT ?
Ten days earlier ...
...an unusual letter had arrived at the Central Library.
A certain man, on clearing a forebear's belongings from an old storehouse, had uncovered a box...
...containing a single tome tattered with age.

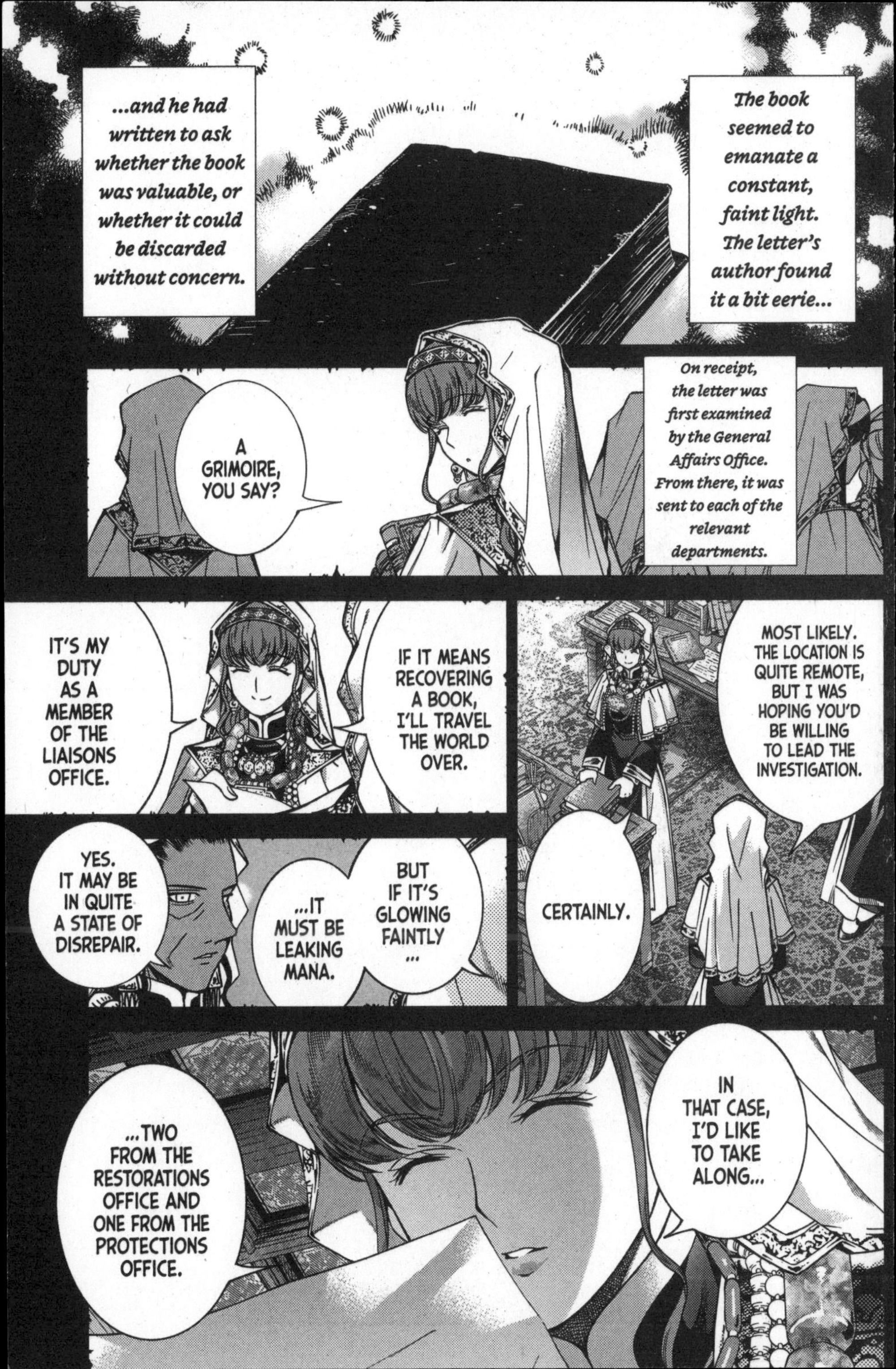
The book seemed to emanate a constant, faint light. The letter's author found it a bit eerie...
...and he had written to ask whether the book was valuable, or whether it could be discarded without concern.
On receipt, the letter was first examined by the General Affairs Office. From there, it was sent to each of the relevant departments.
A GRIMOIRE, YOU SAY?
MOST LIKELY. THE LOCATION IS QUITE REMOTE, BUT I WAS HOPING YOU'D BE WILLING TO LEAD THE INVESTIGATION.
CERTAINLY.
IF IT MEANS RECOVERING A BOOK, I'LL TRAVEL THE WORLD OVER.
IT'S MY DUTY AS A MEMBER OF THE LIAISONS OFFICE.
BUT IF IT'S GLOWING FAINTLY ...
...IT MUST BE LEAKING MANA.
YES. IT MAY BE IN QUITE A STATE OF DISREPAIR.
IN THAT CASE, I'D LIKE TO TAKE ALONG...
...TWO FROM THE RESTORATIONS OFFICE AND ONE FROM THE PROTECTIONS OFFICE.

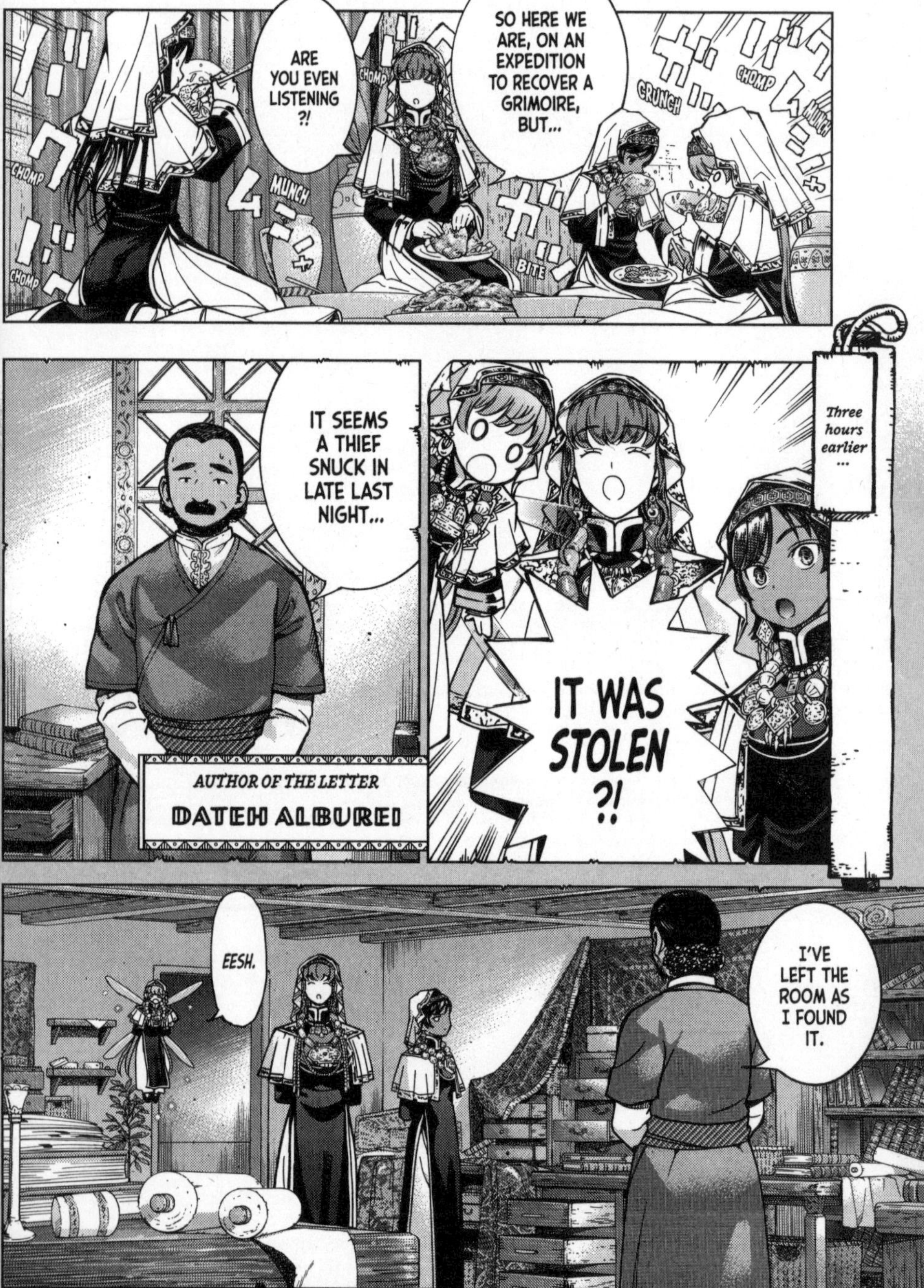
SO HERE WE ARE, ON AN EXPEDITION TO RECOVER A GRIMOIRE, BUT...
CHOMP
MUNCH
CRUNCH
BITE
ARE YOU EVEN LISTENING ?!
CHOMP
MUNCH
CHOMP
CHOMP
Three hours earlier ...
IT WAS STOLEN ?!
IT SEEMS A THIEF SNUCK IN LATE LAST NIGHT...
AUTHOR OF THE LETTER
DATEH ALBUREI
I'VE LEFT THE ROOM AS I FOUND IT.
EESH.

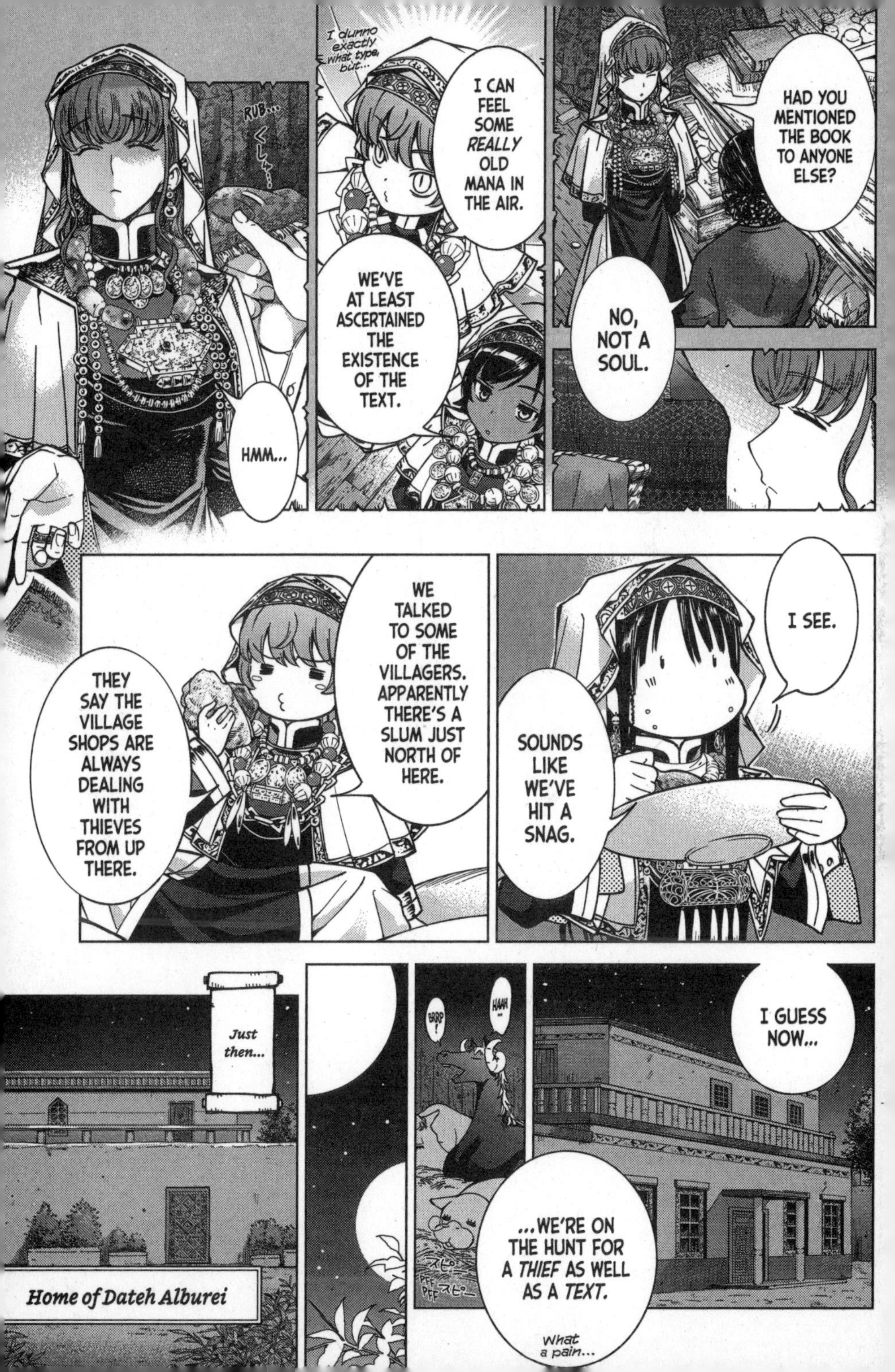
HAD YOU MENTIONED THE BOOK TO ANYONE ELSE?
NO, NOT A SOUL.
I dunno exactly what type, but...
I CAN FEEL SOME *REALLY* OLD MANA IN THE AIR.
WE'VE AT LEAST ASCERTAINED THE EXISTENCE OF THE TEXT.
RUB...
HMM...
I SEE.
SOUNDS LIKE WE'VE HIT A SNAG.
WE TALKED TO SOME OF THE VILLAGERS. APPARENTLY THERE'S A SLUM JUST NORTH OF HERE.
THEY SAY THE VILLAGE SHOPS ARE ALWAYS DEALING WITH THIEVES FROM UP THERE.
I GUESS NOW...
...WE'RE ON THE HUNT FOR A *THIEF* AS WELL AS A *TEXT*.
What a pain...
HAAH...
BRRP!
PFF
PFF
Just then...
Home of Dateh Alburei

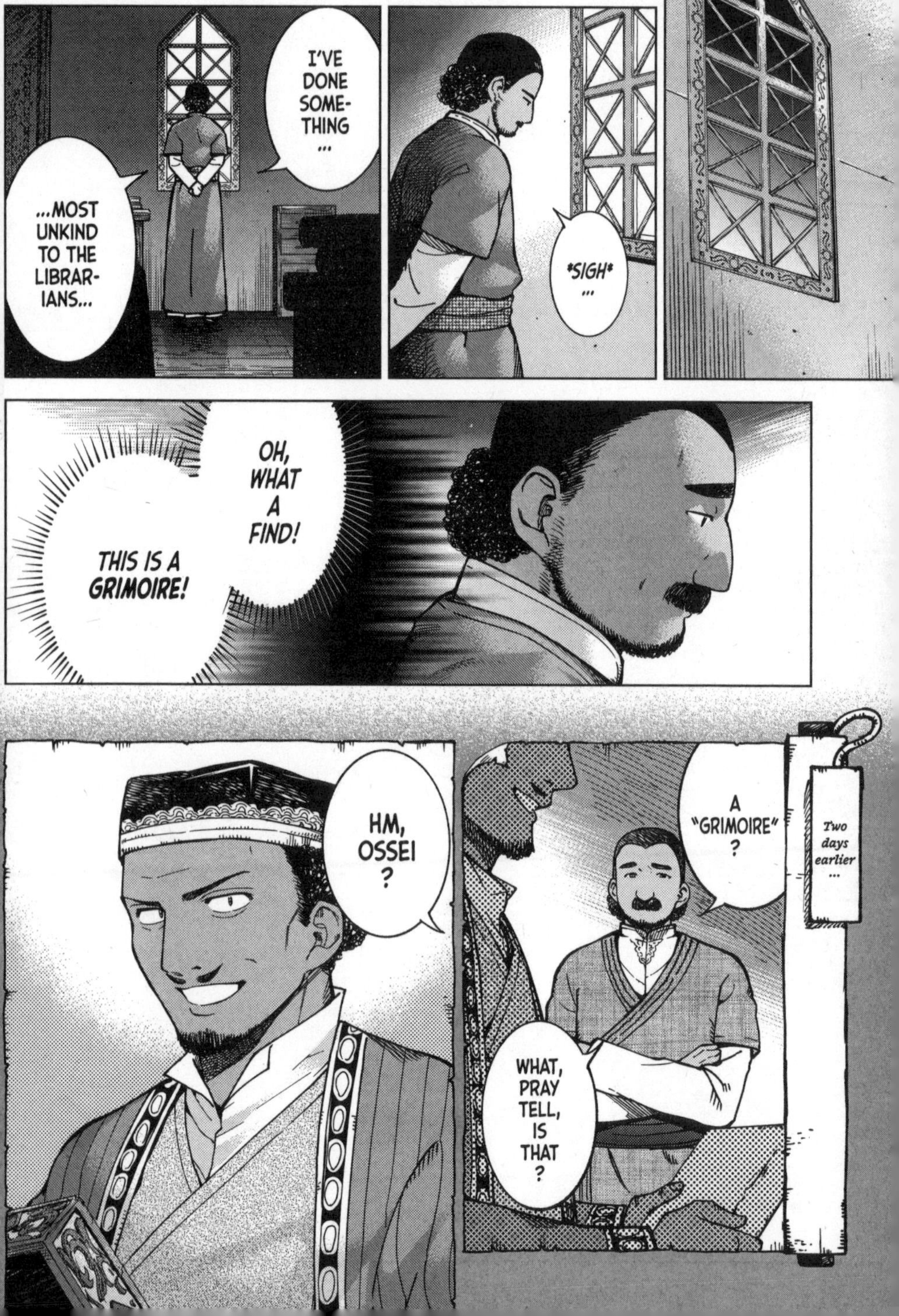
SIGH ...
I'VE DONE SOMETHING...
...MOST UNKIND TO THE LIBRARIANS...
OH, WHAT A FIND!
THIS IS A GRIMOIRE!
Two days earlier...
A "GRIMOIRE"?
WHAT, PRAY TELL, IS THAT?
HM, OSSEI?

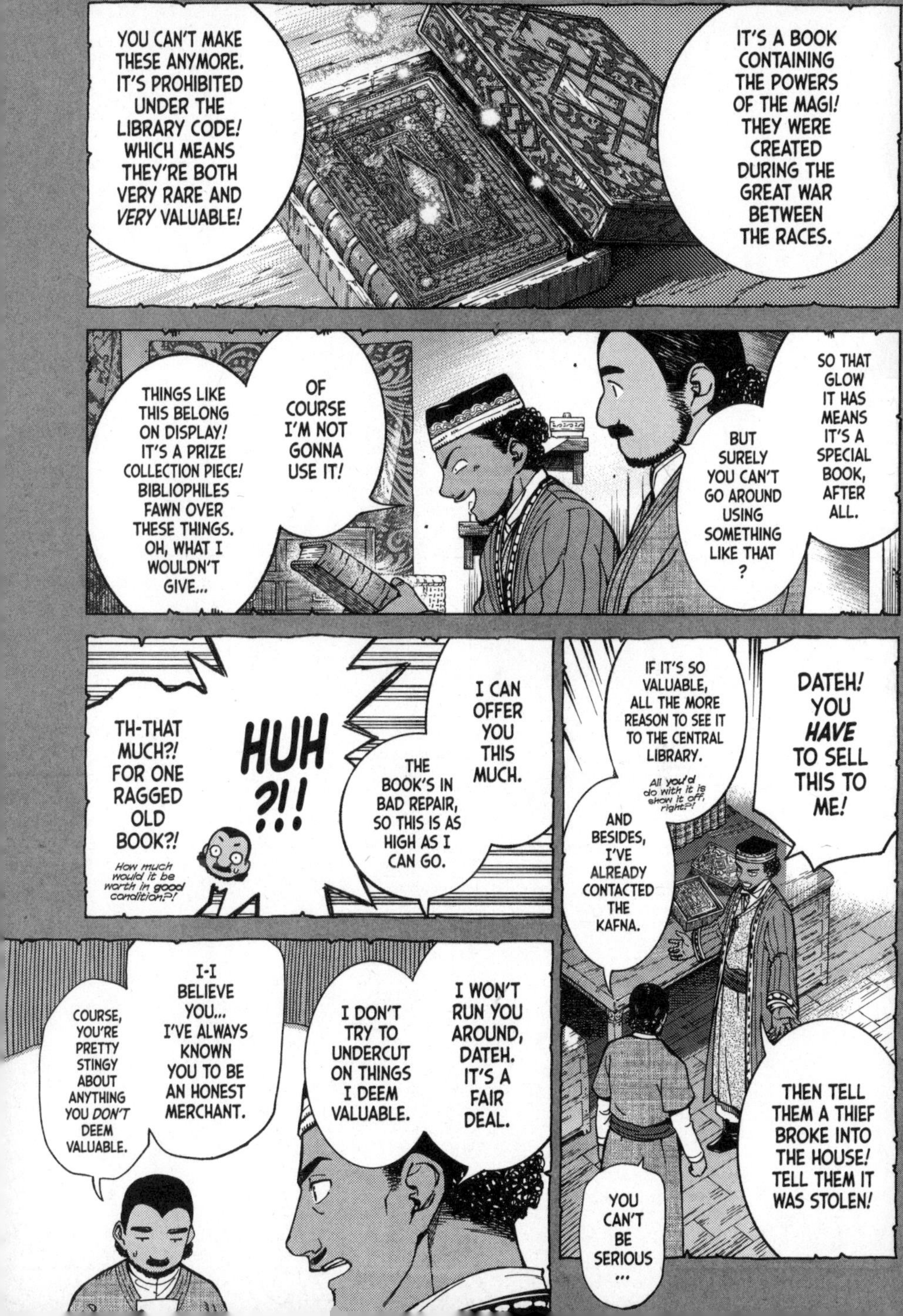
IT'S A BOOK CONTAINING THE POWERS OF THE MAGI! THEY WERE CREATED DURING THE GREAT WAR BETWEEN THE RACES.
YOU CAN'T MAKE THESE ANYMORE. IT'S PROHIBITED UNDER THE LIBRARY CODE! WHICH MEANS THEY'RE BOTH VERY RARE AND VERY VALUABLE!
SO THAT GLOW IT HAS MEANS IT'S A SPECIAL BOOK, AFTER ALL.
BUT SURELY YOU CAN'T GO AROUND USING SOMETHING LIKE THAT?
OF COURSE I'M NOT GONNA USE IT!
THINGS LIKE THIS BELONG ON DISPLAY! IT'S A PRIZE COLLECTION PIECE! BIBLIOPHILES FAWN OVER THESE THINGS. OH, WHAT I WOULDN'T GIVE...
DATEH! YOU HAVE TO SELL THIS TO ME!
IF IT'S SO VALUABLE, ALL THE MORE REASON TO SEE IT TO THE CENTRAL LIBRARY.
All you'd do with it is show it off, right?!
AND BESIDES, I'VE ALREADY CONTACTED THE KAFNA.
THEN TELL THEM A THIEF BROKE INTO THE HOUSE! TELL THEM IT WAS STOLEN!
YOU CAN'T BE SERIOUS...
I CAN OFFER YOU THIS MUCH.
THE BOOK'S IN BAD REPAIR, SO THIS IS AS HIGH AS I CAN GO.
HUH ?!!
TH-THAT MUCH?! FOR ONE RAGGED OLD BOOK?!
How much would it be worth in good condition?!
I WON'T RUN YOU AROUND, DATEH. IT'S A FAIR DEAL.
I DON'T TRY TO UNDERCUT ON THINGS I DEEM VALUABLE.
I-I BELIEVE YOU... I'VE ALWAYS KNOWN YOU TO BE AN HONEST MERCHANT.
COURSE, YOU'RE PRETTY STINGY ABOUT ANYTHING YOU DON'T DEEM VALUABLE.

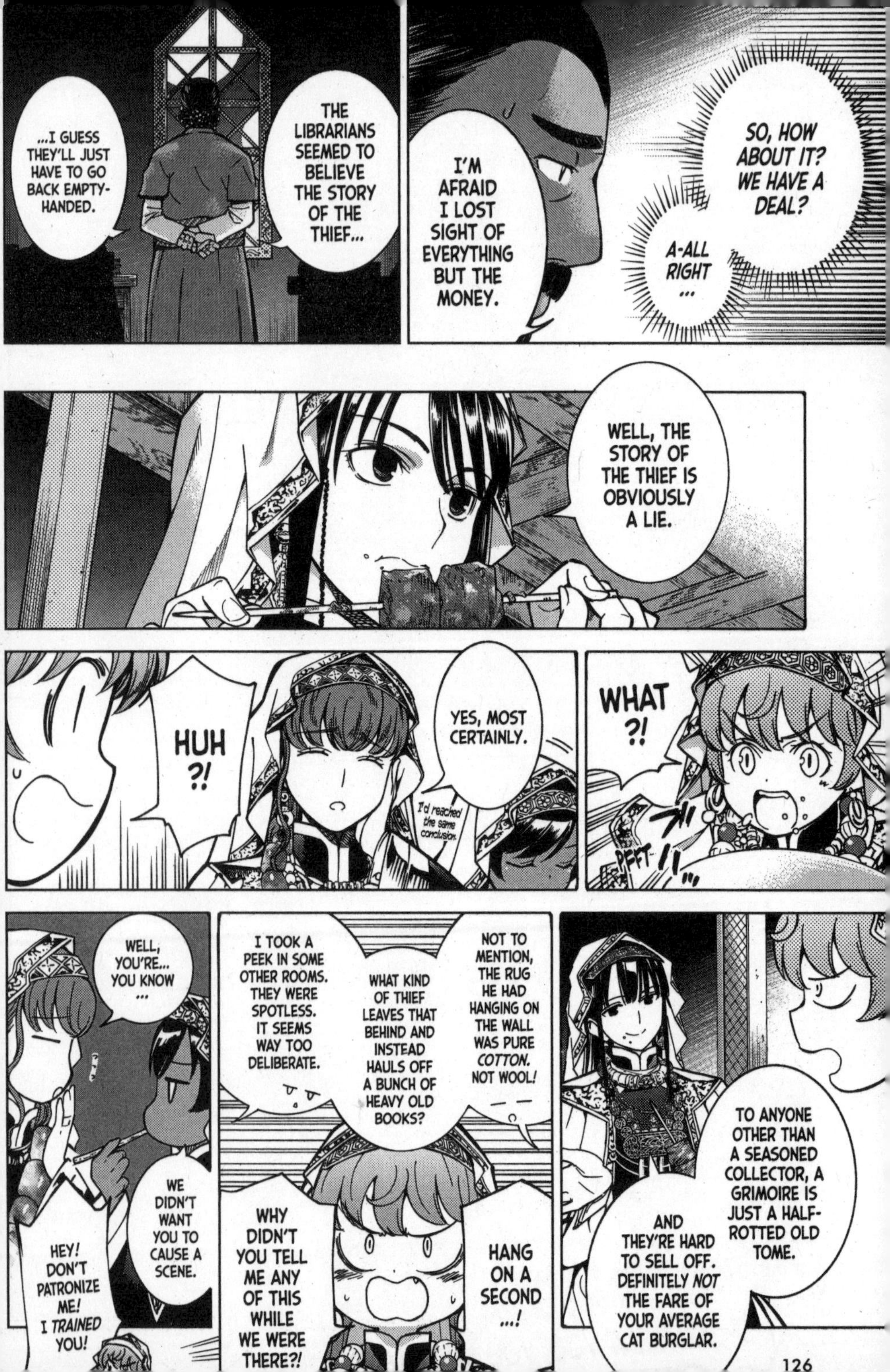
SO, HOW ABOUT IT? WE HAVE A DEAL?
A-ALL RIGHT ...
I'M AFRAID I LOST SIGHT OF EVERYTHING BUT THE MONEY.
THE LIBRARIANS SEEMED TO BELIEVE THE STORY OF THE THIEF...
...I GUESS THEY'LL JUST HAVE TO GO BACK EMPTY-HANDED.
WELL, THE STORY OF THE THIEF IS OBVIOUSLY A LIE.
WHAT ?!
PFFT
YES, MOST CERTAINLY.
I'd reached the same conclusion.
HUH ?!
TO ANYONE OTHER THAN A SEASONED COLLECTOR, A GRIMOIRE IS JUST A HALF-ROTTED OLD TOME.
AND THEY'RE HARD TO SELL OFF. DEFINITELY *NOT* THE FARE OF YOUR AVERAGE CAT BURGLAR.
NOT TO MENTION, THE RUG HE HAD HANGING ON THE WALL WAS PURE *COTTON*. NOT WOOL!
WHAT KIND OF THIEF LEAVES THAT BEHIND AND INSTEAD HAULS OFF A BUNCH OF HEAVY OLD BOOKS?
I TOOK A PEEK IN SOME OTHER ROOMS. THEY WERE SPOTLESS. IT SEEMS WAY TOO DELIBERATE.
HANG ON A SECOND ...!
WHY DIDN'T YOU TELL ME ANY OF THIS WHILE WE WERE THERE?!
WELL, YOU'RE... YOU KNOW ...
WE DIDN'T WANT YOU TO CAUSE A SCENE.
HEY! DON'T PATRONIZE ME! I *TRAINED* YOU!

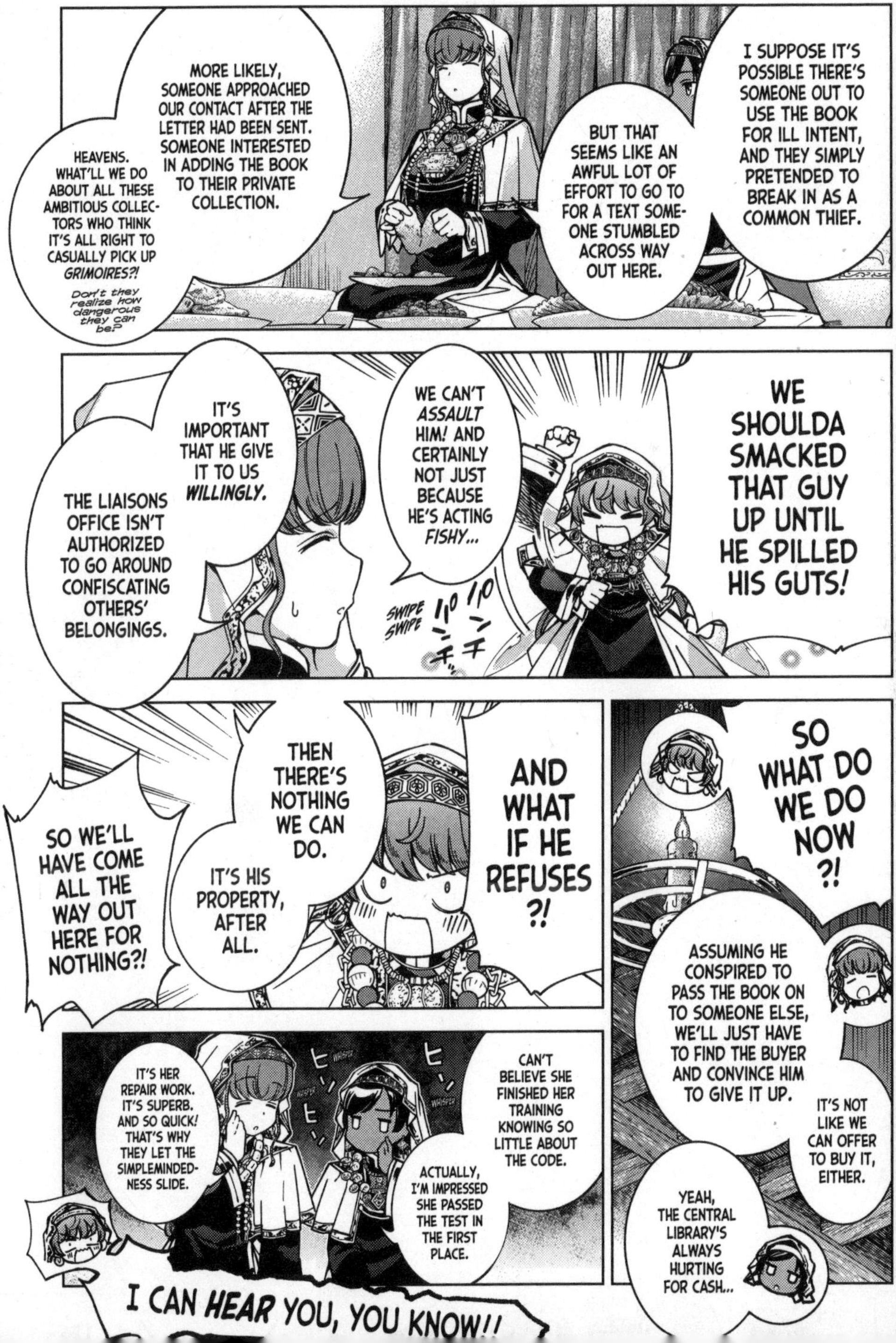
I SUPPOSE IT'S POSSIBLE THERE'S SOMEONE OUT TO USE THE BOOK FOR ILL INTENT, AND THEY SIMPLY PRETENDED TO BREAK IN AS A COMMON THIEF.
BUT THAT SEEMS LIKE AN AWFUL LOT OF EFFORT TO GO TO FOR A TEXT SOME-ONE STUMBLED ACROSS WAY OUT HERE.
MORE LIKELY, SOMEONE APPROACHED OUR CONTACT AFTER THE LETTER HAD BEEN SENT. SOMEONE INTERESTED IN ADDING THE BOOK TO THEIR PRIVATE COLLECTION.
HEAVENS. WHAT'LL WE DO ABOUT ALL THESE AMBITIOUS COLLEC-TORS WHO THINK IT'S ALL RIGHT TO CASUALLY PICK UP *GRIMOIRES?!*
Don't they realize how dangerous they can be?
WE SHOULDA SMACKED THAT GUY UP UNTIL HE SPILLED HIS GUTS!
WE CAN'T *ASSAULT* HIM! AND CERTAINLY NOT JUST BECAUSE HE'S ACTING *FISHY*...
SWIPE SWIPE
IT'S IMPORTANT THAT HE GIVE IT TO US *WILLINGLY.*
THE LIAISONS OFFICE ISN'T AUTHORIZED TO GO AROUND CONFISCATING OTHERS' BELONGINGS.
SO WHAT DO WE DO NOW?!
ASSUMING HE CONSPIRED TO PASS THE BOOK ON TO SOMEONE ELSE, WE'LL JUST HAVE TO FIND THE BUYER AND CONVINCE HIM TO GIVE IT UP.
IT'S NOT LIKE WE CAN OFFER TO BUY IT, EITHER.
YEAH, THE CENTRAL LIBRARY'S ALWAYS HURTING FOR CASH...
AND WHAT IF HE REFUSES?!
THEN THERE'S NOTHING WE CAN DO.
IT'S HIS PROPERTY, AFTER ALL.
SO WE'LL HAVE COME ALL THE WAY OUT HERE FOR NOTHING?!
CAN'T BELIEVE SHE FINISHED HER TRAINING KNOWING SO LITTLE ABOUT THE CODE.
ACTUALLY, I'M IMPRESSED SHE PASSED THE TEST IN THE FIRST PLACE.
IT'S HER REPAIR WORK. IT'S SUPERB. AND SO QUICK! THAT'S WHY THEY LET THE SIMPLEMINDED-NESS SLIDE.
I CAN *HEAR* YOU, YOU KNOW!!

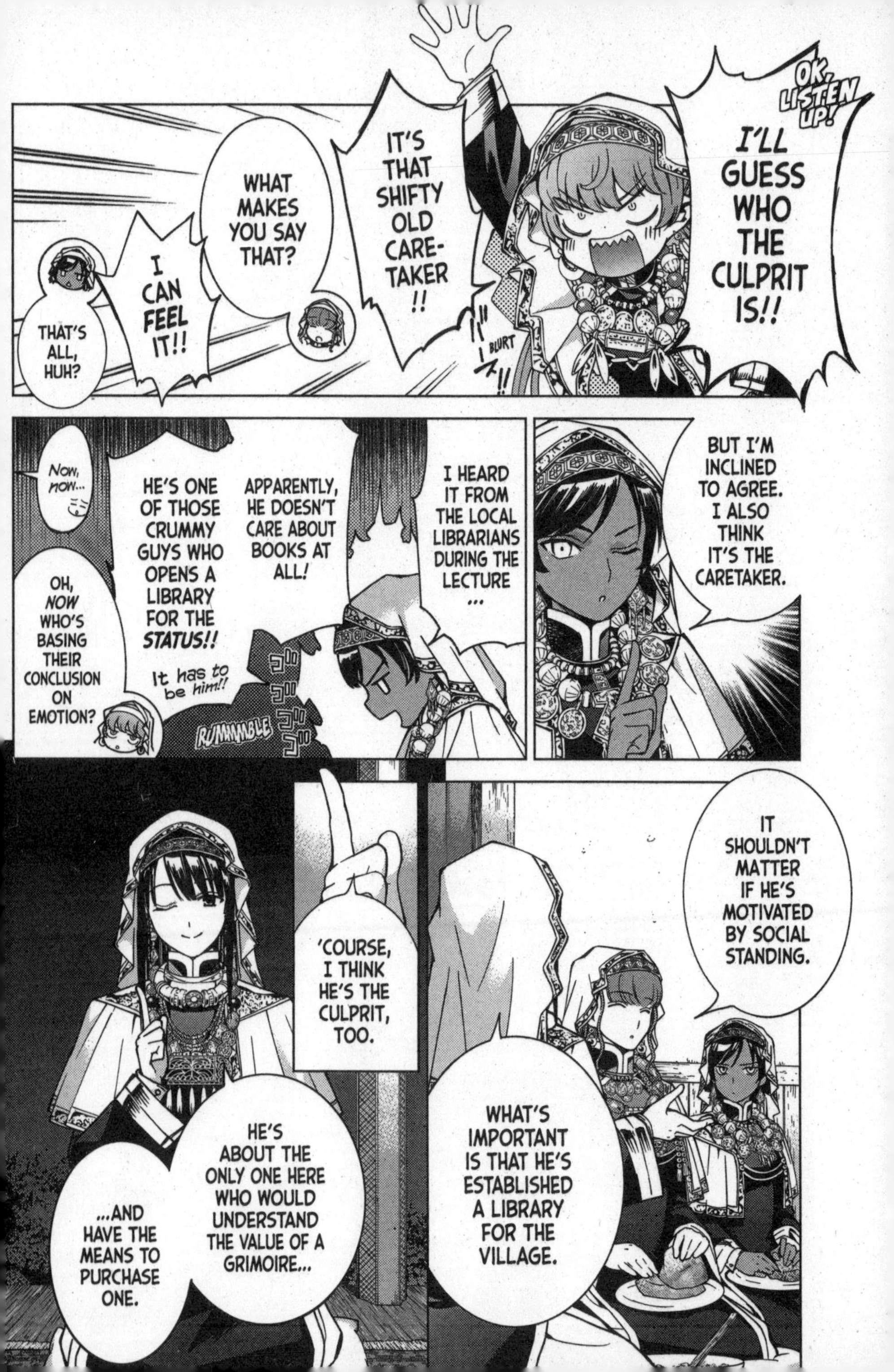
OK, LISTEN UP!
I'LL GUESS WHO THE CULPRIT IS!!
BLURT
IT'S THAT SHIFTY OLD CARE-TAKER!!
WHAT MAKES YOU SAY THAT?
I CAN FEEL IT!!
THAT'S ALL, HUH?
BUT I'M INCLINED TO AGREE. I ALSO THINK IT'S THE CARETAKER.
I HEARD IT FROM THE LOCAL LIBRARIANS DURING THE LECTURE...
APPARENTLY, HE DOESN'T CARE ABOUT BOOKS AT ALL!
HE'S ONE OF THOSE CRUMMY GUYS WHO OPENS A LIBRARY FOR THE STATUS!!
RUMMMBLE
It has to be him!!
Now, now...
OH, NOW WHO'S BASING THEIR CONCLUSION ON EMOTION?
IT SHOULDN'T MATTER IF HE'S MOTIVATED BY SOCIAL STANDING.
WHAT'S IMPORTANT IS THAT HE'S ESTABLISHED A LIBRARY FOR THE VILLAGE.
'COURSE, I THINK HE'S THE CULPRIT, TOO.
HE'S ABOUT THE ONLY ONE HERE WHO WOULD UNDERSTAND THE VALUE OF A GRIMOIRE...
...AND HAVE THE MEANS TO PURCHASE ONE.

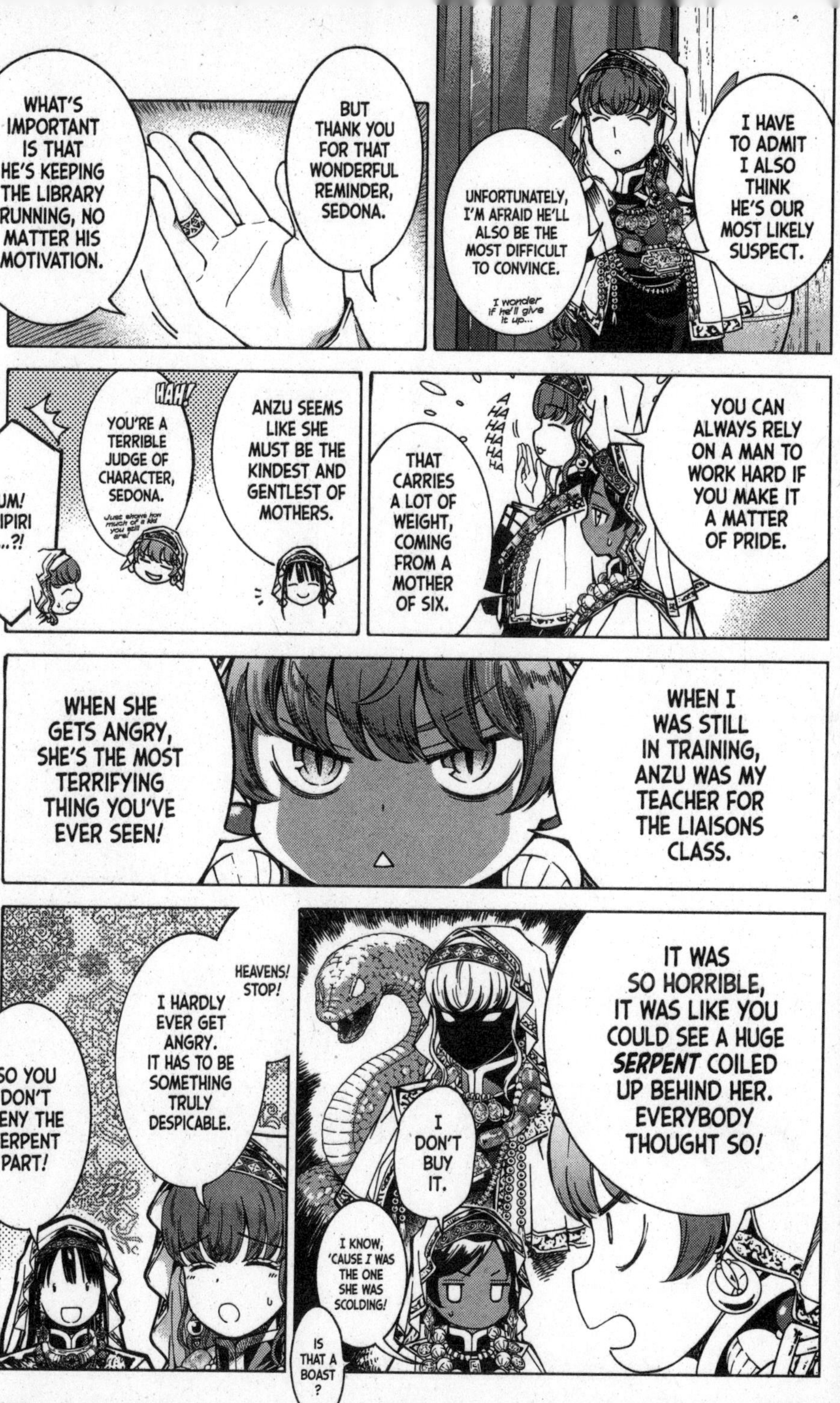
I HAVE TO ADMIT I ALSO THINK HE'S OUR MOST LIKELY SUSPECT.
UNFORTUNATELY, I'M AFRAID HE'LL ALSO BE THE MOST DIFFICULT TO CONVINCE.
I wonder if he'll give it up...
BUT THANK YOU FOR THAT WONDERFUL REMINDER, SEDONA.
WHAT'S IMPORTANT IS THAT HE'S KEEPING THE LIBRARY RUNNING, NO MATTER HIS MOTIVATION.
YOU CAN ALWAYS RELY ON A MAN TO WORK HARD IF YOU MAKE IT A MATTER OF PRIDE.
A HA HA HA HA HA HA
THAT CARRIES A LOT OF WEIGHT, COMING FROM A MOTHER OF SIX.
ANZU SEEMS LIKE SHE MUST BE THE KINDEST AND GENTLEST OF MOTHERS.
HAH!
YOU'RE A TERRIBLE JUDGE OF CHARACTER, SEDONA.
Just shows how much of a kid you still are!
UM! PIPIRI ...?!
WHEN I WAS STILL IN TRAINING, ANZU WAS MY TEACHER FOR THE LIAISONS CLASS.
WHEN SHE GETS ANGRY, SHE'S THE MOST TERRIFYING THING YOU'VE EVER SEEN!
IT WAS SO HORRIBLE, IT WAS LIKE YOU COULD SEE A HUGE SERPENT COILED UP BEHIND HER. EVERYBODY THOUGHT SO!
I DON'T BUY IT.
I KNOW, 'CAUSE I WAS THE ONE SHE WAS SCOLDING!
IS THAT A BOAST?
HEAVENS! STOP!
I HARDLY EVER GET ANGRY. IT HAS TO BE SOMETHING TRULY DESPICABLE.
SO YOU DON'T DENY THE SERPENT PART!

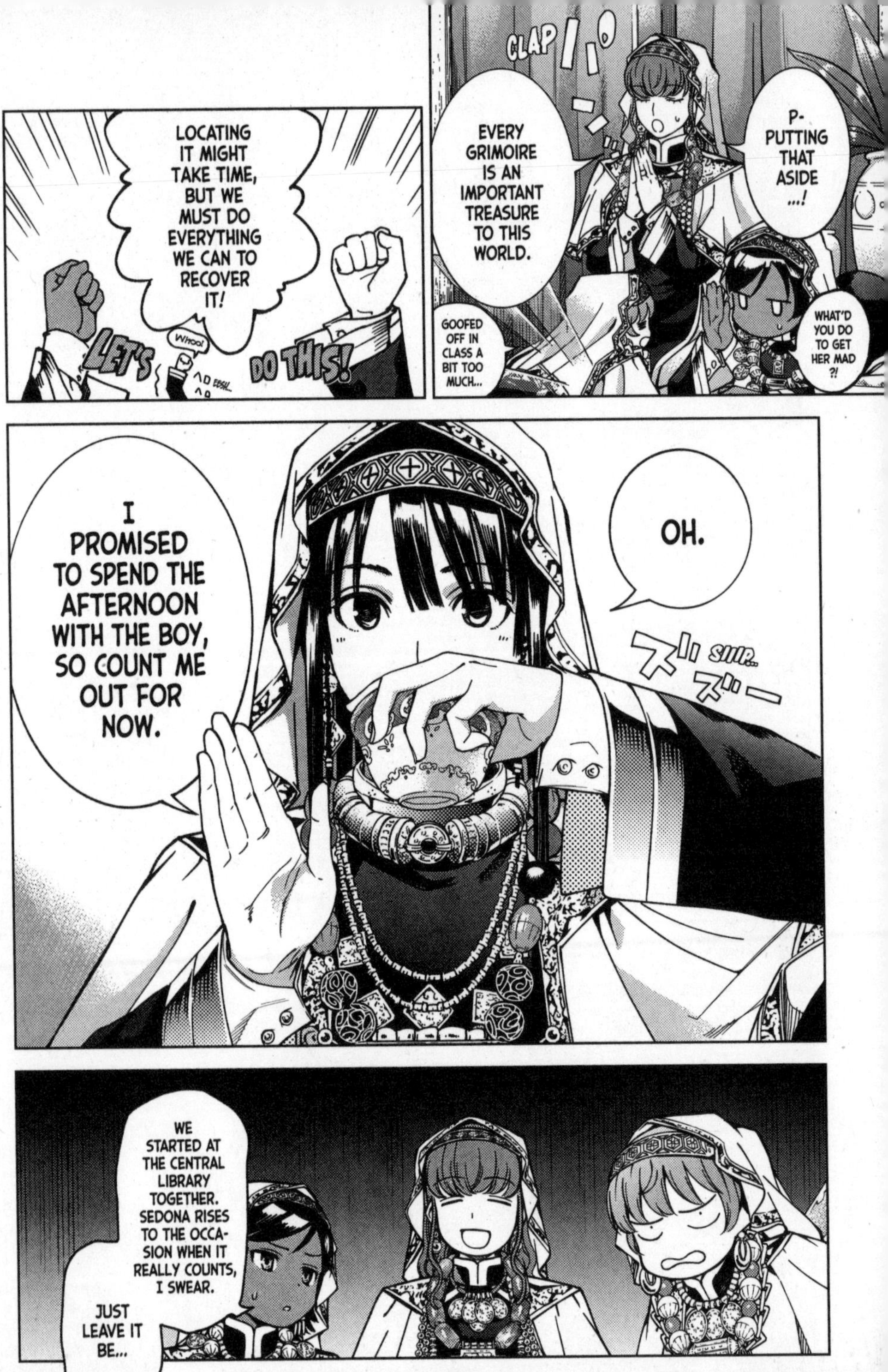
CLAP
P-PUTTING THAT ASIDE...!
EVERY GRIMOIRE IS AN IMPORTANT TREASURE TO THIS WORLD.
WHAT'D YOU DO TO GET HER MAD?!
GOOFED OFF IN CLASS A BIT TOO MUCH...
LOCATING IT MIGHT TAKE TIME, BUT WE MUST DO EVERYTHING WE CAN TO RECOVER IT!
LET'S DO THIS!
Whoo!
OH.
SLURP...
I PROMISED TO SPEND THE AFTERNOON WITH THE BOY, SO COUNT ME OUT FOR NOW.
WE STARTED AT THE CENTRAL LIBRARY TOGETHER. SEDONA RISES TO THE OCCASION WHEN IT REALLY COUNTS, I SWEAR.
JUST LEAVE IT BE...

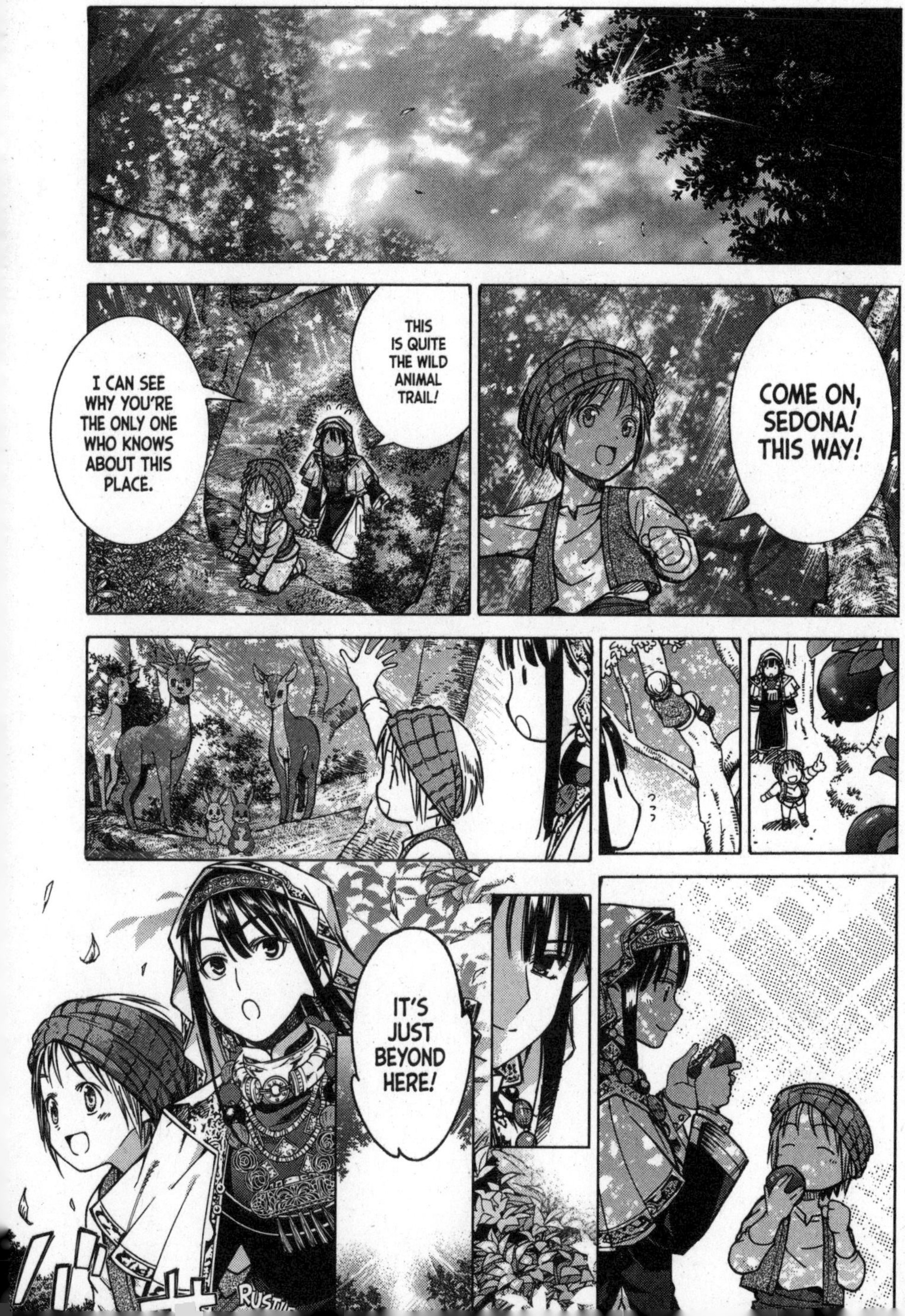
COME ON, SEDONA! THIS WAY!
THIS IS QUITE THE WILD ANIMAL TRAIL!
I CAN SEE WHY YOU'RE THE ONLY ONE WHO KNOWS ABOUT THIS PLACE.
IT'S JUST BEYOND HERE!

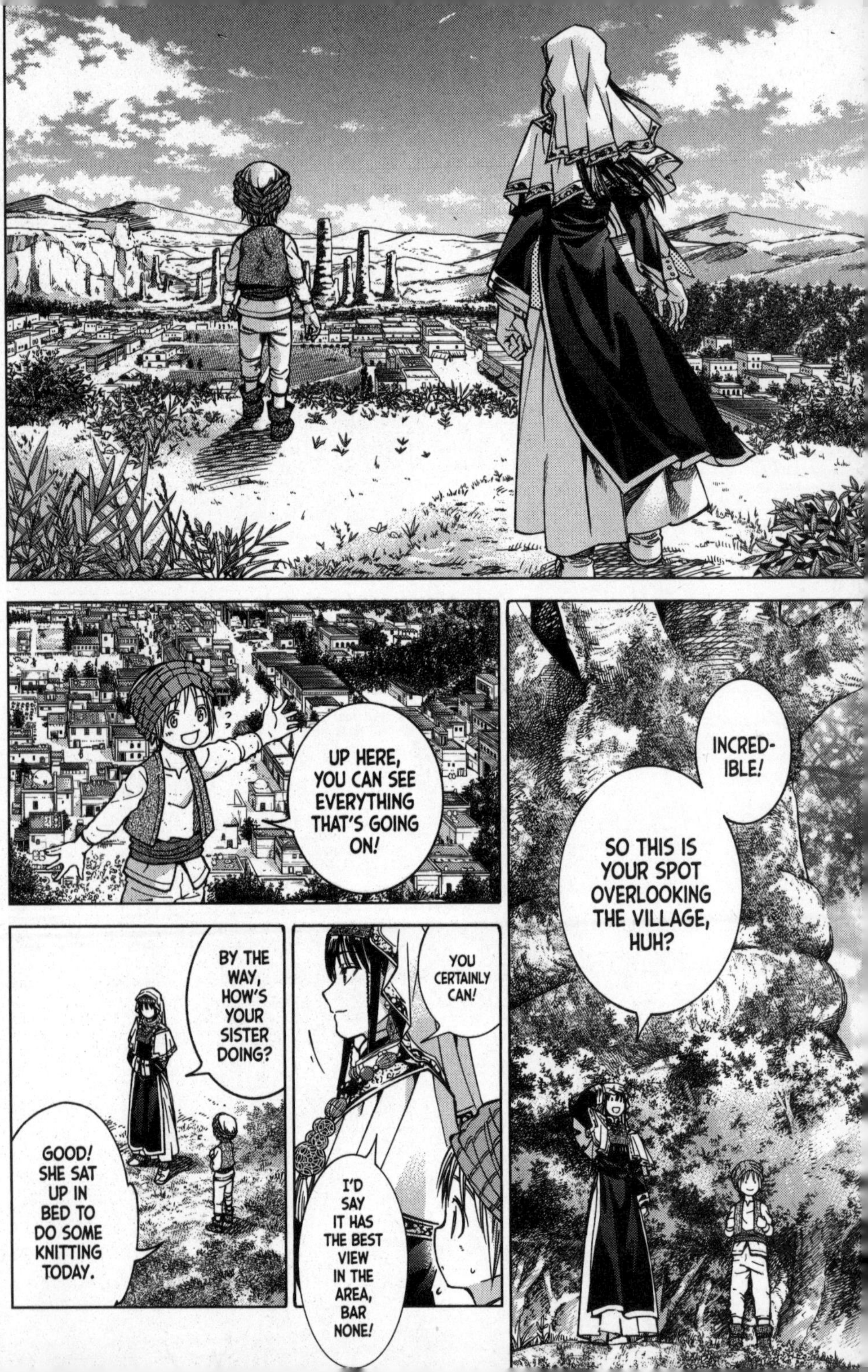
INCRED-IBLE!
SO THIS IS YOUR SPOT OVERLOOKING THE VILLAGE, HUH?
UP HERE, YOU CAN SEE EVERYTHING THAT'S GOING ON!
YOU CERTAINLY CAN!
I'D SAY IT HAS THE BEST VIEW IN THE AREA, BAR NONE!
BY THE WAY, HOW'S YOUR SISTER DOING?
GOOD! SHE SAT UP IN BED TO DO SOME KNITTING TODAY.

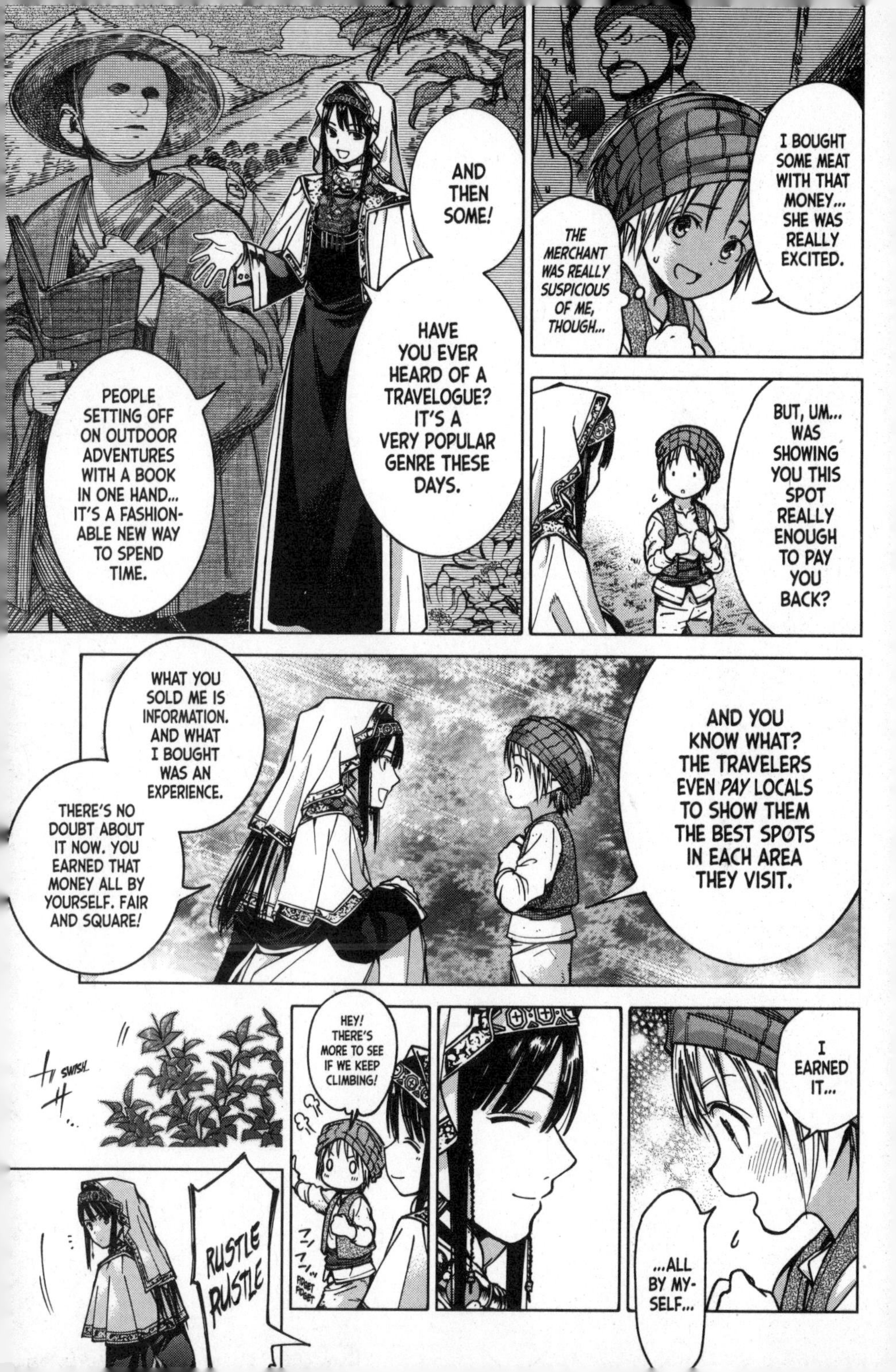
I BOUGHT SOME MEAT WITH THAT MONEY... SHE WAS REALLY EXCITED.
THE MERCHANT WAS REALLY SUSPICIOUS OF ME, THOUGH...
BUT, UM... WAS SHOWING YOU THIS SPOT REALLY ENOUGH TO PAY YOU BACK?
AND THEN SOME!
HAVE YOU EVER HEARD OF A TRAVELOGUE? IT'S A VERY POPULAR GENRE THESE DAYS.
PEOPLE SETTING OFF ON OUTDOOR ADVENTURES WITH A BOOK IN ONE HAND... IT'S A FASHION-ABLE NEW WAY TO SPEND TIME.
AND YOU KNOW WHAT? THE TRAVELERS EVEN *PAY* LOCALS TO SHOW THEM THE BEST SPOTS IN EACH AREA THEY VISIT.
WHAT YOU SOLD ME IS INFORMATION. AND WHAT I BOUGHT WAS AN EXPERIENCE.
THERE'S NO DOUBT ABOUT IT NOW. YOU EARNED THAT MONEY ALL BY YOURSELF. FAIR AND SQUARE!
I EARNED IT...
...ALL BY MY-SELF...
HEY! THERE'S MORE TO SEE IF WE KEEP CLIMBING!
FIDGET FIDGET
SWISH
RUSTLE RUSTLE

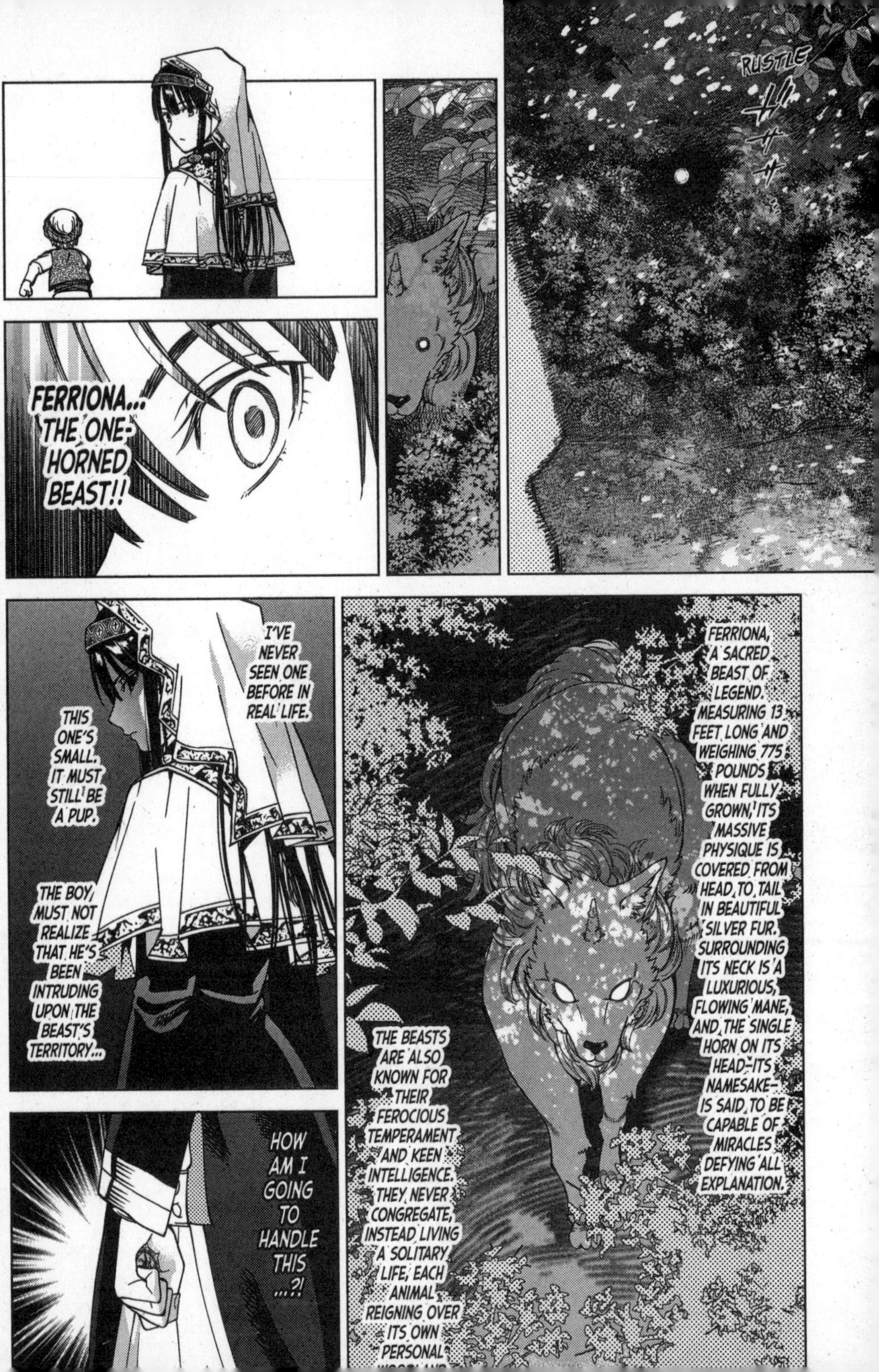
RUSTLE
FERRIONA... THE ONE-HORNED BEAST!!
FERRIONA, A SACRED BEAST OF LEGEND. MEASURING 13 FEET LONG AND WEIGHING 775 POUNDS WHEN FULLY GROWN, ITS MASSIVE PHYSIQUE IS COVERED FROM HEAD TO TAIL IN BEAUTIFUL SILVER FUR. SURROUNDING ITS NECK IS A LUXURIOUS, FLOWING MANE, AND THE SINGLE HORN ON ITS HEAD—ITS NAMESAKE—IS SAID TO BE CAPABLE OF MIRACLES DEFYING ALL EXPLANATION.
THE BEASTS ARE ALSO KNOWN FOR THEIR FEROCIOUS TEMPERAMENT AND KEEN INTELLIGENCE. THEY NEVER CONGREGATE, INSTEAD LIVING A SOLITARY LIFE, EACH ANIMAL REIGNING OVER ITS OWN PERSONAL
I'VE NEVER SEEN ONE BEFORE IN REAL LIFE.
THIS ONE'S SMALL. IT MUST STILL BE A PUP.
THE BOY MUST NOT REALIZE THAT HE'S BEEN INTRUDING UPON THE BEAST'S TERRITORY...
HOW AM I GOING TO HANDLE THIS ...?!

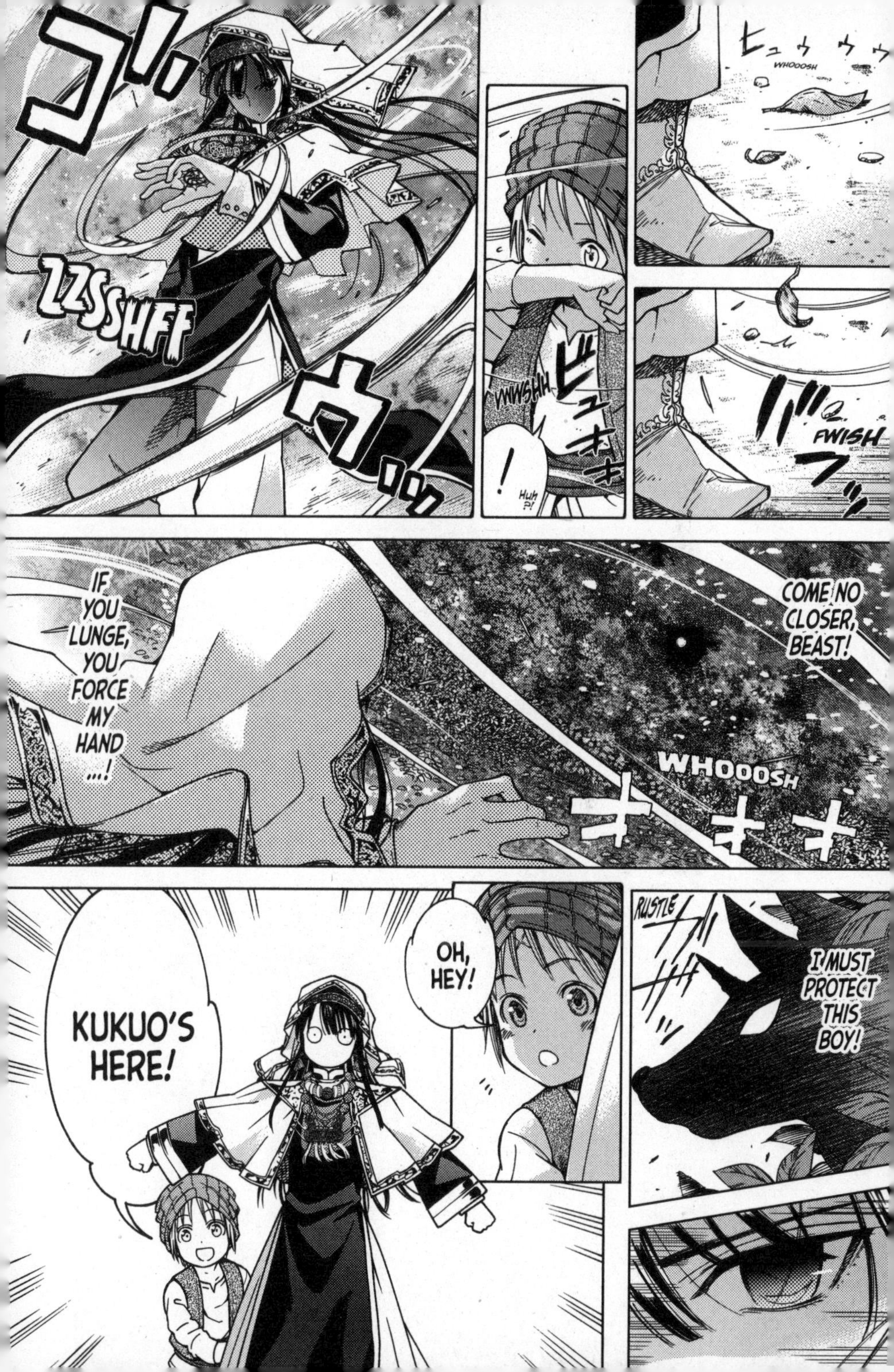

ヒュウウウ
WHOOOSH
バッ
FWISH
ビュオオ
VWWSHH
!
Huh?!
ZZSSHFF
COME NO CLOSER, BEAST!
WHOOOSH
IF YOU LUNGE, YOU FORCE MY HAND ...!
RUSTLE
I MUST PROTECT THIS BOY!
OH, HEY!
KUKUO'S HERE!

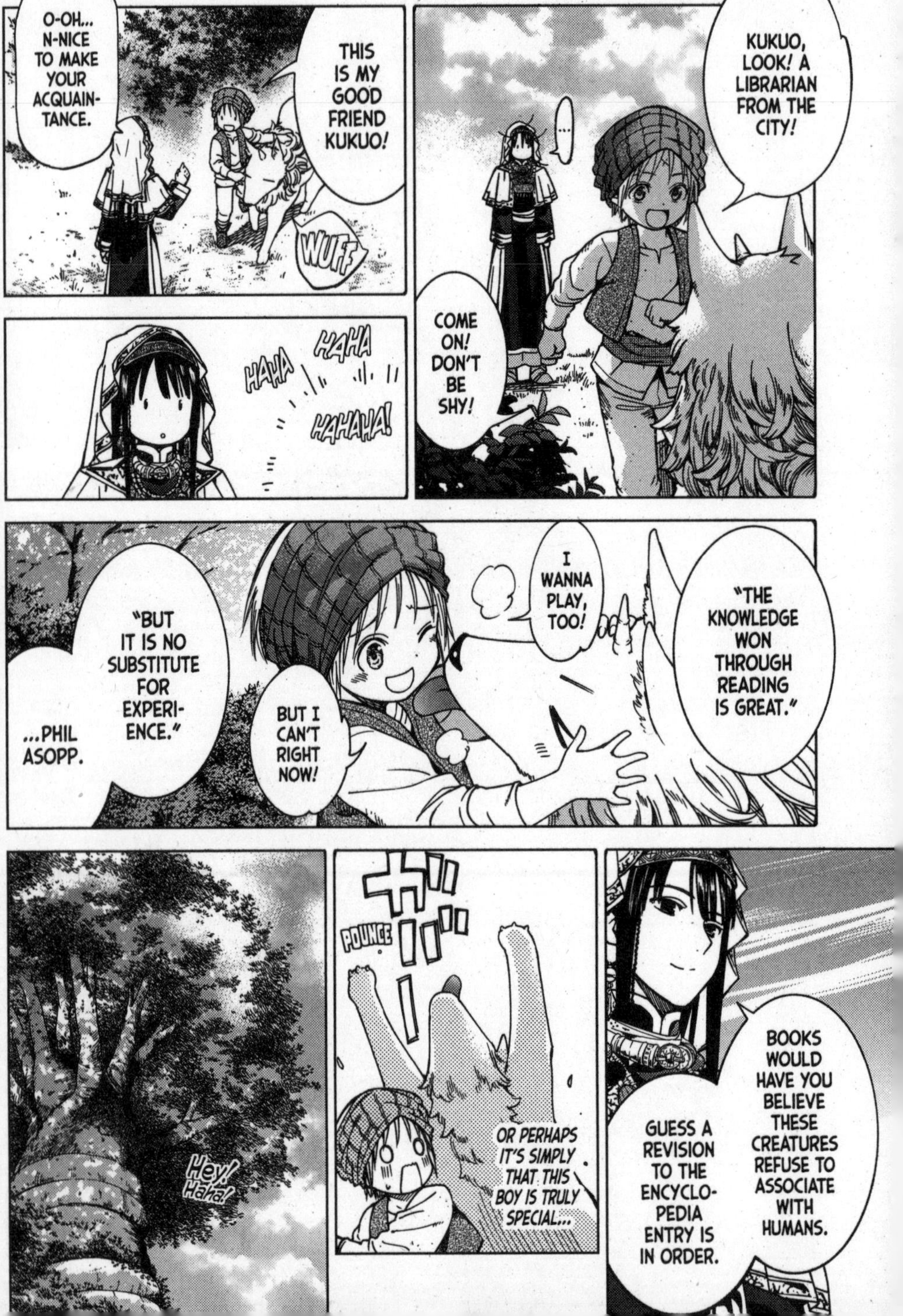
KUKUO, LOOK! A LIBRARIAN FROM THE CITY!
...
COME ON! DON'T BE SHY!
THIS IS MY GOOD FRIEND KUKUO!
WUFF
O-OH... N-NICE TO MAKE YOUR ACQUAIN-TANCE.
HAHA
HAHA
HAHAHA!
"THE KNOWLEDGE WON THROUGH READING IS GREAT."
I WANNA PLAY, TOO!
BUT I CAN'T RIGHT NOW!
"BUT IT IS NO SUBSTITUTE FOR EXPERI-ENCE."
...PHIL ASOPP.
BOOKS WOULD HAVE YOU BELIEVE THESE CREATURES REFUSE TO ASSOCIATE WITH HUMANS.
GUESS A REVISION TO THE ENCYCLO-PEDIA ENTRY IS IN ORDER.
POUNCE
OR PERHAPS IT'S SIMPLY THAT THIS BOY IS TRULY SPECIAL...
Hey! Haha!

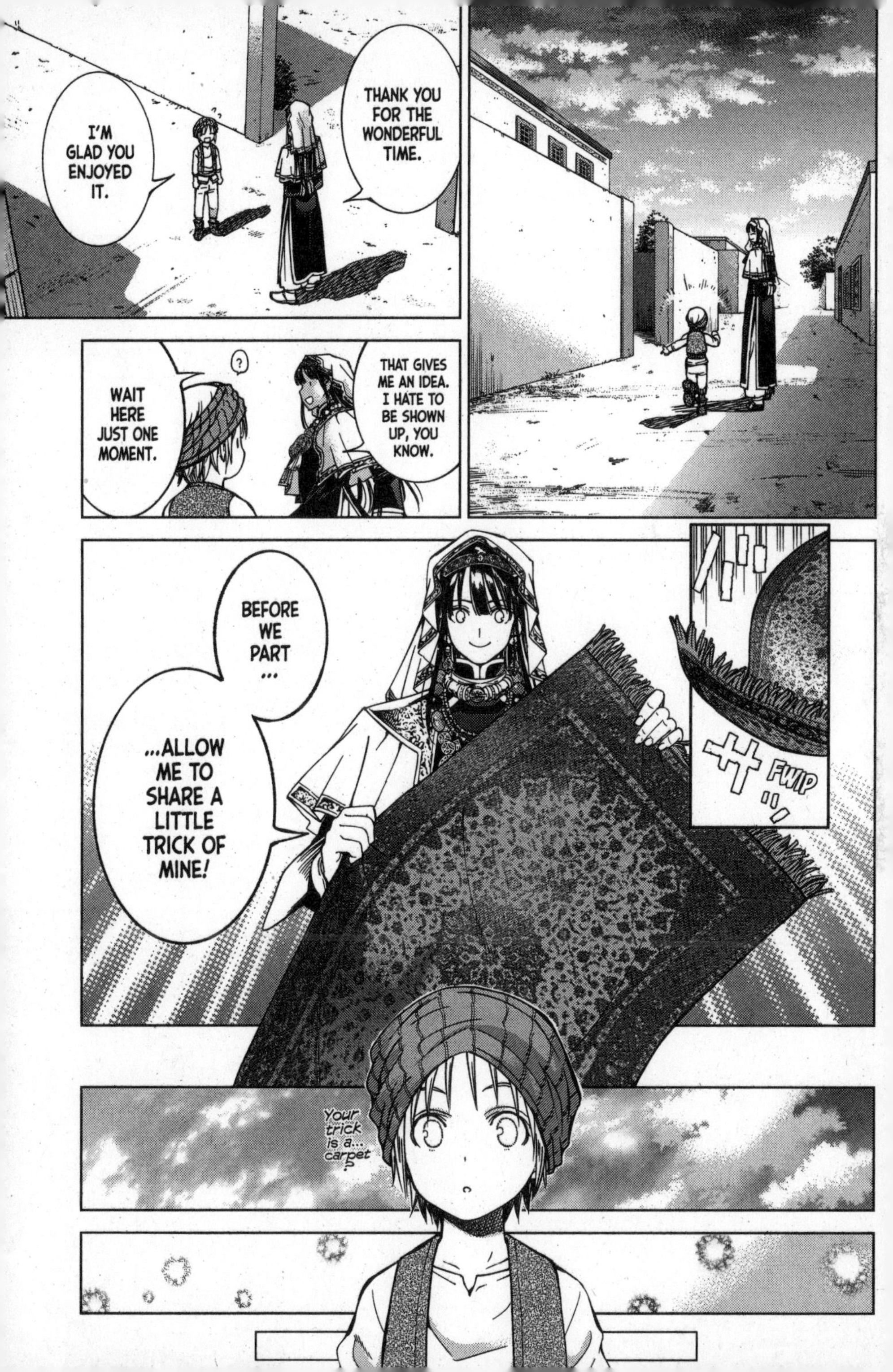
THANK YOU FOR THE WONDERFUL TIME.
I'M GLAD YOU ENJOYED IT.
THAT GIVES ME AN IDEA. I HATE TO BE SHOWN UP, YOU KNOW.
?
WAIT HERE JUST ONE MOMENT.
FWIP
BEFORE WE PART ...
...ALLOW ME TO SHARE A LITTLE TRICK OF MINE!
Your trick is a... carpet?

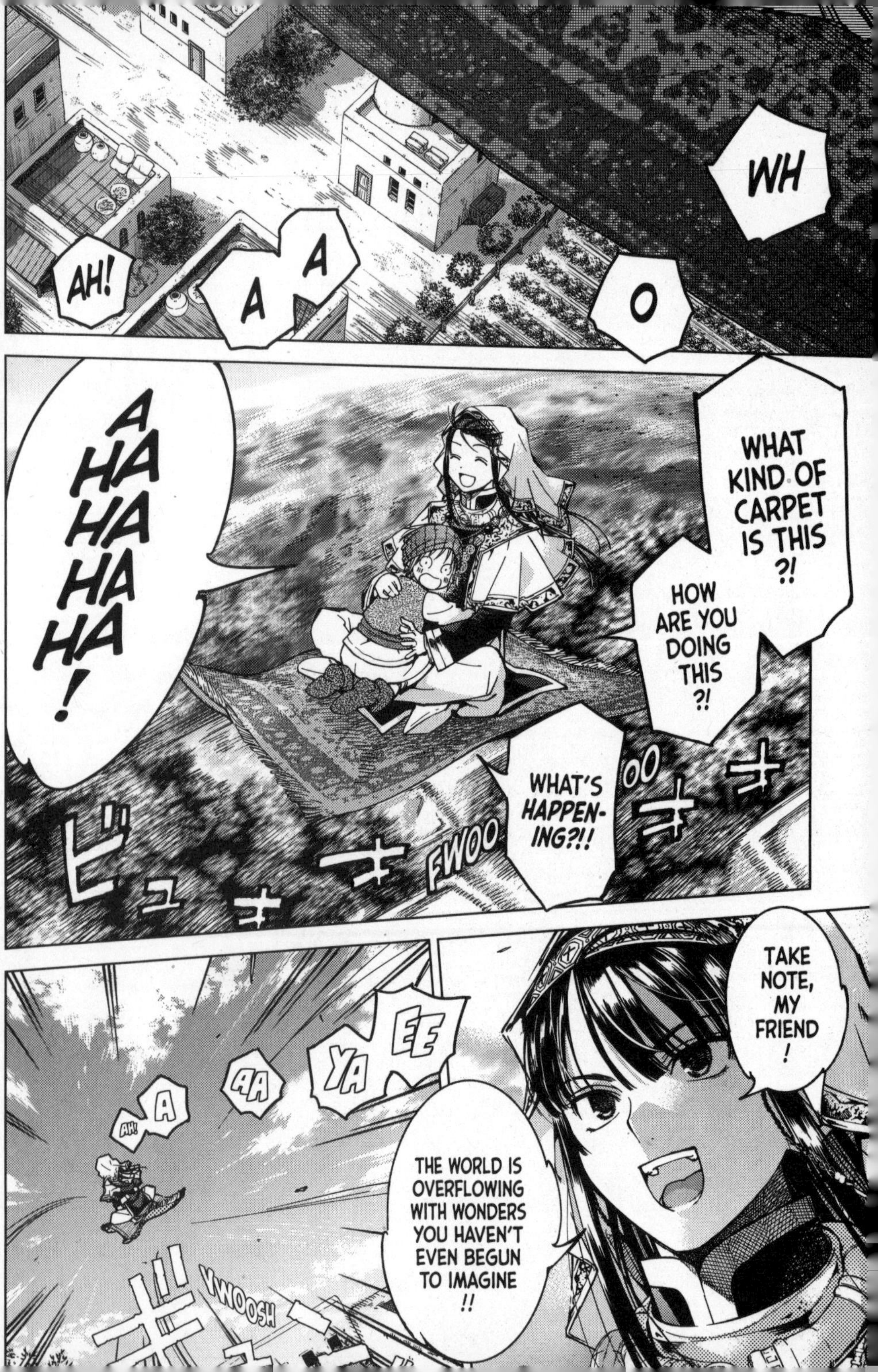
WH
O
A
A
AH!
WHAT KIND OF CARPET IS THIS?!
HOW ARE YOU DOING THIS?!
WHAT'S HAPPEN-ING?!!
OO
FWOO
AHAHAHAHAHA!
TAKE NOTE, MY FRIEND!
THE WORLD IS OVERFLOWING WITH WONDERS YOU HAVEN'T EVEN BEGUN TO IMAGINE!!
EE
YA
AA
A
AH!
VWOOSH

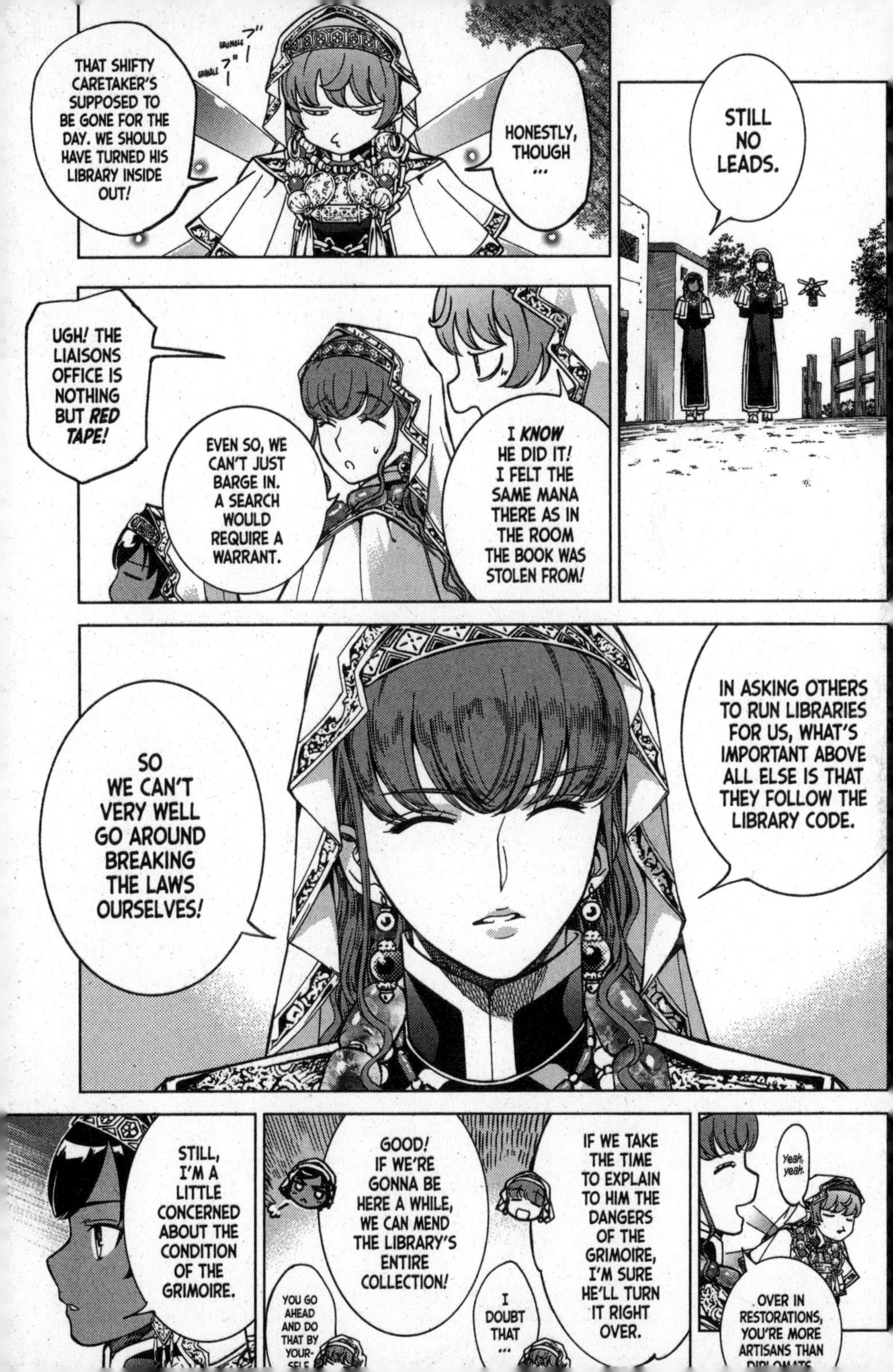

STILL NO LEADS.
HONESTLY, THOUGH ...
THAT SHIFTY CARETAKER'S SUPPOSED TO BE GONE FOR THE DAY. WE SHOULD HAVE TURNED HIS LIBRARY INSIDE OUT!
GRUMBLE GRUMBLE
UGH! THE LIAISONS OFFICE IS NOTHING BUT *RED TAPE!*
I *KNOW* HE DID IT! I FELT THE SAME MANA THERE AS IN THE ROOM THE BOOK WAS STOLEN FROM!
EVEN SO, WE CAN'T JUST BARGE IN. A SEARCH WOULD REQUIRE A WARRANT.
IN ASKING OTHERS TO RUN LIBRARIES FOR US, WHAT'S IMPORTANT ABOVE ALL ELSE IS THAT THEY FOLLOW THE LIBRARY CODE.
SO WE CAN'T VERY WELL GO AROUND BREAKING THE LAWS OURSELVES!
Yeah, yeah.
OVER IN RESTORATIONS, YOU'RE MORE ARTISANS THAN
IF WE TAKE THE TIME TO EXPLAIN TO HIM THE DANGERS OF THE GRIMOIRE, I'M SURE HE'LL TURN IT RIGHT OVER.
I DOUBT THAT ...
GOOD! IF WE'RE GONNA BE HERE A WHILE, WE CAN MEND THE LIBRARY'S ENTIRE COLLECTION!
YOU GO AHEAD AND DO THAT BY YOUR-
STILL, I'M A LITTLE CONCERNED ABOUT THE CONDITION OF THE GRIMOIRE.

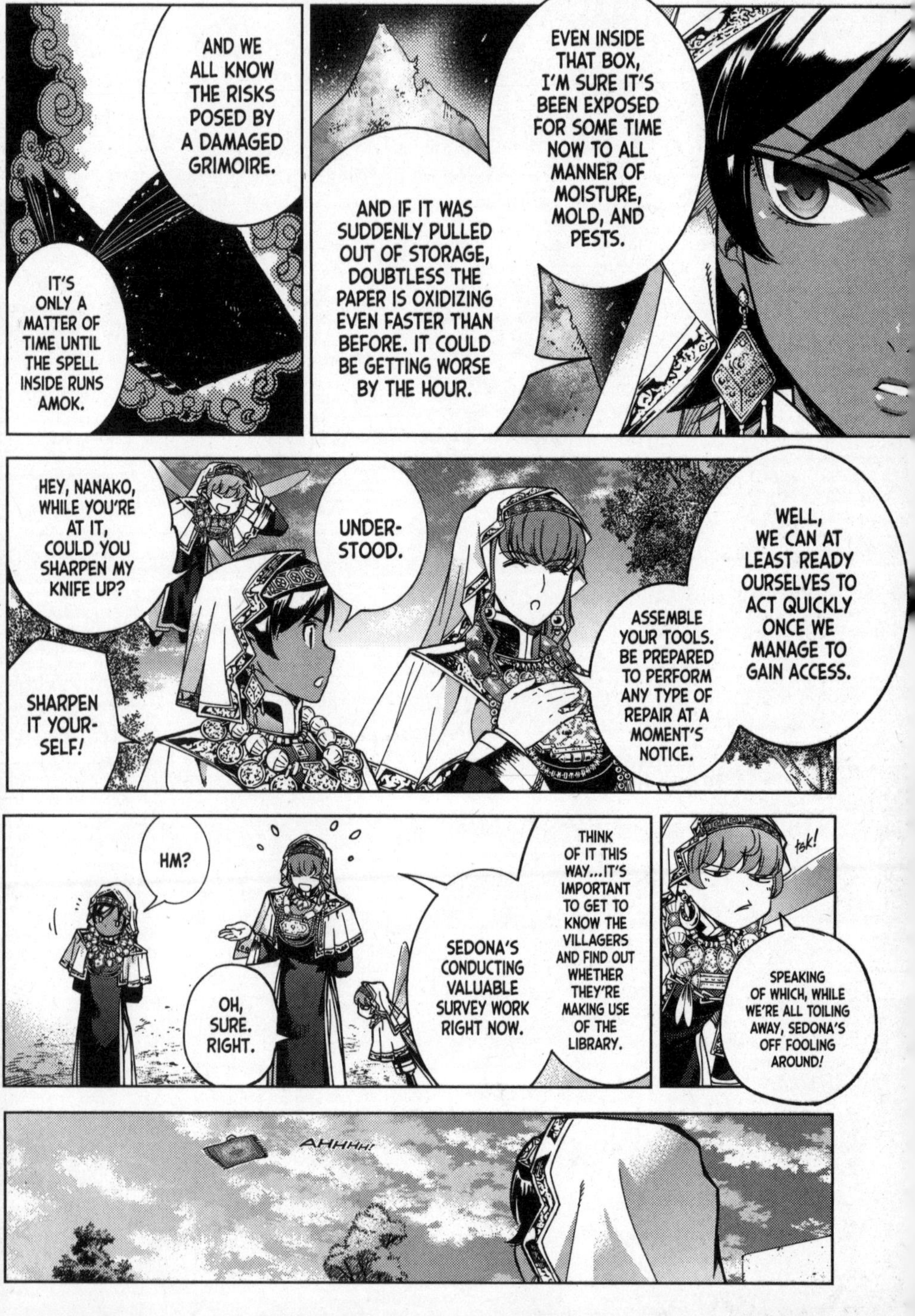
EVEN INSIDE THAT BOX, I'M SURE IT'S BEEN EXPOSED FOR SOME TIME NOW TO ALL MANNER OF MOISTURE, MOLD, AND PESTS.
AND IF IT WAS SUDDENLY PULLED OUT OF STORAGE, DOUBTLESS THE PAPER IS OXIDIZING EVEN FASTER THAN BEFORE. IT COULD BE GETTING WORSE BY THE HOUR.
AND WE ALL KNOW THE RISKS POSED BY A DAMAGED GRIMOIRE.
IT'S ONLY A MATTER OF TIME UNTIL THE SPELL INSIDE RUNS AMOK.
WELL, WE CAN AT LEAST READY OURSELVES TO ACT QUICKLY ONCE WE MANAGE TO GAIN ACCESS.
ASSEMBLE YOUR TOOLS. BE PREPARED TO PERFORM ANY TYPE OF REPAIR AT A MOMENT'S NOTICE.
UNDER-STOOD.
HEY, NANAKO, WHILE YOU'RE AT IT, COULD YOU SHARPEN MY KNIFE UP?
SHARPEN IT YOUR-SELF!
tsk!
SPEAKING OF WHICH, WHILE WE'RE ALL TOILING AWAY, SEDONA'S OFF FOOLING AROUND!
SEDONA'S CONDUCTING VALUABLE SURVEY WORK RIGHT NOW.
THINK OF IT THIS WAY...IT'S IMPORTANT TO GET TO KNOW THE VILLAGERS AND FIND OUT WHETHER THEY'RE MAKING USE OF THE LIBRARY.
HM?
OH, SURE. RIGHT.
AHHHH!

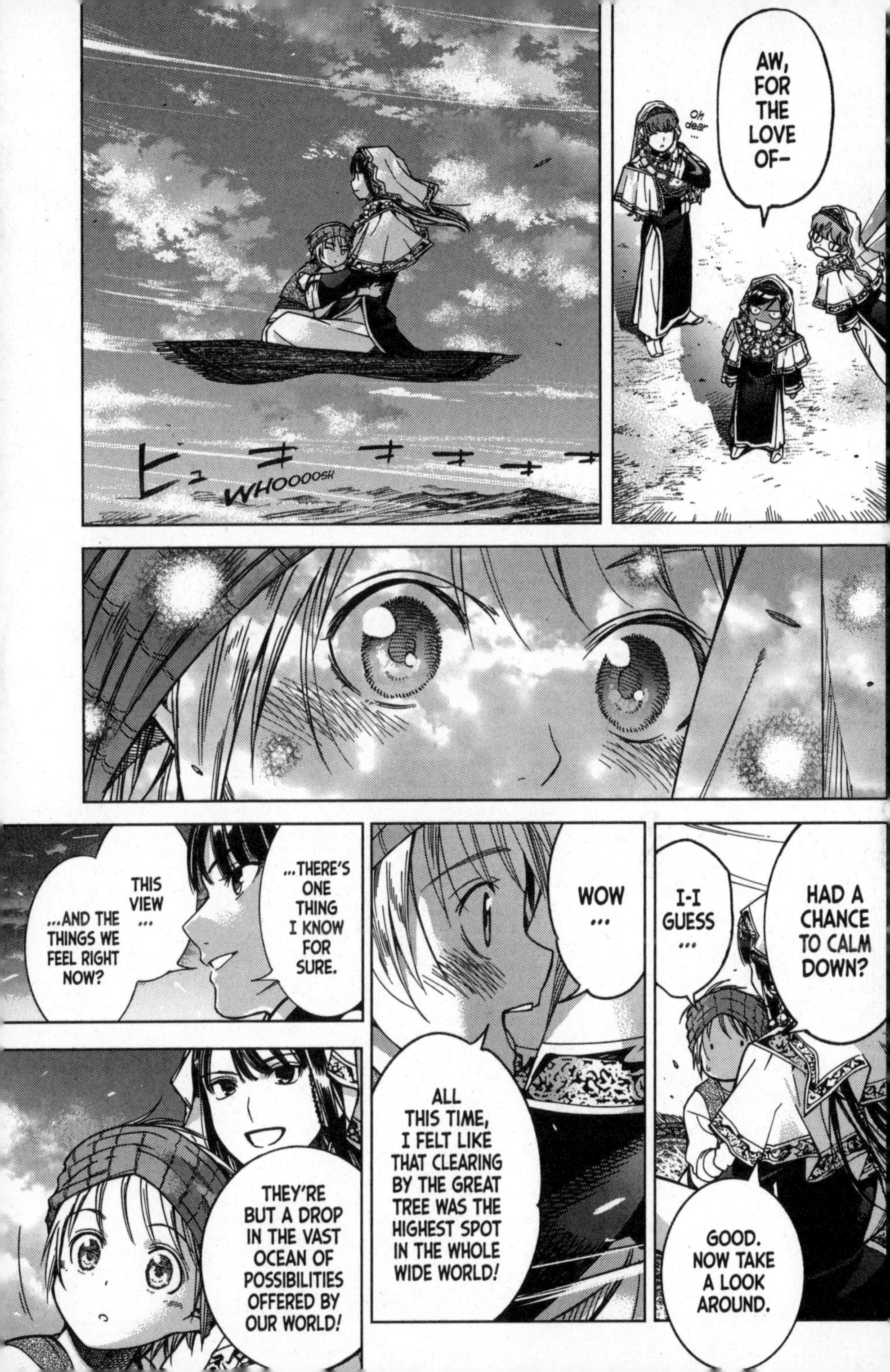
AW, FOR THE LOVE OF–
Oh dear ...
ヒュオオオオオ
WHOOOOSH
HAD A CHANCE TO CALM DOWN?
I-I GUESS ...
GOOD. NOW TAKE A LOOK AROUND.
WOW ...
ALL THIS TIME, I FELT LIKE THAT CLEARING BY THE GREAT TREE WAS THE HIGHEST SPOT IN THE WHOLE WIDE WORLD!
...THERE'S ONE THING I KNOW FOR SURE.
THIS VIEW ...
...AND THE THINGS WE FEEL RIGHT NOW?
THEY'RE BUT A DROP IN THE VAST OCEAN OF POSSIBILITIES OFFERED BY OUR WORLD!

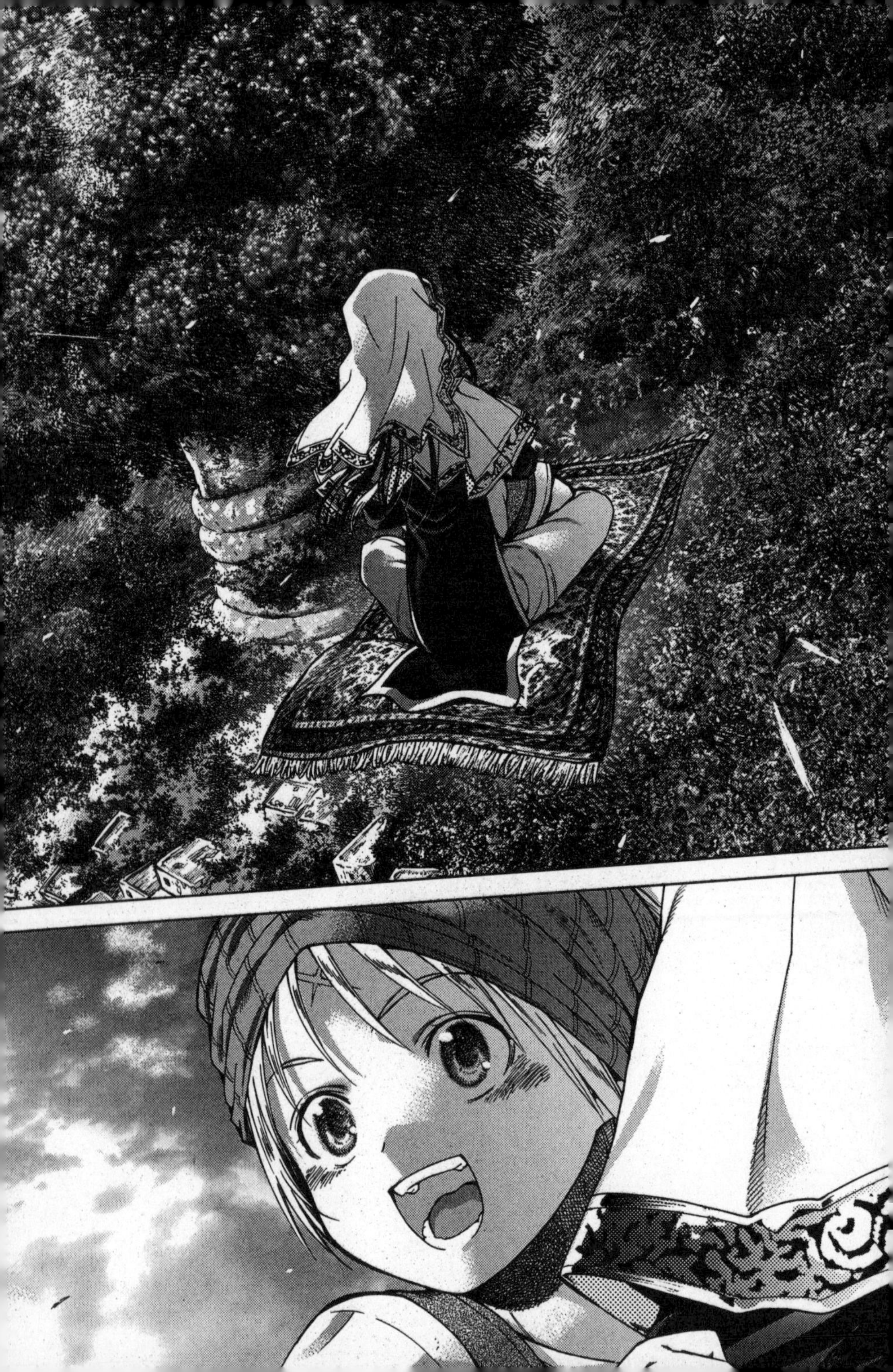

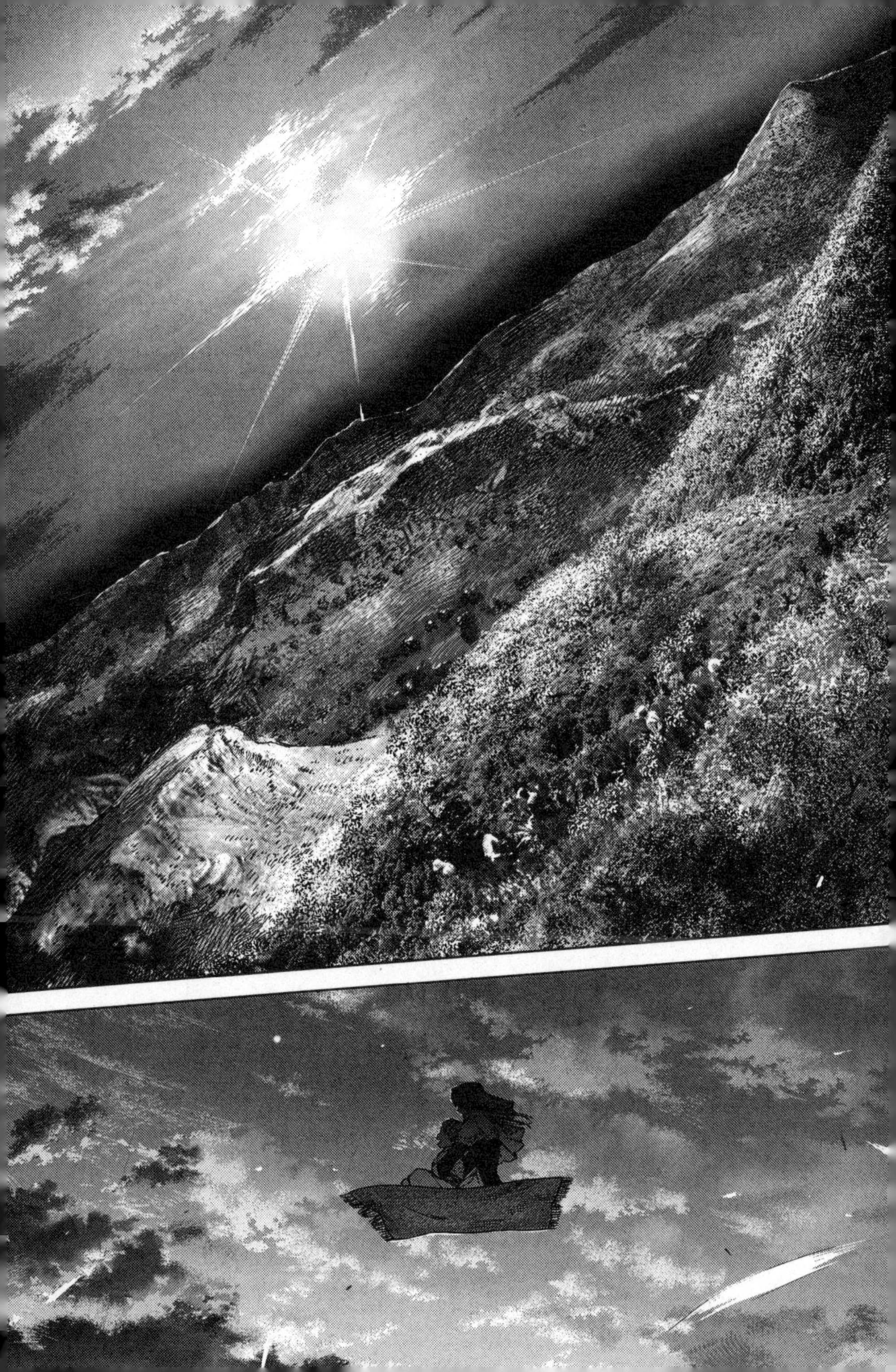

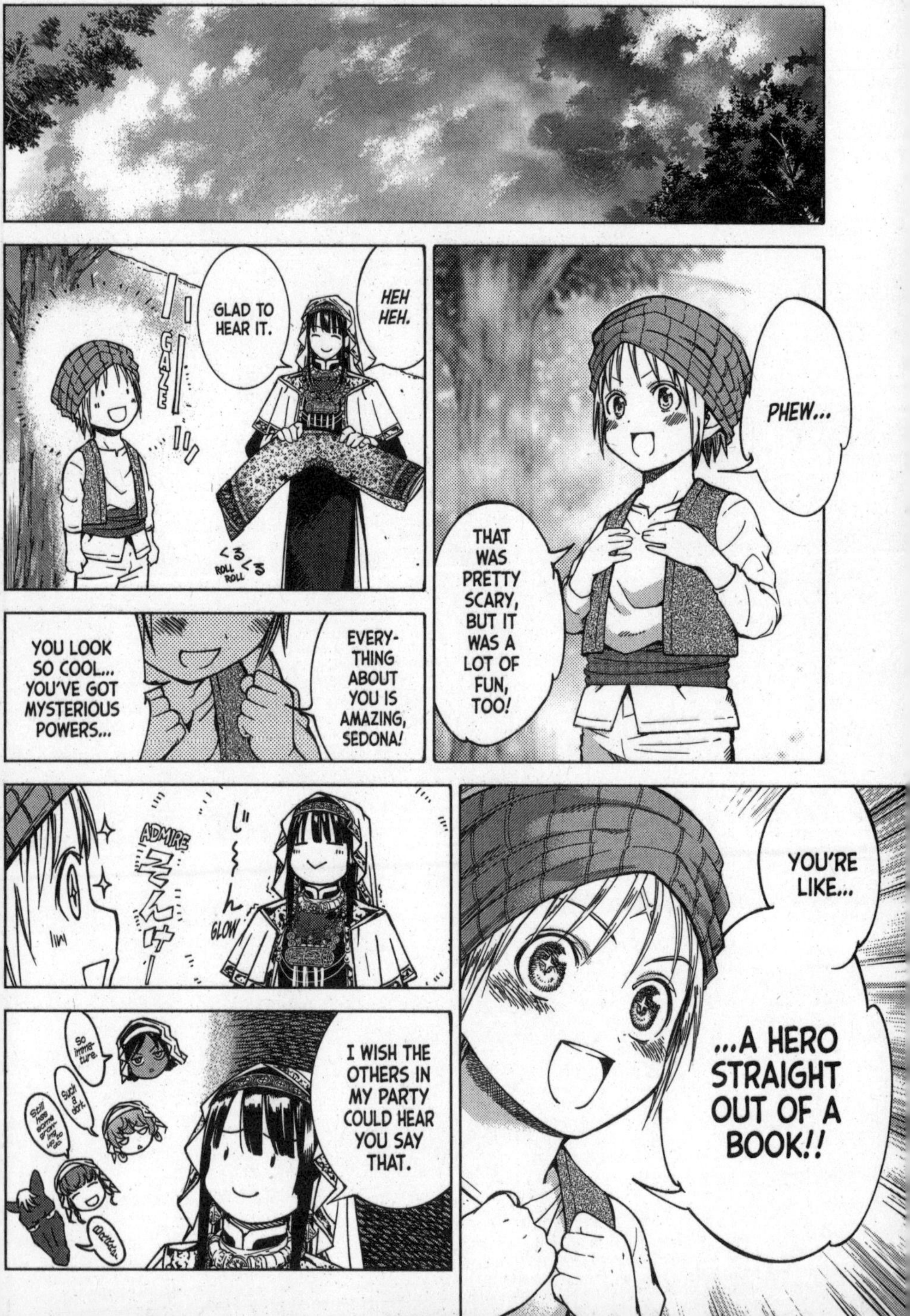
PHEW...
THAT WAS PRETTY SCARY, BUT IT WAS A LOT OF FUN, TOO!
HEH HEH.
GLAD TO HEAR IT.
GAZE
くるくる ROLL ROLL
EVERYTHING ABOUT YOU IS AMAZING, SEDONA!
YOU LOOK SO COOL... YOU'VE GOT MYSTERIOUS POWERS...
YOU'RE LIKE...
...A HERO STRAIGHT OUT OF A BOOK!!
ADMIRE そんけー
じ〜ん GLOW
I WISH THE OTHERS IN MY PARTY COULD HEAR YOU SAY THAT.
So immature.
Such a dork.
Still has some growing up to do.

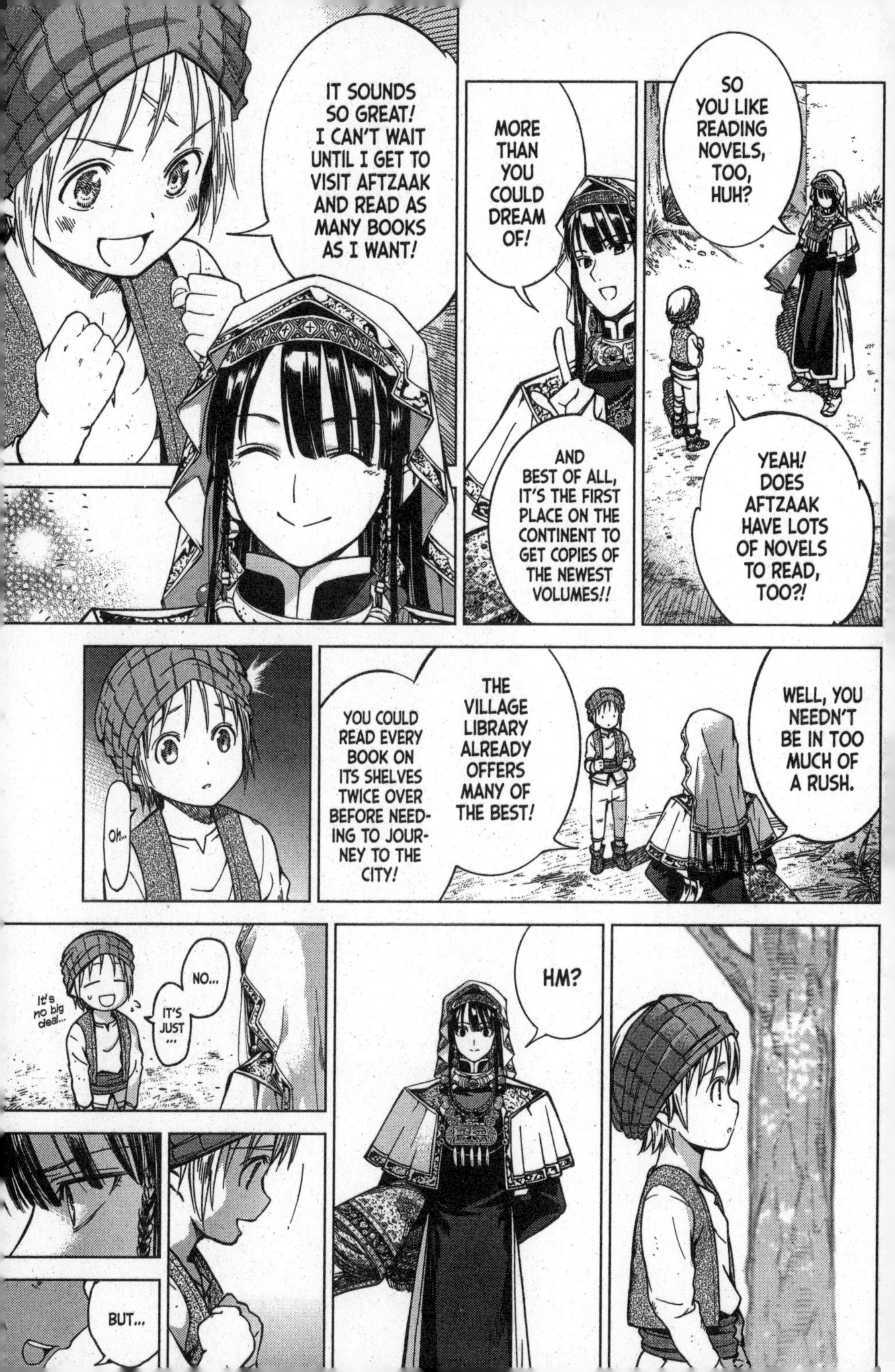

SO YOU LIKE READING NOVELS, TOO, HUH?
YEAH! DOES AFTZAAK HAVE LOTS OF NOVELS TO READ, TOO?!
MORE THAN YOU COULD DREAM OF!
AND BEST OF ALL, IT'S THE FIRST PLACE ON THE CONTINENT TO GET COPIES OF THE NEWEST VOLUMES!!
IT SOUNDS SO GREAT! I CAN'T WAIT UNTIL I GET TO VISIT AFTZAAK AND READ AS MANY BOOKS AS I WANT!
WELL, YOU NEEDN'T BE IN TOO MUCH OF A RUSH.
THE VILLAGE LIBRARY ALREADY OFFERS MANY OF THE BEST!
YOU COULD READ EVERY BOOK ON ITS SHELVES TWICE OVER BEFORE NEEDING TO JOURNEY TO THE CITY!
Oh...
HM?
NO...
IT'S JUST ...
It's no big deal...
BUT...

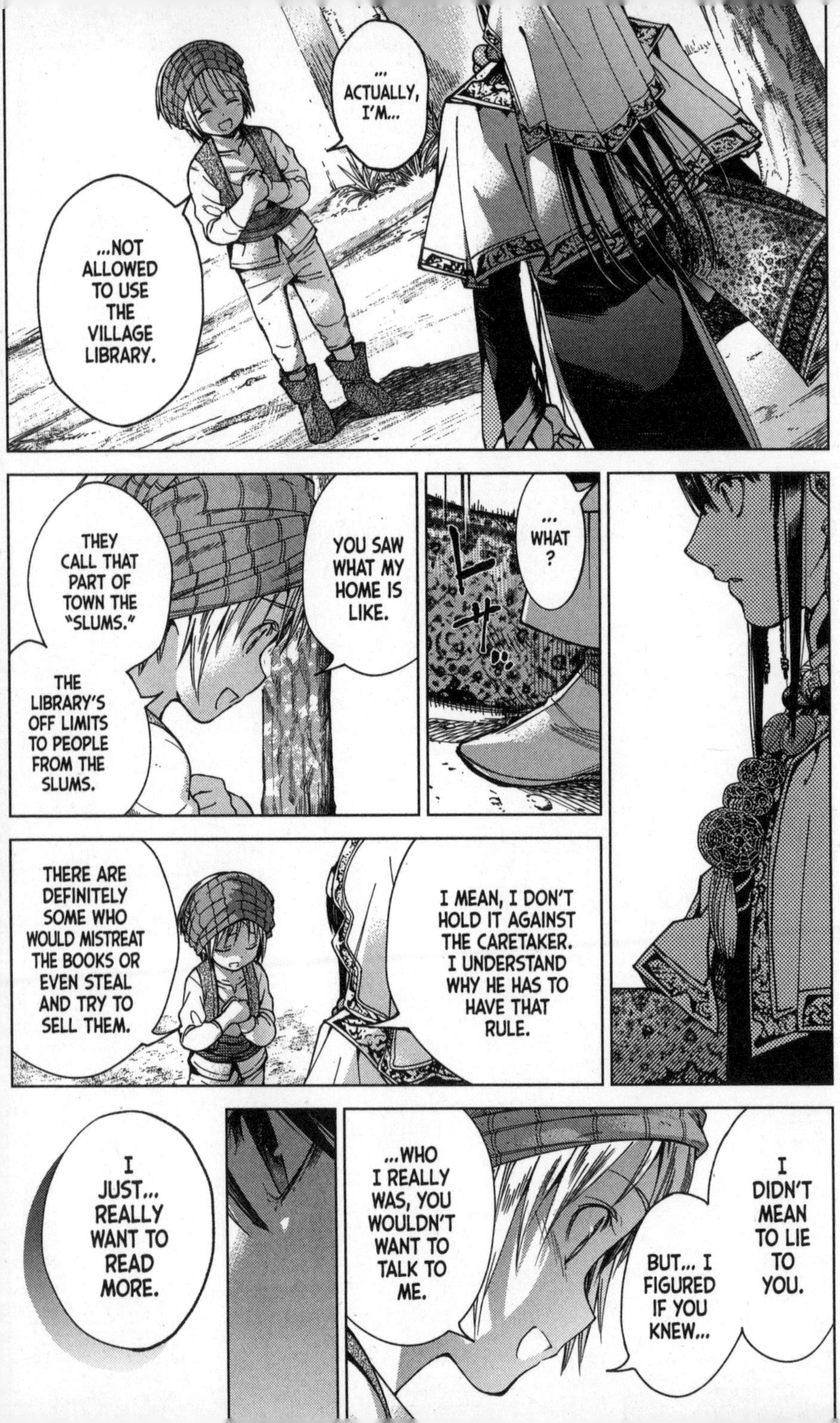
... ACTUALLY, I'M...
...NOT ALLOWED TO USE THE VILLAGE LIBRARY.
... WHAT ?
YOU SAW WHAT MY HOME IS LIKE.
THEY CALL THAT PART OF TOWN THE "SLUMS."
THE LIBRARY'S OFF LIMITS TO PEOPLE FROM THE SLUMS.
I MEAN, I DON'T HOLD IT AGAINST THE CARETAKER. I UNDERSTAND WHY HE HAS TO HAVE THAT RULE.
THERE ARE DEFINITELY SOME WHO WOULD MISTREAT THE BOOKS OR EVEN STEAL AND TRY TO SELL THEM.
I DIDN'T MEAN TO LIE TO YOU.
BUT... I FIGURED IF YOU KNEW...
...WHO I REALLY WAS, YOU WOULDN'T WANT TO TALK TO ME.
I JUST... REALLY WANT TO READ MORE.

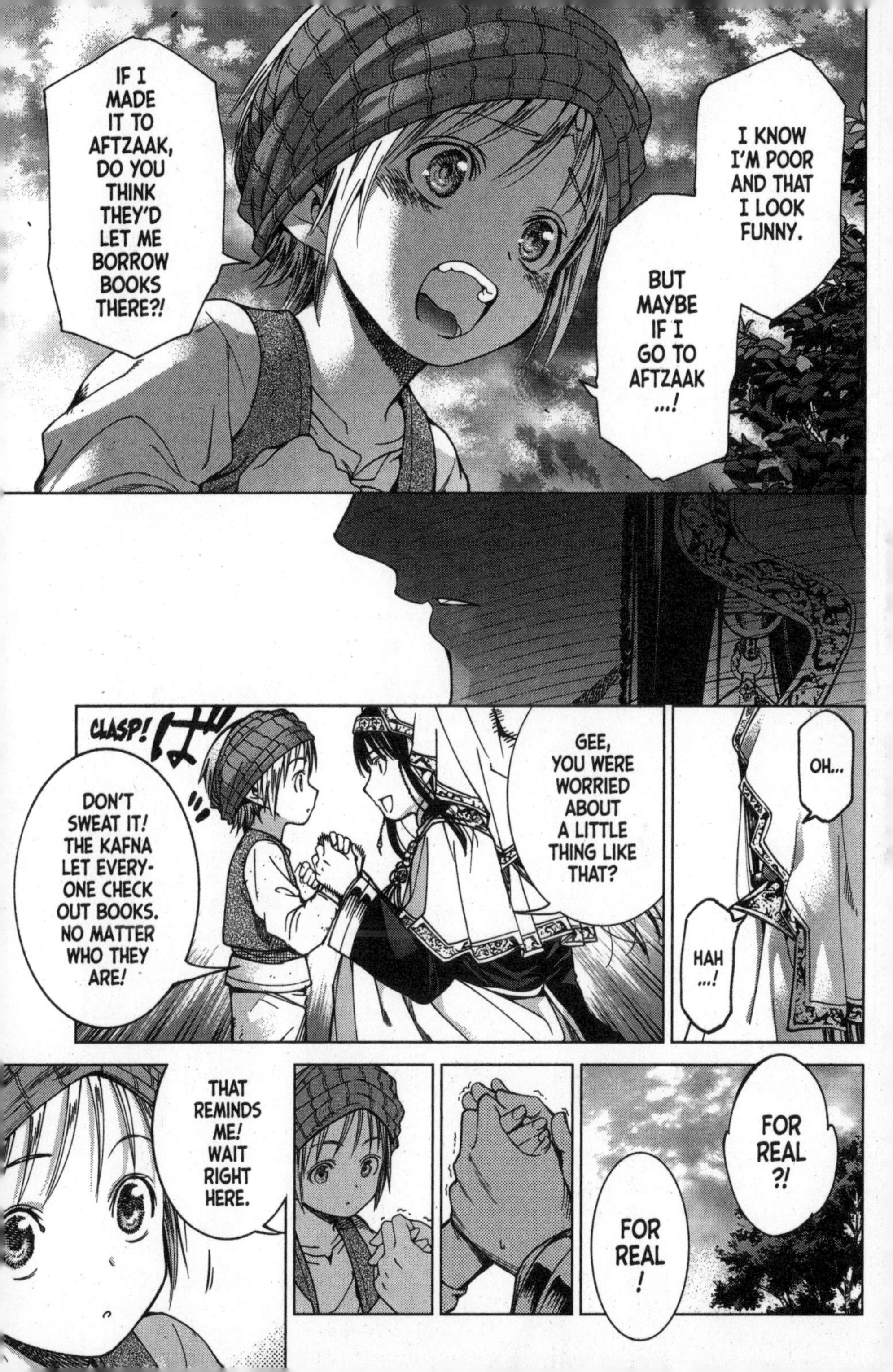
I KNOW I'M POOR AND THAT I LOOK FUNNY.
BUT MAYBE IF I GO TO AFTZAAK ...!
IF I MADE IT TO AFTZAAK, DO YOU THINK THEY'D LET ME BORROW BOOKS THERE?!
OH...
HAH ...!
GEE, YOU WERE WORRIED ABOUT A LITTLE THING LIKE THAT?
CLASP!
DON'T SWEAT IT! THE KAFNA LET EVERY-ONE CHECK OUT BOOKS. NO MATTER WHO THEY ARE!
FOR REAL ?!
FOR REAL !
THAT REMINDS ME! WAIT RIGHT HERE.

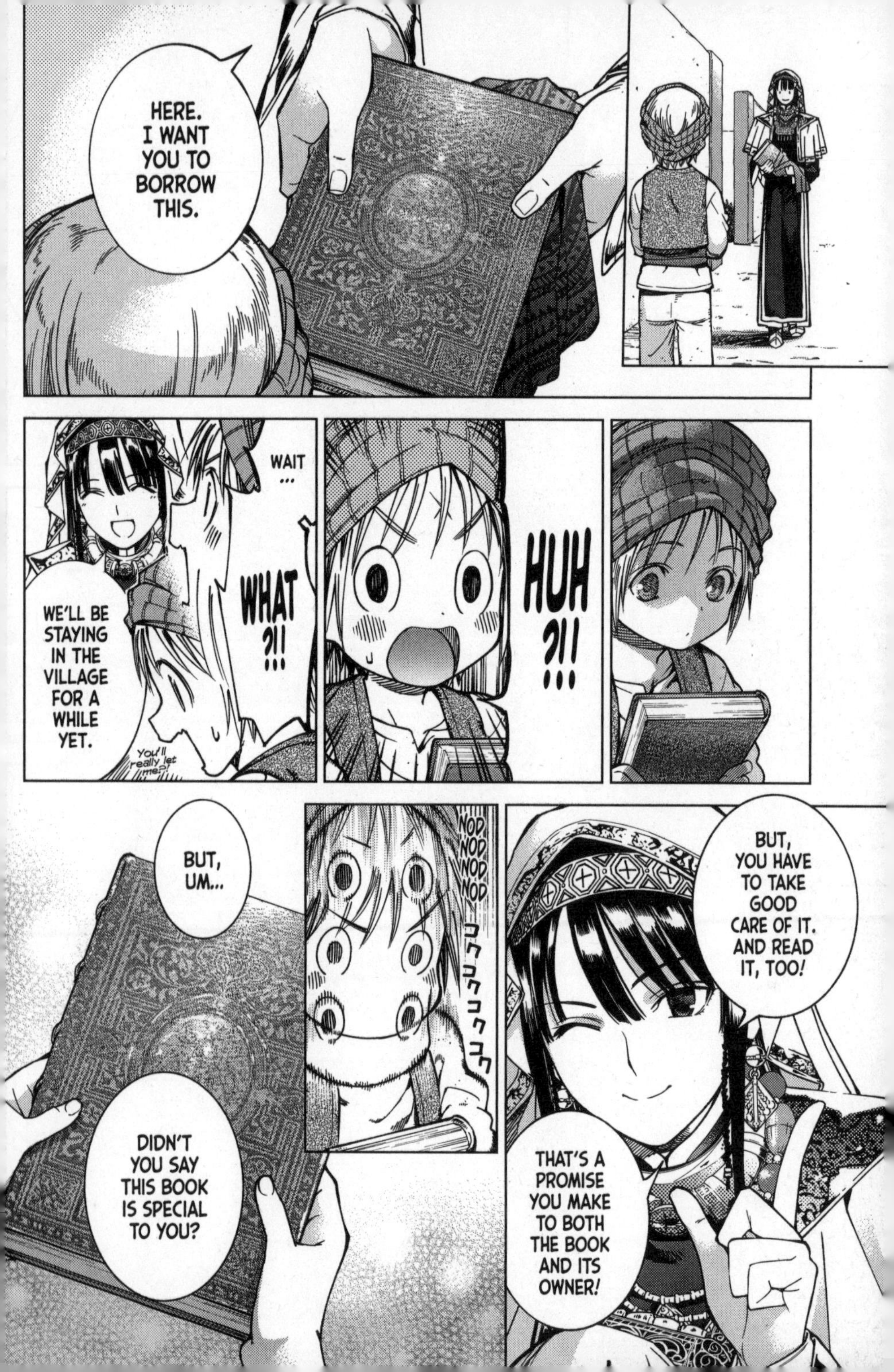
HERE. I WANT YOU TO BORROW THIS.
HUH ?!!
WAIT ...
WHAT ?!!
WE'LL BE STAYING IN THE VILLAGE FOR A WHILE YET.
You'll really let me?!
BUT, YOU HAVE TO TAKE GOOD CARE OF IT. AND READ IT, TOO!
THAT'S A PROMISE YOU MAKE TO BOTH THE BOOK AND ITS OWNER!
NOD NOD NOD NOD
コクコクコクコク
BUT, UM...
DIDN'T YOU SAY THIS BOOK IS SPECIAL TO YOU?

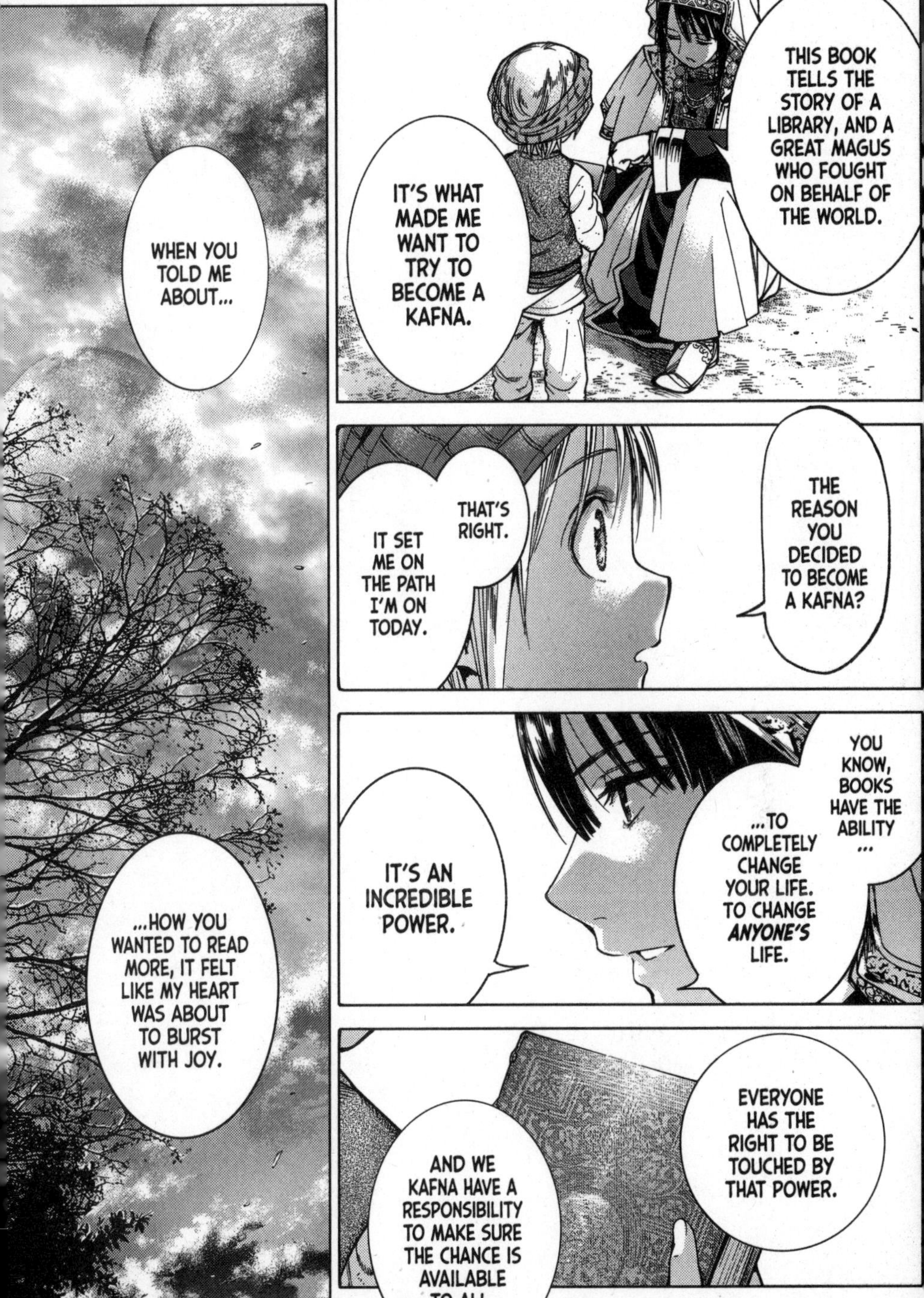
THIS BOOK TELLS THE STORY OF A LIBRARY, AND A GREAT MAGUS WHO FOUGHT ON BEHALF OF THE WORLD.
IT'S WHAT MADE ME WANT TO TRY TO BECOME A KAFNA.
THE REASON YOU DECIDED TO BECOME A KAFNA?
THAT'S RIGHT.
IT SET ME ON THE PATH I'M ON TODAY.
YOU KNOW, BOOKS HAVE THE ABILITY...
...TO COMPLETELY CHANGE YOUR LIFE. TO CHANGE *ANYONE'S* LIFE.
IT'S AN INCREDIBLE POWER.
EVERYONE HAS THE RIGHT TO BE TOUCHED BY THAT POWER.
AND WE KAFNA HAVE A RESPONSIBILITY TO MAKE SURE THE CHANCE IS AVAILABLE TO ALL.
WHEN YOU TOLD ME ABOUT...
...HOW YOU WANTED TO READ MORE, IT FELT LIKE MY HEART WAS ABOUT TO BURST WITH JOY.

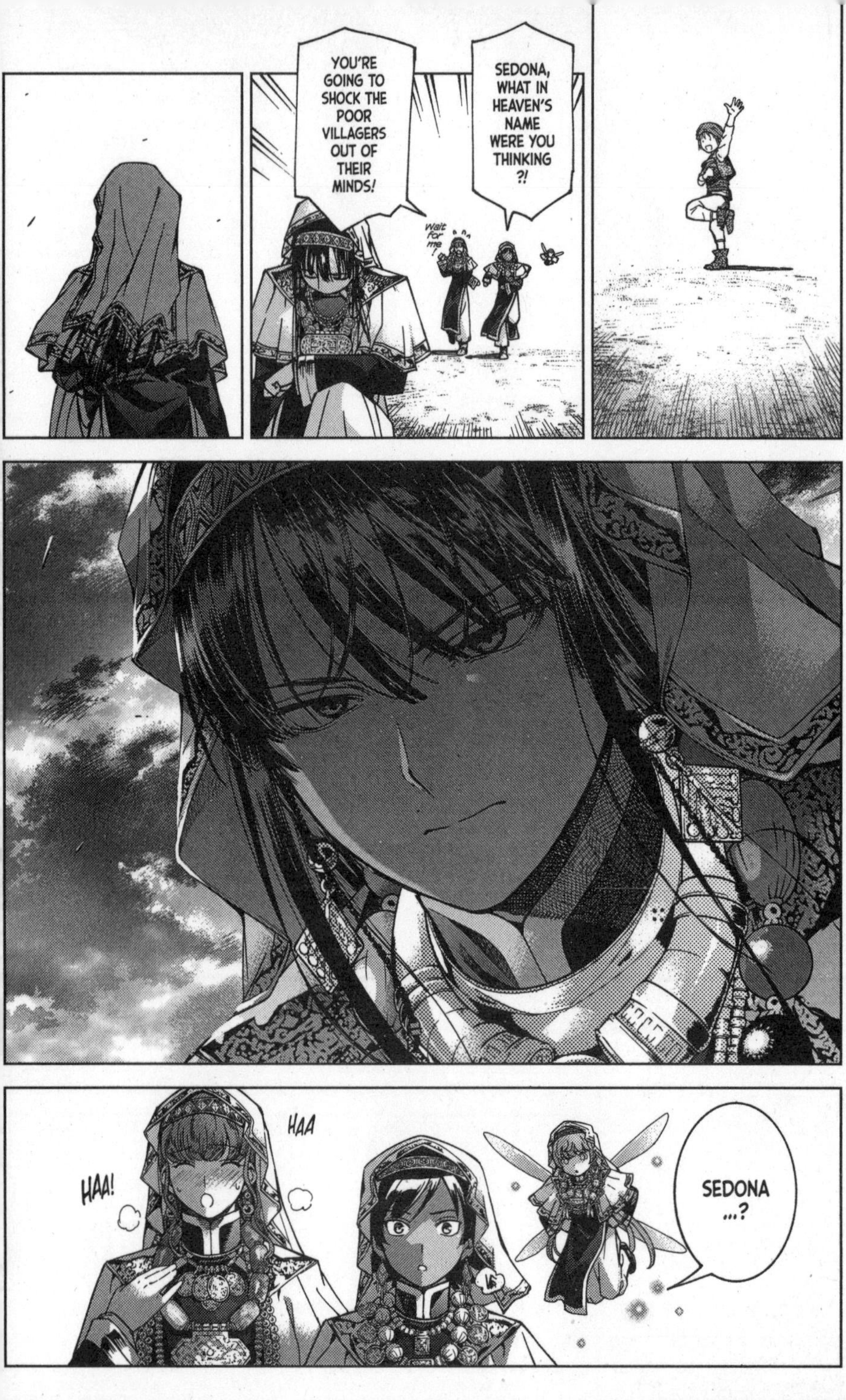
SEDONA, WHAT IN HEAVEN'S NAME WERE YOU THINKING?!
YOU'RE GOING TO SHOCK THE POOR VILLAGERS OUT OF THEIR MINDS!
Wait for me!
SEDONA ...?
HAA
HAA!

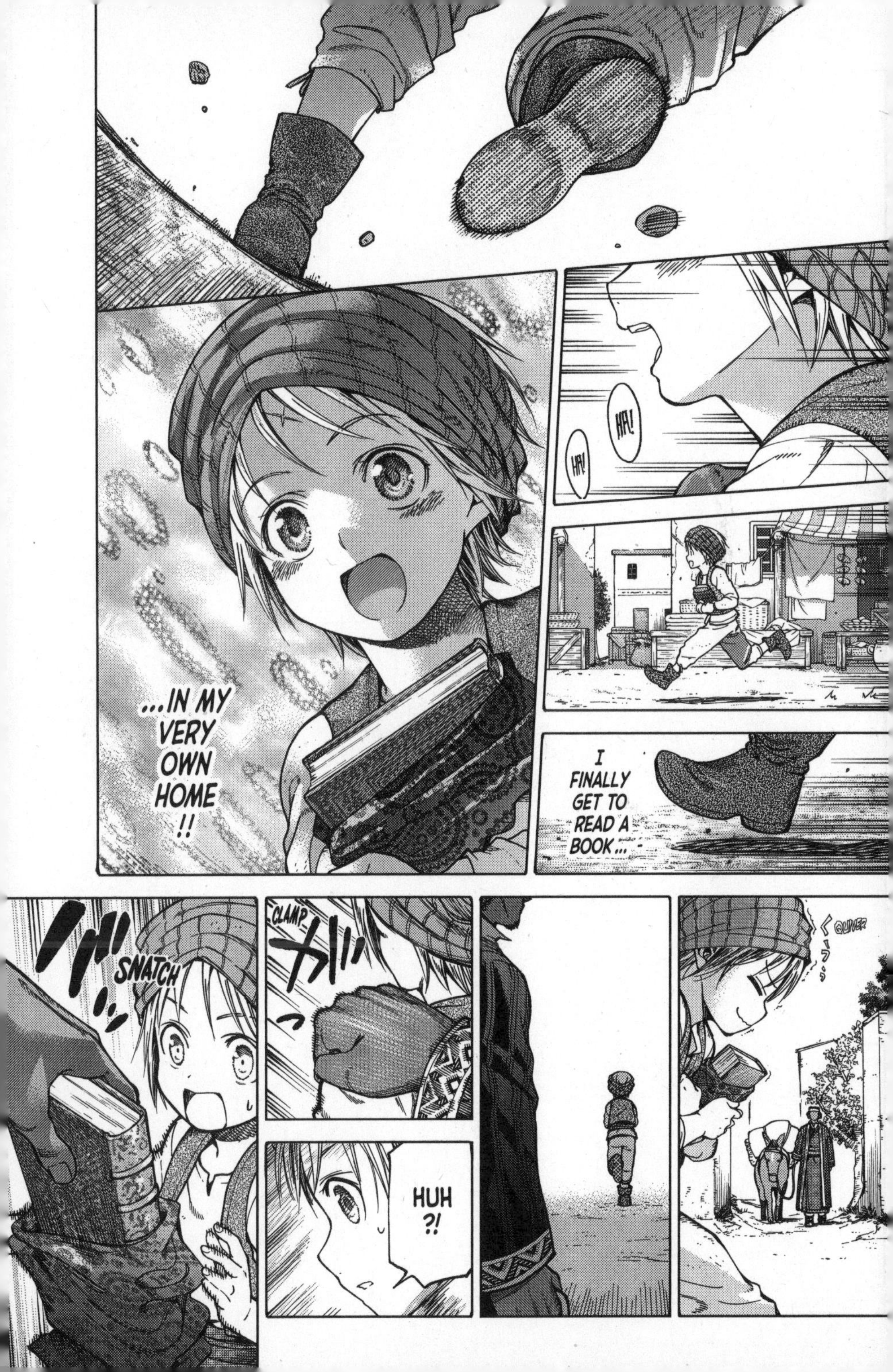
HA!
HA!
I FINALLY GET TO READ A BOOK...
...IN MY VERY OWN HOME!!
QUIVER
CLAMP
HUH?!
SNATCH

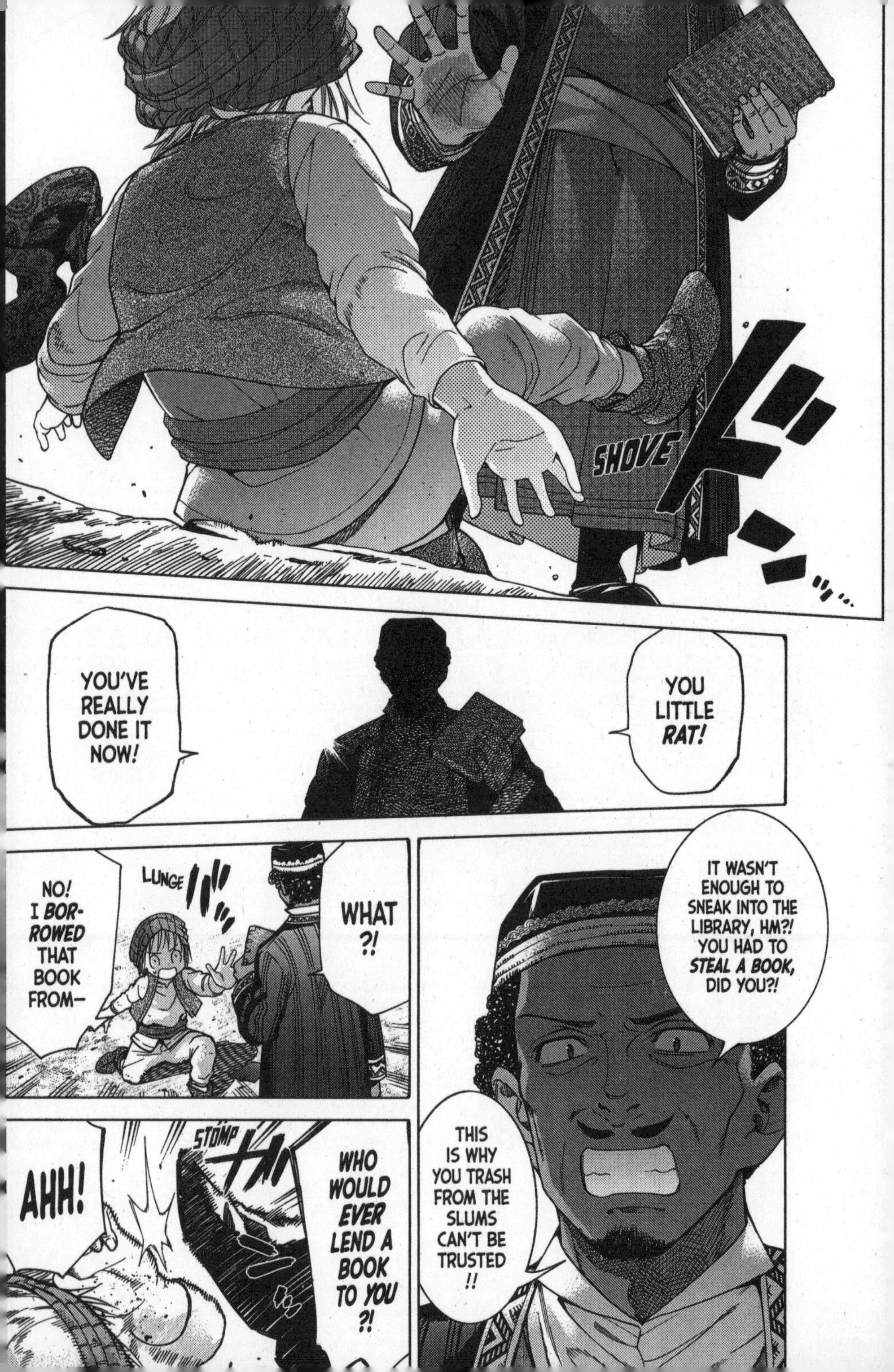
SHOVE
YOU LITTLE RAT!
YOU'VE REALLY DONE IT NOW!
IT WASN'T ENOUGH TO SNEAK INTO THE LIBRARY, HM?! YOU HAD TO STEAL A BOOK, DID YOU?!
THIS IS WHY YOU TRASH FROM THE SLUMS CAN'T BE TRUSTED!!
WHAT?!
LUNGE
NO! I BORROWED THAT BOOK FROM—
STOMP
WHO WOULD EVER LEND A BOOK TO YOU?!
AHH!

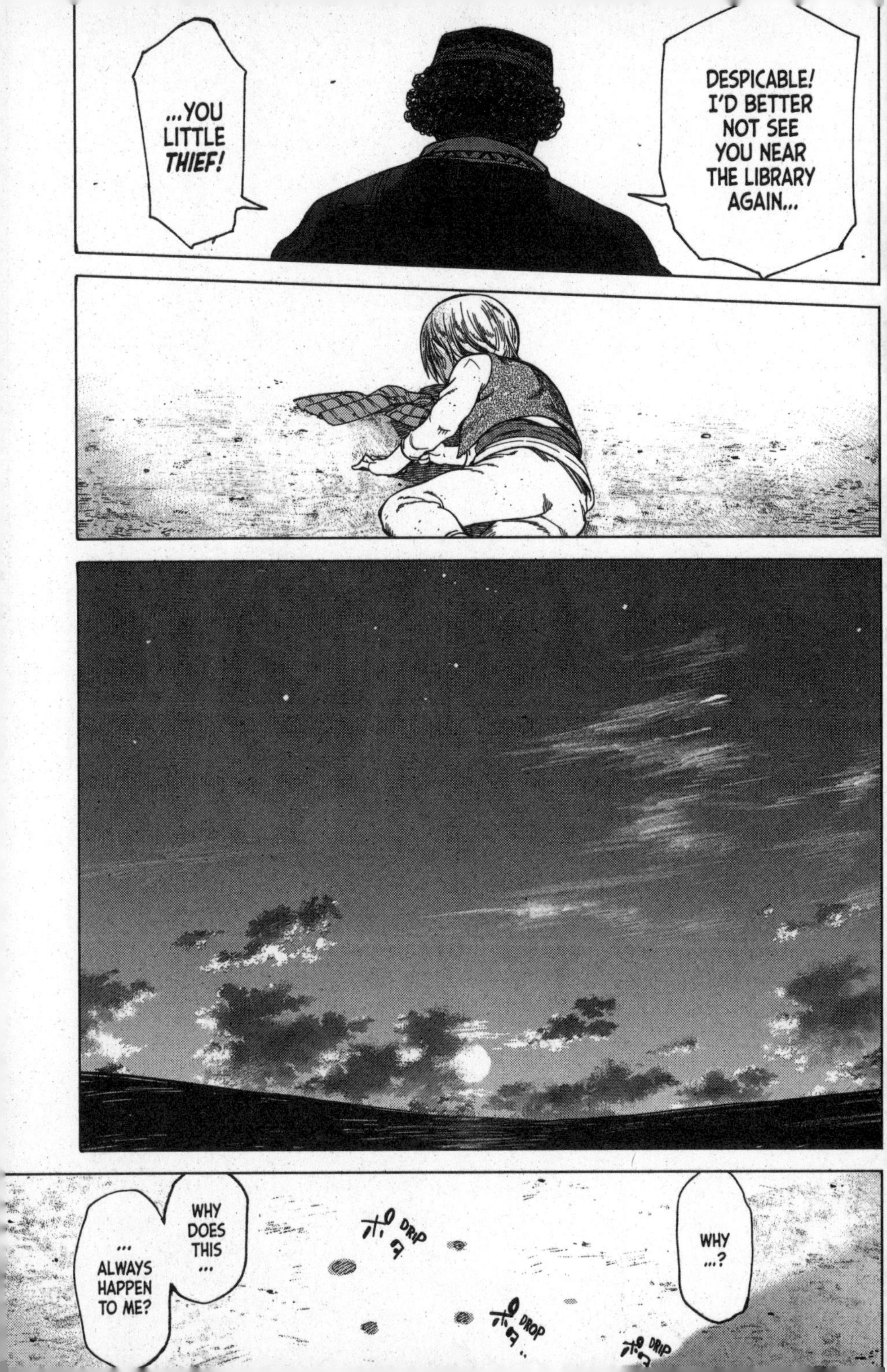
DESPICABLE! I'D BETTER NOT SEE YOU NEAR THE LIBRARY AGAIN...
...YOU LITTLE *THIEF!*
WHY ...?
DRIP
DROP
DRIP
WHY DOES THIS ...
... ALWAYS HAPPEN TO ME?

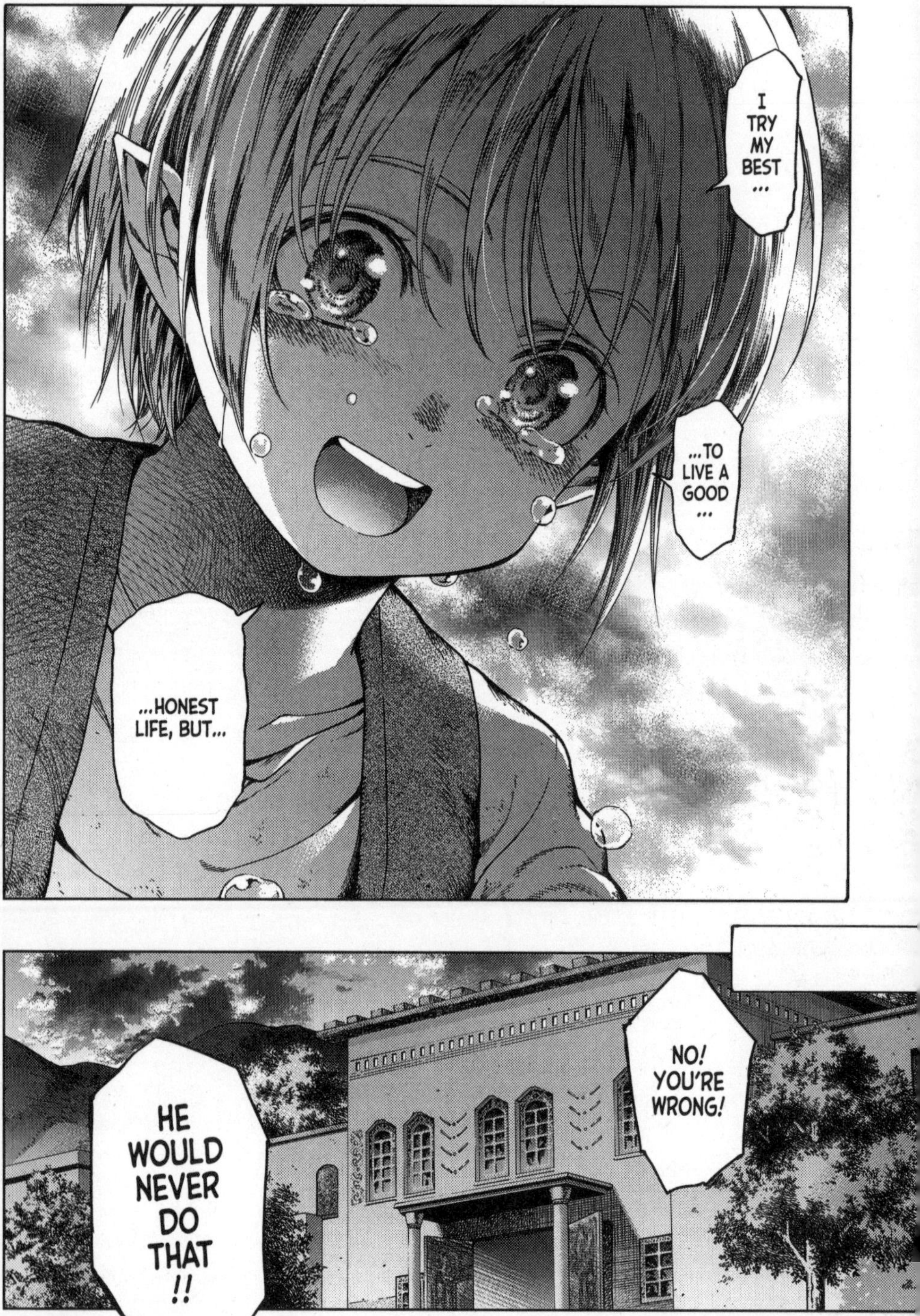
I TRY MY BEST...
...TO LIVE A GOOD...
...HONEST LIFE, BUT...
NO! YOU'RE WRONG!
HE WOULD NEVER DO THAT!!

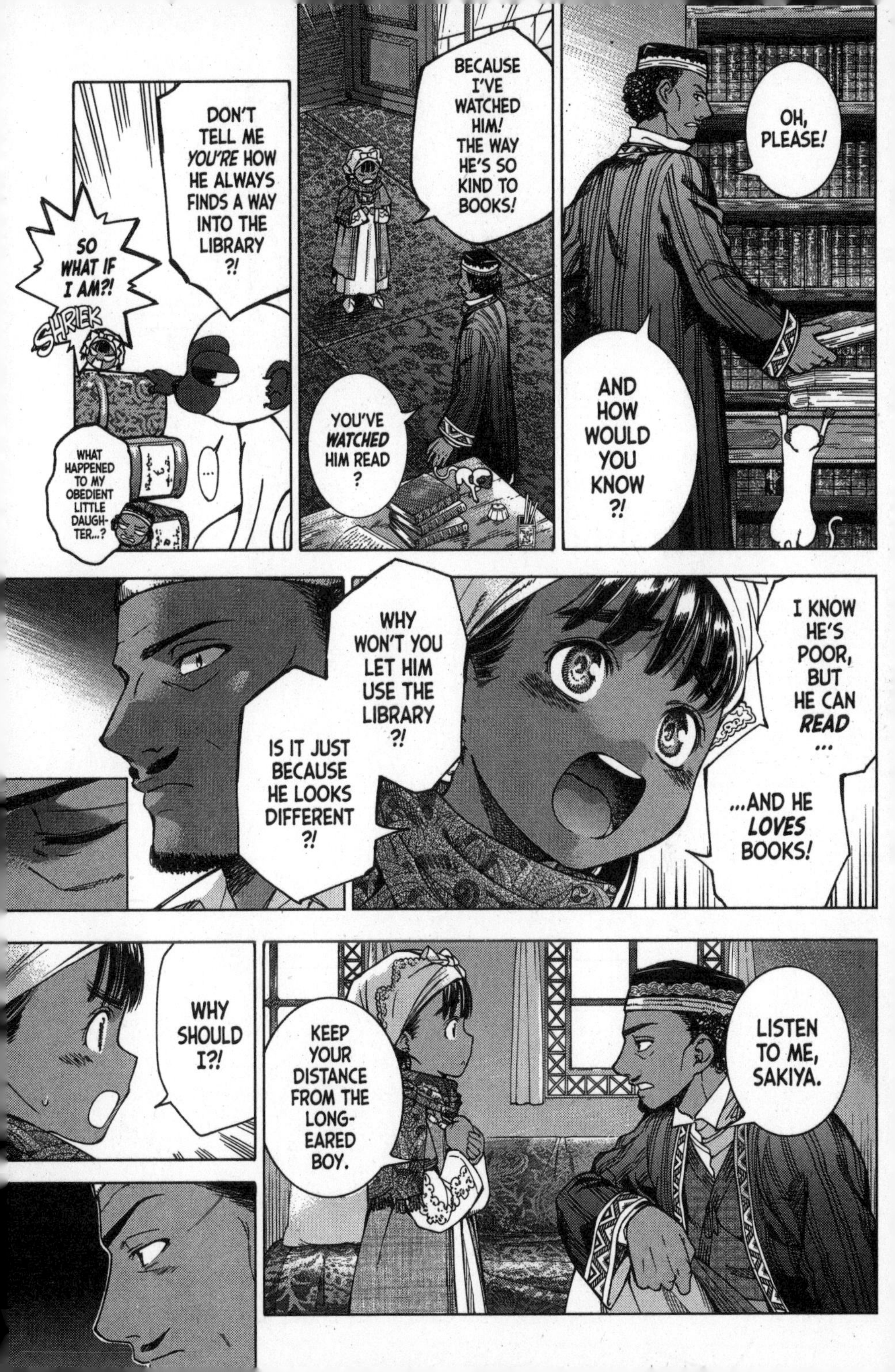
OH, PLEASE!
AND HOW WOULD YOU KNOW?!
BECAUSE I'VE WATCHED HIM! THE WAY HE'S SO KIND TO BOOKS!
YOU'VE WATCHED HIM READ?
DON'T TELL ME YOU'RE HOW HE ALWAYS FINDS A WAY INTO THE LIBRARY?!
SO WHAT IF I AM?!
SHRIEK
...
WHAT HAPPENED TO MY OBEDIENT LITTLE DAUGHTER...?
I KNOW HE'S POOR, BUT HE CAN READ...
...AND HE LOVES BOOKS!
WHY WON'T YOU LET HIM USE THE LIBRARY?!
IS IT JUST BECAUSE HE LOOKS DIFFERENT?!
LISTEN TO ME, SAKIYA.
KEEP YOUR DISTANCE FROM THE LONG-EARED BOY.
WHY SHOULD I?!

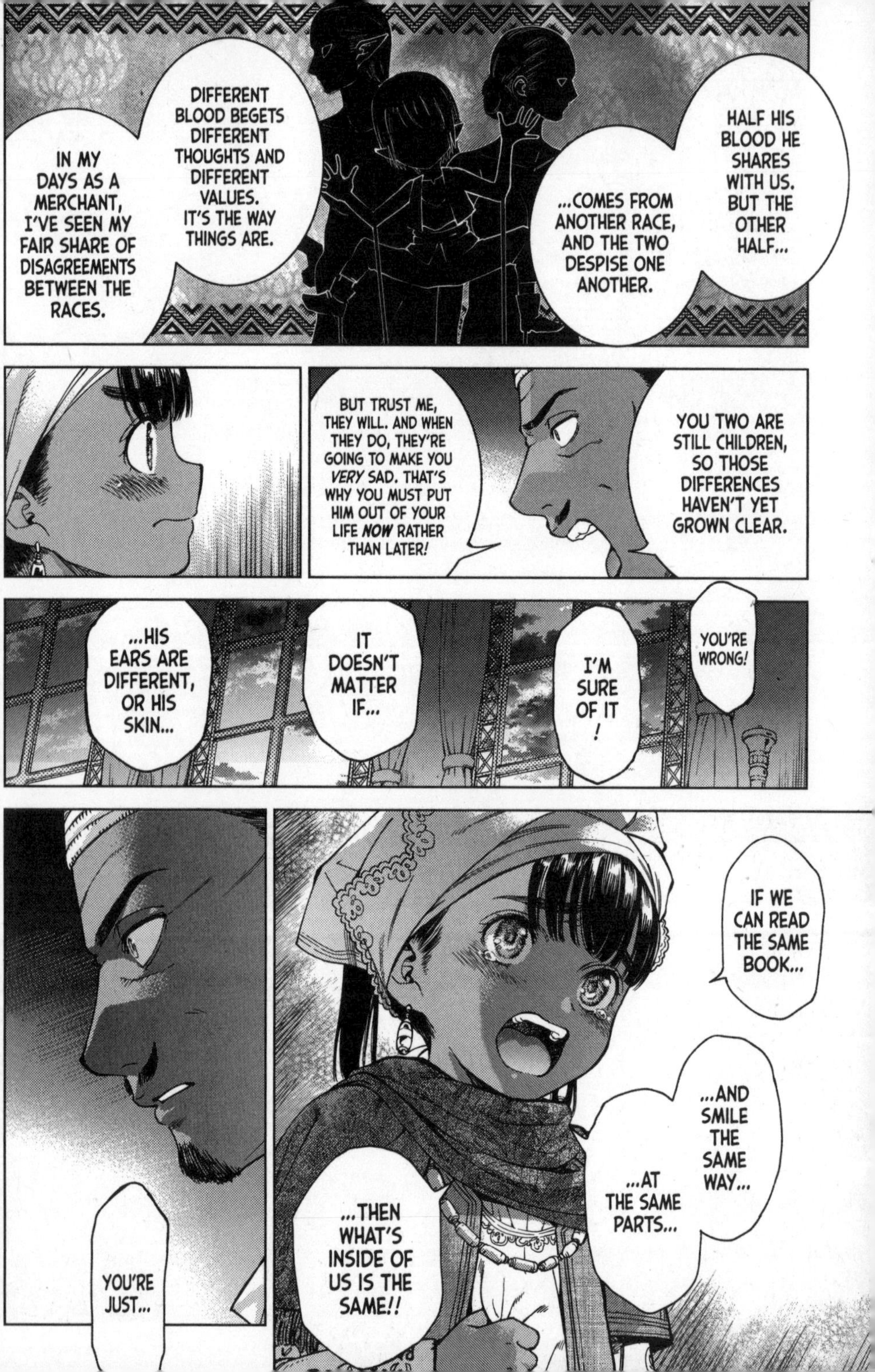
HALF HIS BLOOD HE SHARES WITH US. BUT THE OTHER HALF...
...COMES FROM ANOTHER RACE, AND THE TWO DESPISE ONE ANOTHER.
DIFFERENT BLOOD BEGETS DIFFERENT THOUGHTS AND DIFFERENT VALUES. IT'S THE WAY THINGS ARE.
IN MY DAYS AS A MERCHANT, I'VE SEEN MY FAIR SHARE OF DISAGREEMENTS BETWEEN THE RACES.
YOU TWO ARE STILL CHILDREN, SO THOSE DIFFERENCES HAVEN'T YET GROWN CLEAR.
BUT TRUST ME, THEY WILL. AND WHEN THEY DO, THEY'RE GOING TO MAKE YOU *VERY* SAD. THAT'S WHY YOU MUST PUT HIM OUT OF YOUR LIFE ***NOW*** RATHER THAN LATER!
YOU'RE WRONG!
I'M SURE OF IT!
IT DOESN'T MATTER IF...
...HIS EARS ARE DIFFERENT, OR HIS SKIN...
IF WE CAN READ THE SAME BOOK...
...AND SMILE THE SAME WAY...
...AT THE SAME PARTS...
...THEN WHAT'S INSIDE OF US IS THE SAME!!
YOU'RE JUST...

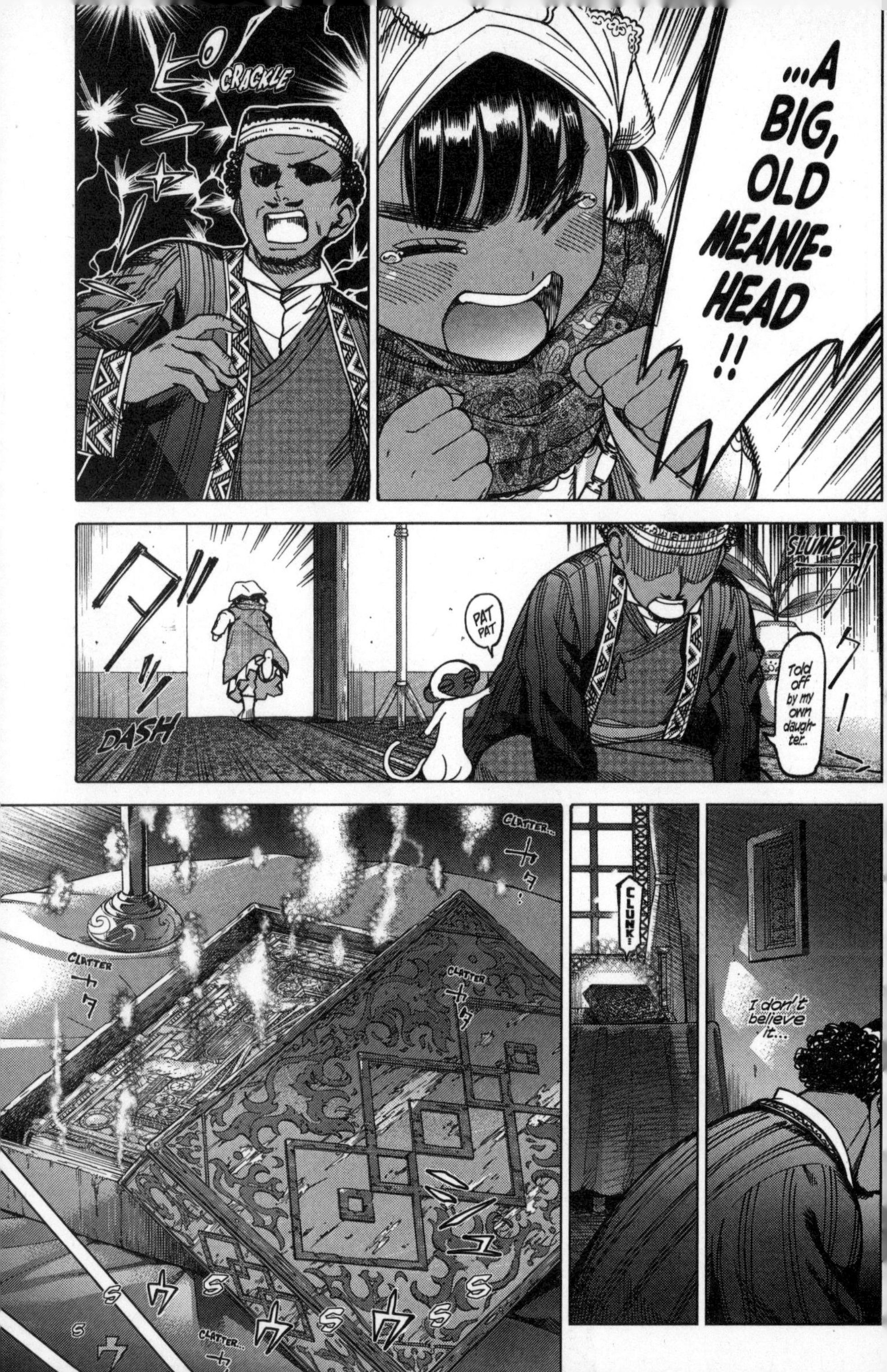
...A BIG, OLD MEANIE-HEAD !!
CRACKLE
SLUMP
Told off by my own daughter..
PAT PAT
DASH
I don't believe it...
CLUNK!
CLATTER...
CLATTER
CLATTER
CLATTER...

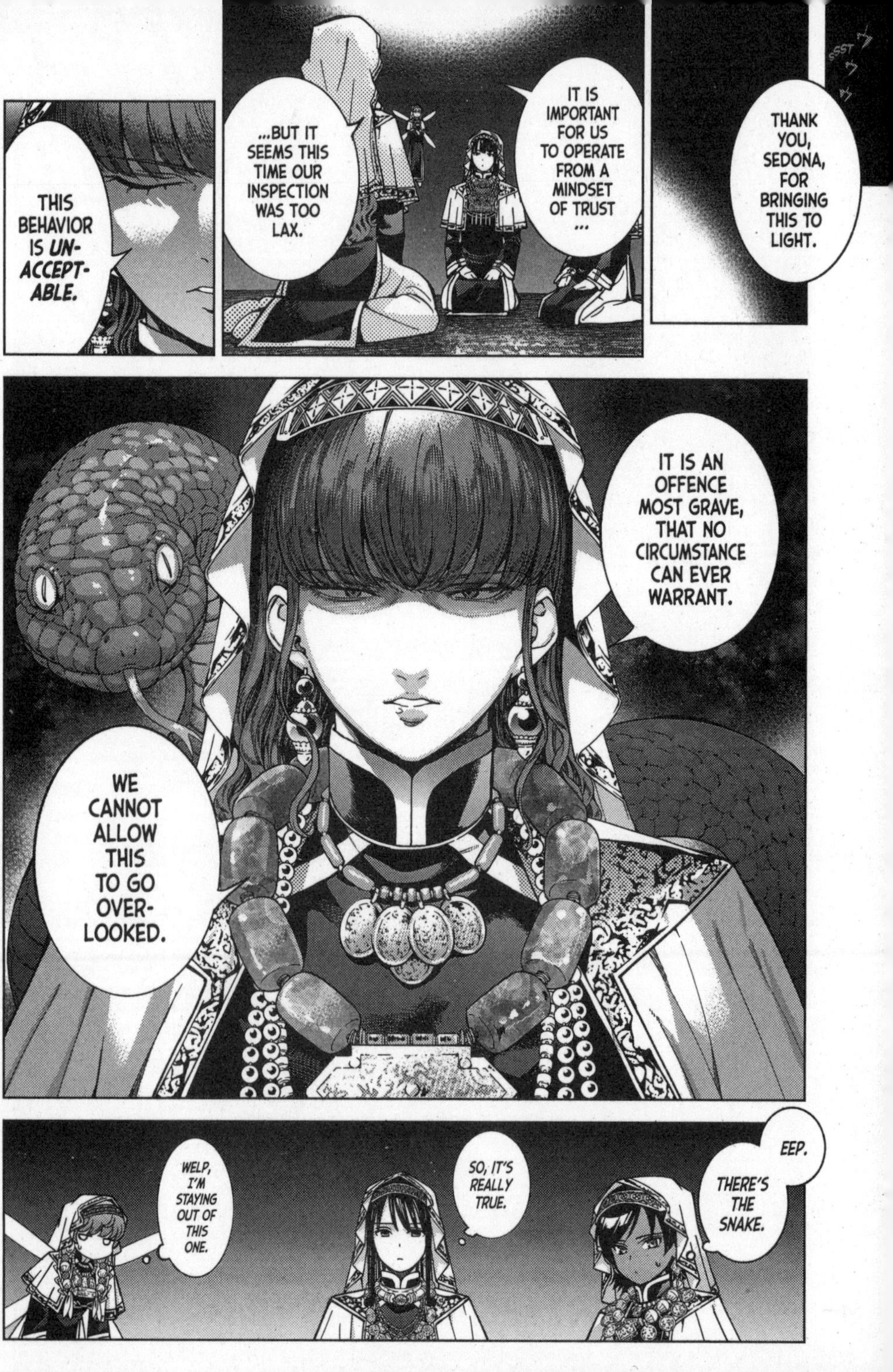

SSST
THANK YOU, SEDONA, FOR BRINGING THIS TO LIGHT.
IT IS IMPORTANT FOR US TO OPERATE FROM A MINDSET OF TRUST...
...BUT IT SEEMS THIS TIME OUR INSPECTION WAS TOO LAX.
THIS BEHAVIOR IS *UNACCEPTABLE.*
IT IS AN OFFENCE MOST GRAVE, THAT NO CIRCUMSTANCE CAN EVER WARRANT.
WE CANNOT ALLOW THIS TO GO OVERLOOKED.
EEP.
THERE'S THE SNAKE.
SO, IT'S REALLY TRUE.
WELP, I'M STAYING OUT OF THIS ONE.

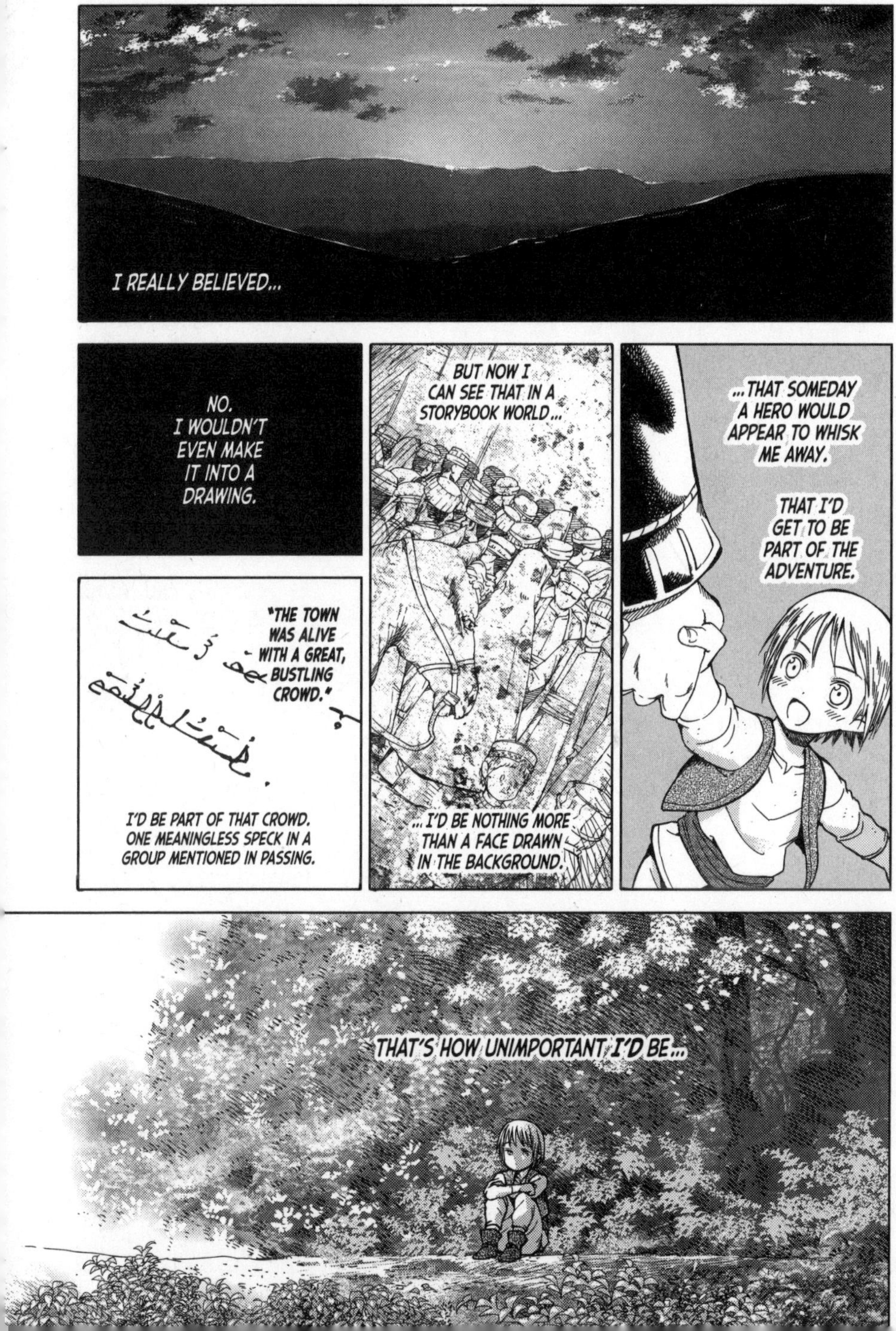
I REALLY BELIEVED...
...THAT SOMEDAY A HERO WOULD APPEAR TO WHISK ME AWAY.
THAT I'D GET TO BE PART OF THE ADVENTURE.
BUT NOW I CAN SEE THAT IN A STORYBOOK WORLD...
...I'D BE NOTHING MORE THAN A FACE DRAWN IN THE BACKGROUND.
NO. I WOULDN'T EVEN MAKE IT INTO A DRAWING.
"THE TOWN WAS ALIVE WITH A GREAT, BUSTLING CROWD."
I'D BE PART OF THAT CROWD. ONE MEANINGLESS SPECK IN A GROUP MENTIONED IN PASSING.
THAT'S HOW UNIMPORTANT I'D BE...

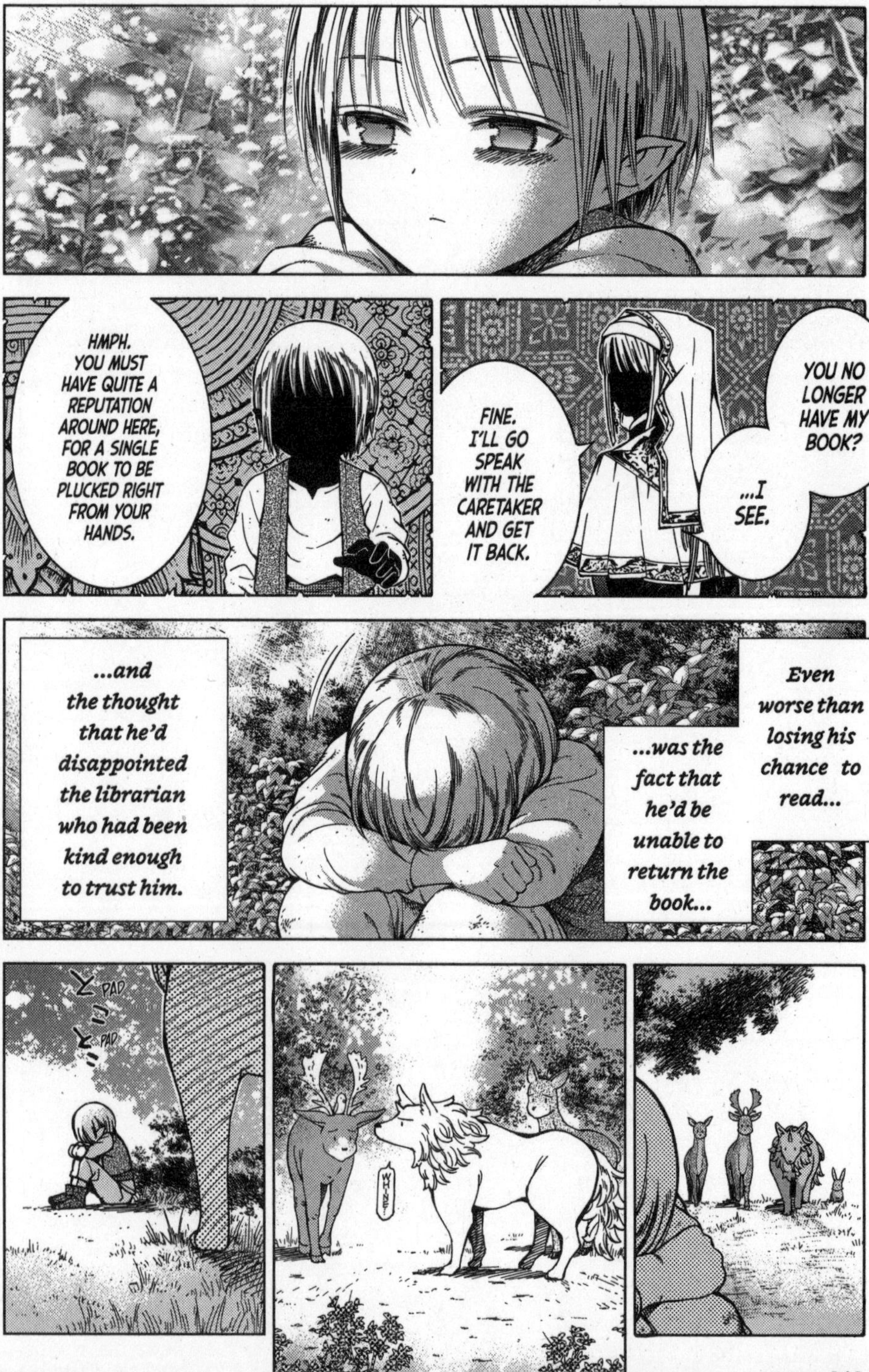
YOU NO LONGER HAVE MY BOOK?
...I SEE.
FINE. I'LL GO SPEAK WITH THE CARETAKER AND GET IT BACK.
HMPH. YOU MUST HAVE QUITE A REPUTATION AROUND HERE, FOR A SINGLE BOOK TO BE PLUCKED RIGHT FROM YOUR HANDS.
Even worse than losing his chance to read...
...was the fact that he'd be unable to return the book...
...and the thought that he'd disappointed the librarian who had been kind enough to trust him.
WHINE!
PAD
PAD

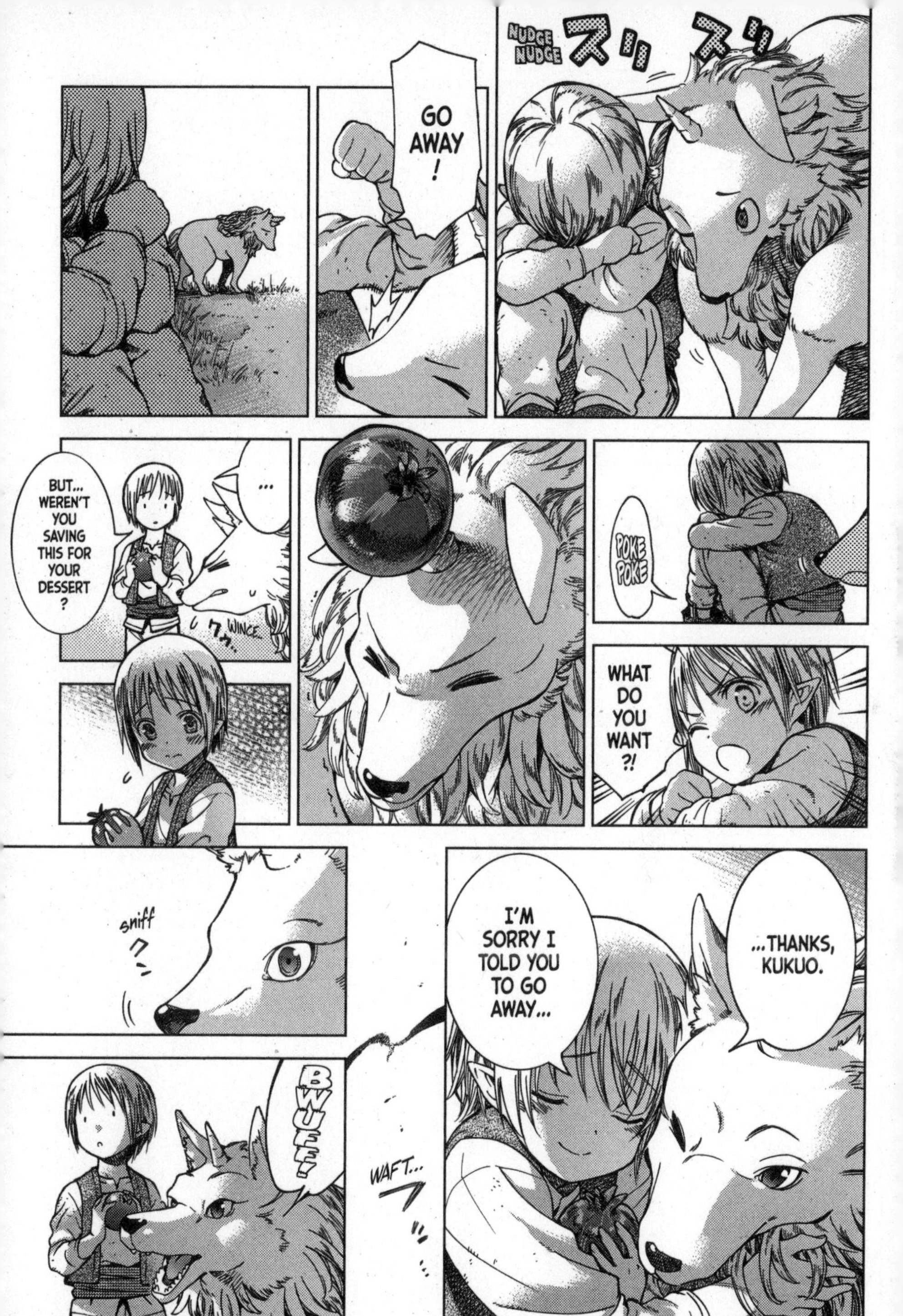
NUDGE NUDGE
スリ スリ
GO AWAY!
POKE POKE
WHAT DO YOU WANT?!
...
BUT... WEREN'T YOU SAVING THIS FOR YOUR DESSERT?
WINCE
...THANKS, KUKUO.
I'M SORRY I TOLD YOU TO GO AWAY...
sniff
BWUFF!
WAFT...

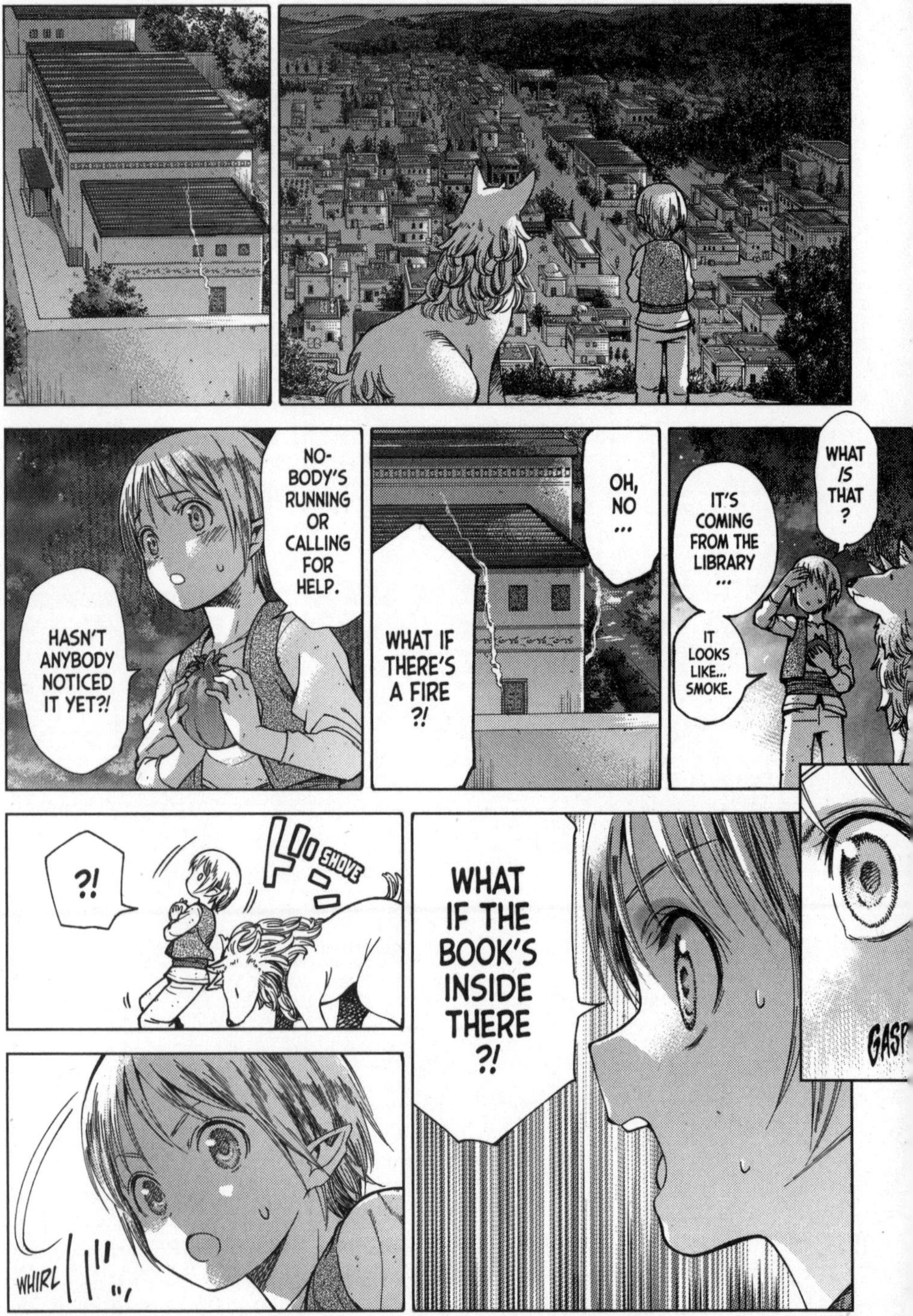
WHAT IS THAT?
IT'S COMING FROM THE LIBRARY...
IT LOOKS LIKE... SMOKE.
OH, NO...
WHAT IF THERE'S A FIRE?!
NO-BODY'S RUNNING OR CALLING FOR HELP.
HASN'T ANYBODY NOTICED IT YET?!
GASP
WHAT IF THE BOOK'S INSIDE THERE?!
SHOVE
?!
WHIRL

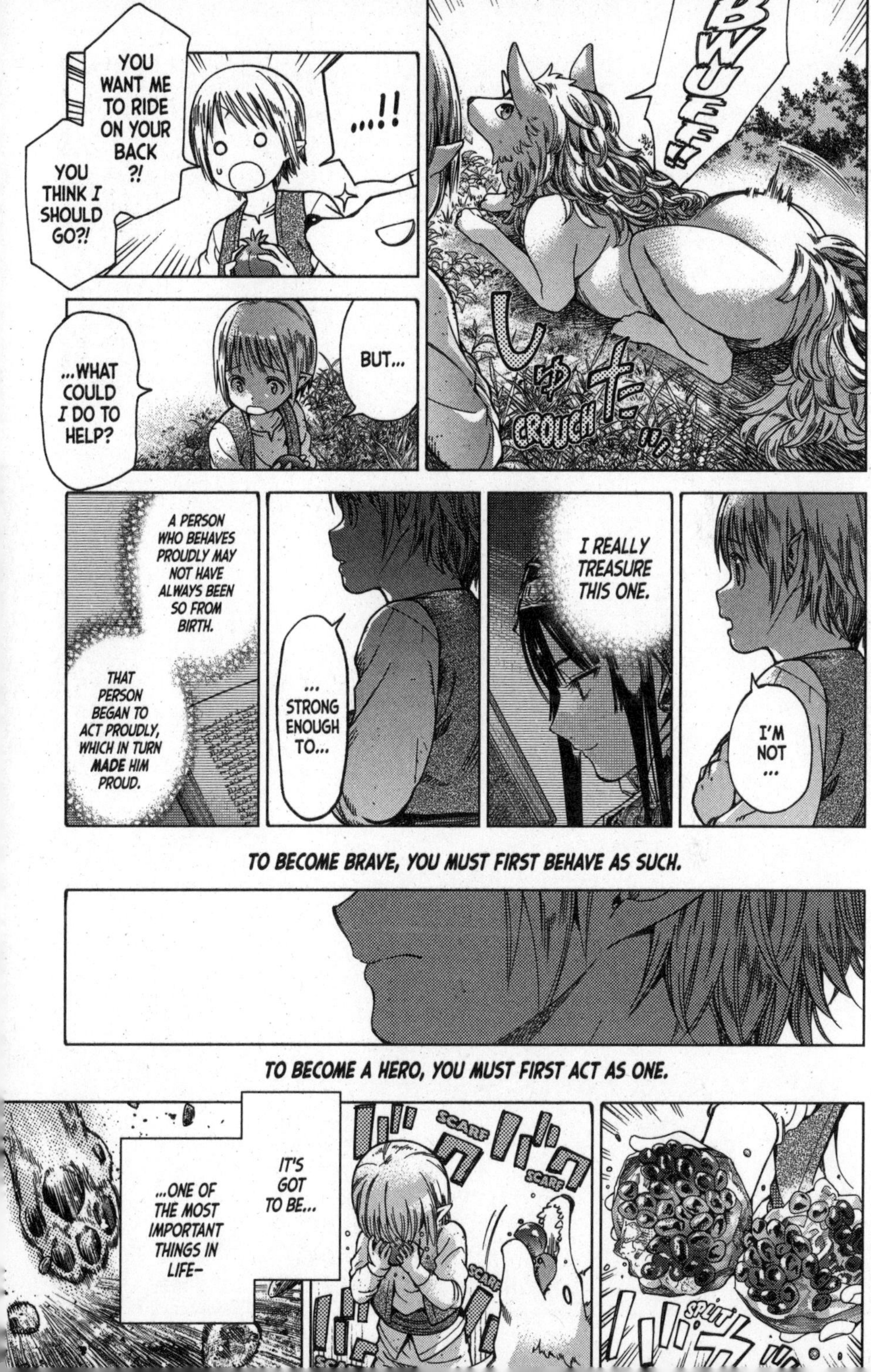
BWUFF!!
CROUCH
...!!
YOU WANT ME TO RIDE ON YOUR BACK ?!
YOU THINK I SHOULD GO?!
BUT...
...WHAT COULD I DO TO HELP?
I'M NOT ...
I REALLY TREASURE THIS ONE.
... STRONG ENOUGH TO...
A PERSON WHO BEHAVES PROUDLY MAY NOT HAVE ALWAYS BEEN SO FROM BIRTH.
THAT PERSON BEGAN TO ACT PROUDLY, WHICH IN TURN MADE HIM PROUD.
TO BECOME BRAVE, YOU MUST FIRST BEHAVE AS SUCH.
TO BECOME A HERO, YOU MUST FIRST ACT AS ONE.
SPLIT
SCARF
SCARF
SCARF
IT'S GOT TO BE...
...ONE OF THE MOST IMPORTANT THINGS IN LIFE–

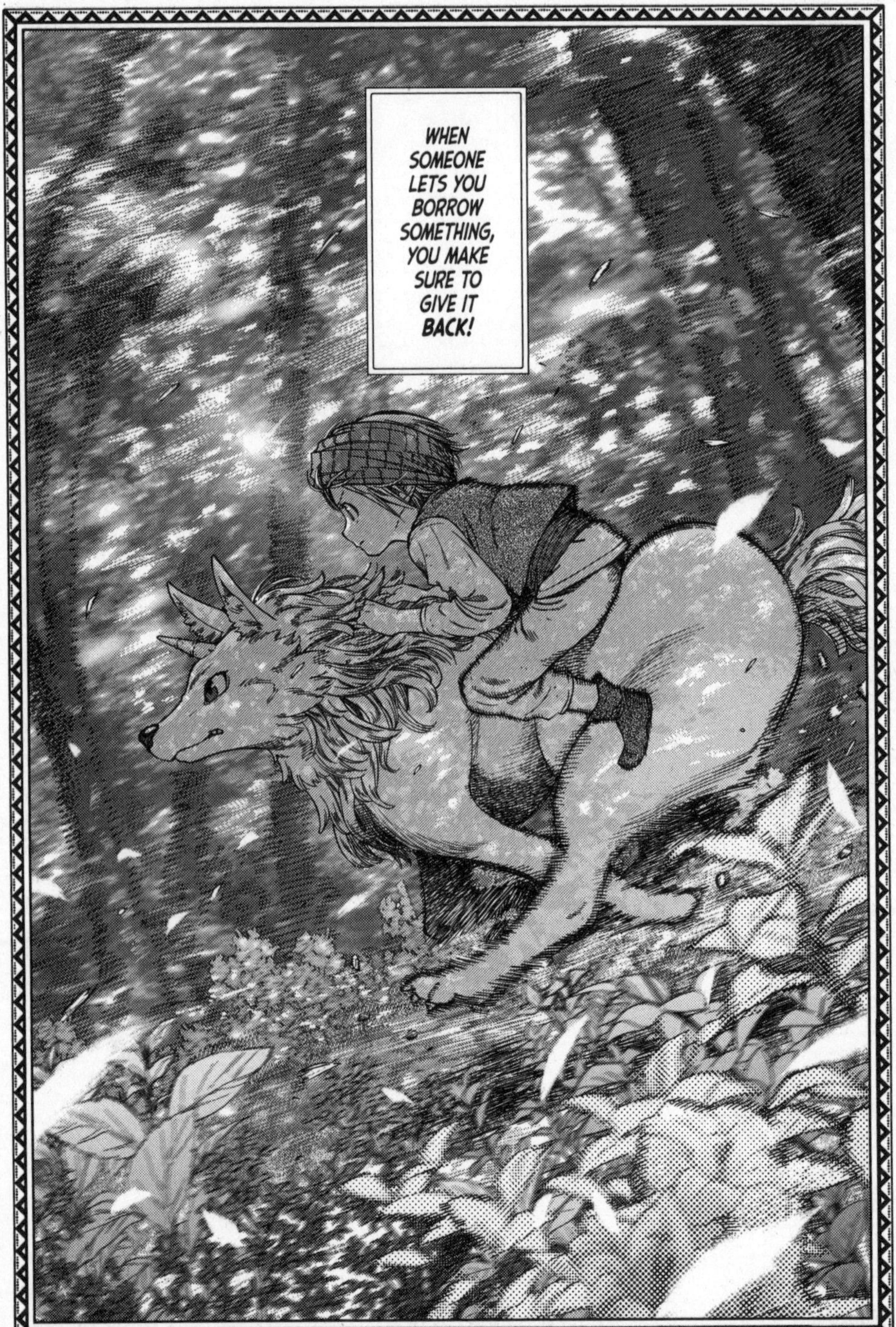
WHEN SOMEONE LETS YOU BORROW SOMETHING, YOU MAKE SURE TO GIVE IT BACK!

Magus of the Library

Salazar

Jei-jei

Birou

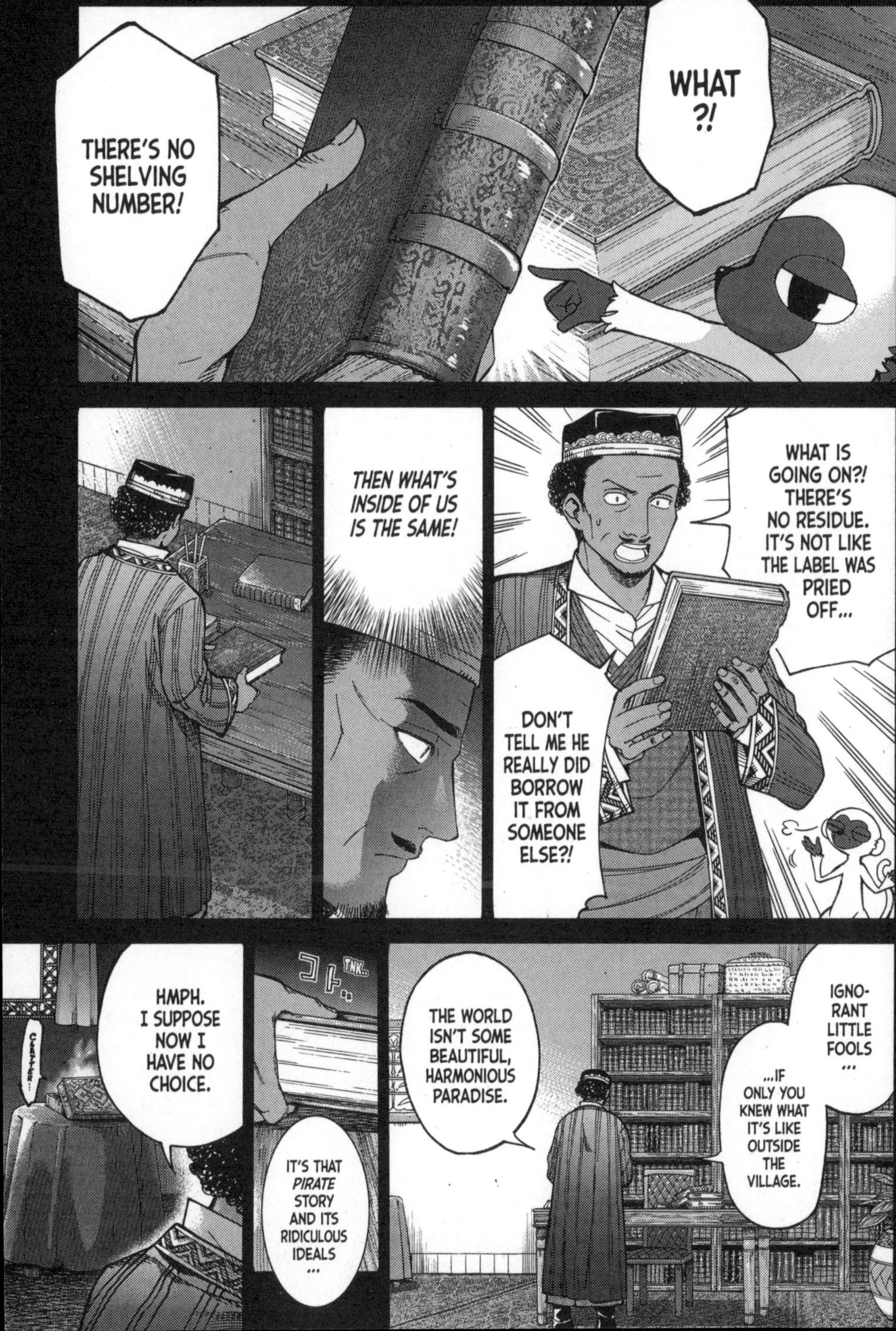
WHAT ?!
THERE'S NO SHELVING NUMBER!
WHAT IS GOING ON?! THERE'S NO RESIDUE. IT'S NOT LIKE THE LABEL WAS PRIED OFF...
DON'T TELL ME HE REALLY DID BORROW IT FROM SOMEONE ELSE?!
THEN WHAT'S INSIDE OF US IS THE SAME!
IGNORANT LITTLE FOOLS ...
...IF ONLY YOU KNEW WHAT IT'S LIKE OUTSIDE THE VILLAGE.
THE WORLD ISN'T SOME BEAUTIFUL, HARMONIOUS PARADISE.
TNK..
IT'S THAT PIRATE STORY AND ITS RIDICULOUS IDEALS ...
HMPH. I SUPPOSE NOW I HAVE NO CHOICE.
CLATTER...

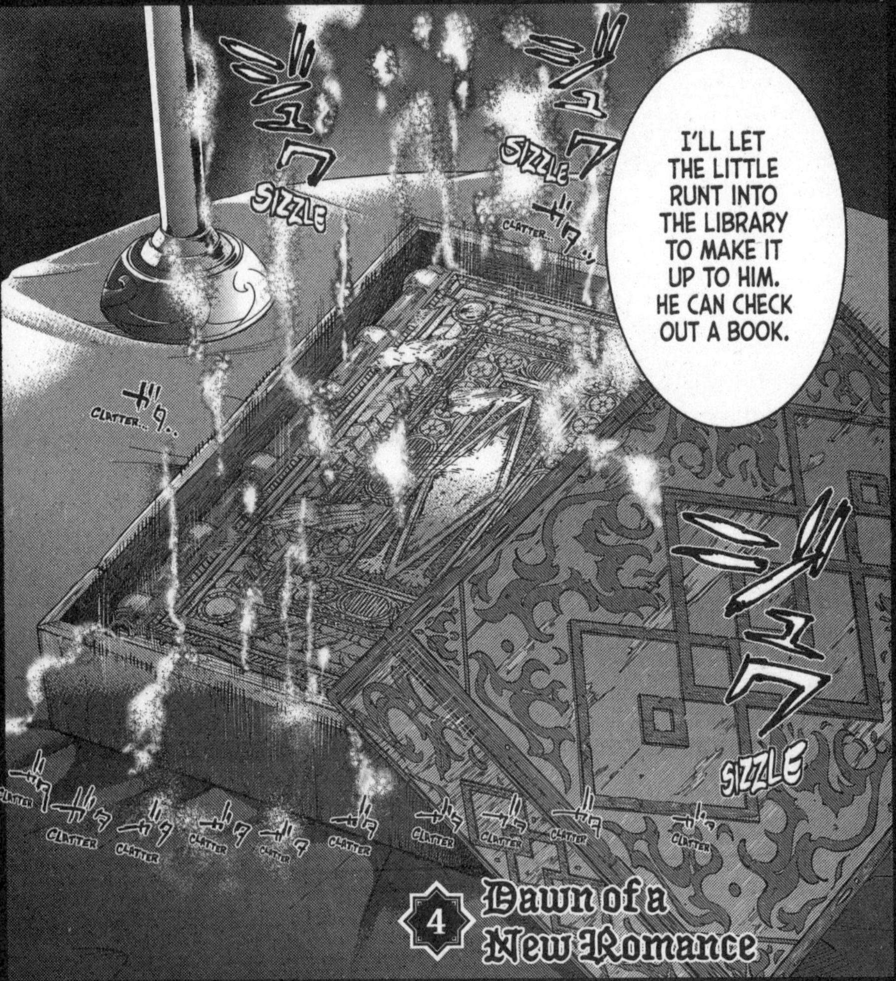
I'LL LET THE LITTLE RUNT INTO THE LIBRARY TO MAKE IT UP TO HIM. HE CAN CHECK OUT A BOOK.
SIZZLE
CLATTER...
SIZZLE
CLATTER...
SIZZLE
CLATTER
CLATTER
CLATTER
CLATTER
CLATTER
CLATTER
CLATTER
CLATTER
CLATTER
CLATTER
4
Dawn of a New Romance

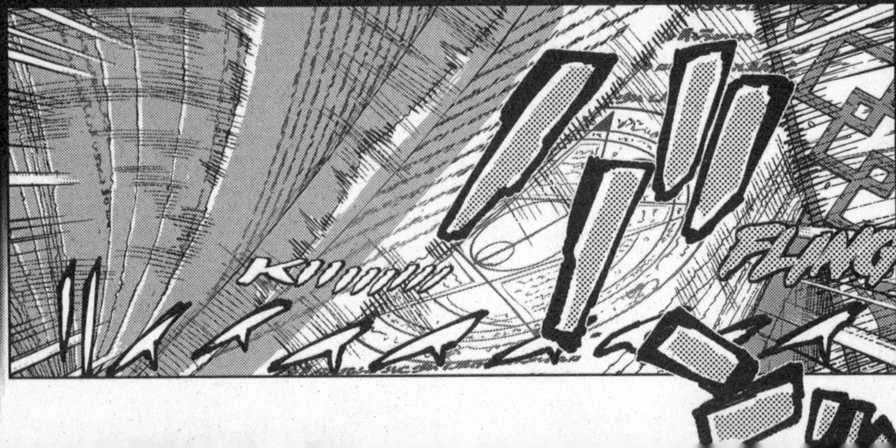
FLING
KIIIIIIIN

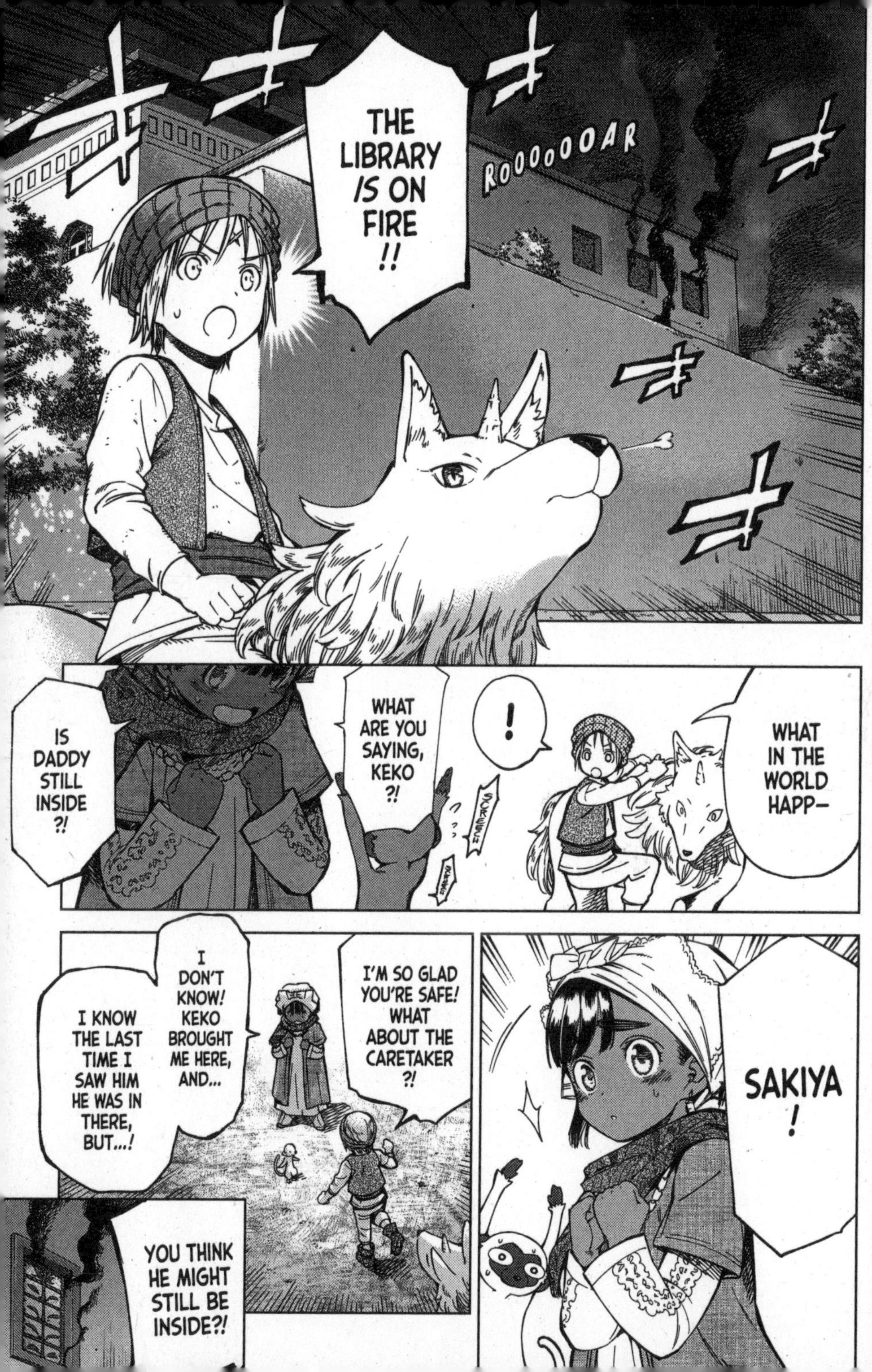
THE LIBRARY IS ON FIRE !!
ROOOOOOAR
WHAT IN THE WORLD HAPP–
!
SCREECH
WHAT ARE YOU SAYING, KEKO ?!
IS DADDY STILL INSIDE ?!
SAKIYA !
I'M SO GLAD YOU'RE SAFE! WHAT ABOUT THE CARETAKER ?!
I DON'T KNOW! KEKO BROUGHT ME HERE, AND...
I KNOW THE LAST TIME I SAW HIM HE WAS IN THERE, BUT...!
YOU THINK HE MIGHT STILL BE INSIDE?!

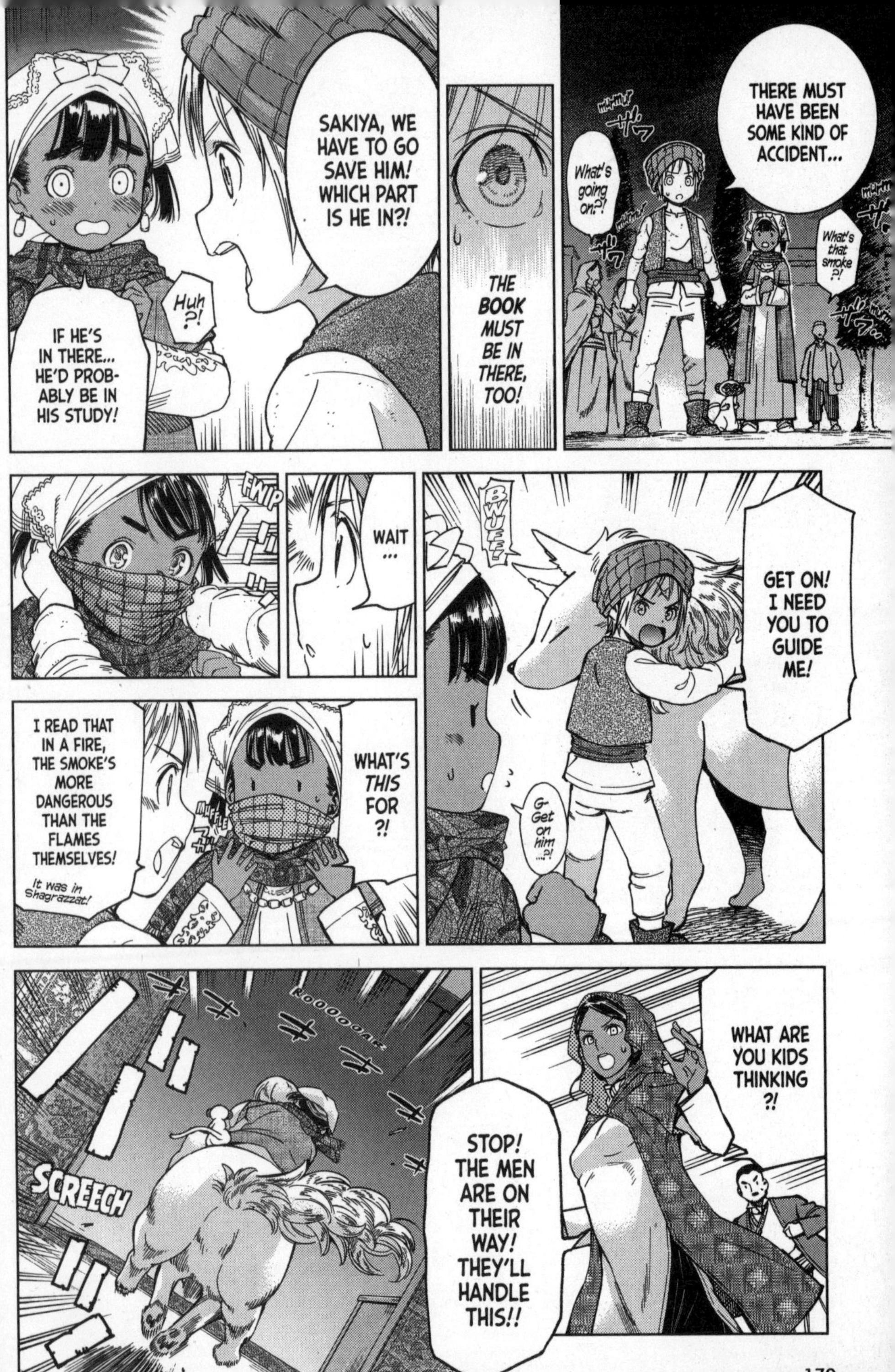
THERE MUST HAVE BEEN SOME KIND OF ACCIDENT...
What's going on?!
What's that smoke?!
THE BOOK MUST BE IN THERE, TOO!
SAKIYA, WE HAVE TO GO SAVE HIM! WHICH PART IS HE IN?!
Huh?!
IF HE'S IN THERE... HE'D PROBABLY BE IN HIS STUDY!
BWUFF!
GET ON! I NEED YOU TO GUIDE ME!
G-Get on him...?!
WAIT...
FWIP
WHAT'S THIS FOR?!
MUFFLE
I READ THAT IN A FIRE, THE SMOKE'S MORE DANGEROUS THAN THE FLAMES THEMSELVES!
It was in Shagrazzat!
WHAT ARE YOU KIDS THINKING?!
STOP! THE MEN ARE ON THEIR WAY! THEY'LL HANDLE THIS!!
ROOOOOAR
SCREECH

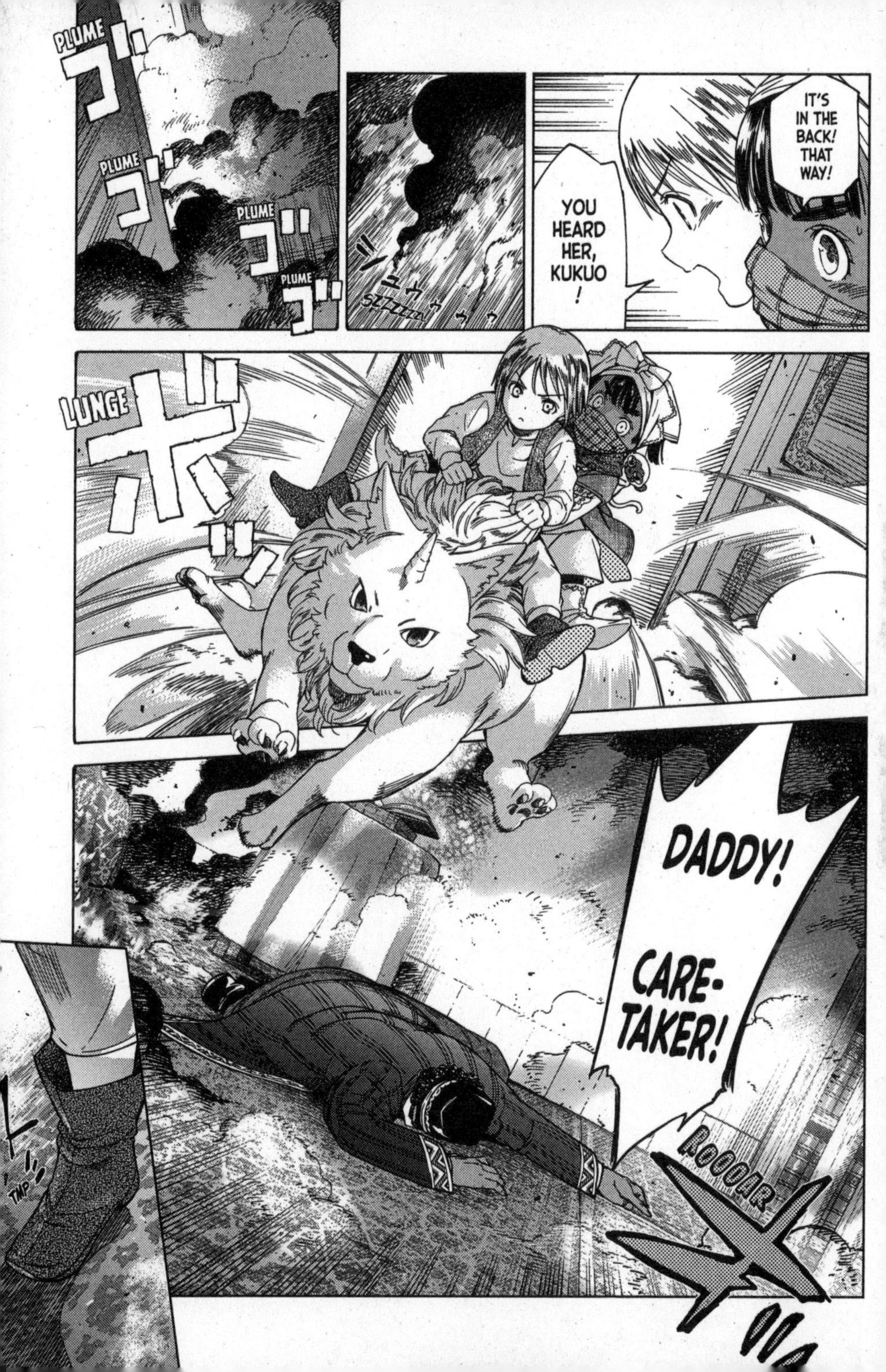
IT'S IN THE BACK! THAT WAY!
YOU HEARD HER, KUKUO!
SZZZZZZ
PLUME
PLUME
PLUME
PLUME
LUNGE
DADDY!
CARE-TAKER!
ROOOAR
TMP

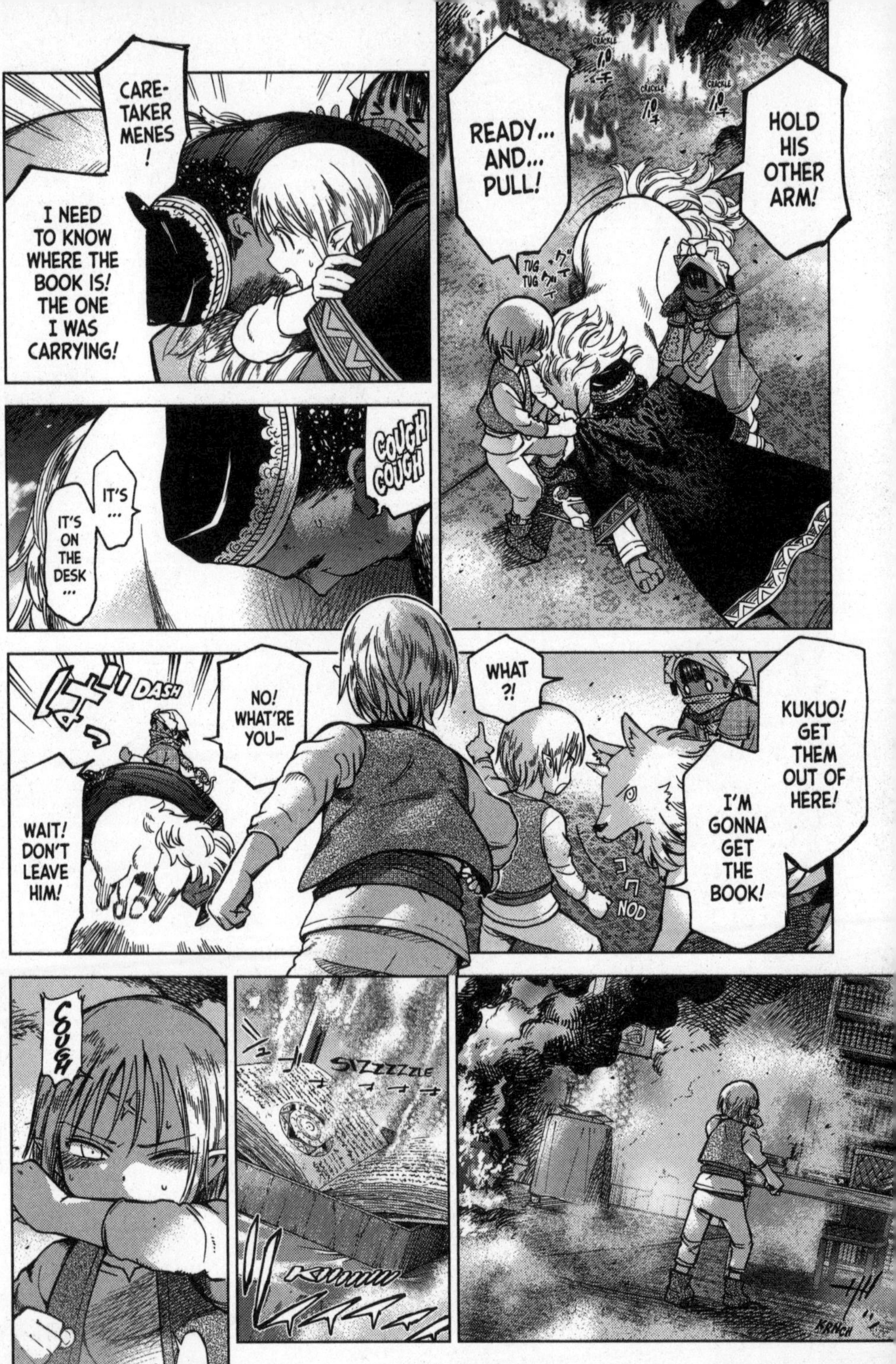

CRACKLE
CRACKLE
CRACKLE
HOLD HIS OTHER ARM!
READY... AND... PULL!
TUG TUG
CARE-TAKER MENES!
I NEED TO KNOW WHERE THE BOOK IS! THE ONE I WAS CARRYING!
COUGH COUGH
IT'S...
IT'S ON THE DESK...
KUKUO! GET THEM OUT OF HERE!
I'M GONNA GET THE BOOK!
WHAT?!
NOD
NO! WHAT'RE YOU-
DASH
WAIT! DON'T LEAVE HIM!
KRNCH
SIZZZZZLE
COUGH
HFF..

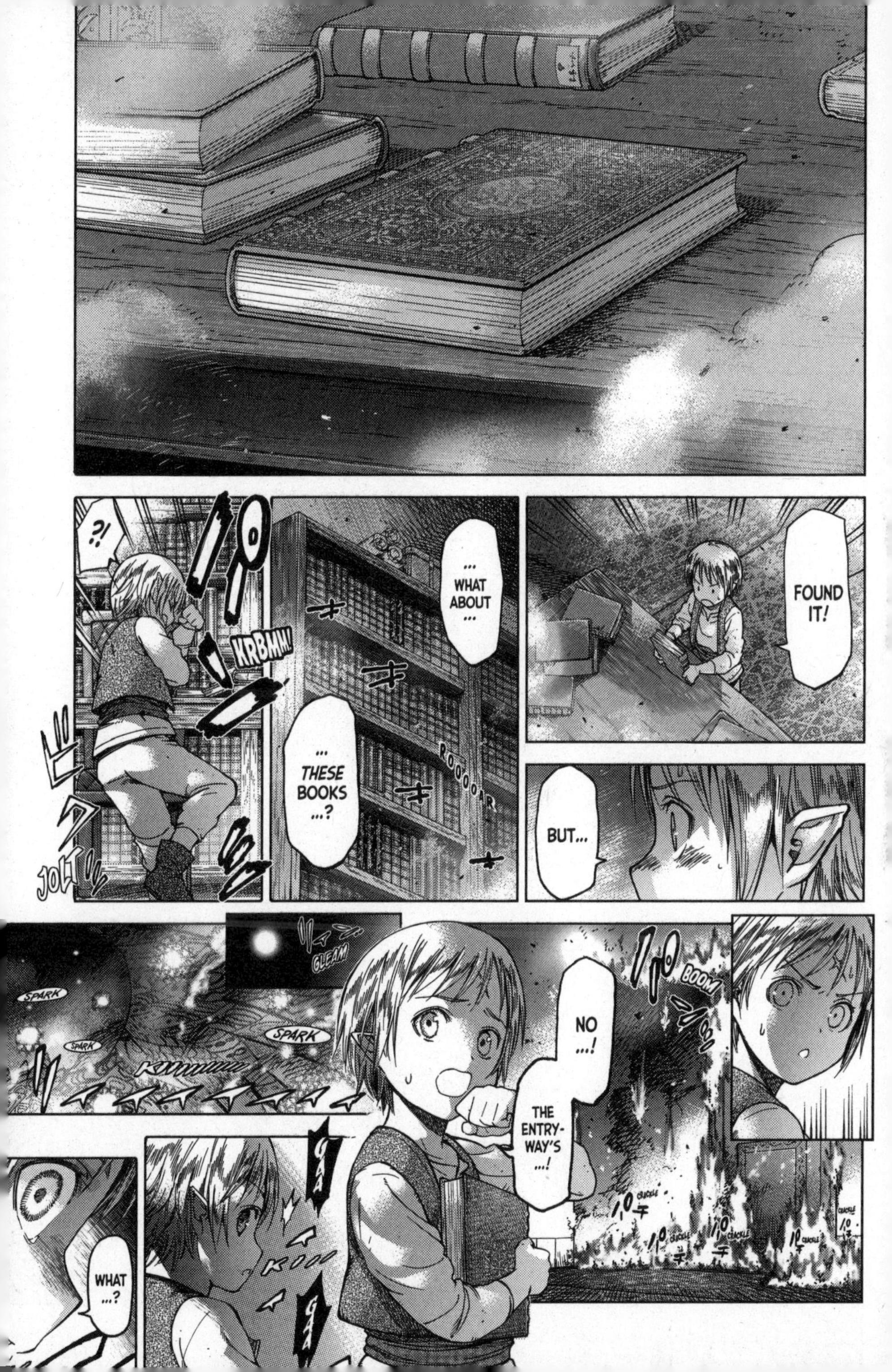
FOUND IT!
BUT...
... WHAT ABOUT ...
... THESE BOOKS ...?
ROOOOAR
?!
KRBMM!
BOOM
NO ...!
THE ENTRY-WAY'S ...!
CRACKLE
CRACKLE
CRACKLE
CRACKLE
GLEAM
SPARK
SPARK
SPARK
WHAT ...?

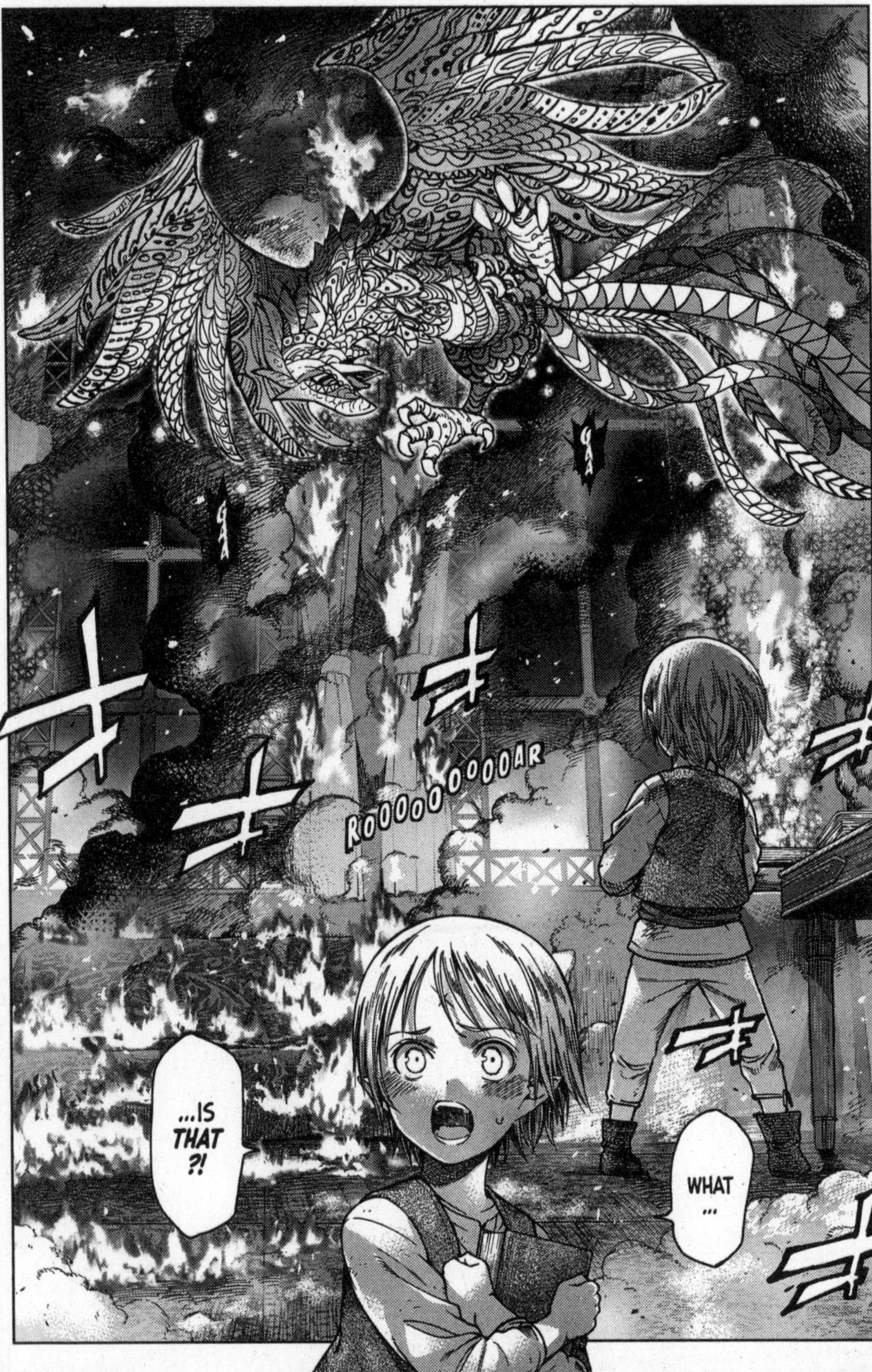
GAA
GAA
ROOOOOOOOOAR
WHAT ...
...IS THAT ?!

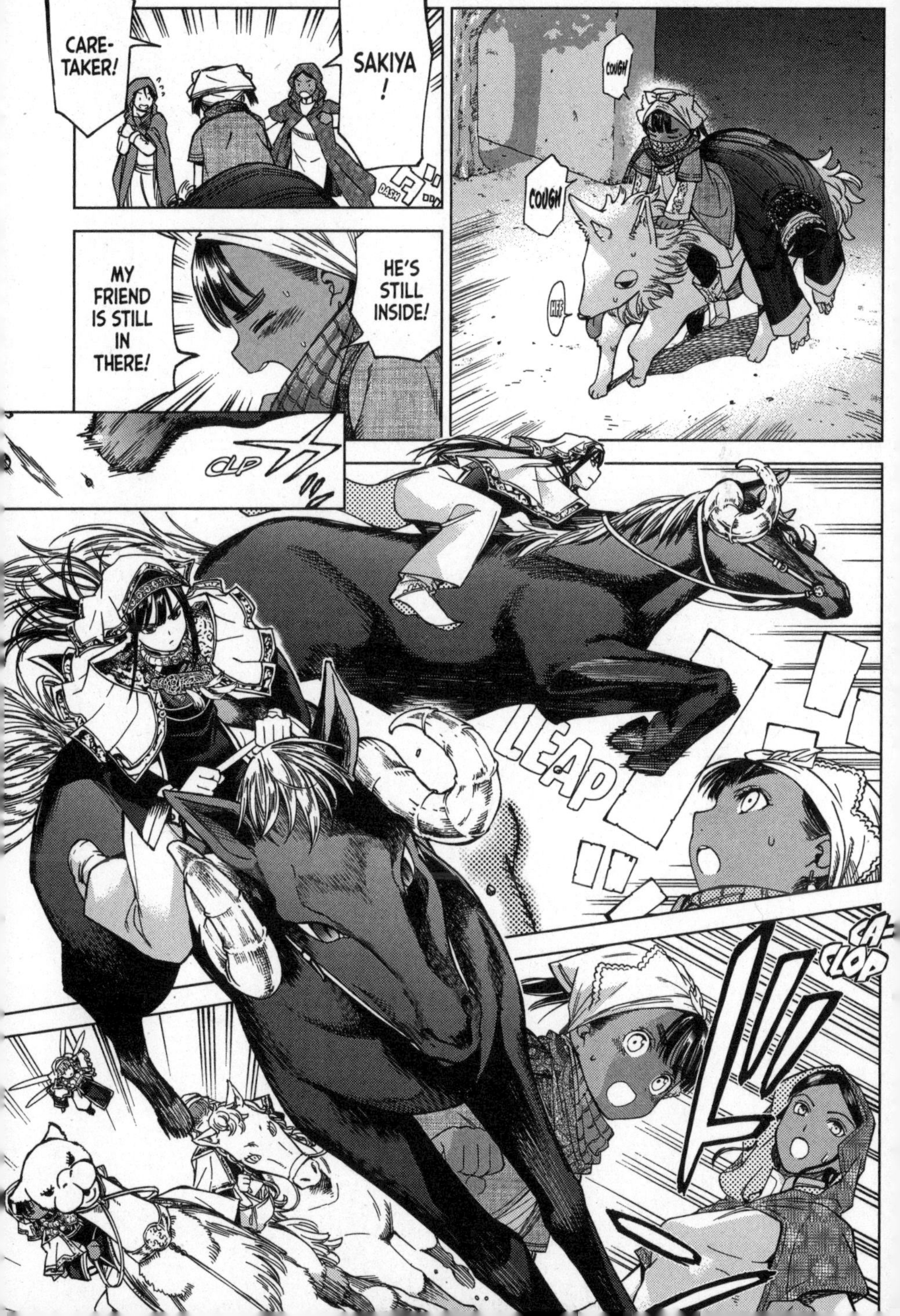
COUGH
COUGH
HFF
SAKIYA!
CARE-TAKER!
DASH
HE'S STILL INSIDE!
MY FRIEND IS STILL IN THERE!
CLP
LEAP
CA-CLOP

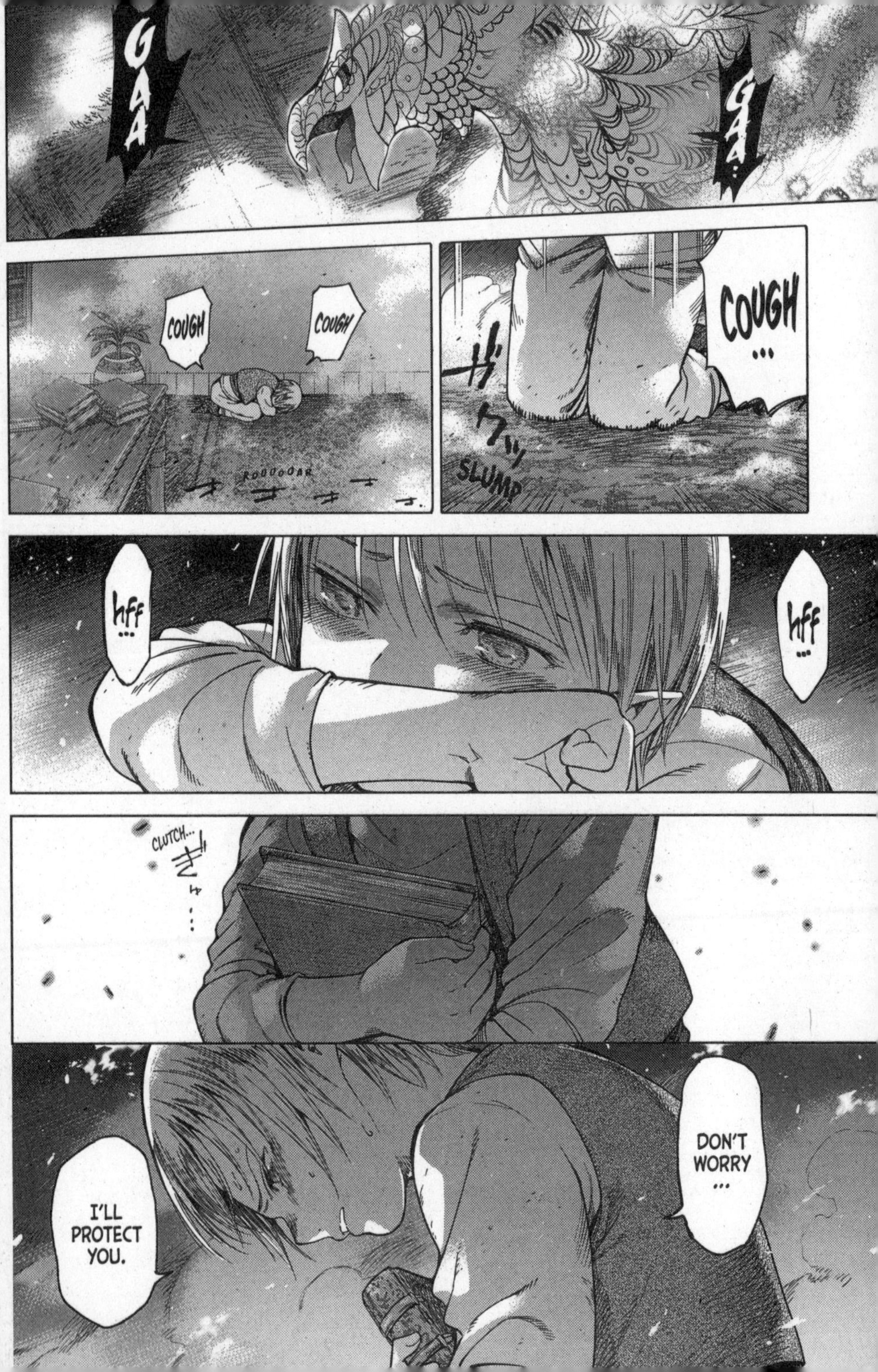

GAA
GAA
COUGH...
SLUMP
COUGH
COUGH
ROOOOOAR
hff...
hff...
CLUTCH...
DON'T WORRY...
I'LL PROTECT YOU.

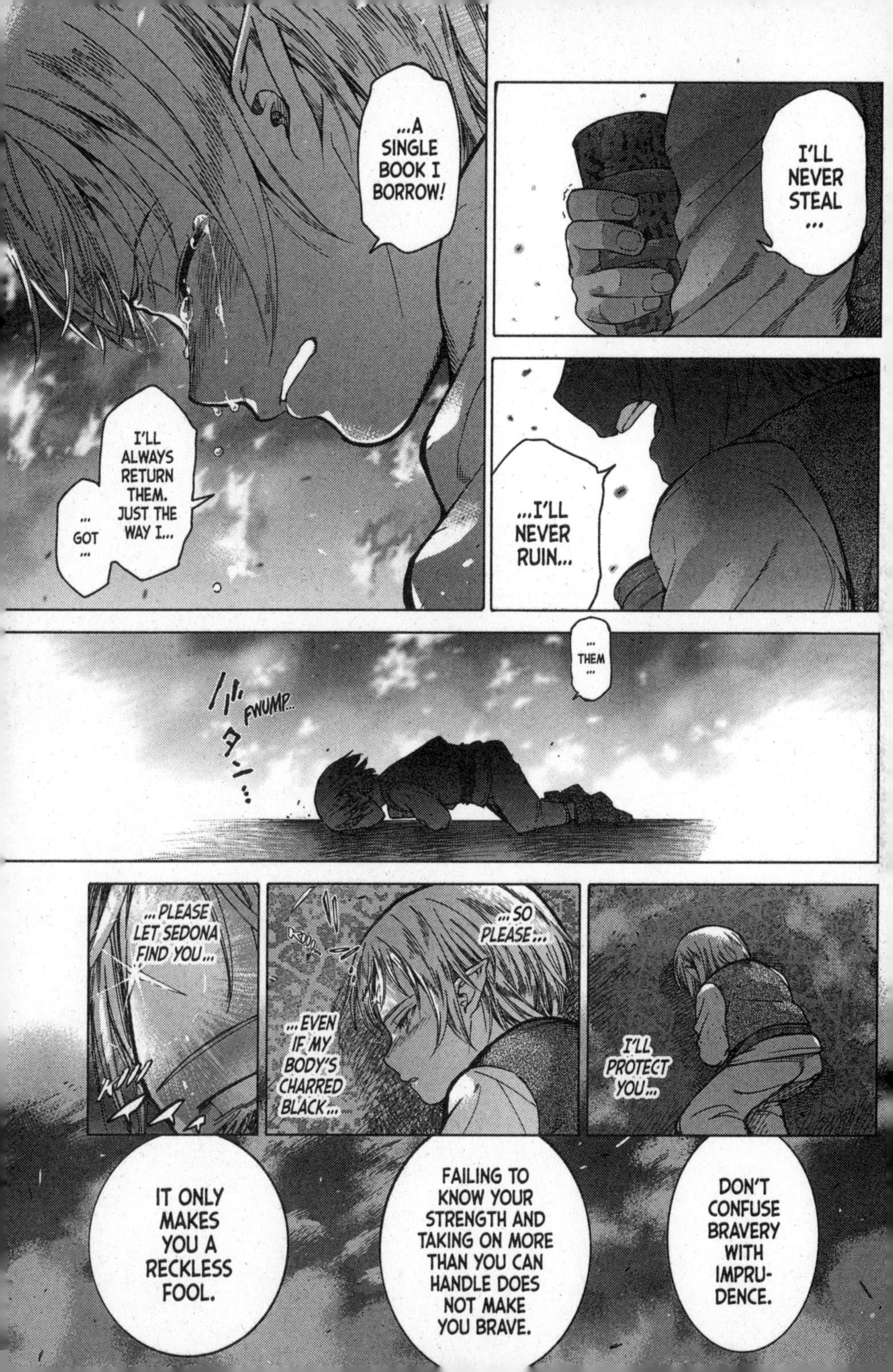
I'LL NEVER STEAL...
...I'LL NEVER RUIN...
...A SINGLE BOOK I BORROW!
I'LL ALWAYS RETURN THEM. JUST THE WAY I...
...GOT...
...THEM...
FWUMP...
I'LL PROTECT YOU...
...SO PLEASE...
...EVEN IF MY BODY'S CHARRED BLACK...
...PLEASE LET SEDONA FIND YOU...
DON'T CONFUSE BRAVERY WITH IMPRU-DENCE.
FAILING TO KNOW YOUR STRENGTH AND TAKING ON MORE THAN YOU CAN HANDLE DOES NOT MAKE YOU BRAVE.
IT ONLY MAKES YOU A RECKLESS FOOL.

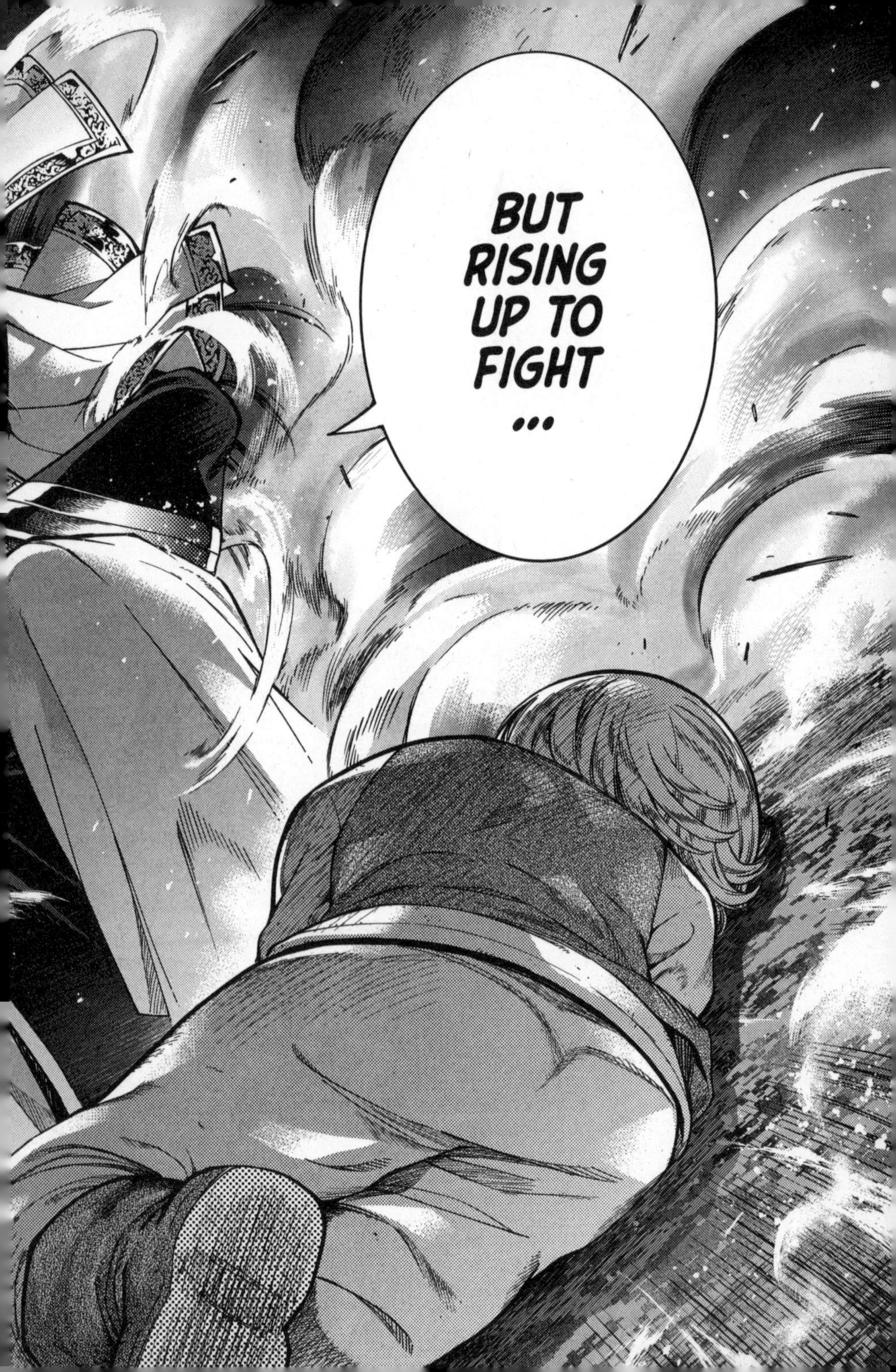
BUT RISING UP TO FIGHT ...

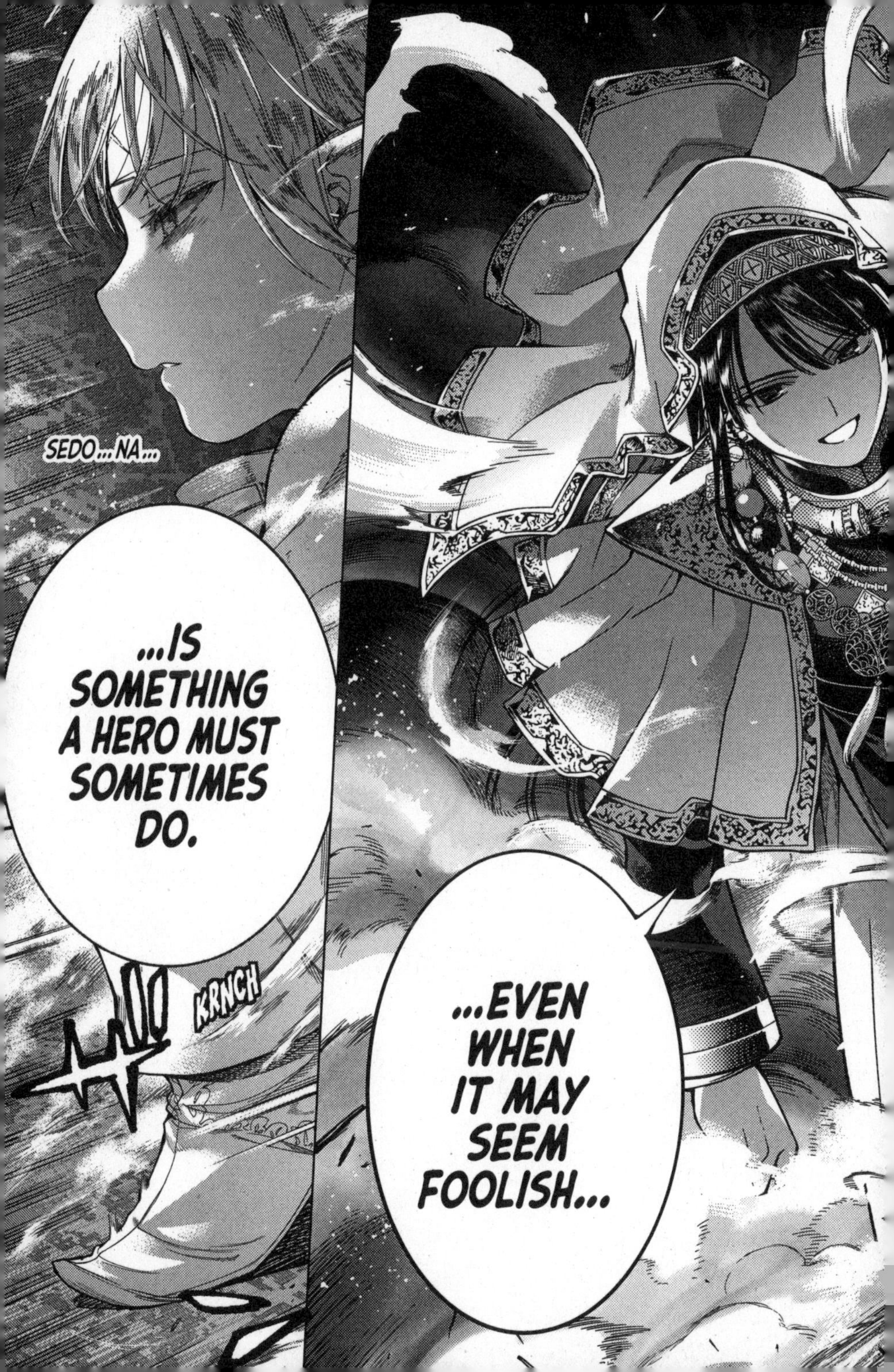
...EVEN WHEN IT MAY SEEM FOOLISH...
SEDO...NA...
...IS SOMETHING A HERO MUST SOMETIMES DO.
KRNCH

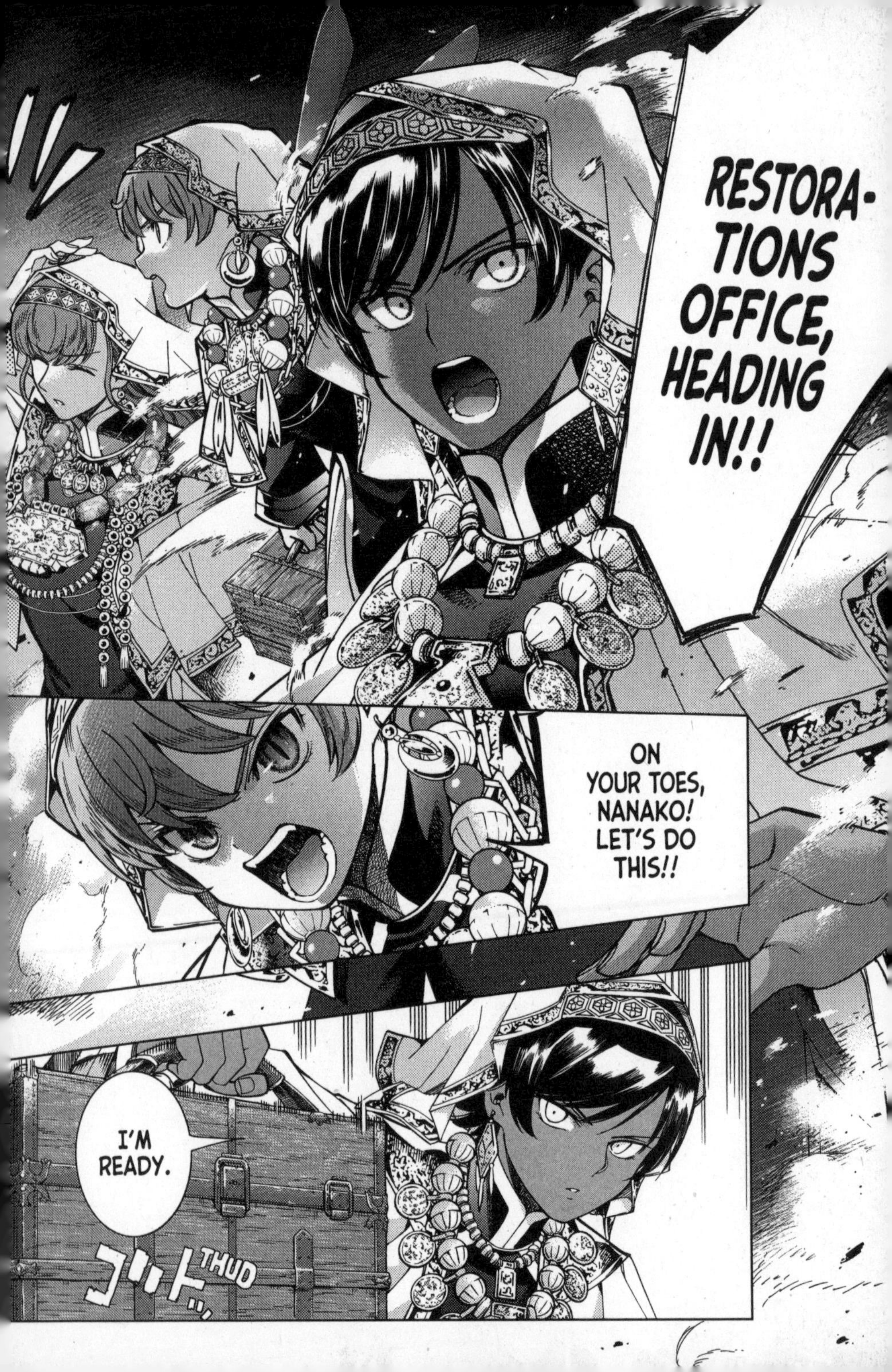
RESTORATIONS OFFICE, HEADING IN!!
ON YOUR TOES, NANAKO! LET'S DO THIS!!
I'M READY.
ゴット
THUD

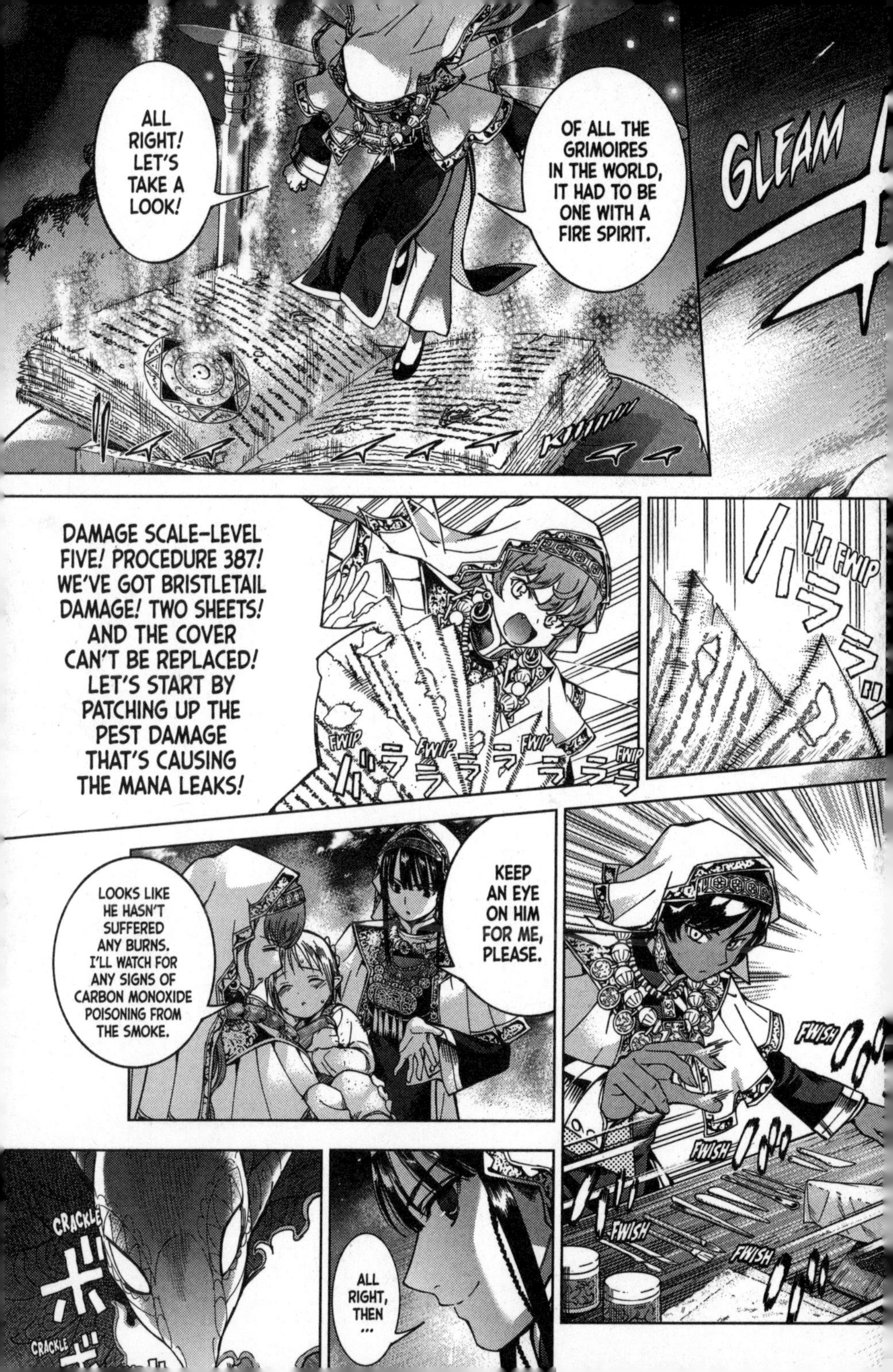
GLEAM
OF ALL THE GRIMOIRES IN THE WORLD, IT HAD TO BE ONE WITH A FIRE SPIRIT.
ALL RIGHT! LET'S TAKE A LOOK!
FWIP
DAMAGE SCALE-LEVEL FIVE! PROCEDURE 387! WE'VE GOT BRISTLETAIL DAMAGE! TWO SHEETS! AND THE COVER CAN'T BE REPLACED! LET'S START BY PATCHING UP THE PEST DAMAGE THAT'S CAUSING THE MANA LEAKS!
FWIP FWIP FWIP FWIP
FWISH
FWISH
FWISH
FWISH
KEEP AN EYE ON HIM FOR ME, PLEASE.
LOOKS LIKE HE HASN'T SUFFERED ANY BURNS. I'LL WATCH FOR ANY SIGNS OF CARBON MONOXIDE POISONING FROM THE SMOKE.
ALL RIGHT, THEN...
CRACKLE
CRACKLE

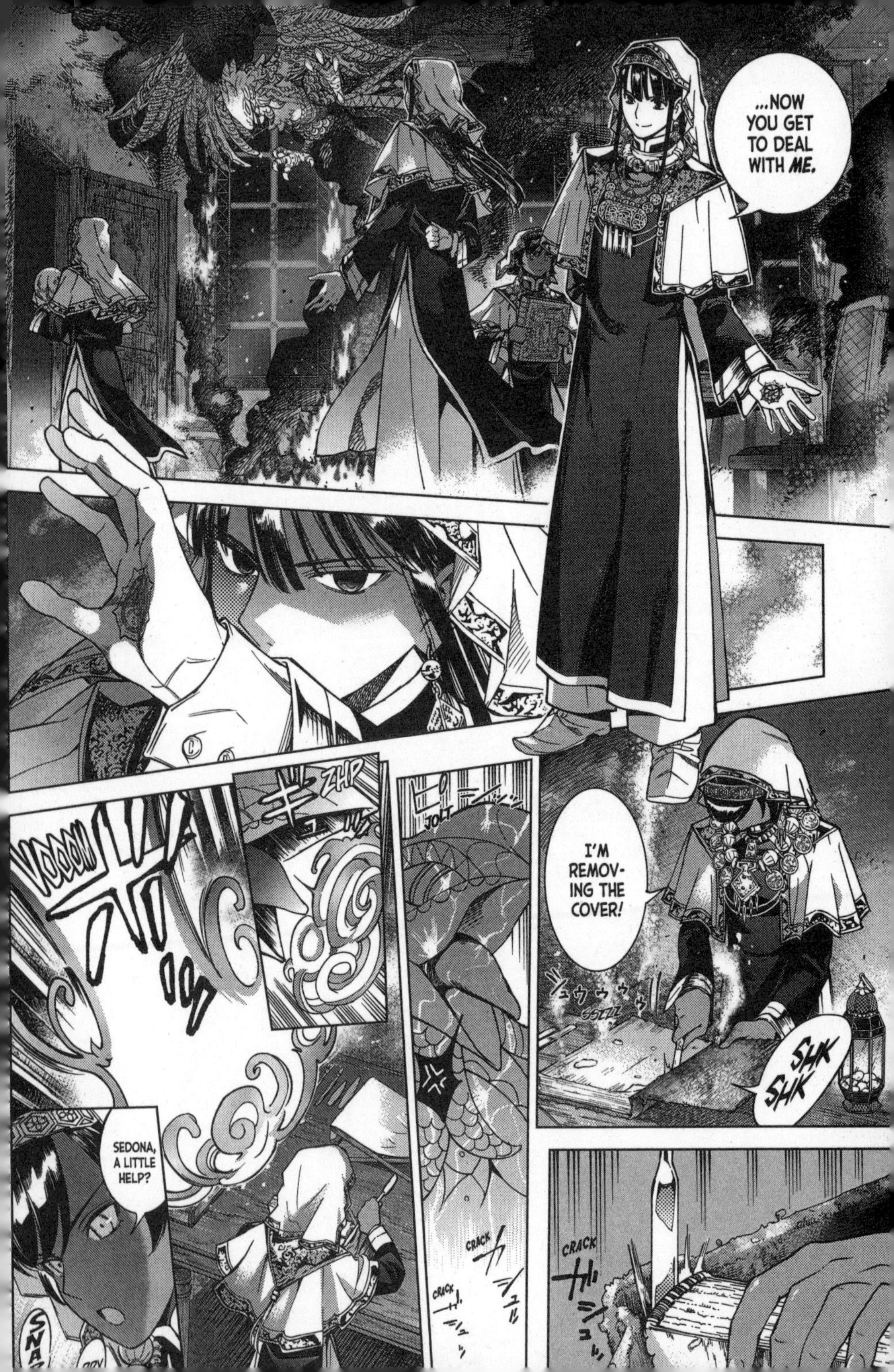
...NOW YOU GET TO DEAL WITH ME.
I'M REMOVING THE COVER!
SSZZZ
SHK SHK
ZHP
JOLT
VOOOOM
CRACK
CRACK
SEDONA, A LITTLE HELP?
CRACK

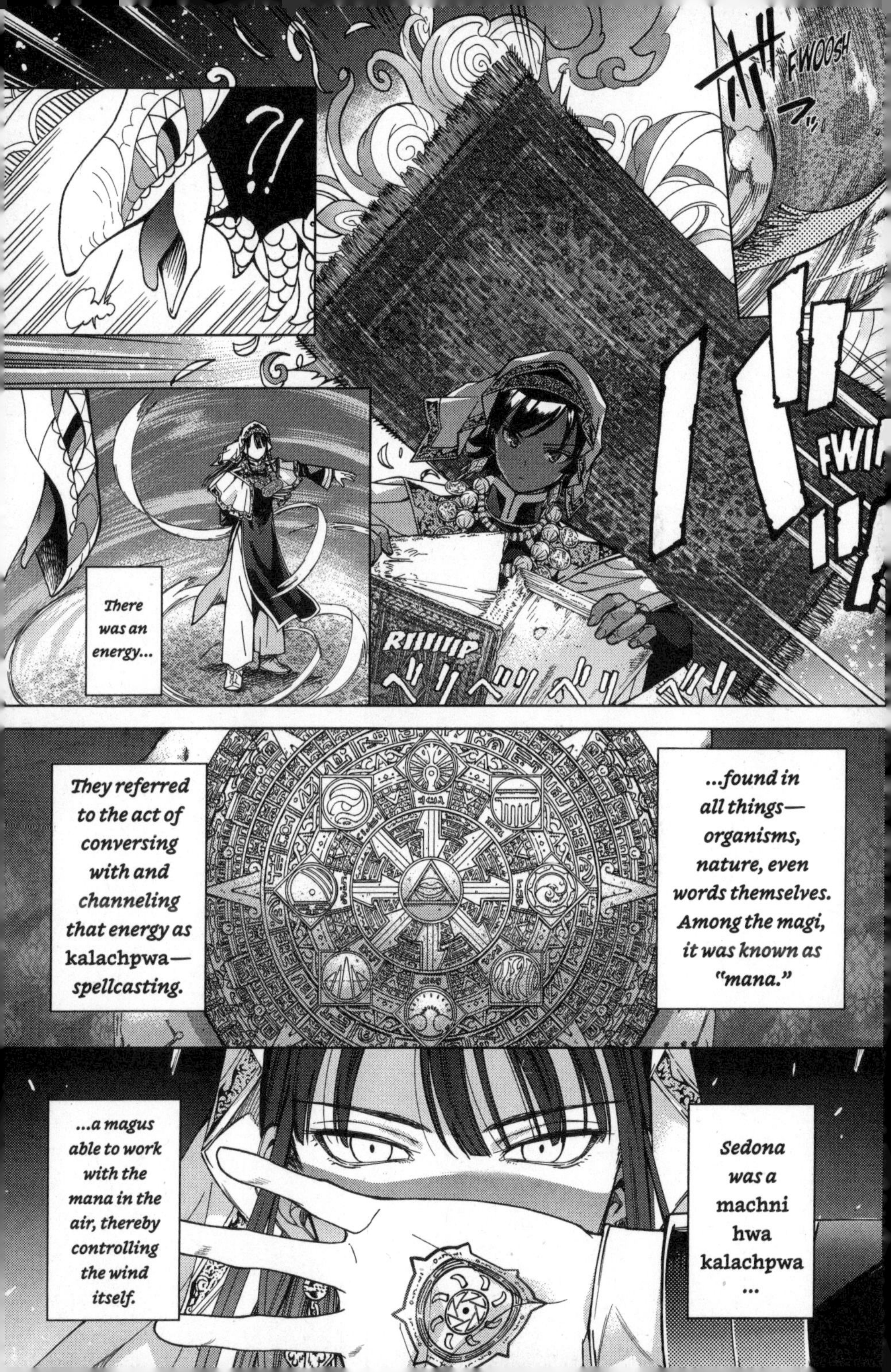
FWOOSH
?!
FWI
RIIIIIP
There was an energy...
...found in all things—organisms, nature, even words themselves. Among the magi, it was known as "mana."
They referred to the act of conversing with and channeling that energy as kalachpwa—spellcasting.
Sedona was a machni hwa kalachpwa...
...a magus able to work with the mana in the air, thereby controlling the wind itself.

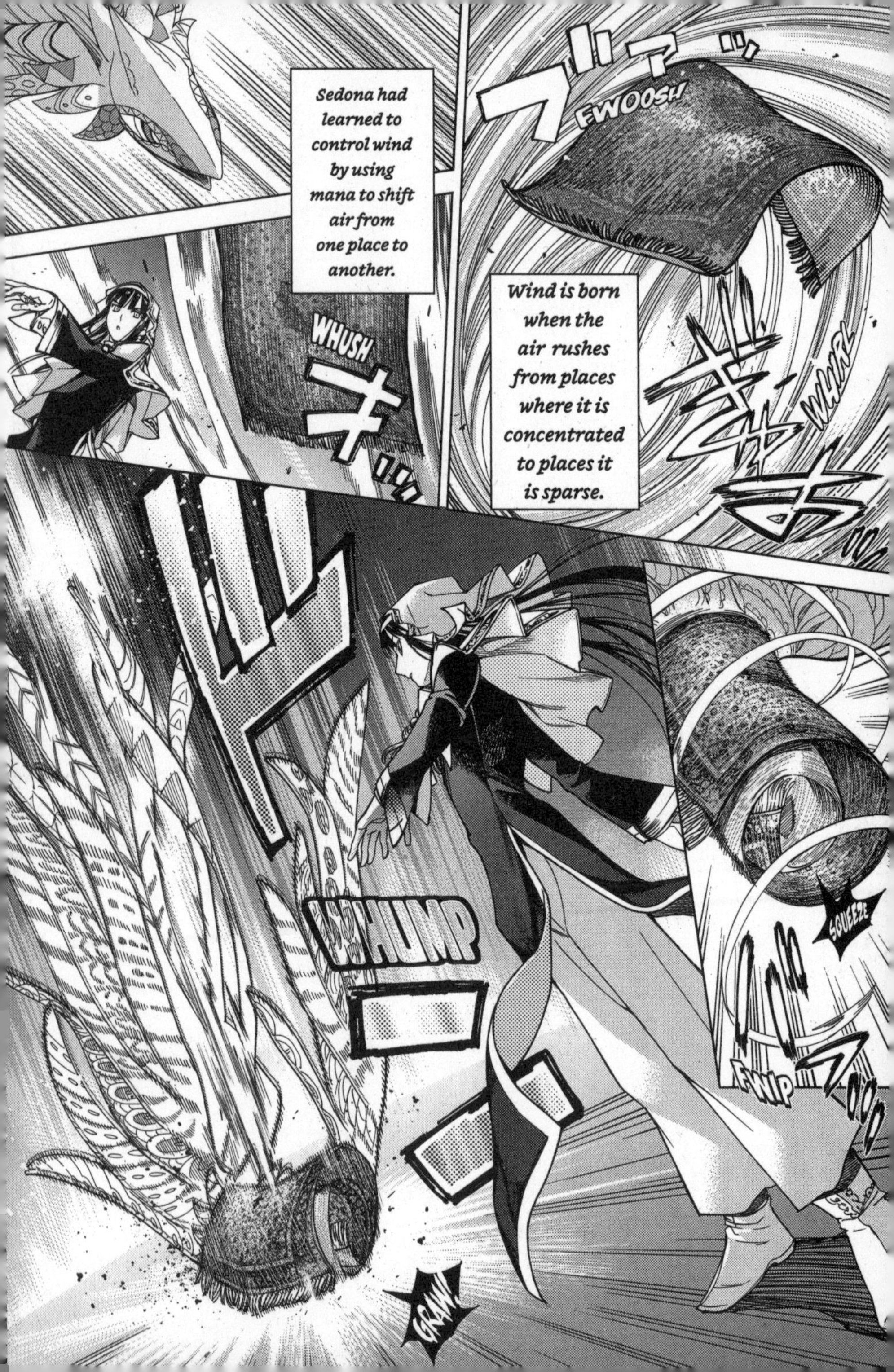
FWOOSH
Wind is born when the air rushes from places where it is concentrated to places it is sparse.
WHIRL
Sedona had learned to control wind by using mana to shift air from one place to another.
WHUSH
SQUEEZE
FWIP
WHUMP
GRAW

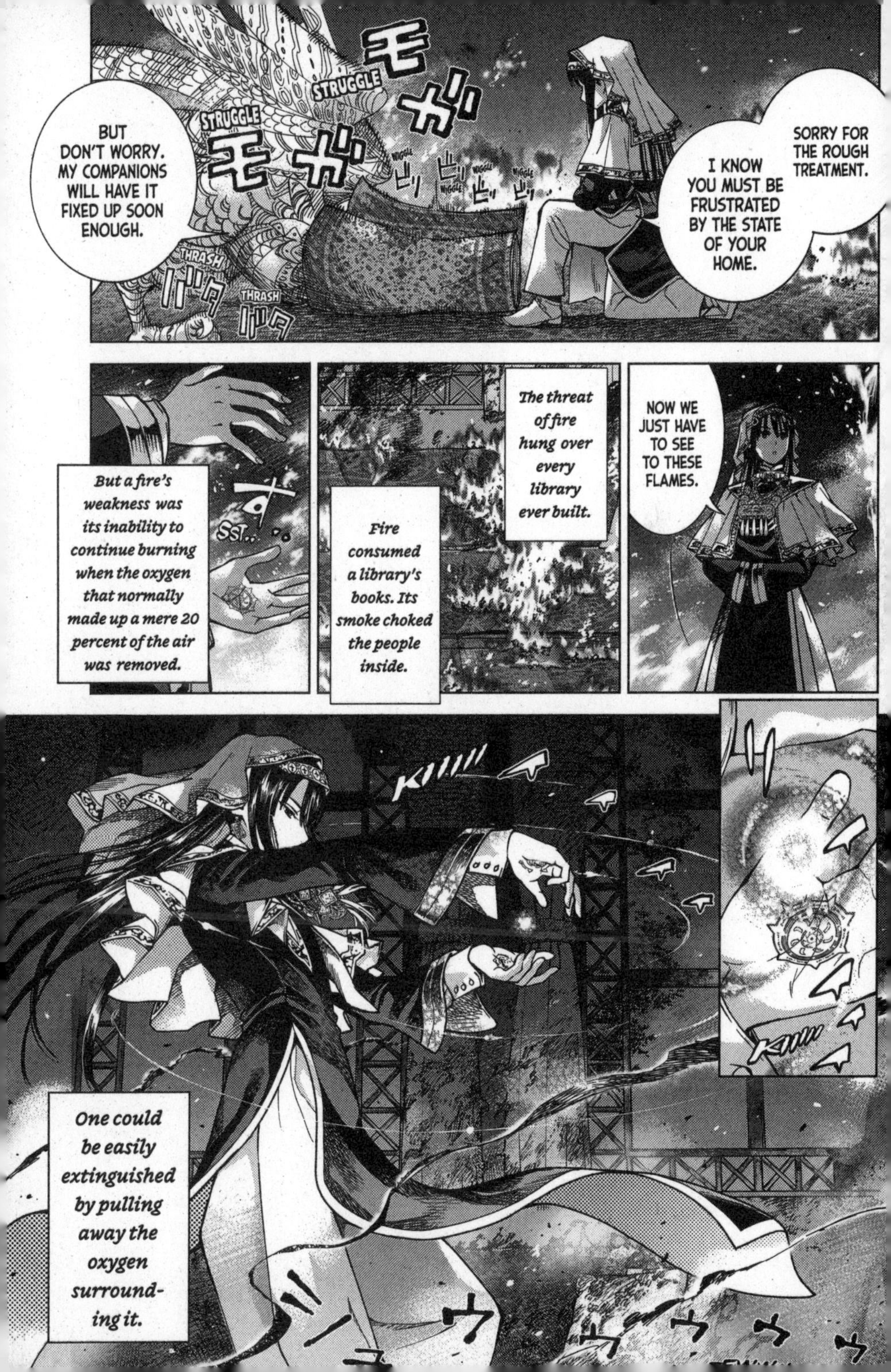

SORRY FOR THE ROUGH TREATMENT.
I KNOW YOU MUST BE FRUSTRATED BY THE STATE OF YOUR HOME.
STRUGGLE
STRUGGLE
WIGGLE
WIGGLE
WIGGLE
WIGGLE
BUT DON'T WORRY. MY COMPANIONS WILL HAVE IT FIXED UP SOON ENOUGH.
THRASH
THRASH
NOW WE JUST HAVE TO SEE TO THESE FLAMES.
The threat of fire hung over every library ever built.
Fire consumed a library's books. Its smoke choked the people inside.
SST..
But a fire's weakness was its inability to continue burning when the oxygen that normally made up a mere 20 percent of the air was removed.
One could be easily extinguished by pulling away the oxygen surrounding it.

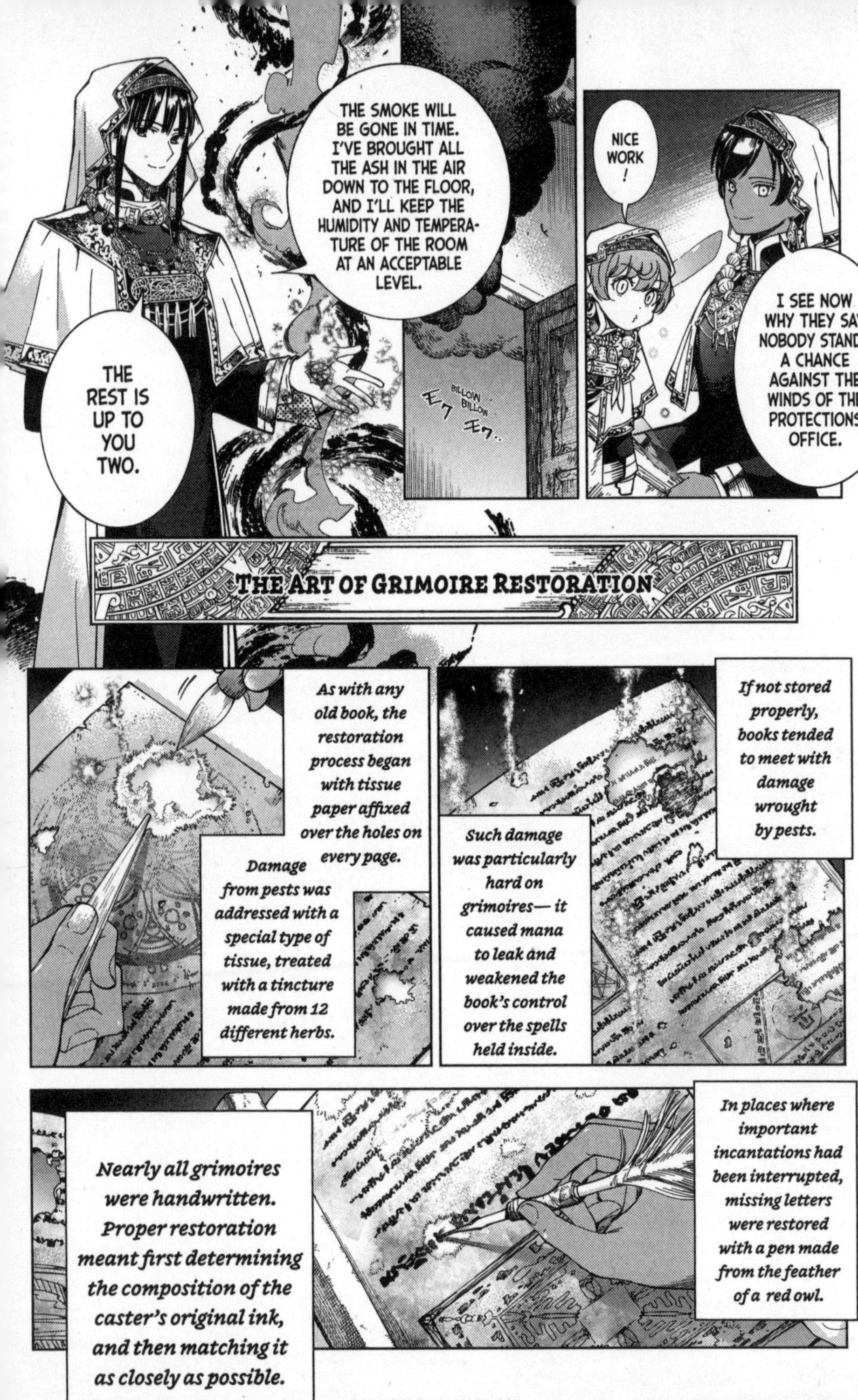
NICE WORK !
I SEE NOW WHY THEY SAY NOBODY STANDS A CHANCE AGAINST THE WINDS OF THE PROTECTIONS OFFICE.
THE SMOKE WILL BE GONE IN TIME. I'VE BROUGHT ALL THE ASH IN THE AIR DOWN TO THE FLOOR, AND I'LL KEEP THE HUMIDITY AND TEMPERATURE OF THE ROOM AT AN ACCEPTABLE LEVEL.
BILLOW BILLOW
THE REST IS UP TO YOU TWO.
THE ART OF GRIMOIRE RESTORATION
If not stored properly, books tended to meet with damage wrought by pests.
Such damage was particularly hard on grimoires— it caused mana to leak and weakened the book's control over the spells held inside.
As with any old book, the restoration process began with tissue paper affixed over the holes on every page.
Damage from pests was addressed with a special type of tissue, treated with a tincture made from 12 different herbs.
In places where important incantations had been interrupted, missing letters were restored with a pen made from the feather of a red owl.
Nearly all grimoires were handwritten. Proper restoration meant first determining the composition of the caster's original ink, and then matching it as closely as possible.

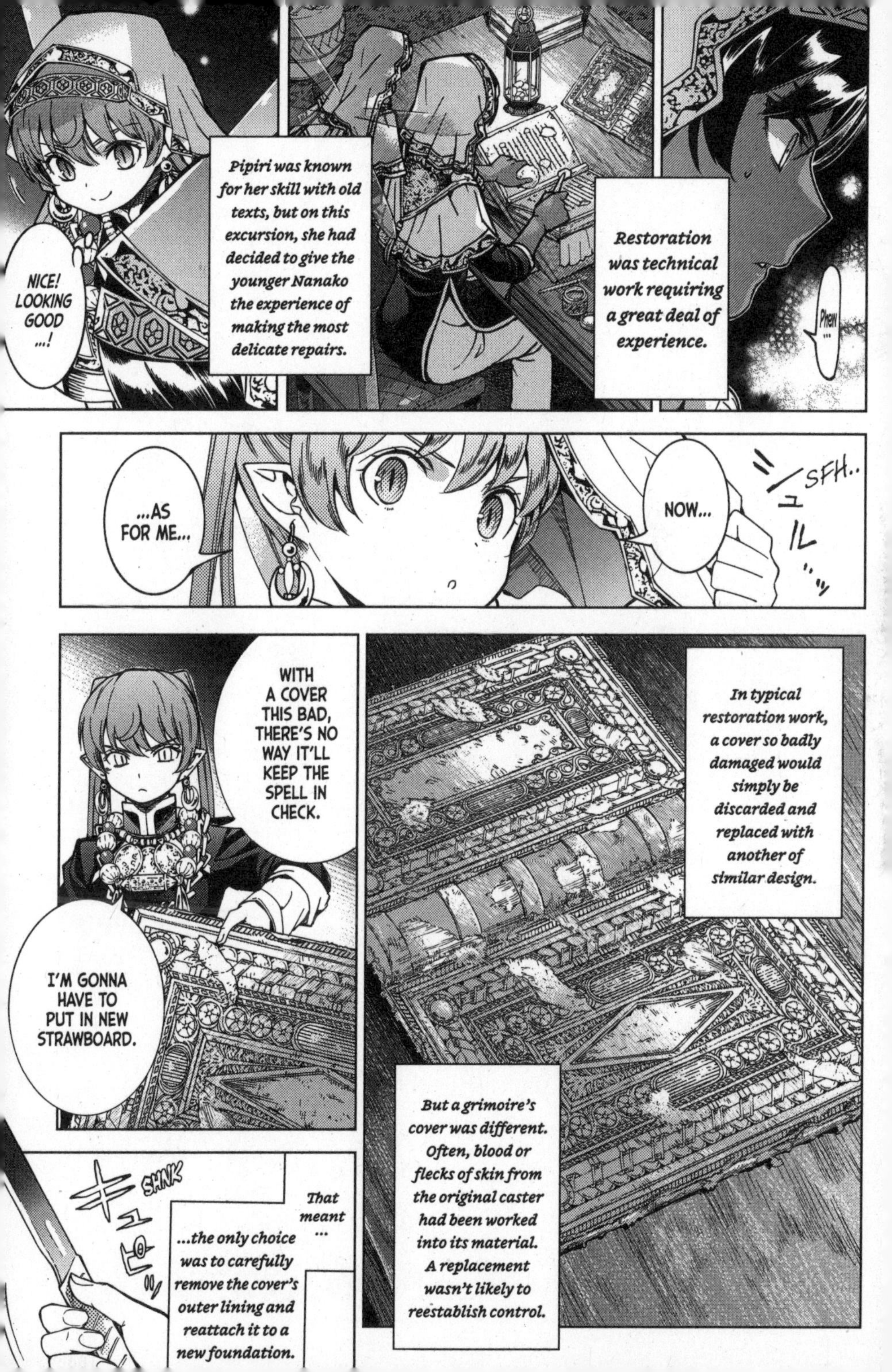

Restoration was technical work requiring a great deal of experience.
Phew ...
Pipiri was known for her skill with old texts, but on this excursion, she had decided to give the younger Nanako the experience of making the most delicate repairs.
NICE! LOOKING GOOD ...!
SFH..
NOW...
...AS FOR ME...
In typical restoration work, a cover so badly damaged would simply be discarded and replaced with another of similar design.
But a grimoire's cover was different. Often, blood or flecks of skin from the original caster had been worked into its material. A replacement wasn't likely to reestablish control.
WITH A COVER THIS BAD, THERE'S NO WAY IT'LL KEEP THE SPELL IN CHECK.
I'M GONNA HAVE TO PUT IN NEW STRAWBOARD.
SHNK
That meant ...
...the only choice was to carefully remove the cover's outer lining and reattach it to a new foundation.

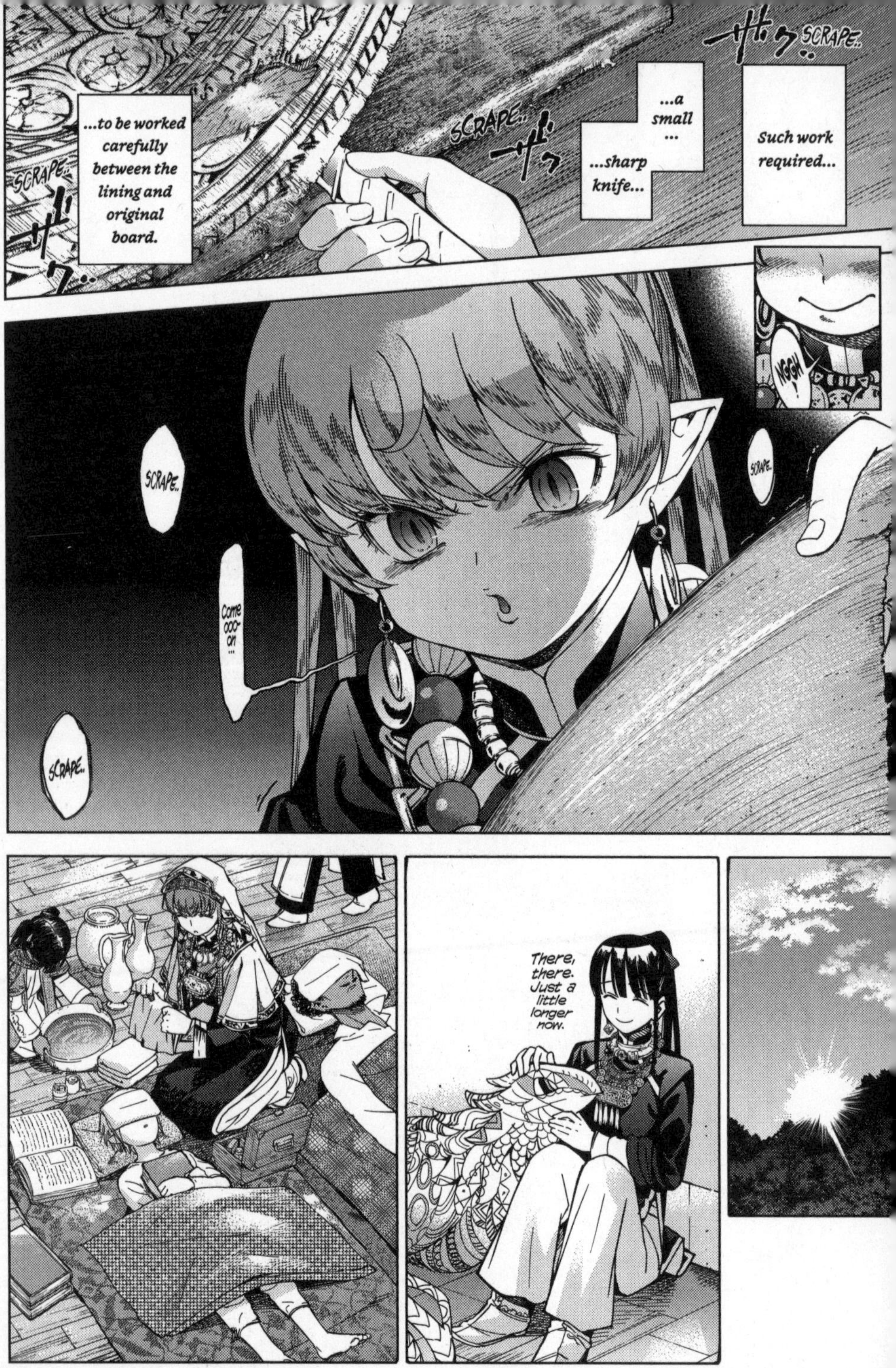
ザク SCRAPE..
Such work required...
...a small ...
...sharp knife...
SCRAPE.. ザク
...to be worked carefully between the lining and original board.
SCRAPE.. ザグ
NGGH!
SCRAPE..
SCRAPE..
Come ooo-on ...
SCRAPE..
There, there. Just a little longer now.

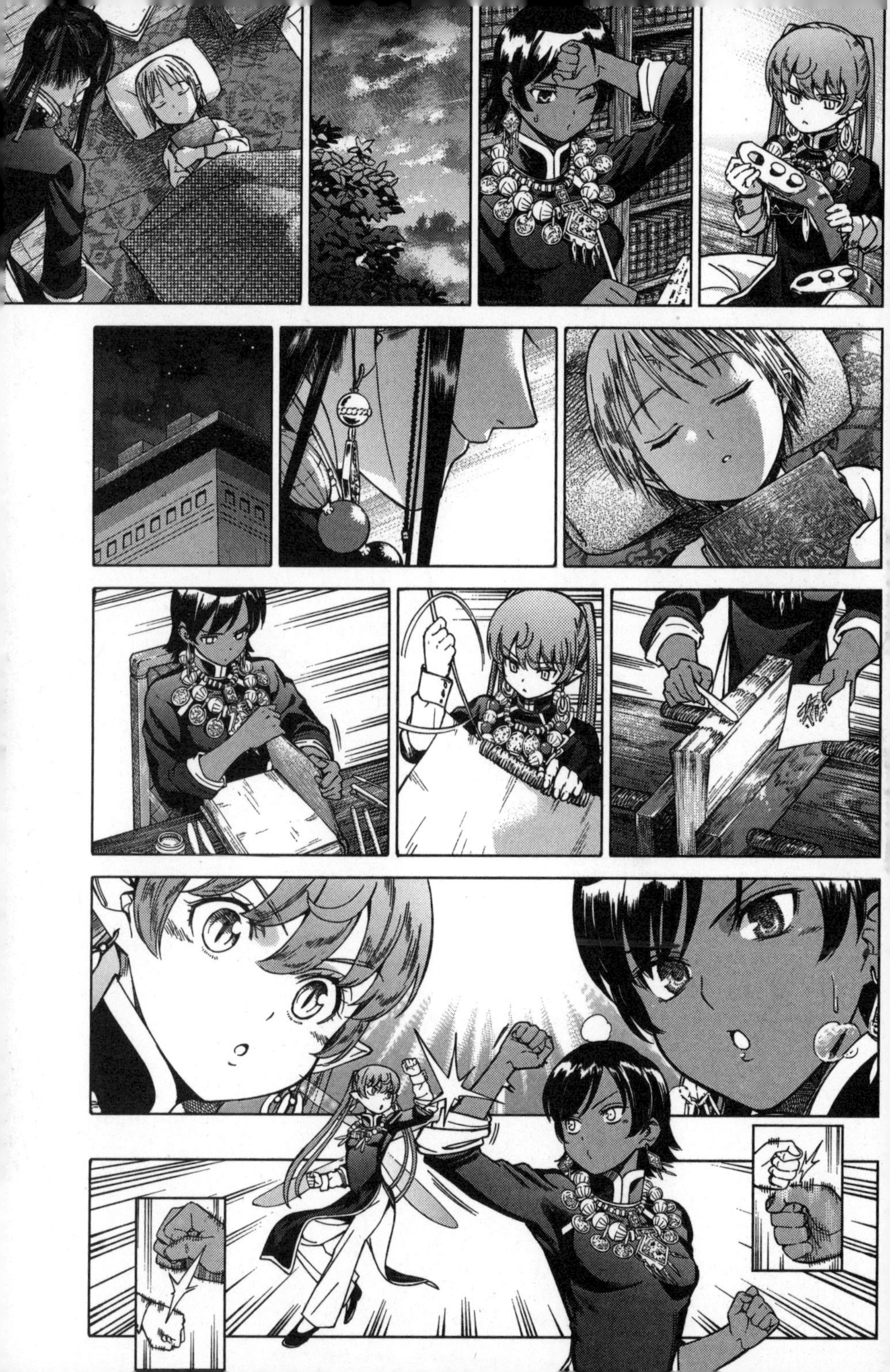

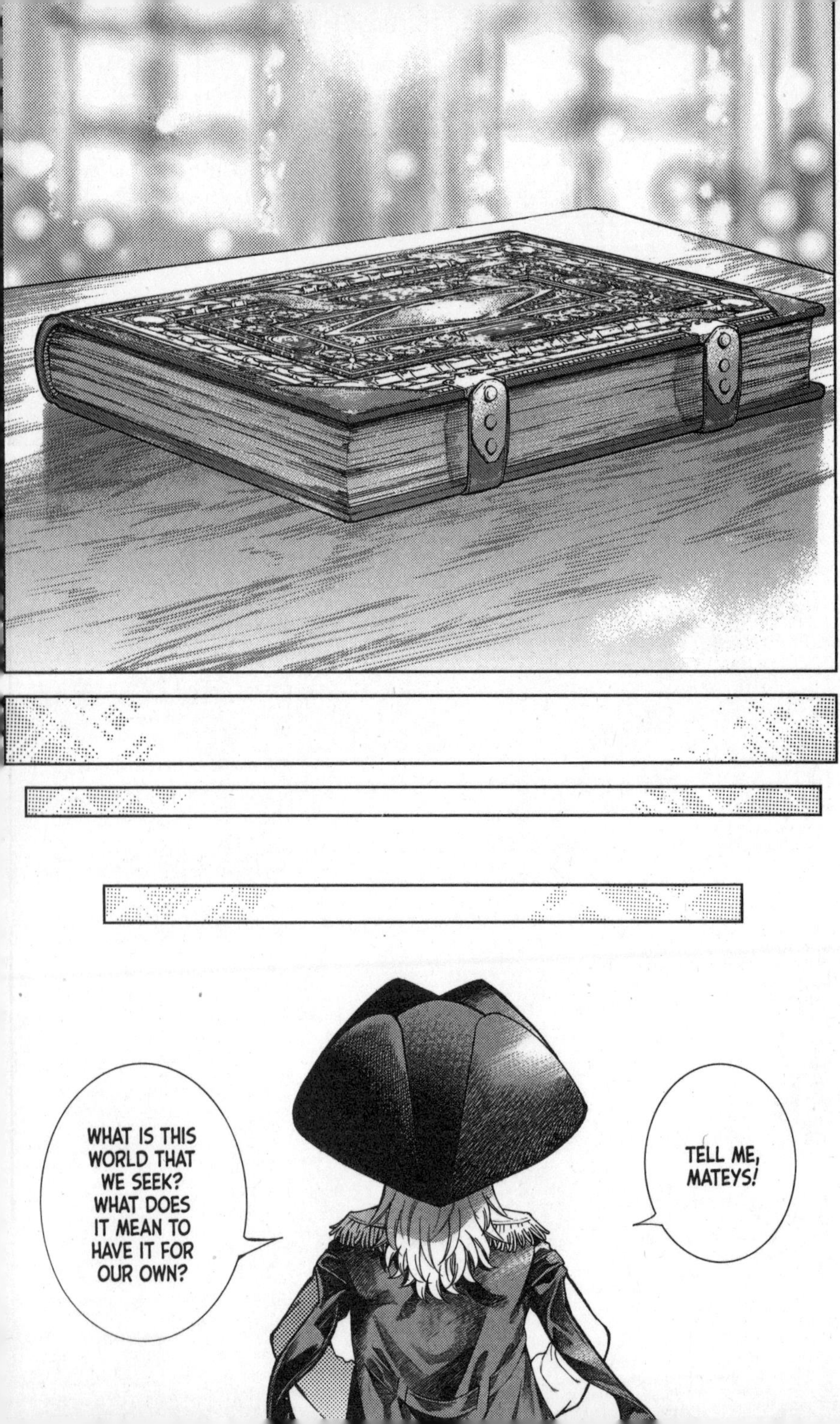
TELL ME, MATEYS!
WHAT IS THIS WORLD THAT WE SEEK? WHAT DOES IT MEAN TO HAVE IT FOR OUR OWN?

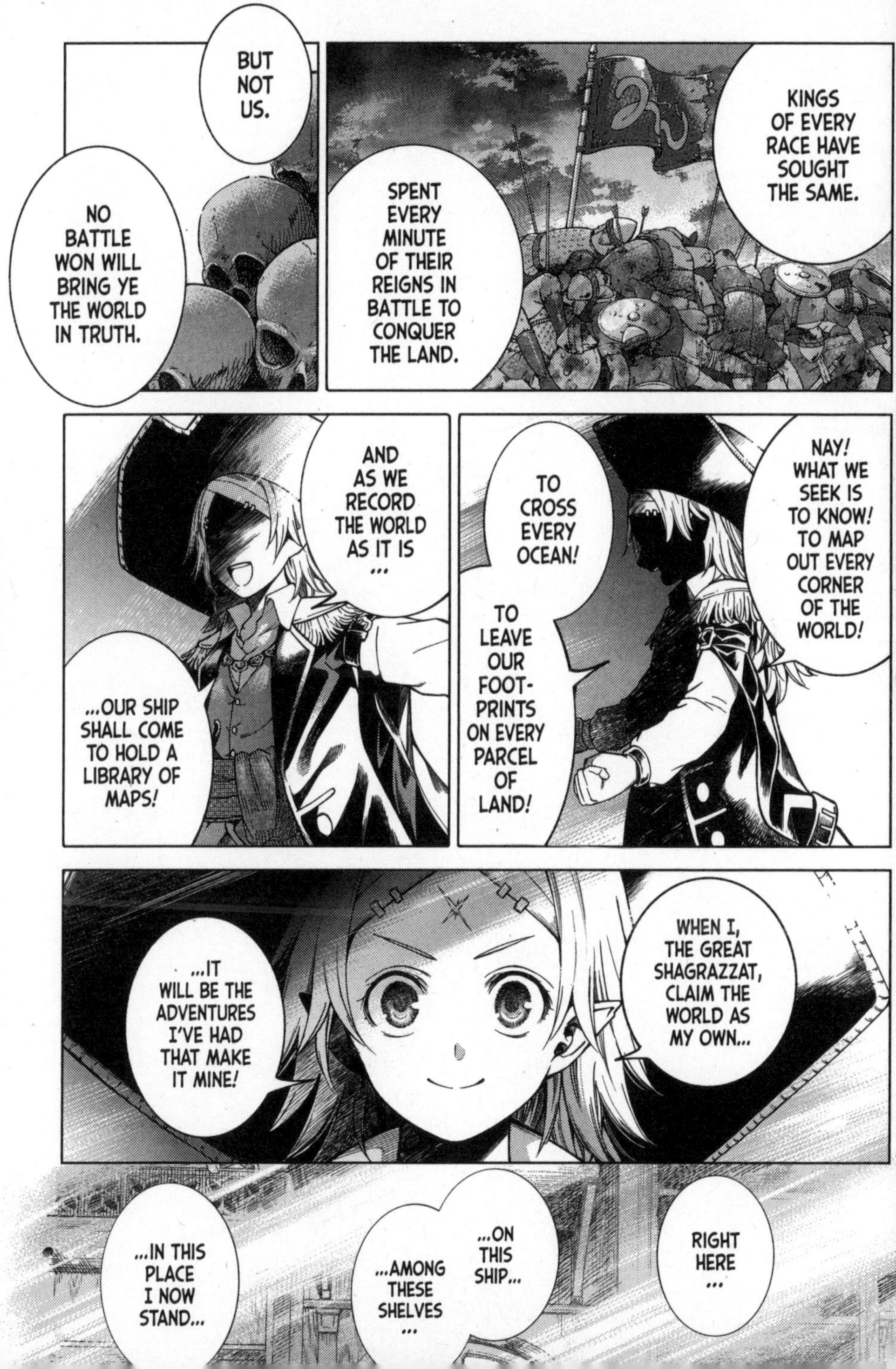
KINGS OF EVERY RACE HAVE SOUGHT THE SAME.
SPENT EVERY MINUTE OF THEIR REIGNS IN BATTLE TO CONQUER THE LAND.
BUT NOT US.
NO BATTLE WON WILL BRING YE THE WORLD IN TRUTH.
NAY! WHAT WE SEEK IS TO KNOW! TO MAP OUT EVERY CORNER OF THE WORLD!
TO CROSS EVERY OCEAN!
TO LEAVE OUR FOOT-PRINTS ON EVERY PARCEL OF LAND!
AND AS WE RECORD THE WORLD AS IT IS ...
...OUR SHIP SHALL COME TO HOLD A LIBRARY OF MAPS!
WHEN I, THE GREAT SHAGRAZZAT, CLAIM THE WORLD AS MY OWN...
...IT WILL BE THE ADVENTURES I'VE HAD THAT MAKE IT MINE!
RIGHT HERE ...
...ON THIS SHIP...
...AMONG THESE SHELVES ...
...IN THIS PLACE I NOW STAND...

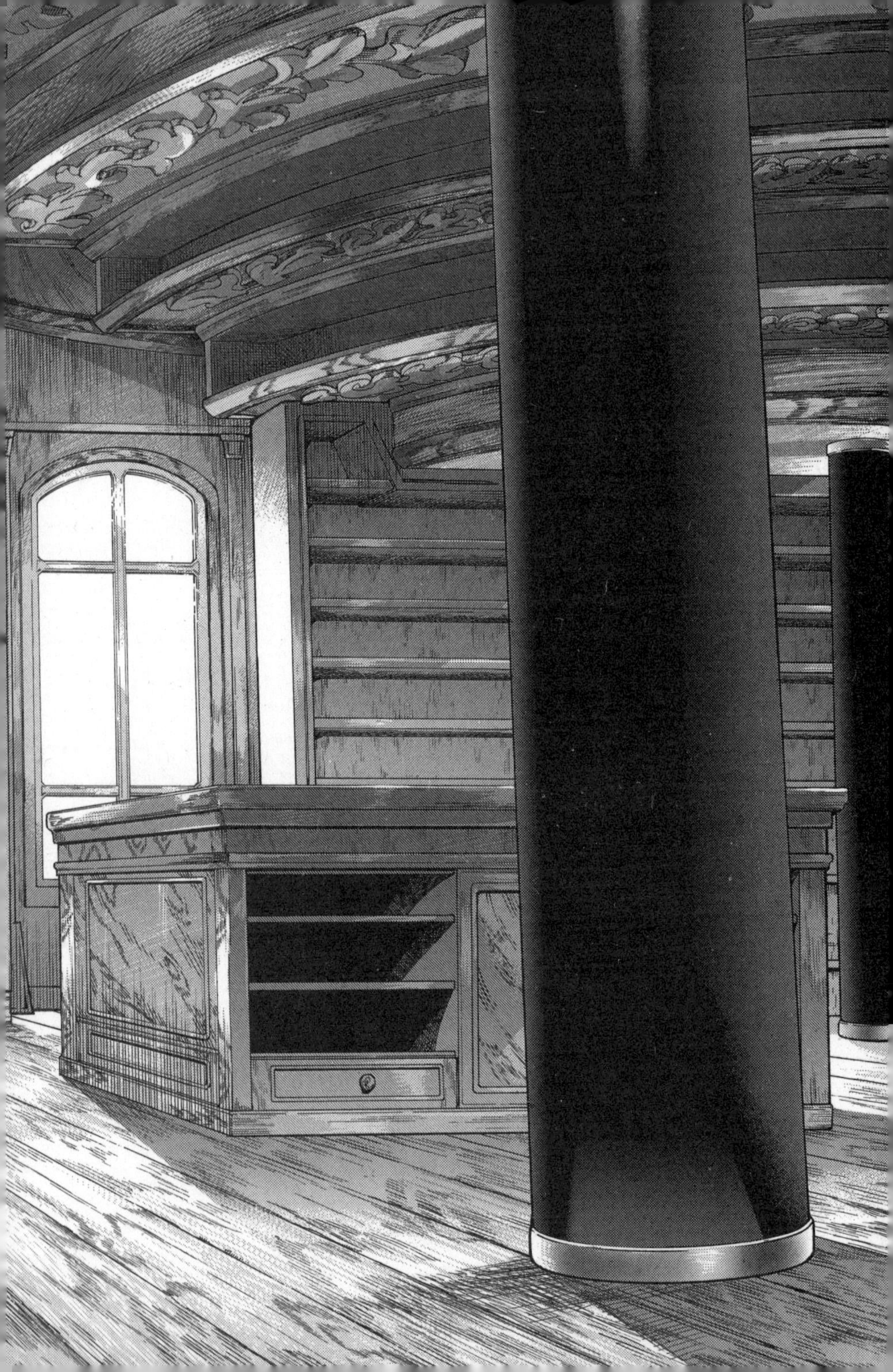

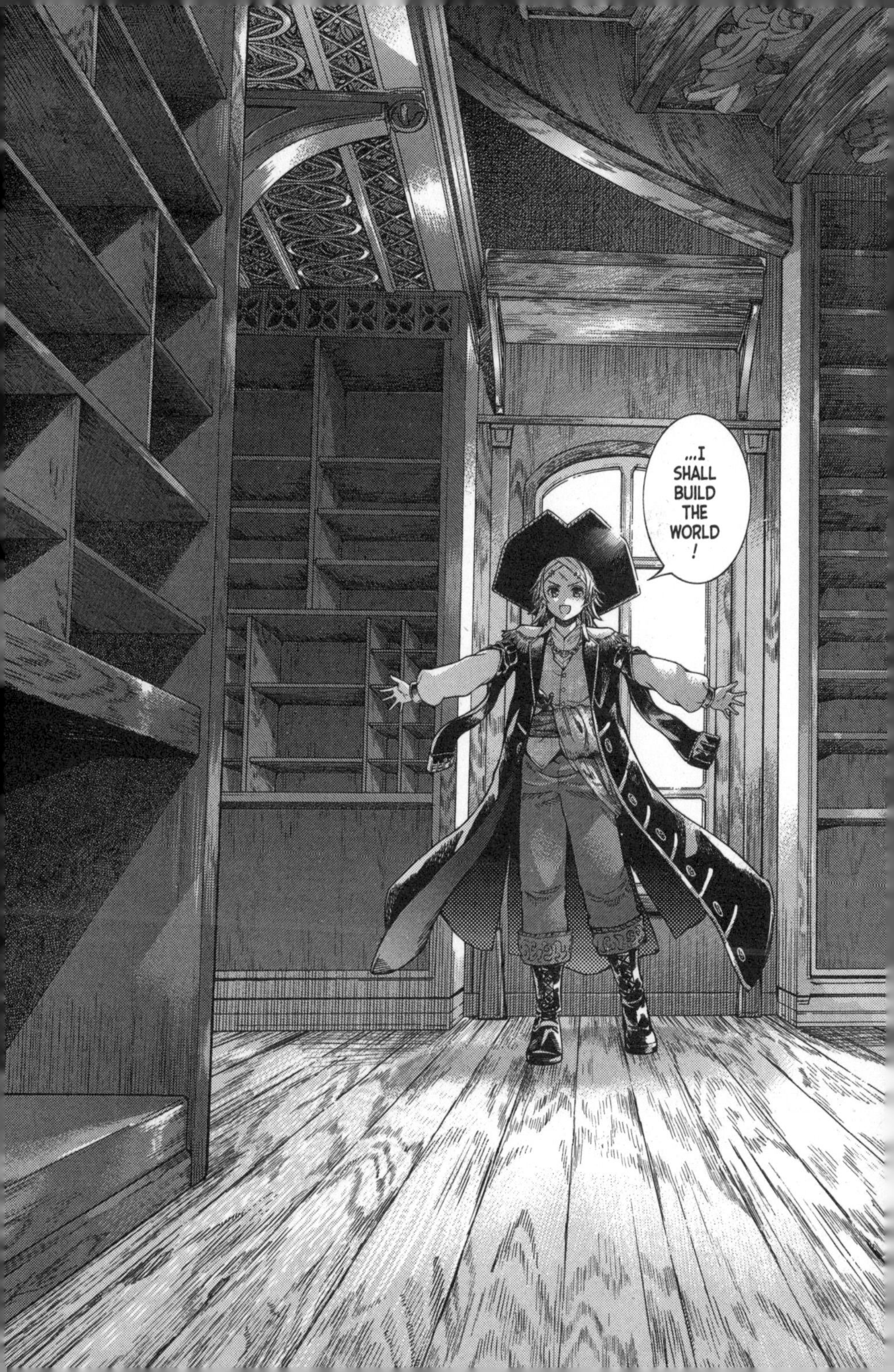
...I SHALL BUILD THE WORLD!

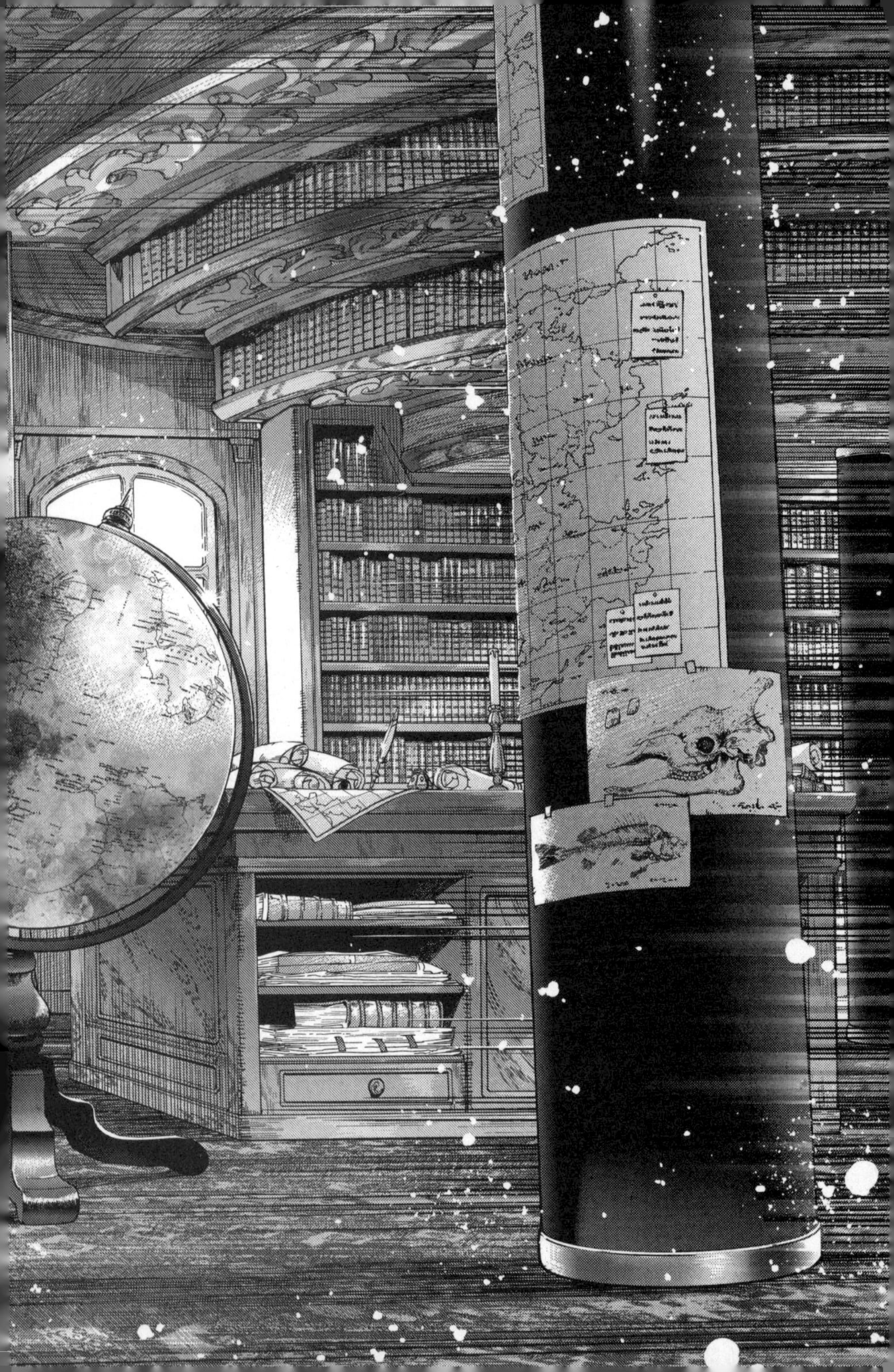

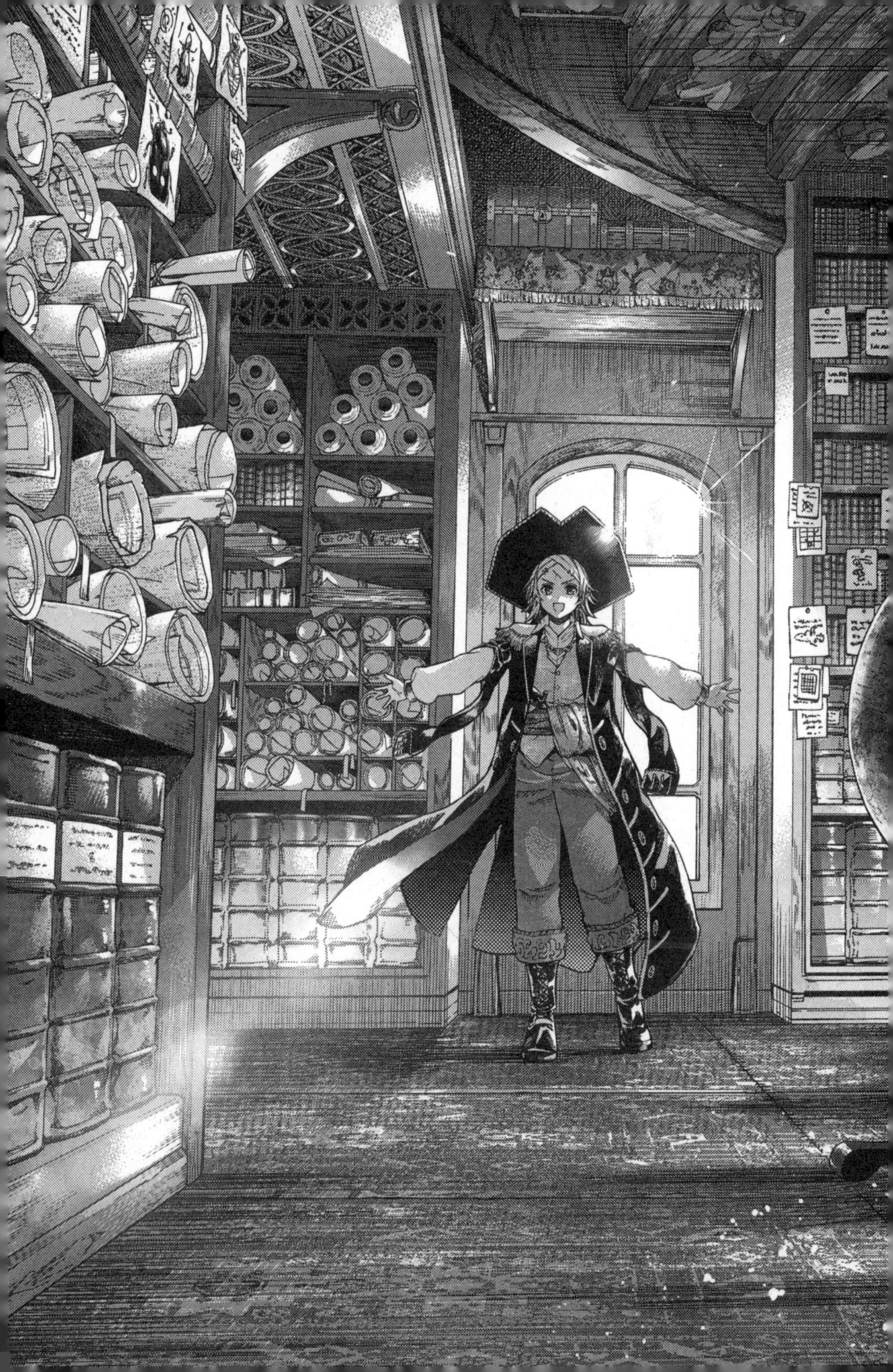

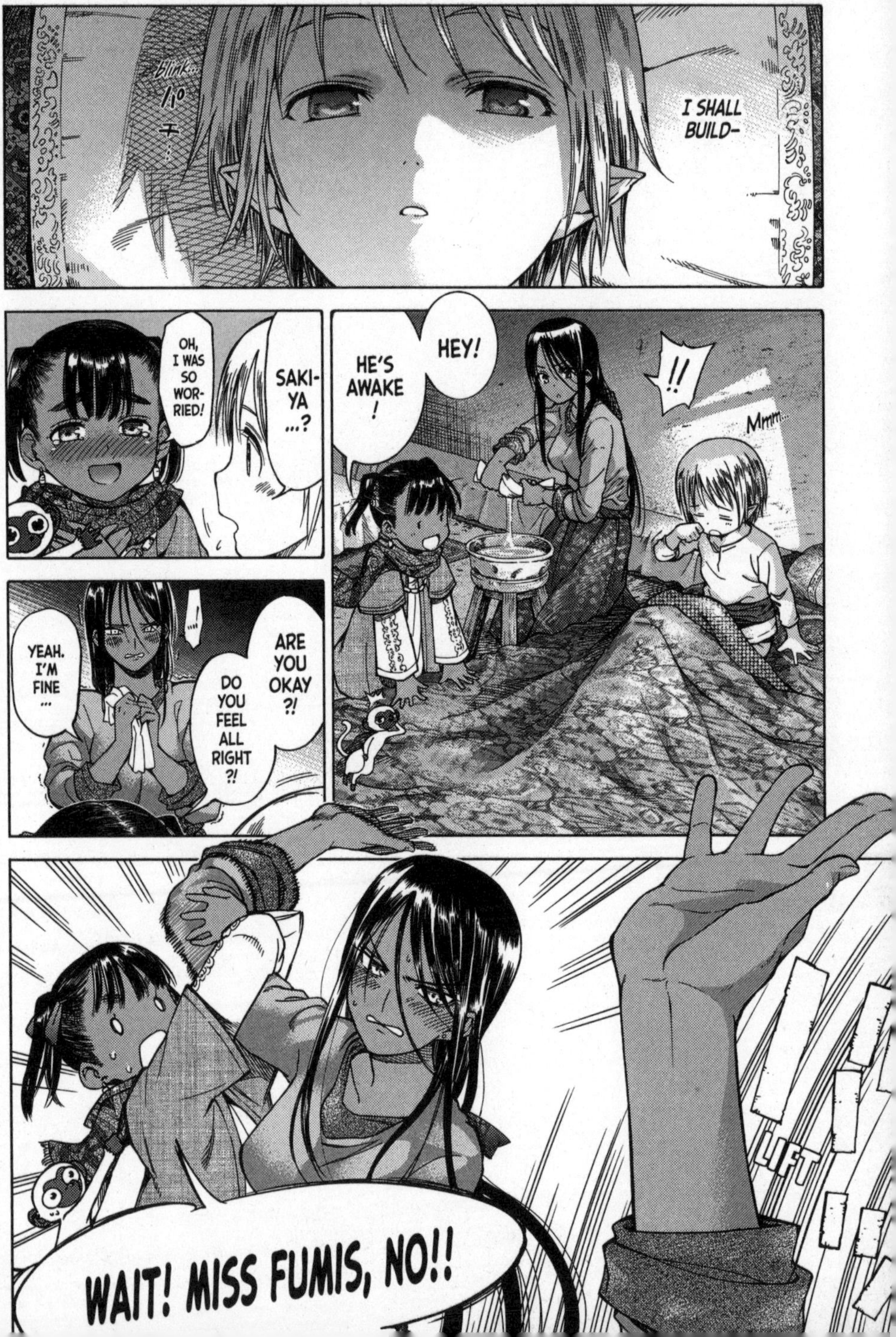
I SHALL BUILD-
blink...
パチ…
!!
Mmm...
HEY!
HE'S AWAKE!
SAKI-YA...?
OH, I WAS SO WOR-RIED!
ARE YOU OKAY?!
DO YOU FEEL ALL RIGHT?!
!....
YEAH. I'M FINE...
LIFT
WAIT! MISS FUMIS, NO!!

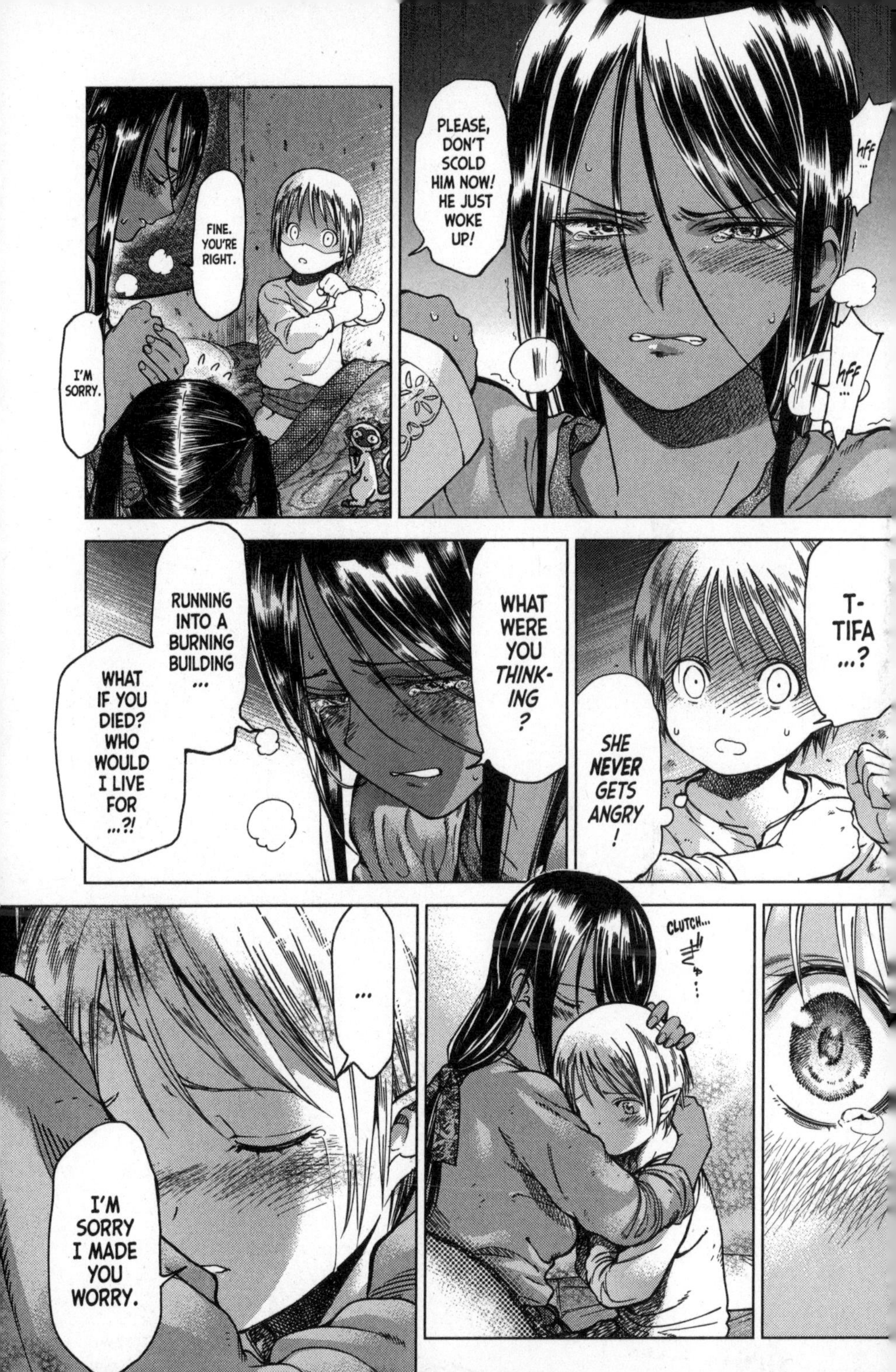
hff...
PLEASE, DON'T SCOLD HIM NOW! HE JUST WOKE UP!
hff...
FINE. YOU'RE RIGHT.
I'M SORRY.
T-TIFA...?
SHE NEVER GETS ANGRY!
WHAT WERE YOU THINKING?
RUNNING INTO A BURNING BUILDING...
WHAT IF YOU DIED? WHO WOULD I LIVE FOR...?!
CLUTCH...
...
I'M SORRY I MADE YOU WORRY.

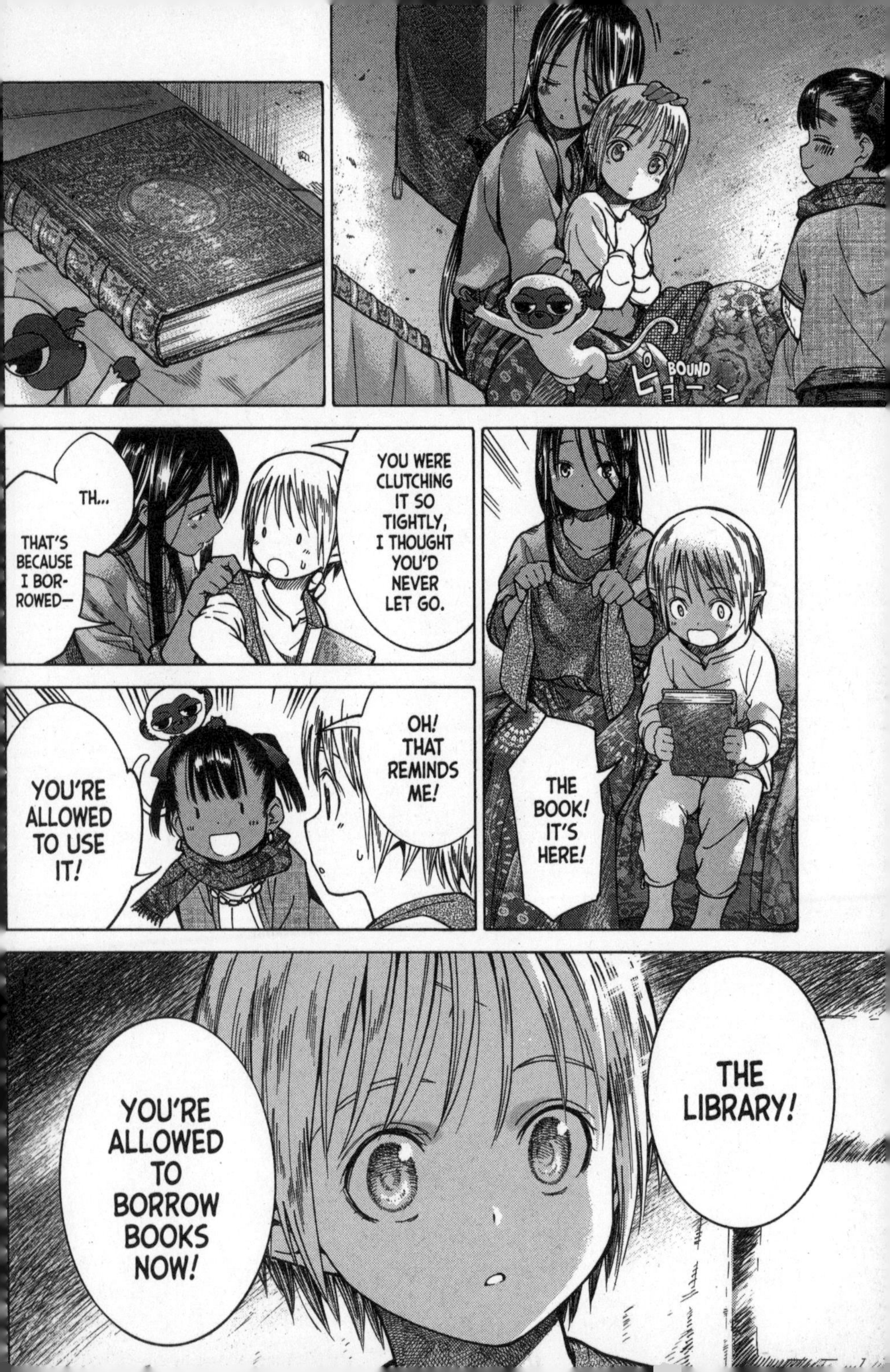
BOUND
THE BOOK! IT'S HERE!
YOU WERE CLUTCHING IT SO TIGHTLY, I THOUGHT YOU'D NEVER LET GO.
TH...
THAT'S BECAUSE I BORROWED—
OH! THAT REMINDS ME!
YOU'RE ALLOWED TO USE IT!
THE LIBRARY!
YOU'RE ALLOWED TO BORROW BOOKS NOW!

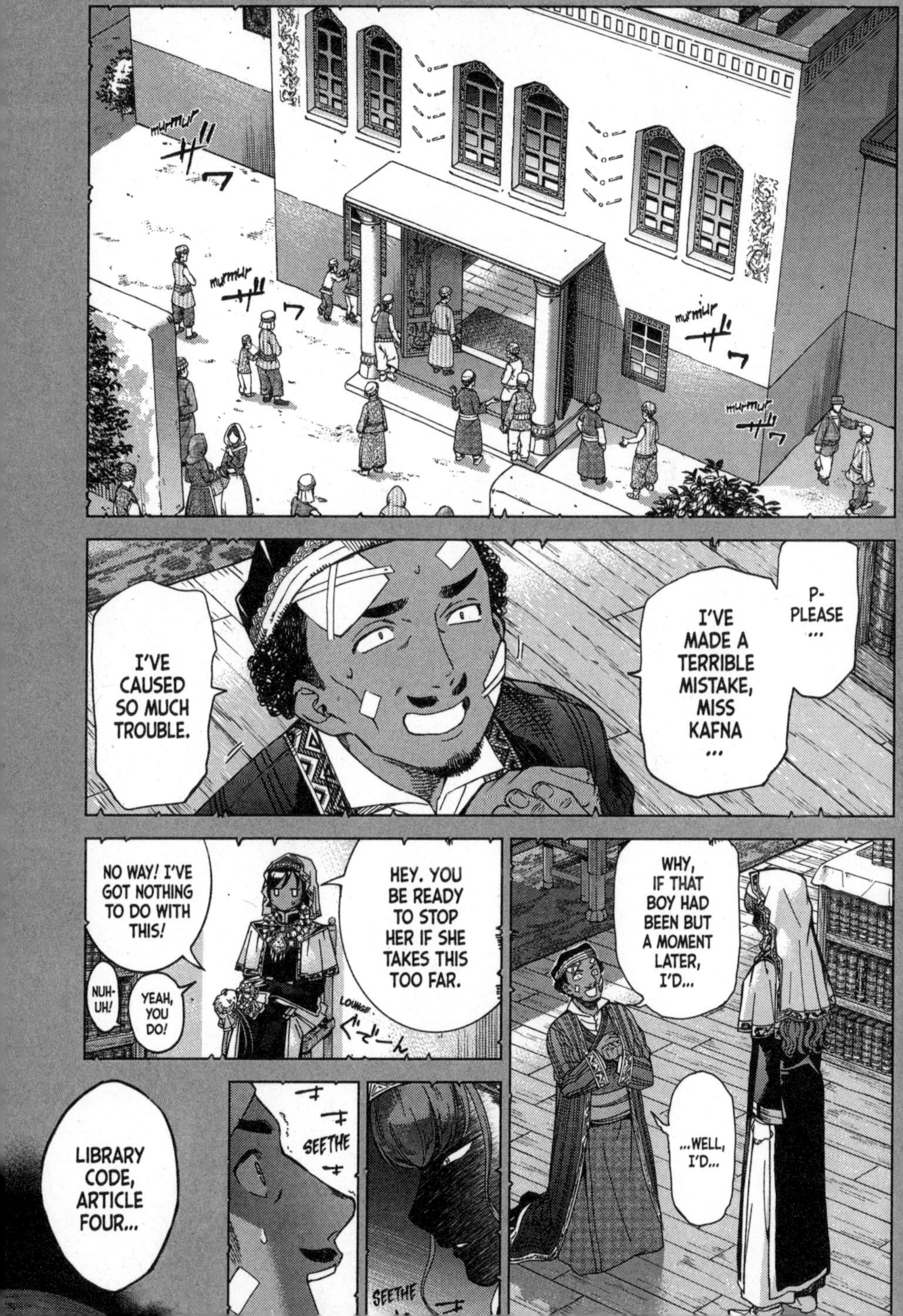
murmur
murmur
murmur
murmur
P-PLEASE...
I'VE MADE A TERRIBLE MISTAKE, MISS KAFNA...
I'VE CAUSED SO MUCH TROUBLE.
WHY, IF THAT BOY HAD BEEN BUT A MOMENT LATER, I'D...
...WELL, I'D...
HEY. YOU BE READY TO STOP HER IF SHE TAKES THIS TOO FAR.
NO WAY! I'VE GOT NOTHING TO DO WITH THIS!
YEAH, YOU DO!
NUH-UH!
LOUNGE
ぐでーん
SEETHE
SEETHE
LIBRARY CODE, ARTICLE FOUR...

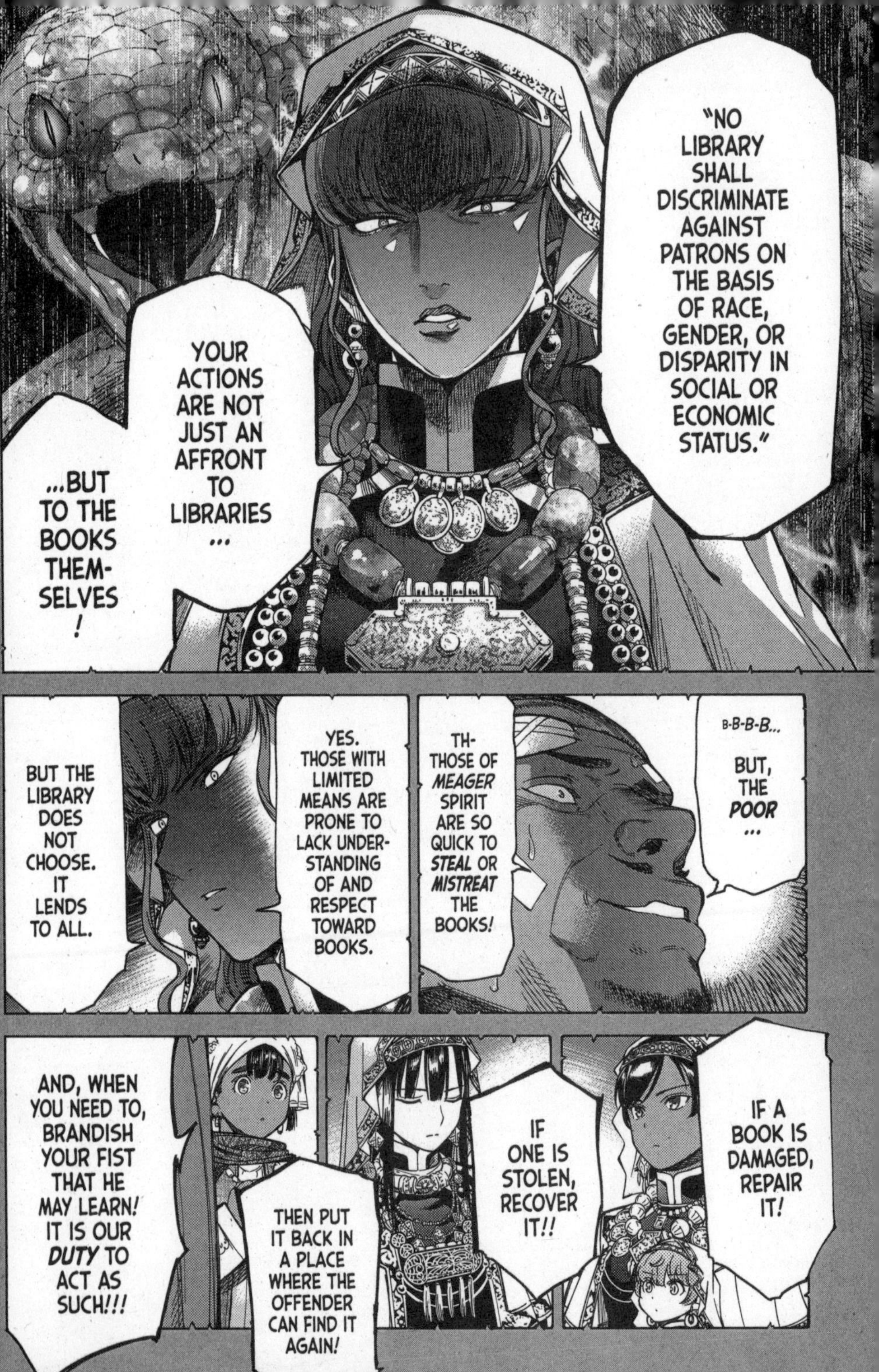
"NO LIBRARY SHALL DISCRIMINATE AGAINST PATRONS ON THE BASIS OF RACE, GENDER, OR DISPARITY IN SOCIAL OR ECONOMIC STATUS."
YOUR ACTIONS ARE NOT JUST AN AFFRONT TO LIBRARIES...
...BUT TO THE BOOKS THEMSELVES!
B-B-B-B...
BUT, THE *POOR*...
TH- THOSE OF *MEAGER* SPIRIT ARE SO QUICK TO *STEAL* OR *MISTREAT* THE BOOKS!
YES. THOSE WITH LIMITED MEANS ARE PRONE TO LACK UNDERSTANDING OF AND RESPECT TOWARD BOOKS.
BUT THE LIBRARY DOES NOT CHOOSE. IT LENDS TO ALL.
IF A BOOK IS DAMAGED, REPAIR IT!
IF ONE IS STOLEN, RECOVER IT!!
THEN PUT IT BACK IN A PLACE WHERE THE OFFENDER CAN FIND IT AGAIN!
AND, WHEN YOU NEED TO, BRANDISH YOUR FIST THAT HE MAY LEARN! IT IS OUR *DUTY* TO ACT AS SUCH!!!

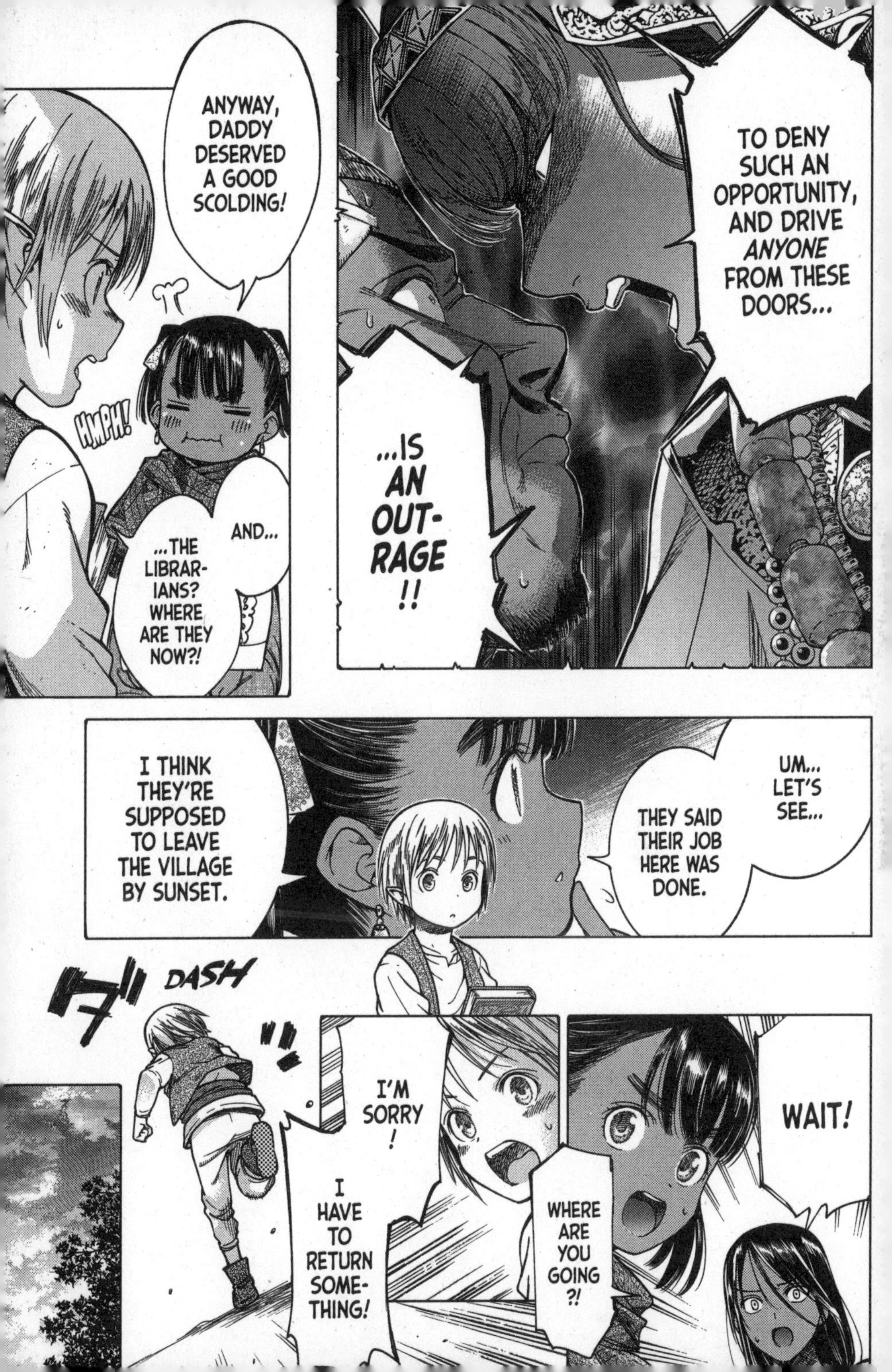
TO DENY SUCH AN OPPORTUNITY, AND DRIVE *ANYONE* FROM THESE DOORS...
...IS **AN OUTRAGE**!!
ANYWAY, DADDY DESERVED A GOOD SCOLDING!
HMPH!
AND...
...THE LIBRARIANS? WHERE ARE THEY NOW?!
UM... LET'S SEE...
THEY SAID THEIR JOB HERE WAS DONE.
I THINK THEY'RE SUPPOSED TO LEAVE THE VILLAGE BY SUNSET.
WAIT!
WHERE ARE YOU GOING?!
I'M SORRY!
I HAVE TO RETURN SOMETHING!
DASH

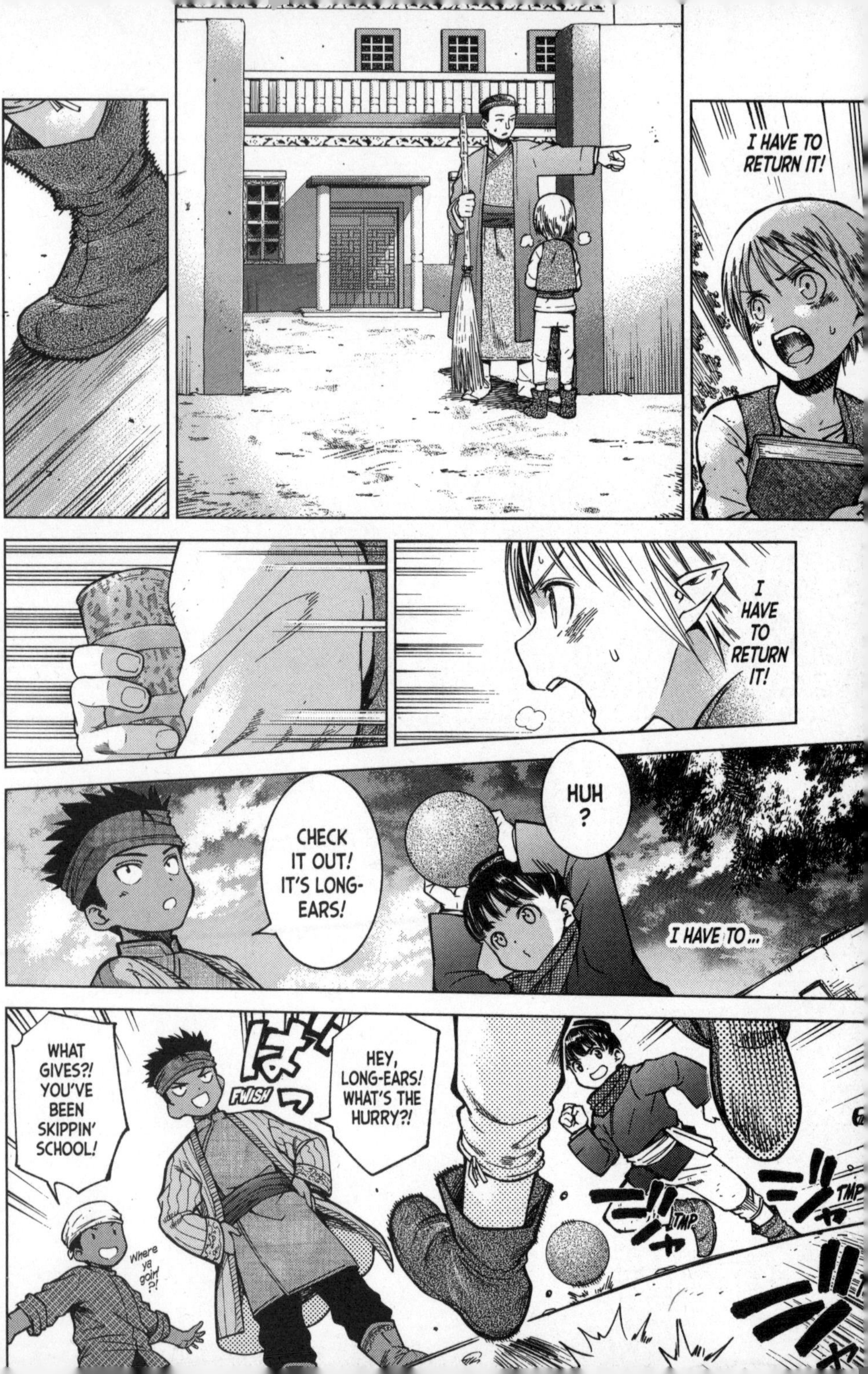
I HAVE TO RETURN IT!
I HAVE TO RETURN IT!
HUH ?
I HAVE TO...
CHECK IT OUT! IT'S LONG-EARS!
TMP
TMP
HEY, LONG-EARS! WHAT'S THE HURRY?!
FWISH
WHAT GIVES?! YOU'VE BEEN SKIPPIN' SCHOOL!
Where ya goin' ?!

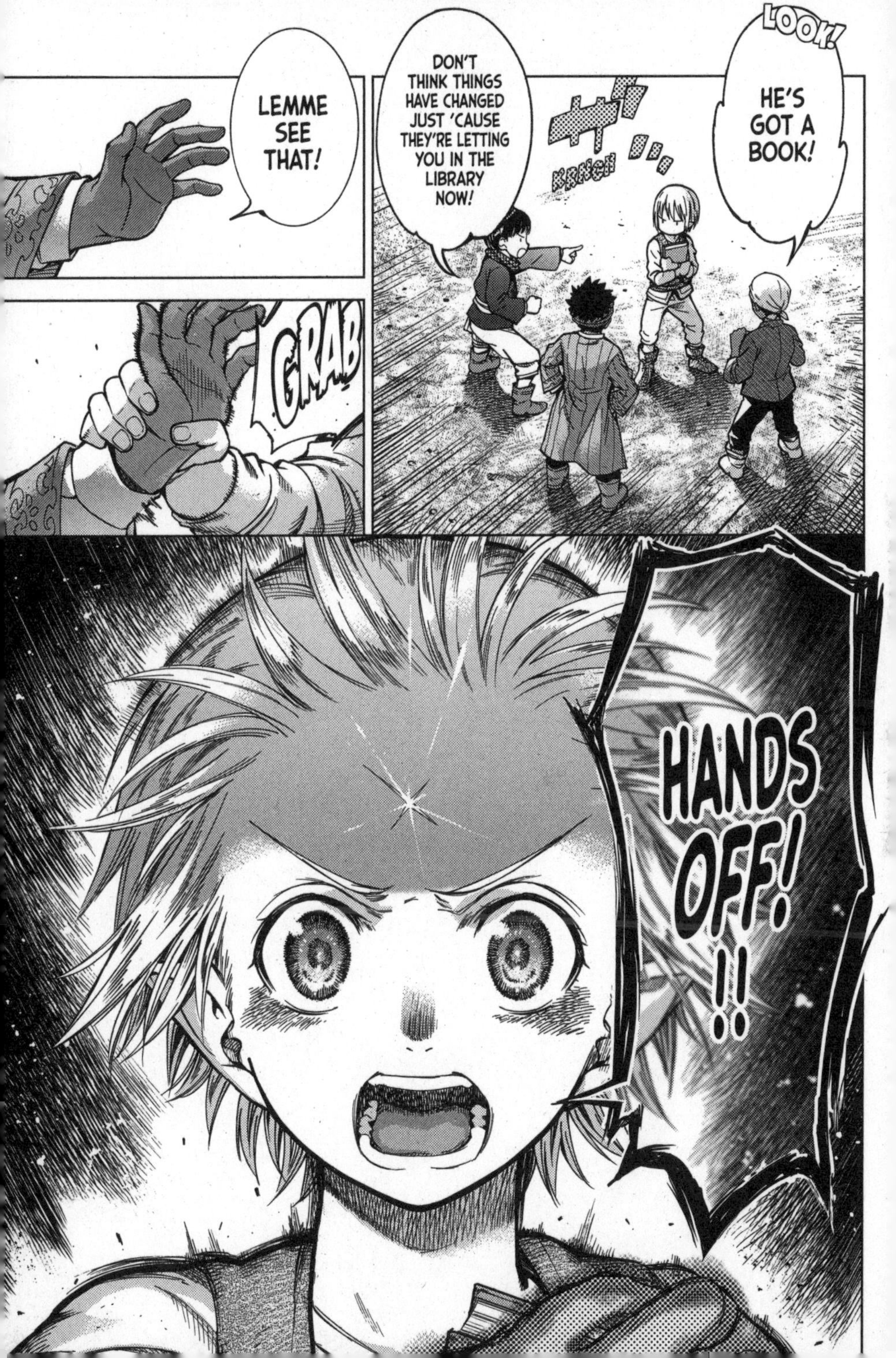
LOOK!
HE'S GOT A BOOK!
DON'T THINK THINGS HAVE CHANGED JUST 'CAUSE THEY'RE LETTING YOU IN THE LIBRARY NOW!
LEMME SEE THAT!
GRAB
HANDS OFF!!!

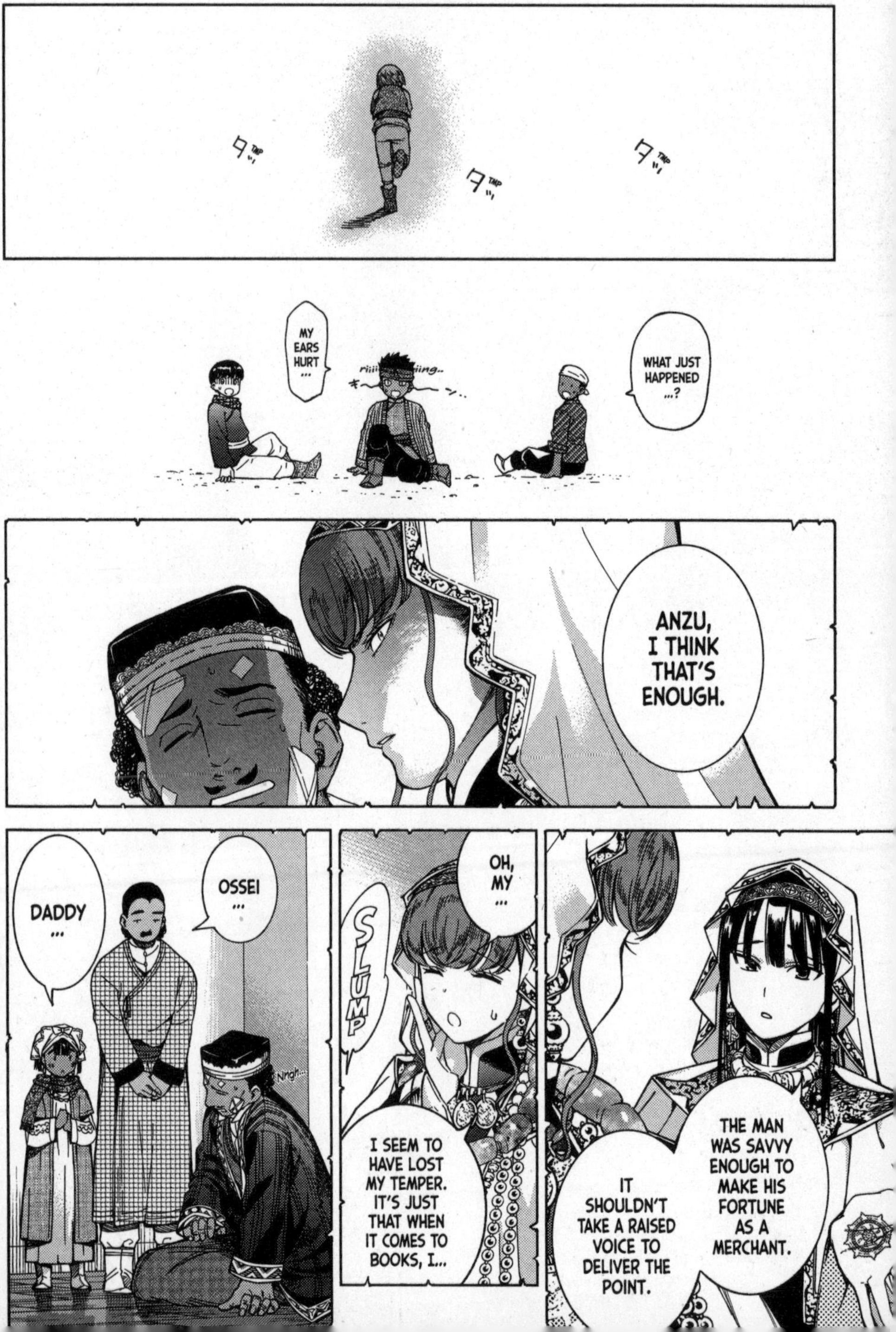

タッ TMP
タッ TMP
タッ TMP
WHAT JUST HAPPENED ...?
riiiiiiiiiing.. キ〜ン..
MY EARS HURT ...
ANZU, I THINK THAT'S ENOUGH.
THE MAN WAS SAVVY ENOUGH TO MAKE HIS FORTUNE AS A MERCHANT.
IT SHOULDN'T TAKE A RAISED VOICE TO DELIVER THE POINT.
OH, MY ...
SLUMP
I SEEM TO HAVE LOST MY TEMPER. IT'S JUST THAT WHEN IT COMES TO BOOKS, I...
OSSEI ...
DADDY ...
Nngh...

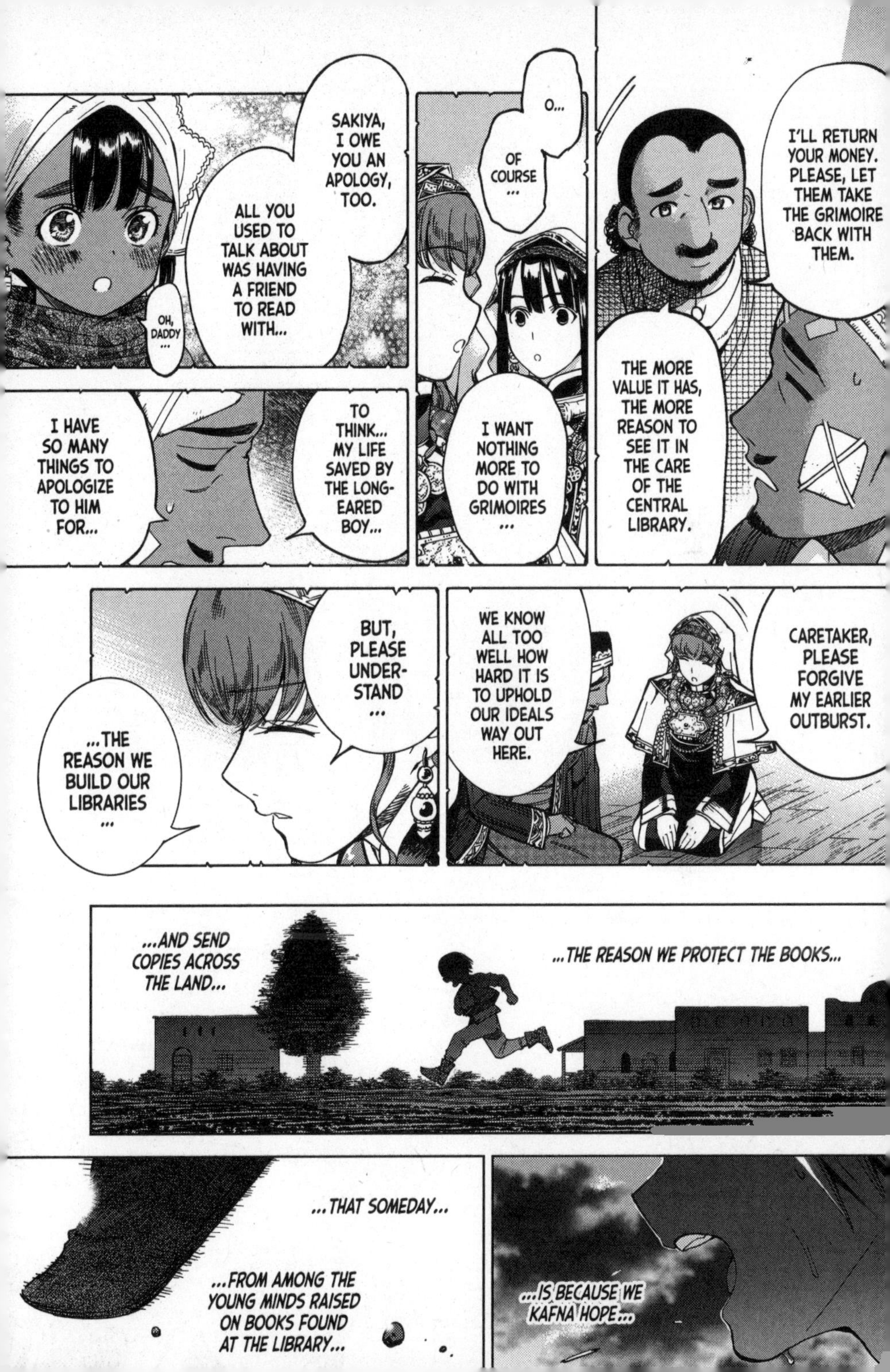
I'LL RETURN YOUR MONEY. PLEASE, LET THEM TAKE THE GRIMOIRE BACK WITH THEM.
THE MORE VALUE IT HAS, THE MORE REASON TO SEE IT IN THE CARE OF THE CENTRAL LIBRARY.
O...
OF COURSE...
I WANT NOTHING MORE TO DO WITH GRIMOIRES...
SAKIYA, I OWE YOU AN APOLOGY, TOO.
ALL YOU USED TO TALK ABOUT WAS HAVING A FRIEND TO READ WITH...
OH, DADDY...
TO THINK... MY LIFE SAVED BY THE LONG-EARED BOY...
I HAVE SO MANY THINGS TO APOLOGIZE TO HIM FOR...
CARETAKER, PLEASE FORGIVE MY EARLIER OUTBURST.
WE KNOW ALL TOO WELL HOW HARD IT IS TO UPHOLD OUR IDEALS WAY OUT HERE.
BUT, PLEASE UNDERSTAND...
...THE REASON WE BUILD OUR LIBRARIES...
...THE REASON WE PROTECT THE BOOKS...
...AND SEND COPIES ACROSS THE LAND...
...IS BECAUSE WE KAFNA HOPE...
...THAT SOMEDAY...
...FROM AMONG THE YOUNG MINDS RAISED ON BOOKS FOUND AT THE LIBRARY...

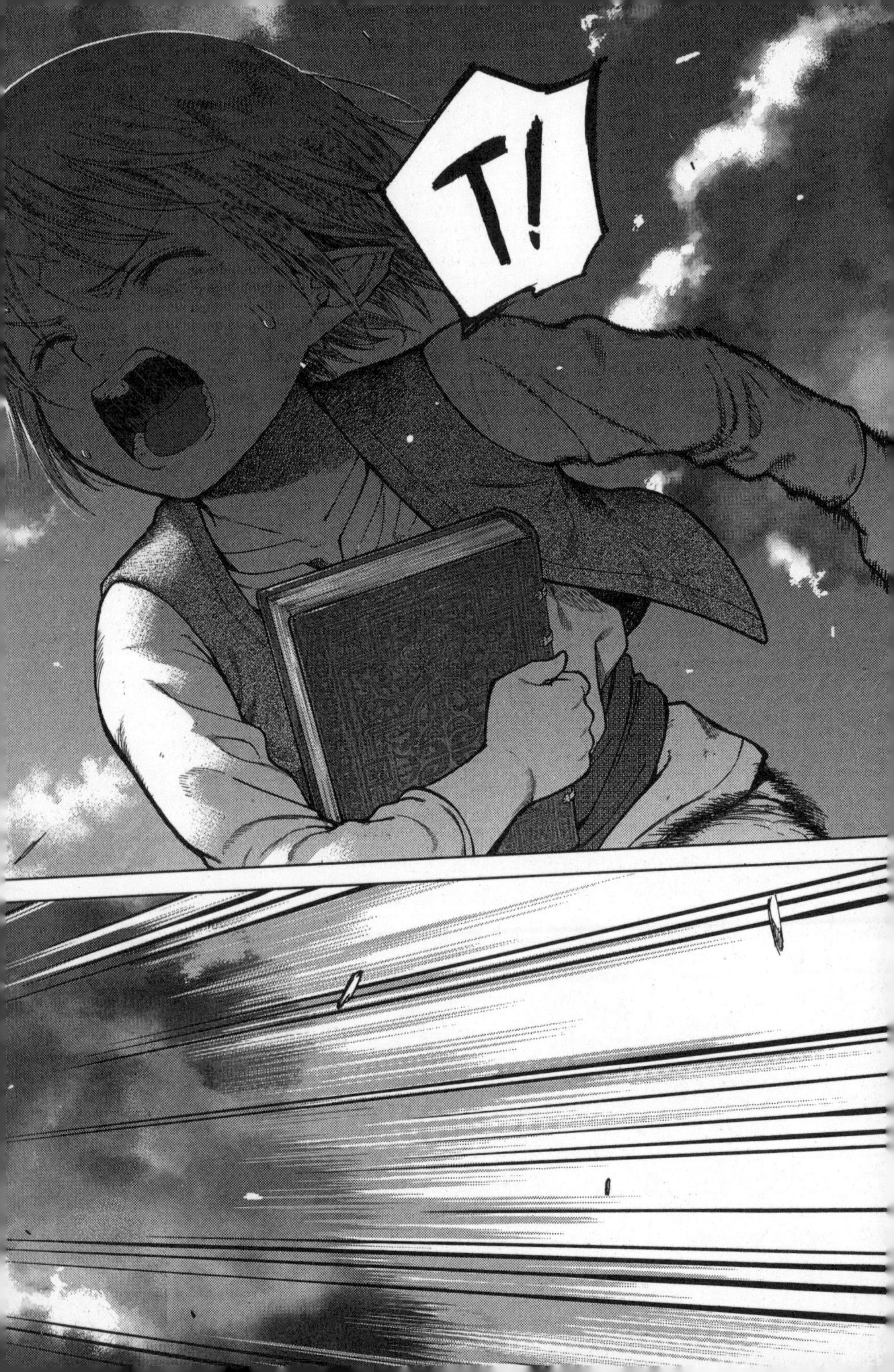
T!

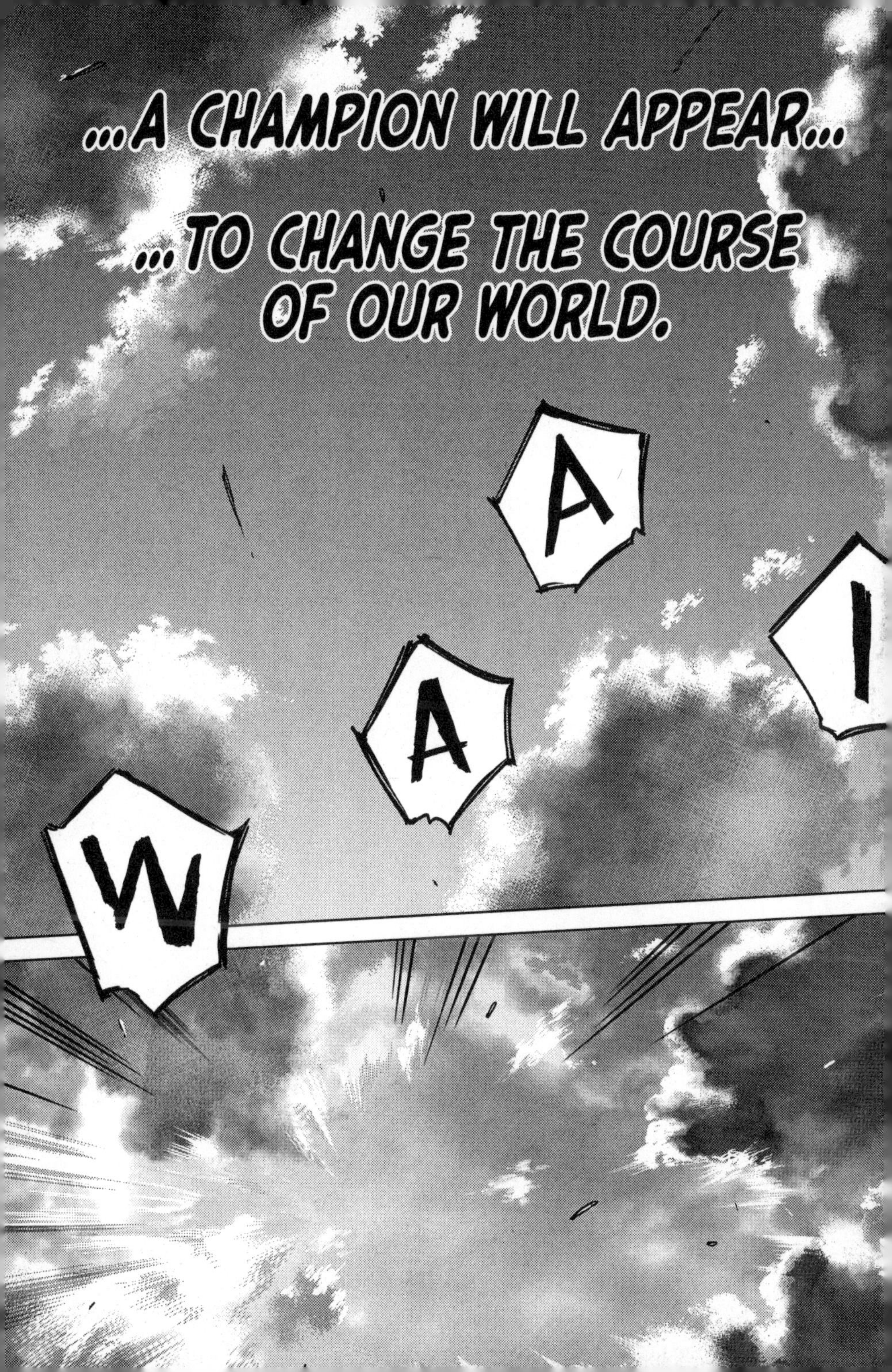
...A CHAMPION WILL APPEAR...
...TO CHANGE THE COURSE OF OUR WORLD.
WAAI

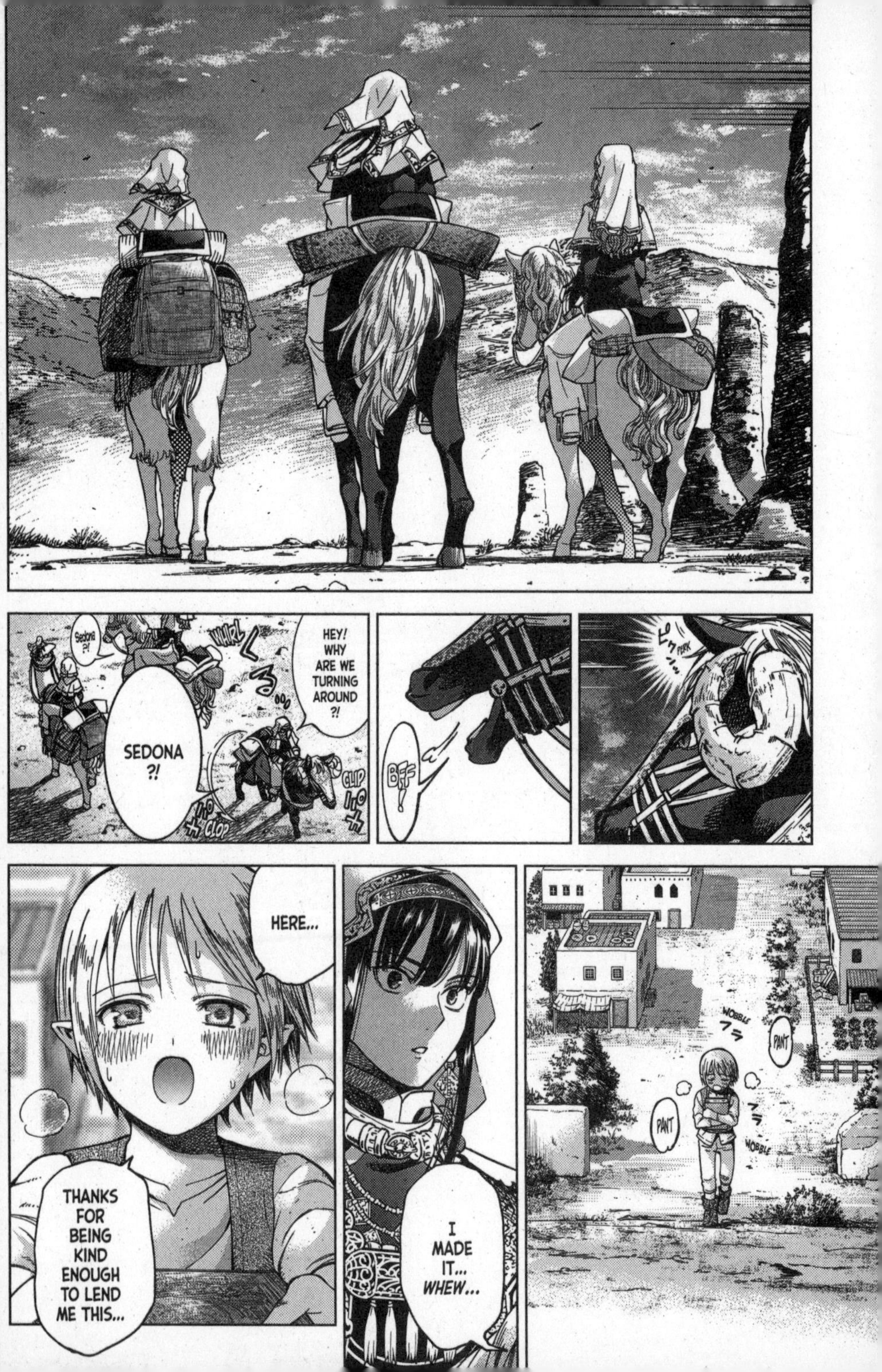
PERK
BFF!
HEY! WHY ARE WE TURNING AROUND?!
Sedona ?!
WHIRL
SEDONA ?!
CLIP
CLOP
WOBBLE
PANT
PANT
WOBBLE
I MADE IT... WHEW...
HERE...
THANKS FOR BEING KIND ENOUGH TO LEND ME THIS...

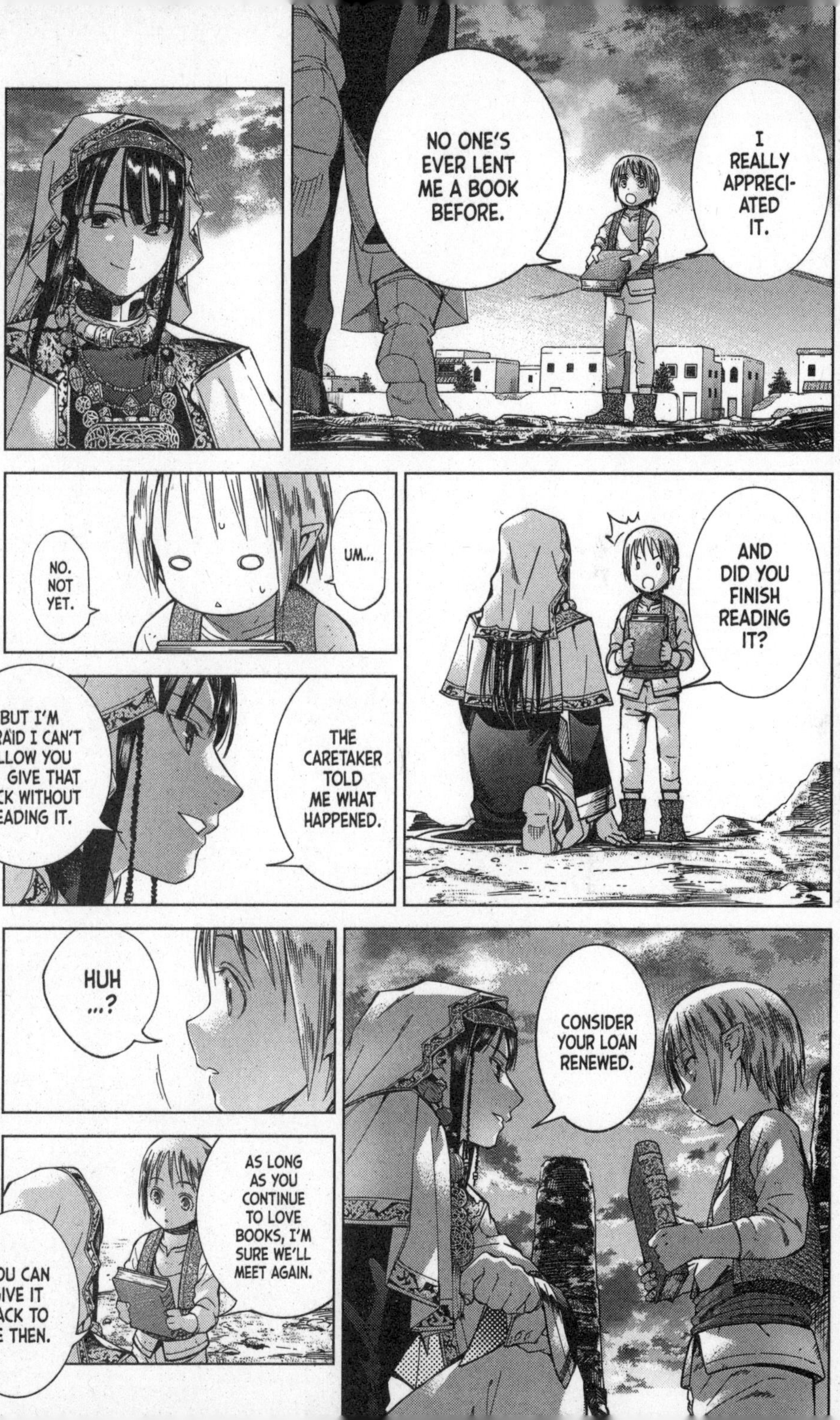
I REALLY APPRECIATED IT.
NO ONE'S EVER LENT ME A BOOK BEFORE.
AND DID YOU FINISH READING IT?
UM...
NO. NOT YET.
THE CARETAKER TOLD ME WHAT HAPPENED.
BUT I'M AFRAID I CAN'T ALLOW YOU TO GIVE THAT BACK WITHOUT READING IT.
CONSIDER YOUR LOAN RENEWED.
HUH ...?
AS LONG AS YOU CONTINUE TO LOVE BOOKS, I'M SURE WE'LL MEET AGAIN.
YOU CAN GIVE IT BACK TO ME THEN.

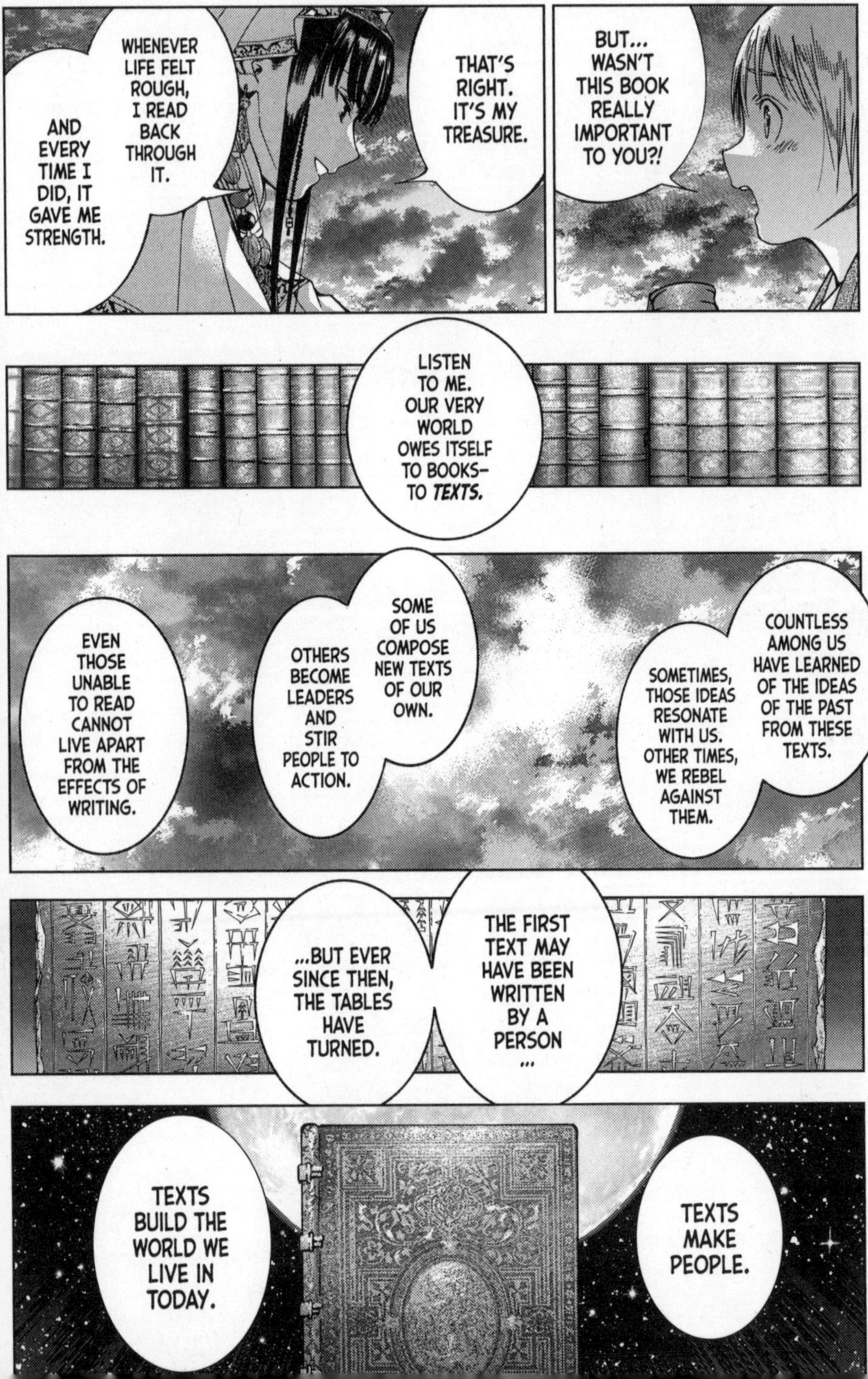
BUT... WASN'T THIS BOOK REALLY IMPORTANT TO YOU?!
THAT'S RIGHT. IT'S MY TREASURE.
WHENEVER LIFE FELT ROUGH, I READ BACK THROUGH IT.
AND EVERY TIME I DID, IT GAVE ME STRENGTH.
LISTEN TO ME. OUR VERY WORLD OWES ITSELF TO BOOKS— TO *TEXTS.*
COUNTLESS AMONG US HAVE LEARNED OF THE IDEAS OF THE PAST FROM THESE TEXTS.
SOMETIMES, THOSE IDEAS RESONATE WITH US. OTHER TIMES, WE REBEL AGAINST THEM.
SOME OF US COMPOSE NEW TEXTS OF OUR OWN.
OTHERS BECOME LEADERS AND STIR PEOPLE TO ACTION.
EVEN THOSE UNABLE TO READ CANNOT LIVE APART FROM THE EFFECTS OF WRITING.
THE FIRST TEXT MAY HAVE BEEN WRITTEN BY A PERSON ...
...BUT EVER SINCE THEN, THE TABLES HAVE TURNED.
TEXTS MAKE PEOPLE.
TEXTS BUILD THE WORLD WE LIVE IN TODAY.

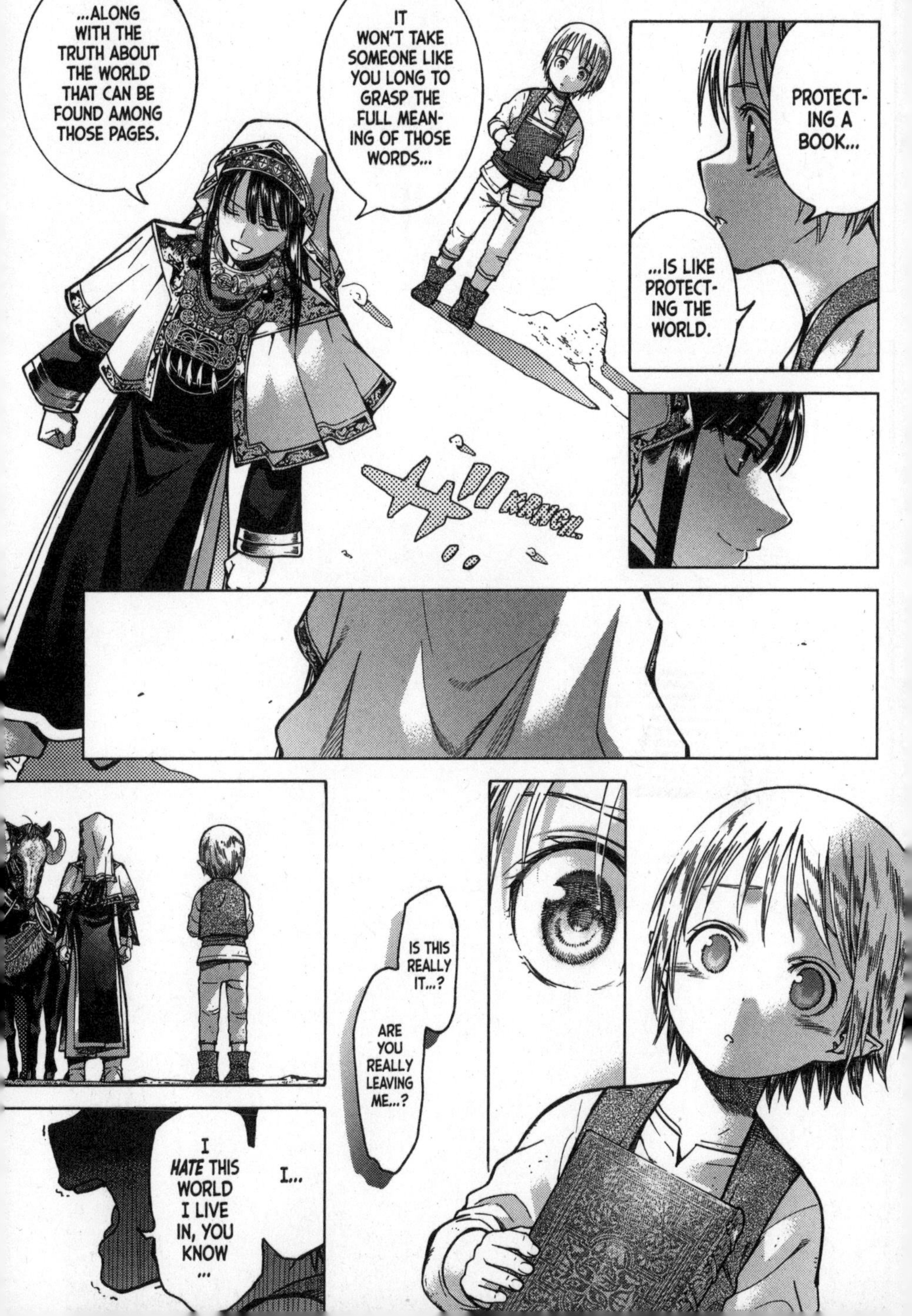
PROTECTING A BOOK...
...IS LIKE PROTECTING THE WORLD.
IT WON'T TAKE SOMEONE LIKE YOU LONG TO GRASP THE FULL MEANING OF THOSE WORDS...
...ALONG WITH THE TRUTH ABOUT THE WORLD THAT CAN BE FOUND AMONG THOSE PAGES.
KRNCH..
IS THIS REALLY IT...?
ARE YOU REALLY LEAVING ME...?
I...
I *HATE* THIS WORLD I LIVE IN, YOU KNOW...

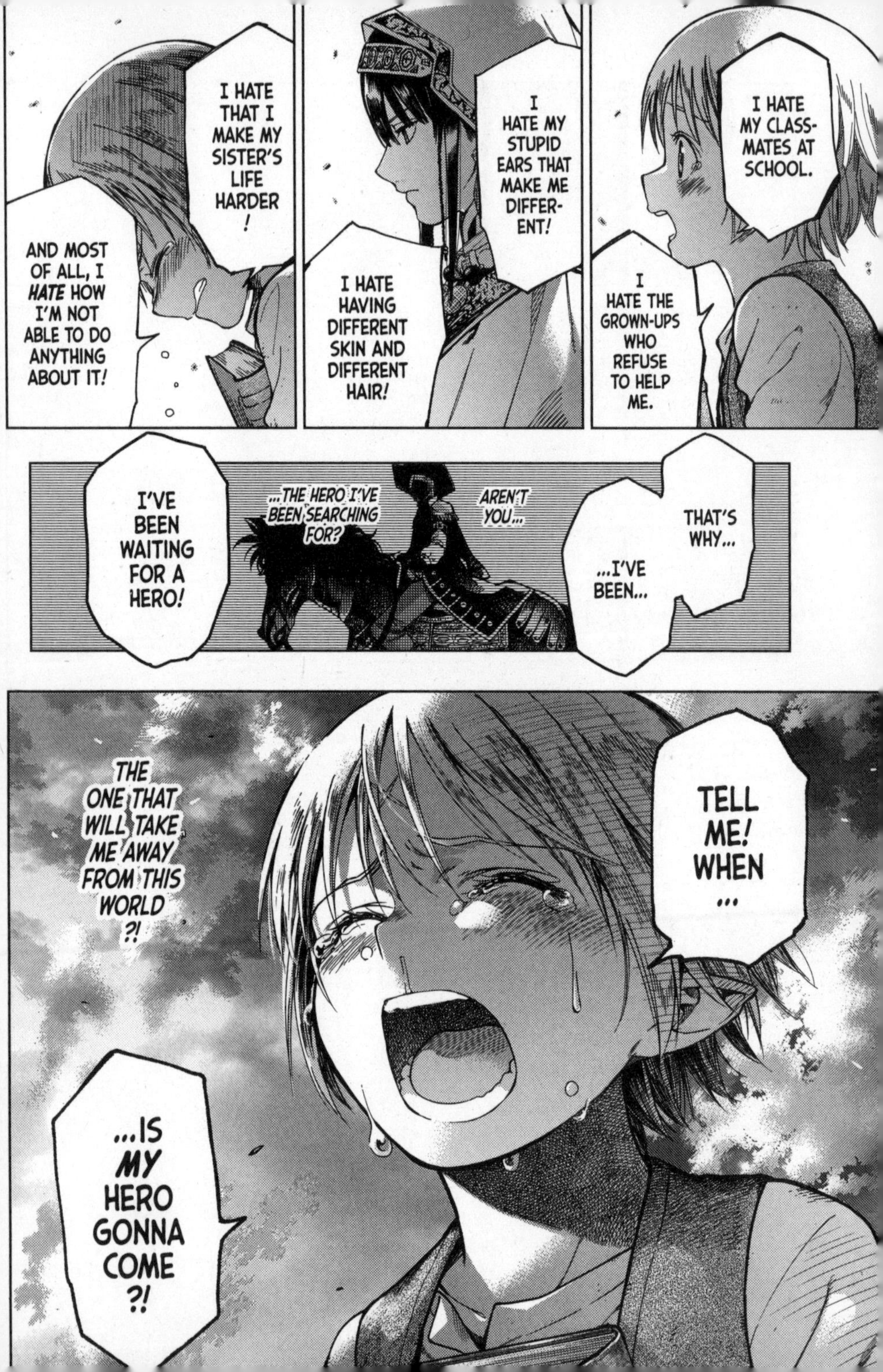
I HATE MY CLASSMATES AT SCHOOL.
I HATE THE GROWN-UPS WHO REFUSE TO HELP ME.
I HATE MY STUPID EARS THAT MAKE ME DIFFERENT!
I HATE HAVING DIFFERENT SKIN AND DIFFERENT HAIR!
I HATE THAT I MAKE MY SISTER'S LIFE HARDER!
AND MOST OF ALL, I *HATE* HOW I'M NOT ABLE TO DO ANYTHING ABOUT IT!
THAT'S WHY...
...I'VE BEEN...
AREN'T YOU...
...THE HERO I'VE BEEN SEARCHING FOR?
I'VE BEEN WAITING FOR A HERO!
TELL ME! WHEN...
THE ONE THAT WILL TAKE ME AWAY FROM THIS WORLD?!
...IS *MY* HERO GONNA COME?!

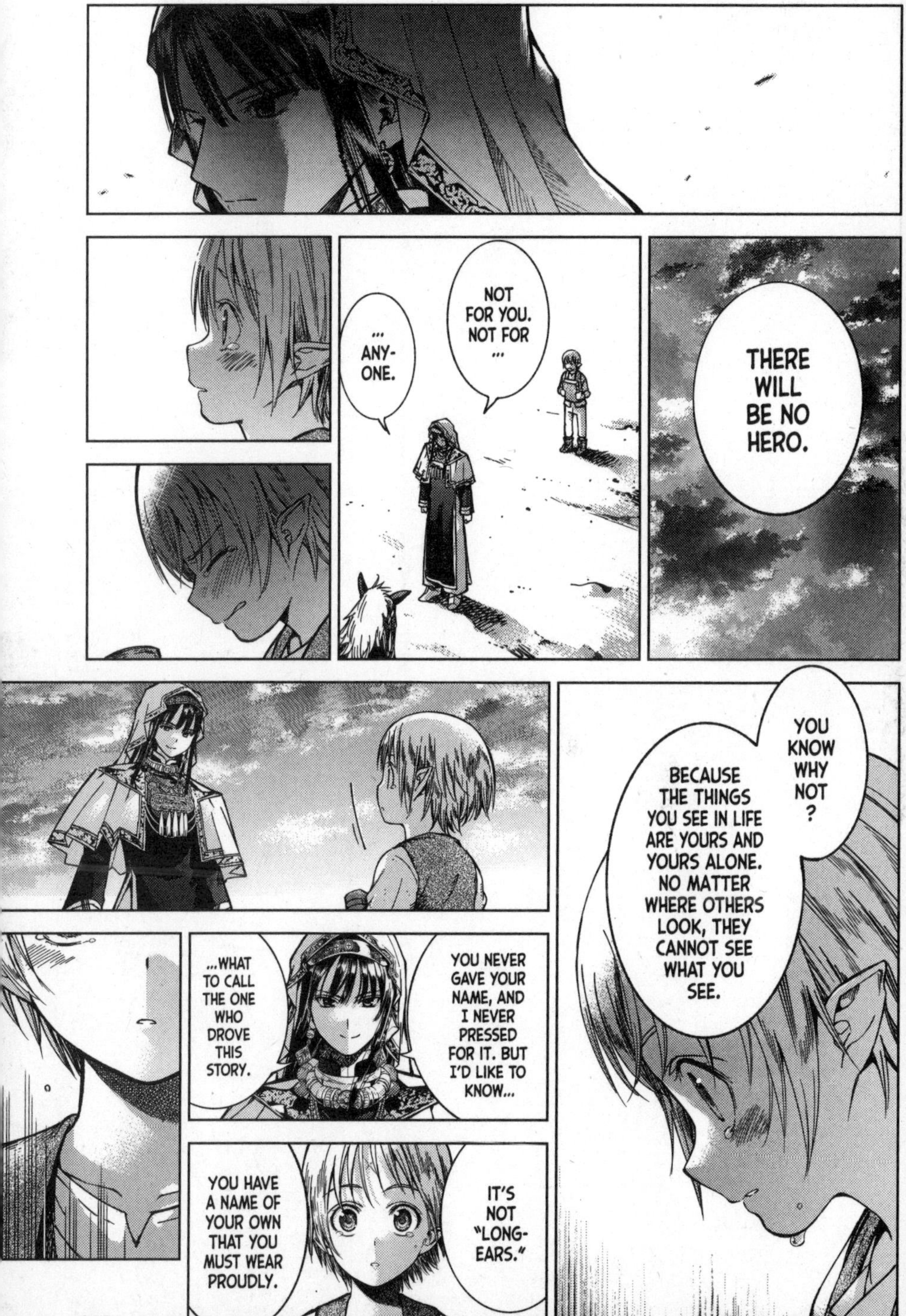
THERE WILL BE NO HERO.
NOT FOR YOU. NOT FOR ...
... ANY-ONE.
YOU KNOW WHY NOT?
BECAUSE THE THINGS YOU SEE IN LIFE ARE YOURS AND YOURS ALONE. NO MATTER WHERE OTHERS LOOK, THEY CANNOT SEE WHAT YOU SEE.
YOU NEVER GAVE YOUR NAME, AND I NEVER PRESSED FOR IT. BUT I'D LIKE TO KNOW...
...WHAT TO CALL THE ONE WHO DROVE THIS STORY.
IT'S NOT "LONG-EARS."
YOU HAVE A NAME OF YOUR OWN THAT YOU MUST WEAR PROUDLY.

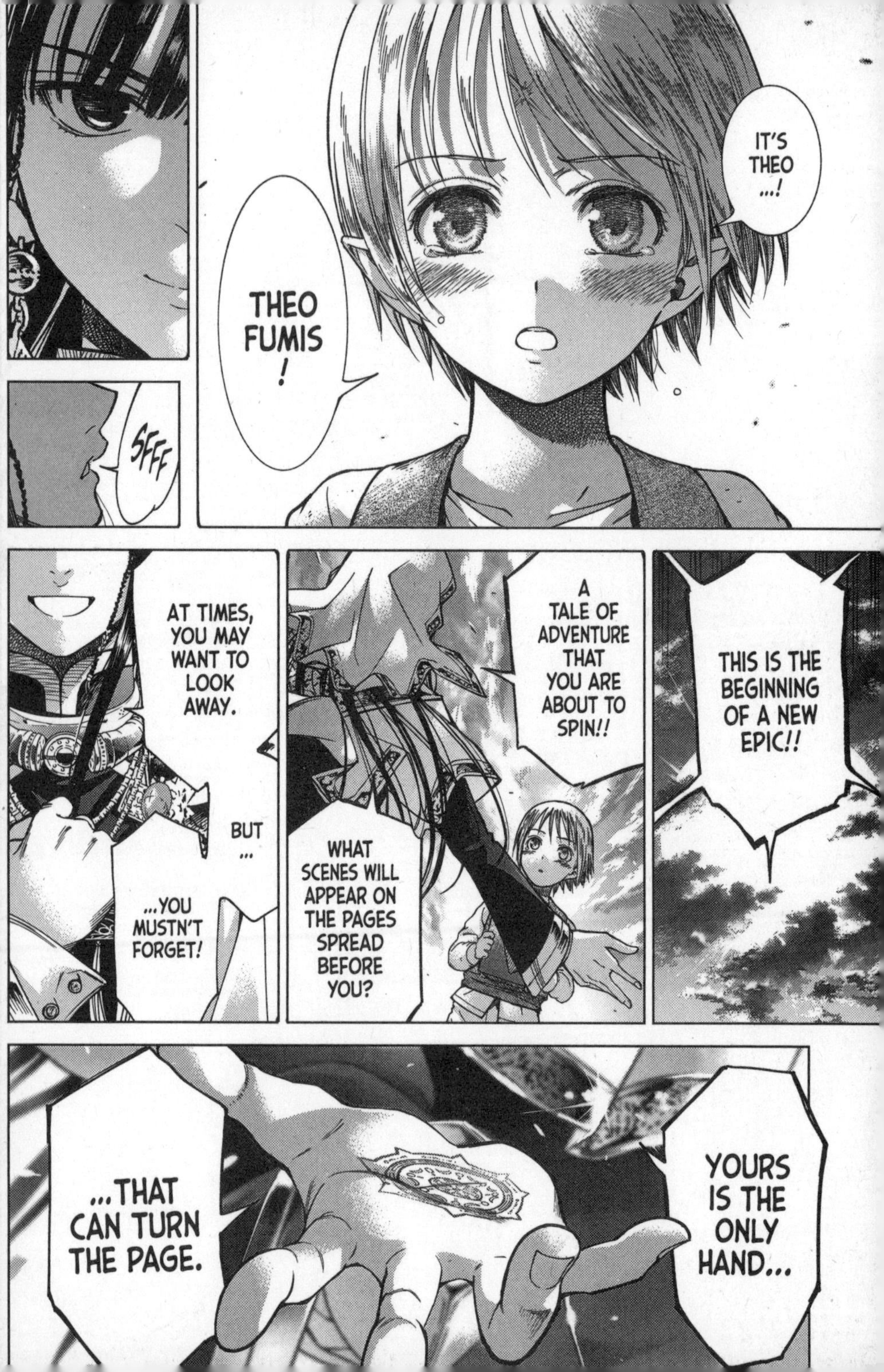
IT'S THEO ...!
THEO FUMIS!
SFFF
THIS IS THE BEGINNING OF A NEW EPIC!!
A TALE OF ADVENTURE THAT YOU ARE ABOUT TO SPIN!!
WHAT SCENES WILL APPEAR ON THE PAGES SPREAD BEFORE YOU?
AT TIMES, YOU MAY WANT TO LOOK AWAY.
BUT ...
...YOU MUSTN'T FORGET!
YOURS IS THE ONLY HAND...
...THAT CAN TURN THE PAGE.

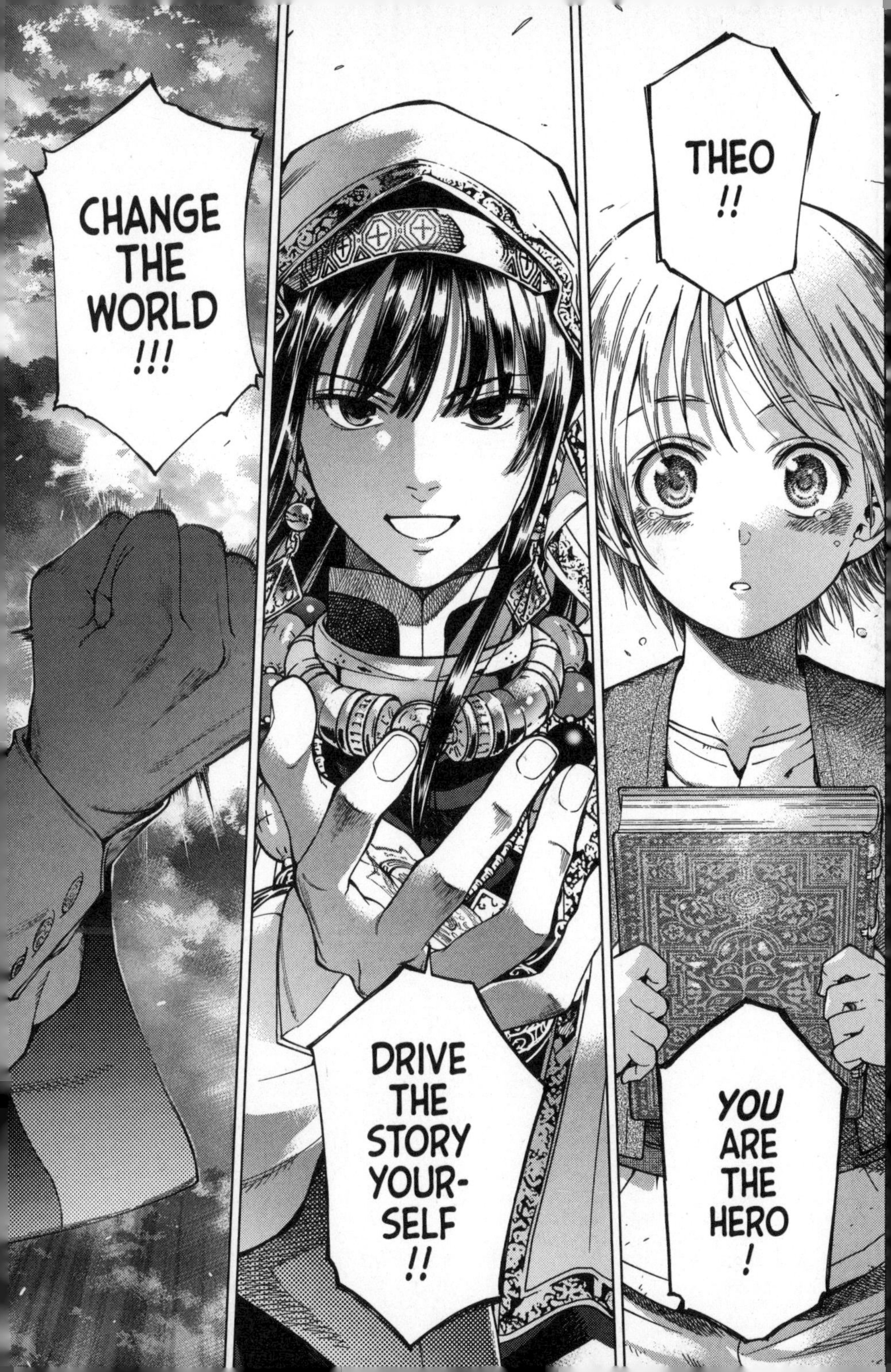
THEO !!
YOU ARE THE HERO !
DRIVE THE STORY YOUR-SELF !!
CHANGE THE WORLD !!!

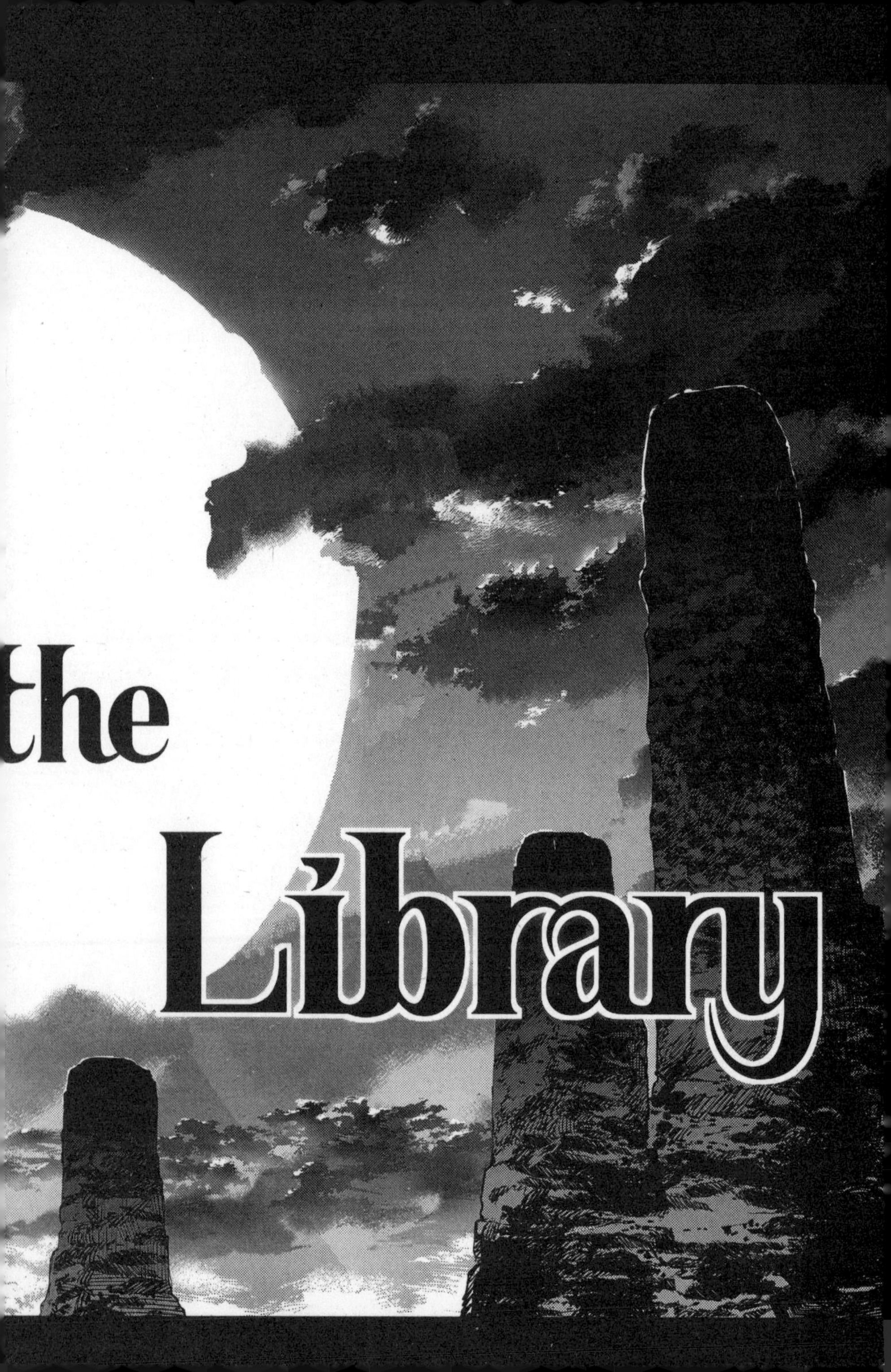
the Library

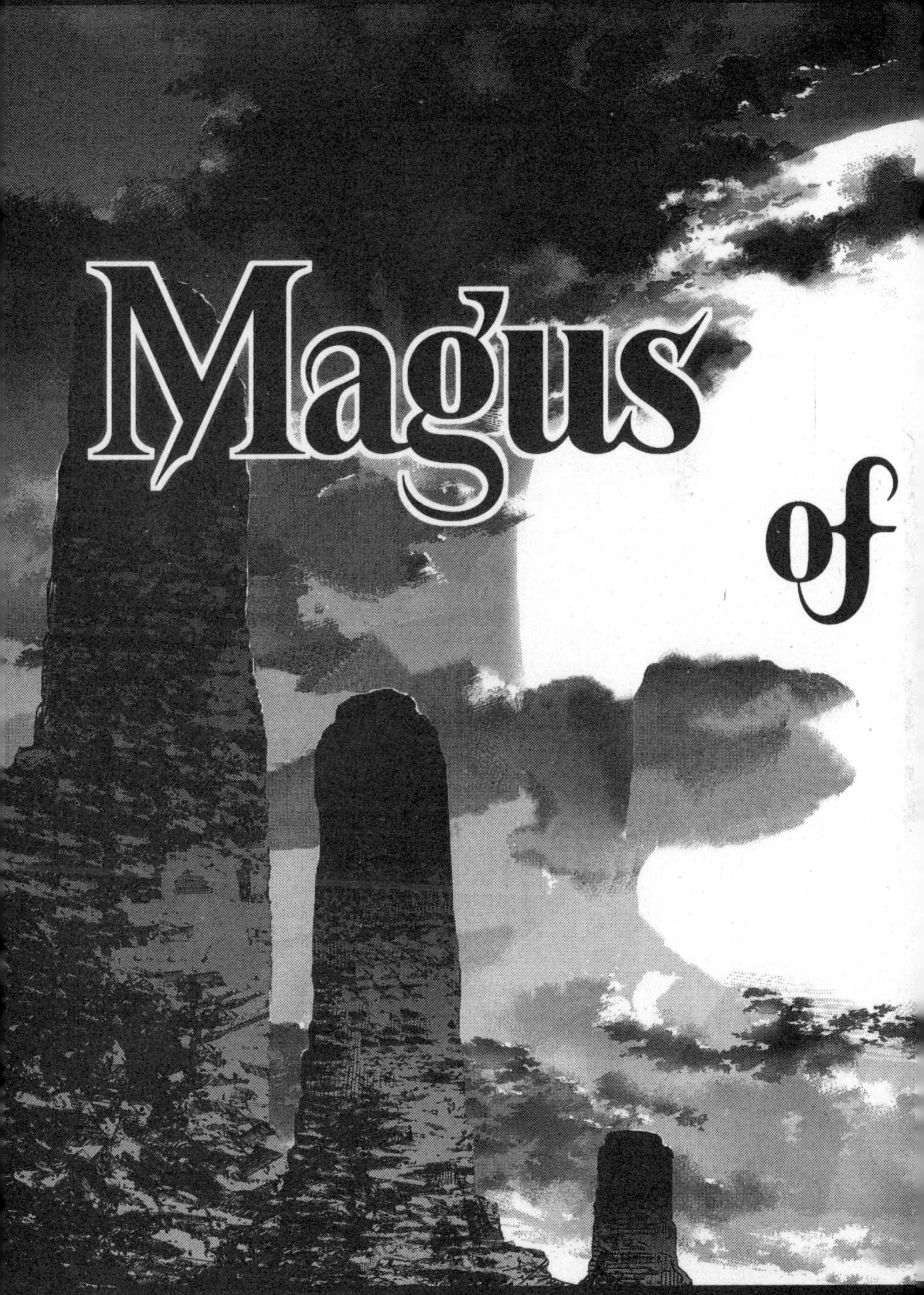
Magus
of

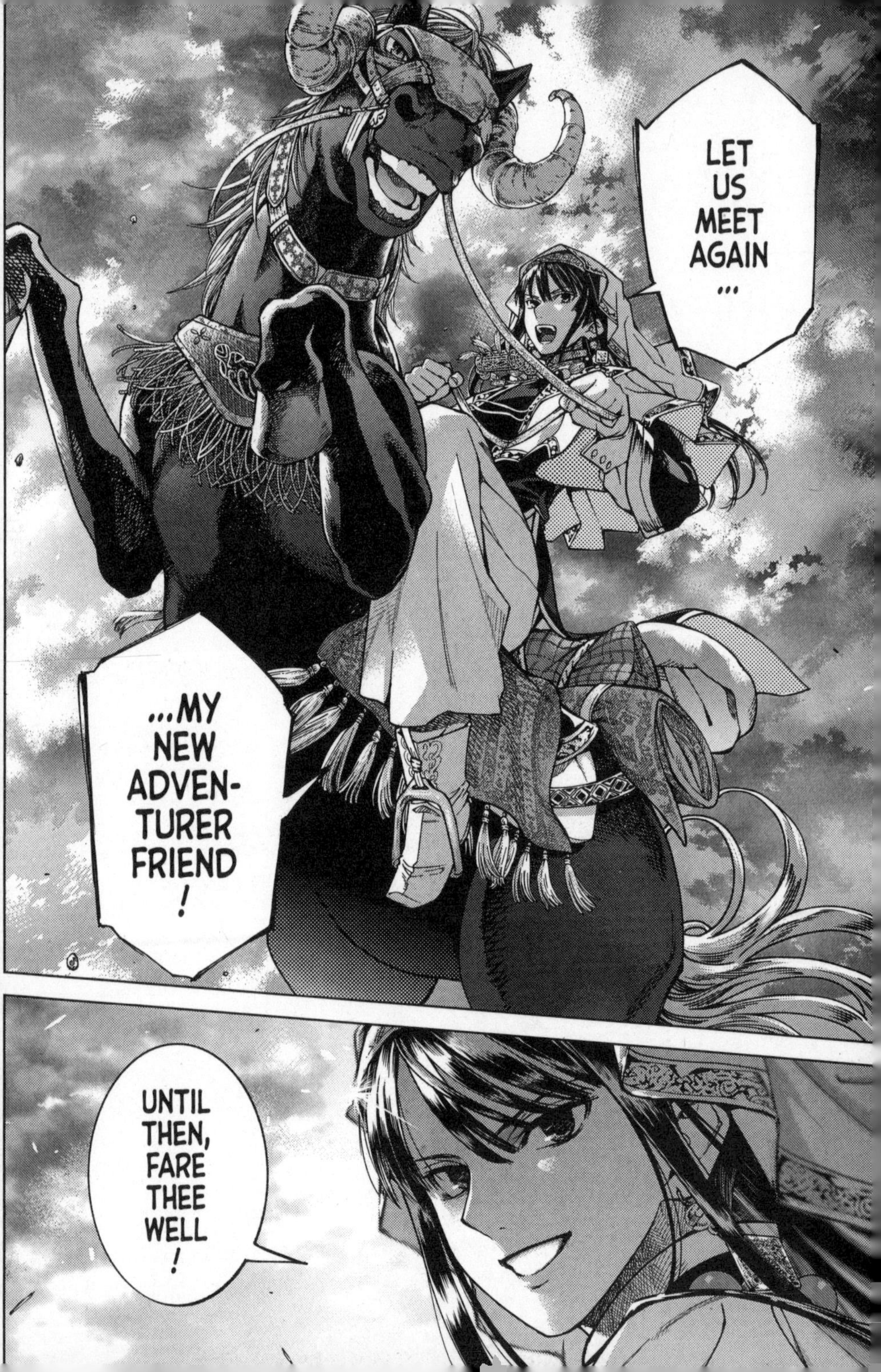
LET US MEET AGAIN...
...MY NEW ADVENTURER FRIEND!
UNTIL THEN, FARE THEE WELL!

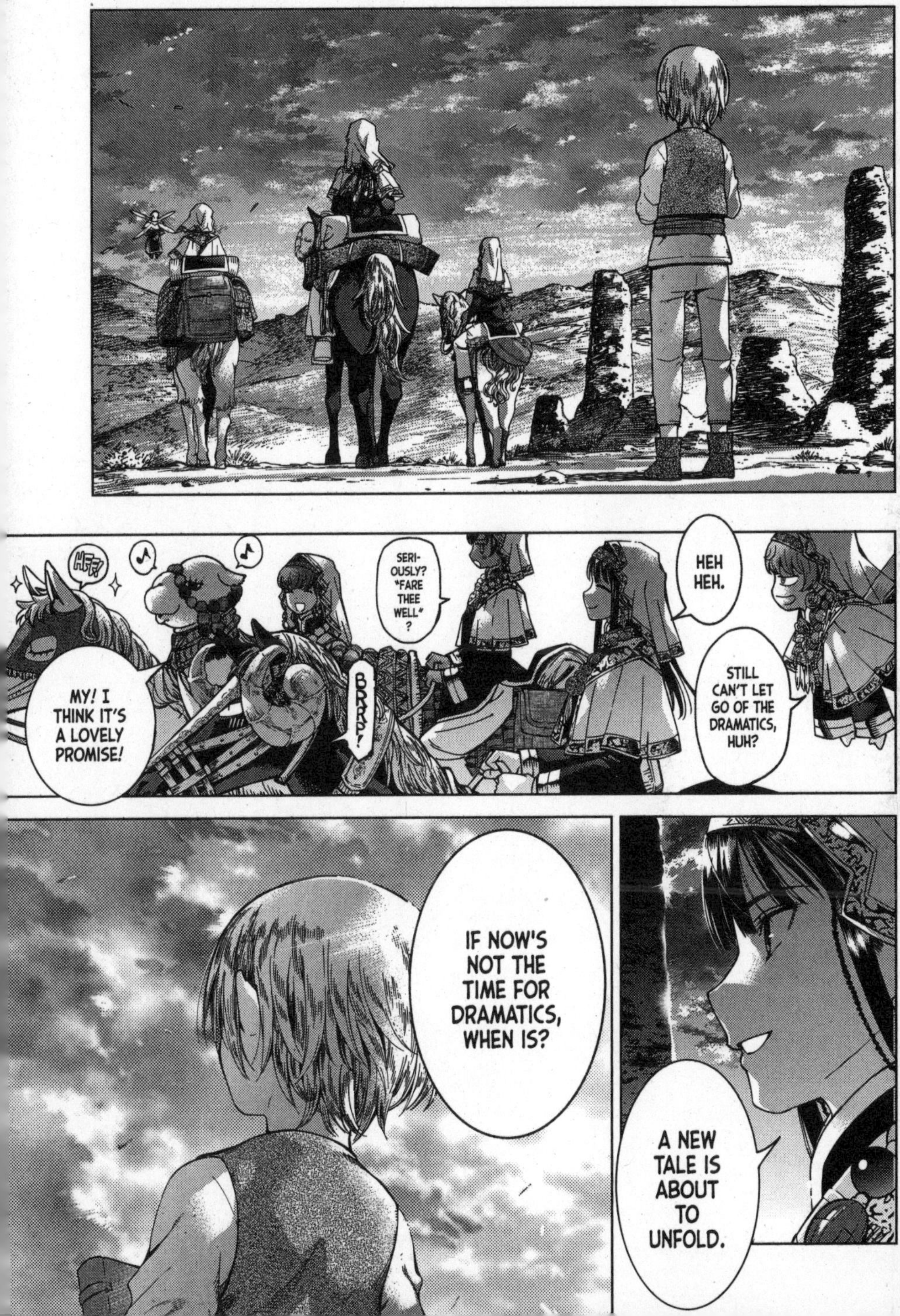
HEH HEH.
STILL CAN'T LET GO OF THE DRAMATICS, HUH?
SERI-OUSLY? "FARE THEE WELL"?
HFF!
BRRRP!
MY! I THINK IT'S A LOVELY PROMISE!
A NEW TALE IS ABOUT TO UNFOLD.
IF NOW'S NOT THE TIME FOR DRAMATICS, WHEN IS?

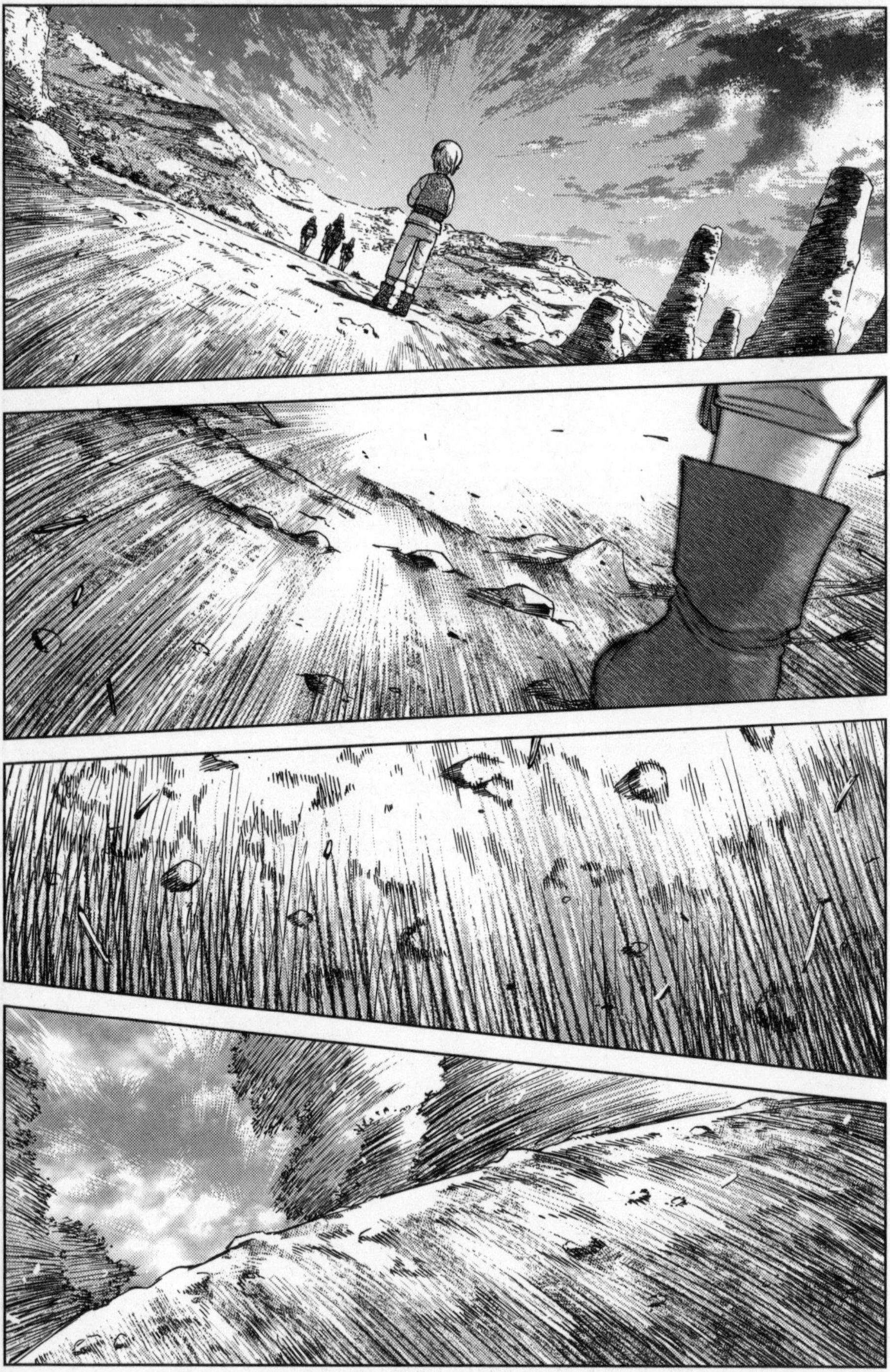

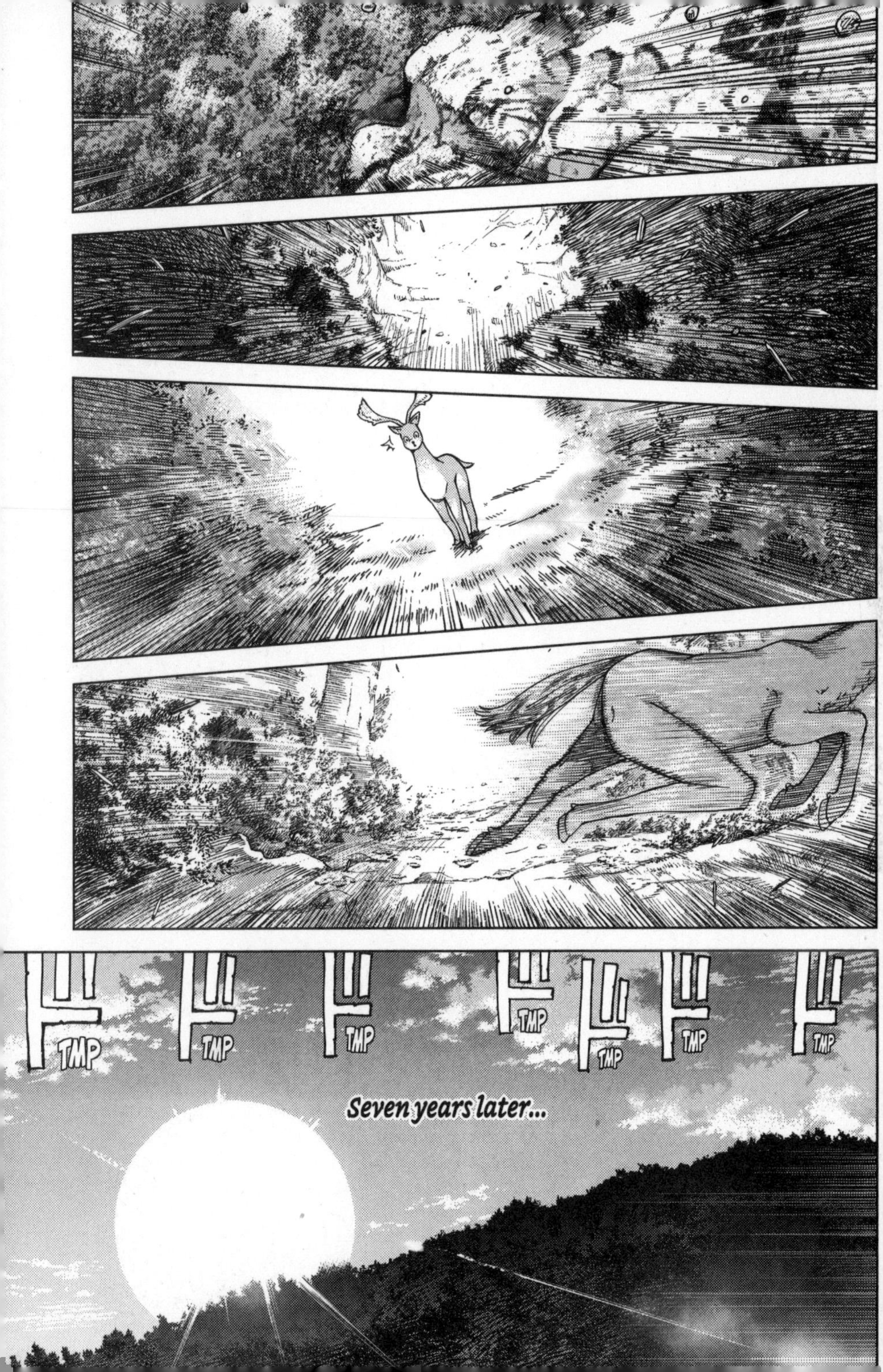
ド TMP
ド TMP
ド TMP
ド TMP
ド TMP
ド TMP
ド TMP
Seven years later...

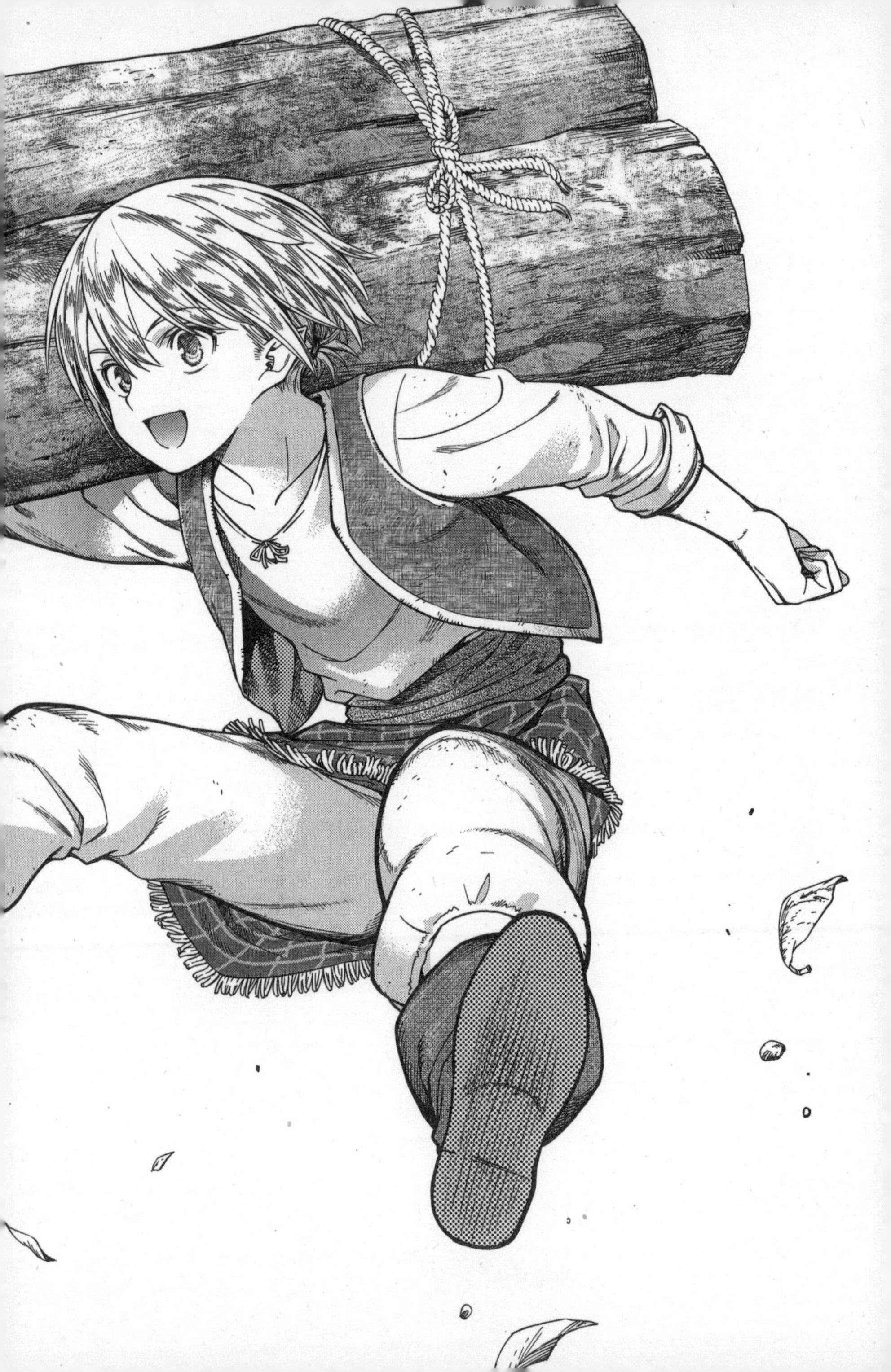

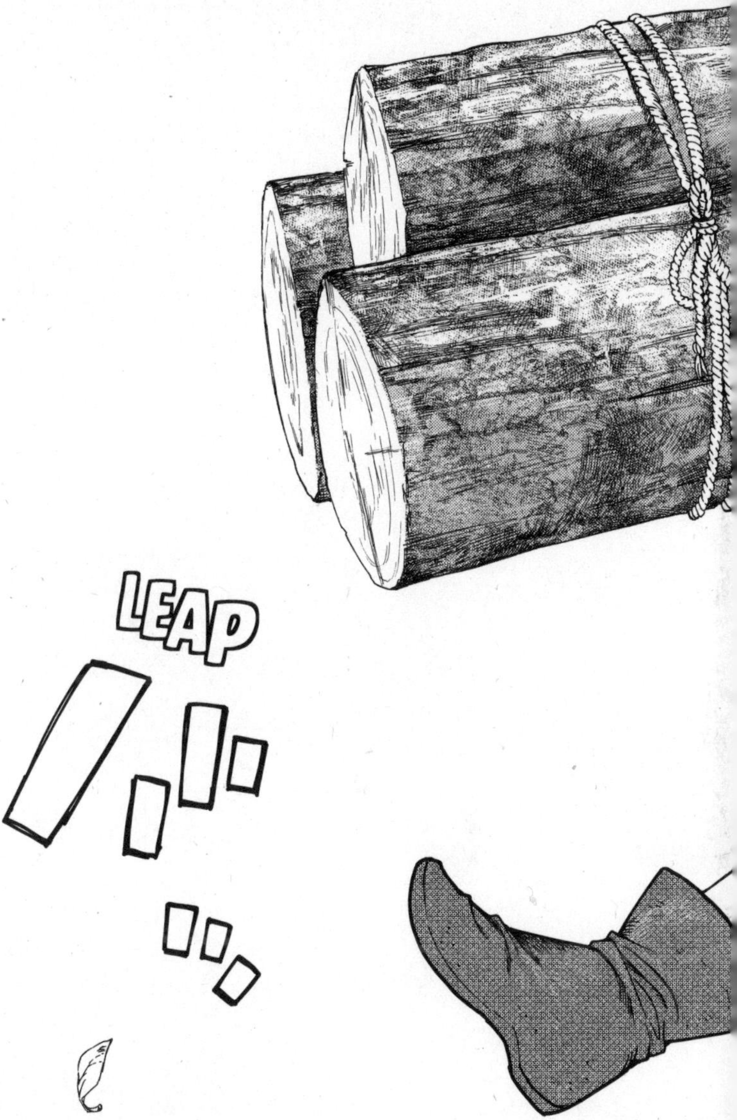
LEAP

Theo Fumis

Age 13

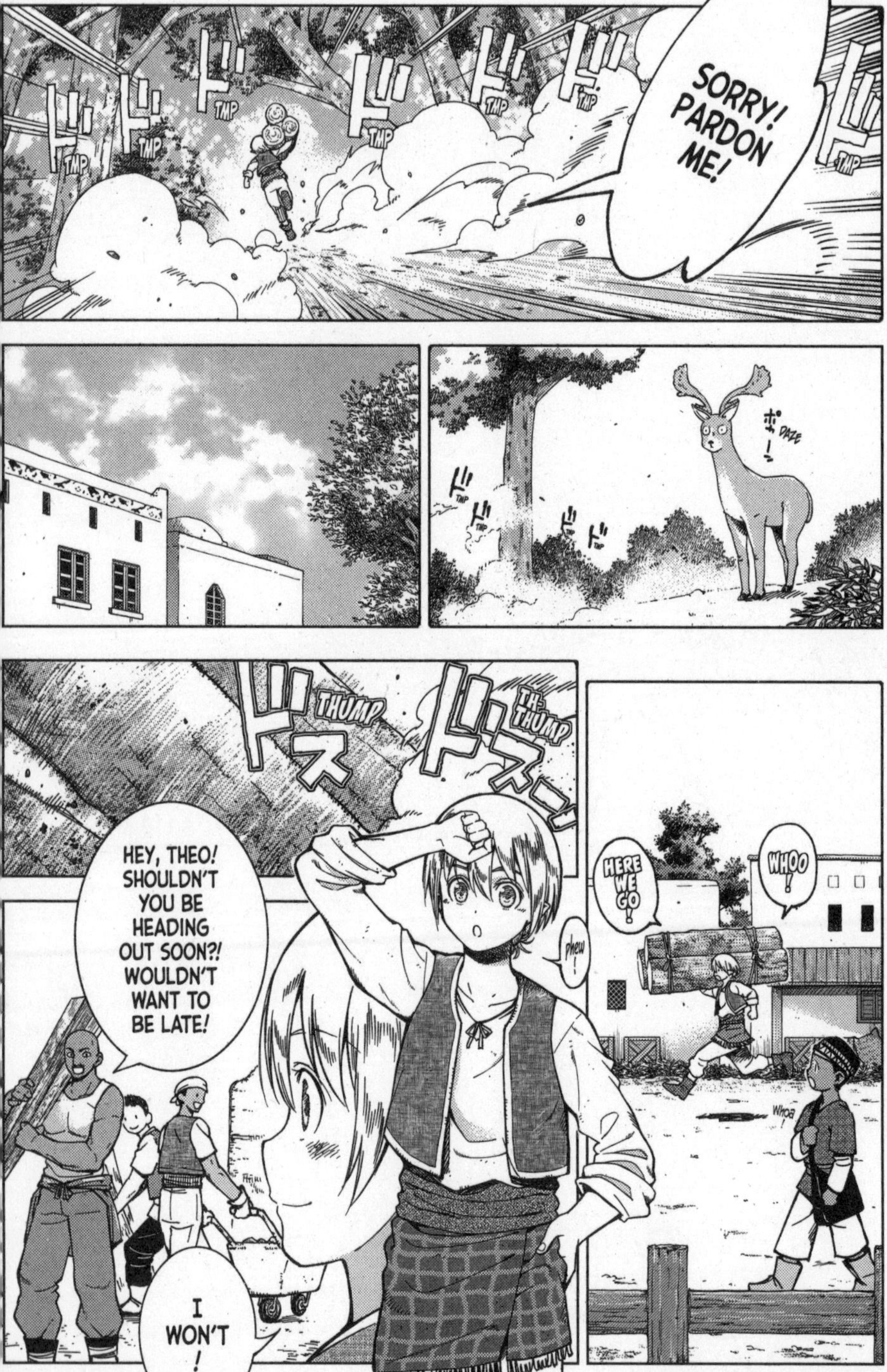

TMP
TMP
SORRY! PARDON ME!
TMP
TMP
TMP
TMP
TMP
DAZE
TMP
TMP
TMP
TMP
WHOO!
HERE WE GO!
Whoa!
THUMP
TH-THUMP
phew!
HEY, THEO! SHOULDN'T YOU BE HEADING OUT SOON?! WOULDN'T WANT TO BE LATE!
I WON'T!

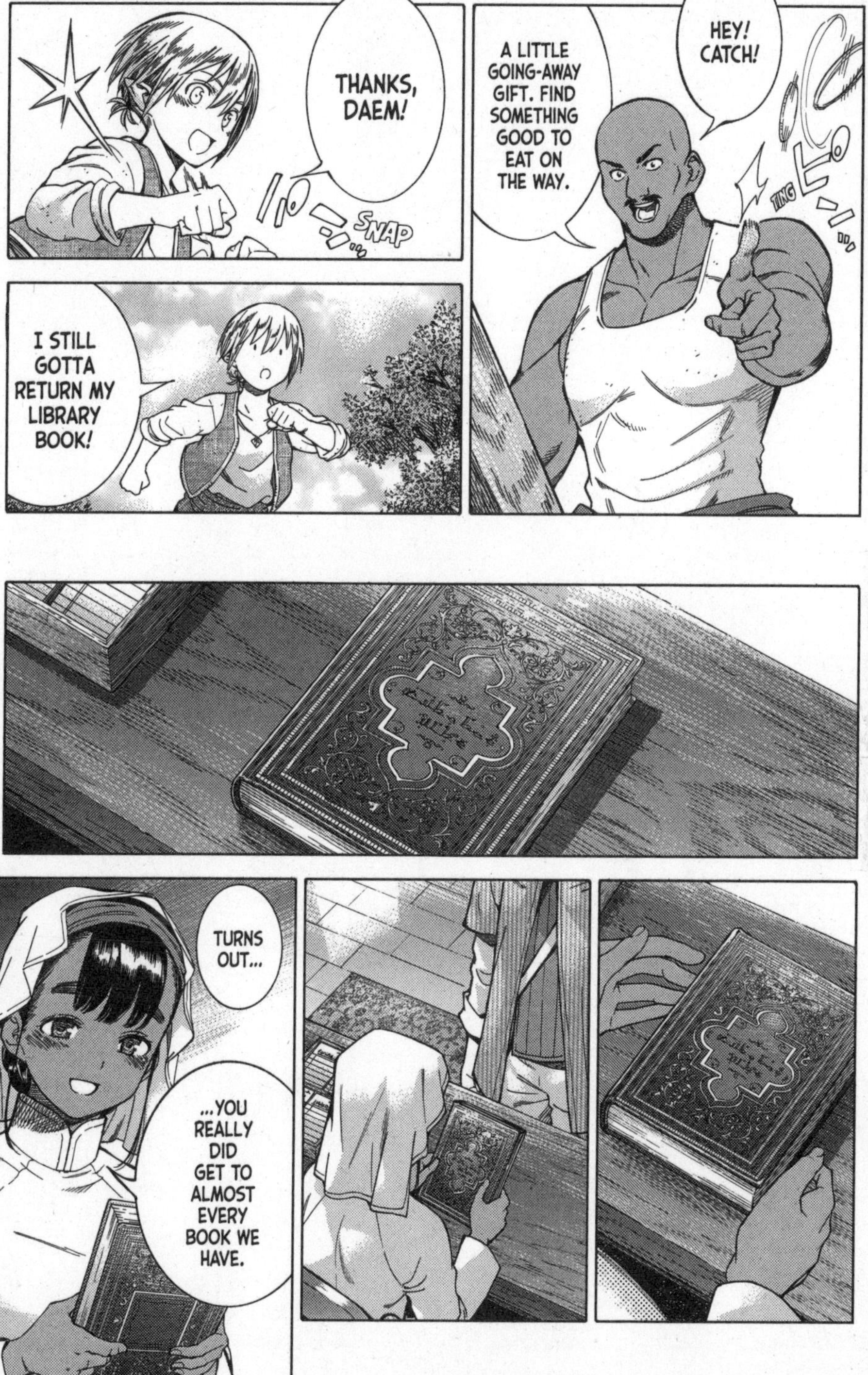
HEY! CATCH!
A LITTLE GOING-AWAY GIFT. FIND SOMETHING GOOD TO EAT ON THE WAY.
TING
THANKS, DAEM!
SNAP
I STILL GOTTA RETURN MY LIBRARY BOOK!
TURNS OUT...
...YOU REALLY DID GET TO ALMOST EVERY BOOK WE HAVE.

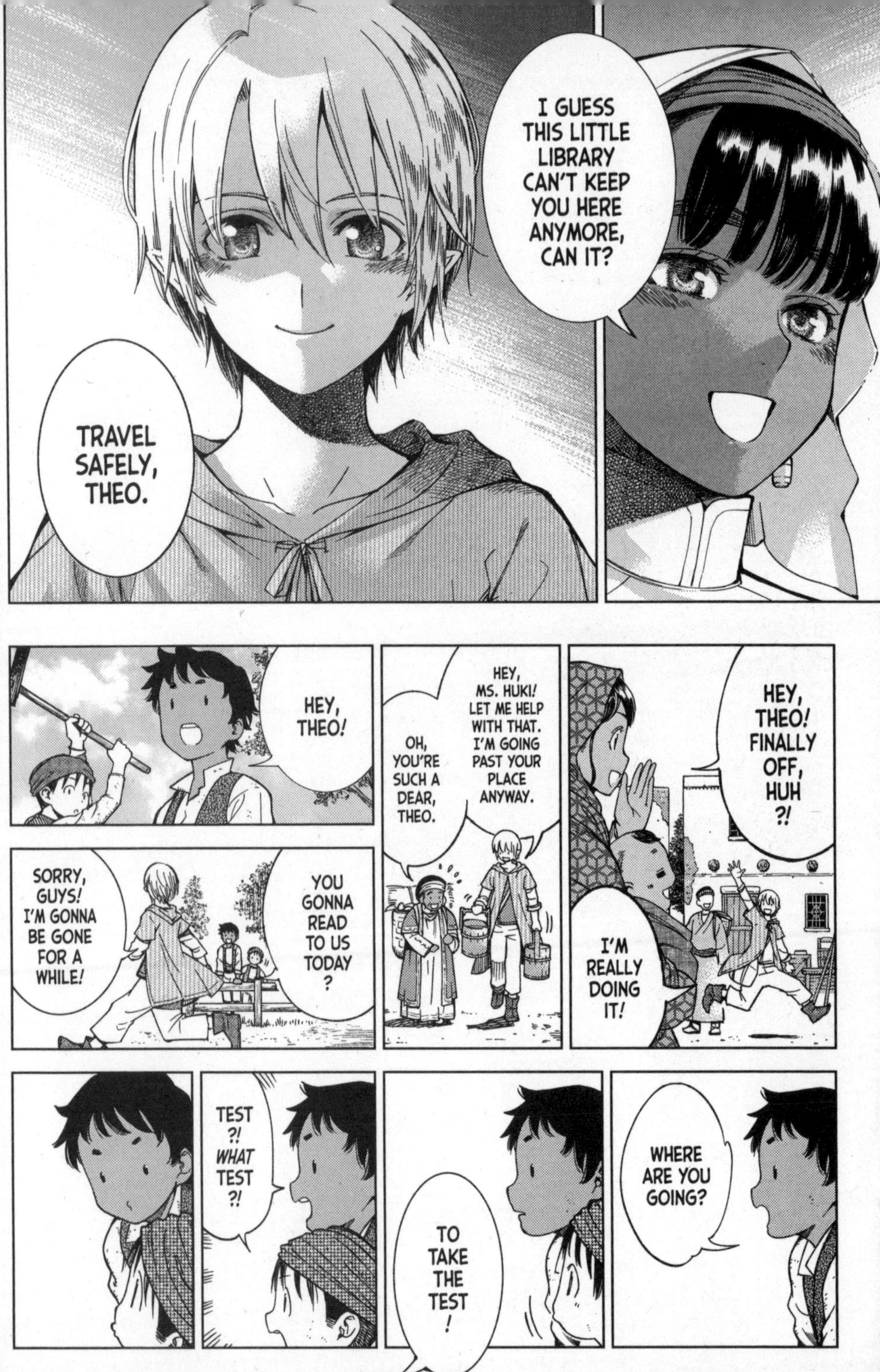
I GUESS THIS LITTLE LIBRARY CAN'T KEEP YOU HERE ANYMORE, CAN IT?
TRAVEL SAFELY, THEO.
HEY, THEO! FINALLY OFF, HUH?!
I'M REALLY DOING IT!
HEY, MS. HUKI! LET ME HELP WITH THAT. I'M GOING PAST YOUR PLACE ANYWAY.
OH, YOU'RE SUCH A DEAR, THEO.
HEY, THEO!
YOU GONNA READ TO US TODAY?
SORRY, GUYS! I'M GONNA BE GONE FOR A WHILE!
WHERE ARE YOU GOING?
TO TAKE THE TEST!
TEST?! *WHAT* TEST?!

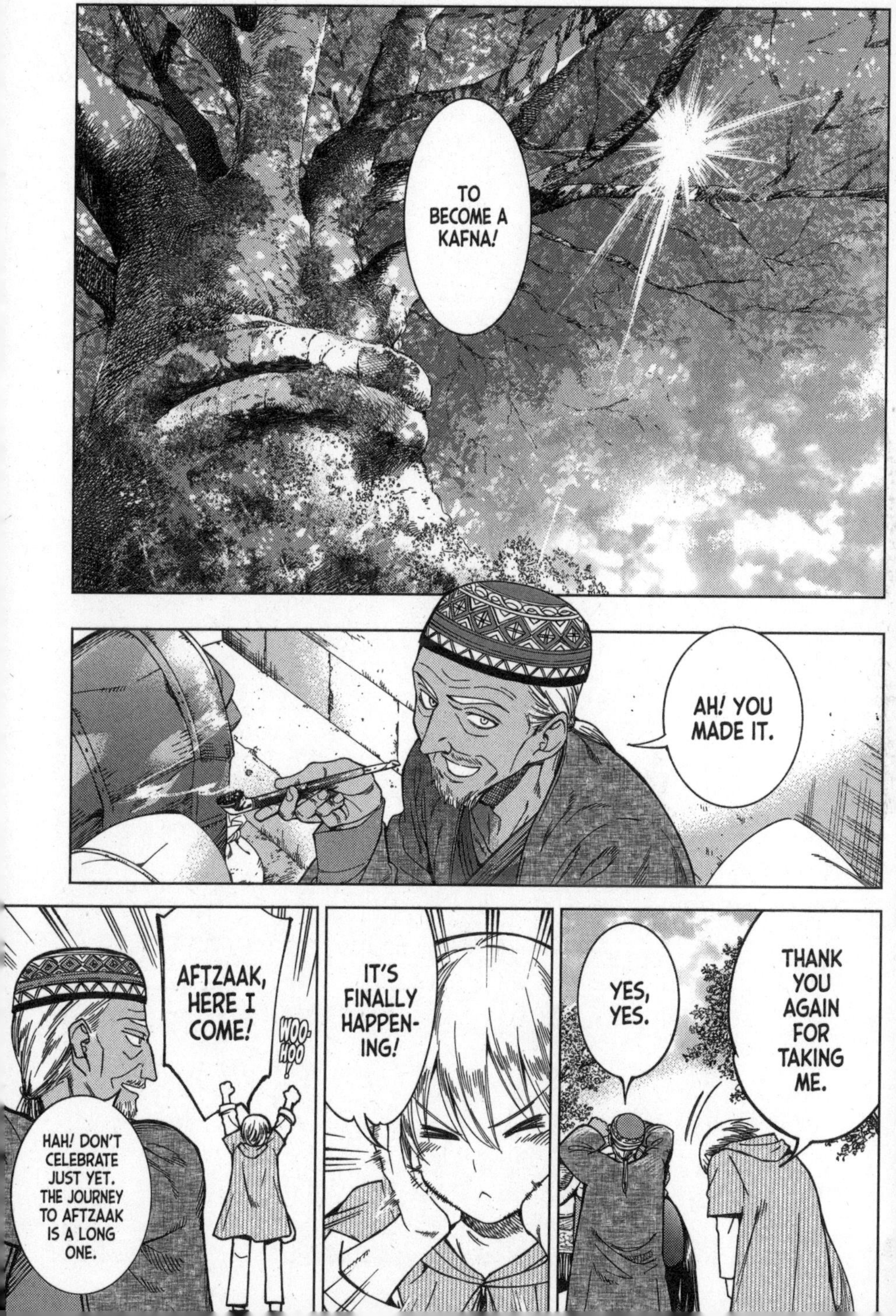
TO BECOME A KAFNA!
AH! YOU MADE IT.
THANK YOU AGAIN FOR TAKING ME.
YES, YES.
IT'S FINALLY HAPPENING!
AFTZAAK, HERE I COME!
WOO-HOO!
HAH! DON'T CELEBRATE JUST YET. THE JOURNEY TO AFTZAAK IS A LONG ONE.

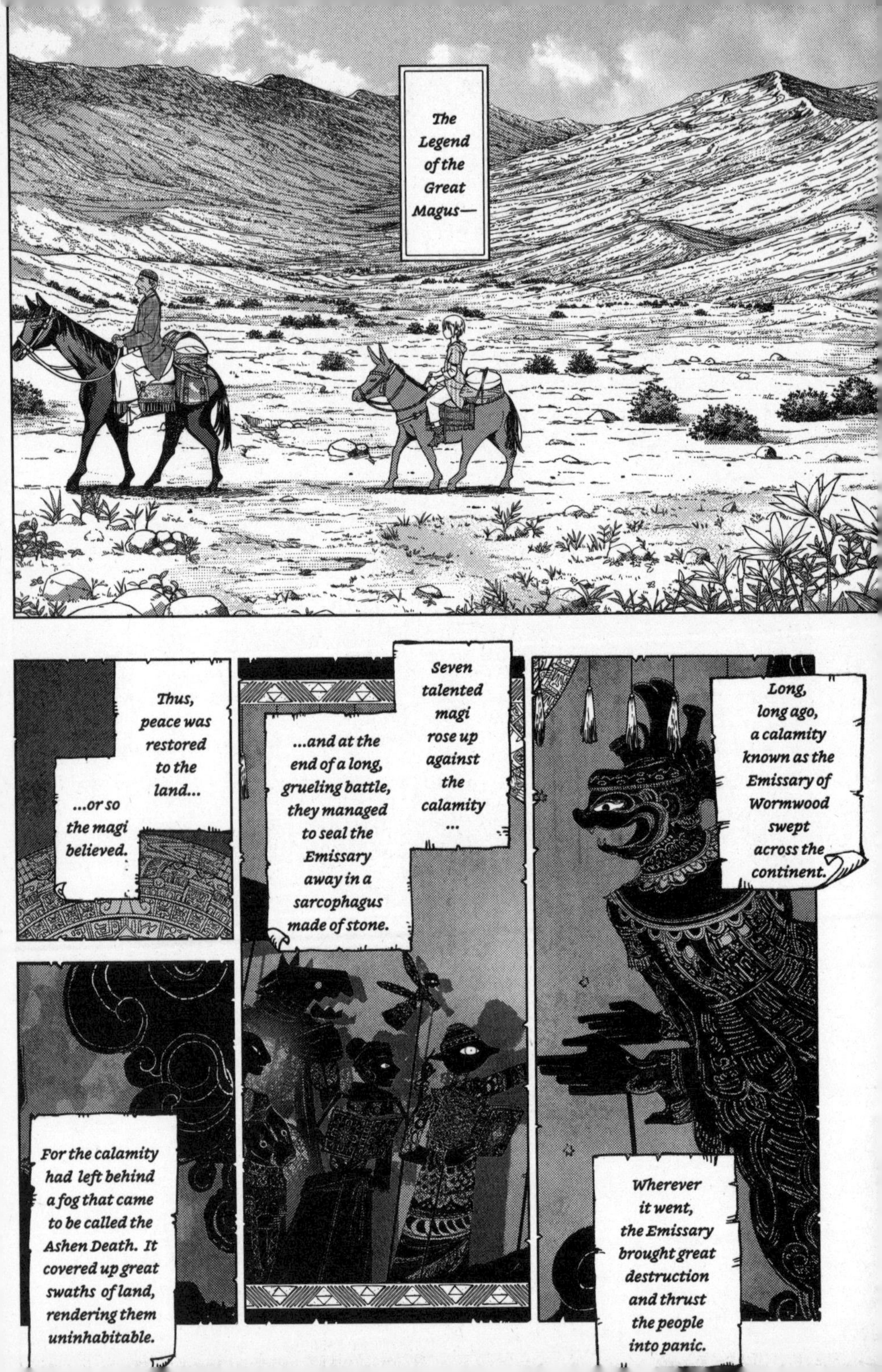
The Legend of the Great Magus—
Long, long ago, a calamity known as the Emissary of Wormwood swept across the continent.
Wherever it went, the Emissary brought great destruction and thrust the people into panic.
Seven talented magi rose up against the calamity...
...and at the end of a long, grueling battle, they managed to seal the Emissary away in a sarcophagus made of stone.
Thus, peace was restored to the land...
...or so the magi believed.
For the calamity had left behind a fog that came to be called the Ashen Death. It covered up great swaths of land, rendering them uninhabitable.

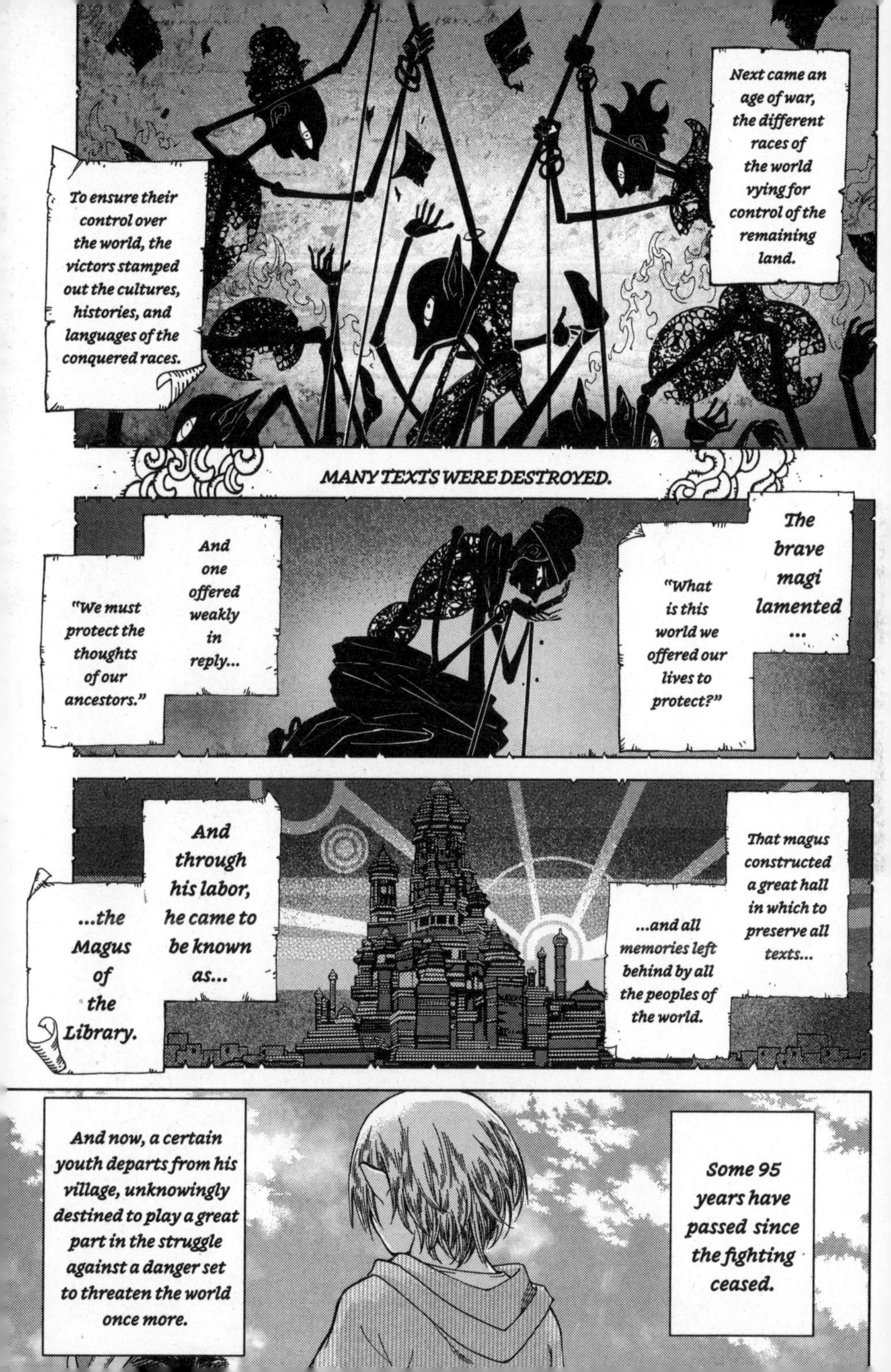
Next came an age of war, the different races of the world vying for control of the remaining land.
To ensure their control over the world, the victors stamped out the cultures, histories, and languages of the conquered races.
MANY TEXTS WERE DESTROYED.
The brave magi lamented...
"What is this world we offered our lives to protect?"
And one offered weakly in reply...
"We must protect the thoughts of our ancestors."
That magus constructed a great hall in which to preserve all texts...
...and all memories left behind by all the peoples of the world.
And through his labor, he came to be known as...
...the Magus of the Library.
Some 95 years have passed since the fighting ceased.
And now, a certain youth departs from his village, unknowingly destined to play a great part in the struggle against a danger set to threaten the world once more.

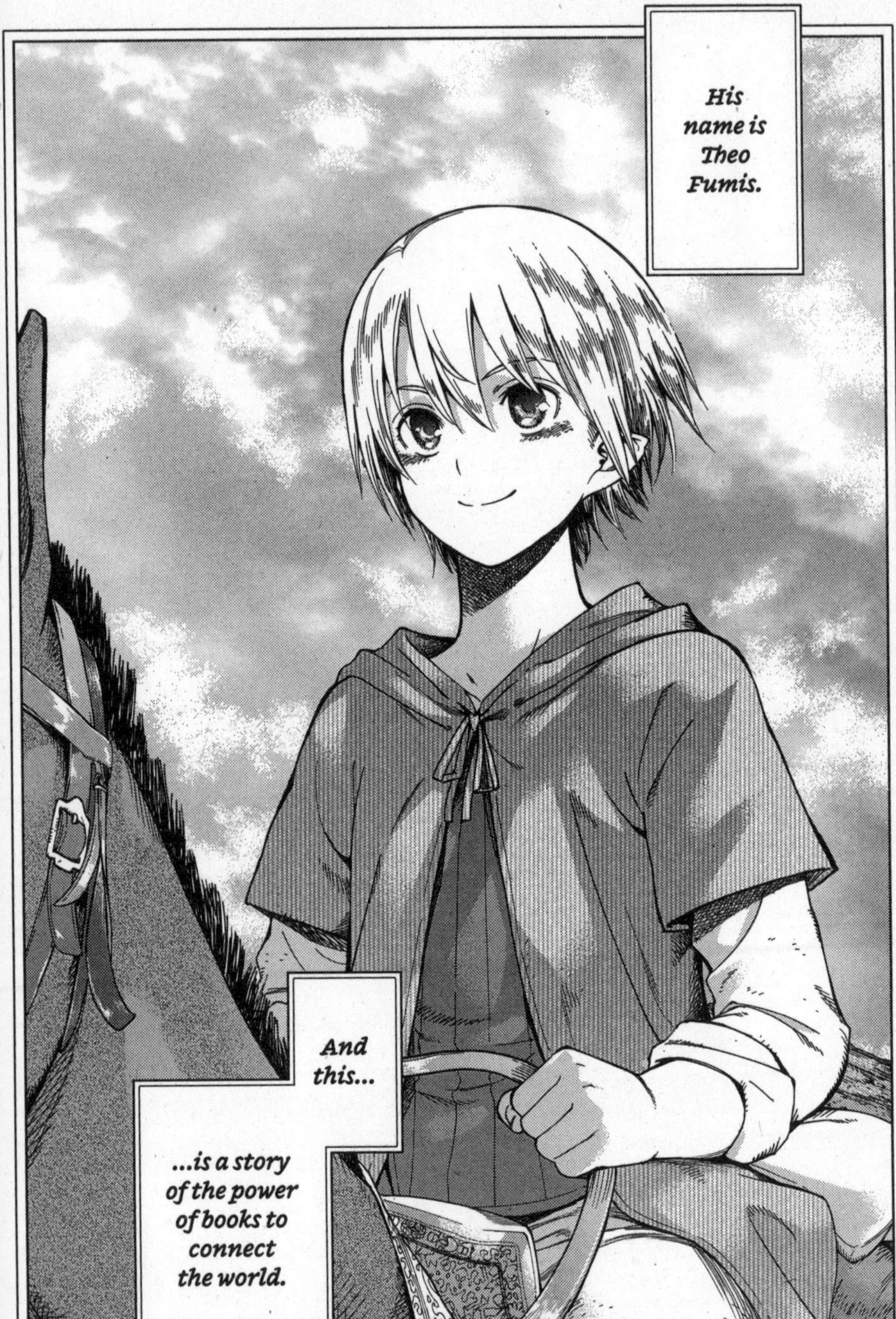
His name is Theo Fumis.
And this...
...is a story of the power of books to connect the world.

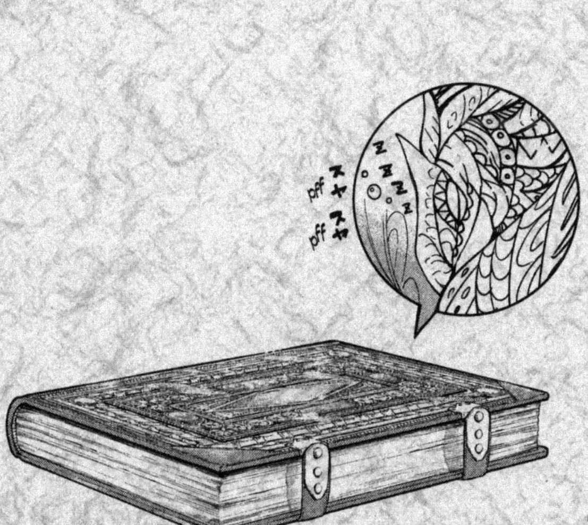
pff
pff

To be continued.

PRIOR TO THE VISIT

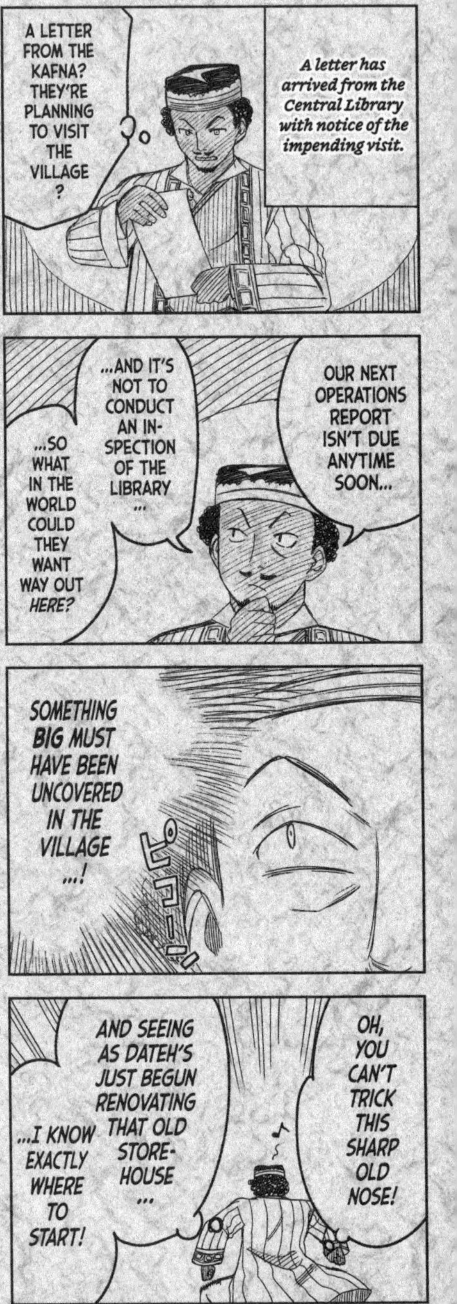
A letter has arrived from the Central Library with notice of the impending visit.
A LETTER FROM THE KAFNA? THEY'RE PLANNING TO VISIT THE VILLAGE?
OUR NEXT OPERATIONS REPORT ISN'T DUE ANYTIME SOON...
...AND IT'S NOT TO CONDUCT AN INSPECTION OF THE LIBRARY...
...SO WHAT IN THE WORLD COULD THEY WANT WAY OUT HERE?
SOMETHING BIG MUST HAVE BEEN UNCOVERED IN THE VILLAGE...!
ピコーン!
OH, YOU CAN'T TRICK THIS SHARP OLD NOSE!
AND SEEING AS DATEH'S JUST BEGUN RENOVATING THAT OLD STOREHOUSE...
...I KNOW EXACTLY WHERE TO START!

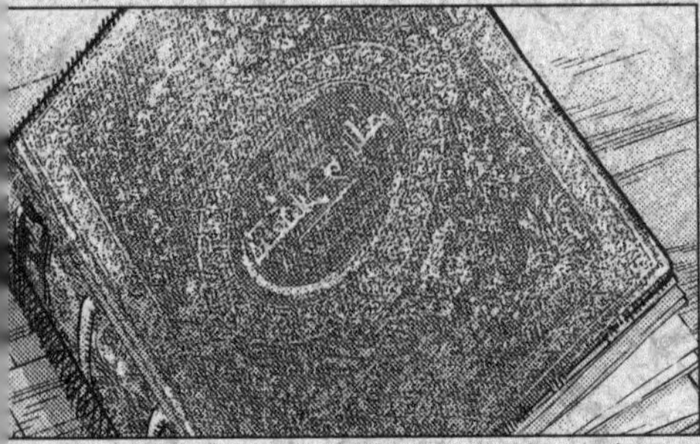

THE ADVENTURES OF SHAGRAZZAT

A series of adventure novels set among the high seas. It tells the story of the pirate captain Shagrazzat and his quest to claim the world for his own. Traveling with him is an eclectic crew composed of peoples from every land he visits. In Theo's world, a great, sweeping fog known as the "Ashen Death" has rendered the seas unnavigable. The fog set in sometime after the arrival of the Emissary of Wormwood, and because of it, those born following the Great War have never witnessed the ocean with their own eyes. The mystique of the sea is one factor driving the immense popularity of these oceangoing tales.

However, the Central Library also conspires to see Shagrazzat widely read: Hoping to ease tension between the races, the Library has carefully selected this tale of different peoples working together to overcome their difficulties. The librarians use it as a primary text in promoting intercultural harmony and in forming good reading habits among young minds.

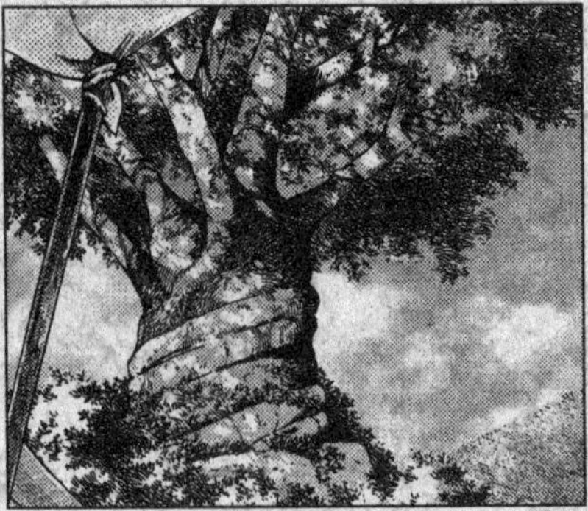

THE TONA TREE

A grand tree towering above the Village of Amun. It is said to have long ago protected the land nearby from the Emissary of Wormwood. The mana bursting forth from its branches has greatly affected Theo over his many hours spent playing nearby.

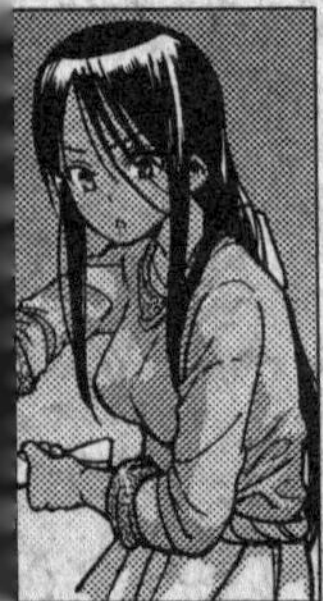

TIFA FUMIS *AGE 15*

Tifa arrived in Amun six years ago, at the end of an arduous journey. She is regarded by the villagers as a strange young woman who dedicates herself to the care of a half-blood boy.

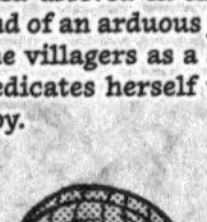

THEO FUMIS
AGE 6

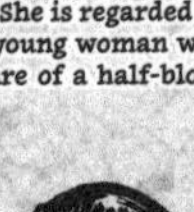

SAKIYA MENES
AGE 7

PREPARING FOR DEPARTURE

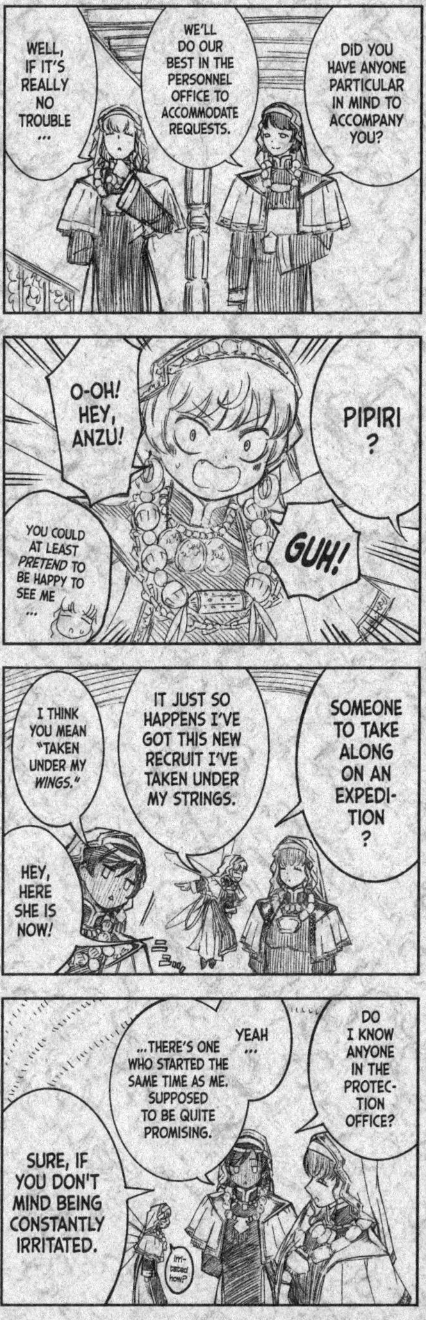
DID YOU HAVE ANYONE PARTICULAR IN MIND TO ACCOMPANY YOU?
WE'LL DO OUR BEST IN THE PERSONNEL OFFICE TO ACCOMMODATE REQUESTS.
WELL, IF IT'S REALLY NO TROUBLE ...
PIPIRI ?
O-OH! HEY, ANZU!
GUH!
YOU COULD AT LEAST *PRETEND* TO BE HAPPY TO SEE ME ...
SOMEONE TO TAKE ALONG ON AN EXPEDITION ?
IT JUST SO HAPPENS I'VE GOT THIS NEW RECRUIT I'VE TAKEN UNDER MY STRINGS.
I THINK YOU MEAN "TAKEN UNDER MY *WINGS*."
HEY, HERE SHE IS NOW!
DO I KNOW ANYONE IN THE PROTECTION OFFICE?
YEAH ...
...THERE'S ONE WHO STARTED THE SAME TIME AS ME. SUPPOSED TO BE QUITE PROMISING.
SURE, IF YOU DON'T MIND BEING CONSTANTLY IRRITATED.
Irri-tated how?

Longer *lipine* (decorative head coverings) indicate higher ranks.

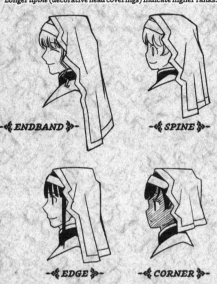

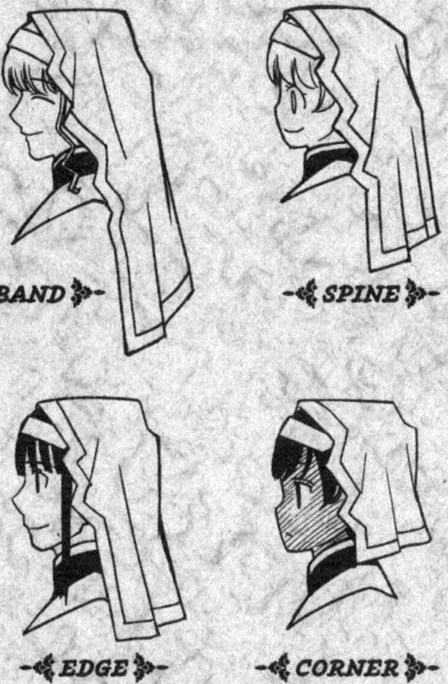
ENDBAND
SPINE
EDGE
CORNER

Patterned crests on the *kaachni* (decorative bands worn across the forehead) indicate assigned office.

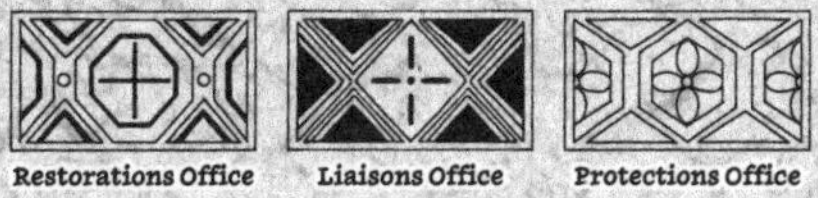
Restorations Office
Liaisons Office
Protections Office

SEDONA'S SPELL SEALS

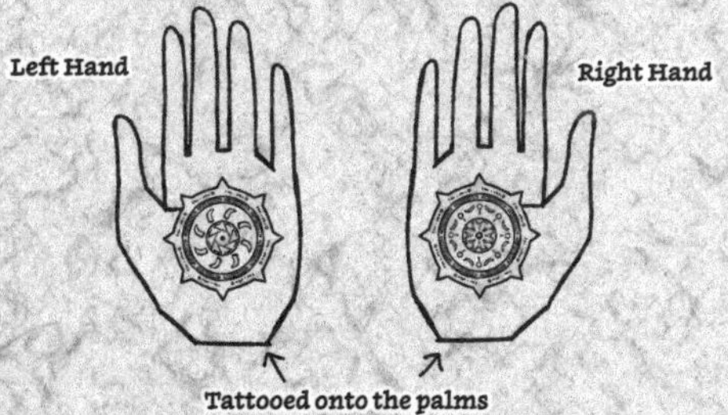
Left Hand
Right Hand
Tattooed onto the palms

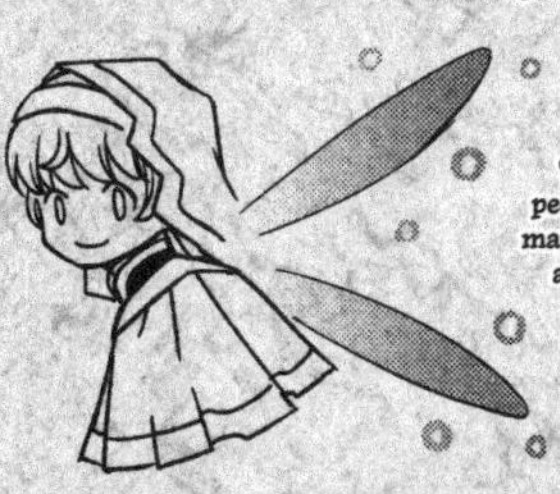

The wings of the *Kokopa* people are tangible slivers of mana; they can be manifested and extinguished at will.

◀ KAMOME ▶
SHIRAHAMA

Witch Hat Atelier

A magical manga adventure for fans of Disney and Studio Ghibli!

Witch Hat Atelier © Kamome Shirahama/Kodansha Ltd.

The magical adventure that took Japan by storm is finally here, from acclaimed DC and Marvel cover artist Kamome Shirahama!

In a world where everyone takes wonders like magic spells and dragons for granted, Coco is a girl with a simple dream: She wants to be a witch. But everybody knows magicians are born, not made, and Coco was not born with a gift for magic. Resigned to her un-magical life, Coco is about to give up on her dream to become a witch...until the day she meets Qifrey, a mysterious, traveling magician. After secretly seeing Qifrey perform magic in a way she's never seen before, Coco soon learns what everybody "knows" might not be the truth, and discovers that her magical dream may not be as far away as it may seem...

KC
KODANSHA
COMICS

Acclaimed screenwriter and director Mari Okada (*Maquia*, *anohana*) teams up with manga artist Nao Emoto (*Forget Me Not*) in this moving, funny, so-true-it's-embarrassing coming-of-age series!

When Kazusa enters high school, she joins the Literature Club, and leaps from reading innocent fiction to diving into the literary classics. But these novels are a bit more...*adult* than she was prepared for. Between euphemisms like fresh dewy grass and pork stew, crushing on the boy next door, and knowing you want to do that *one thing* before you die—discovering your budding sexuality is no easy feat! As if puberty wasn't awkward enough, the club consists of a brooding writer, the prettiest girl in school, an agreeable comrade, and an outspoken prude. Fumbling over their own discomforts, these five teens get thrown into chaos over three little letters: S...E...X...!

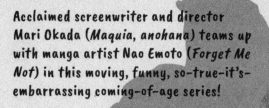

O Maidens in your Savage Season

Anime coming soon!

Mari Okada   Nao Emoto

A dark and sexy body-horror action manga perfect for fans of *Prison School* and *High School of the Dead*!

Shuichi Kagaya is a smart kid, and most smart kids his age would be thinking about college. Shuichi is also a monster, and he's smart enough to know that monsters don't go to college. But after he uses his monstrous form to save his classmate Claire Aoki, it doesn't matter what his plans for the future were, because he's not the one making the decisions anymore. Now that the seductive, sadistic Claire knows Shuichi's secret, she's got her own ideas about what a monster is good for—because he's not the first monster she's met...

GLEIPNIR

You and me together...we would be unstoppable."

THE HIGH SCHOOL HAREM COMEDY WITH FIVE TIMES THE CUTE GIRLS!

"An entertaining romantic-comedy with a snarky edge to it." —Taykobon

Futaro Uesugi is a second-year in high school, scraping to get by and pay off his family's debt. The only thing he can do is study, so when Futaro receives a part-time job offer to tutor the five daughters of a wealthy businessman, he can't pass it up. Little does he know, these five beautiful sisters are quintuplets, but the only thing they have in common...is that they're all terrible at studying!

THE QUINTESSENTIAL QUINTUPLETS

negi haruba

ANIME OUT NOW!

KC/ KODANSHA COMICS

The slow-burn queer romance that'll sweep you off your feet!

10 DANCE
Inouesatoh presents

"A FANTASTIC DEBUT VOLUME... ONE OF MY FAVORITE BOOKS OF THE YEAR..."
— AiPT!

"10 DANCE IS A MUST-READ FOR ANYONE WHO'S ENJOYED MANGA AND ANIME ABOUT COMPETITIVE DANCE (ON OR OFF THE ICE!)."
—Anime UK News

Shinya Sugiki, the dashing lord of Standard Ballroom, and Shinya Suzuki, passionate king of Latin Dance: The two share more than just a first name and a love of the sport. They each want to become champion of the 10-Dance Competition, which means they'll need to learn the other's specialty dances, and who better to learn from than the best? But old rivalries die hard, and things get further complicated when they realize there might be more between them than an uneasy partnership...

KC KODANSHA COMICS

Yuri Is My Job!

miman

JOIN US FOR AFTERNOON TEA WITH EQUAL PARTS YURI, ROM-COM, AND DRAMA!

Hime is a picture-perfect high school princess, so when she accidentally injures a café manager named Mai, she's willing to cover some shifts to keep her façade intact. To Hime's surprise, the café is themed after a private school where the all-female staff always puts on their best act for their loyal customers. However, under the guidance of the most graceful girl there, Hime can't help but blush and blunder! Beneath all the frills and laughter, Hime feels tension brewing as she finds out more about her new job and her budding feelings...

KC KODANSHA COMICS

"A quirky, fun comedy series... If you're a yuri fan, or perhaps interested in getting into it but not sure where to start, this book is worth picking up."
— Anime UK News

A Kodansha Comics Trade Paperback Original.

Published in the United States by Kodansha Comics,
an imprint of Kodansha USA Publishing, LLC, New York.

Publication rights for this English edition arranged through Kodansha Ltd., Tokyo.

First published in Japan in 2018 by Kodansha Ltd., Tokyo,
as *Toshokan no Daimajutsushi* volume 1.

ISBN 978-1-63236-823-2

Printed in the United States of America.

www.kodanshacomics.com

9 8 7 6 5 4 3 2 1

Translation: Stephen Kohler
Lettering: Evan Hayden
Editing: Paul Starr
Kodansha Comics edition cover design: Phil Balsman